Critics of Henry George

Also by ROBERT V. ANDELSON:

Imputed Rights

Critics of Henry George

A Centenary Appraisal
of Their Strictures on
Progress and Poverty

Edited by
ROBERT V. ANDELSON

Rutherford ● *Madison* ● *Teaneck*
Fairleigh Dickinson University Press

London: Associated University Presses

Associated University Presses, Inc.
Cranbury, New Jersey 08512

Associated University Presses
Magdalen House
136-148 Tooley Street
London SE1 2TT, England

330.09
C

Library of Congress Cataloging in Publication Data
Main entry under title:

Critics of Henry George.

    Includes bibliographical references.
    1. George, Henry, 1839-1897. Progress and poverty—
Addresses, essays, lectures. I. Andelson, Robert V., 1931-
HB171.G3C74   330'.092'4   78.66791
ISBN 0-8386-2350-6

PRINTED IN THE UNITED STATES OF AMERICA

to
Violetta G. Graham
(known professionally as V.G. Peterson),
wise counselor,
untiring mentor,
and
cherished friend,
this book is fondly dedicated

Errata:

Page 22 —line 4 from bottom: After *power,* insert *(other than through external imposition).*

Page 25 —line 10 under *III*: For *chief d'oeuvre,* read *chef-d'oeuvre.*

Page 27 —first line of note 11: For *Bromwell,* read *Bramwell.*

Page 30 —line 23: For *symthesis,* read *synthesis.*

Page 39 —line 3: For *effeciency,* read *efficiency.*

Page 40 —line 26: After *beginning,* delete *of.*

Page 40 —line 30: After *roots to the,* insert *alienation of the public domain by predatory seizures, doubtful.*

Page 86 —line 26: For *milion,* read *million.*

Page 132—line 12: For *temporal,* read *ecclesiastical.*

Page 197—first line of footnote: For *p. 238n.,* read *p. 255n.*

Page 201—third line of footnote: For *regards,* read *rewards.*

Page 204—line 8: Delete second *at.*

Page 220—last line of note 47: Interchange parenthesis and bracket.

Page 255—line 17: Insert *not* after *Does it.*

Page 260—note 19: For *Simgle,* read *Single.*

Page 271—last line of note 4: Insert end parenthesis after *1975.*

Page 308—line 27: For *observers,* read *observes.*

Page 381—line 14: For *the,* read *that.*

Page 384—line 27: For *three,* read *four.*

Page 385—line 8: For *he facts,* read *the facts.*

Contents

Acknowledgments

The decision to undertake the labors of which this book is the fruition would never have been made had it not been for the encouragement of my friend, colleague, and department head, Professor Delos B. McKown, who was unfailingly supportive at each step of its development.

Funds that made its publication possible were generously provided by the Robert Schalkenbach Foundation of New York, and Basic Economic Education, Inc., of San Diego. Mr. P. I. Prentice, president of Schalkenbach, and Miss V. G. Peterson, its longtime executive secretary until her recent retirement, deserve special mention in this regard, as does Mr. Everett J. Seeley, chairman of the board of B.E.E.

Auburn University released me from my classroom obligations so that I could devote the spring quarter of 1977 solely to the project, and made available a grant for secretarial and research assistance. Dr. Taylor D. Littleton, vice-president for academic affairs, and Dr. Chester C. Carroll, vice-president for research, were particularly helpful in facilitating these favors.

The authors all took time from busy and demanding schedules to prepare their chapters, contributing their efforts gratuitously, patiently suffering my sometimes importunate demands, and graciously acquiescing in revisions that they may privately have considered brash.

Professors Alexander R. Posniak and José A. Madrigal of the Auburn department of foreign languages kindly donated many hours of assistance with translation, and the staff of Ralph Brown Draughon Library at the university was helpful beyond the call of duty. I wish to note in particular the extraordinary efforts of Mrs. Frances Honour and Mr. David N. King, both of whom have since moved on to new locations and pursuits.

The preparation of the typescript was primarily the work of Mrs. Anne C. Clark, whose dedication and efficiency cannot be overpraised. Mrs. Hildegaard Wolverton also gave able and conscientious service to this task when her departmental responsibilities permitted.

I have had the benefit of valuable comments (and, in several cases, other courtesies) from the following persons who read portions of the manuscript: Messrs. Victor H. Blundell and Richard Grinham of the Economic and Social Science Research Association (London); Mr. Weld S. Carter, executive secretary of the Committee on Taxation, Resources and Economic Development; Mr. Robert Clancy, president of the Henry George Institute, and acting president of the International Union for Land Value Taxation and Free Trade; Professors Robert B. Ekelund, Jr., Richard Higgins, Stephen O. Morrell, and Richard Saba of the Economics Department at Auburn; Professor James E. Green of the Economics Department at the University of Georgia; Mr. Gordon

Hoover of Los Angeles; Professor Carl McGuire of the Economics Department at the University of Colorado; Professor Raj Mohan of the Sociology Department at Auburn, editor of the *International Journal of Contemporary Sociology*; Miss Peterson of Schalkenbach, whom I have already mentioned in another connection; Mr. Harry Pollard, president of the Henry George School of Los Angeles; Mr. William O. Ranky of Chicago; Miss Frances Soriero of Schalkenbach and Professor Bruce Yandle of the Economics Department at Clemson University. Some of my literary contributors, notably Professors Gaffney, Hébert, and Schwartzman, also provided useful advice or other help. Of course, culpability for the defects of the volume rests ultimately with me.

Mr. Julien Yoseloff, president of Associated University Presses, Inc., extended himself in many ways to be accommodating.

Finally, these acknowledgments would be sadly incomplete if they omitted reference to my lady, who accepted the husbandly neglect that was an inevitable aspect of my more than four years of intense involvement with this volume. Were it possible to report honestly that she did so uncomplainingly, I should have reason to be apprehensive.

R.V.A.
July 1978

I wish to thank the following for having given permission to quote from published works:

The American Journal of Economics and Sociology, for permission to quote chapter 24, originally titled "Msgr. John A. Ryan's Critique of Henry George," published in vol. 33, no. 3 (July 1974):273-86; and section I of chapter 19, adapted from my article "Where Society's Claim Stops: An Evaluation of Seligman's Ethical Critique of Henry George," pulished in vol. 27, no. 1 (January 1968):41-53.

Harvard University Press, for permission to quote from Thomas Nixon Carver, *Essays in Social Justice*, 1915.

Macmillan Administration (Basingstoke) Ltd. and The Free Press, a division of Macmillan Publishing Co., Inc., for permission to quote from Alfred Marshall, *The Early Economic Writings of Alfred Marshall, 1867-1890,* edited and introduced by J. K. Whitaker, 1975.

Oxford University Press, for permission to quote from Joseph Schumpeter, *History of Economic Analysis,* edited by Elizabeth Boody Schumpeter, 1954.

Random House, Inc., and Alfred A. Knopf, Inc., for permission to quote from *Essays in Economic Theory*, edited by Rexford C. Tugwell, 1924.

The Robert Schalkenbach Foundation, for permission to quote from Henry George, *Progress and Poverty*, 75th anniversary edition, 1954.

The executors of the estate of Eustace Seligman, for permission to quote from Edwin R. A. Seligman, *Essays in Taxation*, 9th ed., 1923.

Critics of Henry George

Part I
Prolegomena

1

Introduction

BY ROBERT V. ANDELSON

I

"People do not argue with the teaching of George, they simply do not know it." This sentiment, expressed by Tolstoy in 1905,[1] had a degree of validity even then. The writers of economic textbooks in particular, when deigning to mention George at all, have tended to dismiss his contribution with a few patronizing sentences that, more often than not, display a lamentable absence of real acquaintance with his thought.[2]

Henry George was one of a long succession of political economists—including Adam Smith, Malthus, the two Mills, Ricardo, Chalmers, Sidgwick, and Marx—with no official training in the discipline. Like that of most of the other members of this line, moreover, his pursuit of the subject was merely a particularization of broader social and even metaphysical concerns. It was his misfortune, however, to have launched his theory just as economics was becoming a specialized profession, as signaled by the founding of the American Economic Association in 1885 by scholars, many of whom had done postgraduate study in Germany. Henceforth, at least in the United States, he who presumed to write on economic theory without having first armed himself with advanced degrees in the field would run the risk of being disparaged as an amateur in academic circles. And George held no degrees at all—advanced or otherwise! His response to the coolness elicited by his ideas in these circles was scarcely calculated to dispel it. It was perhaps both understandable and inevitable that this self-taught reformer, who believed with passionate sincerity in the unassailability of his logic and the imperative necessity of his social program, should impute motives of intellectual cowardice to his scholarly detractors. "George's unwarranted suspicion, even contempt, for the academic world, an attitude duplicated by many of his followers, undoubtedly created much antagonism for him among the very people whose endorsement he desperately needed."[3] And this antagonism all too often manifested itself in contemptuous silence or peremptory dismissal.

Yet there have been those who, Tolstoy to the contrary notwithstanding, *have* argued with the teaching of George. Not all of their arguments have been

15

sketchy, crude, or ill-informed; several have been detailed, closely reasoned, and based upon a careful study of his works. Had most of his disciples in this century taken Tolstoy's assertion (justifiably a commonplace among them) less literally, they might have discovered not a few criticisms worthy of their analysis and possible refutation, together with some areas in which the master's legacy could profit from judicious modification or supplementation.

I do not, of course, wish to impart the impression that George's thought met with only hostile or indifferent response among the literati. A formidable list of testimonials, ranging from Tolstoy and Sun Yat-sen to Nicholas Murray Butler and John Dewey, could be cited to show the opposite.[4]. The list would, in fact, contain statements from some prominent economists, although not many have accorded unqualified approval to the Georgist doctrine. Even George's most dedicated opponents have, almost without exception, paid tribute to the eloquence of his literary style and the luminous nobility of his intentions, and some have credited him with calling needed attention to abuses, with awakening their interest in economic problems, and with performing yeoman service in exposing certain hoary fallacies.[5] Joseph Schumpeter, to mention but one recent economist of great distinction, spoke appreciatively of George in no uncertain terms in his last book, *History of Economic Analysis*, posthumously published.*

My purpose here, however, is not to rehearse encomia; that task may be left to the various periodicals of the Georgist movement without fear that they will be in the least delinquent in fulfilling it. Rather, on this centenary of George's magnum opus, I am convinced that the highest tribute we can pay his memory, and the one that he himself would cherish most, is to present as fairly as possible the arguments of his most significant critics, and to weigh them in the scales both of abstract reason and of empirical evidence.

Heretofore this has not been done in any comprehensive way. During

---

*It may be instructive to quote Schumpeter's remarks, especially insofar as they relate to the question of George's technical competence:

He was a self-taught economist, but he *was* an economist. In the course of his life, he acquired most of the knowledge and of the ability to handle an economic argument that he could have acquired by academic training as it then was. In this he differed to his advantage from most men who proffered panaceas. Barring his panacea (the Single Tax) and the phraseology connected with it, he was a very orthodox economist and extremely conservative as to methods. They were those of the English "classics," A. Smith being his particular favorite. Marshall and Bohm-Bawerk he failed to understand. But up to and including Mill's treatise, he was thoroughly at home in scientific economics; and he shared none of the current misunderstandings or prejudices concerning it. Even the panacea—nationalization not of land but of the rent of land by a confiscatory tax—benefited by his competence as an economist, for he was careful to frame his "remedy" in such a manner as to cause the minimum injury to the efficiency of the private-enterprise economy. Professional economists who focused attention on the single-tax proposal and condemned Henry George's teaching, root and branch, were hardly just to him. The proposal itself, one of the many descendents of Quesnay's *impot unique*, though vitiated by association with the untenable theory that the phenomenon of poverty is entirely due to the absorption of all surpluses by the rent of land, is not *economically* unsound, except that it involves an unwarranted optimism concerning the yield of such a tax. In any case, it should not be put down as nonsense. If Ricardo's vision of economic evolution had been correct, it would even have been obvious wisdom. And obvious wisdom is in fact what George said in *Progress and Poverty* (ch. 1, Book ix) about the economic effects to be expected from a removal of fiscal burdens—if such a removal were possible. [Joseph A. Schumpeter, *History of Economic Analysis,* ed. Elizabeth Boody Schumpeter (New York: Oxford University Press, 1954), p. 865.]

George's lifetime he published rejoinders to a few of his critics, notably
Herbert Spencer, the Duke of Argyll, and Edward Atkinson;[6] and Thomas
Shearman attempted to refute several animadversions in a brief article, and
later in the last part of his *Natural Taxation*.[7] Max Hirsch's *Democracy and
Socialism* contains chapters that deal with the objections of Atkinson and
Francis A. Walker, and shorter discussions that address those of Lord
Bramwell, J. C. Spence, W. E. H. Lecky, Thomas H. Huxley, H. M. Hyndman, John A. Hobson, and an anonymous Fabian pamphleteer.[8] As far as the
number of critics covered is concerned, by far the most ambitious effort along
these lines is Steven B. Cord's *Henry George: Dreamer or Realist?*, but it is
more of an evaluative survey than an analysis in depth, and is limited to the
treatment of George by American economists and historians. Otherwise, to my
knowledge, examination and appraisal of George's critics have been confined
to incidental passages and to articles occasioned by individual attacks.

This book does not, of course, purport to be exhaustive. In view of the vast
bulk of the literature on George, such would be neither feasible nor desirable.
It does strive, however, to cover all of the most significant critiques, except
for those by Spencer and Argyll. To these latter, George's replies, both of
them substantial, are still in print and readily available.[9] Although I have attempted to research the entire literature in English and the other major European tongues except for Russian, some works were not available to me, while
others may well have escaped my notice.

II

I have used an editor's discretion in deciding what constitutes a
"significant" critique, and my judgments in this respect may to some students
appear arbitrary in various instances. They have been guided by such criteria
as originality, subtlety, influence, brilliance of organization and expression,
and, in at least one case (Alcázar), sheer length. Of necessity there will be a certain amount of overlapping, because many of the same arguments, or approximations thereof, have been employed by more than one critic. When an argument was first advanced in germinal form by a writer who did not essay a sustained critique of George, I have tried to see to it that it is presented and
evaluated in its most developed manifestation, with indication given as to its
original source.

There are a number of critiques that might, for one reason or another, have
arguably justified consideration in these pages, but that I have not included.
Let me mention some of these, together with my reasons for their omission:

In 1881 and 1882 *Progress and Poverty* was the subject of review in three
learned German periodicals by Adolf Wagner (*Zeitschrift für die Gesammte
Staatswissenschaft* [Tübingen] 37 [1881]: 619-24), E. Heitz (*Jahrbucher für
Nationalokonomie und Statistik* [Jena] 4 [1882]: 120-26), and Gustav
Schmoller (*Jahrbuch fur Gezetzgebung, Verwaltung und Volkswirtschaft*
[Leipzig] 6 [1882]: 354-59), respectively. Wagner and Schmoller, in particular,
were famous and influential scholars, but each review is but six pages in
length—substantial enough as an expression of the medium but too brief to be
classed as a critique for purposes of this study.

Viewed solely from the standpoint of their author's eminence, the essays by

William Graham Sumner that appeared in *Harper's Weekly* during the early months of 1883, and that were gathered and reprinted under the title *What Social Classes Owe to Each Other*, would surely warrant treatment. Yet it is only in the loosest sense that they may be considered a critique of George, for although a few passages suggest that Sumner bore *Progress and Poverty* in mind, the essays deal sweepingly with broad social issues, touching in only the most general way upon some elementary premises of George's system without ever naming him or any of his writings. (Two years earlier Sumner had specifically reviewed *Progress and Poverty* in an unsigned editorial in *Scribner's Monthly*, but it was only a page in length and consisted wholly of unsupported ridicule.) Although this series gave rise to a rival one by George in *Frank Leslie's Illustrated Newspaper* (collected and republished with additional material as *Social Problems*), it was, as Barker puts it, "a competitive venture, not a controversy."[10]

The pamphlet review of *Progress and Poverty* by that "fine old crusted Tory" Lord Bramwell[11] went into seven editions from 1883 through 1895, hence one may assume that the Liberty and Property Defense League, under whose imprint it appeared, must have considered it an unusually effective attack. But, although vigorously written, it is a relatively trivial piece of work; its fiften pages focus mainly upon a small number of passages in isolation from their context, and demonstrate a decidedly less than perfect understanding of George's argument.

Altogether different in tone is the thirty-page scholarly discussion devoted chiefly to George's theory by the distinguished French economist Charles Gide.[12] So fairly and even persuasively does he elucidate the strengths of George's thesis that one almost expects him to conclude with an unequivocal endorsement. Yet he rejects it, for reasons that he states in a surprisingly cursory, almost offhand fashion, recommending instead a trial of the scheme of land reform advocated by the Belgian socialist Baron de Colins. Gide concedes on the one hand that land is an especially appropriate subject for taxation, yet claims on the other that the problem of separating land values from improvement values is insoluble—a contention denied by many experts, Kenneth Back being a recent example.[13] To Gide probably belongs the dubious honor of having been the first to argue that if the state were to confiscate through taxation the unearned increment of land, it would be unjust if it did not also indemnify landowners when land decreased in value. Commenting on the same objection as put by other critics, Charles F. Collier remarks that under the existing system, although the tax liability of one who suffers financial reverses may decrease, "there is no tax which *reimburses* people for loss of income. . . .It is surely misleading, if not unfair, to single out one tax for criticism based on a property shared by all alternative taxes."[14]

The two lectures on George given in 1883 at St. Andrews Hall, London, by Arnold Toynbee, Oxford economist and eponymous uncle of the noted historian, represented Toynbee's last intellectual effort. In the words of one who heard them, they betrayed "unmistakeable signs of nervous exhaustion and physical collapse";[15] a few weeks after their delivery the speaker died at the early age of thirty-one, without having had an opportunity to check or revise the shorthand transcript of them. Their criticisms, which are complicated and difficult to follow, center upon alleged inconsistencies in George's wage theory. According to Philip Wicksteed, who was also present, Toynbee's concessions were "large and significant."[16] His objections are subjected to friendly but unfavorable analysis by H. Llewelyn Davies in an article[17] that appeared soon after the republication (as an appendix to the 1894 edition of Toynbee's famous *Lectures on the Industrial Revolution*) of the transcript.

Arthur Crump, in a thirty-two page onslaught ominously entitled *An Exposure of the Pretensions of Mr. Henry George*,[18] upon examining the first three books of *Progress and Poverty*, finds them such a "confused mass of inconsistencies, contradictions, fallacies, and absurdities" that he concludes that it would be a waste of time to bother with the other seven. This effusion is utterly splenetic, and the reliability of its interpretation of George may be judged by the fact that it upbraids him for "preaching against capitalists," which, of course, he never did.

In 1884, the same year as Crump's attack, Isaac B. Cooke published *Progress and Poverty: A Reply to Mr. George*.[19] This twenty-two page pamphlet is characterized by a courteous, dignified tenor that contrasts pleasantly with Crump's shrillness. Cooke begins by accepting George's contention that poverty has accompanied progress, and calls the problem "one of surpassing importance, worthy of our deepest study." Yet the last half of his work is almost wholly devoted to denying the existence of the problem that he had earlier declared to be so vital. Some of his arguments are complacent in the highest degree. For example, he holds that "the simple difference between those who habitually spend less than and those who habitually spend all that they earn, will account for most of the discrepancy between luxury and squalor"; that insofar as the increase of wealth in Britain did not diminish pauperism, it was because of the free choice of the people, who, though they "had the opportunity of improvement, . . .preferred the increase of numbers to improvement in condition"; and that laborers need only "raise themselves to the rank of capitalists" in order to be "enabled to form eligible terms of co-partnership in the undertakings in which they obtain employment. . . ." He also holds that even if the entire yield of all production came to landlords in the form of rent, most of it, being perishable, could not be stored indefinitely and would have to be distributed in exchange for labor, and that, in fact, "in ordinary circumstances, the shares appropriated to rent and interest are eventually distributed almost wholly as wages." He misconceives George as defining wages only as the share of production received by the agricultural laborer, so that "the mechanics and artisan classes are left without provision"—a notion that has no basis in any of George's writings. Cooke does venture two more promising lines of criticism: The first is that human labor can create nothing, but can only modify natural materials. Hence George's doctrine, strictly interpreted, cannot justify the ownership of *anything*. (Curiously, Murray Rothbard uses essentially the same argument to justify the ownership of *everything* to which labor has been applied, including land.[20]) The second is that land ownership is not properly stigmatized as monopolistic so long as land is available for purchase in the open market. These ideas, however, are merely thrown out in passing. Had they been adequately developed, Cooke's critique might have been of genuine importance.

More worthy of consideration, if for no other reason than that its author eventually came to occupy the highest office in the British government, is a little-known paper by Arthur J. Balfour, then a mere M.P., presented at the London Industrial Remuneration Conference of 1885, and carried in the report of its proceedings published the same year. Entitled "Land, Land Reformers, and the Nation," this work includes nine pages of scathing attack on George's reasoning, some important subtleties of which, however, Balfour appears to have overlooked (perhaps deliberately for forensic reasons). Thus he scores George for inconsistency in holding that the return given by nature to capital over and above that which accrues to the labor expended in its use or exchange, may be with justice privately appropriated, while that given to land may not—a reproach that ignores the key points: (a) that capital, unlike land, is produced by labor; (b) that the private appropriation of its yield does not represent a toll upon access to natural opportunity; and (c) that, according to George, the added return arising from the active powers of nature in certain modes of production is equalized to capital in all modes. One of Balfour's most sarcastic arguments is that the full application of George's principles would extinguish any right to property acquired by the sale of land. "The receiver of stolen goods clearly should not be allowed to retain the wealth which he enjoys only through having passed on those goods to somebody else." He evidently did not know that four years previously George had anticipated and rebutted this attempt at reductio ad absurdum in "The Great-Great Grandson of Captain Kidd," a chapter of *The Irish Land Question.*

Also included in the annals of the conference is "Social Remedies," a paper by Frederic Harrison,* a prolific litterateur and leader of the London Society of Positivists. In 1908 it was reprinted by Macmillan of New York in *National and Social Problems*, a collection of Harrison's essays. While expressing strong appreciation of George's powers as a critic of the status quo, and while sympathetic to the idea of taxing land values more heavily, the author rejects George's "pretended panacea" as "chimerical and futile." As with Balfour's argument just cited, much of his gravamen was anticipated and dealt with in "The Great-Great Grandson of Captain Kidd." Otherwise his main objection seems to be either that George contemplated the confiscation of improved and not just "prairie" land values, or that the prairie value of land, at least in Britain, would be seriously inadequate as a basis for taxation. His illustrations are limited to farms, and he evidently assumes that all improvements that "merge with the soil" are attributable to landowners' outlays.

In 1884 George's own British publisher, Kegan Paul, brought out *The Nationalisation of Land*, an expanded version of a twenty-three-page article in the *Contemporary Review* the previous year by Samuel Smith. Because of the misconception signaled by the title, much of Smith's criticism has little bearing on what George actually proposed. Somewhat incongruously, after roundly condemning what he takes to be George's program, this Liberal M.P. concedes that "property in land ought not to be as absolute as property in chattels," and deplores the granting away of vast tracts to speculators in the New World, and the garnering of unearned increments by suburban landowners in the Old.

Next to be noted is *Progress and Robbery*,[21] an elaborate (seventy-page) but superficial assault by J. Bleeker Miller, consisting largely of three speeches

*Not to be confused with Fred Harrison, the contributor to this volume.

delivered on behalf of the Tammany opposition during George's New York mayoralty campaign of 1886. It accuses George of having borrowed, without attribution, his ideas from Considérant and his phraseology from Proudhon, and labels him a "demi-communist," while (one observes with amazement) paying respectful compliments to Lassalle and Marx. Small wonder that of this work Barker remarks that "there is little, indeed, to be said about quality."[22]

In 1887 Charles H. Kerr & Company, the Chicago firm that has since come to be identified with Marxist publications, brought out *Progress from Poverty: Review and Criticism of Henry George's "Progress and Poverty" and "Protection or Free Trade"*, a work that, far from being Marxist, was not even reformist in character. The author was one Giles Badger Stebbins, and it ran to sixty-four pages, but they were of less than duodecimo size. This book contains numerous misrepresentations, holding, for example, that George advocated land nationalization, denied property rights in improvements, excluded brainwork from his definition of labor, apologized for chattel slavery, and sought "to make the laborer the master and monarch over the capitalist." It also advances the erroneous idea that taxes on land are shifted to the tenant. For the rest, it consists mainly of paraphrases and extracts from other critics, especially George Basil Dixwell.

The same year saw the publication by Hill and Harvey, a Baltimore firm, of a rambling indictment of the "socialism" of Henry George and Herbert Spencer(!)—*Ownership and Natural Right*, by R. P. I. Holaind, S.J., a professor at Woodstock College. This feeble work of 176 pages, prefaced by an effusive letter of commendation from Archbishop Corrigan of New York (George's adversary in the McGlynn affair) amounts to little more than a pastiche of extracts from Roman and canon law as well as from more modern sources—in some cases (e.g., Locke) selected in such a way as to give a distorted impression. It is worth mentioning here only because it was, for some reason I cannot fathom, regarded as sufficiently important to warrant a French edition, *Le Socialisme americain. La Propriété et le droit naturel* (Paris and Brussels, 1900), which is the only edition listed in most catalogues. Interestingly, although French was Holaind's native tongue, the translation was done by one Edmond J. P. Buron.

Alluring Absurdities: Fallacies of Henry George was the work of M. W. Meagher, published by the American News Company, New York, in 1889. One hundred and ninety-three pages in length, this book is devoted largely to a minute critical analysis of selected passages by George, and manages to score a number of debater's points against him, which is scarcely surprising since its author was founder of the National Debating Association, with offices at Cooper Union. These points are, however, for the most part fairly trivial, and some even puerile in their superficiality. Meagher delights in exposing petty contradictions and imperfect analogies (often taken out of context), but nowhere does he really come to grips with George's central arguments. The book exhibits some of the more unpleasant characteristics of the forensic approach: captious logic-chopping and a tone of arrogant pomposity.

The March 1892 issue of the *Annals of the American Academy of Political and Social Science* carried "The Basis of Interest: A Criticism of the Solution Offered by Mr. Henry George." It was the product of Dwight M. Lowrey, who found George's doctrine of interest "little more than a tissue of fallacies," while acclaiming George as *"facile princeps* among all American economists" in almost every other area of economic analysis. Were it not for the restricted nature of its topic and for the fact that it undertakes to overthrow a theory that few have ventured to defend, this keenly argued paper would warrant more than a mere notice here.

An unlikely parallel is drawn by Arthur Kitson in his "Criticism of Henry George's Single Tax Theory" (*American Journal of Politics*, October 1894) between George and the arch-protectionist, William McKinley, on the grounds that both advocated the use of taxation (quite apart from the revenue produced therefrom) to effect "socialistic" remedies for economic ills. Like R. C. Rutherford (to whose more sizable attack Collier has devoted chapter 15 in the present work), Kitson cites chapter and verse of *Progress and Poverty* to try to show that it is self-refuting. His chief argument is that if a man has, as George contends, a right to the full product of his labor, it is just as unjust for him to have to pay rent to the community for the use of land as to a private owner. Kitson was answered by three writers in the course of the following year. The first, Isaac Feinberg, admitted inconsistencies in George, but claimed that they did not invalidate the merits of the single-tax idea. The second, R. W. Joslyn, agreed with many of Kitson's criticisms, but applauded the single tax (perhaps with tongue in cheek) because he imagined that it would do away with all sale and rental of lands. The last, George Bernard, defended George against Kitson's charge of inconsistency, citing a passage in *Progress and Poverty*[23] to demonstrate that George had anticipated and disposed of the principal chain of reasoning on which the charge was based.[24]

Fred Harrison, in a note to his chapter 14 on Marxist critics of George in the present book, expresses chagrin that he was unable to examine and discuss Algie M. Simons's *Single Tax vs. Socialism* (Chicago: Charles H. Kerr & Company, 1899), for it is considered by Geiger to be among the most effective presentations of the Marxist position on the subject. (Simons was editor of the *International Socialist Review*.) After protracted searching, I finally located (at the Walter Reuther Library at Wayne State University) a copy of this scarce work sturdy enough to allow duplication. Perusal of it left me mystified as to the basis for Geiger's evaluation, and convinced that Harrison need have wasted no regrets over the book's unavailability to him. Save for its plain language and clear organization, this twenty-nine-page screed has little to commend it, for almost its whole argument rests upon such Marxist dogmas as the dialectic and the class struggle, which are simply asserted without so much as an attempt at proof. Simons ridicules the Georgist "landophobia," as he calls it, holding that inasmuch as land has been long since surpassed by capital as the dominant factor in production, "to insist on again raising it to prominence is to advocate the relapse to barbarism." The coming fundamental social change, he pronounces, will be the seizure of capital by the workers when, in the fullness of time, the capitalist system has ripened to the point of rottenness. Unfortunately for the cogency of this thesis, Marxism has never yet come to power in an advanced capitalist society, but only in places where the paramount feature of the economy was the concentration of land ownership in the hands of a small segment of the population.

In 1900 there appeared *Taxation of Land Values and the Single Tax*

(Glasgow: James MacLehose and Sons, 1900), a slim book by that British popularizer of the Austrian school of economics, William Smart, professor of political economy at the University of Glasgow. As admitted in the preface, this work "does not profess to be a contribution to economic science," and only the last twenty-seven pages of it deal specifically with George's doctrine. The rest is primarily taken up with the hostile evaluation of two concrete proposals for legislation (the London County Council Resolutions, and the Glasgow Land Value Assessment Bill), Smart's analyses of which have to do largely with complicated peculiarities of English and Scottish land tenure. The author speaks from the standpoint of the "equal sacrifice" theory of taxation and condemns George's proposal as confiscatory.

"The Economics of Henry George's 'Progress and Poverty,' " by Edgar H. Johnson, was published in the *Journal of Political Economy*, November 1910. After twenty pages of highly technical analysis accusing George of inconsistency, special pleading, and inattention to empirical facts, this critic concludes by acknowledging the truth of three of the most salient Georgist principles: that land is the gift of nature rather than the product of human toil; that its value is owing to the activities of the community rather than of the owner; and that a tax upon it is not, generally speaking, a burden on industry.

In 1912 one E. B. Silvers brought out in Kansas City a 105-page broadside, *Single Tax A Fallacy: a Refutation of the Theory of Single Taxation as Announced by Henry George*. It was evidently published by himself. Most of its criticisms are the standard ones, but it deserves a reference because of its ingenious argument that since, according to George, wages and interest are determined at the margin, the single tax, by leaving the landowner only that portion of his product classifiable as wages and interest, would condemn him to a marginal existence. Thus he would have no inducement to make his land produce more than a bare living. For all his recurrent emphasis upon the margin, Silvers does not seem to understand its functional role in George's system, nor to take account of any of the qualifications or subtleties in George's treatment of it. He simply introduces it mechanically, oblivious to context, whenever he feels inclined to deal a particularly devastating blow.

A ripple of attention was attracted by Alvin S. Johnson's "The Case Against the Single Tax," which appeared in the *Atlantic Monthly* of January 1914 as one in a series of three articles on the subject of the Henry George plan. Johnson contended that the lure of unearned increment is essential to development (a notion readily susceptible of empirical refutation), and that the main burden of the plan would fall upon the middle class (as if, even if this were so, the same is not notoriously true of our existing system). Although ably formulated and thus not without surface plausibility, the piece is far too slight (ten pages) to constitute a very thoroughgoing critique. Several pages are devoted to the refutation of Johnson's article by Charles B. Fillebrown in *The Principles of Natural Taxation*.[25]

The first decade and a half of this century witnessed a series of unsuccessful campaigns in Washington and Oregon to introduce by ballot various approaches to the single tax. A Seattle newspaper editor, Charles H. Shields, rose to the fore as leader of the opposition. By 1914 his *Single Tax Exposed* (published by The Trade Register, Inc., Seattle) had gone into seven editions and reached 190 pages. Forcefully written but surprisingly free of ad hominems, this polemic had great impact in bringing about the defeat of Georgist measures in 1912 and 1914. However, its argument rests to a large extent upon the false assumptions that the single tax would destroy *all*, not merely speculative, land values; that George anticipated that under his sytem land titles would revert to the government; and that land monopoly is a problem peculiar only to agrarian society. The latter part of the book is devoted to showing that the spectacular development of Western Canada immediately after 1910, which Georgist propaganda had attributed to the exemption of improvements from taxation, was really owing to other causes, and had, in any case, come to a halt. While Shields was correct in faulting single taxers for having used the Western Canadian boom to illustrate the efficacy of their program, by the same token, the recession that followed it cannot be cited to demonstrate the program's failure. For, as he himself observes, although improvements were indeed exempted, land-value taxes were kept even lower than in most cities below the border.

The Fallacies of Henry George, reprinted from *The Malthusian* by the Malthusian League, London, around 1922, and written by its president, Dr. C. V. Drysdale, represents the sort of tendentious approach that one might expect from such a source. Drysdale seeks not only to refute George's attack upon Malthusianism, but also to resuscitate, long after its abandonment by John Stuart Mill, the theory of the wages-fund, erroneously assuming that George, because of his opposition to this theory, regarded the capitalist as an exploiter of labor. Drysdale's argument (which runs to forty-two pages) is persuasively expressed, but contains little that had not been said before.

The year 1922 also saw Mario de Tezanos Pinto issue his 351-page volume *El impuesto unico y la exención de impuesto a las mejoras: Exposición y critica del georgismo y de las doctrinas que lo fundamentan*, brought out by Pedro García of Buenos Aires. This massive work is sympathetic to several aspects of Georgism, especially the untaxing of improvements, and advocates a substantially higher tax on land values. But the author (who held a doctorate in law and social sciences) takes issue with many of George's arguments. Most of his criticisms, however, are secondhand. Part of the book is devoted to problems of applicability in Argentina, and particularly in Buenos Aires Province, where a Georgist political party was then campaigning with considerable temporary success.

Hugh Wheeler Sanford, a Knoxville ironworks owner, devoted part of the first volume of his book *The Business of Life: Economics for Business Men* (New York: Oxford University Press, 1924) to an unfavorable examination of George's theory of rent. Because Sanford used nonstandard terminology, his critique gives the appearance of being more original than it actually was; one of his main arguments goes back at least as far as Isaac Cooke.

Influential economists such as Henry Fawcett, Frank Fetter, M. Slade Kendrick, Henry Rogers Seager, Frank Taussig, and many others gave brief critical attention to George, often in textbooks; their comments are succinctly reviewed in Steven Cord's useful *Henry George: Dreamer or Realist?*.

There are numerous other works that could be included in this catalogue if space permitted. But before moving on to another topic, I do wish to indicate my personal regret that it was not deemed advisable to devote a chapter to *Progress and Poverty Reviewed, and Its Fallacies Exposed*, by my late friend

Spencer Heath,[26] whom I remember with esteem, and who would have welcomed even a harsh examination of his views. Since Heath's ideas have achieved currency only to the extent that they are reflected in the work of Murray Rothbard, I felt that they could more appropriately be considered briefly in the context of chapter 25 below, primarily devoted to Rothbard.

III

In the eighteen years of life remaining to George after the completion of *Progress and Poverty*, he delivered himself of seven other substantial literary efforts: *The Irish Land Question* (1881), *Social Problems* (1883), "The 'Reduction to Iniquity' " (which first appeared as an article in *The Nineteenth Century* in 1884), *Protection or Free Trade* (1886), *The Condition of Labor, an Open Letter to Pope Leo XIII* (1891), *A Perplexed Philosopher* (1892), and the unfinished *Science of Political Economy* (posthumously published in 1898). In these other works the ideas of *Progress and Poverty* are supplemented, approached from somewhat different angles, and accorded varying emphases, but never appreciably altered.[27] It remains his chief d'oeuvre. In it, Geiger remarks, his economic thoughts "reached their highest development,"[28] and in it his philosophy finds its most complete and systematic expression. According to Jacob Oser it "probably had the greatest circulation of any non-fiction book in the English language before 1900 except for the Bible."[29] Understandably, therefore, it is upon this work that most of the critiques of George's doctrine are focused, the more so inasmuch as it was through it that the doctrine first gained worldwide notice and attracted critical comment. That a like emphasis should be exhibited by the present volume is thus not to be explained merely by a wish to commemorate the centenary.

Few, if any, of George's ideas had not been advanced by earlier thinkers, although he arrived at his fundamental thesis independently.[30] He disclaimed novelty for his beliefs, averring that "social truth never is, never can be new. . . ."[31] Never before, however, had these beliefs been brought together in such a powerful synthesis nor stated so impressively. In the words of one of his more enlightened critics, "The sublimity his transformations impart to the commonest doctrines remind one that the accusation of plagiarism was brought against Handel,"[32] a comment endorsed by Geiger as "probably the best statement of this whole matter of the precise degree of George's originality."[33]

Without being dogmatic "true believers," the authors of the ensuing chapters are all sympathetic, more or less, to George's contribution. No apology need be made for this; since his most ardent current antagonist has acknowledged "great respect for many aspects of Henry George,"[34] it would be today a singularly narrow and ignorant commentator who could not find something to appreciate in the sweep and richness of his thought. No attempt has been made to impose uniformity of viewpoint upon the contributors to this volume, and the attentive reader will descry some points of disagreement among them. They have approached their topics in the spirit that George himself commended when, at the outset of his great essay, he declared: "I propose to beg no question, to shrink from no conclusion, but to follow truth wherever it may lead.''[35] Neither has there been any effort to impose uniformity of style. For example, the method of subdividing chapters has been left up to each individual contributor, and the British spellings (e.g. ''Georgeist'') of Douglas and Harrison have been retained.

A few words in defense of the format of this volume may be in order. Had the study been intended simply as a typological analysis of the various possible arguments against George, it would have lent itself to topical arrangement. But since it was meant to be an evaluative review of arguments that have, in fact, been historically advanced by specific critics, a topical arrangement would have had the disadvantage of failing to convey the structural pattern of each man's overall critique. Feeling that understanding often suffers when an argument is lifted from its matrix in a person's thought, I decided to eschew the topical approach as prone, in this context, to be artificial and misleading. Attempts to organize the chapters under ideological headings fell foul of the fact that some critics overlap ideological categories while others argue on technical grounds that do not admit of ideological classification. It therefore seemed advisable to adopt the chronological-geographical format revealed in the table of contents. If the reader is disconcerted to find Hyndman, Marx, and Engels discussed in a chapter listed under the heading of ''American Critics,'' the answer is that it was logical to treat them in connection with Gronlund, whose two tracts against George represent the most considerable Marxist effort to refute him. (Although Danish-born, Gronlund was a naturalized citizen of the United States, and his attack was deliberately geared to distinctively American considerations.) As for authors such as Seligman, whose criticisms of George continued well into the twentieth century, and Ely and Davenport, whose began in the nineteenth, their placement has been determined by the dates of their most extensive writings on the subject.

The concluding chapter is not meant to be a summary, but is rather an expression of my own views as to the necessary modifications, current relevance, and future prospects of the doctrine that is the subject of this work. Although it in some measure reflects the judgments of my contributors, it does not presume to speak for them, and any faults it contains are my responsibility alone.

Notes

1. Count Leo Tolstoy, ''A Great Iniquity,'' *The Public* (Chicago), 19 August 1905, p. 18. Reprinted from the *London Times*, 1 August 1905.

2. This assertion is documented in a painstaking survey by Steven B. Cord, *Henry George; Dreamer or Realist?* (Philadelphia: University of Pennsylvania Press, 1965). See especially pp. 171-80 and 186-91.

3. Ibid., p. 243.

4. For Tolstoy, see above, n. 1. For Sun Yat-sen, see his interview with American journalists as reported in *The Public* (Chicago), 12 April 1912, p. 349, in which he is quoted as saying: ''The teachings of your single-taxer, Henry George, will be the basis of our program of reform.'' For Nicholas Murray Butler, see his 1931 commencement address at Columbia University, printed under the auspices of the office of the secretary of the university (New York, 1931). For John Dewey, see the following statement from his ''An Appreciation of Henry George,'' the introduction to *Significant Paragraphs from Progress and Poverty*, edited by Harry Gunnison Brown (New York: Robert Schalkenbach Foundation, 1929): ''His is one of the great names among the world's

social philosophers. It would require less than the fingers of the two hands to enumerate those who from Plato down rank with him. . . . No man, no graduate of a higher educational institution, has a right to regard himself as an educated man in social thought unless he has some first-hand acquaintance with the theoretical contribution of this great American thinker."

5.   The word *almost* should be noted. J. Bleeker Miller and Arthur Crump (whose works are briefly characterized later in this introduction) make George out to be a plagiarist and a charlatan, respectively. The charge of plagiarism is also brought by George's disgruntled associate, James L. Sullivan, in "Ideo-Kleptomania, the Case of Henry George," *Twentieth Century*, 10 October 1889, and by Alexander del Mar in his *Science of Money* (London: G. Bell and Sons, 1885), pp. 98-99 n.

For tributes from four of George's unequivocal opponents, see Edward Atkinson, "A Single Tax on Land," *Nineteenth Century*, July 1890, p. 394; John Bates Clark, *Distribution of Wealth* (New York: Macmillan, 1899), p. viii; Richard T. Ely, *The Labor Movement in America* (New York: Macmillan, 1886), p. 126; and Francis A. Walker, "The Tide of Economic Thought," *Publications of the American Economic Association* 6 (1891): 20.

6.   George's work on Spencer, *A Perplexed Philosopher,* first published in 1892, runs to 276 pages in the Robert Schalkenbach Foundation edition of 1946. His reply to the Duke of Argyll, "The Reduction to Iniquity," originally appeared in *Nineteenth Century,* July 1884. It is included, together with the Duke's arraignment and two other essays by George, in *The Land Question* [and Other Essays] (New York: Robert Schalkenbach Foundation, 1953). His reply to Atkinson was carried, along with Atkinson's fullest critique, in *Century Illustrated Monthly Magazine* 40 (July 1890): 385-403.

7.   Thomas Shearman's article, "Henry George's Mistakes," *Forum* 8 (1889): 40-52, dealt with criticisms advanced by the Duke of Argyll, W. H. Mallock, Abram Hewitt, Edward Atkinson and W. T. Harris. The objections of E. R. A. Seligman are among those treated in Shearman's *Natural Taxation* (New York: Doubleday and McClure, 1888).

8.   Max Hirsch, *Democracy versus Socialism,* 4th ed. (New York: Robert Schalkenbach Foundation, 1948). The chapters on Atkinson and Walker are pt. 5, chaps. 6 and 7, respectively. The shorter discussions are found in pt. 5, chaps. 2, 4, and 5. *Democracy versus Socialism* first appeared in 1901.

9.   See n. 6.

10.   Charles Albro Barker, *Henry George* (New York: Oxford University Press, 1955), p. 426.

11.   George William Wilshere, 1st Baron Bromwell, *Nationalisation of Land: A Review of Mr. Henry George's "Progress & Poverty"* (London).

12.   Charles Gide, "De quelques nouvelles doctrines sur la propréte foncière," *Journal des Économistes,* 4th ser., 22 (1883):169-99.

13.   Kenneth Back, "Land Value Taxation in Light of Current Assessment Theory and Practice," in D. M. Holland, ed., *The Assessment of Land Value* (Madison, Wis.: University of Wisconsin Press, 1970).

14.   Charles F. Collier, "Henry George's System of Economics: Analysis and Criticism," Ph. D. Dissertation, Duke University, 1976, p. 215. Collier is here directly addressing a statement by Thames Williamson, but he mentions it as typical of a line of argument also set forth by Francis A. Walker, Henry Fawcett, Robert Flint, Arthur T. Hadley, Roland R. Renne, and Richard T. Ely (with George R. Wicker).

15.   H. Llewelyn Davies, "Arnold Toynbee and Henry George," *Free Review* (London) 4 (1895): 34. The lectures of George were first published by K. Paul, Trench & Co., 1883.

16.   Philip Wicksteed in a letter to Henry George, 4 February 1883. Cited by Barker, *Henry George*, p. 392.

17.   See n. 15.

18.   Arthur Crump, *An Exposure of the Pretentions of Mr. Henry George, as Set Forth in his Book "Progress and Poverty"* (London: Effingham Wilson, 1884).

19.   Isaac B. Cooke, *Progress and Poverty: A Reply to Mr. George* (Liverpool: Young, 1884).

20.   See Murray Rothbard, *For a New Liberty* (New York: Macmillan, 1973), p. 34.

21.   J. Bleeker Miller, *Progress and Robbery and Progress and Justice. An Answer to Henry George the Demi-Communist* (New York: Baker & Taylor, 1887).

22.   Barker, *Henry George*, p. 554.

23.   Henry George, *Progress and Poverty*, 75th anniversary ed. (New York: Robert Schalkenbach Foundation, 1954), p. 343.

24.   The replies by Feinberg, Joslyn, and Bernard appeared in 6: 1-12 and 312-16, and 7: 425-39, respectively, of the *American Magazine of Civics*, successor to the *American Journal of Politics*.

25.   Charles B. Fillebrown, *The Principles of Natural Taxation* (Chicago: A. C. McClurg, 1917), pp. 201-7.

26.   Spencer Heath, *Progress and Poverty Reviewed, and Its Fallacies Exposed* (Baltimore, Md.: Science of Society Foundation, 1952).

27.   See Henry George, *The Science of Political Economy* (1897; reprint ed. New York: Robert Schalkenbach Foundation, 1962), p. 203.

28.   George Raymond Geiger, *The Philosophy of Henry George* (New York: Macmilan, 1933), p. 81 n.

29.   Jacob Oser, *Henry George* (New York: Twayne Publishers, 1974), p. 68.

30.   See Samuel Milliken, "Forerunners of Henry George," *Single Tax Year Book*, Joseph Dana Miller, ed. (New York: Single Tax Review Publishing Co., 1917), pp. 306-43; Arthur Nichols Young, *The Single Tax Movement in the United States* (Princeton, N.J.: Princeton University Press, 1916), chap. 1; and Geiger, *The Philosophy of Henry George*, chap. 4.

31.   In his reply to an oral criticism at Oxford by Alfred Marshall. See Anna George de Mille, *Henry George: Citizen of the World*, Don C. Shoemaker, ed. (Chapel Hill, N.C.: University of North Carolina Press, 1950), p. 130.

32.   Robert Scott Moffat, *Mr. Henry George the "Orthodox"* (London: Remington & Co., 1885), p. 5.

33.   Geiger, *The Philosophy of Henry George*, p. 213 n.

34.   Murray N. Rothbard, *A Reply to Georgist Criticisms* (Irvington-on-Hudson, N.Y.: Foundation for Economic Education, July 1957), p. 3.

35.   George, *Progress and Poverty*, p. 13.

2

The Essential Henry George

BY LOUIS WASSERMAN

I agreed to undertake this assignment from motives practical and pedagogical, though not entirely without a touch of sentiment. There was an occasion in my undergraduate days when my academic progress depended upon a forty-minute report concerning an American philosopher. Through one of those fortuities which illumine the paths of even the dull-witted, I stumbled upon Henry George. Thereupon, as I remember, lights shone and bells rang. I proceeded to make myself the advocate of the single tax, and—since no one in class had heard of it before—my report was a resounding success. That was in the 1930s, and I have learned since how to temper my enthusiasms and moderate my aims. But such moments of discovery are to be treasured; they come far too seldom in academic life. Perhaps, then, the following summary of *Progress and Poverty* may serve to shine a light or to ring a bell for some student of this present generation.

It was the role of land in society that constituted the massive preoccupation of Henry George, and the fact that the publication of his major work in 1879 generated sympathetic rumblings throughout much of the world indicated that he had touched upon a fundamental theme of political economy. It is strange, then, that the subject of land economics, particularly in its theoretical aspects, receives such scant attention at present. Perhaps this is because of the inertia that attends upon a long-institutionalized social arrangement, as differentiated from the otherwise fluid elements of an industrial economy. But it may also be that economists have simply neglected that which seemed to George of such paramount concern: the relationship of land rent to fiscal policy and the impact of both upon industrial development, income distribution, urban growth, and the like.

The land, according to both Genesis and geology, preceded the advent of man into the world, and there is no doubt that landed wealth has enjoyed a more persistent history than any other form. Even today, when a sophisticated economics has transmuted every kind of wealth into some variety of liquid capital, the land has continued to play its unique role. It is the very assumption upon which human existence is based, and the taken-for-granted foundation of all productive activity; it can be modified by man, but not created or destroyed except in tiny patches, and its essential qualities are impervious to either boom or depression.

If—as the dictum prescribes—a book should be so written that its message can be presented in a single sentence, the argument of *Progress and Poverty* might be stated thus: that the natural land ought everywhere to be regarded as a community, rather than as a private, resource and that its rental value should accordingly be recaptured as public revenue by the community, thereby eliminating the need of any taxes upon productive enterprise.

It is by no means adventitious that this statement combines an ethical propostion with an economic prescription. Henry George was primarily a social philosopher (the greatest this country has had, according to John Dewey) rather than a professional economist. But it was precisely the core of his conviction that the two realms of man's life, the moral and the material, must be brought into harmony. If men are degraded by the conditions of their labor, if their wages can buy no more than animal existence, or if some part of their effort is appropriated by nonproducers, then how, George asks, can such an economic system accord with either natural or human justice? He is confident that it is possible to find rational, and therefore just, principles that can be made to govern the production and distribution of wealth in society.

It is the search for such economic principles that George undertakes in his *Progress and Poverty*. In the course of nearly six hundred pages he makes an exhaustive analysis of the principal economic categories of his time: wealth, value, labor, capital, interest, and land. His writing, it may be observed, shows evidence not only of an immense erudition but of an uncommon capacity for inductive observation and creative symthesis. His emphasis on the role of land resources in wealth production was not original—it had been formulated often since biblical days—but he gave to that theme perhaps its definitive statement. It would be difficult to discuss any aspect of land and its treatment today without touching upon the issues he raised.

The "sovereign remedy" that George proposed as the way to end poverty was to shift the entire burden of taxation from the products of labor and capital to the socially created rental value of land. Such a simplistic scheme was bound to repel many sober minds, and this fact doubtless contributed to consigning George's writings to near oblivion in economic circles. If so, it was an untimely fate. The full single tax is not a serious fiscal proposal today, if only because there are no political prospects for its adoption anywhere on a national scale. But George's central principle—that the incidence of taxation should bear on the value of land rather than upon productive enterprise and improvements—remains a lively issue of fiscal reform. Under the generic title of "land-value taxation" this principle has received wide application in such forms as the following: taxation of the land at a higher rate than the improvements thereon; full or partial exemption of improvements, the lost revenue being made up by an increased levy on the land; a surtax on absentee land-ownership; and, in the effort to reduce speculation, a high rate of tax on the profits derived from land sales. Such practices are common in Australia and New Zealand, with scattered local applications to be found in Western Canada, the Union of South Africa, and elsewhere.[1] Denmark provides generous exemptions on improvements, offsetting this by both a higher rate on the land and a national tax on the increment of land values.

In the United States the common practice is to include a tax on the raw land as a component of the general property tax, which otherwise bears most heavily on improvements. Beyond this there is a scattering of "single-tax" enclaves in Delaware, New Jersey, and Alabama, and in the irrigation districts of California, as well as the graded tax plans of Pittsburgh and Scranton, Pennsylvania. A series of campaigns to enact land-value measures in several states of the Union during the first two decades of this century failed of success. Yet the movement to effect tax reform along some such lines continues to show an enduring vitality—nourished, at bottom, by the twin irritants of rising land costs and onerous taxes on production. What is typically sought by land-value taxers today is a modest advance along Georgist lines, such as the enactment of local option laws, which would enable municipalities to free from taxation some or all of the value of improvements by transferring the tax to the unimproved value of the land.

The statement of George's doctrine that follows will focus primarily upon that which distinguishes his work and which remains of contemporary interest—that is, his contribution to land economics and fiscal policy. Those sections of *Progress and Poverty* which treat at length of classical economic theories now outmoded or of little relevance will, accordingly, be touched upon but briefly.

The Problem

George's economic analysis is set in the context of America's industrial development of the late nineteenth century. The "paradox" of that development, as he saw it, lay in the persistence of widespread poverty in the face of an unparalleled increase of wealth. The use of machine technology had expanded production, cheapened costs, and multiplied gross income; for the first time in human history the prospect of material well-being for all had come within the range of possibility. But the actual consequence, wherever industry flourished, was to enhance the contrast between rich and poor: a small class lived in ostentatious luxury while the working class survived in wretched poverty. Despite long hours of work and rising productivity, the wages of labor rose little or not at all, and it was, unaccountably, in the oldest centers of manufacturing that the worst conditions prevailed. Industrial booms periodically gave way to industrial collapse, with workers and enterprisers alike suffering from the breakdown. Was it possible that poverty must inevitably accompany technical progress, or did the explanation lie in man's faulty provisions for the production and distribution of wealth?

George examined the prevailing economic doctrines of his day, in particular the wages-fund theory and the Malthusian thesis, but he found in them no satisfactory explanation of the problem. As opposed to the former, he contended that wages are produced, not out of a preexisting fund of capital, but by the labor for which they are paid. As opposed to the latter, he sought to demonstrate that there is no warrant, either in experience or analogy, for the assumption that there is any natural tendency in population to increase faster than subsistence. Moreover, he rejected entirely the argument that there existed an inherent conflict between labor and capital, or that either the growth of industrial monopoly or an excess of competition was responsible for the persistence of poverty.

The Rewards of Production

Following the pattern laid down by the classical economists, George proceeded to identify three factors of production: the land and its resources (as natural opportunity); labor (as every form of human effort, mental as well as physical); and capital (as wealth used to produce more wealth). Among these he found labor to be the primary force; from its application to the resources of the land comes all that is tangibly produced, processed, and transported by man. Capital, though it may be identified as a separate factor of production, is actually the product of previously accomplished labor that has not been directly consumed but is stored up for further use. The forms assumed by capital are various—machinery, stocks of merchandise, warehouses, railway terminals, investment funds, and the like—but all are simply at one or more remove the products of prior human labor.

The production of goods and services, then, is wholly accomplished by the combination of labor and capital working on the land. But this third factor, the land, while it is indispensable to all human effort, is itself wholly a passive agent. The site upon which labor is performed does not engage in the process of production; it is rather the physical surface upon which human effort is enabled to move, build, mine, drill, fabricate, and harvest its products.

But what is the situation when the rewards of production come to be distributed? Although only labor and capital participate in the process, the income therefrom must be apportioned into three shares: as wages to labor, as interest to capital, and as rent to the landowner. Yet, as George repeatedly points out, the landowner, simply as owner, contributes no effort to the product; he is paid for possession alone. Just as he did not, in the first instance, create the land to which he holds title, so he takes no part in that which the farmer, enterpriser, or laborer produces upon that site. Nevertheless, under existing conditions, it is the landowner who controls access to the physical basis of production, and it is only after his claim to ground rent has been satisfied that the remainder of what has been produced goes to labor and capital.

As the cost of land rises, morever, the tribute paid to the landowner increases, thus serving to reduce the gains that labor and capital might expect through improved technology and productivity, ". . .hence, no matter what be the increase in productive power, if the increase in rent keeps pace with it, neither wages nor interest can increase."[2] Put alternatively: only to the extent that the rate of technical progress succeeds in outstripping the rise in land values will labor and capital be able to benefit from their increased productivity.

In summary, then, George finds the clue to the persistence of poverty in the improper distribution of production income; the fault, his analysis reveals, lies in the privilege granted to landowners to share in the rewards of production without themselves having contributed to that process.

The Special Character of Land as a Factor of Production

George defines the term *land* broadly to embrace the whole of man's natural physical environment: it includes not only the cultivable soil but the solid earth everywhere, fertile or infertile; all building sites, residential, commercial, and industrial; the natural resources of the earth, including minerals, petroleum, forests, and wildlife; the waterfronts with their natural beaches and harbors; the oceans, lakes, and rivers and all the natural goods therein; and even air space and air waves.[3] (It is in this broadly conceived sense that the term *land* will accordingly be used.)

All this, as George perceives it, is the gratuitous gift of nature to mankind, and the common endowment of the community that occupies it. In its natural state the land embodies no human labor and no capital investment. Rather, it represents economic and social opportunity, the indispensable condition upon which human beings are enabled to live, to build, to manufacture the needs of life—and beyond that, to create the amenities of their civilization. George's concept of the land is ecological in character; he views it as the natural milieu in which communities exist in interrelationship with the surrounding environment, animate and inanimate. The atmosphere, sunlight, and water—alike the gifts of nature—are contributing elements.

It is of the essence of George's argument to distinguish clearly between (a) the raw land, the physical endowment described above, and (b) the works of man that have been wrought upon the face of the earth. The first, be it repeated, is the common heritage, antecedent to man and provided for his benefit. But the works of man are, by contrast, the things of his own creation: the crops he has cultivated, the houses, barns, shops, theaters, office buildings, and industrial plants he has built; the railroads, mine shafts, piers, refineries, and the multitude of other goods with which he has adorned his civilization. All these products and "improvements" are the fruit of human labor, of man's mind and muscle, exerted individually or in cooperation with his fellow men. George summarizes thus the critical distinction he makes between human production and the raw land:

The essential character of the one class of things [man-made products] is that they embody labor, are brought into being by human exertion, their existence or non-existence, their increase or diminution, depending on man. The essential character of the other class of things [land] is that they do not embody labor, exist irrespective of human exertion and irrespective of man; they are the field or environment in which man finds himself, the storehouse from which his needs must be supplied, the raw material upon which and the forces with which alone his labor can act.[4].

Further, whereas human productivity is potentially unlimited, subject only to man's creative efforts, the amount of land, except for minor changes, is fixed and nonreproducible. (Technically, according to George, "made land" is not really land but wealth—and usually that form of wealth defined as capital.)

Land Value as a Social Creation

What is it that gives value to a piece of natural land? It is, George asserts, the result of the growth and development of the aggregate community. Without a population to occupy an area, to cultivate and build upon it or to utilize its products, there is no value in land; an isolated cultivator can do no more than wrest a subsistence from it. But as the community grows and prospers, as it diversifies its functions, augments its output, widens its markets, and expands its public services, the value of the land within its jurisdiction increases. A growing population means an enhanced demand for property, whether for homes, offices, markets, oil wells, or manufacturing—thus causing land prices to rise and marginal areas to be brought into profitable use. An acre in a remote farming district might be valued at only two hundred dollars, but a plot of equal size in more populous centers would show a scale of comparative values something like this: in a nearby town, five thousand dollars; in an urban residential section twenty to fifty thousand dollars; in the same city's business center, perhaps one hundred thousand to one million dollars. The wide range of site costs within a community's borders derives from such special factors as location, use, zoning provisions, available utilities, street improvements, transportation facilities, growth expectations, and the like—but these are all aspects of the community at large, the level of its population, and the opportunities it presents for residence and livelihood.

"The value of land," George asserts, "expresses in exact and tangible form the right of the community in land held by an individual."[5] It is the collective product of the community, to which all its constituent members have jointly contributed. The landowner, simply as legal title holder, has no control over the process of land-value creation—the acreage he owns will find its price level as surely when he is physically absent as present. (He may, of course, by speculative withholding, help to give his land an artificial value.) If he is a worker or enterpriser as well, however, he contributes to production in the same manner as other individuals, and like them deserves to receive the full yield of his efforts.

The Nature of Land Rent

George employs the term *rent* in a precise and explicit sense, to designate only that portion of income that accrues to landowners by virtue of their title to the raw land (or, if the site yields no income, what they would have to pay another for its use if they did not hold title to it).[6] He is at pains here to distinguish clearly between two kinds of payments that, in popular parlance, are usually combined. When an apartment-house tenant, for example, speaks of paying $200 a month "rent" to his landlord, he is in reality making two distinct payments at once: one part, say $140, is for use of the apartment itself, which is the "improvement" erected on the land; the remaining $60 is payment for the use of raw land, the ground site, and this alone is what George refers to by the term *rent*. If the apartment-house owner happens to own the land as well, he will retain the entire $200; if he does not, he must remit the $60 portion to the landowner as part of his payment for leasing the land. In either event it is possible to ascertain the share of the ground rent alone by determining what return the land site, if it were not built upon, would yield when leased to the highest bidder.

The only kind of rent George is concerned with, then, is ground rent, that which derives from the land alone. How does such rental value come about? George gives his full endorsement to the formulation expressed by the economist Ricardo: "The rent of land is determined by the excess of its produce over that which the same application [of labor and/or capital] can secure from the least productive land in use."[7] Production use is, of course, not limited to agriculture; every commercial and industrial activity must be performed upon some land site, for the use of which a ground rental must be paid its owner. Since the supply of land is limited and nonreproducible, this rental value depends upon what its users are required to pay for it in relation to marginal areas.

Land rent, accordingly, is established entirely by demand, irrespective of its inherent qualities. "Wherever land has an exchange value there is rent in the economic meaning of the term."[8] If the demand for a particular piece of land increases, its rent will increase. (George notes that this is not always the case with goods that are produced by labor: commodity prices may sometimes go down as well as up, depending upon the conditions of supply coupled with an elastic demand.)

George elaborates three principal factors that conduce to rent increase. The most important is that of population growth, which not only exerts demand pressure upon central and marginal areas but also carries with it a qualitative enrichment of community life. A second factor is the continuous improvement of industrial techniques, whose effect is to expand the production of wealth, to broaden the potential markets for goods and services, and thus to enhance the value of available land sites. Finally, there is the artificially induced factor of land speculation, the withholding of land from use in the expectation of higher sale price. This, George was convinced, was the principal cause of the disastrous boom-and-depression cycles that afflicted the economy:

> Given a progressive community, in which population is increasing and one improvement succeeds another. . .land must constantly increase in value. This steady increase naturally leads to speculation in which future increase is anticipated, and land values are carried beyond the point at which, under the existing conditions of production, their accustomed returns would be left to labor and capital. Production, therefore, begins to stop. . .owing to the failure of new increments of labor and capital to find employment at the accustomed rates.[9]

In brief, the practice of land speculation serves to compound the existing injustice: to the share already extracted by the landowner from the produce of labor and capital is added a bonus that discounts the rewards of future production. The effect of land speculation is that of enforcing "a lockout of labor and capital by landowners."[10]

The Sources of Taxation

It is notably in the field of fiscal policy, George contends, that the private appropriation of land rent is seen in its most mischievous form. Public revenue must somehow be obtained to support government services, but it is of the utmost consequence that the burden be assessed with equity and with the least detriment to the economy. Yet existing tax systems, George finds, perversely impose the heaviest burdens upon those who labor to produce, while at the same time bearing lightly upon the nonproducing landowners.

When workers and enterprisers combine their skills, savings, and inventiveness to produce goods and services, these are precisely the efforts that are penalized by current fiscal policies. If new machinery is obtained to speed production, or a swamp drained to build upon, or a house modernized to make it more livable, the tax collector levies upon the improvement as if it were a public nuisance. The result is that enterprise is discouraged, workers denied employment, improvements postponed, and land often debarred from its highest use. Symbolically as well as actually, the tenement appears a more attractive investment than a new structure.

By contrast, the landowner is treated with undeserved solicitude. He adds nothing to production, yet is taxed but lightly on the ground rent that the community has generated for him. And if he chooses to withhold his land from use, he is abetted in this by a lighter assessment.

George's strictures upon landlordism, however, do not indicate his primary concern. The thrust of his argument is that each man should receive the full reward of his individual production, however that share is competitively determined, and that no part of what he has produced should be taken from him in the form of taxation. The obverse of this is that no individual has the right to appropriate privately that which is the product of the collective community— namely, the rental value and increment of the land. Placing the two principles in conjunction, George concludes that the only tax that will not penalize individual effort and that will bear equitably upon all is a full (or nearly full) recapture tax on the common product of community development, the value of its land.

The Single-Tax Remedy

He puts the matter concisely thus: "What I, therefore, propose. . .is—*to appropriate rent by taxation.* . . .[and] *To abolish all taxation save that upon land values.*"[11] There is no need, George declares, to nationalize the land; it would neither be purchased nor expropriated by the state. Private titles would remain undisturbed, no owner or tenant would be dispossessed, and no limit would be put upon the amount of land that could be held by anyone.

> I do not propose either to purchase or to confiscate private property in land. The first would be unjust; the second, needless. Let the individuals who now hold it still retain, if they want to, possession of what they are pleased to call *their* land. Let them continue to call it *their* land. Let them buy and sell, and bequeath and devise it. . . .*It is not necessary to confiscate land; it is only necessary to confiscate rent.*[12]

The machinery of property assessment and taxation, George points out, is already everywhere at hand. In those states where the value of land is now assessed separately from its improvements, no further preparation is needed; elsewhere, a separate assessment would be undertaken as the first step. Then, in accordance with the enacted legislation, the tax rate on the raw land would be increased by stages until, on completion of the program, approximately the full annual ground rent would thus be recaptured as public revenue. (In order to minimize the administrative costs and dislocation that might accompany the new system, George suggests a practical expedient: that the landowners retain title to their land, and in return for their collection services be given "a percentage of rent which would probably be less than the cost and loss involved in attempting to rent lands through State agency. . . ."[13]) Coordinately with each stage, other existing taxes—those on improvements, personal property, commodities and services, private and corporate income, and so on—would be commensurately reduced until they were eliminated entirely.

The Canons of Taxation

George proceeds to test the validity of his proposal against four accepted "canons of taxation." Any measure that seeks to raise public revenue, he asserts, should conform as closely as may be feasible to these requirements: (1) that the tax fall as lightly as possible upon productivity; (2) that it be simply and inexpensively collected; (3) that it be certain in its incidence; and (4) that it bear equally upon all. He finds the tax on ground rent confirmed in each case.

With respect to (1): it would not only put no burden on production but also serve to remove those burdens presently imposed by other taxes:

> Tax manufactures, and the effect is to check manufacturing; tax improvements, and the effect is to lessen improvement; tax commerce, and the effect is to prevent exchange; tax capital, and the effect is to drive it away. But the whole value of land may be taken in taxation, and the only effect will be to stimulate industry, to open new opportunities to capital, and to increase the production of wealth.[14]

Land value, which is itself a reflection of community development, neither increases nor decreases the rate of production. Consequently, since a tax on land value cannot be shifted but must be absorbed by the owner, it can be imposed up to the point of the land's annual rental return without penalizing either wages or capital. Indeed, the imposition of the tax will act to create added opportunities for productive enterprise by making unimproved land available for use.

(2) Ease and cheapness of collection would be assured. The machinery of land assessment and tax collection being already a part of every fiscal system, it would be no more difficult to collect the full revenue of the land than just a portion of it as at present. Moreover, as other tax-gathering agencies were eliminated, the community would benefit from large savings in the costs of administration.

(3) Certainty of collection could be expected "with a definiteness that partakes of the immovable and unconcealable character of the land itself."[15] Periodic assessments of the land would be based on the ground rental value of each site, and the tax would be collected from the registered owner or—if the land is held by the community—from the lessee. The land tax is also more certain, George declares, because it is not subject to the iniquities that accompany other forms of taxation, such as evasion, fraud, smuggling, and the bribery of officials.

(4) Finally, the land tax would bear equally upon all members of the community, since it would be drawn from the social product to which all had contributed in common. This condition, George asserts, is true only of land values. All other taxes bear unequally, either because they cannot be apportioned to the actual needs of those who pay them, or because they lack preci-

sion in discriminating between the rewards of productive effort and those of unearned appropriation.

Anticipated Benefits of the Land-Value Tax

The remedy he proposed was simple but its favorable effects, George was confident, would reach into every sector of the economy. No longer would industrial enterprise be forced to undergo the chain reaction set up by heavy taxes on production—the sequence of increased costs that led to lessened demand, reduced output, and fewer jobs with lower wages for labor. Production would at last be free to respond with its full resources to the burgeoning needs of the population. The prices of goods and services could be expected to fall to the extent that the taxes upon them were removed, thus leading to an increase in purchasing power. Labor and capital alike would receive the full reward of their contribution to production, minus only that share which would be deducted by government in the form of land tax—and this share would be returned to all in the form of public services.

Since there would be little or no profit to be had through land speculation, this major cause of economic imbalance would be removed. House builders and businessmen would no longer need to invest heavy outlays of capital to purchase land, since secure possession and use could be managed simply by payment of the annual land tax. Capital thus liberated would be available to build upon a wide range of land sites, including those which speculators no longer found it profitable to hold out of use. A marked upswing in building construction could therefore be anticipated. New housing and other improvements, free of taxation, would tend to replace the tenements and other outmoded structures that now persist only because of their low tax liability.

But George expected even more than these tangible economic results—and here it is necessary to venture into the wider reaches of his social philosophy. The "progress" he was concerned with in his long search was not simply economic growth, much less mere fiscal reform.[16] What he was seeking was rather the means by which the human being could best realize his intellectual and moral capacities. It was this that led him inescapably to the realm of economics. Man can fulfill himself as a human being, George believed, only within the context of his social and material life—it is first necessary to live, before one can aspire to live well. In a condition of poverty not only is man deprived of his opportunity to develop, but also he must use up so much of his energy in the sheer struggle for existence that little of it remains to express his higher potentialities.

An economic system can be successful only when it does justice to men's incentives and capabilities. This requires that opportunities to produce shall be equally available to all, that each worker receives the full return of his work, and that no one profits from special privilege. But each of these conditions George found to be violated through the private appropriation of land rent.

The socialization of rent would therefore finally bring about a harmony of economic development and human progress. Free of both the tax collector and the land monopolist, each man would be able to labor to his capacity and to reap the full reward of his effort. The community, in its turn, having created its own value in the form of ground rent, would collect that income and use it for community needs. In such a situation no individual is any longer penalized and none is unjustly enriched. Ethical rightness becomes merged with economic effeciency, to their mutual benefit and support. Upon such a firm base, George concludes, human beings will be able to exercise their highest moral and intellectual capacities.

Effect upon Particular Groups

What effect would the proposed socialization of ground rent have upon particular income groups of the community?

Clearly, the overall consequence would be that all who received rental income from landholdings would henceforth lose all but a small percentage of that income. Therefore the land would cease to have speculative value. It would, however, retain use value, reflected in its rent, which would go almost entirely to the community. Legal title would not be affected: the owner would retain his title as long as he paid his land-tax.

A. THE HOME OWNER, POSSESSING HIS HOUSE AND LOT: in market terms, the selling value of his lot would diminish, like that of every other plot of land. But his possession and use, or sale, of his property, would remain unaltered. In exchange for the annual tax on the value of his lot, he would be free from taxation on his house, personal property, private earnings, and other tax levies. If he should wish to buy or build another dwelling he could, of course, expect to receive relatively little from the sale of his original lot apart from its improvements; but he would not have to invest a large sum in a new lot, since land could be purchased cheaply by anyone willing to pay most of its ground rent to the community.

B. THE FARMER: at present he carries a disproportionately heavy burden, George believes, because of the high ratio of visible property upon which he is taxed—his crops, dwellings, barns, livestock, machinery, and the like. All that makes his production possible is now levied upon, directly and indirectly. When he improves his land he is taxed more heavily for it, even while high-priced but unimproved land in the towns is assessed at a minimum. The farmer would benefit under George's proposal in two principal ways: first, by being liberated from the oppressive levies upon his production and improvements; and second, because his land would be assessed at a low rental value since it is on the margin of the demand area. Moreover, since the purchase of the land he works would no longer require a large investment, he could engage in farming with much less capital and use his earnings to improve his (tax-free) buildings, equipment, and livestock.

C. THE LARGE PROPORTION OF THE POPULATION WHO POSSESS NO LAND AT ALL: they would have no taxes to pay directly. They would, however, absorb, in the price of the goods and services they buy, that share of production costs which represents the ground rent of the producing enterprise. But two changes would have taken place: first, the ground rent would have become public revenue instead of landowners' income, and would, accordingly, be utilized to pay for the costs of government; second, the price of goods and services would no longer be burdened with the multitude of taxes upon production that were hitherto passed on to consumers.

D. THE GROUP OF LARGE LANDOWNERS WHOSE INCOMES ARE DERIVED

SOLELY OR PREDOMINANTLY FROM THEIR HOLDINGS OF LAND AND SUCH NATURAL RESOURCES AS MINERAL OR PETROLEUM DEPOSITS: would thus bear the major loss resulting from the transition. Their deprivation would be measured roughly by the extent to which their rent income is a greater share than the other elements of their total income. The capital value of their landed investments would be wholly, or almost wholly, forfeited. However, as George contends, all landowners, great and small, would benefit directly from the abolition of taxes on improvements, personal income, investments in productive enterprise, and the like. He asserts that even the largest landowners, though they will suffer immediate loss of ground rent, will profit in common with all other groups in the long-run advantages of the reform.

Despite this, the question is raised, on ethical as well as material grounds, whether landowners should not be compensated for the loss of their investment in land. George recognizes not only that the practice of private landownership has long enjoyed legal and social sanction, but also that present owners have in numerous cases purchased their holdings with capital acquired by acceptable means. But he answers to this that "if landowners are to lose nothing of their special privileges, the people at large can gain nothing," and that "to buy up individual property rights would merely be to give the landholders in another form a claim of the same kind and amount that their possession of land now gives them."[17] The practical difficulties involved in such a proceeding would likewise be formidable, chiefly because the market value of land generally incorporates a factor of projected future increment.

But the issue as George sees it is much more fundamental. If taken on an ethical basis, the private appropriation of land values constituted from the beginning of an unnatural and pernicious act against the community. Private land ownership itself, George reminds us, originated in force, fraud, and conquest, and it was perpetuated by those who inherited or acquired this private power to exact rent as tribute from others. Many of the greatest fortunes in America, as elsewhere, trace their roots to the grants of title, and subsequent political connivance in such acts.[18] Even though ownership today has been acquired by appropriate payment, there is still no ethical right to its earnings. The community creates land-value and the whole community should reap its benefits. The fact that private appropriation has been long sanctioned by society is no more final, George argues, than that chattel slavery was for many generations an approved practice. When an established social institution is found to be morally injurious, it is the duty as well as the right of society to correct it.

Furthermore, if the matter be considered on practical grounds, it will be seen that the effect of private appropriation has been to enrich nonproducers, to deny labor its rightful earnings, and to hold back normal economic growth. It is possible to regard every form of tax as a partial confiscation of the income upon which it is imposed. The tax that is now levied everywhere upon the raw land, whatever its rate, reduces the capital value of that land to some extent. An increase in rate would utilize the same principle, except that a correspondingly larger part of the capital value would revert from the landowner to the community. In such an event, George believes, the most appropriate form of compensation would be the benefit that all of society would obtain from the reform.

George's Replies to Certain Objections

OBJECTION: that ground rental and increased land values are not the only form of "unearned income" in our economy; why then single out the land and landowners exclusively?

George concedes that it may be possible to identify other elements of unearned income, but he insists that, even if this is so, the increment of land value remains a unique phenomenon. Each form of investment capital, even if inherited rather than earned, is engaged in producing reproducible things or services by means of human labor and equipment; thereby it earns a return, large or small, reflecting the economic decisions of producers and consumers. But the natural land, unlike capital, does not constitute either immediate or stored-up labor; it is not a manufactured product; it is not reproducible; and its unimproved value does not depend in any way upon the decisions of the owner. The value of landed property derives from the socially created opportunities it affords for production and residence. As such, the return it yields represents social, rather than private, increment. Accordingly, even if it were possible to isolate other forms of capital income as unearned, this might provide a case for suitable fiscal measures, but it would in no way lessen the propriety of recapturing land values.

OBJECTION: that it is often difficult, if not impossible, to separate the value of the raw land from the improvements made upon it.

George denies that this presents any untoward difficulties. Many states already provide separate assessments of the land and its improvements, even though the two are often merged for imposition of a uniform tax rate. The cost of buildings and other man-made additions is generally known; the balance of the assessed value of the property is that which represents the bare land.

It is, of course, recognized that certain modifications of the land itself, such as swamp drainage, hill terracing, and the like, become eventually indistinguishable from the original site. Improvements of this sort, effected by human effort and capital, would be exempted for an interval of time from taxation; ultimately they would be considered as having fused into the site of the land itself.

OBJECTION: that the increased tax on land would simply be shifted to tenants or consumers in the form of higher rents or commodity prices.

George replies that this would not occur, because land is not a man-made product subject to greater or lesser output. The amount of land available is fixed in extent; hence the effect of an added tax is to decrease the net rental retained by the landowner. To support his position, George cites the then (and now) prevailing view of economists that a land tax (unlike other taxes) cannot be shifted by the owner, that he must absorb the increase himself.

OBJECTION: that an exclusive tax upon land would be too inelastic to provide for the changing requirements of public revenue, particularly in the light of extraordinary expenditures for defense and welfare purposes.

At the time he wrote, George calculated that a single tax on land values would yield a sufficient revenue for all the purposes of government, local, state, and national.[19] He contended, moreover, that the land tax was inherently elastic because its amount would increase directly with the growth of population and the concomitant enhancement of land values. He was confident, as well, that his remedy would so strongly stimulate business, employment, and real income that the heavy welfare costs of government would be sharply diminished or eliminated.

OBJECTION: that the full land tax would, in effect, put an end to the individual ownership of land, erase the sense of security that comes from such possession, and thus destroy a man's incentive to care for the land and put it to its best use.

George reiterates that neither the title nor the use of the land would be disturbed as long as the annual land-value tax was paid. The situation would remain unchanged except that all but a fraction of the rental income would flow from either the owner or user to the community, instead of to the landowner. The user of the land is always motivated to put the property to its best use, since that is the surest way to make it profitable for himself; this is less the case with the landowner who, if his tax rate is low, may choose to keep his property unimproved until it will fetch a higher price.

The security and incentive that people really want, George concludes, is the assurance that what they cultivate and build and earn by their own efforts will not be taken from them. This the land-value tax would effectuate through the removal of all other taxes.

Forty years after my first encounter with *Progress and Poverty* I continue to find its message enduringly sane and timely. During that period taxes have multiplied, the public debt has grown inexorably, and proud states have approached the edge of insolvency—yet with little or no effort made to correct that most palpable of inequities, the indulgence of landownership at the expense of production. The thought occurs: what if one of the newly emergent nations of our time had had the foresight to install the single tax on land as its public revenue source—how would its people have responded? Would their opportunity and enterprise have been encouraged thereby? Would their tax-free crops and industries have burgeoned? their arts and sciences have flourished? their rewards made commensurate to their efforts? land speculation quashed? the government and bureaucracy confined to their income?

Henry George would have been confident of the result. And how instructive such an example would be to his critics and advocates alike!

Notes

1. Brief reports from eleven countries, including the United States, appear in H.G. Brown et al., eds., *Land Value Taxation Throughout the World* (New York: Robert Schalkenbach Foundation, 1955).

2. Henry George, *Progess and Poverty*, 75th anniversary ed. (New York: Robert Schalkenbach Foundation, 1954), p. 171.

3. Ibid., p. 38.

4. Ibid., pp. 337-38.

5. Ibid., p. 344.

6. Ibid., pp. 165-66.

7. Ibid., p. 168.

8. Ibid., p. 166.

9. Ibid., p. 264.

10. Ibid., p. 270.

11. Ibid., pp. 405-6. Some have made the point that what George proposes is not a tax at all in the traditional sense, and that it should rather be construed as a process by which the community would collect annually the social increment that it alone is capable of producing and would use to defray its own expenses. This, it is contended, involves no levy at all upon the productive powers of labor.

12. George, *Progress and Poverty*, p. 405.

13. Ibid.

14. Ibid., p. 414.

15. Ibid., p. 418.

16. This concern, central to George's philosophy, is developed at length in bk. 10 of *Progress and Poverty*.

17. George, *Progress and Poverty*, p. 360.

18. George deals with this issue at some length in bk. 7, chap. 4, "Property in Land Historically Considered," and chap. 5, "Of Property in Land in the United States."

19. George, *Progress and Poverty*, p. 406. Some Georgists today are prepared to approve inheritance and income taxes as supplementary sources of revenue in the event the land tax is inadequate for legitimate and necessary purposes. George himself said nothing about this.

Part II
Nineteenth-Century British and Continental Critics

3

Laveleye: The Critic Ripe for Conversion

BY ROY DOUGLAS

Émile de Laveleye (1822-1892), professor of political economy at the University of Liège, and later Baron de Laveleye, was a Belgian scholar and publicist, whose observations on Henry George first appeared in a brief article published in January 1880 in the *Revue scientifique de la France et de l'étranger*.[1] Later he wrote a much longer commentary which appeared in the London *Contemporary Review* of 1882.[2]

Laveleye's first article adopts a somewhat ambivalent position in relation to George. The beginning and the end are highly laudatory: "il m'a instruit et m'a fait refléchir," he writes of *Progress and Poverty* near the beginning, while towards the end he waxes enthusiastic for the "single tax" doctrine: "Elle est si simple et d'une si grande portée pour l'avenir, qu'elle aurait chance d'être accueillie." Indeed, in his very last sentence Laveleye claims to have justified and developed the idea himself in an earlier work, to which I shall have need to refer later.

Yet there is a passage in the middle which appears more critical. George is taken to task for not considering the burden of military expenditure and of other government exactions upon labour: this ignores such sections as book 9, chapter 4. There is a part of the article, however, which is distinctly socialistic in its tendency, and to this too I shall later return.

Laveleye's second article is also by no means hostile, although it contains certain undeniably critical passages. As C. A. Barker noted in his biography of George, "Except for a private communication which this reviewer presently sent the author, it would be hard to say to which side his judgment leaned. But he assured George that in his net opinion *Progress and Poverty* was a book to be admired, and he offered compliments on the huge success of the English editions."[3]

Laveleye's arguments fall under several heads. He commences by making some interesting comments on the nature of economics as a science, and its connexion with morality. He then raises criticisms of George which relate to the Malthusian and "wage fund" theories. These criticisms are largely similar to those raised more fully by later writers, but introduce a few points of Laveleye's own. George, he argues, "is wrong in stating that this increase [i.e., the increase in rent] is the sole cause of the inequality of conditions," contending that the "constant increase of capital [is] no less important."[4] Finally, Laveleye moves from the posture of a negative critic to advocate a position of his own, for he was the author of important works on historical analysis and social theory, whose conclusions he contrasts with those of George. It is convenient to examine the "wage fund" arguments in the chapter which is mainly concerned with the views of W. H. Mallock, while the other points will be discussed here.

Laveleye's discussion of the nature of economics as a study is perhaps least vital to the argument, since it is quite possible to agree with his views in toto without dissenting from any important conclusions drawn by Henry George. Nevertheless, the topic has some fascination. George is taken to task for the proposition that economics is "as much a science as geometry."[5] The parallel may be closer than either George or Laveleye realised. Euclidian geometry and most of George's economics turn on a priori reasoning. The geometer discusses the properties of (say) lines and triangles, although there is no such thing in the whole order of nature as a line or a triangle as he defines those terms. George's a priori approach to economics contrasts sharply with the a posteriori approach which is now so common in the social sciences.

The a priori approach common to George and the geometer has much to commend it. Suppose, for example, that the modern economist with his a posteriori reasoning wishes to study the relationship between inflation rates and economic growth. He may examine societies with different inflation rates, and compare their economic growth. Yet the relationship which he claims to have established will almost certainly be criticised by another economist who argues that the effect was really due in part or whole to something else: different technological inputs; the discovery of fuel reserves; the fiscal policy of another country. In contrast with the condition in most natural sciences, controlled experiments cannot be applied to determine the matter. Such difficulties by no means destroy the value of a posteriori investigations in economics, but they render the method a good deal less convincing than in a science like chemistry.

The a priori approach—whether of George or of the geometer—does not operate in a vacuum. The proposition that the angles of a triangle always add up to 180 degrees is accepted not merely because it is based on an elegant and intellectually satisfying theorem, but because it helps engineers to design bridges. The attraction of George's economics is not just the lucidity of his reasoning, but the fact that observed economic effects are consistent with his arguments.

Laveleye comes very close to George when he comments: "Political economy. . .treats of the production of riches—that is to say, of the things that satisfy men's wants; and men's wants, and their working activity, vary in accordance with the ideas of happiness and duty, or concerning their destiny in this life and the next. . . .Consequently Mr. George is by no means wrong when he gives great importance to the religious element in his study of social questions."[6] The product of man's activities, in other words, will be determined in part by what sort of thing man considers valuable, and this will not be conditioned exclusively by considerations of wealth, whether of an individual or of a community. Although economics as a science takes no cognisance of morality, the decision as to what economic results are desirable is a profoundly moral one.

The second criticism advanced by Leveleye which calls for discussion here is of a different kind. He does not deny George's contention that increasing the rent which passes to a landowner tends to produce inequality, but he argues that increase of capital (or rather in the remuneration of capital) operates in a similar fashion.

> It is true, the workman gains somewhat by industrial progress, for as the use of machinery lowers the price of many wares he is better provided for than formerly; but the forestalments absorbed by capital are far more rapid. When corn was ground by hand, as in olden times, nearly the full value of the grinding was paid in wages. If, to grind by steam, only one-third of the hands previously employed are necessary, their wages will absorb but one-third of the profit of the operation of the grinding; the other two-thirds will become the remuneration of realized capital.[7]

In his earlier article, Laveleye gives what is perhaps an even clearer illustration.[8] To carry a hundred tons in Africa required two thousand porters and no capital; to carry the same load in Belgium required two men and a very expensive train, consisting of a locomotive and ten wagons. In the first case, no interest was paid on capital; in the second a great deal of interest was paid.

Laveleye's development of the same argument, however, hints at its own weakness: "The immense fortunes amassed so rapidly in the United States, like those of Mr. Gould and Mr. Vanderbilt, now proverbial, were the results of railway speculation, and not the greater revenue or value of land."[9]

What, may we ask, was the nature of the transactions entered by Messrs. Gould and Vanderbilt? In the first instance they acquired long, narrow strips of land, on which they were authorised to build railroads. Second, they acquired a de facto state monopoly not merely of those particular strips of land, but of other land connecting the settlements which the railroads joined, so that others could not construct rival railroads. The vast profits of the great railway entrepreneurs could be secured only because the organs of government granted those two monopolies. As the communities linked by the railroads grew in size and economic importance, the land on which the railroads were built became exceedingly valuable. Let us suppose that all of the capital of one of the railroads was suddenly destroyed: the railway lines, the station buildings, the rolling stock, and so on; but Mr. Gould or Mr. Vanderbilt retained ownership of the long, narrow strips of land, and also retained the state monopoly of building rail communications between the towns in question. Would that radically have diminished the fortunes of the railroad kings? Surely not. They would have replaced the capital in a very short time, and at a cost which represented only a small proportion of their fortunes. These fortunes were mainly built, not on the value of capital, but on the value of land, and the value of state monopoly.

The example drawn by Laveleye in his earlier work brings this point out. Railway engines and wagons are capital. They were made by the labour of men who won iron ore and coal; who turned the coal into coke; who smelted the ore; who fashioned the crude ingots of metal into engines, and so on. The man who demands remuneration for the use of rolling stock is making a wholly reasonable claim for recompense in respect of the labour expended in its manufacture. His position differs not in degree but in kind from that of the landlord, under whose possession the coal and iron ore originally lay. Neither that landlord nor his predecessors contributed anything to the minerals. The value received by the landlord derives from the accident that minerals happen to lie under his land.

The steam-grinding example is not wildly different. Laveleye supposes that workers would continue to work in the steam mills at roughly the same rate of remuneration as they had originally secured as independent hand-grinders. This is the paradox which George sets at the beginning of his inquiry: "that discovery upon discovery, and invention after invention, have neither lessened the toil of those who most need respite, nor brought plenty to the poor." Today, for reasons which the present author discusses in chapter 6 below, this proposition (which to George was self-evident) can no longer be maintained without qualification; yet it clearly retains considerable force. The phenomenon is far older than capitalism, and it is difficult to see how the capitalist could by himself bring about the impoverishment of labour even if he so desired.

Here we come close to the fundamental fallacy of socialist analysis. Socialists have correctly perceived the contrast between the wealth of many capitalists and the poverty of many workmen, and have pointed out that this disparity is incomparably greater than any disparity of their contributions to the general good of the community might justify. From this observation they have jumped to the conclusion that it is something in the nature of capitalism which brings about this disparity of wealth. They have failed to ask sufficiently closely by what *mechanism* capitalists become rich and labourers poor.

Insofar as those whom we call "capitalists" are truly deriving their wealth from the use of capital, they are claiming a just recompense for some value which they have created which is beneficial to labour. Often, however, as the example of Mr. Vanderbilt so clearly shows, an individual who is loosely called a "capitalist" performs two or more quite different functions. He acts as a true capitalist, for which he derives a just remuneration, but he also acts as a landlord or as a monopolist. The first kind of remuneration very likely sets him in better circumstances than most of his fellows, and deservedly so, but it is the second and third kinds of remuneration which make him rich beyond the dreams of avarice—and impoverish many other people in the process.

Labour with access to land may create new capital in what are for all practical purposes limitless quantities. If the remuneration of capital is high, then it would seem natural for labourers to purchase—or to hire—capital. Yet in practice this apparently simple expedient is frequently impossible.

Parallels with this situation are surely very ancient. In innumerable societies—long before the advent of *capitalism* as we usually understand the term—moneylenders grew rich and other people grew poor. This often led people to murder moneylenders, or to drive them out of business by legislation. These expedients, however, did not abate poverty: indeed, if anything, they tended to increase poverty. When people who had got rid of the old moneylenders fell upon bad times, or when they sought capital to improve their productiveness, then either the capital could not be secured at all because no one had sufficient incentive to lend it—or else the loan of capital acquired a large element of risk, and therefore capital commanded a very high rate of interest.

Capital, by itself, cannot exploit labour. Let us assume that a capitalist, however wealthy, is operating in a society where land is of free access, and where the state refuses privileges like the grant of tariffs against foreign competitors—or the exclusive power to build railroads between human settlements. The only means by which that capitalist can secure the services of labour is by offering people more attractive conditions than they had enjoyed before he came. If the interest rate seems high, then others will set up in business in competition with him, and speedily bring it down by that competition. What exploits labour is not capital, but monopoly in land, or some other privilege.

Most of Laveleye's criticisms of George are either fallacious, or else have little effect on the main thesis, even should we concede their validity. In one direction, however, he makes a real contribution to the whole discussion: for in the review he reminds us of his own extremely important book, *Primitive Property*, which George cites extensively in *Progress and Poverty*.[10]

Laveleye's work, originally issued in French, ran into several editions, including an English translation published in 1878. The author investigates the "land question" in many different societies, and perceives common patterns of development. This sociohistorical approach is clearly important. If George was right in arguing that the land question is absolutely crucial to an understanding of the causes of poverty, then surely there should be abundant historical evidence corroborative of that fact. The argument on which Laveleye's book turns is encapsulated in a passage which deserves to be quoted *in extenso*.

So long as primitive man lived by the chase, by fishing or gathering wild fruits, he never thought of appropriating the soil; and considered nothing as his own but what he had taken or contrived with his own hands. Under the pastoral system, the notion of property in soil begins to spring up. It is, however, always limited to the portion of land which the herds of each tribe are accustomed to graze on, and frequent quarrels break out with regard to the limits of these pastures. The idea that a single individual could claim a part of the soil as exclusively his own never yet occurs to any one; the conditions of pastoral life are in direct opposition to it.

Gradually, a portion of the soil was put temporarily under cultivation, and the agricultural system was established; but the territory which the clan or tribe occupies, remains its undivided property. . . . Subsequently the cultivated land is divided into parcels, which are distributed by lot among the several families, a mere temporary right of occupation being thus allowed to the individual. This is the system still in force in the Russian commune; and was, in the time of Tacitus, that of the German tribe.

By a new step of individualisation, the parcels remain in the hands of groups of patriarchal families dwelling in the same house and working together for the benefit of the association, as in Italy or France in the middle ages, and in Servia at the present time.

Finally, individual property appears. It is, however, still tied down by the thousand fetters of seignoral rights, *fideicommissa, retraits-lignages*, hereditary leases, *Flurzwang* or compulsory system of rotation, etc. It is not until after a last evolution, sometimes very long in taking effect, that it is definitely constituted and becomes the absolute, sovereign, personal right, which is defined by the Civil Code, and which alone is familiar to us in the present day.[11]

Laveleye proceeds to discuss the mechanism by which this drastic and final change was effected. In some countries—like France and England and Italy—there were invasions which resulted in foreigners establishing themselves as a land-owning aristocracy. This experience, however, was not universal, and in particular it did not apply in Germany. "Originally we see in Germany a society of equal and independent peasants, like the inhabitants of Uri, Schwitz and Unterwalden (cantons of Switzerland) at the present day. At the close of the middle ages we find in the same country a feudal aristocracy resting more heavily on the soil and a rustic population more completely enslaved than in England, Italy or France."[12] He argues that various historical mechanisms operated to produce this effect. When new land was won from forest, it passed absolutely to the man who first cultivated it. When land was bequeathed to the Church, the Church took it free from the ordinary obligations owed by secular occupiers towards the local commune. When particular individuals contrived by various means to get others to cultivate their lands for them, those individuals acquired the leisure necessary to develop into a warrier aristocracy which could thereafter enforce its privileges by force of arms. Thus may we perceive a complex process, spread over centuries, developing at different speeds in different countries, with infinite local variations, by which the concept of land shifted from the original idea of something *publici juris* to the later view of land as a freely alienable and heritable entity, essentially similar to moveable property.

So very far does the analysis of Laveleye seem to conform with the picture which a Georgeist might expect, that it may seem astonishing to discover Laveleye baulking at George's conclusions. He hints at rather than develops the points which lay at issue between them: "The Universities of Oxford and Cambridge, as corporate bodies, are in possession of large plots of land, the revenue of which is devoted to the public good. Generalize this system, and the plan of Mr. George is accomplished. The State owns the Saarbruck collieries in Germany, and in Belgium the railways. Ownership in both these cases present many more difficulties than the mere possession of the soil."[13] Private land ownership may operate to the public good; state ownership of land is likely to present great difficulties.

It is useful to examine Laveleye's second point first. The term *land nationalization* was still being used by the advocates of George's proposals and in at least one place[14] by George himself. It was all too easy to associate this idea with "nationalization" of entities like mines or railways—things which contain an element of land but also an element of capital. "Nationalization" of these things, as commonly understood, involves state control of their operations. Experience, whether in Bismarckian Germany or in twentieth-century Britain, suggests that the state is often exceedingly inefficient in its management of commercial enterprises. Even the term *land nationalization* was (and is) often used to mean state control of the use of land as well as state acquisition of the economic rent. Laveleye here does not so much disagree with George as misunderstand what George sought to do. He was certainly not the last man to make that mistake.

The other point at which Laveleye detects a difference from George is one where their analyses are truly different. "In my opinion," the critic declares, "there is but one true cure for the social evil; it is individual property generalized and assured to all.''[15] If by *property* Laveleye confined himself to personalty, then it might be difficult to dissent from his proposition, but it appears from the context that he envisages the maxim applying to land as well. He appears to look towards some kind of system which in its rural form would be called "peasant-proprietorship."

Laveleye certainly had no sympathy for the system of minute peasant tenancies which then existed in parts of Europe. George himself was fully conscious of that fact: "M. de Laveleye. . .states in his paper on the Land Systems of Belgium and Holland, printed by the Cobden Club, that the condition of the laborer is worse under this system. . .than it is in England; while the tenant farmers. . .are rack-rented with a mercilessness unknown in England and even in Ireland. . . .''[16] What he evidently favoured, however, was a system in which the peasants would be owners of their holdings, without obligation towards either landlord or state.

In Ireland, where the ideas of Henry George made great initial headway, there was always a dichotomy between those land reformers like Davitt who saw land as a public thing, and those like Parnell who visualised its division into separate and absolute holdings.[17] This dispute was to a large extent obscured because the disparate land reformers were overwhelmingly conscious of the need to cooperate against the British Government and Anglo-Irish landlords. Yet the issue remained, and in the end it was the "peasant proprietors" who won, and whose ideas were enshrined in a series of legislative measures culminating in Wyndham's great Land Purchase Act of 1903.

"Peasant proprietorship" appears so similar to the ideas of Henry George that many hardly perceived the difference. Yet in fact that difference is fundamental. In the first place, peasant proprietorship does not by itself provide any guarantee against the later concentration of land into fewer hands, and still less does it prevent the peasant landowner who happens to live close to some industrial or urban development from arrogating publicly created land values to the detriment of his neighbours. In the second place, it makes no provision for the man who happens to have no land. In 1880 there was probably very little economic difference between the rack-rented Irish tenant farmer and the landless labourer. Yet a succession of Land Acts and Land Purchase Acts made the difference fundamental. The man who acquired ownership of his peasant holdings became a prosperous farmer. Even the peasant with a tiny, uneconomic holding in one of the "Congested Districts" of the West was enabled to receive a share of those *latifundia*, the cattle ranches, while the man who had had no land at all received nothing, and became a pauper.

Thus in place of the old system where the social division lay between a small, wealthy landlord class and a vast mass of impoverished peasants and labourers, a new system appeared. The landholders could now be numbered by the hundred thousand, but so also could landless men. It was relatively easy for the mass of the nation to struggle against a small class of great landowners; it was impossible for the landless men to struggle against a vast class of peasant-proprietors. Thus the ingenious measures by which the old landlords were bought out did not suffice to remove poverty from Ireland, or to abate the manifold social and political ills which have flowed, and continue to flow, from that poverty. Modern Dublin still shows much that is redolent of the

1930s; modern Belfast is still torn by feuds in which frustrated labourers wreak their anger upon each other. In that sense, Laveleye's vision of peasant proprietorship may prove even more damaging and persistent than the system which preceded it.

Perhaps the real basis of Laveleye's criticism lies in a matter which George's latter-day followers have not always been willing to acknowledge. Although Henry George deals at considerable length with the principle of land-value taxation in *Progress and Poverty*, the bulk of the book is concerned more (as the title suggests) with showing the relationship between land ownership and poverty, and how this persists despite technological and other advances. A very large part of *Progress and Poverty* was therefore wholly acceptable to people who concurred with George's destructive analysis, but were groping towards completely different proposals for remedies. In many minds, ideas like peasant proprietorship, the taxation of land values, and land nationalization had not been sharply differentiated. In the pages of that remarkable periodical of the 1880s, the *Christian Socialist*, we may trace the gradual appreciation by socialists of the gulf which lay between George and themselves;[18] in the dialogue between George and H. M. Hyndman we may trace a similar—and simultaneous—realisation by two leading individuals.[19] In the very early 1880s, it was easy for a man who perceived the inequity and social folly of land ownership in its crudest form to fail to appreciate the complete incompatibility between different remedies proposed. George (as we have seen) writes in at least one place about "land nationalization," meaning thereby what he and his followers later called "nationalization of rent" or "land value taxation"; Alfred Russel Wallace uses the same term, *land nationalization*, to mean state control as well as ownership of land.[20] When Davitt spoke of the land of Ireland reverting to the people of Ireland he thought of something like George's proposals; when Parnell used practically the same language he thought of peasant proprietorship. Even as the differences gradually became clear to the thoughtful, publicists whose overriding concern was to draw attention to the iniquities of the current land system were not always eager to emphasise their differences from others who made similar destructive criticisms of the status quo, but advocated profoundly different remedies. In politics, it is often very difficult to decide on both moral and practical grounds how far log-rolling is a legitimate activity.

Laveleye's attack on George must therefore be seen in its historical context. *Progress and Poverty* made a "splash" even greater than that of George's later works. In *Progress and Poverty* George was particularly concerned to show the inherent importance of the land question; in the later works he found it necessary to bring out in sharper relief the difference between his remedies and those of others. Perhaps if those works had been available to Laveleye, he would have discovered that his own ideas could be reconciled with those of George on some matters where he took issue, while on others he might well have come to prefer George's views to his own earlier doctrines. Laveleye's value as a trailblazer for historical analysis of the land question is incomparable, and there is little doubt that he will be remembered as the author of *Primitive Property* rather than as the somewhat hesitant critic of Henry George.

Notes

1.   Émile de Laveleye, "La Propriété terrienne et le pauperisme," *Revue scientifique de la France et de l'étranger*, no. 30, 24 January 1880, pp. 708-10

2.   E. de Laveleye, " 'Progress and Poverty.' A Criticism," *Contemporary Review,* November 1882, pp. 786-806. (Hereinafter referred to as *C.R.*)

3.   C. A. Barker, *Henry George* (New York: Oxford University Press, 1953), p. 385.

4.   *C.R.*, p. 795.

5.   Ibid., p. 788.

6.   Ibid., pp. 788-89.

7.   Ibid., p. 795.

8.   "La Propriété terrienne," p. 709.

9.   *C.R.*, p. 796.

10.   Henry George, *Progress and Poverty*, 75th anniversary ed. (New York: Robert Schalkenbach Foundation, 1954), pp. 371-74.

11.   Émile de Laveleye, *Primitive Property*, trans. G. R. L. Marriott (London: Macmillan, 1878), pp. 3-4.

12.   Ibid., p. 222.

13.   *C.R.*, p. 799.

14.   Henry George, *The Land Question* [and Other Essays] (New York: Robert Schalkenbach Foundation, 1965), p. 64. "The Land Question" was first published in the early part of 1881, under the title of "The Irish Land Question."

15.   *C.R.*, p. 804.

16.   *Progress and Poverty*, pp. 325-26.

17.   See T. W. Moody, "Michael Davitt and the British Labour Movement," *Transactions of the Royal Historical Society* 5th ser. (1952-53): 58-60; F. S. L. Lyons, "The Economic Ideas of Parnell," *Historical Studies* 2 (1959): 64; also discussion by Roy Douglas in *Land, People and Politics* (London: Allison & Busby; New York: St. Martin's Press, 1976), pp. 43 ff.

18.   See in particular *Christian Socialist*, August 1883, p. 38 and January 1884, p. 114.

19.   See E. P. Lawrence, *Henry George in the British Isles* (East Lansing: Michigan State University Press, 1957), passim.

20.   See, e.g., A. R. Wallace, *Land Nationalization: Its Necessity and Its Aims* (1882); *My Life* (1908); pamphlets of the Land Nationalization Society, 1881 et seq.

4

Marshall: A Professional Economist Guards the Purity of His Discipline

BY ROBERT F. HÉBERT

I. Background

In 1883 the name of Henry George was more familiar on both sides of the Atlantic than that of Alfred Marshall. Marshall was to achieve lasting recognition a decade later as the foremost British economist of his day, but George's *Progress and Poverty* had already achieved an unusual measure of success for a work in political economy. Sales of that volume reached one hundred thousand in the British Isles a few years after its appearance in a separate English edition. This popularity (in a period when "best sellers" were less well received than now) was undoubtedly one measure of the British sentiment for land reform—a sentiment that had been carefully nurtured for several decades, especially by John Stuart Mill and Alfred R. Wallace. Additional sympathy for George and his ideas was also stirred by his controversial arrests in Ireland in 1882.[1]

Most economists of the late nineteenth century paid little attention to the lively subject of land reform, but Marshall was an exception. Intellectually, he was akin to John Stuart Mill—both were simultaneously attracted and repelled by socialist doctrine. Marshall admitted a youthful "tendency to socialism," which he later rejected as unrealistic and perverse in its effect on economic incentives and human character.[2] His early writings, however, clearly identify him as a champion of the working class. Marshall cultivated this reputation in his correspondence, and he continued to take socialism seriously, even after his "flirtation" with it ended.

In the winter of 1883 Marshall gave a series of public lectures at Bristol on "Henry George's subject of Progress and Poverty." These lectures have only recently become accessible to American readers.[3] In retrospect they appear to be Marshall's first deliberate attempt to renounce his socialist "ties," such as they were. Still, Marshall was a reluctant critic—a fact seemingly denied by his open antagonism to George, but affirmed by his personal correspondence. Urged by a colleague, Henry Foxwell, to publish the George lectures, Marshall politely replied:

56

As general propositions I maintain that it is more important to establish truth than to confute error; & that controversy should be left to people with sound digestions.

It seems to me infinitely more important that I should solve difficulties which still perplex me than that I should tilt at a successful rhetorician. The one thing that he [George] says which is important, I think, is that economists are—to outward appearance at least—at loggerheads with one another. I would rather put in one brick just where it should be in the slowly rising economic edifice than plant a hundred brickbats with the utmost dexterity between the eyes of Mr. George.

Still the book has had so many buyers (though I doubt whether one in fifty of them has read to the end) that I almost determined to publish something about him. My weak point was that I did not know what to attack: a book as large as his own would be wanted to refute all his fallacies. But I hope[d] that I should find out, in the course of my lectures at Bristol, which of his fallacies had stuck. I failed utterly. Trying to refute George in Bristol was like throwing oneself against a door that is not fastened. There was no resistance anywhere. There was plenty of enthusiasm for nationalisation of the land: if I had gone on fighting against that, I could have had opposition for ever. But there was no opposition to my attacks on George; & I practically had to leave him entirely out of the argument. . . .

When I go to Oxford[4] I shall hold out to my pupils there the same challenge that I held out to my pupils at Bristol. I shall defy them to shew me anything in George that is new & true; also to shew me any attack of his on Mill's doctrines that is even verbally valid against that rendering of Mill's doctrines that is to be found in the [E]conomics of [I]ndustry. (It seems to me that very few even of George's false sayings are less than fifty years old). . . .

Well, by this means I shall find out which of George's fallacies are worth attacking, & if I find that the book is not already fast losing its hold (which I expect) I shall probably write a review article or two at Xmas or Easter.[5]

The review articles alluded to never came, probably because Marshall was busy with his new duties at Oxford, and because he soon resumed work on his *Principles of Economics*.[6] However, Marshall's move to Oxford afforded a chance for a personal confrontation between himself and George. The occasion was a public lecture given by George at the Clarendon Hotel, Oxford, on the eve of 14 March 1884. In an audience consisting mainly of university students and faculty unsympathetic to George, Marshall led the questioning from the floor. In his initial foray, Marshall made so many points that George complained he was "piling them a little too thick." Marshall protested George's neglect of productivity and thrift; his failure to see the interdependence between land and other forms of property, to "prove his proofs," and to understand the authors he had undertaken to criticize. George was irresponsible, said Marshall, and he had "instilled poison" in the minds of his listeners. After Marshall rephrased a single question concerning thrift and productivity, George answered that thrift alone would be rendered ineffective by the monopoly privilege of land ownership, which would drive wages down to subsistence. Repeated attempts by Marshall to establish the competitive nature of the supply of land elicited no appreciation from George of the theoretical issues involved. Thereafter Marshall relinquished the floor. In all likelihood neither antagonist was especially pleased with the outcome of the confrontation. Nevertheless, the event clearly demonstrated George's ability to arouse passionate controversy. George was rudely treated by the audience, and the meeting, which became increasingly disorderly as the evening wore on, was adjourned early.[7]

The intellectual cleavage between Henry George and Alfred Marshall is revealing in several respects, not the least of which is the ambivalence of Marshall toward questions of land tenure. This study seeks to analyze the essence of the intellectual differences between these two antagonists, relegating to a minor place any personality traits that may have intruded on the "debate" (if it can be called that). Properly understood, the disagreement, as perceived by Marshall, was over the scope and logical method of economic science.

II. Georgist Lemmas and Marshallian Criticism

As he indicated in his letter to Foxwell, Marshall did not attempt in his lectures on *Progress and Poverty* to refute every detected fallacy in George's system. He declared his intention to address George's "subject," and to test for resistance to his specific criticisms of George. This section concentrates on four basic propositions found in George's *Progress and Poverty*, and analyzes Marshall's criticisms of each.

Lemma 1: Progress Causes Poverty

In *Progress and Poverty* George argued that the lowest class of society did not generally share the fruits of economic and technical progress. There is a meaningful sense in which Marshall shared George's concern for this pauper class, although the tenor of Marshall's comments in his first Bristol lecture was calculated to deflate George's argument. Citing increases in real wages, Marshall argued that living conditions had improved among the British working class during the eighteenth and nineteenth centuries. "On the whole," he calculated, "a shilling now [1883] will purchase nearly as much of the labourers' necessaries, comforts, and luxuries of life as two shillings would then [1803]."[8] Marshall cited national income statistics to the effect that labor's relative share of total income had also increased, from roughly one-fourth of total income in 1688 to over one-third of total income in 1883.[9] These facts do not literally contradict George's argument, but Marshall insisted that they placed the problem of poverty in better perspective. He concluded:

> Mr. George says that progress drives a wedge into the middle of society, raising those that are above it but lowering those that are below it. If this is true at all, I think it is clear that the great body of the working classes are above the wedge, and that progress is pushing them upwards, though unfortunately at a very slow rate. If there are any whom the wedge of progress is pushing down, it is the lowest stratum of all. The existence of a large pauper class is a disgrace to the age; but there is no use in making even this evil appear greater than it is. Pauperism is the product of freedom. No sensible man gives insufficient food to his horses, and slaves are managed on exactly the same principles as horses.[10]

Changes in labor's share of total output over long periods are difficult to measure because of virtually insurmountable statistical problems involved in identifying functional shares of national income.[11] Therefore, over time, economic history has often focused on the behavior of real wages. Much of the "evidence" on this issue remains in the realm of unsupported assertion. However, studies employing the more sophisticated econometric techniques seem to support Marshall's claim that real wages were increasing during the eighteenth and nineteenth centuries.[12] Since modern Georgists have generally conceded the weak empirical foundations of George's premise, the issue retains little more than historical interest. Nevertheless, Alfred Marshall was an economist who had a reputation for "getting his facts right," and his opinion of other economists was undoubtedly colored by whether or not they did the same.

Lemma 2: High Rents Cause Low Wages and Interest

The *theory* of income distribution—as against the historical change in relative shares—affords a more substantive issue on which to compare George and Marshall. George's criticism of the wages-fund doctrine was extensive and cannot concern us here in all its detail. Much of it was "empty" in the sense that George's rendering of the doctrine simply does not stand up to a careful reading of the classical economic literature. Still, almost from its inception the doctrine was subject to much confusion—a situation greatly exacerbated by John Stuart Mill's eleventh-hour "recantation" in 1869.[13] Taussig captured the significance of George's role in the lengthy controversy when he wrote:

> As to the wages fund doctrine, George's attacks are chiefly significant of the ease with which the old statements could be shaken, and of their failure to put in any clear light the basis of truth and fact on which the doctrine might rest.[14]

The basis of truth and fact on which the doctrine rested concerns the following propositions: (1) In advanced, capitalist economies, production is not instantaneous, so that a stock of produced goods must exist at any point of time in order to enable future production to be carried on; (2) The amount of such goods available for the support of labor provides a rough-and-ready measure of the aggregate demand for workers' services; and (3) The "average wage" in the economy will depend on the relationship of the aggregate demand for labor to its aggregate supply (the classical economists used population as a proxy for the latter).

George's criticisms of the *popular* notion of the doctrine were timely and in many respects justified by the failure of economists to clarify the issues involved. However, his reaction was to throw out the (analytical) baby with the bathwater. In other connections, George at least paid lip service to demand and supply. But in this case he ignored the crudely formulated demand/supply framework of the wages fund and made the determination of wages (as a functional share) depend entirely on the behavior of land rents (another functional share). This raises a host of analytical questions. If the determination of one functional share depends on the prior determination of another, which is determined first, and how? George had no problem supplying an answer to these questions because of the primacy of land in his system. Marshall, however, opted for a general analytical framework that would allow all functional shares to be determined on the same principles and more-or-less simultaneously. He found this framework in the demand/supply apparatus of the received wages-fund doctrine.[15] Marshall's acquaintance with, and respect for, the "ancients" served him well in this regard, and his conviction that analytical progress in economics is the consequence of an evolutionary process is demonstrated in his passionate defense of the intellectual tradition of classical political economy. Still, Marshall did not treat George fairly. He maintained on more than one occasion that there was nothing new and true in George's writings. What he overlooked in George's criticisms of the wages fund was the American's valuable insight that production is a continuous, value-added process rather than the point-input, point-output process assumed by the classical economists. Even though the rigid "yearly harvest" notion of classical economics is not a logical necessary requirement of the wages fund, George may well have been the first writer to explicitly suggest a continuous production function.[16] The ramifications of this notion cannot be fully explored here, but it has proved useful in certain neoclassical developments in economics, notably in the theory of capital.

The analytical differences between George and Marshall are placed in bold relief when one considers the effects of population growth. Given an increase in population, George's theory reasons that the margin of cultivation will be extended (to meet the increased demand for food), thereupon land rents will rise and average wages will fall. In a related argument, George also asserted that the increased settlement accompanying population growth will further drive rents up and wages down. Without the rudder of a supply-demand apparatus to guide it, George's analytical ship literally runs aground. The primacy of land is complete and total. For George, changes in the nonland shares of income derived from prior changes in the value of land, falling as land values rise and rising as land values fall.

Marshall's reaction was that this theory confused cause and effect. While lower average wages may accompany economic progress, they are not caused by prior changes in land values. Rather, wage changes are explained by the theory of competitive markets: an increase (decrease) in demand for labor will raise (lower) wages, *ceteris paribus*; an increase (decrease) in supply of labor will lower (raise) wages, *ceteris paribus*. It was in his *Principles of Economics* (1890) that Marshall gave the fullest expression to the theory of competitive markets, but the outline of this theory was already present in his lectures on *Progress and Poverty*. Thus Marshall wrote:

> the great law of distribution is that the more useful one factor of production is, and the scarcer it is, the higher will be the rate at which its services are paid. . . .if the numbers of unskilled labourers were to diminish sufficiently, then those who did unskilled work would have to be paid good wages.[17]

The theory of competitive markets is more general and heuristically more appealing than George's land-based theory, and Marshall used it to expose some of the economic fallacies in George's analysis, such as George's general "law" that interest and wages are always high together and low together.[18]

Marshall argued, correctly, that like the wage rate, the interest rate is determined by the supply of capital relative to the other factors, so that "whenever population is plentiful and capital scarce, interest is high and wages low."[19]

Once such analytical differences between George and Marshall are exposed, their policy differences take on new perspective. Since George saw higher land rents essentially crowding out labor's share of income, he derived a policy to eliminate those differential advantages of land which produced higher rents. For his part, Marshall emphasized policies that would have the effect of raising the demand for labor or of reducing its supply. The hope of the poor, he felt, lay in increasing their productivity as workers or in restricting their numbers relative to the other factors of production. In a general sense, Marshall seemed to believe that poverty could be "educated" out of existence.[20]

Lemma 3: Land Rent Is a Monopoly Price

Even though most economists no longer hold the notion that land rent is a monopoly price, there is established precedent in the history of economic thought for doing so. The idea was conveniently stated by Adam Smith, whose conclusion that "the rent of land. . .is naturally a monopoly price"[21] was based on an observed conflict between his own theory of competitive markets and the actual existence of ground rents. The theory of competitive markets asserted that the long-run equilibrium price of each good and each economic resource was determined by its average cost of production. In its natural state, however, land was regarded as a free gift, namely, a resource provided by nature having literally zero costs of production. By Smith's value theory, therefore, the rent of land should have been zero. Since this contradicted experience, Smith concluded that land must be supplied under conditions other than those of competition. That is, rent must be a monopoly price. He went on to infer that as a monopoly price, rent was not a payment necessary for production to occur. In this way, classical rent theory made land rent eminently suitable for taxation.

Ricardo advanced the classical theory of rent by adding the principle of diminishing returns. But he also recognized that the value of land does not depend on the amount of labor expended on it, and to reconcile this fact with his empirical labor theory of value,[22] he regarded land as a special agent of production. Subsequent treatments of value in classical economics generally deferred to Smith or Ricardo, thus reinforcing the notion that land is a unique factor of production, and that payment for it is not an economic cost.

This classical view of land rent ceased to be dominant once it was generally recognized that land commonly has alternative uses. For then a payment (in the form of opportunity costs) must be forthcoming in order to secure land for a particular use, and this payment is a necessary economic cost of production. George did not seem fully aware of the analytical subtleties involved here: he clung to the classical conclusion that land rent is not a necessary cost, while simultaneously discarding the classical assumption that land has no alternative uses. Yet his two positions are mutually exclusive, as demonstrated by the logical structure of economic theory.

There is another sense in which George exceeded the limits of classical rent theory: He rooted his own doctrine of rent in ethics rather than in economics. Undoubtedly a large measure of George's popular appeal, in his day as well as our own, stems from his knack for combining economic analysis with moral outrage. But George's ethics often intruded on his economics, leaving certain strictly economic issues muddled in a wake of passionate declamation. One example of this concerns the very issue of land rent as a monopoly price. In *Progress and Poverty*, George asserted:

> The value of land does not express the reward of production. . . .It expresses the exchange value of monopoly. And the value of land expressing a monopoly, pure and simple, is in every respect fitted for taxation. That is to say, while the value of a railroad or telegraph line, the price of gas or of a patent medicine, may express the price of monopoly, it also expresses the exertion of labor and capital; but the value of land, or economic rent, . . . is in no part made up of these factors, and expresses nothing but the advantage of appropriation.[23]

There are really two separate issues in this passsage that deserve consideration. The first is the strictly moral issue of land ownership and its legitimacy. Because George's position on this topic is discussed in section III of this paper, let us pass over it for the moment. The second issue concerns the question of whether or not land is supplied under conditions of monopoly. From an economic standpoint, George used the term *monopoly* loosely, as did most thinkers in the classical tradition. He did not bother to distinguish between monopoly and ownership, so that his writings frequently gave the impression that exclusive ownership is a necessary *and* a sufficient condition for monopoly. Yet the difference between monopoly and ownership is one of substance. Monopoly is a *market* phenomenon. It refers to the absence of actual or potential rivalry in the sale of goods. Ownership is a *legal* phenomenon that refers to the right to use (or not use) resources. Ownership can be absolute— which means that the owner's choice of how a particular right will be exercised dominates the decision process that governs actual use. But even absolute ownership does not necessarily imply monopoly. Absolute ownership can be diffuse or concentrated. Diffuse ownership is conducive to competition, whereas concentrated ownership is conducive to monopoly. The reason concentrated ownership conveys monopoly power in the marketplace is that it enables the owner to restrict the number of substitutes for the monopolized resource. Thus, if individual A owns one square block of French Quarter land in New Orleans and there are forty-nine other blocks of French Quarter land owned by forty-nine other owners, A can exclude others from using his block, but there is no meaningful sense in which he has a land monopoly, since there are forty-nine reasonably good substitutes for his block. If, on the other hand, A owned all fifty blocks of French Quarter property, he would have an effective monopoly to the extent that only imperfect substitutes exist for the said property.

George was not sympathetic to this view because he tended to define land in terms of location instead of in terms of use. The reason he could argue that taxation of economic rent cannot diminish production is that he held the supply of land to be perfectly inelastic. This view is correct only insofar as land is defined in terms of location. Given the fixed location of individual parcels of land, there can be no real supply response to changes in the price (i.e., rent) of each parcel. But if land is defined in terms of its *use*, higher rents will call forth additional supply as long as each plot of land has alternative uses. Marshall seemed to be aware of this last point and he therefore saw a degree of competition in the supply of land that George would not admit, possibly because George insisted in classifying every product or resource not according to its economic function but according to whether or not it was the product of labor and capital. In their Oxford confrontation, Marshall attempted to get George to see that as long as land has alternative uses and many owners it comes to be supplied under conditions approaching competition. That is, a number of available, but not perfect, substitutes exist for each plot of land in a specific use, so that the buyer of land is not at the mercy of any one seller. However, the argument was lost on George. He continued to assert that land rent is a monopoly price, citing Adam Smith as his authority.[24]

In his *Principles*, Marshall raised other objections, although indirectly, to George's characterization of land rent as a monopoly return. Marshall admitted that land rent was monopolistic to the extent that it represented a return to the uniqueness of location or fertility. But the observed value of land commonly includes the reward to foresight and, since foresight comes under the broad rubric of entrepreneurial talents, its reward may be economically justified. The difficulty of separating that portion of rent which represents the return to foresight from that which represents the return to uniqueness appeared insurmountable to Marshall, and he felt that George had overstated his case by identifying rent purely and simply as a monopoly return. He was either unaware of, or chose not to recognize George's proposal to allow landowners to retain part of their annual rent as a sort of "agency fee."[25]

Lemma 4: Land-Value Taxes Stimulate Production

The exclusive ownership of land raised another Georgian bugbear: land speculation. George's attack on land speculation was two-pronged. First, he based his theory of business cycles on the proposition that the speculative advance of rents that accompanies economic development drives down the earnings of labor and capital, thus producing industrial depressions. Second, speculators generally hold land out of use, thereby curtailing production. The first conclusion is based on a questionable theory of income distribution, which Marshall made an earlier point of attack. As we have seen, Marshall argued that high or low ground rents do not of themselves cause income fluctuations; instead, these fluctuations are the outcome of changes in the demand and/or supply conditions of the agents of production.

George's second argument was of more concern, and in his *Principles* Marshall admitted that "antisocial" forms of speculation posed a potential threat to economic progress. Yet he saw a side to speculation that George never acknowledged:

It has been well observed that a speculator, who, without manipulating prices by false intelligence or otherwise, anticipates the future correctly; and who makes his gains by shrewd purchases and sales. . .generally renders a public service by pushing forward production where it is wanted, and repressing it where it is not: but that a speculator in land in an old country can render no such public service, because the stock of land is fixed. At the best he can prevent a site with great possibilities from being devoted to inferior uses in consequences of the haste, ignorance, or impecuniosity of those in control of it.[26]

Marshall thus shared George's distrust of speculators, but unlike George, he was not willing to condemn all land speculation out of hand. In fact, he thought that great harm usually came from "hasty attempts to control speculation by simple enactments."[27]

In any event, Marshall never regarded land speculation as a main issue of George's analysis. More fundamental was the question of whether a Georgist program would stimulate production and economic growth or merely redistribute income. George defended the first proposition; Marshall the latter. Marshall noted:

> I do not say that the working classes would not be better off if those who had become owners of land would distribute its rent among the rest. What I say is that this would not make much difference. The diminishing productiveness of the free soil has a greater influence in lowering wages than the payment of rent fees. But even this has not a very important influence. So long as the population is not excessively thick, it is counterbalanced by the advantages for manufacturing and other purposes arising from the closeness of population. It need not make wages fall if the efficiency of the population can be kept up.[28]

Marshall followed this with numerical estimates of national income, showing that in the year 1883 the transfer of taxes from labor and capital to land would have amounted to a per capita saving for workers of "less than a penny in the shilling on their income."[29] On the other hand, he estimated the social costs to be enormous:

> For the sake of this [meager gain] Mr. George is willing to pour contempt on all the plans by which working men have striven to benefit themselves; he is willing arbitrarily to bring to ruin numberless poor widows and others who have invested their little all in land; he is willing to convulse society and run the dangers of civil war; and he is willing to run the risk of driving away capital and business ability so that their aid in production cannot be got by labour except on most onerous terms.[30]

Possibly these remarks were calculated to strike terror in the hearts of the laborers to whom Marshall was speaking and who were, in his view, most susceptible to George's arguments. Nevertheless, they do not represent Marshall at his best. He did not bother to explain why George's tax program would have the above consequences, and in this respect he did not measure up to John Stuart Mill, who signaled the adverse allocative effects to be expected from a restructuring of property rights.[31] We must recall, however, that Marshall did not choose to publish these lectures—probably because he recognized his performance therein as in many respects mediocre.

Ultimately, the question of whether or not a general land-value tax will lead to an increase in production remains problematical. It is not, however, crucial to a defensible neo-Georgist position on taxation. Given existing property rights, a sufficiently strong argument in favor of a land-value tax is the analytically sound proposition that such a tax does not disturb production and consumption as much as other kinds of taxes. Marshall himself continued to affirm this proposition throughout his professional career.[32]

III. Land Tenure, Property Rights, and the Nature of Rent

George explicitly grounded his theory of taxation in the ethics of ownership. He argued that ownership is legitimate only if the property claimed as one's own was the product of human labor. The uniqueness of land, for George, is that it is *not* the product of human exertion, and therefore its value should accrue to the state. The labor theory of ownership thus provided the ethical foundation of George's single tax. It should be noted, however, that among land reformers, George was one of the most conservative. In order to secure the ownership of capital improvements already in place, and so as not to discourage future improvements, he would preserve, pro forma, existing property rights in land. The *benefits* of private property would nevertheless be transferred from individuals to the community.

Marshall's ethical presuppositions were much less obtrusive. Nevertheless, his explicit statements on property rights present some clues to his attitude. In the following passage, for example, Marshall almost seemed to have George in mind:

> The rights of property, as such, have not been venerated by those master minds who have built up economic science; but the authority of the science has been wrongly assumed by some who have pushed the claims of vested rights to extreme and antisocial uses. It may be well therefore to note that the tendency of careful economic study is to base the rights of private property not on any abstract principle, but on the observation that in the past they have been inseparable from solid progress; and that therefore it is the part of responsible men to proceed cautiously and tentatively in abrogating or modifying even such rights as may seem to be inappropriate to the ideal conditions of human life.[33]

This passage betrays Marshall's conviction that sudden economic and social change is suspect, but it does not provide much in the way of an ethical theory of property. This was undoubtedly intentional on Marshall's part, for where George was concerned he wished to focus attention on the economic rather than the ethical aspects of land tenure.

On strict economic grounds, the differences between George and Marshall on this subject were mainly taxonomic. The incidence of a land-value tax was treated by Marshall in much the same way as George had done. Moreover, Marshall's discussion of rent was bifurcated in an way that George might have found congenial if he had fully understood it. Rent is a surplus, Marshall argued, but land rent is merely one form of a more general genus. All economic surpluses are explained by either scarcity or differential advantages. There is dissimilarity between land and the other agents of production insofar as land is a permanent and fixed stock—at least in old countries. But there is similarity, Marshall maintained, insofar as some of the other agents of production cannot be produced quickly, so that in the short run their stock is practically fixed. The short-run payments to nonland factors of production (Marshall's "quasi-rent") therefore stand in the same relation to the value of the products they produce as does land rent to the value of the products produced by land.[34] On the other hand, differential advantages may persist in the long run, and such advantages of situation or fertility are often the result of the growth and dispersion of population or of industrial development. Marshall termed this part of the annual value of land (the result of human action, but not of the individual landholder) its "public value," and he argued correctly that this rent could be taxed away without adverse effects on production or consumption.[35]

In recognizing land's public value and in insisting that land is unique among the factors of production, Marshall stood closer to George than he does to modern neoclassical economists. However, Marshall was careful to set forth certain *obiter dicta*. He made the helpful distinction between the supply of land in the aggregate and the supply of land for a particular use; and he investigated the effects of a land-based tax on each. While the aggregate supply of land is (perfectly) inelastic, the output from land (e.g., living units) is not, even though it is subject to diminishing returns. The effects of a tax on land therefore depends on whether it is a tax on the general capabilities of land or a tax on a particular use. Marshall argued that a tax on the value of output from land may have the effect of deterring improvements. He wrote:

> If an improved method of cultivation develops latent resources of the soil, so as to yield an increased return much in excess of what is required to remunerate the outlay with a good rate of profits; this excess of net return above normal profits belongs properly to true rent: and yet, if it is known, or even expected, that a very heavy special tax on true rent will be made to apply to this excess income, that expectation may deter the owner from making the improvement.[36]

This argument does not necessarily undermine George's tax proposal, but it does place a heavy burden on the technical expertise required to separate, administratively, "true rent" from aggregate rent payments, and the "public value" of land from its "private value." Marshall reserved the latter term for the part of rent that can be traced to the work and outlay of individual landholders.

For his part, George argued that the whole of true rent is a community value. He recognized what Marshall called the "private value" of land, but he insisted that this be classified under interest rather than under rent. He further concluded that after long periods of time this "private value" becomes "public." His examples are of swamps drained or of hills terraced by the ancient Romans.[37]

This taxonomic difference regarding the nature of rent led to an impasse between George and Marshall on the matter of compensation. George was adamant that compensation be denied, since to allow it would be a violation of the labor theory of ownership. Marshall meanwhile insisted that landowners be compensated in the amount of the private value of land.[38] The compensation issue thus presents a curious example of how debates over taxonomy and terminology (however necessary in the development of science) sometimes serve to impede mutual understanding, and possibly even the pace of analytical progress.

It should be emphasized that Marshall often spoke in favor of land-value taxation and changes in land tenure. The most startling revelation in this regard is found in his lectures on *Progress and Poverty*. There he qualifiedly endorsed a plan whereby all land would become the property of the state after one hundred years. Under this plan the state would sell the usufruct of the land for one hundred years, thereafter taking it for public use, or again selling the usufruct with any new contractual conditions deemed desirable by the public. The advantage, Marshall noted, was that the plan would enable adopting countries "to dispense with the tax-gatherer."[39] This endorsement presents a genuine puzzle for the Marshallian scholar. It provides for a more explicit restructuring of property rights than even George proposed, while revealing none of Mill's awareness of the dangers to economic incentives inherent in such a plan.[40] Marshall must have thought better of the idea, for he never returned to it at a later date. But the fact that he entertained the notion in 1883 shows how far he was willing to accept change in land tenure even while simultaneously denouncing George's program.

Marshall was more guarded when he wrote for the record, but he held out the prospect of land reform again in his *Principles*. There he wrote:

> From the economic and from the ethical point of view, land must everywhere and always be classed as a thing by itself. If from the first the State had retained true rents in its own hands, the vigour of industry and accumulation need not have been impaired, though in a very few cases the settlement of new countries might have been delayed a little. Nothing at all like this can be said of the incomes derived from property made by man.[41]

Finally, Marshall supported Lloyd George's budget of 1909, with its proposals for taxing land values. In a letter to the *Times* (16 November 1909), Marshall wrote:

> In so far as the Budget proposes to check the appropriation of what is really public property by private persons, and in so far as it proposes to bring under taxation some income, which has escaped taxation merely because it does not appear above the surface in money form, I regard it as sound finance.[42]

It would appear, therefore, that not only did Marshall follow with interest the lively subject of land reform; he seemed never to have lost hope that meaningful land reform would be accomplished. The question of what reform meant to Marshall, is, however, ambiguous. To Mill it meant stronger land tenure, namely, the widest possible distribution of property rights. By contrast, Marshall at least flirted with the idea of state ownership of land.

IV. Conclusion

Despite the fact that he regarded sudden change pernicious, Alfred Marshall was not opposed to land-value taxation on economic or ethical grounds. What he attacked most vehemently was the Georgist notion that under nineteenth-century systems of land tenure, poverty was the inevitable result of progress. For Marshall, history and sound logic denied this proposition, as it did other crucial points in George's advancement of "reforms" under the aegis of economics, which in the more "scientific" state to which Marshall was seeking to raise it, did not support George's conclusions. Marshall's complaint against George can therefore be best appreciated as the defense of a professional economist against attacks on the integrity of his discipline. Marshall made this plain enough in his lectures on *Progress and Poverty*, although his remarks have usually been dismissed as mere intellectual snobbery. He called George "a poet, not a scientific thinker," amplifying his meaning a bit later by declaring that George "was not a man of science because he said erroneous things."[43] While these remarks could just as easily be overemphasized as underemphasized, I submit that they reveal Marshall's candid evaluation of George. There is, of course, no reason why Marshall should have felt personally threatened by George or his popularity, and I do not think that he did feel so threatened. George's shortcomings as an economist were obvious to Marshall, and he considered them serious. In Marshall's eyes, George argued from weak or invalid empirical premises; he stumbled badly at several points in his analytical structure; he was insensitive to the long-run implications of economic change; and most important, he did not seem mentally equipped to handle the theory of competitive markets, which was to Marshall the essence of economic analysis.

Recent investigations of Marshall's social thought have focused on Marshall's personal traits as the source of his aggressiveness toward George. Anastasios Petridis has underlined Marshall's personal sensitivity to criticism of economics (which George freely supplied); his abhorrence of controversy; and his strong distaste for socialism (with which he associated George).[44] Rita Tullberg has cited Marshall's "obsessive fear of change"[45] as a source of resistance. There is no doubt that Marshall was hostile, and that each of these claims has some degree of validity, but nevertheless they both seem to miss the essence of the entire Marshall-George episode in the history of economic thought. I believe that the explanation offered here accords more with Marshall's accepted stature in that history. For while historians of every stripe may be more prone than others to hero-worship, the *choice* of heroes is not a random process. Marshall has received a higher place than George in the common list of heroes simply because in the minds of the "faithful" he was a better economist.

George was a social reformer whose commitment to economics seemed to his critics to be of smaller consequence than his zeal for reform. By contrast, not even the severest of Marshall's critics questioned his commitment to economics. Marshall saw economics as a powerful tool for effecting meaningful and lasting improvements in the quality of life. In many respects, his zeal for social reform matched George's, and his own economic thought pushed him toward much the same kind of policy that George advocated. Therein lies the irony of the Marshall-George episode in the history of economic thought. For Marshall refused to accept George's organon. Marshall insisted that to be truly and lastingly useful, economics must be built on rigorously thoughtful theoretical foundations. George, he felt, had moved too hurriedly, and had consequently built on sand. For his part, George (and others) interpreted Marshall's hostility as intellectual snobbery, and responded predictably. But to Marshall the issue cut much deeper. Against George, he spoke out in defense of scientific method and professional integrity.[46]

George's influence was nevertheless wide-ranging. On the one hand, he was claimed as a champion by the Fabian Socialists (the kind of influence Marshall should have welcomed). His pregnant suggestion of a continuous production function seems to have been ignored, but the idea resurfaced in later economic literature. F. W. Taussig, a frequent critic of George, wrote that "the stimulating effect of his writings on economic discussion during the last twenty years is too obvious to need mention."[47]

It has not been the purpose of this paper to defend either Marshall or George in a debate that is now a century old. The chief aim of this inquiry has been to shed light on the nature and essence of the disagreement between Henry George and Alfred Marshall. There was no real debate between them in any meaningful sense. Marshall's lectures on *Progress and Poverty* were not published during his lifetime nor during George's. Obviously, therefore, George could not "respond," and the attack remained somewhat one-sided. But the nature of the disagreement between the two antagonists, however late revealed, raises questions concerning the scope and method of economics that are still alive to controversy. The reader will have to decide for himself whether or not George and his analytical system fit the mold in which they were cast by Marshall. He must decide, too, the import of Marshall's criticisms. He would do well, however, to reflect on the historical record. George stirred the emotions of the general public in his day and was very popular with a certain segment of the population. At the same time, Marshall's influence impacted with great force upon the appointed guardians of the "new" science of economics. Marshall had perhaps as little impact in George's sphere of influence as George had in Marshall's. Possibly this reveals much about the stuff of which heroes are made, and about the people who make heroes of particular individuals.

Notes

1.   E. P. Lawrence, *Henry George in the British Isles* (East Lansing: Michigan State University Press, 1957), p. 8.

2.   Alfred Marshall, *Industry and Trade* (London: Macmillan, 1919), p. vii; also Rita McWilliams-Tullberg, "Marshall's 'Tendency to Socialism,' " *History of Political Economy* 7 (Spring 1975): 75-111; also Talcott Parsons, "Wants and Activities in Marshall," *Quarterly Journal of Economics* 46 (November 1931): 101-40.

3.   See [Ronald Coase], "Three Lectures on Progress and Poverty by Alfred Marshall," *Journal of Law and Economics* 12 (April 1969): 184-226.

4.   Upon Arnold Toynbee's sudden demise in 1883, Marshall left Bristol College to assume the historian's duties at Oxford, which included a lectureship to the Indian Civil Service Probationers at Balliol.

5.   Alfred Marshall to Henry Foxwell, 22 July 1883. Reprinted in J. K. Whitaker, *The Early Economic Writings of Alfred Marshall, 1867-90* (New York: The Free Press, 1975), 1: 24-25.

6.   Three weeks after his last public lecture on George, Marshall enthusiastically wrote to Foxwell: "I am looking forward to nearly 6 months almost uninterrupted work on my book. I

shall not spare the time that would be wanted for publishing my lectures on Progress & Poverty." Whitaker, *Early Economic Writings*, 1:86.

7. As reported in [Coase], "Three Lectures," pp. 217 ff.

8. Ibid., p. 188.

9. Ibid., p. 187.

10. Ibid., p. 188.

11. For a review of economic research in this area and a discussion of some of the statistical problems involved in measuring functional shares of national income, see Irving B. Kravis, "Income Distribution: Functional Shares," *International Encyclopedia of the Social Sciences,* ed. D. L. Sills, 8: 132-43.

12. See E. H. Phelps Brown and S. V. Hopkins, "Seven Centuries of the Prices of Consumables, Compared With Builders' Wage Rates," *Economica*, n.s., 23 (November 1956): 296-314.

13. J. S. Mill, "Thornton on Labour and Its Claims," *Fortnightly Review* 29 (1 May 1869). For a perceptive analysis of the issues and substance of the doctrine as well as Mill's role in its formulation, see R. B. Ekelund, Jr., "A Short-Run Classical Model of Capital and Wages: Mill's Recantation of the Wages-Fund," *Oxford Economic Papers* 28 (March 1976): 66-85.

14. F. W. Taussig, *Wages and Capital* (1896; reprint ed. New York: Augustus M. Kelley, 1968), p. 289.

15. Marshall criticized Mill for "putting his main theory of wages before his account of supply and demand, . . .[thus] cut[ting] himself off from all chance of treating that theory in a satisfactory way" (Alfred Marshall, *Principles of Economics*, 8th ed. [London: Macmillan, 1964], p. 678). Charles Collier (Henry George's System of Economics: Analysis and Criticism, Ph.D. dissertation, Duke University, 1976, p. 185), has recently complained that Marshall emphasized supply factors to the exclusion of demand. Strictly speaking, this charge is inaccurate, although in his lectures on George, Marshall was preoccupied with the supply side. In this he was trying to restore balance to the classical doctrine of the wages fund, which, he felt, "laid excessive stress on the side of demand for labour, to the neglect of the causes which govern its supply" (*Principles*, p. 452).

16. Henry George, *Progress and Poverty*, 75th anniversary ed. (New York: Robert Schalkenbach Foundation, 1954), pp. 65, 74. I am indebted to R. B. Ekelund, Jr. for directing my attention to this aspect of George's writings.

17. [Coase], "Three Lectures," p. 193.

18. George, *Progress and Poverty*, p. 223.

19. [Coase], "Three Lectures," p. 195.

20. Ibid.

21. Adam Smith, *An Inquiry into the Nature and Causes of the Wealth of Nations* (New York: Modern Library, 1937), p. 145.

22. This phrase is George Stigler's. See "Ricardo and the 93% Labor Theory of Value," *American Economic Review* 48 (June 1958): 357-67.

23. George, *Progress and Poverty*, pp. 412-13.

24. [Coase], "Three Lectures," Appendix, pp. 223 ff.

25. George himself did not emphasize this proposal in *Progress and Poverty*, but he does provide for landowners "a percentage of rent which would probably be much less than the cost and loss involved in attempting to rent lands through State agency. . ." (p. 405). Given the context of his remarks it seems that what George had in mind was not a payment to entrepreneurial skill but rather a small incentive payment to prevent abandonment of the land by existing owners.

26. Marshall, *Principles*, p. 359 n. Also see the perspicacious discussion of "constructive speculation" in Marshall's *Industry and Trade*, pp. 250-68.

27. Marshall, *Principles*, p. 598.

28. [Coase], "Three Lectures," p. 196.

29. Ibid., p. 208.

30. Ibid.

31. See J. S. Mill, "The Claims of Labour," *Edinburgh Review* 81 (April 1845): 498-525.

32.   See Marshall, *Principles*, p. 360; idem, *Industry and Trade* p. 825.

33.   Marshall, *Principles*, p. 40.

34.   Ibid., p. 358.

35.   Ibid., p. 360.

36.   Ibid.

37.   George, *Progress and Poverty*, pp. 343, 426.

38.   This seems to be the gist of the combined statements in Marshall's *Principles* (pp. 130, 134, 360) and in his earlier lectures on *Progress and Poverty* ([Coase], "Three Lectures," p. 205).

39.   [Coase], "Three Lectures," p. 205.

40.   See n. 31 above.

41.   Marshall, *Principles*, p. 661.

42.   Cited in T. W. Hutchison, "Economists and Economic Policy in Britain After 1870," *History of Political Economy* 1 (Fall 1969): 248-49.

43.   [Coase], "Three Lectures," pp. 186, 199.

44.   Anastasios Petridis, "Alfred Marshall's attitudes to the Economic Analysis of Trade Unions: A Case of Anomalies in a Competitive System," *History of Political Economy* 5 (Spring 1973): 170.

45.   Tullburg, "Marshall's 'Tendency to Socialism,' " pp. 89, 97.

46.   On Marshall's assessment of the rewards to integrity in science, see "Some Aspects of Competition" (1890), reprinted in *Memorials of Alfred Marshall,* ed. A. C. Pigou (London: Macmillan, 1956), p. 264. The duties and responsibilities of economists and economics are discussed in "The Old Generation of Economists and the New" (1897), in ibid., pp. 295-311. On the scope and method of economics see Marshall's *Principles*, bk. 2, chap. 4 and Appendix C.

47.   Taussig, *Wages and Capital,* p. 283 n.

5

Longe and Wrightson: Conservative Critics of George's Wage Theory

BY FRED HARRISON

The wage-fund theory was one of the orthodox theories of political economy taught during the nineteenth century. It sought to explain the source of wages and the principles by which these were distributed. John Stuart Mill embodied a definitive statement of it in his influential *Principles of Political Economy*. Henry George knew that, if he was to offer an explanation of the cause of poverty in industrial society which both challenged the conventional wisdom and stimulated reform, he would have to destroy the theory. This was an aim of the opening chapters of *Progress and Poverty*.

The formula with which we are concerned is this: $W = K/L$. For the classical economists, this explained how wages were settled in a competitive market economy. Wages (W) were a function of the ratio between the size of the labouring population (L) and the portion of circulating capital (K) which was set aside by capitalists to pay out as wages. If, therefore, population rose at a faster rate than capital, the ratio turned against the workers; more of them would be competing against each other for money, and so ruling wage rates would come down.

This was an intensely conservative theory. For Henry George, the most outrageous feature was the way in which it shifted responsibility for poverty onto the sexual proclivities of working men and women. The latter, wrote Mill, "obey a common propensity, in laying the blame of their misfortunes, and the responsibility of providing remedies, on any shoulders but their own."[1] Their reproductive habits and shortsightedness, rather than institutional factors, were the cause of hunger, poor shelter, bad education—the whole gamut of deprivation. In Mill's revealing phrase, labourers may momentarily enjoy a higher living standard, but they tended to "people down to their old scale of living."[2] From this it followed that poor living standards were built into the framework of the economy. For, given a growing population, today's work force relied on the capital created by yesterday's labour: "a stock, previously accumulated, of the products of former labour," wrote Mill.[3] Since yesterday's work force (which created the capital out of which today's wages are paid) was smaller than today's work force, it followed that the rate of growth of the labouring work force was normally ahead of the growth of the wage fund. Ergo, the tendency to beat down wages in the long run, unless people were wise enough to learn that they were their own worst enemies. Capitalist and landowner were absolved of responsibility. Economic reforms which reduced the cost of living were of little use if marriages and fertility were not prudently controlled.[4]

Pursuing a Malthusian chain of reasoning, Mill argued that the labouring class tended to deploy increased wealth not in enjoying higher per capita living standards, but in having more children.[5] Thus, only by restraining births would this class improve its condition, "and every scheme for their benefit, which does not proceed on this as its foundation, is, for all permanent purposes, a delusion."[6] The real choice was a simple one: "Wherever population is not kept down by the prudence either of individuals or of the state, it is kept down by starvation or disease."[7]

Henry George was one of those whom Mill would have counted among "the enemies of the population principle."[8] For by a painstaking description of the productive process, he showed that wage earners did not rely on a previously accumulated wage fund for their income. In fact, they created their own wages as they laboured. Employees were paid out of current production. They were sometimes paid at the end of the day, or the week, or the month; but while the time scale varied, the principle did not: they were paid only if they demonstrated that they had contributed to the process of wealth creation. Workers therefore, did not rely on the goodwill of capitalists and their fictitious wage fund. They manufactured their own wages. But if this was correct, George had to account for low living standards and involuntary unemployment. For if people financed their own day-to-day living, why was it that a technologically progressive economy was associated with poverty? At least Mill was free to argue, with some degree of superficial plausibility, that poverty was the result of an increasing population competing for a share in a wage fund which lagged behind in its growth. What competing thesis could George advance to explain how men created their own wages and yet account for the apparent paradox of involuntary poverty?

George argued that Mill failed to integrate his law of wages with those laws which determined the size and distribution of rent and interest, thus producing a fatal incoherence. The American therefore embarked on a lengthy process of defining economic concepts, describing capitalist production, and accounting for those discontinuities in the productive process which created unemployment, low wages, and human misery. His central thesis was that land monopoly was the fundamental cause of poverty and that the margin of cultivation established the base rate for wages.[9] A free man would not agree to switch to wage labour unless his income was going to equal what he could earn at the margin of cultivation, where he could apply his labour without paying rent. Employers, on the other hand, under the pressure of competition, would not offer wages higher than those which were just sufficient to attract labour away from self-employment on the land and into manufacturing and commerce.

George's two key propositions, therefore, were these:

(1) Wages depend upon the margin of production, or upon the produce which labour can obtain at the highest point of natural productiveness open to it without the payment of rent.

(2) Where natural opportunities are monopolized, wages may be forced by the competition among labourers to the minimum at which they can reproduce.

Two Britishers, Francis D. Longe and Francis Wrightson, lost little time in publishing what they thought were refutations of this alternative theory of the wage determination process. Longe, an Oxford educated barrister, occupied various minor governmental posts. He had been the author of two prior economic monographs, and later wrote on other subjects. No information about Wrightson seems to be available, apart from his claim to have had "practical experience of land" in both Britain and California, and the fact that "Ph.D." appears after his name on the title page of his critique.

I

1. *The wage fund*

Francis Longe coupled his attack on Henry George with a restatement of his objections to Mill's wage-fund theory.[10] He had earlier expressed these objections in his *Refutation of the Wage-Fund Theory of Modern Political Economy* (London, 1886). Yet his critique of the wage-fund theory is far less radical than was that of George or even that of Walker; despite his "refutation" of the theory, he continued to accept so many of its assumptions that he may be regarded, for all practical purposes, as a representative of it in the context of his assault on George.

Longe apparently believed the following:

(1) *Labour is dependent on capital for employment*. While labour may originally have fashioned the first pieces of capital equipment, when it comes to "material progress, or the increase of wealth and population, the factor which plays the first part is capital";[11] indeed, "it is the capitalist who provides the materials on which alone the labourer can exert his labour. It is, accordingly, the capitalist, and not the labourer, who commences the process by which wealth is increased."[12] He did not see any possibility of realising Henry George's hypothetical proposition that "where land is free and labour is assisted by capital, wages will consist of the whole produce, less that part necessary to induce the storing up of labour as capital."[13] Longe had evidently not considered either the circumstances under which farmers worked on marginal land, or the conditions under which migrants worked in the early stages of the colonisation of Australia or North America.

(2) *Wage rates are determined by the increase of population*. George's thesis that wage rates were heavily influenced by income earned at the margin was unacceptable to Longe, who held that "it is labourers who are out of employment, not labourers who are actually employed, whose competition lowers wages."[14] If anything, Longe's Malthusianism was stronger than Mill's, for the latter allowed for the possibility that education could enable people to appreciate that lower fertility rates meant higher living standards. For Longe, however, "the tendency of population is to exceed the means of subsistence"; in the long run there was a permanent "excess of candidates for employment."[15] Responsibility, then, lay with the fecund disposition of the labouring class, "and to attribute the whole responsibility to employers or landowners, or some vague abstraction such as the 'social maladjustments that

in the midst of wealth condemn men to want,' is, to say the least, a one-sided and misleading representation of the matter."[16] It was, he pronounced, "fruitless to combat, and pernicious to disguise" the laws of wages and population.[17]

(3) *Labourers depend on capital for their wages.* This third proposition may at first appear controversial. In his analysis of Mill's theory, Longe specifically stated that "if labourers are not paid until after they have done the work for which they are paid, they are certainly not maintained on their employers' capital during the performance of that work."[18] Whence, then, wages? We have seen that Longe ascribed primacy to the role of capital. He reinforced that claim several times. "It may be assumed that *so long as* an increasing amount of wealth can be employed so as to bring to the employer that minimum of profit which Mr. George allows the capitalist, so long will an increasing population find a subsistence in productive trade."[19] If we are not to interpret this as meaning that wages came out of capital, or the profits of capital, his assertion that population can only increase in line with increases in capital accumulation[20] is less ambiguous. But one of the clearest statements is contained in a passage about peasants who had been dispossessed of their land. "While capital buys up the land, or occupies it in large firms, *capital buys off the poor man by wages* which offer him a better living than he can obtain without its assistance." He continued: "For these classes to complain of being excluded from the land by capital, would be to complain of *the very conditions which brought them into existence and supplied them with a means of subsistence which the land could never have given*; and for them to destroy the conditions on which capital lives and thrives would be to destroy *the only condition* on which they can themselves exist."[21] Longe actually believed that a distinct wages fund existed, which consisted of circulating capital.[22] In this he was following Adam Smith, who stated: "That part of the capital of the farmer which is employed in the instruments of agriculture is a fixed, that part which is employed in the wages and maintenance of his labouring servants is a circulating capital."[23] We have seen enough to appreciate that, conceptually, he was very close to Mill, and ipso facto far removed from Henry George. We now turn to the criticisms which he advanced against the American.

2. *Marginalism*

Because of George's general law of wages, he was led—argued Longe—to "the grand fallacy which underlies his entire argument. This fallacy consists in identifying 'product of labour' with 'labour.' "[24] Product of labour, Longe pointed out, was the thing produced, not the labour or work employed in producing it. Longe did not cite evidence for charging George with this confusion. George was meticulous—often to a fault—in defining his terms. Longe's mistaken criticism sheds light on the level of his theoretical reasoning. He asserted that the labourer "does not make or produce the wealth which he receives in wages, any more than the seller of a pig makes the money, or wealth, which the purchaser gives in exchange for the pig," although the self-employed labourer did produce the wealth "with which he is supposed by Mr. George to pay the wages of his own labour."[25] In an exchange economy, it is obvious that a labourer does not receive in wages that which he has produced, and George was well aware of this elementary fact. Why, then, did Longe erroneously perceive a fallacy underlying George's theory? An examination of this point yields some interesting insights into the history of the theory of wages, and so I shall conjecture an answer.

It is wrong, as Longe stated, to confuse "product of labour" with labour itself. But is there no connection at all? George's theory that the lowest wages were determined at the margin of cultivation related units of labour with the physical product which marginal land would yield to the cash wage which a labourer would demand of an employer if he agreed to change his employment. If one week's work yielded one cwt. of wheat which could be sold for £20, the self-employed farmer was not likely to accept less than £20 in wages to work for someone else. The component parts of this equation are *equivalent* in terms of their value: 40 hours work = 1 cwt. weight = £20. Now, this theoretical reasoning anticipated the marginalist revolution in economic theory which is commonly associated with neoclassical economists like Alfred Marshall. Wage theory today still relies on the concept of marginal productivity, but there has been a shift in the perspective. George approached the problem from the supply side: how much a free labourer who had access to marginal land would require in wages before giving up his self-employed status. Today, theorists focus on the demand side: how many workers would be hired by employers at ruling wage rates. But the basic equation remains as George defined it: equilibrium is that point where the marginal *physical* product of labour = marginal revenue to the firm = the marginal wage. Longe simply failed to understand this relationship.

The marginal-productivity theory has been criticised as unrealistic: it relies on the assumption of competition, whereas economies are today disfigured by monopolistic encumbrances. This does not undermine the value of the working model into which one can build modifications for the purpose of deriving predictions. Marginal-productivity theory can be modified to take account, for example, of dominant firms wielding oligopolistic power in the labour market, or trade unions which can intervene in wage bargaining to influence settlements or restrict the productive process by practises designed to protect those already employed in a firm or industry.

Likewise, Henry George appreciated that the theory viewed from his perspective had to be adjusted; land monopoly meant that labour was not, in fact, free—did not enjoy unrestricted access to rent-free land at the margin of cultivation—and was therefore "captive" in the factor market. Dramatically, he characterised wages in those conditions as being no better than those in a society based on slavery.[26] As evidence, I can briefly note the workings of the most complicated wage structure to be found anywhere: society transforming from an economy based on slavery to a reliance on wage labour, within the framework of private property in land. Cuba between the 1840s and 1870s is an example. The cheapest and most suitable form of labour for sugar plantations was the African slave. As the supply of slaves began to dry up, wages of Creole and European workers rose[27]—but not as high as they would have been had the easily cultivated land been freely available to immigrant farmers. Aimes, in his study of the Cuban slave economy, noted that a proposal advanced in 1865 to reform the tax system (which had until then relied on customs duties) would have a beneficial effect: ". . .a direct property tax would help in the problem of immigration because immense tracts of land were held by people who would not develop them nor sell them, because it cost nothing to hold unproductive property, and there seemed to be a difficulty in getting the land into the hands of small owners. A direct tax was ordered by Real Decreto, February 12, 1867, and the collection of this tax in the eastern part of the island directly caused the war of 1868.''[28] But the availability of free land (or of fruit for the picking) created a problem for plantation owners. Aimes recorded that an unhampered supply of African labour would have resulted, by 1860, in all the arable land being owned and cultivated; and this, as George would have pointed out, would have resulted in a captive labour market. Aimes would not only have agreed, but would also have approved. For, he said, "One of the great obstacles to Cuba's tranquillity was that the settled parts of the island adjoined a great backwoods; consequently, society did not react against itself. The great open interior caused a constant evaporation of the labourer class. . . ." Ames did not like the way free men of all breeds exercised their right to avoid the back-breaking work at ruling wage rates on the sugar plantations. "There was always a great plenty of very fertile lands on which an easy living could be obtained. This kind of a life was far more attractive to the ordinary negro, mulatto, and low white than hard steady work in sugar ingenios, and they worked in them enough to get a small amount only of wages, with which to buy a few articles which they could not produce themselves."[29] The easy access to food on this tropical island meant that Negroes and mulattoes were able to enjoy a relatively free and easy life. This led Aimes to express a value judgment: "The free negro or mulatto was generally a parasite. They refused to apply themselves any more than was absolutely necessary to gain sufficient to live on." Clearly, a group of people in Cuba—uninhibited by European cultural constraints—felt disposed to maximise their leisure. This caused problems for the plantation owners, who wanted a hard-working—but cheap—labour force; the absence of such a supply of workers was a brake on their plans for expansion. But they did, of course, have a solution in their hands (or rather, pockets): they could have paid wages which were so attractively high that the workers would have been lured from the back streets of Havana or the highlands of Scotland. But this, of course, would have cut the returns to the landowners.

Such are the complications which a theory of wages needs to encompass. While George's use of marginalism with respect to wages predated its use and development by the neoclassical school, his approach was the richer. For he explained the process of wage determination in full, whereas the later version was simply a theory of the demand for labour.[30] Marginalism has held the centre of the stage since George's time. Longe's rejection of George's theory exposed him as anachronistic; this conclusion supports my attempt to draw a strong parallel between him and the classical economists with whom he thought he disagreed.

3. *Speculation*

Longe believed that there was no intersectoral link in the wage-determination process.[31] This objection to George will be discussed in the section on Wrightson. Here we shall consider Longe's emphasis on what he called the "natural price" of agricultural labour.[32] This was arrived at, he said, through "the unrestrained influence of competition among themselves."[33] This was an unexceptional statement with which George would not have argued; but by itself it said little. We need to know the economic framework within which this competition operated; how, for instance, the rights to natural resources were distributed, and how these were used (or misused) by those who had access to the resources. If land was monopolized by a relatively few people and access to it restricted, the consequences would be wholly different from a regime in which there were fiscal penalties on people who chose to limit access to land for speculative purposes. Longe felt that such considerations did not affect the principle of "unrestrained influence of competition" among agricultural labourers: "This principle, which attributes the reduction of wages to a minimum to the competition of labourers rather than to any action on the part of the wealth-owner, whether employers or landowners, cannot be excluded from any theory of social science, however reluctant the theorist may be to admit a principle which must to a great extent relieve the rich of responsibility for the existence of poverty, even in their midst."[34] Thus landowners were once again absolved of any responsibility for the level of wages. But this was a curious conclusion, for Longe appreciated that in land-abundant colonies wages were high.[35] How did he account for this? Not in terms of the strong bargaining power which labour enjoyed when it had free access to fertile land; for he insisted that "it is the law of the increase of population which underlies the law of natural wages."[36] And so Longe explained these high wages as owing to a high accumulation of capital. Eventually, however, the natural increase of population would drag down these high wages, for "there is at least some truth in the doctrine which asserts that the tendency of population is to exceed the means of subsistence."[37] This Malthusianism may appear plausible when we look at the number of poor people in Third World countries. But it begged an important question: when was poverty experienced *solely* because of ecological insufficiency in relation to demographic growth? It also fails to explain why, in industrial countries, falling birth rates have not removed poverty! In the end, as George repeatedly stressed, poverty was largely a distributional problem, and one could not overlook the institutional framework within which landlords and capitalists operated.

And yet, in the same way that he is difficult to disentangle from Mill's wage-fund theory, so Longe's declamations against George have to be qualified by certain of his admissions which—if they had been pressed to their logical conclusions—would have brought him round to the Georgist thesis. But Longe avoided logical conclusions by introducing special pleading to justify the status quo. I shall note two examples. The first was embodied in the following damaging admission: "Undoubtedly Progress tends to exclude the poor man from the ownership and even occupation of land as a means of living, but if that is an evil who are the sufferers? If that is a grievance on whose behalf is it to be raised? Certainly not on behalf of those industrial classes whom Progress brings into existence, and supplies, on the whole, with a much better living and more means of enjoyment than a poor peasantry can obtain."[38] So here we have it; the "poor"—whether many or few, we are not told—were to be sacrificed in the name of progress. But what did Longe mean by *progress*, which he absolved of blame for poverty?[39] If he meant technological innovations, or improved organisation to facilitate mass production, Henry George never held that these were, in and of themselves, responsible for poverty.

Yet Longe did not mean this. And in referring to the poverty in Chicago, St. Louis, and San Francisco, Longe concluded that it was owing to "the presence and operation of other causes besides increase of population and rent."[40] But what were these causes? Longe could not resist blaming the unemployed for their plight: "the indolent and ne'er-do-wells, the professional beggar and pauper, who hang about wealth as moths round a lamp, and seek to pick up the crumbs which fall from the rich man's table."[41] And yet—and here we come to the second piece of special pleading—Longe felt obliged to take into account the effects of land speculation: " . . .Mr. George has, probably, good ground for attributing the exclusion of the poor population of the thriving American towns from gaining a livelihood as settlers on lands near these towns, to the 'speculation in land values' and the acquisition by the capitalist of the more fertile and best situated land."[42] In admitting this, Longe was conceding defeat. Yet he would not finally throw in the towel. For, he responded, "this action on the part of speculative capitalists appears to be fully recognised as an evil by the politicians of these young communities, and laws restraining it are very general."[43] Historically, this is not correct. But even if it were, Longe was not interested in thoroughgoing reform to remove the evil of idle land going a'begging while beggars went a'wanting. For, he said, "it is clear that the cause of this evil is the 'possessory right' which enables the speculators to exclude others, not rent."[44] Rent, then, is exculpated from responsibility—as if it were unrelated to "possessory rights"!

Longe tentatively suggested a solution (one applicable only, apparently, to "young communities"): "If rent be the object of this practise of engrossing land, the condition of society in these young communities is peculiarly one in which any restriction required by the interests of the community at large might be placed on the powers of the landowners to raise rents, without interfering with vested rights or long-established institutions."[45] Thus, he was willing to ameliorate the evil to the extent of preventing further increases in rent, but would not entertain a radical reform which would have removed altogether the cause of the problems under consideration: vested interests had to be protected.

In a revealing conclusion to what he thought was an attack on Henry George's proposal for land-value taxation, the British writer argued that the institution of private property in land was one which had been adopted in the United States because of its "intrinsic merit." For, he asked, would it otherwise have been acceptable to the wise founding fathers? Would they really have imported an evil institution from Europe?

Certainly no young society can undertake the task of settling the fundamental laws on which the property under its dominion is to be held or occupied with stronger grounds for prejudice against the institution of private property in land, than a society composed largely, if not entirely, of emigrants from other lands, who have been compelled to leave them under the force of those very conditions which this institution is charged with aggravating, if not originating. We find, however, *notwithstanding this reasonable ground for prejudice against it*, the right of private property in land adopted by State after State.[46]

Again he repeated the claim that restrictions were generally imposed on the tendency to land speculation. Yet he admitted, without extrapolating the consequences: "But no restrictions are placed on the prospective wealth which Progress will confer on the fortunate Rip Van Winkles from the rent of the lands they purchase."[47]

In view of his admissions, one is tempted to conclude that Longe had ideological, rather than honest scientific reasons for opposing Henry George. How else do we explain his attempt to ridicule George's claim that economic growth arising from technological innovations tended to increase land values? George was quoted as stating that "this being the case, every labour-saving machine, whether it be a steam plough, a telegraph, a perfecting printing press, or a sewing machine, has a tendency to raise rent."[48] Longe responded sarcastically: "When an author himself supplies such a forcible *reductio ad absurdum* to his own argument it is needless to take up further time in showing its fallacy."[49] And yet, on page 29, he felt obliged to admit that "the ground rent of land occupied by our factories, ironworks, and shipyards, is undoubtedly raised by the progress of trade." Time and again Longe set up an objection and then destroyed it himself!

One of the sharpest differences between the two economists lay in the emphasis each placed on the importance of land, labour and capital. For George these were interdependent and equally important in the productive process, and no one component could be understood properly if studied in isolation. For Longe, however, primacy went to capital, which created land values[50] and brought the industrial classes into existence.[51] Because of his false emphasis on capital, Longe was bound to reject the validity of George's solution: a tax on land values. And this brings us to yet another admission by Longe: "That the condition of the industrial classes who are brought into existence and maintained by capital is fraught with liabilities of which disappointment, poverty, and want are the outcome, no one can dispute."[52] Yet, said Longe, a tax on land values would multiply and intensify this unhappy situation. For "the industrial classes under his system would be just as much 'slaves' to capital as they are now." He embellished this claim with several assertions which he did not adequately elaborate. For example, employment would be no more certain or regular under land-value taxation than without it.[53] To sustain that claim, Longe had to show that the removal of speculation, through a tax on land values, would *not* help to eliminate the economic crises which periodically caused unemployment. He did not even discuss the issue.

He did, however, claim that toiling labourers would have as much reason to feel embittered by the sight of wealth and "the lavish expenditure of the rich" in a Georgist society as under the existing system. Admittedly, no human society could expect to remove all of the base emotions. For instance, in a society which forcibly ensured that everybody received precisely the same income, people capable of contributing more than the average in creative effort would resent the coercion which enforced strict equality; this would embitter some of them toward less capable people who received more than they contributed. But in the system advocated by Henry George, inequalities of wealth would only represent the differential contributions of individual people to the wealth-creating process through the exercise of physical or mental effort or entrepreneurial skills. No one would enjoy the benefits of unearned income from land. Longe could not perceive this, and so his objections to land-value taxation failed to allow for the transformation of public attitudes arising from a reform of the economic system. In fact, he would have considered the attitudinal effect of income redistribution irrelevant. For he argued that the accumulation of wealth in the hands of capitalists and landowners was not at the expense of the portion going to labourers, who therefore had no justifiable right to feel aggrieved. This was a consistent conclusion for the wage-fund theorist, but one which produced all kinds of confusions and no logical solutions to economic problems like the presence of poverty in the midst of plenty.

II

1. *The Theory of Rent*

Francis Wrightson wrote that after reading *Progress and Poverty* twice he suspected that there was something wrong, "but could not lay [his] finger on the spot." The third time lucky, he discovered "a palpable falsehood masquerading as truth."[54] On this discovery hung his attempted refutation of Henry George's book. The falsehood, however, lay with Wrightson. His mistake perhaps lay in his initial overconfidence:

> That I have arrived, starting from the same principles and adopting the same theory so far as it was applicable, at the contrary conclusion to that of Henry George, viz:—that *Poverty and low wages are NOT caused by landowners taking all the surplus wealth*, is due perhaps to the fact, that I have had the advantage both of scientific training and of some practical experience of land, both in this country, and in the frequently referred to country of California—of which experience there is internal evidence in George's book to show he has had none.[55]

So the "prophet of San Francisco" who spent so many of his formative years in California was wrong. And what verities did the British critic offer the world? Precisely none! "I am not so rash; I do not believe in the existence of any *law* with regard to rent," he declared.[56] And in the penultimate of his thirty-six pages he confessed abjectly: "The evil of the unequal distribution is still to be solved." The powers of this scientific training, it would appear, were limited, and this revealed itself in his critique of Henry George.

Wrightson argued that George made two fundamental errors. The first was in generalising a theory of rent which was relevant only to the agricultural sector. The second was in explaining wages as being determined at the margin of cultivation. We shall first consider the law of rent which was so crucial to *Progress and Poverty*.

Wrightson rested his critique on the assertion that the element which determined rent was soil fertility, "the *inherent* and *permanent* property of *fertility* in *the soil*, for if this were temporary or accidental, easily lost or diminished, no fixed rent would be possible."[57] He cited Ricardo and J. S. Mill as his authorities.

Wrightson did not quibble with George's initial definition of the rent of land as being "determined by the excess of its produce, over that which the same application (of labour and capital) can secure from the least productive land in use rent free."* His central objection was George's claim that the law also operated in the urban, industrialized sector.[58] George was under the impression that the law of rent per se was not a controversial one. "Mr. George is obviously wrong in this," wrote Wrightson, "as Ricardo *strictly* limits the rent law, or 'margin of cultivation' to agriculture; to the 'inherent indestructible powers of the soil,' of its varying fertility. And I think Mr. George can quote no writer who extends the law as he has done."[59] Wrightson was mistaken. Fertility was no doubt the defining characteristic of the law of rent which an economist in a largely agrarian economy would single out for prominence and repetition, but *location* was also crucially important. Transport costs were part of the cost of production; they therefore helped to determine the amount which a landowner could claim as being "surplus" to the total costs of an enterprise, whether agricultural, commercial, or industrial. A plot of land, therefore, whatever its use—rural or urban—had ascribed to it a value depending on whether it was close to, or far from, the markets or places of employment.

Nor was Wrightson correct in claiming that his authorities employed only his narrow definition. Mill, in noting the high quality of land used in the United States, said this was so "except sometimes in the immediate vicinity of towns, where a bad quality is compensated by a good situation."[60] This was a throwaway observation, in parenthesis, so that we might forgive Wrightson for overlooking it. But his failure to take account of Ricardo's analysis of the importance of location in determining rent is not so easily tolerated. Ricardo said that if all land was of equal fertility, in theory there would be no rent; but that since some land would be further away from the markets and was therefore burdened with the costs of carriage, rent would be a measure of locational advantage.[61] Marginal land would be the least advantageously situated land which the demands of a community required to be brought into use. Ricardo, admittedly, was not always comprehensive in his definitions. For example, he stated that "whenever I speak of the rent of land, I wish to be understood as speaking of that compensation, which is paid to the owner of land for the use of its original and indestructible powers." He did not include the locational element here. Nonetheless, Ricardo soon extended his definition and theory in the following clear terms: "If all land had the same properties, if it were unlimited in quantity, and uniform in quality, no charge could be made for its use, *unless where it possessed peculiar advantages* of situation. It is only, then, because land is not unlimited in quantity and uniform in quality, and because, in the progress of population, land of an inferior quality, *or less advantageously situated*, is called into cultivation, that rent is ever paid for the use of it."[62] From that point on there was no reason why Wrightson should have overlooked location in the theory of rent. Ironically, however, he did indirectly admit that location was relevant, for in dealing with international competition he referred to "the smaller expense of placing [produce] in the English markets," which had an effect on production costs and therefore on rents![63]

---

*Wrightson gratuitously added "rent free" to George's definition in bk. 3, chap. 2 of *Progress and Poverty*. Actually, George equated the least productive land in use with the *most* productive rent-free land.

Since Wrightson rejected the relevance of the law of rent in the nonagricultural sector, how did he explain the payment of rent for urban land? This, he declared, was compensation to the landowner for destroying the agricultural value of the land, and for "putting a dirty, smoky factory thereon."[64] There was no competition for land on which to erect buildings for manufacturing or any other purpose but agriculture, he asserted. "In fact, one has only to observe the notice boards all round the suburbs of towns to see that it is building land which goes a begging for tenants, and the landowner who should try to stipulate for even a one hundredth part of the 'surplus produce' on the faith of George's theory, would simply be laughed at as a lunatic!"[65] In this sentence, Wrightson added, in parenthesis, a damaging admission. The unused plots, he said, were "frequently not held for speculation." Perhaps so; but he was conceding that, in some cases, speculation *was* the motive! What advantage was there in speculatively holding land idle if the owner could expect compensation only for damage done through pollution? There are other problems with Wrightson's eccentric theory. The difference between urban and rural rents could not be accounted for in terms of the loss of the agricultural use of an acre of land in, say, New York's Broadway or London's Mayfair. Nor could Wrightson explain why two plots of urban land of equivalent size, with identical disfigurements upon them (say, two-storey detached houses of similar appearance), yield different rents. The difference, of course, must be ascribed to location, which landowners exploit because of their monopoly power.

2. *Intersectoral Competition*

We now return to the problem of wage determination. Soil fertility, and cultivation at the margin, may determine agricultural wages, said Wrightson.[66] But these had nothing to do with the wage of the industrial worker, for whom "competition there may be, between himself and his skilled fellow artisans, but it will be independent of 'the margin of cultivation,' and can have no relation thereto; therefore the general law of wages, as stated by Mr. George, is as fallacious as the general law of rent."[67]

At the base of the labour force was what Henry George called "the lower and wider strata" of workers whose wages were the lowest. These wages were on, or above, subsistence levels, depending on whether the ruling land-tenure system was a rational one, working for the benefit of the whole community, or an irrational one, working for the good of the relatively few monopolists. These wages were determined in the following manner:

Now, the primary and fundamental occupations, upon which, so to speak, all others are built up, are evidently those which procure wealth directly from nature; hence the law of wages in them must be the general law of wages. And, as wages in such occupations clearly depend upon what labor can produce at the lowest point of natural productiveness to which it is habitually applied; therefore, wages generally depend upon the margin of cultivation, or, to put it more exactly, upon the highest point of natural productiveness to which labor is free to apply itself without the payment of rent.[68]

Wrightson considered this proposition of doubtful validity.[69] Yet today's agricultural workers, in all European countries, as a group receive the lowest wages. Firms seeking unskilled workers are hardly likely to offer wages greatly in excess of what they needed to pay to attract labour from the farming sector. Just how much these would have to be depends upon the various factors which George outlined, and taking into account the obstacles to mobility (such as the availability of housing, which to an important extent is a function of the way property rights in land are exercised).

But Henry George was referring to workers in all of the primary industries, not just the agricultural sector, and the wages of British miners are higher than for many in the manufacturing sector. This presents no problem to George's theory. It can be explained in terms of monopoly power. The mines having been nationalized under one employer (the government, ultimately), the workers simply had to organise themselves into a single powerful union to be able to exercise reciprocal power. So strong has the National Union of Mineworkers become that they were able to challenge and topple the Conservative government in 1974, and successfully negotiate a high wage claim under the incoming Labour government as an allegedly "special case." Agricultural workers, on the other hand, are so scattered as to be unable to wield the same kind of power; for them, wage bargaining has to operate within the context of the imperfectly free market.

But the kind of exception exemplified by the British miners does not invalidate the underlying tendencies which George isolated into economic laws. To see how his theory of wages operates, we can take a look at the relationship between peasants and artisans vis-a-vis landlords and urban employers following the Black Death in the fourteenth century.

The plague decimated the working population of Europe, and this left large tracts of land vacant. What happened? Not surprisingly, we learn from historians that the custom of searching for better working conditions became more common after the Black Death. Peasants who remained in the agricultural sector moved to better land yielding them higher returns. The revenue of landlords declined, for their bargaining strength weakened in favour of the peasants. Landlords who wanted to repopulate their land had to agree to pay higher wages or (what amounts to the same thing) agree to lower rents. As a result, bondage almost totally disappeared in Western Europe.[70]

The movement of workers and wages in rural areas affected urban employment. Labour mobility equalised wages between the two sectors. Trout Rader states that "there is no reason to believe there were any significant wage differentials between town and country—except possibly to account for cost of living."[71] Landlords had no doubts that workers could influence wage rates, which was why the Statutes of Labourers were passed in Britain—to try and restrict the mobility of labour, and so diminish the need to compete with other employers in the labour market.

3. *National Income*

Having failed to perceive any connection between agricultural wages and those paid in the industrial sector, and having no alternative theoretical framework to offer, Wrightson tried to win his argument by being scathing. He drew isolated sentences from *Progress and Poverty* and relied on sarcasm to try to win his points. George had been led to the "utterly false conclusion, that *all* wealth is going into the pockets of landowners," he observed.[72] George had "levelled *all* wages down to what a man could earn at [the] margin."[73] George had drawn the general conclusion that "*all* the surplus wealth over the *bare* 'margin of cultivation' goes to swell the plethoric pockets of the landowners; while all labour is ground down to starvation point," and "neither increase of population, nor improvements in the arts and sciences, can increase wages or diminish poverty."[74] Wrightson had no difficulty in contradicting *this* account with evidence that rents had declined in the face of international competition,[75] and that there had been an increase in the income of a nonlandlord class (he did not make clear whether he was referring to workers or capitalists).

Whether this distortion arose out of maliciousness, or whether Wrightson had simply misread the published material (which he had done with Ricardo and Mill) we cannot determine, though so crude was his representation of the contents of *Progress and Poverty* that we are strongly inclined to believe that he deliberately sought to be mischievous. W. H. Mallock, whom Wrightson cited in verification of his arguments,[76] must be placed in the same category. Before digressing to look at Mallock's interpretation of George's theory, we need to clarify terminology used by the American which could give rise to confusion if not considered carefully.

George occasionally failed to make clear, in his discussions on the production of wealth and distribution of income, whether he was referring to individual productive enterprises on specific plots of land, or to the economy as a whole. Both, for example, are wrapped up in the following sentence: "Thus, increase of population, as it operates to extend production to lower natural levels, operates to *increase rent and reduce wages as a proportion*, and may or may not reduce wages as a quantity; while it seldom can, and probably never does, reduce the *aggregate production of wealth* as compared with the aggregate expenditure of labor, but on the contrary, increases, and frequently largely increases it."[77] In the first half of this sentence George drew attention to the effects on wages and rents at the microeconomic level as a result of the operation of the economic laws, which he defined, at the margin of production. In the second half of the sentence he alluded to total income in the economy. Mistakes arise if these two are confused. I illustrate the point in the following way.

Let us assume a two-factor (land and labour) economy, in which a plot of marginal land yields no rent. Then, following George, let us assume an increase of population which extends to new marginal land. Because of the lower returns, owing to poorer soil fertility or higher transportation costs, the income of the labourer is reduced to what we can hold to be the minimum subsistence level. This, *ceteris paribus*, drags down the *level* of wages on all other land and raises rent. This was what Henry George emphasised, and it is the only economic effect which would matter to people at the bottom end of the wage-earning scale (who would not care about aggregate wages). Mallock chose to take this as representing the whole of George's theory, rather than just the beginning (albeit a vital beginning) to his exposition. By limiting himself to this one proposition, Mallock deduced, and attributed to Henry George, the conclusion that landowners took a growing proportion of *aggregate* income.

But George's example showing how the general rate of wages coincided with the margin of production, falling as it fell and rising as it rose, contained no reference to aggregate wages in the country. His references were to the general rate of wages; wages (rates) as a proportion to rent in specific locations; and wages as a quantity received by the industrial labourer. With an extension of the margin because of increased population and an increase in the arts of production, the aggregate wage bill of a country might rise or fall as a proportion of the total produce of the country or rise or fall in relation to rent, but none of this is relevant to George's thesis. Thus, even if it could be shown that the aggregate wages of a community had increased in quantity and/or as a proportion of total output, it would not destroy George's argument.

In 1884, the year before Wrightson published his tract, Mallock drew up a chart of national income[78] showing the proportion going to landlords if Henry George's theory—as he interpreted it—was correct. Given a gross income of £1,200 million, Mallock revealed that the theory contained in *Progress and Poverty* was such that large landed proprietors ought to be receiving £900 million, and the rest of the nation £200 million. In fact, one of the "truths' which he offered was this: "The rental of the landed aristocracy, instead of being, as Mr. George and various agitators imagine, something over 900 millions, is in reality under 45 millions."

Thus George was exposed as a charlatan, a man seeking to distort reality for his own ends, a trouble-maker who refused to test his hypotheses against the facts. For an understanding of how Mallock deduced George's "supposed" position, let us turn to a book he published in 1914. *Social Reform*[79] provided a repeat performance of the statistical exercise, but by now national income had grown to £2,000 milion. According to George—declared Mallock—the bulk of the population of Britain and Ireland should have been subsisting on £500 million, while the owners of the unimproved soil should be appropriating £1,500 million. In fact, he triumphantly revealed, the actual rental income, after deducting that portion which was interest on buildings, did not total £80 million, while the great landowners themselves received less than half that sum.[80] Furthermore, the proportion of national income going to landowners had decreased from twenty percent of £180 million in 1801 to four percent of £2,000 million in 1914.[81]

Mallock's reading of *Progress and Poverty* was of the same simplistic order as Wrightson's. The core of his understanding of George's work, which underlay his statistics, was this:

> in whatever ratio the income of any progressive country increases, the portion of it which is taken by landowners as the rent of crude land, or land-rent as distinct from interest on human improvements, constantly increases in a ratio greater still. If the total income within a given period doubles itself, land-rent will within the same period continue till 'the earnings of capital' (as he put it) no less than 'the wages of labour' are so far absorbed by land-rent that the landowners appropriate the entire and increasing difference between the total of the national product, no matter how great, and the amount which is *just sufficient to keep the rest of the* population alive.[82]

I shall note two points which not only render Mallock's debunking exercise null and void, but indicate how unreliable his own figures were. First, he used statistics which represented *income actually received* in the United Kingdom. These were the only figures of interest to the taxation authorities, who worked on the Smithian precept of taxing people according to their ability to pay. But when it came to rent, George was interested in only one figure: the *potential* income and tax yield from all land. Therefore, Mallock's statistics, if they were to be a fair test, would have to be adjusted to include rents imputed to the owners of freehold land. For landowners either (a) used the land themselves, and therefore theoretically paid themselves rent in their capacity as landowners, or (b) held the land idle, for whatever reason, and so were choosing not to realise potential income. To calculate this "income," a new Domesday Book exercise would need to be instituted.

The second point is this. What if, after completing the valuation of all land in the economy, it was found that Mallock was right—that rent (as defined by Henry George) *was* diminishing as a proportion of national income? This in itself would prove nothing at all, for we can envisage a situation in which a growing population pushes up production by extending cultivation outwards; this increases total output in such a way that, while wage *levels* on particular plots may drop, total wages may *increase* as a proportion of national income. Conversely, while rental *levels* increase, the *share* of rent in the economy's total output may decrease. So while the wages bill may have increased as a whole, who could deny that, in per capita terms, the landlords were the better-off class? It may be objected that this relies on an extensive use of land: is this realistic when dealing with land, which is in finite supply? The objection causes us no difficulty, for George did not rely on an indefinite outward extension of the margin of cultivation. In fact, at the end of book 4, chapter 2, he revealed that he believed that concentration of economic activity on localised centres was by far the most important cause of increases in land values. In his chapter on the law of wages (bk. 3, chap. 6) he noted how rents *and* wages can both rise with "the advance of the arts or the economies that become possible with greater population." He continued: ". . . the relative fall of wages will not be noticeable in any diminution of the necessaries or comforts of the laborer, but only in the increased value of land and the greater incomes and more lavish expenditure of the rent-receiving class." Here he dealt specifically with the rise of rents relative to wages on particular plots of land. We now know from experience that where there have been striking advances in the "arts" of production, and benefits accruing from further growth of population, aggregate wages paid out in the economy can increase enormously (which Mallock thought was fatal to George) while at the same time the growth of the level of rents outstrips the growth of wage rates (the point which George knew caused problems for many wage earners). It was the failure to distinguish between rates of wages and total wages, and the reciprocal reactions of rent and interest, which misled many of George's critics, like Wrightson, and caused others to appear foolish because—like Mallock—they pushed their satirical criticisms to absurd lengths.

But was there no warrant for saying that everybody other than the landowner would receive an income "which is just sufficient to keep . . . alive?" In the preface to the fourth edition of *Progress and Poverty*, written in 1880, George did briefly outline a model which, if it reflected a real economy, would produce a close approximation to such a result. By holding technical progress constant, and assuming a growing population, the rising demand would push hard against an inelastic supply of land and so "increase the proportion of the aggregate produce which is taken in rent, and reduce that which goes as wages and interest." But even if we assume, along with Mallock, that this was the situation for the United Kingdom in 1801, it is impossible to envisage a transformation of the share taken by rent over the course of a century from twenty percent to the seventy-five percent which he attributed to George's theory in 1914: the Malthusian influences favoured by Mill would most certainly have come into play with a vengeance to retard such a shift!

George's hypothesis was a simple theoretical model for testing the relationships and responses between given variables. It was not unrealistic: it was a legitimate construct for the purpose of scientific analysis of real-world problems, where these were limited to the specified variables. He elaborated on the analysis in book 4, chapter 2. Such reasoning, for example, would have enabled one to predict the consequences of the Black Death in the fourteenth century. But George did not intend this hypothesis to be his paradigm of nineteenth-century Europe or North America. Indeed, the very title of his book placed technical progress at the centre of his problematic. In book 3, chapter 6, he accounted for wages and salaries which were above subsistence level. He described the differential structure of income paid to the working class. Wage rates, he wrote—following Adam Smith—adjusted to allow for

Distributive Shares as Percent of Home-Produced National Income: UK Decennial Averages*		
	Wages and Salaries	Rent**	Profits
1876-1885	55.7	14.8	29.5
1886-1895	59.4	13.8	26.8
1896-1905	59.2	12.4	28.4
1906-1913	56.5	11.8	31.8
1926-1935	66.9	9.3	23.8
1936-1945	61.7	7.5	30.8
1946-1955	62.5	4.6	32.9
1956-1965	65.1	5.8	29.1

SOURCES: E. H. Phelps Brown and P. E. Hart, "The Share of Wages in National Income," *Economic Journal* (1952); L. C. Hunter and D. J. Robertson, *Economics of Wages* and Labour (New York: Augustus M. Kelley, 1969), p. 348.

*Except for 1906-1913, which is for an eight-year period.
**This category does not represent economic rent. It includes interest payments on capital (e.g., houses and factories) and does not include the rental income which can be imputed to the owners of freehold land.

innate abilities, the disagreeableness of certain occupations, the cost of acquiring special skills, the security of employment, and special factors (such as where an employer had to repose trust in an employee). These considerations pushed up the wages of some people above minimum standards, and the list has not been improved upon by contemporary textbooks on economics.[83]

Nonetheless, if Wrightson and Mallock were alive today they would point to trends in national income distribution over the one hundred years since *Progress and Poverty* was published and claim that they had been vindicated: that Henry George was wrong in attributing special status to the power of the landowning class in the industrial economy. For the trends apparently show rent declining as a percentage of national income. (See table opposite.)

If we accepted these trends at face value, we could still account for them in a way quite consistent with George's theories: in particular, the rapid capital accumulation, technological innovation and the empire-building military adventures of European states. The increasing use of capital as a substitute for land has had an enormous effect. Chemicals, for instance, facilitate an increase in the yields of fixed acreages; the rewards for this are paid out as interest on capital, although land values (and therefore rental income) can be pushed up as a result. For instance, the Green Revolution, which scientists hoped would increase crop yields in Asia and so reduce prices and poverty, also had the effect of pushing up the value of land which was well irrigated and therefore suitable for the new seeds.[84]

European landowners, furthermore, found themselves competing with the new lands as settlers followed the gunboats and opened up the four continents of the world. The nineteenth century was unique for the way in which one part of the globe was able to enjoy access to, and plunder, resources in the rest of the world at very low cost. The economic effect was to severely temper the results of a interaction between rising demand and the relatively inelastic supply of land in Europe. In the twentieth century rental income has been held back for a variety of additional reasons. Institutional controls, for example, such as the freeze on rents during times of war or economic crisis, have held back income to landowners. Technical progress has necessitated fresh capital formation at an ever-faster rate, and a result of this, as J. S. Mill forecasted, was that the "tendency of profits to fall, is from time to time counteracted."[85] And many workers have raised their wages on the basis of what has been considered to be new socially acceptable minimum living standards, or because of the higher rewards which have to be paid for the higher skills required to operate modern machines in the computer age.[86]

But we would be entitled to reject the trends revealed in existing national income statistics as being neither relevant nor fatal. We have already noted that annual income from land is not fully reflected in the statistics. But even if we restricted ourselves to considering the figures as given, we find that they present us with no embarrassment.

The share going to wages and salaries is shown in the table as having increased by ten percent; profits, although periodically dropping, ended up at the same level at which they were a century earlier. So the decline in the proportion of rent over one hundred years has been just ten percent: a small margin indeed. This shift may be explained by a variety of factors. One is that, for most of this period, rents paid by many leaseholders have been below true economic levels (because of undervaluations and the use of long leases with fixed rents). Another reason is the extension of land ownership. For instance, most British people now own their homes. Owner occupiers have increased from ten percent before 1914 to about 53 percent in 1977. They do not pay rent; therefore, the rental value of their land is "hidden" from the national income statistics which are collated for taxation purposes.* If all rental income had been taxed (including rents which people qua landlords "paid" themselves for using land which they owned) the decline in the share shown in the rent column would have been either much smaller or wiped out. Indeed, given the astronomical rise in the values of a great deal of land, we might get a rising proportion going to rent!

These national income statistics do not settle a question which Wrightson and Mallock thought was vital: namely, whether a drop in the share going to landowners necessarily meant that workers were receiving higher wages. For although the "decline" in rents is shown as having favoured labour, this does not mean that all workers have necesarily been raised by the economic system above subsistence level. For wages remained at an almost constant rate of forty percent; the apparent improvement in income distribution was wholly to the advantage of those who received salaries. Wage rates, for many people, have in fact remained at subsistence level.

Conclusion

I shall end this dicussion of the problem of wage determination by making three points. The first is located in the past, the second in the present, and the third in the future.

George's critics did not succeed in demolishing his account of how "the rate of wages in one occupation is always dependent on the rate in another, and so on, down, until the lowest and widest stratum is reached, in occupations where the demand is more nearly uniform and in which there is the greatest freedom to engage."[87] We have only to note the way groups of workers use widening or narrowing differentials in the pay structure to argue for wage increases to see the truth of George's statement. As for those at the lowest end of the wage scales, they have the weakest bargaining hands and so are glad of poorly paid menial jobs. At these levels wages were and often still are at bare subsistence levels. Throughout the industrial world millions of people earn barely enough to meet the minimum requirements of biological, let alone civilized social living; many millions of them rely on transfers of income from others to supplement their wages and pensions, to ensure that they receive subsistence incomes. Poverty, as Henry George repeatedly emphasised, is the attendant of progress.

This review of the wage-fund theory controversy exemplifies the continual need to critically question conventional wisdom, and especially that which invites people to resign themselves to degradation and exploitation. For inertia

---

*The same shift can be seen in the agricultural sector, where over half of the land in Britain is now owner-occupied. At the start of this century, nearly ninety percent of land under crops and grass was rented; this figure had dropped to fifty-one percent by 1960.

is at the centre of those conservative attitudes which justify and propagate human suffering, especially where these are held to be "natural," inevitable, and therefore unalterable. Henry George, if he were alive today, would turn his iconoclastic powers onto the modern version of the wage-fund theory: the belief that the number of jobs is both given and inadequate when divided by the size of the working population. Hence the fatalistic policy prescriptions designed, allegedly, to deal with the troublesome economic events which disrupted the industrial world in the mid-seventies. Economists and politicians preach paternalism, the need to institute job-creating projects financed out of public funds. Social reformers are once again falling back on charity (early retirement, for example, is supposed to leave over some of the work for others to do). Trade unions, not surprisingly, are among the most conservative institutions—among their solutions are the "closed shop," restrictive make-work practises, and opposition to higher-productivity machines which threaten jobs. Political parties have divided themselves into predictable postures. The Left proposes closed economy solutions, such as tariff walls and quota restrictions on imports; and the Right resorts to naked prejudice (immigrants, for example, "take jobs from our own people"). These attitudes reflect a reactionary conservatism and superficial understanding of the industrial economy which makes Henry George's critique (the subtitle of *Progress and Poverty* in part reads *An Inquiry into the Cause of Industrial Depressions*) as relevant today as it was one hundred years ago.

Finally, let us turn to the use of statistics. These are often used to reinforce prejudices and obscure the theoretical insights which advance knowledge, as we have seen in the cases of Wrightson and Mallock. There is, however, a need for new research in this area, in order to test hypotheses. It is not sufficient to argue that available data do not refute George's theories. In order to press George's prescriptions—a tax on land values with a simultaneous reduction in taxes on earned income, to produce a free and flourishing economic system—we need to strengthen the case by means of quantification. Clearly, no one person or private organisation can hope to finance or carry out a full valuation of all the land within the territorial boundaries of a state: this could only be conducted (quite easily) by the responsible public authorities. Nonetheless, there is a great deal of partial work which can be carried out by individuals. One concern expressed forcibly by George is adequately documented: the degree of poverty associated with a technologically progressive industrial society. But for his other formulations we have had to rely largely on logic and impressionistic evidence. Some work on quantification is available in the existing literature. Take, for instance, the claim that in an advancing economy, while living standards for many workers may rise, and while profits may be high for some firms, landowners enjoy a rate of return rising disproportionately faster than that of the owners of the other factors of production. In their important study of "Accumulation, Productivity and Distribution," Phelps Brown and Weber[88] disaggregated the rate of return on capital. They confirmed the well-established theory that, in the long run, the rate of return on industrial capital declined. But they found that, for buildings, the rate of return consistently increased between 1870 and the beginning of the Second World War (except for the period of the First World War and its aftermath). This conclusion was reached by calculating the ratio of the total of rents (so far as this was recorded by Schedule A income tax assessments) to a total replacement value reckoned by valuing the physical stock of buildings at current building costs. Now, there is no reason why brick-and-mortar buildings should be more efficient, in terms of yields, than metal machines. The rising rate of return, then, can be explained only in terms of increasing land values. As wealth is accumulated, so an ever-larger slice is creamed off by the landowners in the form of rising rents.

Regrettably, however, the level and trends in land values are almost totally ignored by governments and those private organizations (universities, policy research centres, and the like) which presume to instruct the rest of us on how to run our lives. The impact of such phenomena as land speculation, therefore, on vital areas—such as the construction industry and the business cycle—is neglected. Is it surprising that industrial economies lurch from one crisis to another?

Notes

1.   John Stuart Mill, *Principles of Political Economy*, 3d ed. (1852), bk. 2, chap. 11, sec. 6.

2.   Ibid., 7th ed. (1871), bk. 2, chap. 11, sec. 2. All subsequent references to the *Principles* are also to the seventh edition, the last revised by Mill himself.

3.   Ibid., bk. 1, chap. 4, sec. 1.

4.   Mill wrote: "I cannot, therefore, agree in the importance so often attached to the repeal of the corn laws, considered merely as a labourer's question. . ." (Ibid., bk. 2, chap. 11, sec. 2).

5.   Ibid., bk. 4, chap. 3, sec. 4.

6.   Ibid., bk. 2, chap. 11, sec. 3.

7.   Ibid.

8.   Ibid., sec. 6.

9.   Henry George, *Progress and Poverty*, 75th anniversary ed. (New York: Robert Schalkenbach Foundation, 1954), bk. 3, chap. 6.

10.   Francis D. Longe, *A Critical Examination of Mr. George's 'Progress & Poverty' and Mr. Mill's Theory of Wages* (London: Simpkin & Marshall, 1883). Mill renounced the wage-fund theory in 1869, in an article in the *Fortnightly Review*.

11.   Ibid., p. 20.

12.   Ibid., p. 21.

13.   Ibid., p. 8.

14.   Ibid., p. 17.

15.   Ibid., p. 18.

16.   Ibid., p. 19.

17.   Ibid., p. 18.

18.   Ibid., p. 45.

19.   Ibid., p. 20; emphasis added.

20.   Ibid., p. 20.

21.   Ibid., p. 32; emphasis added.

22.   Ibid., pp. 47, 48.

23.   Adam Smith, *The Wealth of Nations*, bk. 2, chap. 1.

24.   Longe, *Critical Examination*, p. 6.

25.   Ibid.

26.   George, *Progress and Poverty*, bk. 7, chap. 2.

27.   H. H. S. Aimes, *A History of Slavery in Cuba 1511 to 1868* (New York: Knickerbocker Press, 1907), p. 170.

28.   Ibid., p. 218.

29.   Ibid., p. 261.

30. L. C. Hunter and D. J. Robertson, *Economics of Wages* and *Labour* (New York: August M. Kelley, 1969), p. 229.

31. Longe, *Critical Examination*, pp. 14, 27.

32. Ibid., p. 16.

33. Ibid., p. 9.

34. Ibid.

35. Ibid., p. 16.

36. Ibid., p. 17.

37. Ibid., p. 18.

38. Ibid., p. 32.

39. Ibid., p. 35.

40. Ibid.

41. Ibid., p. 36.

42. Ibid.

43. Ibid.

44. Ibid.

45. Ibid., p. 37.

46. Ibid.; emphasis added.

47. Longe, *Critical Examination*, p. 37.

48. George, *Progress and Poverty*, bk. 4, chap. 3.

49. Longe, *Critical Examination*, p. 14.

50. Ibid., p. 32.

51. Ibid., p. 33.

52. Ibid.

53. Ibid.

54. Francis Wrightson, *Henry George's 'Progress and Poverty': The Cause—The Remedy. An Analysis and a Refutation* (Birmingham: Cornish Brothers, 1885), p. 3.

55. Ibid., p. 17; original emphasis.

56. Ibid., p. 33; original emphasis.

57. Ibid., p. 5; original emphasis.

58. Ibid., p. 7.

59. Ibid., p. 20; emphasis added.

60. Mill, *Principles of Political Economy*, 7th ed., bk. 4, chap. 3, sec. 5.

61. David Ricardo, *Principles of Political Economy and Taxation*, in *The Works of David Ricardo*, ed. J. R. McCulloch (London: John Murray, 1888), pp. 35, 36. Johann von Thunen, in *The Isolated State*, published the first scientific treatment of the role of location in the formation of rent.

62. Ricardo, *Principles*, pp. 35, 36; emphasis added. See also chap. 14.

63. Wrightson, *Henry George's 'Progress and Poverty'*, p. 34.

64. Ibid., p. 9.

65. Ibid.

66. Ibid., p. 21.

67. Ibid., p. 22.

68. George, *Progress and Poverty*, bk. 2, chap. 6.

69. Wrightson, *Henry George's 'Progress and Poverty'*, pp. 21, 22.

70. See papers by Sylvia Thrupp and Georges Duby in *The Middle Ages*, ed. Carlo M. Cipolla (London: Fontana, 1972), esp. pp. 182, 213, 268. See also Rodney Hilton, *Bond Men Made Free* (London: Methuen, 1977), pp. 153-57, and R. Faith, "Peasant Families and Inheritance Customs," *Agricultural History Review* (1966).

71. Trout Rader, *The Economics of Feudalism* (New York: Gordon and Breach, 1971), p. 108.

72. Wrightson, *Henry George's 'Progress and Poverty,'* p. 17; emphasis added.

73. Ibid., p. 22.

74. Ibid., p. 25; emphasis added.

75. Ibid., p. 33.

76.   Ibid., p. 18.

77.   George, *Progress and Poverty*, bk. 4, chap. 2; emphasis added.

78.   W. H. Mallock, *The Landlords and the National Income* (London: W. H. Allen & Co., 1884).

79.   W. H. Mallock, *Social Reform* (London: John Murray, 1914).

80.   Ibid., p. 204.

81.   Ibid., p. 203.

82.   Ibid., p. 301-02; emphasis added.

83.   E. Nevin, *Textbook of Economic Analysis*, 3d ed. (London: Macmillan, 1967), chap. 15, sec. 4.

84.   The conservatism of the landlord class has in the past led it to adopt a reactionary attitude to scientific and technological advances which, they felt, retarded the rise in their incomes. In the seventeenth century, for example, during the time of striking advances in agriculture, the landlords believed that innovations injured their income; agricultural improvements, wrote Sir William Petty, "be grumbled against by landlords, as the way to depress the price of victuals" (as a result of the increase in the supply of produce). W. Petty, *Political Arithmetick* (London, 1690), pp. 69-70. Their attitude was conditioned by the correct belief that "corn is not high because a rent is paid, but a rent is paid because corn is high" (Ricardo, *Principles*, p. 39). See also Mill, *Principles of Political Economy*, bk. 4, chap. 3, sec. 4.

85.   Mill, *Principles of Political Economy*, 7th ed., bk. 4, chap. 3, sec. 3.

86.   See the interesting study by Gerhard Bry and Charlotte Boschan, "Secular Trends and Recent Changes in Real Wages and Wage Differentials in Three Western Industrial Countries: The United States, Great Britain and Germany," in *Second International Conference of Economic History*, Aix-en-Provence, 1962 (Paris: Mouton & Co., 1965).

87.   George, *Progress and Poverty*, bk. 3, chap. 6.

88.   E. H. Phelps Brown and B. Weber, "Accumulation, Productivity and Distribution in the British Economy, 1870-1938," *Economic Journal*, (1953).

Mallock and the "Most Elaborate Answer"

BY ROY DOUGLAS

The publication of *Progress and Poverty* exerted an early and enormous effect upon opinion in the British Isles. One of George's first English theoretical critics was the litterateur and publicist William Hurrell Mallock (1849-1923), whose book *Property and Progress* was based on earlier essays, and published as a complete work in 1884. Mallock's attentions were not directed at George alone, but George was his most serious target. One twentieth-century commentator has gone so far as to describe *Property and Progress* as "the most elaborate answer to Henry George ever written."[1] Although Mallock's criticisms were essentially destructive in character, he was concerned to reason rather than indulge in empty polemics, and—unlike many of George's critics—genuinely sought to understand the gravamen of George's arguments and in places made important concessions to them. Above all, Mallock refused to accept the almost hysterical and highly personal denunciations which were much in vogue among the more comfortable social classes at the time: "There has been a strong disposition among certain English critics to regard Mr. George as though he were nothing more than a charlatan, and to think, upon that ground, that a passing sneer will dispose of him. In both these views we consider them wholly wrong: but even were the first of them never so well founded, we shall fail to see in it the least support for the second."[2] Mallock sought to meet George's principal economic arguments by an implied defence of the status quo.

The dialogue between George and Mallock was partly, though by no means entirely, concerned with the arguments advanced by T. R. Malthus. "Malthusianism" in its most sweeping form is seldom advanced by serious disputants today; but many people are still prone to adopt attitudes which contain a substantial Malthusian element, particularly when they are considering—for example—very poor people or societies.

All creatures, the Malthusian argument runs, tend to increase in geometrical progression. The lives of most wild animals will be terminated by violence, by starvation, or by disease. Man also tends to reproduce at an exponential rate, and the natural forces which keep his reproductive proclivities in check are similar to those which apply to the rest of nature. Whatever technological or economic improvements we make, the great mass of mankind will continue to live at around the level of subsistence. As we find ways of growing more corn, so do more mouths appear to consume it. If the Malthusian view is correct, then any argument—whether of George or anyone else—which turns on the contention that the economic condition of the mass of mankind is susceptible of prolonged improvement, appears to be in vain.

Mallock quoted the apparently devastating reply which George delivered to Malthus:

> Of all living things, man is the only one who can give play to the reproductive forces, more powerful than his own, which supply him with food. Both the jay hawk and man eat chickens, but the more jay hawks the fewer chickens, while the more men the more chickens. . . . Within the limits of the United States alone, there are now forty-five millions of men, where there were only a few hundred thousand; and yet there is now within that territory much more food *per capita* for the forty-five millions than there was for the few hundred thousand. It is not the increase of food that has caused the increase of men, but the increase of men that has brought about the increase of food. . . . In short, while all through the animal and vegetable kingdoms the limit of subsistence is independent of the thing subsisted, with men the limit of subsistence is, within the final limits of earth, water and sunshine, dependent upon man himself.[3]

Mallock was compelled to admit the force of much of George's argument. With one small exception, he confessed, "Mr. George is as true as he is lucid." The fault of George's reasoning, in Mallock's view, was a "sin not of commission but of omission."

Mallock suggests that the limits of subsistence may be compared with the bow of Odysseus: a bow which may indeed be drawn, but only with great difficulty and by a man of exceptional strength. "Many men starve in their own country," he declared, "because they love it too well to leave it, or because they are too weak to make the effort required to do so. Many men starve, not because there is no work to be done, but because they do not know where the work is. . . . In extending the indiarubber rings, some pressure has to be always exerted, and . . . on the average a certain proportion of people are always injured by the pressure before they are able to release it."[4]

Here is something not really very different from the challenge-and-response theory of history, developed so impressively in our own day by Toynbee.

Where, then, are the victims of these population pressures to be seen, in actual experience? Mallock quotes without confutation George's assertion that "the globe may be surveyed and history may be reviewed in vain for any evidence of a considerable country in which want can be fairly attributed to an increasing population."[5] Yet George is also quoted in his admission that, in some isolated communities—he suggests Pitcairn Island—which are "cut off from communication with the rest of the world," Malthusian pressures may exist. The present author has examined much evidence which suggests that such pressures did indeed exist in parts of the Scottish Hebrides in the late nineteenth century—in communities where the people suffered from the considerable disadvantages of bad communications with the mainland, an incapacity to speak any language but Gaelic, an intense emotional attachment to a group of beautiful but barren islands, and the ruin of their economy through technological changes elsewhere.

This seems to suggest the kind of limits within which the Malthusian view possesses a degree of validity. There may well be, indeed, there certainly are, some particular areas where conditions of living would be better if the population within that area were smaller. People are deterred from leaving those places and migrating to others for a variety of reasons: sentiment, linguistic difficulties, ignorance, bad or expensive communications, or by action of the organs of government in their own states or others. Even within places where these general disadvantages are absent, there will be isolated examples where poverty contains a certain Malthusian element in a family of exceptional size, or among people with exceptionally low physical or mental capabilities, among people suffering from disease or pathological addictions, and so on. In such cases, an extra child may very well mean serious economic distress, for an extra child will present a demanding mouth long before the accompanying hands are able to produce food.

Where the Malthusian argument falls down is in its general application. As George argued so cogently, there is no evidence whatever which suggests that human reproduction has outstripped the supply of materials which man requires—or of his capacity to utilise those materials. Indeed, there is much evidence which shows the very reverse: the general effect of increasing the number of human beings has been and will probably continue to be, to increase the per capita productivity of all. In spite of the anxieties of our own time, there seems no reason to rehabilitate Malthusianism except within the very limited field which George was disposed to leave to it. Yet even if we were inclined to accept Mallock's contention on the Malthusian question as valid, he certainly had in no way demonstrated that it was inherently impossible to introduce great improvements in the condition of the mass of mankind; and perhaps he did not even seek to do so. It is one thing to say that the population pressures may harm some human individuals; it is a very different thing indeed to say that they foredoom to failure all devices for improving the lot of the great mass of mankind.

While Mallock's defence of Mathus is much less than wholehearted, he is disposed to set a good deal more weight on another "pessimistic" economic theory, which is not unrelated to Malthusianism, although either theory may be defended independently of the other. This is the "wage-fund" theory: an idea which seems at first sight rather collateral to George's most important economic contentions, but which is really highly relevant to the question whether public policy may be called into action to deal with poverty.

Mallock summarises the wage-fund theory in the following terms: "Wages [are] fixed by the ratio between (a) the number of labourers and (b) the amount of capital devoted to the employment of labour."[6]

Like Malthusianism, the wage-fund theory will probably find few defenders today; nevertheless discredited economic theories have a curious habit of reviving themselves later in a new form, and so it is perhaps worth giving the matter some attention.

If the wage-fund theory is correct, then any substantial change in the remuneration of labour can result only from variations in either the number of labourers or the quantity of capital devoted to their employment; therefore, nothing can vary wages except insofar as it varies one or both of those factors. From this Mallock deduced that it would be futile for workers to anticipate any benefit from the application of George's proposals, evidently not realizing (or perhaps refusing to believe) that such application would stimulate investment in productive enterprise. No doubt the validity of that deduction would be challenged today, even if the wage-fund theory were accepted; but it probably would have secured general acceptance in the nineteenth century, when few people envisaged the possibility that the state would deploy either capital or labour on a modern scale. The wage-fund theory is defended not only by Mallock but also by such prominent thinkers of the period as T. H. Huxley, and Émile de Laveleye. Huxley's more strictly "biological" criticisms of George are examined in chapter 9, but it is convenient here to consider the arguments of the three men together insofar as they relate to the wage-fund theory. Huxley introduces some arguments which Mallock did not employ but his most powerful contributions seem to be drawn, directly or indirectly, from what Mallock had to say.

Huxley challenges George's definition of *capital*, while the criticisms by Mallock, and perhaps by Laveleye too, are applicable to *capital* as George understood the term. It is, of course, always futile to argue over definitions; the only essential requirement of a definition is that it should be as clear as possible, and that it should be rigorously adhered to by the disputants. As different usages of the word *capital* exist, however, we need to discover in what sense George used it, in order to perceive the substance of the disagreement between him and his critics.

Capital, as George used the term, is a species of "wealth," which in turn he defines as "natural products that have been . . . modified by human exertion, so as to fit them for the gratification of human desires."[7] Thus "wealth" excludes natural resources ("land"). George, like other economists, had more difficulty in finding a satisfactory definition of *capital*, and finally arrived at a double definition. It included wealth used to produce further wealth, and also "wealth in course of exchange, understanding exchange to include not merely the passing from hand to hand, but also such transmutations as occur when the reproductive or transforming forces of nature are utilised for the increase of wealth."[8] *Capital* being a species of wealth, must necessarily contain an element of modification or translocation by human activity.

George recognizes three factors in production: "land" (i.e., nature), "labour" (by which he means all human effort), and "capital." Huxley's attack on George is in many places rhetorical, but his most serious argument on that score is that "capital" may sometimes grade into "land." For this reason Huxley refuses to accept the distinction between the words. An example suggested by Huxley may perhaps be modified somewhat to illustrate this point. Suppose that a stone-age man picks up the nearest pebble, hurls it at an animal, and thereby kills that animal for his dinner. Is the pebble "capital"? When it falls to the ground, it becomes indistinguishable from all the other pebbles lying around, which we should not hesitate—following George—to call "land." Yet suppose that the man instead flakes the pebble into a stone dart before aiming it at the animal. The dart is certainly "capital" and will remain "capital" after it has struck the animal for it may be used repeatedly for a similar purpose. How many blows, the sophist might ask, are needed to turn a stone from "land" into "capital"? We are back at the ancient question about how many hairs a man must have on his chin in order to possess a beard! It is probably best to give Huxley his point, for what it is worth: that truly marginal cases exist, whose allocation between "land" and "capital" is arbitrary. Such minor concessions, however, certainly do not warrant Huxley's triumphant assertion: ". . . There really is no fundamental distinction between land and capital."[9]

In the great majority of cases there can be little doubt into which category a thing should be allocated, just as the existence of a few intersexes does not derogate from the convenience of dividing humans into males and females. To avoid argument over marginal cases—and to avoid discussing the possibility that certain forms of capital do exist which are not used in production—we may give the word *capital* a somewhat narrower sense than George employed, and—for the purposes of the present discussion only—confine the term to kinds of wealth (as defined above) which are designed for use to facilitate the production of other kinds of wealth. This definition does not cover all the things which George called capital, nor does it meet all the points where Huxley disagreed with George's definition; nevertheless, it is useful so to define capital in order to investigate the substantial questions at issue between George on one side and Mallock, Huxley, and Laveleye on the other.

Huxley seems to add nothing to the understanding of the problem by further taking issue over the definition of *wages*: "As 'child' implies 'mother,' so does 'hire' or 'wages' imply a 'hirer' or 'wage giver.' Therefore, when a man in 'the original state of things' gathered fruit or killed game for his own subsistence, the fruit or the game could be called his wages only in a figurative sense."[10] The word *wages* may, of course, be employed however one wishes; but if we use it in the sense that Huxley requires, then neither George nor the main defenders of the wage fund were talking about *wages*, but about something else. For convenience of discussion it is far better to follow the technical usage of the word which George and most other economists seem to adopt, and comprehend within it all the reward which labour draws from its activity, whether the "wages" be paid by another or directly drawn by the labourer himself.

We may now return to the main point at issue: whether wages are drawn from capital or not. Mallock studies the process of constructing a ship, and Huxley somewhat embellished the same example. Suppose, Mallock argues, the whole operation takes two years, and costs £10,000. Each week, the shipowner is advancing £100 in wages, and it is only right at the end of the whole construction process that the vessel is of the slightest use as a piece of capital—for carrying freight or passengers. Wages, on this argument, are therefore drawn from the shipowner's financial capital before new capital—the ship—is created. If, for some reason, the ship proves unseaworthy at the end, a useless vessel may scarcely be said to have been the source of the 70,000 dinners which the workmen have already eaten, which they purchased from their wages. Thus, Mallock contends, wages have been drawn from capital.

This argument requires examination from several angles. In the first place, the capital of the shipowner, in the shape of the new vessel, is in fact developing in value throughout the construction process. While it is true that a half-built ship would not be navigable, it would probably be saleable to another shipowner. If the shipowner died at that stage, his executors would assuredly be required to declare its existence as an asset of the estate for taxation purposes. The labour exerted upon the ship has been adding to the shipowner's capital throughout the process of construction. The labour, in fact, was employed for the sole purpose of adding to his capital. Of course, there is always the possibility that the whole venture will fail: that the shipowner will end by having paid for a lot of dinners, and with only a more-or-less worthless lump of timber to show for it. To say that is no more than to say that the purpose of any business transaction may be frustrated by some miscalculation.

Another way of looking at the same case is to consider shipbuilding as a process of exchange which is going on daily. The employer, notionally, gives the workman an unshaped plank of wood, and receives in return a plank which has been sawn and nailed. For this augmentation of his capital, the employer might give the workman bread and beer; but instead—for mutual convenience—he gives the workman money, which may then be exchanged for bread and beer. Whether we go with George in his assertion that the payment of wages cannot even temporarily diminish capital, really turns on our exact definition of capital; but in any case it scarcely matters. What does matter is that wages (in the economist's sense of the term) may be earned—and in some societies they assuredly are earned—with the use of little or no capital; that capital, which ultimately derives from the action of labour upon land, tends to increase the productivity of labour, and therefore the wages which labour may draw; and that if labour has access to land it may generate its own capital therefrom.

A rather different form of the wage-fund argument is adduced by Émile de Laveleye (" 'Progress and Poverty,' A Criticism," *Contemporary Review* [1882], pp. 790-91):

> Even if I pay a workman by giving him a share in the harvest, capital has made the advance to him of the food and nourishment necessary to enable him to plant and gather it in. If I pay him at the expiration of a week or a fortnight, he has been obliged to live in the meantime, and he has lived either on provisions of his own, or, as is more frequently the case, he has purchased on credit. Either he or the tradesman, therefore, has advanced capital, and the wages paid go to repay the capital advanced. . . .The strength which the worker expends on his work has been drawn from the produce of previous labour; that is to say, from capital.

This argument is apparently more attractive and incisive than Mallock's case of the shipbuilders. Yet, on reflection, it is not really any more satisfactory. Suppose, we may ask, the traders refused to advance credit, and the workers had no capital of their own. Would the whole operation of wage-earning described by Laveleye become impossible? Surely not. The master might be compelled to pay the first instalment of wages after a few hours rather than at the end of a week, and then further instalments at very short intervals. This would be annoying and inconvenient for master and servant alike, but it would not make the operation impossible, as one would expect to be the case if the wage-fund theory were true. The advance of capital to the worker is a convenience to him, for which he may find it worth while to pay interest; but it is not essential for the earning of wages.

How, we might ask, were men as intelligent as Mallock, Huxley, and Laveleye led into such an unsatisfactory theory as the wage-fund? Perhaps the answer runs like this. If one could imagine a situation in which access to land was unrestricted and taxation nonexistent, then the reward of labour over a short period might be related quite closely to the amount of capital available at the commencement.

Even within this narrow context, though, the wage-fund theory would not really be valid, for labour could secure some wages without using capital at all, and increase of capital beyond a certain point would not increase the productivity of labour. A more fundamental objection to the wage-fund theory, however, is that it fails to account for the power of labour to generate its own capital.

Objectionable as the wage-fund theory appears when we define *capital* and *wages* in terms broadly consistent with those employed and understood by both George and Mallock, we are led into further errors of understanding if we do not stick to a single definition of *capital* and *wages* but vacillate between the definitions employed by George and those employed by Huxley. By the verbal sleight-of-hand which uses the word *capital* to include "land," Huxley tries to bring the "landlord"—who assuredly has not created land—on to the same moral and economic footing as the "capitalist," in the usual sense of the term, who *has* created capital—either himself or through a predecessor in title. The labourer, who (by Huxley's astonishing definition) cannot draw "wages" without the assistance of another person, is apparently constrained to be equally grateful to the man who has truly advanced the productive powers of labour, and to the man whose sole contribution to the transaction has been to require labour and capital alike to pay a ransom for access to something which no man produced.

We now pass to the next limb of Mallock's criticism: directed, oddly enough, to a matter on which (though for utterly different reasons) George and Malthus agree. This is the proposition that most human beings are now, and will remain "unless something is done about it," at a very low level of existence. More precisely, Mallock sees George to be arguing that "as the proportion of wealth increases, the share to the labouring class grows less."[11] This matter is examined by Mallock, but it is also discussed—sometimes rather better—by W. E. H. Lecky. It will be convenient here to refer to the arguments of the two men in conjunction.

Lecky summarizes George's views in slightly different terms from those of Mallock:

> That all the profits of production of every kind must ultimately centre on the possessors of land (who must in consequence be reaping the most enormous wealth) is a doctrine which belongs more distinctly to Mr. George; but

his statements that wages are steadily tending to the minimum of subsistence, the conditions of the working class steadily deteriorating, and society rapidly dividing into the enormously rich and the abjectly poor, have been abundantly made in Europe, and will, no doubt, continue to be repeated, in spite of the clearest demonstrations of their falsehood.[12]

This seems on its face one of the most telling arguments which could possibly be set against George. In Britain, at least, there could be no serious doubt that the general trend of wages was upwards during the second half of the nineteenth century, although this progress was by no means uninterrupted. If George's argument led to a contrary view, then this seems to demonstrate a fundamental defect in the proposition which he sought to maintain.

Some of George's assertions may fairly be cited in support of the summaries which Mallock and Lecky recorded. Lecky, for example, was able to draw this extract from *Progress and Poverty*: "Every increase in the productive power of labour but increases rent. . . . All the advantages gained by the march of progress go to the owners of land, and wages do not increase. Wages cannot increase."[13]

Yet when we seek the place in *Progress and Poverty* where this contention is first introduced, we discover the astonishing fact that it is not set forth as a matter of debate at all, but as a proposition which George could expect his readers to take as self-evident from their own experience, and to require no further proof: "The cause which produces poverty in the midst of advancing wealth is evidently the cause which exhibits itself in the tendency, everywhere recognized, of wages to a minimum. Let us, therefore, put our inquiry into this compact form: *Why, in spite of increase in productive power, do wages tend to a minimum that will give but a bare living?*"[14]

George and Mallock were both writing books aimed, not at the "faithful" but at unconvinced, and even hostile readers. Why, then, do we find this remarkable disparity on a simple point of fact? The answer is revealing, and will need further consideration later; but for the moment it is important to note the word *tend*.

In economics, as in all social sciences, it is seldom possible to perform the sort of "controlled experiment" which is available in—say—physiology. It is therefore far more difficult in the social sciences to demonstrate convincingly that a particular effect is owing to a certain cause. By the same token, the prophecies which the social scientist may make are far less certain of fulfillment than those of most natural scientists, since innumerable uncontrolled and uncontrollable factors may intervene and destroy or even reverse the anticipated conclusion. Thus, we might assert, on either a priori or a posteriori grounds, that scarcity of a commodity will tend to produce a rise in its price. Yet, for a variety of reasons, this tendency may be overborne, and the anticipated rise not observed. Perhaps something better has come on to the market. Perhaps a general economic depression has made the people who normally buy that commodity so poor that they have no money left to buy it, and the vendor finds it exceedingly difficult to sell. Perhaps the commodity is put on rations, or its sales are subsided. Other possible factors may be imagined, almost without limit, which could prevent the anticipated price rise. All economic prophecies must therefore be hedged with the implicit or explicit qualification, "other things remaining unchanged." The economist is a scientist, not a soothsayer.

Still retaining Mallock's and Lecky's criticisms in mind, let us now look at the real point which George was trying to make: a point which he sets down in terms substantially different from the passages to which they take exception:

> When land is all monopolised . . . rent must drive wages down to the point at which the poorest paid class will be just able to live and reproduce, and thus wages are forced to a minimum fixed by what is called the standard of comfort—that is, the amount of necessaries and comforts which habit leads the working classes to demand as the lowest on which they will consent to maintain their numbers. This being the case, industry, skill, frugality and intelligence can avail the individual only in so far as they are superior to the general level.[15]

The difference between that statement and those to which Mallock and Lecky quite reasonably take exception is no mere quibble. On the assumption that our real concern is with the substance of George's message and not with whether he always expressed himself to the best effect, it is better now to concentrate on the passage just quoted, and later to examine the more sweeping statements, mainly to understand why some of his assertions, or prophecies, were proved wrong.

George, in the latest quotation, was avowedly considering the situation which would arise "when all land is monopolised." The supply of land is inelastic. The productivity of a piece of land may be vastly increased; the quantity of land is virtually unalterable. The word *monopolised*, however, admits of two possible meanings. In the first sense it may be taken as a synonym for "owned privately," in which case most of the highly productive land certainly is monopolised. The word may also be read in another way. My own motor car is assuredly "monopolised," for I am its absolute owner; but I do not monopolise motor cars. If I seek to sell or hire my car, I am in competition with many other people who are willing to sell or hire theirs, and this sets me in a very different position indeed from that which I should occupy if mine were the only motor car in the world. In that sense, land is not "monopolised," for there is often a great deal of competition between landowners, which necessarily reduces the reward which a particular landowner may secure for the sale or hire of his land. If, for example, a mineral is discovered on one man's land, it is likely that the same mineral will also be found on the land of many other men, and as a result each of them will be able to claim a reward which is far less than he could obtain if he were the sole provider. Again, one urban landlord may indeed "monopolise" the most favoured site in town; but if that landlord makes demands which are too exorbitant, the man who would like to build a shop or an office upon that land will reluctantly turn to another site somewhat less favoured; and the knowledge that this is likely to happen will operate to reduce the rent which the landlord may demand.

It would seem likely (although this is not the place to attempt proof of such a proposition) that the districts where poverty is most severe would correspond closely with those where—for all practical purposes—the labourer has no choice but to hire land from a specific landowner; while wages tend to be much higher in societies where there are many moderate-sized landowners in competition with each other.

George's "standard of comfort" point is also important. During boom conditions—when labour is scarce—the "standard of comfort" will tend to rise; and if economic depression then supervenes, it will not prove possible to depress wages to the level at which they had stood before the boom. The "standard of comfort" will vary from age to age; but, as technology advances, that standard will tend steadily to rise. Not least of the operative considerations here will be the rising education of the workers. Because they are literate, because they have access to "the media," they are aware of the standards which other people enjoy, and are unwilling to assume that the order which their own predecessors accepted is fixed immutably for all time. They are conscious of the power which collective organization gives them. All of these factors must tend to raise the "standard of comfort" which workers are prepared to accept—even those workers whose "industry, skill, frugality and intelligence" are not "superior to the general level."

Education and technological improvement have also produced a further and even more important effect, which evidently comes within the ambit of George's assertions. Increased industrial sophistication and complexity have increased the demand for specialized skills, and placed a premium upon the services of those possessing them. A nineteenth-century employer who sought (say) a farm labourer, or a factory hand, might well have been free to enroll almost any unhired man in his district to do the job. A modern employer who seeks (say) a research chemist, or a computer operator, will find that only a very small number of the unemployed workers in his area could possibly do the job without weeks, months, or even years of training—if, indeed, they could ever be trained to do the job at all. Even the so-called unskilled jobs would not be within the capacity of all—or even the majority—of the workers who are on the lists at the local Labour Exchange. The activities of trade unions, prescribing both terms of employment and also who may be employed, have reduced the employer's choice even further. There are indeed places in the world where the recompense of labour is still miserably small; where it often stands at around the subsistence level, in the narrowest sense of that term. These are the places where there is little job specialization; where one worker is interchangeable with any other; where trade union activities are minimal or absent; where the habitual expectation of workers—their "standard of comfort"—is, and always has been, exceedingly low.

We are now free to examine the astonishing paradox noted earlier: that George could not only regard any substantial augmentation of real wages as impossible without some kind of radical land reform, but also call his readers to witness that this proposition was confirmed in their own experience; while, with equal confidence, Mallock and Lecky could affirm the contrary, and also appeal to their readers' experience as the most telling possible evidence.

Lecky provides some hint of how this disparity of experience arose, by reference to what might be called the "prepauperisation" stage in America and other places: "Mr. George . . . thought of the high wages in some new countries . . . . The explanation of those high wages, is, surely, that the labourers are few, and that, if they do not wish to work for an employer, they have other and easy ways of acquiring a comfortable subsistence."[16] The operative point, however, is not that labourers were few (for labourers even then were far more numerous than they had been in pre-Columbian times, yet their renumeration per capita was far greater). The essential difference between the "pioneer" days and the later period of "pauperisation" was that land was available for the taking in the first period but not in the second. "Pauperisation" coincided closely with the point where land ceased to be freely available.

George, writing not merely as an American, but as a Californian, at the end of the eighth decade of the nineteenth century, could validly point out that the technological improvements of the previous quarter or half century had not been accompanied by improved wages. This was exactly the result which would be expected on his analysis when on the one hand land was becoming privately owned, while on the other hand labour was undifferentiated and unorganized. Broadly, this was also the experience of other "new" countries, and among undifferentiated working classes, such as the peasantry, in "old" countries at that time.

The British experience, however, was markedly different. In that connection I may note that another book by Mallock, entitled *Social Reform*,[17] which appeared thirty years after *Property and Progress*, devotes several pages to criticisms of George; but these pages are exclusively concerned with one argument: to show that the income of landowners relative to other persons in the United Kingdom had not increased, but had greatly declined; while the income of the poorer members of the community had greatly increased. Mallock contends, for example, that in 1801 the land rent of England and Wales was 20 percent of the total income of £180 millions; while in 1914 the land rent was only four percent of a total income of £2,000 millions.[18] In the same period, he declared, the per capita income of the poorer classes had more than doubled.[19] At times it is difficult to trace Mallock's sources, and one suspects that his figures are open to the severest criticism; but even if we take them at face value they prove only that devices appeared which mitigated the exactions of the landlords, not that those exactions were innocuous.

The reason for the striking difference between George's experience and that of Mallock appears therefore to be that British labour differentiation and industrial organization were both exceptionally advanced, particularly in the industrial districts. George may be fairly criticised for not giving as much attention as he should have done to such considerations; although it may be said in extenuation that he did not entirely ignore them, and in any event they lay largely outside his experience.

The most deleterious effect of landlordism may well derive not so much from the quantity of rent which landlords are able to extract from the activities of other people, but from the economic distortion which "landlordism" causes. In nineteenth-century Ireland, for example, it was widely believed that a peasant who improved his holding would be likely to face a demand for more rent. The actual quantity of extra rent extracted by landlords in consequence of tenant improvements was probably quite tiny; yet the knowledge, or even the suspicion, that landlords could behave in that way if they wished had a profoundly deleterious effect on the whole economy of the country, for tenants frequently refrained from making improvements. In the same way, there were doubtless innumerable cases in Britain where—for example—men decided not to make building developments because they were convinced that the landlord would soon soak up most of the benefit through increased rent. The proposition that landlords were not enormously enriched may well be sustained; the proposition that the rest of the community was not impoverished by their presence would be far harder to defend. Another apparent discrepancy between George's argument and actual experience was noted by Lecky, who called him to task for the following passage: "Wherever you may find land relatively low, will you not find wages relatively high? And whenever land is high, will you not find wages low? As land increases in value, poverty deepens and pauperism appears."[20] The historian's retort seemed crushing: "It is obvious that, according to this law, wages must be far lower in London than in Dorsetshire or Connemara; far lower in England and France than in Hungary, or Poland, or Spain!"[21]

This state of affairs manifestly did not apply. Here again the "tendency" of landlordism was not merely overcome but reversed by other processes. In the late nineteenth century, labour was far more differentiated, more sophisticated, and more organized in London than in Dorset or Connemara; more organized and differentiated in England and France than in Hungary, Poland, or Spain.

There remains one further line of argument advanced by Mallock which calls for attention. Henry George had contended that the taxation of land values would produce four benefits:

1. Taxation of labour products could be abolished, thus making living cheaper.
2. A surplus would be produced, over the current requirements of the state, which could be returned in some form or other to the community.
3. It would cease to be profitable to hold land out of use in the expectation of a rise in value, and thus the community would benefit by more land becoming available.
4. Rents would be reduced.

The first two advantages relate to the "single-tax" theory, which was eagerly advanced by George and his supporters in the late nineteenth and early twentieth centuries. At the scale of public expenditure which then existed, a one hundred percent land vaue tax might well have sufficed to meet all government requirements, and perhaps leave a substantial surplus for distribution. Mallock and the other contemporary critics of George did not confute that assertion.

Mallock's answer to George's first anticipated advantage was that the fall in living costs would prove of only brief benefit; for wages would soon fall as well, and things would revert to their previous condition. If this proposition is to be taken as argument rather than mere assertion, then it seems to be founded on the demonstrably invalid Malthusian or wage-fund theories.

The second point is so unlikely to apply today that it may seem unnecessary to examine it; nevertheless, for the sake of completeness it may be useful to do so. Mallock replied that the distribution of land-value surplus would take the form of providing either new public amenities—like libraries and museums—or, alternatively, the issue of general largesse. In the former case poverty would not be alleviated, while in the second he feared those baleful results which comparable eleemosynary activities are alleged to have produced on the "city mob" of ancient Rome. To what extent the Romans were truly corrupted by the "corn dole" would be best to leave to today's social historian of classical antiquity—whose assertions on the subject may perhaps be somewhat less dogmatic than those of his nineteenth-century predecessor. Be that as it may, it appears unlikely that the problem will arise; and if it should do so, there is not likely to be any difficulty in devising useful public works, whose provision would be generally appreciated.

George's third argument, that land could not be withheld for speculative purposes, is met by Mallock with the somewhat weak reply that this would not benefit people who sought land in a district already fully occupied, or those who were too poor to pay rent at all. There can be few districts of any size where substantially all land is set to productive use—or, indeed, to any use. Mallock does not dispute the argument that a tax on land values would tend to force land into the most productive use, which would presumably redound to the general advantage. As for the second limb of his reply, it depends on the fallacy that the quantity of rent demanded is related to the wealth or poverty of the individual tenant. A poor man is driven on to marginal land; he is not suffered to live on good land at a low rent. George's proposals would bring unused, or underused good land into productive use, and would thus make more of it available, which would be of particular benefit to the poor man. The added productivity of other land would also benefit him, as, indeed, it would benefit other people too.

The final argument, that rents would be reduced, is not really met at all, although Mallock does contend that "the State would be harder than the land-lords and middlemen would be harder than the State." A "landlord" usually performs two quite distinct functions: he receives rent for land, and he controls the use of that land. George demanded that the state should receive rent, but not that it should control land use. The "harshness" or otherwise of the state would therefore apply exclusively in the state's function as *rentier*.

The present author confesses himself quite incapable of understanding why or how the activities of middlemen would be increased. And since the state's capacity as landlord would be limited to its receipt of rent, its "harshness' could scarcely consist in anything other than the insistence that it receive full market value—that is, the refusal to give something for nothing. But such behaviour is normative in economic life; to call it harshness is to indict the market concept and indeed the whole idea of reciprocity upon which that concept rests.

We are now in a position to examine the overall effect of Mallock's arguments upon the thesis which George sought to maintain. I have noted that there are ways in which the bad effects which (George argued) "tended" to follow from landlordism have in fact been reduced. These points are not only sound and valid in themselves; they are also salutary warnings to George's less-critical adherents that little good is done to any cause by repeating assertions which run counter to experience. The followers of Henry George were correct in recognizing and emphasizing the universal relevance of his essential teachings, but they would have served their purpose better if they had shown a clearer understanding of the work of men like Mallock.

Surely the most important contribution which Mallock made to the discussion was to draw attention obliquely to devices which have reduced the adverse tendencies of landlordism. In our own century devices which performed that function in the late nineteenth century have been enormously multiplied. Proposals designed to deal with poverty which springs ultimately from the land system range from socialism, fascism, and communism to the welfare state, trade union restrictive practices, and state economic planning.

These multitudinous devices function much like analgesic drugs in pharmacy. They reduce the pain suffered by the patient, but do not touch the core of his disease. They frequently produce side effects which may be even more deleterious than the original affliction. They require frequent and expensive application, and are often addictive.

Where Mallock assuredly failed was in the main task which he set himself. He failed to show that there was any overriding economic law which would make it impossible for workers to secure a great increase in their own rewards through political action. Mallock failed to disprove that the application of George's proposals would be of great benefit to the community as a whole, and to its poorest members in particular. He won some battles, but he lost the war.[22]

Notes

1.   C. A. Barker, *Henry George* (New York: Oxford University Press, 1955), p. 393.

2.   W. H. Mallock, *Property and Progress* (London: John Murray, 1884), p. 1.

3.   Henry George, *Progress and Poverty*, quoted by Mallock, *Property and Progress*, pp. 37-38.

4.   Mallock, *Property and Progress*, p. 46.

5.   Henry George, *Progress and Poverty*, quoted by Mallock, *Property and Progress*, p. 42.

6.   Mallock, *Property and Progress*, p. 23.

7.   Henry George, *Progress and Poverty*, 75th anniversary ed. (New York: Robert Schalkenbach Foundation, 1954), pp. 41-42.

8.   Ibid., p. 48.

9.   T. H. Huxley, *Collected Essays* (1890; London: Macmillan, 1894), 9:176.

10.   Ibid., p. 180.

11.   Mallock, *Property and Progress*, p. 17.

12.   W. E. H. Lecky, *Democracy and Liberty* (London: Longman, 1896), 2: 292.

13.   Ibid., p. 296.

14.   George, *Progress and Poverty*, p. 17.

15.   Ibid., p. 304.

16.   Lecky, *Democracy and Liberty*, p. 296.

17.   W. H. Mallock, *Social Reform as Related to Realities and Delusions* (London: John Murray, 1914).

18.   Ibid., p. 203.

19.   Ibid., p. 207.

20.   George, *Progress and Poverty*, p. 288.

21.   Lecky, *Democracy and Liberty*, p. 296.

22.   The author wishes to acknowledge receipt of a grant from the Faculty IV Research Fund of the University of Surrey, which has helped in this work.

7

Moffat's "Unorthodox" Critique

BY GEORGE BABILOT

I. Introduction

Although he wrote a number of articles and two important books on political economy, the contributions of Robert Scott Moffat, British author/essayist (1834-1895), are less well-known than those of many of his contemporaries. He was a lucid, forceful writer whose works were often at odds with the premises of received economic doctrine. In focusing on the shortcomings of orthodox economics his efforts fell outside the classical mainstream, and perhaps this may have been a factor in his receiving less attention than did other writers of his day.

His first book, titled *The Economy of Consumption*, appeared in 1878, and in it Moffat, in the tradition of earlier critics of similar persuasion (Lauderdale, Chalmers, Malthus, Sismondi), questions the efficacy of the competitive industrial organization in general, and the inherent ability of the system to avoid recurrent episodes of general overproduction in particular. Probably because of its length and the fact that it was a rather difficult book to read, it did not enjoy a very wide audience. Even so, the book's impact was of sufficient importance to provoke T. W. Hutchison into recognizing Moffat as one among the very few nonsocialist writers since Thomas Malthus to question the orthodox formula about the "impossibility of general over-production."[1]

The second book, *Mr. Henry George The "Orthodox,"* published in 1885, is a lengthy effort (296 pages) at an "unorthodox" critique of *Progress and Poverty*[2]—an unorthodox critique because Moffat attempts to integrate his appraisal of the economics of Henry George into his objections to the orthodox economics of David Ricardo and J. S. Mill. He chooses this approach because it enables him to expound further on his own reservations concerning orthodox economics, and at the same time provides him with a convenient reference for analysis of George's work. The book, therefore, is designed to serve more than one purpose: as a vehicle to continue his attack on certain tenets of orthodoxy on the one hand, and, on the other, as a critical review of *Progress and Poverty*. Because much of Moffat's criticism of Henry George stems, in fact, from his preoccupation and disenchantment with orthodox economics, not surprisingly, he proceeds to reject methodically those parts of *Progress and Poverty* which he perceives as outgrowths of Ricardo-

Mill principles, providing detailed commentary and explanations and, in the process, often citing his own *The Economy of Consumption* for support. Those portions which he admits have a certain uniqueness, on the other hand, he more often than not is inclined to dismiss as being rhetorical and scientifically or economically unsound.

This distinctive method of critique does not lack thoroughness. Systematically, and in some detail, Moffat discusses each subject in turn: Population, Wages and Capital, Laws of Distribution, Dynamics, book by book, chapter by chapter through book 4. He gives shorter treatment to the chapters on the Remedy and the Laws of Human Progress found in books 5 through 10, evidently feeling that the nature of the topics warranted only a summary evaluation. In a separate section there are an appraisal of George as an economist, a commentary on the theory of rent, and a reference to two "rival theories" of labor and wages. At only one point does Moffat depart from the order of topics as they are arranged in *Progress and Poverty*. He chooses to discuss the theory of population before discussing the topic of wages, maintaining that "a clear view of the problem of population is indispensable to any useful discussion of the problem of wages." More than neatness is implied by this change. In reversing the order of the first and second books Moffat hopes to reveal an error in George's thinking concerning the sequential relationship between the level of wages and growth in population, the source of the labor supply. Noting that George is "the boldest of the opponents to Malthus," he proceeds initially to examine in great length George's objections to the Malthusian theory and its related doctrine, the wages-fund theory.

II. The Malthusian Population Doctrine and Related Matters

It is well to keep in mind that Moffat's outlook is thoroughly Malthusian. This is evident not only in his views on population growth—approximately one-third of the book is on this subject—but also in his views concerning competitive organization of industry and the problem of recurrent overproduction ("gluts"). At only one point does he seriously differ from Malthus, and that is on the meaning of wealth. Unlike Malthus and the Classical School, he does not confine his definition to material commodities alone. He defines wealth as physical well-being that includes services as well as material commodities, and only in this sense would he agree that wealth is the central subject of political economy. Moffat claims classical economics to be in error for defining wealth so narrowly, and in even greater error for failing to tie in the theory of wealth with the theory of population. The broader view of wealth, he believes, makes the theory of population the most fundamental doctrine of political economy. Moreover, he is of the opinion that a theory of wealth not consistent with a theory of population is incapable of providing a scientific political economy.

Moffat is puzzled at the persistent unpopularity of the Malthusian doctrine, particularly since he feels its unpopularity has mistakenly tended to stifle its development in conjunction with other theoretical doctrines. What is even more disconcerting to him is that while the doctrine is recognized by the most respected economists, "the recognition has been accompanied by many practical *caveats* calculated to stand off the responsibility for a strict application of it to existing circumstances, and so to save the credit of the acceptors without diminishing the odium of its original form. Even of those who have accepted it most unequivocally, most, if not all, have wholly missed its true purport and application."[3] He observes that the doctrine itself is not new—he traces it back through Adam Smith to the time of Plato and Aristotle—but what makes it applicable in contemporary times, according to Moffat, can be ascribed to the transition by civilized societies from war-making to industrial pursuits. Evidently, it was an idea whose time had come: "The period of predominance of industry in civilized society [which] was preceded by a period of predominance of war, marks both the time and the place in which it was natural that the theory of Malthus should appear. . . . As long as men slaughter each other freely, and for the purpose, among others, of appropriating their means of maintenance, there is no need of codes to induce them to restrain the growth of population."[4] Claiming that "the constitution of civilized society is Malthusian," meaning that in peaceful industrial environments population growth needs to be restrained, Moffat apparently chooses to view the appearance of the doctrine as more opportune than novel.

Just as he maintains that the doctrine itself is not new, so he finds George's arguments in opposition to it "old and familiar." He makes a distinction between George's position, which rejects totally the doctrine of population, and the position of those who recognize the doctrine theoretically but practically erode it by believing its consequences to lie in the too remote future to occupy their attention now. To the latter group he offers this admonition: "The doctrine of population does not mean that when the whole surface of the earth is covered with human beings, there will begin to be a danger of overpopulation. It means that such a danger exists now and will continue to exist, in every settled community."[5] To Henry George he gives dubious credit for a theoretical position diametrically opposite in view: "As far as Malthus can extend the capability of the human species to grow, so far does Mr. George extend the adequacy of the provision for its growth."[6] By placing George's theory in juxtaposition to Malthus's doctrine, Moffat claims the basic issue involved reduces to whether the actual capacity for development of the human race is finite (Malthus) or infinite (George). More to the point, if a choice had to be made between the two alternatives, which would be the more desirable? For Moffat the choice is not difficult: "If it is one of the conditions of our existence that the number of our race should be unlimited, surely it is not a desirable condition and if we value our own peace of mind we must wish the victory to Malthus."[7] But this standard for comparison, while understandable from Moffat's point of view, is unfortunate because it is misleading. Not only does it bring to the center matters of only peripheral importance in George's overall thesis, but it also tends to divert attention from George's chief concern about the Malthusian theory, which is simply to show that the theory is not necessarily proved by the reasoning offered in its support.

The alternatives as contrived by Moffat would have to be rejected by George both on the basis of appropriateness and on the basis of relevance. If issues must be drawn and choices made, George would surely argue for a more appropriate basis to contrast him with Malthus, such as, for example, which is the more desirable: to accept poverty and misery as the immutable results of natural instinct, or to view poverty and misery as the unnecessary products of society's material advance, controllable by humankind? Moffat cites from

Progress and Poverty, "the earth could maintain a thousand billions of people as easily as a thousand millions," as justification for his inference of a population of infinite size.[8] The quotation does reveal George's confusion of the returns of scale and the principle of diminishing returns, and on that score deserves criticism.[9] That granted, the statement as used by Moffat is not along those lines, however, nor is it germane to the alternatives advanced by him, which imply in contrast that George offers a theory that admits to a population so great it is restrained *only* by the limits of space. It is useful to note that the quotation cited is contained in a passage that has as its main point a discussion of the life-sustaining and cycling properties of matter, which George views as an ongoing, endless process, and from which he concludes that the only technical limit to population is the limit of space. It is this remote possibility of the human race's pressing upon space that, according to George, gives to the Malthusian theory its self-evident character. He denies even this remote possibility to the Malthusian doctrine, however, carefully pointing out that, unlike vegetable and animal life, human beings do not have a tendency to press against the limits of space. George, in clear contradiction to Moffat's inference, offers in place of the positive and prudential checks of Malthus a check on population that cannot be disassociated from rising standards of living, intellectual development, and society's overall advancement:

> If the real law of population is thus indicated, as I think it must be, then the tendency to increase, instead of being always uniform, is strong where a greater population would give increased comfort, and where the perpetuity of the race is threatened by the mortality induced by adverse conditions; but weakens just as the higher development of the individual becomes possible and the perpetuity of the race is assured. In other words, the law of population accords with and is subordinate to the law of intellectual development, and any danger that human beings may be brought into a world where they cannot be provided for arises not from the ordinances of nature, but from social maladjustments that in the midst of wealth, condemn men to want.[10]

Considering the reasons offered by Moffat for preferring Malthus's theory as a alternative—because it demands "only that in the propagation of our species as in all other things, we shall go about the business, whether of maintaining or increasing population with prudence and moderation"[11]—by the same standard he might as easily have chosen George's position. Moffat instead accuses George of demagoguery. He thinks that George, in rejecting the Malthusian doctrine, is purposely attempting to win popular favor by trying to show that the depressed millions are depressed from some cause beyond their own control, and by charging their misery to landlords and governments, and thereby implying further that, to remove it, no sacrifice or effort will be needed on their part. This is Moffat's reaction to what he regards as George's implacable stand against the notion of prudential restraint.

George's reference to repressive government activities and the rack-rent practices of absentee landlords, rather than overpopulation as the cause of poverty and misery in India and Ireland, brings forth a not-unexpected divergent response from Moffat. He states that it is a matter of indifference to the country from which rents are received whether the rent is spent in that country or out of the country.[12] Then, claiming that rents in Ireland are lower than in England, he tries to dispose of the matter by posing this question: "If it is asserted that there is an indefinite margin of productiveness for the support of additional population, why is there not margin enough to support a small number of landlords at a moderate rent?"[13] The first statement, even if it were correct, which, of course, it is not, misses the point. Rent as an unearned claim against the nation's product means that those left with reduced earned incomes owing to the drain of rents are forced to accept a smaller bundle of goods than that bundle which is actually warranted by their productivity. Two comments are in order with respect to the second statement. What is meant by a moderate rent? George estimates that at least a fourth of the net produce from the land of Ireland went to absentee landlords.[14] Elsewhere he also argues that where land is held as a monopoly, the tendency is for rent to take a larger proportion of net product as productivity increases.[15] Therefore, in the absence of monopolized land holdings, according to George, additions to population theoretically could be sustained by their own productiveness. But Moffat, as before, strays from George's central point, which is that, whether moderate or not, rent is an unearned income and as such represents an unwarranted drain on earned incomes, which are derived from productive activity in contrast to rent, which goes to the landowner simply by virtue of his ownership and not because of his contribution to production.

Moffat's evaluation of George's criticism of Malthusian population doctrine cannot be divorced from his own version of population theory and his own views concerning recurring economic crises. Before we take a look at these, one area he discusses in criticism of George is instructive for it reveals a characteristic pattern of unevenness in his analysis where part is correct and quite perceptive and part is incorrect and fuzzy. The "unlimited resources" argument of George he handles with good perception of the confusion over diminishing returns and returns to scale (without using these terms, of course). At a time when the concept of returns to scale was not well understood, he, by suggesting the notion of "increased organization" as the explanation for George's observation of economies of production and distribution accompanying population growth, was implicitly expounding the principle of increasing returns to scale. In the process of suggesting this he does not deny George's claim that aggregate wealth is greatest in the most civilized and densely peopled countries. "That it is to growth of organization and not to mere increase of numbers that increased productiveness is due, is obvious. . . . Growth of population may contribute to growth of organization; but if it is passed, organization must retrograde. . . . Thus the resources of distribution of labour and of organization will steadily diminish if population grows more rapidly than improvement in industrial art."[16] Two other observations are somewhat less perceptive. Moffat is of the opinion that the benefits of division of labor—in response to George's "the denser the population, the more minute becomes the subdivision of labour, the greater the economies of production and distribution"—are virtually exhausted and the practical limits to this advantage have been reached. As to the possibilities of technology and inventions causing per capita output to increase by growing at a rate faster than the rate of growth of population, he is pessimistic. He observes, "The physical wealth of modern Europe is due to the most labour-saving appliances, resulting from the great scientific discoveries and mechanical inventions of the last two or three centuries. The effects of these in increasing the productiveness of labour are not yet exhausted; but as each advance is made, population steadily follows in its wake and comes to press upon the limit permitted by the actual organization of industry to each class of the community."[17] Moffat concludes that "if we take our inventions and discoveries in the aggregate, we shall also find that though much still remains to be done fully to utilize them, the prospect of any equally fruitful cycle of improvement in the future, is a faint one."[18] He perceived correctly a limitation on the returns to scale ("increased organization") but failed to sense the importance of technological change on productivity and the possibility of technological change's advancing at a rate more rapid than population growth in certain areas of the world, permitting an ever-rising per capita output. Though George uses a variety of arguments, some more sound than others, to substantiate this, it is this very possibility of rising per capita output that forms the key to his rejection of the Malthusian doctrine.

Moffat is inclined to agree with George that something is apparently amiss with the operation of the economic system. But he charges that George's total rejection of the theory of population blinds him to the true nature of the difficulty. Moffat's own theory of population set forth in *The Economy of Consumption* clearly reflects the influence of Malthus on his thinking.[19] He holds that the fundamental law of population is that population is distributed mainly in accordance with the fertility or natural resources of the region. There are conditions or circumstances that may modify this law: (1) the element of chance, (2) the compensation variable—the natural conditions of life may summon up the maximum human effort when the natural environment demands it, (3) the habits of human nature—the attachment to a locality and its institutions offsets migratory behavior, so that population will expand slower if conditions are poor, or people will suffer all sorts of privations before electing to migrate. Moffat notes that the effect of competition on the law of population is to encourage increases in the laboring classes to a point beyond which they are no longer productive. Since the wealthy and powerful profit from workers' pressing upon the means of subsistence, they do nothing to discourage population growth or to alleviate the misery and privation it brings in its wake. The inevitable result is one of two things:"If the excess of the numbers is not great enough to force a change of habits on the class, it will be eliminated, as the result of an unequal struggle, by natural agents of destruction; if it is great enough the habits of the class will be changed."[20] If custom and conditions of society dictate that the worker should be properly housed and clothed and that his children be educated, "the labourer who cannot comply with these conditions will be warred against by natural forces, and eliminated from the industrial system, as surely as if what he had failed to provide were the barest necessaries of life."[21]

In rejecting George's reasons for affluence and luxury existing side by side with poverty and privation, Moffat offers in their place an explanation of his own, one familiarly Malthusian in overtones. Poverty and privation amidst affluence and luxury, he maintains, are the inevitable consequence of the tendency for population to press upon the subsistence level (a level determined by the customs and mores of society) and of the competitive organization of industry, which tends to encourage the process or at least does nothing to restrain it.

Moffat also uses the population doctrine and competition in his criticism of George's law of wages, and as the basis for an alternative explanation for why wages tend to a minimum.

III. The Wage/Capital Relationship

It becomes clearer from his comments on George's treatment of wages and capital why Moffat chose to engage in an extended discussion of population theory beforehand. As suggested earlier, the law of population, or rather its lack, is the issue in much of his criticism of George. This is particularly apparent in his reaction to the reasons George gives for repudiating the wages-fund doctrine, and it is equally apparent in his rejection of George's alternative explanation of why wages tend toward a minimum.

George's disavowal of the wages-fund doctrine—that wages are determined by the ratio between capital and the number of workers—can be traced directly to his objections to the Malthusian population doctrine. He in fact held that the Malthusian doctrine was at the root of the received doctrine of wages, and therefore needed to be dispelled first before the wages-fund notion could be effectively dislodged.[22] Moffat does not agree that a relationship necessarily exists between the two. He thinks that "by getting rid of the doctrine of population, it is possible he [George] may get rid of the obnoxious doctrine of wages, but it is also possible that, by establishing the doctrine of population, he might render the amendment of that doctrine imperative."[23] While Moffat agrees with George that the wages-fund doctrine is unacceptable and factually incorrect, he is less inclined to agree that the doctrine ever held as firm a grip on the public mind as George supposed it did.

He thinks that George's counterprinciple that wages derive from the produce of labor and are not drawn from capital is based on a faulty premise. The faulty premise Moffat alludes to is what George calls the "fundamental truth" of economic organization. It is the thread George uses to relate pristine and modern economies, maintaining that the most advanced economy and the most primitive economy share a common basis. The "fundamental truth" finds its clearest expression in the following:

> And so, if we reduce to their lowest terms all the complex operations of modern production, we see that each individual who takes part in this infinitely subdivided and intricate network of production and exchange is really doing what the primeval man did when he climbed the trees for fruit or followed the receding tide for shellfish—endeavoring to obtain from nature by the exertion of his powers the satisfaction of his desires. If we keep this firmly in mind, if we look upon production as a whole—as the co-operation of all embraced in any of its great groups to satisfy the various desires of each, we plainly see that the reward each obtains for his exertions comes as truly and as directly from nature as the result of that exertion, as did that of the first man.[24]

Moffat labels the "fundamental truth" a "prodigious blunder," noting that what may be true of a simpler time is not necessarily applicable to a more advanced, complex time. In other words, that primeval man got his food, clothing, and shelter by his own exertions, and therefore, that his labor generated his wages, may be accepted as fact; however, expanding the observation to apply to a more complex, interdependent monetary-exchange economy involves a faulty extension of that fact. Moffat puts it this way: "If you have a few factors, you may deduce from them a few elementary principles; and it is true that where these factors remain, these principles will persist. But if you add new factors, you find that along with new combinations, you have new principles of combinations; so that the laws of the original combination do not exclusively control the extended groups." Then, contrary to George, he concludes that "it is because the labourer co-operates with the capitalist that he receives present maintenance, not because his own labour produces it; for as maintenance is not contained in the product of his labour, it cannot be 'drawn' from it."[25]

George, in offering his alternative principle, no doubt was thinking along lines of a much simpler socioeconomic system than what is generally described as modern industrial capitalism. The system he envisioned was one that most likely would have permitted the individual worker/craftsman to identify more closely with the product of his efforts; one made up of mostly local community markets serviced by local merchants, small scale manufacturers, and modest-size farms. It was not a vision of complex national markets serviced by absentee owners, nor of giant impersonal corporations and bonanza-size corporate-owned farms. Accordingly, what he had in mind probably does have more in common with early primitive economy than with twentieth-century or even late nineteenth-century industrial capitalism. If in a normative sense one can be "right," then George's vision is correct, for it directs attention to what "ought to be." Who could deny that many, if not most people would, on economical, environmental, or ecological grounds, prefer his optimistic vision to what exists today? But while the "fundamental truth" is perhaps more attuned to what "ought to be," it is incorrect as a description of "what is." The principle that wages derive from the produce of labor and are not drawn from capital may be applicable in certain circumstances, but it is not universally applicable. There may be quite a gap in time between the value generated by labor and the transforming of that value into a monetary flow via sale of the finished product. The validity of Moffat's criticism, therefore, rests implicitly on the recognition that labor is paid for the value it adds to the product, but the payments made to labor in many production processes may precede by many months or even years the monetary flow back to the owners of capital from sale of the finished product.

The repudiation of the population and wages-fund doctrines is a necesary ground-clearing operation preparatory to presenting George's own proposition on why wages tend to a minimum, a proposition that forms an integral part of his overall view of why poverty accompanies progress. Moffat likewise rejects the wages-fund doctrine but contrariwise accepts the population doctrine, since he regards it as crucial to all economic analysis. He is being consistent, therefore, when he rejects George's alternative version of why wages tend to a minimum. He, like George, has his own theory, but in it he disdains a single-cause explanation.

Wages, according to George, are determined by what a worker unassisted by capital could get from unappropriated no-rent land (marginal land). This means that where land is free, the whole produce must go to labor, and if the worker is assisted by capital, then that portion of the product remaining after payment of interest for capital constitutes wages of labor. However, where land is not free and private ownership derives rent payments from the land, wages then are fixed by what workers could earn on no-rent land (marginal land). Hence it follows that where workers are without access to unappropriated land—where, for example, all land is monopolized—competition for employment among workers forces their wages down to the minimum subsistence level.[26] That is the substance of George's alternative explanation of why wages tend to a minimum. Since George reasons that the proportion of total produce going to wages and interest is determined by what remains after rent payments are subtracted from total output, then the greater proportion that goes to rent, the smaller the proportion available for wages. As to the poverty that is seen accompanying economic growth, George attributes its cause to land owners' appropriating proportionately greater amounts from each advance in material output thus rendering an ever-declining percent of total produce available for distribution as wages of labor.

Moffat agrees that there is a downward tendency of wages, although he thinks the evidence available is not uniformly supportive of the idea. Moreover, he thinks that while it may be natural on a priori grounds to assume a single cause, as George does, the facts suggest otherwise. Moffat believes that there are distinct causes for the phenomenon, different in both direction and origin. He cites two in his own theory of why wages tend to a minimum. One cause he regards as evil, the other benign. The benign cause is the operation of the law of population:

> As long as labour, whether on the labourer's own account, or on account of an employer, can be made productive of a maintenance, that is, the means of providing for a family, labourers will be found to give that labour. It consequently follows that if labour will always be done that yields only a maintenance, the labour that receives least remuneration will seldom, and that only exceptionally, earn more than a maintenance. This law is not an evil. It simply means that natural resources are fully utilized for the good of man.

The evil cause is the operation of competition:

> Competition, taking advantage of the willingness of labourers to work for a maintenance, organizes enterprises in anticipation of the natural growth of industrial development, and which ultimately fail to yield a maintenance to those engaged in them. This is the natural tendency of competition. It constantly pushes its enterprises in advance of normal development, and is only arrested in doing so by the failure of its enterprises, in the form of cessation of profit, and consequent failure of capital. This is an evil to capitalists and labourers alike. It is the great specific evil of the competitive organization of industry.[27]

Once again, the omission of the doctrines of population and competitive organization is the basis on which Moffatt's criticism turns. This time it is directed to George's theory of wages. In addition to citing what appear to him to be errors of omission, he is critical of George's theory in its own right as well. Much of it harks back to remarks cited earlier on the "fundamental truth'' and the corollary that wages are not drawn from capital. There are two additional points he makes relative to the "natural" wage—the wage a worker could get by his own efforts on no-rent land. The first is that the product even of no-rent land is the output of both labor and capital combined, not simply labor alone. Moffat argues that workers without capital would be unable to work the land, and that therefore access to marginal land by workers without capital would not assure to them a wage unless their exertions were assisted by capital. The produce then would have to be recognized as being composed of both wages and interest. The second point is that in situations where it is needed there is no unappropriated land available. Where the land is already owned, therefore, workers cannot freely avail themselves of moving onto land and of applying their efforts to it. The implication is that George's assumption does not conform to reality.

The first point is not necessarily in conflict with George's argument. In effect it reduces to a problem of imputation. As long as what remains after allowance is made for a return to capital is at least equal to a subsistence level, it creates no great difficulty. If it is intended as something more fundamental than that, whatever it is can probably be set in proper perspective by noting that both land and labor must exist before capital goods can exist, and consequently, for analytical purposes both can be treated independently of capital goods. The second point is somewhat puzzling unless what Moffat intends is to separate the basis for the "natural" wage from George's explanation of why wages tend to a bare minimum. In such case he is saying that since there is no unappropriated land available there can be no "natural" wage, or at least it cannot be measured by the method George suggests. But the two cannot logically be separated in George's model. The very fact that land is already appropriated (monopolized, according to George) forces wages to a bare-minimum subsistence. The object of Moffat's criticism—lack of access to land and its produce—is the crux of George's explanation of why wages of labor tend to a minimum.

IV. The Laws of Distribution and the Remedy

Moffat's objection to George's treatment of wages independently of capital is not unrelated to his overall rejection of George's laws of distribution. His criticism is targeted on two areas: (1) the definition of wages, interest, and rent, and (2) the assumed relationship between wages, interest, and rent from which George's laws of distribution emerge. With reference to the former, Moffat maintains that the meanings George attaches to the terms *wages, interest,* and *rent* may deny their implied mutual exclusion. According to him, the evidence of overlap would have been readily apparent had George explicitly allowed for a profit return. All elements of profit would have been made manifest, not just the lone element that George recognizes as wages of superintendence. Perhaps not coincidental is that Moffat's notion of profit as he presents it in his *The Economy of Consumption* contains an element of wages in the form of a return for superintendence, an element of interest denoted by the return to capital above replacement, an element for risk-taking, and at times he would include an element of rent.[28] Ignoring all elements of profits except wages of superintendence weakens, he claims, George's explanation of why wages tend to a minimum. In other words, by incorporating the return for superintendence into his wages concept George makes less convincing his argument that all wages tend to a minimum. "Profit, though not, in the narrowest sense, distinctively the remuneration of capital, is a remuneration attached to capital, and not a remuneration attached to labour."[29] Because of this Moffat contends: "Any deductions Mr. George may draw from his classification, therefore, will not apply to wages as actually distinguished, and as alone capable of being observed. They will not apply to the wages in which he has observed a tendency to a minimum, capable of yielding only a bare subsistence."[30] Putting profits into the category of wages as compensation for superintendence, and maintaining in addition that in the matter of distribution wages and interest move in the same direction, creates, according to Moffat, "the absurdity of attempting to account for present poverty by the assumption that it is shared by capitalists, or that they owe their exemption from it to rent."[31]

It seems clear from the above that, while Moffat rejects the wages-fund doctrine as a causative factor in the distribution of wealth (income), he is not ready to abandon totally the notion of an inherent conflict in interests between the owners of capital and those of hired labor. There exists a fundamental difference between his view and George's view of the forces at work influencing distribution. Moffat sees the basic conflict as more likely a conflict between owners of capital and labor rather than, as George sees it, a conflict between labor and owners of capital on one side and owners of land on the other. Hence it is not unexpected that he should question George's method of arriving at the sums going to wages and interest—the combined residual remaining after rent is subtracted from the total product. Of greater concern to him, however, is the implication of this method that, as the rent share as a proportion of total product rises, the share going to wages and interest as a proportion must necessarily decline. Moffat agrees that mathematically whatever is subtracted from total product yields the amount available to other factors. But what is chosen to be subtracted, according to Moffat, might just as readily be profits from the total product, the remainder going to wages, interest, and rent, or wages and interest could be taken as a subtraction from total product, the remainder going to rent and profit. "If the produce remains constant the fall of rent necessarily means the rise of the other two in the aggregate but not necessarily of both separately, just as the fall of wages means the rise of rent *plus* profit, and the fall of profit the rise of rent *plus* wages."[32]

George's method of arriving at the laws of distribution via the subtraction of rent from total product is simply a restatement of his central thesis that the basic conflict in the distribution of income is between the landowner on one side and the capital owner and labor on the other. This, according to George, is also the root cause of depressions and the harbinger of chronic poverty amidst plenty. Contrary to what Moffat appears to suggest, whether or not wages and interest move in the same direction and whether or not rent is a rising proportion of total product as total product increases, are matters that can be resolved only by appeal to empirical evidence and cannot be established on a priori grounds alone.[33] With regard to the apparent omission of a profit return in the relationship, George's explanation for this is quite straightforward. The elements of profit found in the conventional notion are absorbed into the factors identified.

> Of the three parts into which profits are divided by political economists—namely, compensation for risk, wages of superintendence, and return for use of capital—the latter falls under the term interest, which includes all the returns for the use of capital, and excludes everything else; wages of superintendence falls under the term wages, which includes all returns for human exertion, and excludes everything else; and compensation for risk has no place whatever, as risk is eliminated when all the transactions of a community are taken together.[34]

Moffat is not at all comfortable with George's explanation of the source of and rationale for interest, and he is even more disturbed with his unqualified acceptance of the Ricardian rent concept. He believes that George is being inconsistent in his justification for the private receipt of interest while rejecting the same justification when it is applied to the private receipt of rent. What Moffat is alluding to is George's reference to the legitimacy of interest as originating in the inherent powers of nature—the same powers, according to Moffat, that George attributes to land. "Thus interest springs from the power of increase which the reproductive forces of nature, and the in effect analogous capacity for exchange, give to capital. It is not an arbitrary, but natural thing, it is not the result of a particular social organization, but of laws of the universe which underlie society. It is, therefore, just."[35] George's "principle of growth or reproduction" explanation for interest brings forth a comment by Moffat not untainted with irony:

> This is Mr. George's discovery, and he announces it with the air of a man whose penetration has been profoundly exercised to reach it. . . .Clearly the modesty of a Newton could not have sufficed to announce such a discovery in a less ostentatious way, and we shall find that even the dexterity of Ricardo could not more rapidly have turned a conjecture into a certainty. What is most remarkable about this singular theory is that its one trait of originality lies in its application. Mr. George having no occasion to account for the legitimate existence of rent, which he purposes to deny altogether, takes the physiocratic theory of the source of rent, and converts it to the use of "interest." What is strange is that he does not see that in doing this he transfers to interest the very objection to the legitimacy of rent. It is because the produce due to the natural increase of the soil is supposed to be constituted without the exertions of the landlord that so many theorists have objected to rent; now Mr. George tells us that the source of interest is the reproductive forces of nature. Thus while it is unlawful for a man who pretends to be an owner to appropriate these, it is quite lawful for a man who professes to be a borrower to do so.[36]

If land were the creation of human effort as capital goods must be, then Moffat's point would not be without merit. However, he was aware of the difference when, in an earlier discussion of the basis for trading between capitalists and labor he recognized the capitalist's interest in acquiring "labour stored"—capital goods.[37] There is a distinction to be made between the natural resource, land, and the stored-labor notion of capital goods that absolves George from the accusation of inconsistency. Capital goods are the products of human endeavor and as human-made instruments they are clearly designed for the furtherance of production. Land's contribution to production, on the other hand, is independent of human exertion, and in that sense rent, if taken as the measurement of this productivity, must be regarded as an unearned addition to the earned components of personal income.

Moffat's repudiation of Ricardian principles extends, of course, to the Ricardian rent concept. While he claims that George is also Ricardian in other matters—for example, in his methodology and in his acceptance of competitive industrial organization—it is the adaptation of the rent concept that convinces Moffat that George is basically if not totally Ricardian in his approach to economics.[38] Though he readily acknowledges the almost universal acceptance of the Ricardian theory of rent, Moffat maintains that "no more insinuating doctrine was ever presented to human reason."[39] He argues at great length against the Ricardian rent concept without offering an alternative theory of his own. He believes that Ricardo and George erred in not recognizing rent as a necessary cost of production. Moffat attributes the error to the logical outcome of Ricardo's principle of equality of profits—the notion that the returns to alternative investments in different industries are equalized throughout the economy on the assumption of the tendency toward a steady state: "Ricardo, in following up this generalization, has committed an oversight singular even for him, and in which he has been followed by Mr. George. He has not only. . .made rent gradually absorb profit and arrest the increase of wages while Mr. George, more consistent than Ricardo, makes it crush out wages also; but both of them having eliminated rent from the cost of production, keep it out of sight to the extent of forgetting it as an element of the wealth of the community."[40] The tone and vigor of his remark about Ricardo's principle of equality of profits is indicative of his attitude toward almost anything Ricardian. This is what he has to say: "The theory of equality of profits, as propounded by Ricardo, is not only one of the most stupendous blunders ever committed in systematic economy, prolific as it is in blunders, but perhaps the most stupendous blunder ever committed in any science."[41]

Moffat offers a potpourri of arguments for treating rent as a socially necessary cost of production and as a determinant element of price (value). There is some confusion on Moffat's part between the Ricardian-Georgist social view of rent as an unnecessary cost of production and rent as viewed by the individual producer. The following is representative of his position and of his confusion.

Rent. . .enters as a distinctive element into value. It may either enter as a positive or a negative element. That is to say the relative quantity of produce brought to the market may be diminished by the necessity of contributing something to the support of landlords, or it may be increased by the speculation of landlords to increase rents. Ricardo's standard is a delusion.[42]

The standard or self-sustaining cost of production includes rent adequate to the maintenance of the capital necessary to the due performance of the functions of the landlord.[43]

Before the landlord can use land for his amusement, he must live by it, and the more expensively he lives, the more he must get out of it.[44]

The landlord in improving land uses capital and acts as a capitalist.[45]

Agricultural rent. . .is only a share of the gross profit of raw material.[46]

Moffat states that rent is a necessary payment to the landlord to reward him for his functions. But nowhere does he describe these functions in a manner to preclude their adequate compensation via wages, interest, or profits. He claims that rent is a necessary payment to the landlord so as to provide him with adequate capital to make improvements, and as a profit on raw materials. Why should profits and interest be assumed deficient and incapable of accomplishing this? In a similar way he maintains that the landlord must receive a rent to enable him to "use the land for his amusement." But again, why suppose that the wages, interest, and profits accruing to the landlord would be insufficient to support such diversions? Finally, he states that rent is a necessary cost of production determining value, while at the same time recognizing that produce does flow from no-rent (marginal) lands. The price/cost on the market of produce from no-rent lands is by his own definition exclusive of a rent "cost."

Given his views for justifying the private receipt of rent, and the virtues he ascribes to private ownership of land, it is not at all unexpected that Moffat should disavow George's solution to poverty and economic crises, namely, the socialization of rent. Much of Moffat's reaction to George's remedy reflects his contrary view concerning rent, and when this is not the case his statements reduce to forcefully expressed subjective evaluations—assertions wholly lacking in analytical substance. His refusal to regard rent as a surplus, and his unusual views concerning the taxation of rent, in which he apparently assumes that a tax on land can be shifted forward to the tenant or to the consumer and is not, therefore, capitalized, show through in the following sampling of statements on the Remedy:

If one man works on rich land, another on poor, ought their rewards be equalized? If they ought, neither receives "the earnings of his labour," and if all rewards are equalized, what becomes of competition? If, on the other hand, the rewards are not equalized, the land is not made common property.[47]

if everything belongs to everybody, the reward of labour cannot possibly be, as Mr. George asserts, the produce of labour, but can only be some pittance presumed to be consistent with common ownership. . . .After all his elaborate efforts to reconcile it with a free competitive organization, Mr. George's scheme thus relapses, by the retributive harmony of natural logic into the impotence of socialistic communism.[48]

If Mr. George's theory is sound, the man who has produced anything at any time stole the material of which it was made.[49]

whether the rent was fixed or differential they would have power to re-levy it on the community, and no individual would escape his natural share of taxation. The State tenants would simply be proprietors and farmers of the revenue, with an insecure title based on popular caprice.[50]

[The occupiers] with only a rent to pay to the state which they would re-levy from the consumers.[51]

in a country where cultivation was protected the landlords would re-levy the whole taxation from the public.[52]

Then finally in response to George's:

It is the greater that swallow up the less not the less that swallow up the greater,[53]

as the equitable prescription where some might be harmed by the change, Moffat states:

It is also worse to rob on behalf of the many than of the few, because it is the robbers, and not the robbed, that robbery corrupts and destroys.[54]

These remarks speak for themselves and are sufficiently representative of his intransigent position concerning the Remedy that further elaboration does not seem necessary. However, it is perhaps worthwhile again to point out that his mistaken view of ground rent as a necessary cost of production leads him to the other error—that of assuming a tax levied on ground rent would be shifted from the landowner to the consumer and/or to the tenant through the pricing process.

Moffat's statements concerning the Remedy, although based on a total rejection of the Ricardian theory of rent, stand, nevertheless, as expressions of personal opinion. His inclination was to view the chapters on the Remedy as "rhapsodic rhetoric" and his manner of treatment may simply be a reflection of this. It is evident here, perhaps even more clearly than elsewhere, that the full significance of Henry George's *Progress and Poverty* eluded him. Why this is so can be a matter only for conjecture. Throughout the book his attention is drawn to the critique of orthodox economics, and his thoroughly Malthusian outlook with respect to the Ricardian idea of the inherent ability of the classical system to avoid recurrent episodes of general overproduction, adds to his mistrust of anything related to Ricardian principles. Moffat mistakenly sees George as little more than a developer of Ricardian economics. In his eyes George is a more faithful developer of Ricardian economics than even J. S. Mill. No doubt contributing to this misconception of George's work were his own strongly held views concerning the cause of poverty and economic crises, views dramatically different from those of George. The cause, according to him, is to be found in the Malthusian theory of population growth, the competitive organization of industry, the vagaries of consumer demand, and in the classical assumption that human wants are unlimited. His disenchantment with orthodox economics, his overdrawn association of George with Ricardian principles, his rejection of the Ricardian rent concept, his Malthusian frame of reference, and his own views concerning the cause of poverty and economic crises—all tended to divert him. This preoccupation probably had an influence on his perception, so that when finally his attention was turned to the task of appraising *Progress and Poverty* he could relate only to segmented parts. The whole as an integrated system escaped him, and with it the essence of George's thought.

Notes

1.   T. W. Hutchison, *A Review of Economic Doctrines. 1870-1929.* (Oxford: Clarendon Press, 1953), p. 356.

2.   The full title of this book of Robert Scott Moffat is *Mr. Henry George the "Orthodox": An Examination of Mr. George's Position as a Systematic Economist; And a Review of the Competitive and Socialistic Schools of Economy* (London: Remington & Co., 1885).

3.   Moffat, *Mr. Henry George*, p. 16.

4.   Ibid., p. 12.

5.   Ibid., p. 17.

6.   Ibid., p. 18.

7.   Ibid., p. 21.

8.   Henry George, *Progress and Poverty*, 75th anniversary ed. (New York: Robert Schalkenbach Foundation, 1954), p. 133.

9.   A clear exposition of this is offered in Jacob Oser, *Henry George* (New York: Twayne, 1974), pp. 56-62.

10.   George, *Progress and Poverty*, pp. 138-39.

11.   Moffat, *Mr. Henry George*, p. 21.

12.   Ibid., pp. 44-45.

13.   Ibid., p. 45.

14.   George, *Progress and Poverty*, p. 128.

15.   Ibid., p. 319.

16.   Moffat, *Mr. Henry George*, p. 68 n.

17.   Ibid., p. 68.

18.   Ibid., p. 69.

19.   It is interesting to note Moffat's reaction to the way his theory was received: "The first attempt, that I am aware of, to base the theory of wealth directly upon the theory of population was made in my, "The Economy of Consumption," published in 1878, which, on this very account, has been subjected to much hostile, and I must add, to much inappreciative and scandalously inaccurate criticism" (*Mr. Henry George*, p. 75).

20.   Moffat, *Mr. Henry George*, pp. 79-80.

21.   Ibid., p. 80.

22.   George, *Progress and Poverty*, p. 91.

23.   Moffat, *Mr. Henry George*, p. 23.

24.   George, *Progress and Poverty*, p. 27.

25.   Moffat, *Mr. Henry George*, p. 101.

26.   George, *Progress and Poverty*, p. 213.

27.   Moffat, *Mr. Henry George*, p. 93.

28.   Ibid., pp. 142-44.

29.   Ibid., p. 144.

30.   Ibid.

31.   Ibid., p. 176.

32.   Ibid., p. 175.

33. Appeal to the facts thus far yields mixed results partly because the statistical measurements are confronted with the difficulty of identifying and isolating the factor meaning of interest and rent. Because of the difficulties of imputation, what is actually measured may not always conform to George's definition of these terms. This aside, the empirical evidence does not universally support a declining proportion of total product as going to wages. For example, labor's share in the U.S. has over time remained a consistently stable percentage of total output. It appears that the share going to labor does not decline in developed and rapidly developing areas. But in environments where land is in fact monopolized—in lesser developed areas—the tendency may be observed for the rent share to rise and the wages share to decline as a proportion of total product. Wages and interest in the early growth of the U.S. could be observed moving in the same direction. They also moved in the same direction during the depression years of the 1930s, but at other times and in other places the evidence is inconclusive.

34. George, *Progress and Poverty*, pp. 161-62.

35. Ibid., p. 188.

36. Moffat, *Mr. Henry George*, pp. 157-58.

37. Ibid., p. 99.

38. Moffat states: "Again and again I have pointed out how faithfully in his economic reasoning Mr. George follows the method of Ricardo. Now Ricardo, as I have said, is the systematizer of orthodox English economy. For this school, as the reader is already aware I have no high veneration" (*Mr. Henry George*. p. 200). He goes on also to say: "But Mr. George, when his doctrines are reduced, as I have indicated, is not a mere imitator, but he is a developer of Ricardo. . .a far more legitimate developer of Ricardo than John Stuart Mill" (ibid., p. 209).

39. Moffat, *Mr. Henry George*, p. 217.

40. Ibid., p. 242.

41. Ibid., p. 238.

42. Ibid., p. 228.

43. Ibid., p. 222.

44. Ibid., p. 227.

45. Ibid., p. 232.

46. Ibid., p. 242.

47. Ibid., p. 268.

48. Ibid., p. 292.

49. Ibid., p. 272.

50. Ibid., p. 286.

51. Ibid., p. 278.

52. Ibid., p. 287.

53. George, *Progress and Poverty*, p. 343.

54. Moffat, *Mr. Henry George*, p. 272.

8

Cathrein's Careless Clerical Critique

BY ROBERT V. ANDELSON

Perhaps the most influential Continental European critic of Henry George was Father Victor Cathrein (1845-1931), a Swiss-born Jesuit who wrote extensively on ethics, jurisprudence, and political economy, as well as on purely religious themes. His impact may be gauged by the fact that two of his works, *Der Sozialismus* and *Moralphilosophie*, went into twenty or more editions; the great Protestant theologian and social ethicist, Emil Brunner, cites him in *The Divine Imperative* no less than fourteen times as a definitive representative of Roman Catholic thought.

Cathrein's attack on George originally appeared in 1887 as a series of articles in the *Stimmen aus Maria-Laach*, published by the German Fathers of the Society of Jesus. It was preceded in the same journal five years earlier by a series in which Cathrein sought to refute Émile de Laveleye's contention that private ownership of land is a relatively recent and unnatural development. The *New York Freeman's Journal* issued an English translation of both series, from February 18th to April 28th, 1888, and the following year they were updated, enlarged, and brought together in a single volume by President J. U. Heinzle, S. J., of Canisius College in Buffalo. It is to this volume, approved by Cathrein and entitled, *The Champions of Agrarian Socialism*, that we shall be referring in the ensuing pages.

With the first chapters of the work we need not concern ourselves, for they deal with Laveleye and his historical research. George, it is true, accepted the conclusions of this research but, as Cathrein concedes,[1] his chief arguments do not rest upon it.

Cathrein opens his critique of George with an attempt to "give the Devil his due," saying that "in unflinching consistency and in powers of agitation" the author of *Progress and Poverty* "leaves all his predecessors far behind." He credits him with "a clear mind" and "extensive knowledge," with a "luminous" and "eloquent" style, and with having "occupied himself seriously with the study of the questions he proposes."[2] He then attempts to show in the forty-eight remaining pages that George was muddled, inconsistent, and either ignorant of or oblivious to obvious economic facts.

I

George's main arguments are based upon considerations of political economy, on the one hand, and of ethics, on the other. The arguments from political economy with which Cathrein takes issue are those which hold that with increasing productive progress an ever-increasing portion of a nation's wealth flows to the proprietors of land, to the prejudice of both labor and capital.

The demonstration for this is treated by Cathrein under the form of two proofs, one of them taken from "Ricardo's Law of Rent," which the priest recognizes as being accepted as correct by most economists.[3] According to this law, the rent of land is determined by the excess of the produce of a given parcel over that which the least productive land will yield with the same application of productive power. Therefore, reasons George, the return of the poorest land in use represents the highest limit of that portion of the product which generally goes to labor and capital even in the best locations. Everything above the limit goes to the landowner as ground rent. As more and more land is utilized due to the growth of population and the increase in economic activity, less and less desirable land is increasingly brought into use, and wages and interest drop accordingly while rent goes up.[4]

Cathrein begins by attempting to show that this account is factually inaccurate. He produces statistics (derived from the second edition of G. Schoenberg's *Handbuch der politischen Oekonomie*) to establish that notwithstanding a vast advance in population and total revenue in Great Britain over the preceding four decades, the share of national wealth going to income from landed property had sharply decreased. (What is true of Britain, he says, may also be asserted of continental Europe, adducing as evidence the complaints of landed proprietors, both great and small, in Germany and France.)

The reliability of these statistics is open to dispute, for one cannot but question whether they reflect the rent of all land or merely land devoted mainly to agricultural production. For example, Cathrein separates the income from "houses" (buildings in general) from the income from land alone, but does not specify under which category he subsumes the income from the land upon which the houses stand. Since all of his examples and remarks pertain to husbandry,[5] and since the discrete valuation of sites and improvements is a practice that did not come into common use until a later date, it is by no means improbable that he (or Schoenberg) made the error of including with income from houses considerable revenue that ought to have been attributed to land.

Cathrein goes on to say that George takes a one-sided view of the case, considering only the causes that raise rent, while almost entirely losing sight of those which make it decline. His discussion here relates exclusively to agricultural lands, and clearly betrays his persistant failure (shared by Father Juan Alcázar Alvarez, another priestly European critic of George dealt with in this volume) to bear in mind that it is not agricultural but rather urban and industrial sites that yield the highest rent. An adequate critique of George on this point would have required that Cathrein demonstrate that rent is subject to forces that cause its diminution in *all* locations, not just in those where it is normally relatively marginal in any case.

Our cleric then turns his attention to George's second proof that rent tends, with progress in production, to swallow up an ever-larger percentage of the national wealth. This is the contention that, in spite of increasing productivity, interest and wages as a relative portion of the total revenue do not increase, and that consequently rent *must* increase.

With respect to interest, Cathrein maintains that if by interest is understood the return to any particular capital investment, the statement may be correct. But if by interest is understood the aggregate return to all existing capital, the statement "taken in its generality" is untrue. He asserts that while the *rate* of interest may decrease because of decreasing risk, the *amount* may increase because of increased capital investment.

Cathrein's reasoning in this passage contains three flaws: First, George, following accepted practice in political economy, explicitly excludes the rewards of risk from his definition of interest.[6] Second, if one ignores Cathrein's mistaken explanation for the decrease in the rate of interest, and simply accepts his observation that the rate may decrease while the amount increases, the observation, far from refuting George's argument, merely underscores the fact, emphasized by him, that capital, unlike land, is elastic, and that its return per unit diminishes with enhanced supply. Finally, Cathrein confuses *amount* with *proportion*. George never denied that the total amount of interest may expand with greater capital investment. He was instead concerned to show that the proportion of the total product going to interest decreases relative to that going to rent. In asserting the former idea, Cathrein thinks that he has destroyed an argument that actually he leaves untouched.

Having, as he believes, dispatched George's teaching on the decrease of interest, Cathrein assails his teaching on the decrease of wages as equally unsound. This contention is based solely upon the accusation that George is guilty of an inexcusable confusion of terms when he claims that wages, in spite of the increase in productive power, tend to a minimum that will give but a bare living.[7] Cathrein holds that in political economy the word *wages* properly refers only to *compensation for hired labor*, whereas George uses it to mean *all earnings of exertion*. Yet it is, in fact, the latter which, as George notes,[8] is the standard sense in which the term is used by most political economists. Cathrein, who cites Lassalle as his authority,[9] evidently confounds socialist usage with orthodox usage!

"We would be at a loss," he comments, "to name a political economist who ever dared to affirm that all income from labor falling to manufacturers, merchants, bankers, etc., tends to a minimum which will give the bare necessaries of life. They affirm this only of those *working for hire*, especially of operatives in factories."[10] George, in point of fact, does implicitly affirm precisely that which no political economist, to Cathrein's knowledge, dares affirm.[11] But to say that all earnings of exertion *tend to* such a minimum is not to say that they all reach or equally approach it. One need but peruse George's discussion of the differences between wages in different occupations to understand why those who engage in certain callings are protected from the full impact of this tendency. As for the wages of superintendence in mercantile pursuits, George remarks that they largely resemble the prizes in a lottery, in which the great gain of one is made up from the losses of many others—as evidenced by the phenomenon that over ninety percent of the mercantile firms that commence business ultimately fail.[12]

II

But the presumed negation of George's economic arguments is, for Cathrein, mere prologue. He now assumes his more accustomed role of Christian moral philosopher, and essays to challenge George on grounds of natural right. Here the two are at least agreed upon a common point of reference: the belief that there is such a thing as natural right, stemming from the will of a beneficient Creator—a point of reference that does not obtain between George and some of his other critics, Seligman for one.

Private property in land, says the American theorist, not only exercises a baneful influence upon the distribution of wealth, but is contrary to the dictates of justice. True, he holds that, for pragmatic reasons, land titles should be left in private hands, but he would cancel the monopolistic advantage that accrues from their possession by appropriating (without compensation) all but an insignificant fraction of ground rent to the community. No legitimate claims would, he insists, be violated by such appropriation, for the advantage is ethically indefensible.

This proposition he deduces from the principle, enunciated long before by Locke, that the rightful basis of property is "the right of a man to himself, to the use of his own powers, to the enjoyment of the fruits of his own exertions. . . .As a man belongs to himself, so his labor when put in concrete form belongs to him."[13] George considers that the natural right of an individual to himself and therefore to his labor is the original and exclusive source of legitimate ownership. There can be no other true justification, he avers, because there is no other natural right from which another justification could be derived, and because the recognition of any other justification would be inconsistent with and destructive of this natural right. Since land is not the product of human labor, says George, its private ownership cannot be justified by the right of the individual to the fruits of his labor. Further, "since the right to the produce of labor cannot be enjoyed without the right to the free use of the opportunities offered by nature, . . .to admit the right of property in these is to deny the right of property in the produce of labor. When non-producers can claim as rent a portion of the wealth created by producers, the right of the producers to the fruits of their labor is to that extent denied."[14]

Such is the argument against which Cathrein addresses his forensic efforts, seeking to disprove that labor is either the original or the sole source of ownership. We need not occupy ourselves at length with his comment that because man belongs to God, George errs in affirming that he has a right to himself. The affirmation has to do with temporal relationships, not with man's relationship to his Creator. In this connection it is worthy of note that Locke, in the same work in which he formulates the principle upon which George builds his moral case, flatly proclaims that "men, being all the workmanship of one omnipotent and infinitely wise Maker—all the servants of one sovereign master, sent into the world by his order and about his business—they are his property whose workmanship they are, made to last during his, not one another's pleasure."[15] It is inconceivable that George, whose works are luminous with Christian fervor, did not unreservedly endorse this sentiment.

Labor is not, said Cathrein, the original source of ownership. He grants that all men are divinely endowed at birth with a general right of acquiring property, but this right exists prior to labor, and is not logically restricted to things produced by labor since it is merely a general right that does not apply to the possession of determinate entities.

First occupancy, not labor, Cathrein maintains, constitutes the original title to the permanent possession of determinate goods. He who first appropriates an ownerless good violates by that action nobody's right, but only exercises the right vested in himself of acquiring property. With the death of the first proprietor, the title ceases to be occupancy and becomes hereditary succession. If George wishes to deny the right of inheritance, "he must do so with regard to movable as well as in the case of immovable goods, or at least he must demonstrate why immovables, and not movables, should be inheritable."[16]

Cathrein's terminology here reflects a careless reading of *Progress and Poverty*, where George specifically dismisses as unphilosophical the distinction between things movable and immovable, in favor of that between labor products (wealth) and the gratuitous offerings of nature (land).[17] The reason, of course, why George denies the right of inheritance in land as opposed to labor products is simply that he is unwilling to concede that anybody ever had a right to own it in the first place—if ownership be interpreted to include the retention of whatever ground rent it may possess or acquire. First occupancy may justify security of possession, but, as Locke observes,[18] this can hold only where "there is enough and as good left in common for others,"—that is, as long as the land in question has no market value. Once ground rent, the measure of monopolistic advantage, has arisen, security of possession cannot be rightfully retained, according to George, unless that rent be turned over to the community as a compensation for the deprivation thereby sustained by its other members.

George attacks the principle of first occupancy with striking illustrations: "Has the first-comer at a banquet the right to turn back all the chairs and claim that none of the other guests shall partake of the food provided, except as they make terms with him? Does the first man who presents a ticket at the door of a theater and passes in, acquire by his priority the right to shut the doors and have the performance go on for himself alone?"[19]

Cathrein tries to answer the objection by discussing the second of these illustrations:

> He who appears first in a theatre has not the right to exclude others from the theatre, but he has the right to choose his seat and to hold it against everybody else. Whosoever would remove him from his seat would wrong him. Just so it is with the occupation of this earth. . . .He who makes his appearance on earth first, may choose at pleasure his dwelling place. He may fence in his field and build his house, and call both his own, as long as he lives. Those who come later may likewise choose their dwelling place but they have no right to drive away the first-comer from his house and home.[20]

This seems plausible enough until one considers that in the theater of the earth some have chosen for their exclusive disposal "seats" capable of accommodating hundreds and even thousands, while others must pay them scalpers' prices to be permitted any space in the theater at all.

The same right to choose a place, said Cathrein, belongs to the posterity of the first occupants until the theater is full—until the last spot on earth has found an owner. "Such a time, however," he opines, "is still in the distant future." Today that future does not seem so distant, particularly if one finds no enchantment in the prospect of settling in the Amazon Basin or the Arctic!

Where population increases greatly, admits Cathrein, ground will not, of course, remain free. But in this world it is not necessary for success that a person be a landowner. The recognition of private property in land is not (as George interprets it as being) equivalent to the contention that some have a better right to exist than others. All men have the same right to live. Yet from this right to live it does not follow that all should have a right to the *actual possession of the same means* of securing their existence. "If it is true that he who calls himself the owner of a piece of ground thereby claims a better right to life, the very same is true of mill-owners, of bankers, of business men."[21]

What the learned Father seems to have ignored in his comparison is the fact that ultimately production cannot occur without recourse to land (which term, of course, encompasses all natural resources). The industrialist, the financier, the merchant—all perform useful services in the productive process. But they are permitted to perform them only if they pay a tribute to the landowner. What does he do to earn this tribute? He did not produce the land. It existed before him, and his ownership, as such, does nothing to give it economic utility. His sole function, as owner, is to reap the harvest of monopoly.* Thus would George reply to the last argument.

Cathrein, however, has another string to his bow. Confident that he has proved that labor cannot be the *original* title of ownership, he now sets out to demonstrate that it cannot be the *sole* title either.

"If production," writes George, "gives to the producer the right to exclusive possession and enjoyment, there can rightfully be no exclusive possession and enjoyment of anything not the production of labor, and the recognition of private property in land is a wrong. For the right to the produce of labor cannot be enjoyed without the free use of the opportunities offered by nature, and to admit the right of property in these is to deny the right of property in the produce of labor."[22]

His Jesuit assailant seeks to reduce this proposition to absurdity by setting up the following analogy: "The right of a carpenter to the tables he makes cannot exist without the right of freely felling the timber for their manufacture. Hence no one else can have a vested right to a forest."[23] But does this analogy succeed in its objective? After all, the carpenter's cost of producing the tables must include the price of the wood. To the extent that that price includes in turn a payment to the owner of the forest simply in the capacity of owner, is not his right to the tables indeed impaired? Of course, we are assuming here that the timber is not the result of artificial forestation, for in that case it would be a labor product and could not be subsumed under the

---

*See n. 32 to chapter 24 on Msgr. John A. Ryan.

category of natural opportunity. But if it be virgin, its price, apart from that portion attributable to felling, dressing, and transportation, is clearly an exaction of monopoly.

George, says Cathrein, evidently confounds the right of the produce of labor with the right of producing, that is, of working. Everyone has the right of producing, but if he is not in the possession of any raw material, he must dispose of his labor to another, and then he has the right to wages. "But in this case the produce of his labor belongs not to him, but to the proprietor of the material, who hired him."[24]

Four years after the original publication of Cathrein's critique of George, much the same reasoning as the above appared in a historic document signed by his ultimate temporal superior: Leo XIII's famed encyclical, *Rerum Novarum*. There we read that even though divided among private owners, the earth does not cease to minister to the needs of all, since those who do not possess land can obtain its produce by selling their labor.[25] George has a powerful rejoinder to this assertion.

> Suppose that to your Holiness as a judge of morals one should put this case of conscience:
>
> "I am one of several children to whom our father left a field abundant for our support. As he assigned no part of it to any one of us in particular, leaving the limits of our separate possessions to be fixed by ourselves, I being the oldest took the whole field in exclusive ownership. But in doing so I have not deprived my brothers of their support from it, for I have let them work for me on it, paying them from the produce as much wages as I would have had to pay strangers. Is there any reason why my conscience should not be clear?"
>
> What would be your answer? Would you not tell him that he was in mortal sin, and that his excuse added to his guilt? Would you not call on him to make restitution and to do penance?[26]

Proceeding with his polemic against the idea that labor is the sole justification of ownership, Cathrein discusses George's dictum: "When non-producers can claim as rent a portion of the wealth created by producers, the right of producers to the fruits of their labor is to that extent denied."[27]

"Certainly," he retorts, "*when* this is the case; but it is never the case."[28] This astonishing asseveration he bases upon the truism that "the productiveness, or utility of the soil is a decisive factor in the determination of its value or its rent." He thinks that because George says that rent does not arise from the natural capabilities of land, and simply represents the power of securing a part of the results of production, George denies that these natural capabilities have any bearing upon it. "An estate on the Rhine or on the Meuse is much more valuable than one of the same extent in the Eifel or in the Hartz mountains. Why so? To know the reason, one need have made no deep studies in political economy. Any peasant might teach our economist that this fact arises from the greater productiveness of the land watered by the Rhine and the Meuse."[29]

Yet this caustic sally is to no purpose. For a close reading of the relevant passage makes it evident that George is not claiming that natural utility has no bearing upon rent, but rather that no amount of natural utility can create rent in and of itself. "I may have very rich land, but it will yield no rent and have no value so long as there is other land as good to be had without rent. But when this other land is appropriated, and the best land to be had for nothing is inferior, either in fertility, situation, or other quality, my land will begin to have a value and yield rent."[30]

But Cathrein is not merely guilty of misreading George; he is also guilty of confusing the productivity of land with that of landowners. Even if George had, as Cathrein imagines, claimed that the utility of land has no bearing upon rent, to refute this claim would not prove that the landowner is responsible for that utility. It is his bare capacity as owner, and nothing that he contributes to productiveness, that gives him the power to extract rent. How much rent he is able to extract will depend upon the land's natural utility as compared to the best free land, but his ability to extract it is wholly the result of his ownership. Thus George writes: "Rent. . .is the price of monopoly, arising from the reduction to individual ownership of natural elements which human exertion can neither produce nor increase."[31]

Cathrein's next approach is to attempt to show that activities not classed by George as labor also create a valid title to property. He asserts that George interprets the term *labor* to signify only work involved in material production, and accuses him of ignoring the claims of those whose services do not lead to the cultivation or fabrication of material goods. He attributes this restrictive view to the American author for no reason other than that George declines to acknowledge that the exertion (such as it may be) attendant upon mere occupancy creates just title. But surely Cathrein would not classify the exertions of a thief as labor properly so-called, and George considers occupancy at society's expense a form of theft. He is at pains, on the other hand, to make clear that by labor he understands all exertions creative of value, whether material (goods) or nonmaterial (services).[32] I am at a loss to explain this curious error on Cathrein's part, for even if George had not explicitly recognized the creation of nonmaterial value as a form of labor, his refusal to accord that dignity to occupancy would scarcely demonstrate a denial of it to intellectual, spiritual, and other nonmaterial efforts. Possibly the Jesuit, overlooking George's insistence upon the interchangeability of goods and services in the market, assumes that since George defines wealth as consisting of material goods, only those whose labor produces material goods are considered by him to have a right to acquire wealth.

Cathrein concludes his assault upon the labor theory by denying that "the amount of a man's temporal possessions ought to depend on the amount of his labor, either productive or non-productive." Such a principle, he says, demands an impossibility, and therefore cannot be founded on natural right. For "who is to determine how much and how long everybody has worked, or how much each individual's labor is worth or can demand, in order that the distribution of products be just?"[33]

George, however, does not think of measuring labor in any such mechanical sense. He is satisfied that the just distribution of products could be achieved by that reciprocal exchange of satisfactions which we call the market, if only the monopoly of natural opportunity were done away with.

According to Cathrein, the alleged impossibility of measuring labor is evidence that the Almighty does not wish equality in earthly possessions. But the labor theory of ownership is not a rationale for equality of possessions. What it calls for is equality of natural opportunity—"a fair field and no favor." It does not seek to level down, or to compensate for differences in genetic endowment; all it asks is the abolition of artificial barriers to the use of the resources supplied by God. Cathrein appears to confuse George with Marx by equating the demand for equality of natural opportunity with the demand for equality of possessions.

III

His economic and moral arguments complete, the Reverend Father moves to strictly theological arguments in the final section of his treatise. However, he begins this section with an excursus on the Irish Question to illustrate his claim that first occupancy gives moral foundation to the permanent proprietorship of land, for he thinks it probable that sympathy with the plight of Ireland had much to do with the formation of George's theory. This conjecture may put the cart before the horse; still, it is not altogether implausible. It was in the context of an editorial on the Irish situation that George, the year before his socioeconomic broodings crystallized in the hills above the eastern shore of San Francisco Bay, first published his belief that every individual has a natural right to land.[34]

Cathrein does not hesitate to endorse the proposition that the soil of the Emerald Isle has, in great part, been unjustly taken away from the Irish people, and ought to be restored to them. By this, however, he means not that the land should be owned by the Irish as a community, but that the principle of first occupancy gives them the right (usurped by the British) to own it as individual proprietors. "Undoubtedly," he says, "the primitive settlement of the island took place gradually by immigration and propagation. The first families, as soon as they had settled, took possession of a sufficient piece of land as their private property, and those who came after them did the same, until at length the entire island was peopled." Unfortunately for the relevance of this account, historians tell us that Ireland was conquered from its original inhabitants by the Celts beginning around 400 B.C. Most of the modern Irish, therefore, have little better claim to the land on the basis of first occupancy than do the British.

With the Irish Question out of the way, our cleric devotes his attention in the remaining pages to more narrowly religious considerations. Life on earth, he declares, is but a preparation for the hereafter. Inequality of temporal goods is an important, divinely appointed means for obtaining life eternal. The rich and the poor stand in symbiotic relationship to one another: the existence of each serves to help fit the other for eternity. The rich man needs the poor, not only on account of the services with which their labor provides him, but still more because they afford him occasions for the practice of Christian charity and thus for earning merit toward heaven. The poor man needs the rich to teach him to bow in humility and stretch out his hands for mercy, while his poverty at the same time detaches his heart from earthly things and directs him to the hope of abundance in the life beyond. He who reflects that true piety has to do with motives other than the wish to garner claim-checks on a happy afterlife cannot but be spiritually repelled by the low prudentialism of this passage. After reading it, one finds it easy to understand why Marx called religion "the opiate of the people."

Of course, Cathrein protests that he does not mean to plead for pauperism. *Excessive* poverty, he admits, is no less a source of moral corruption than is excessive wealth, and widespread moderate prosperity is a proper goal of wise social polity. But the complete abolition of involuntary poverty is a foolish because unfeasible enterprise; "the poor you have always with you."

The necessity to work hard for a living, he says, accords with the plan of Divine Providence, and was decreed as a result of Adam's fall. He charges George with wanting to make the masses believe that he has found the means to transform this world into Paradise, fostering useless discontent by misleading them with promises of things impossible.

It must be conceded that George's rhetoric is, in spots, more than slightly overblown. The sober contemporary reader of *Progress and Poverty* would be more comfortable if the program enunciated therein were presented as a method of substantially reducing poverty rather than of wholly extirpating it. And he is not likely to be reassured by the rhapsody in which George identifies the blessings of a triumphant single tax with "the city of God on earth, with its walls of jasper and its gates of pearl!"[35] Still, despite this verbiage (which reflects, at least in part, the tastes of the day in which he wrote), George does not promise a utopia where abundance will prevail without toil. On the contrary, he makes exertion the title to ownership—a far more biblical posture than is presented by Cathrein's first-occupancy theory. According to the latter, Adam and Eve should logically, as first occupants, have remained, even after their fall, the proprietors of Eden and its bounty.

Cathrein closes his book with a homily calling for moral and spiritual regeneration as the only basis for social regeneration. "Society must return," he says, "to Christ." Yet how much easier this is for those of its members who are able to affirm with Henry George that God, far from being the author of human misery and want, has provided in the laws of economics, if rightly understood and implemented, the way to a social order marked by justice and freedom of opportunity for all!

Notes

1. Victor Cathrein, *The Champions of Agrarian Socialism: A Refutation of Émile de Laveleye and Henry George* (translated, revised and enlarged by Rev. J. U. Heinzle, S.J.; Buffalo, N.Y.: Peter Paul & Bro., 1889), pp. 82 f.

2. Ibid., p. 77.

3. Ibid., p. 85.

4. Henry George, *Progress and Poverty*, 75th anniversary ed. (New York: Robert Schalkenbach Foundation, 1954), pp. 171 f. The first edition appeared in 1879.

5. Cathrein, *Champions of Agrarian Socialism*, pp. 79, 85, 88, 89, 91.

6. George, *Progress and Poverty*, p. 194.

7. Ibid., p. 17 and passim.

8. Ibid., pp. 32 f.

9. Cathrein, *Champions of Agrarian Socialism*, p. 95.

10. Ibid.

11. George, *Progress and Poverty*, bk. 3, chap. 6.

12. Ibid., p. 209.

13. Ibid., p. 334.

14. Ibid., p. 336.

15. John Locke, *The Second Treatise of Government*, chap. 2, par. 5. The treatise was originally published in 1690.

16. Cathrein, *Champions of Agrarian Socialism*, p. 106.

17. George, *Progress and Poverty*, p. 337.

18. Locke, *Second Treatise*, chap. 5, par. 27.

19. George, *Progress and Poverty*, pp. 344 f.

20. Cathrein, *Champions of Agrarian Socialism*, p. 107.

21. Ibid., p. 109.

22. George, *Progress and Poverty*, p. 336.

23. Cathrein, *Champions of Agrarian Socialism*, p. 110.

24. Ibid.

25. Leo XIII, *Rerum Novarum*, par. 8.

26. George, "The Condition of Labor: An Open Letter to Pope Leo XIII," pp. 32 f. in *The Land Question* [and Other Essays] (New York: Robert Schalkenbach Foundation, 1953). The pagination in this volume is separate for each essay. George's "Open Letter" first came out in 1881.

27. George, *Progress and Poverty*, p. 336.

28. Cathrein, *Champions of Agrarian Socialism*, p. 111.

29. Ibid.

30. George, *Progress and Poverty*, pp. 166 f.

31. Ibid., p. 167.

32. Ibid., pp. 42, 302 f. and 235-41; George, *The Science of Political Economy* (New York: Robert Schalkenbach Foundation, 1962), p. 325. *The Science of Political Economy*, George's last and slightly unfinished work, was originally published posthumously in 1898.

33. Cathrein, *Champions of Agrarian Socialism*, p. 114.

34. George in the San Francisco *Monitor*, 11 September 1869.

35. George, *Progress and Poverty*, p. 552.

9

Huxley's Critique from Social Darwinism

BY ROY DOUGLAS

The economic doctrines of Henry George attracted the attention of two of the most famous nineteenth-century biologists: Thomas Henry Huxley (1825-1895) and Alfred Russel Wallace. Each of them had played a major part in the development and publicity of Darwinism. Wallace, indeed, had arrived at Darwin's general conclusions quite independently of Darwin. In each case the man's distinction as a biologist guaranteed that his opinions on other subjects would receive serious attention. Wallace was greatly influenced by George, and although his eventual proposals were by no means the same as George's, he held the American's arguments in the highest regard, differing essentially on application rather than principle. Huxley, however, seemed to oppose George almost in toto, and his opposition was based in part on an interpretation or extrapolation of biological evidence—although it was also partly founded on economic, philosophical, or quasi-historical grounds. Some of Huxley's arguments were essentially a repetition, or a development, of the views advanced previously by W. H. Mallock, and these criticisms are examined in chapter 6, which deals with Mallock.

Huxley's biological objections may to a considerable extent be separated from his economic objections; but the former cannot be separated from his attitude to philosophical problems like the existence of "natural rights," or from his criticisms of other authors—notably Jean Jacques Rousseau—who had written about "natural rights" and about land, and whose views on both subjects bore some relationship to those of George. Huxley, indeed, considered that "the doctrine of 'natural rights' is the fulcrum upon which [George], like a good many other political philosophers, during the last 130 years, rests the lever wherewith the social world is to be lifted away from its present foundations and deposited upon others."[1]

Huxley's disagreement with George is therefore expressed partly in attacks on Rousseau. Some of his objections were advanced in a correspondence with Herbert Spencer in *The Times* of November 1889, while his views were more fully developed in a series of articles which appeared in the *Nineteenth Century* not long afterwards and were eventually reprinted in his *Collected Essays*.[2]

Huxley was a very lucid, but also a very prolix writer. His essential "biological" arguments could be summed as follows: Men are not in any meaningful sense equal. *Natural rights*, in the ordinary sense of the term, do not exist; the only sense in which a man, or any other creature, possesses a "natural right" is that he has the "natural right" to do whatever he is capable of doing. Therefore, any economic or social theory which is based on the idea either that people are equal or that they possess *natural rights* (as the term is usually employed) is vain. Insofar as the theory of Henry George is based on the contention that all men possess natural and equal rights, it is valueless.

Huxley's essay *On the Natural Inequality of Men* is specifically directed against Rousseau, but also by implication against George and others who advanced "the revived Rousseauism of our day"—which in Huxley's view, "is working sad mischief, leading astray those who have not the time, even when they possess the ability, to go to the root of the superficially plausible doctrines which are disseminated among them."[3] From whose point of view, or on what moral basis, this "revived Rousseauism" was "working sad mischief" was not explained; presumably Huxley meant that it was in some way inimical to the general prosperity, perhaps the physical survival, of the human race. The doctrine which Huxley attacked, and which he claimed to see in Rousseau's *Le Contrat social* and his *Discours*, was as follows:

1. All men are born free, politically equal, and good, and in the "state of nature" remain so; consequently it is their natural right to be free, equal, and (presumably their duty) to be good.
2. None can have any right to encroach on another's equal right. Hence no man can appropriate any part of the common means of subsistence—that is to say, the land, or any thing which land produces—without the unanimous consent of all other men. Under any other circumstances, property is usurpation, or, in plain terms, robbery.
3. Political rights therefore are based upon contract; the so-called right to conquest is no right, and property which has been acquired by force may rightly be taken away by force.[4]

Part of the foregoing, of course, is no part of George's doctrine, and would probably have been repudiated by George; yet some of the ideas of Rousseau are evidently present in George's teaching.

"What" demanded Huxley, "is the meaning of the famous phrase that 'all men are born free and equal. . .?' " The only "equality" which newly born babies possess is the "equality of impotence." Furthermore,

In what conceivable state of society is it possible that men should not merely be born but pass through childhood and still remain free? Has a child of fourteen been free to choose its own language and all the connotations with which words become burdened in their use by generation after generation? Has it been free to choose the habits enforced by precept and more surely driven home by example? Has it been free to invent its own standard of right and wrong? Or rather has it not been as much held in bondage by its surroundings and driven hither and thither by the scourge of opinion as a veritable slave?[5]

Like all forms of determinist philosophy, this line of argument seems to lead to the conclusion that the philosopher himself is also determined, and that the conclusions which he reaches are therefore the product of his predetermination and not of the free exercise of his reason. But we must follow Huxley's contentions further.

Not only are people not free, Huxley tells us, but they are also not equal.

Among a body of naked wandering savages. . .there may be no property in things, but the witless man will be poverty-stricken in ideas, the clever man will be a capitalist in the same commodity, which in the long run buys all other commodities; one will miss opportunities, the other will make them; and, proclaim human equality as loudly as you will, Witless will serve his brother. So long as men are men and society is society, human equality will be a dream; and the assumption that it does exist is as untrue in fact as it sets the mark of impracticality on every theory of what ought to be, which starts from it.[6]

In this passage, as far as it goes, Huxley is surely on solid ground; for all ordinary experience demonstrates that human capacities and other attributes differ enormously. His criticism, however, is of loose English rather than of loose ideas. The usual sense in which the word *equal* is applied to men is that they are (or should be) equal before some sort of tribunal: that they are, for example, equally important in the eyes of God; or that they should have equal access to a human court of law, which will judge their causes according to precepts which were laid down before their particular claims were formulated.

If Huxley's attack on the "natural right" to "freedom" and "equality" seems to challenge many established notions at their very root, his attack on "natural rights" is pressed elsewhere to even more disturbing lengths. In his essay "Natural Rights and Political Rights," Huxley appears to see men and tigers as part of a common order of nature which is indeed as the poet said, "red in tooth and claw." They are invested with equal rights to destroy, or to inflict pain upon, each other:

If, then, we deny that tigers have a natural right to torment and devour men, we really impeach not the conduct of the tigers, but the order of nature. And if we ourselves, with our notions of right and wrong, are, like tigers, the products of that order, whence comes our competence to deny the existence of their natural rights to those beings who stand upon the same foundation of natural rights as ourselves? To say that a thing exists in nature, and to say that it has a natural right to existence are, in fact, merely two ways of stating the same truth; which is that, in nature, fact and justification of the fact, or, in other words, might and right, are coextensive.[7]

Just as there is no absolute tribunal to which a man and a tiger may appeal, so also is there no absolute tribunal to which two men with conflicting interests may appeal. Suppose, Huxley argues, Robinson Crusoe and another man (whom he calls Will Atkins) have both been shipwrecked on an island, and they happen to be stalking the same goat. They are ". . .in a position identical with two tigers in the jungle slinking after the same Hindoo, so far as the law of nature is concerned. And if each insisted upon exerting the whole of his natural right, it is clear that there would be nothing for it but to fight for the goat."[8]

This may appear to lead to a totally anarchic condition of affairs, in which every man is constantly at war with every other man: a condition which would clearly not conduce to the survival of the human race. Huxley, however, tries to save us from that situation:

> The two men would, in reality, renounce the law of nature, and put themselves under a moral and civil law, replacing natural rights, which have no wrongs, with moral and civil rights, each of which has its correlative wrong. This, I take it, is the root of truth which saves the saying of Paul of Tarsus that "sin came by the law" from being a paradox. The solitary, individual man, living merely under the so-called "law of nature" which cannot be violated and having rights the contradictions of which are not wrongs, cannot sin.[9]

Whether this is really very different from Rousseau's own idea of a "social contract" is perhaps open to doubt. The real problem, however, concerns the question of sanctions. Suppose that Crusoe and Atkins freely agree to some law which will govern the future killing and eating of wild goats on the island, and one of them later violates that agreement. Before what court, and on what ground, should complaint be made? If the offender denies his offence, how may it be proved against him? What remedy should the aggrieved party seek against the other, and how may he enforce it? Huxley's argument seems to imply that, whereas a man may rob or kill another without any turpitude in the absence of contract, yet the establishment of a contract produces a relationship so binding that it is inconceivable that any man should break it.

More difficult still is the situation which arises when a third man lands on the island. Is there any sense in which the Crusoe-Atkins agreement is morally binding on him? Lawyers are usually reluctant to see a *jus tertii* arising out of a contract; yet Huxley seems to imply rights and obligations which will govern all future inhabitants of the island—all springing from the original agreement, and all of such a compelling nature that it is inconceivable that they will be violated.

Thus Huxley's attempt to erect a system of contractual rights in place of "natural rights" must collapse. If his view about the invalidity of "natural rights" is to be taken seriously, then the moral for those who feel themselves aggrieved by existing arrangements is clear enough. As one of Huxley's contemporaneous critics very neatly put it: "All these witty similes about the right of the tiger to eat the Hindoo and that of the Hindoo to shoot the tiger are summed up in that simple argument, very natural in the mouth of the great biologist, that the only right is that of the stronger. To avoid all discussion let us accept that proposition and let us ask Mr. Huxley if he contests the natural right of the people to their soil if they are strong enough to take it from the minority which now has got possession of it."[10]

A philosopher would probably say that Huxley's arguments have not really struck at the notion of "natural rights" at all; what Huxley has done is to show that many writers have used the term loosely and without sufficient thought. The existence or otherwise of "natural rights" is, however, hardly the problem. Unless most people in a society accept, however tacitly, that some sort of "natural rights" exist which must be respected even when they run counter to people's own interests, then the alternative seems to be a chain of violence extending throughout the whole human future: a future which, on that particular hypothesis, is not likely to be a very long one. It is perhaps useful at this stage to make a substantial digression to see what, if anything, may be done to save mankind from supervening chaos if we follow Huxley in discounting "natural rights" and yet cannot accept the alternative ethical system which he offers.

The bearing of Rousseau upon George is oblique. Rousseau's ideas of "natural" equality and rights were much in vogue at the time of the American Revolution. Though Jefferson was no slavish follower of Rousseau, there is surely a Rousseauesque flavour in the rhetoric of the Declaration of Independence: "We hold these truths to be self-evident: That all men are created equal, and that they are endowed by their Creator with certain unalienable rights. . . ." This almost took on the character of infallible Holy Writ for patriotic Americans. George, though writing a century later, proudly proclaimed himself a "Jeffersonian Democrat" and stood fully in the tradition of the men of 1776. The religious views of George were far more orthodox than those of either Rousseau or Huxley, and he would probably have seen the source of "natural rights" in the fiat of God. George, and probably the men who framed the American Constitution, would have meant by the word *equal*, "with souls equally valuable to God." Huxley's criticisms only concerned deductions drawn from secular reasoning. He does not discuss the possibility that the men may be restrained from fighting over the goat because God has implanted in each of them a moral consciousness which—in certain circumstances at least—is powerful enough to hold them from each other's throat. This intellectual position, whether correct or not, is logically unassailable.

Yet, whether a system of natural rights may be derived from a theological basis or not, both Huxley's society and ours contain many people who doubt or deny the validity of that basis. Such a society cannot long survive unless there is some alternative means of persuading people to forgo their own apparent advantage for the benefit of others.

Even before Huxley's critique had been written, another writer, Samuel B. Clarke, sought by a different line of argument to defend the basis to which George appealed:

So many fantastic schemes have been put forward in the name of man's natural rights that there is, undeniably, some excuse for the incredulity with which propositions purporting to have that basis are frequently met. But a little reflection will be apt to lead to a univeral admission that the standard of rights to which George appeals is valid. Little children in their play vaguely perceive and roughly act upon it in adjudging some of their fellows fair and others unfair. Our conduct in matters outside the domain of positive law, in a social club for instance, is governed by it. In desperate emergencies, as at Cape Sabine, we unflinchingly exact the forfeiture of life itself from the man who will not conform to it.[11]

No doubt the modern psychologist would look with some suspicion at any evidence about absolute ethics which derives from such sources as those discussed above. The anthropologist would probably go further still, and tell us that there are some societies where a particular act is forbidden, and other societies where precisely the same act is not merely permitted, but is actually regarded as obligatory. Yet, in spite of all these difficulties, the idea of "fairness" and "unfairness" is almost universally held, and the great majority of human beings seem to agree in the great majority of circumstances as to whether a particular act is fair or not. Huxley himself gives curious and oblique evidence of this, for some of the criticisms he advances against George really amount to the contention that George was morally as well as logically at fault in advancing certain arguments, or advancing them in certain ways: that George, in fact, was being "unfair." At one point Huxley's sense of moral rectitude is so outraged that he can scarcely keep his temper: "The political philosopher who uses his *a priori* lever, knowing that he may stir up social discord, without the most conclusive justification, to my mind comes perilously near the boundary which divides blunders from crimes."[12]

In fact, this wrangle over "natural" rights is of very little significance either to George's case or to Huxley's. It seems strange that Huxley should have bothered to spin out far-fetched and unconvincing myths about marooned mariners and dead goats in order to derive a basis for social behaviour, when a perfectly simple biological explanation lay at his elbow. In man, as in other social animals, individuals frequently exhibit a kind of behaviour which evidently runs counter to the interest of the particular creature concerned, but is of value to the species as a whole. A parent, for example, will often defend its child against a dangerous enemy, at risk to the parent's life, when the parent could easily have made good its own escape by abandoning the child. Often far more complex patterns of "unselfish" behaviour may be observed. Social hymenoptera, for example, will sting an assailant to their hive, even though the particular individual who does the stinging is always likely, and in some species certain, to die as a result. There is every reason to believe that these behaviour patterns are the products of natural selection; they have been preserved because they have proved of advantage to the species, even though of disadvantage to the individual who displays them.

Just as a man is likely himself to practice certain kinds of "unselfish" behaviour, so also does he expect others to conform to the code which he would follow (or thinks he would follow) in comparable circumstances. Whether we call all this a recognition of "natural rights" possessed by others, or whether we call it no more than a common pattern of behaviour preserved by natural selection, is a matter of vast philosophical significance but singularly little practical importance from the point of view of those who need to pronounce on the organization of society. Mankind, it seems, has been saved from the social collapse which seemed to confront him, not by the philosophy of either

George or Huxley, but by his genetic constitution, which disposes him in some ways to cooperate with his fellows.

While Huxley really should have recognized the biological basis of intraspecific cooperation, there is another limb of his "Social Darwinism" which might seem to bring him into conflict with George: his emphasis on the importance of intraspecific competition. This argument is not set out with great clarity by Huxley in the particular works which we are here examining, although it had been put so clearly elsewhere that he might reasonably have assumed that the reader would already be familiar with it. It appears to the present author, however, that this element of "Social Darwinism" explains, more than anything else, why Huxley took general issue with George. Competition between individuals within a biological species is essential to provide that steady biological "improvement" of the species which is necessary for its numerical increase and even for its continuance. This competition produces what is often tautologically described as *survival of the fittest*—an unfortunate term, for the only test of "fitness" is survival power. We may perhaps avoid the tautology by arguing that intense competition between members of a species (including man) would be likely to result in the selective survival of individuals possessing characteristics like physical strength or intellectual ability; while, *ceteris paribus*, individuals not possessing those characteristics would be less likely to survive and leave progeny. If, however, the "weaker" members of human society were preserved by the mitigation of gross poverty—a condition which George and most other social reformers envisaged—then the eugenic effect would be reduced, or even totally destroyed.

The crude and violent logic of this argument, however, depends on the assumption that "desirable" hereditary characteristics are on the whole possessed by the wealthier members of the society and the "undesirable" hereditary characteristics by the poorer members. Happily, however, there seems singularly little evidence that this is the case in civilized human societies, and we are therefore spared some highly unpalatable moral dilemmas. In the vast majority of animal species, the parents of a new individual afford it no sort of special protection once it has reached adulthood. By that time, if not long beforehand, the one gift it retains from the parents is its assembly of genes. In man, however, the effect of economic inheritance is that advantages secured in one generation may be retained for many succeeding generations, and give the possessor a much greater chance of surviving and leaving progeny than would otherwise be the case. This condition prevails whether the succeeding generations retain the biologically desirable characteristics or not.

Thus a large proportion of the people who have occupied positions of high social rank seem to have possessed no recognizable characteristics—intellectual or physical—in any way above the ordinary. Indeed, there are various cases where biologically heritable characteristics of a positively harmful nature (such as haemophilia) have been preserved only because their possessors happened to live in cosseted conditions. Conversely, an intellectual genius arising as a mutation in (for example) a peasant community, or a community of nineteenth-century laborers, would be less likely to survive than an individual less well endowed—if for no other reason than because high mental qualities are not usually consistent with a capacity to perform dull and repetitive work which his station in life demanded. This particular interpretation of "Social

Darwinism," in other words, is not only a very unpleasant doctrine from the point of view of those who happen to be its victims, but also one whose justification, even on the most strictly biological grounds, is dubious in the extreme.

Even if the existence of "natural rights" were conceded, Huxley would apparently disagree with those particular "natural rights" which George claims to perceive. *Progress and Poverty* is quoted: "What constitutes the rightful basis of property? What is it that enables a man to say justly of a thing, 'It is mine'? Is it not primarily the right of a man to himself, to the use of his own powers, to enjoyment of the fruits of his own exertions?"

Huxley argues that a man's qualities are very largely the product, not of his own efforts, but of the efforts of others.

> So that the man's right to himself and to all his powers and to all the products of his labour, which [George] makes the foundation of his system, turns out, if we follow another fundamental proposition of the same author to its logical conclusion, to be a right to a mere fraction of himself and to the exercise of the powers which exclusively belong to that fraction. Surely it would take a greater sage than Solomon to settle the respective claims of mankind in general, the mother and the educators, to the ownership of a child, and when these were satisfied what might remain in the shape of a right to himself would be hardly big enough to form a safe basis for anything, let alone property.[13]

This consideration seems to lie at the root of Huxley's confusion between "land" and "capital," which the present author discusses in chapter 6 on Mallock. Huxley takes an almost mystical view of "capital," which has been summarized recently by Charles F. Collier:

> Huxley's argument was that all life on earth presupposed a prior accumulation of capital. A nursing infant, for instance, was said to "borrow" "capital" from its mother's "savings." In all cases, grass and green plants are the basis of food because, unaided by human labor they produce the basic "work-stuff," the material which provides the energy to do work. "The one thing needful for economic production is the green plant, as the sole provider of vital capital from inorganic bodies." But even green plants need sunlight to grow. That led Huxley to conclude that the sun is "the primordial capitalist as far as we are concerned."[14]

Capital, as Huxley uses the term, thus covers a large part of what George and most other economists include in their definition of *land,* and which they distinguish completely from *capital*. Yet ordinary experience suggests that the exertion of labor upon land does produce a thing, "capital," to which the man who exerted the effort possesses a higher title than does the generality of mankind. If a savage cuts a stick, fashions it into a hook, and uses that hook for pulling down wild fruit—then has not that particular savage some moral right of complaint against another man who takes it from him? Is that complaint any less valid because the first savage, the thief, the hook, and (for that matter) the fruit all depend on solar energy for their existence?

To Huxley, the practical problems were no less grave than the moral ones: "It is a necessary condition of social existence that men should renounce some of their freedom of action; and the question of how much is one that can by no possibility be determined *a priori*. That which it would be tyranny to prevent in some states of society it would be madness to permit in others."[15] Huxley's theoretical and practical objections to George on this score are conveniently considered together.

George, of course, nowhere confutes either the need for some freedoms to be renounced as "a necessary condition of social existence," or the proposition that this necessary quantum will vary widely through time and space. The only serious problem is who should determine the quantum required. Huxley seems to imply that it should be decided by some kind of aristocracy or otherwise privileged individuals. He cites the powers of the Roman paterfamilias and the claim which is made by the state for taxes, or for military service, as demonstrations that "society's existence turns on the fact that its members are not exclusive possessors of themselves." Yet Huxley also seems to realize that this line of argument has more dialectical force than real substance: ". . .However, there is no greater mistake than the hasty conclusion that opinions are worthless because they are badly argued. The principle that 'the exertion of labour in production is the only title to exclusive possession' has a great deal to say for itself if we only substitute 'may be usefully considered to be a' for 'is the only.' "[16]

No harm will be done to George's essential case if we accept Huxley's rephrasing. The argument that men need to renounce some "rights to themselves" as a condition of living in a society must be used with some caution. The presumption, surely, must be that a man has a right to freedom, and to the possession of those things which he has made himself, or has derived by free agreement from those who have. We must go with Huxley in his contention that these rights may sometimes be displaced; but the *onus probandi* lies heavily on the shoulder of him who disputes that claim to possession, not on the man who seeks to defend it.

Here it is perhaps useful to employ a legal parallel. A man who holds a thing is presumed to have a good title to it; the burden of displacing that title lies on the man who challenges it. Even a thief has some title to a stolen chattel; his title, in fact, is good against anyone but the rightful owner; and a third person who without authority takes it from the thief is himself guilty of larceny. Likewise, we may well accept that a man's qualities are largely—even mainly—the products of the efforts of other people. This, however, does not even give "society" as a whole, much less some particular individual who professes to embody the claims and interests of society, the right to take that thing away, unless it is possible to show that he who does the taking away has a better title than the possessor. For reasons already considered, the mere occupation of high office in no way raises the presumption even of biological superiority, let alone that the incumbent possesses altruistic concern for others in the society.

Or perhaps the argument might be put another way. Every man, it is true, has derived benefits, and even his personal qualities, from others; but it is also true that each man has given benefits to others, and contributed to their qualities. Because it is impossible to draw up a satisfactory balance-sheet, the most simple and practical device is to presume that everyone is entitled to those things which he has made, unless it can be shown that some other particular individual is better entitled; or unless it can be shown that compelling reasons exist for the view that the general interest of the whole community really does require that the possessor should be deprived of his possession. In any case, it is very important to distinguish sharply between the true interests of the "society," and the personal convenience—or greed—of those who happen to rule that society.

The tenor of Huxley's argument hereafter is not wholly clear, but he seems to be implying that a priori moral or economic reasoning is so fallible that the best pragmatic rule is to defend as absolute not merely existing titles to things, but also existing powers and privileges. In this he seems to be moved, not so much by any strong conviction that existing arrangements are particularly desirable in themselves, but rather by fear that any deliberate disruption of the existing social order, whether in obedience to George or to anyone else, is likely to present unforeseeable, and probably unpleasant, consequences—not least because it is exceedingly difficult to formulate governing principles for such a society which would be generally accepted. This may well be true. Yet already in Huxley's time, and far more so in our own, large numbers of people have come to challenge the existing distribution of wealth. That challenge would assuredly have been made without assistance from Rousseau, from George, or (for that matter) from any other thinker whose name we may specify; and, for weal or woe, that challenge will assuredly continue to be made. In one sense, it is more the product of technology and science than of any economic or philosophical thinking. Huxley, as we have seen, angrily assails "the political philosopher who uses his *a priori* lever, knowing that he may stir up social discord"; what he fails to appreciate is that the social discord owes singularly little to George or to any other political philosopher. What led to "social discord" was the visible fact of economic change, in the wake of accelerating industrialism; economic change, which caused men to wonder whether the whole order of society, as well as the production and distribution of goods, might not be susceptible of alteration through conscious human effort. In most preindustrial societies, the passage from one class to another was reserved for a few who combined exceptional capacity with exceptional luck, and the great mass of mankind will readily believe:

> The rich man in his castle
> The poor man at his gate,
> God made them high or lowly
> And ordered their estate.

With industrialism, many people found social roles changing rapidly, and began to ask whether those roles could not be changed further.

Yet one is left with the impression that Huxley, in his eagerness as a controversialist, had misunderstood the implications of George's teachings; indeed, if he had understood them better, Huxley might well have found himself in a considerable measure of agreement. If Huxley's "Social Darwinism" meant that the "unfit" should be so ground down in poverty that they, or their progeny, would meet untimely deaths, then it was surely anathema to George's humanitarianism as well as his economics. But if Huxley's "Social Darwinism" was primarily concerned to ensure that those who were possessed of exceptional qualities should be enabled to move speedily up the social scale into positions of leadership, to the advantage of themselves, and ultimately of mankind as a whole, then assuredly this was completely on all fours with George's libertarian approach. Not least of the deplorable features of the economy against which George inveighed was the manner in which it preserved the "unfit" in high social positions, and deprived many others of the opportunity to reach positions where their capacities would be fully utilized. The logical development of Huxley's biological approach was not to defend a system which not merely offended against the growing moral consciousness of his time, but was also palpably inviable; rather should he have sought to canalize the forces of change into directions which would preserve and accentuate opportunity and beneficial competiton.

What George surely demonstrated was that the existing land system, by arbitrarily excluding some individuals from those natural resources which are essential to the full exercise of their capacities, acted not merely as an obstacle to them, but also as a hindrance to mankind as a whole. Nor is it necessary, in order to remedy that cause of complaint, that each individual should have personal access to natural resources—provided that those who do have access compensate the remainder by paying into some common fund the market value of the benefit they receive. This demonstration promoted one of George's arguments in repudiation of the prima facie presumption in favor of existing titles to land. George, it is important to remember, was in no sense a socialist. He demanded *la carrière overte aux talents*; he never preached the disastrous doctrine that social reformers should attempt to establish a dead level of possessions between men whose aptitudes of application were different from each other. *Progress and Poverty* was a book designed to show that certain proposals would dispel poverty, but George's essential arguments could have been directed just as well to people whose principal concern was to ensure the best utilization of human capacities, wherever they might appear, in order to stimulate the advance of all mankind.

Whatever may be said against private ownership of land on the grounds which we have just been considering, the landowner might perhaps be able to defend his title on a different basis, if he could show that land ownership was in all essentials similar to the ownership of chattels. George, like many land reformers, considered that land, unlike chattels, had been common property in early society; that existing land titles were effectively rooted in ancient theft. To this Huxley retorts: ". . .Almost all parts of the world and almost all societies, have yielded evidence that, in the earliest settled condition we can get at, land was held as private and several property, and not as the property of the public, or general body of the nation."[17] Unfortunately, Huxley does not proceed to adduce examples in support of this striking statement. The present author at least must confess himself quite mystified as to the source of the substantive information. The Sumerians, for example, seem to have taken the view that land belonged to the tribal gods. The Hebrew Scriptures set in the mouth of the Almighty the unambiguous assertion: "The land shall not be sold for ever, for the land is Mine; for ye are strangers and sojourners with Me."[18]

In early Roman law the disposal of *res mancipi*—a category including land, but also certain other things—could take place only by a special process which was not necessary for *res non mancipi*. In English Common Law, ownership of land is still vested only in the Crown. The highest title which a subject may possess—a fee simple—is now for all practical purposes tantamount to ownership, but originally this was not the case, and the subject was required to render services or goods to the Crown in consideration of his title to land. In the Scottish Highlands, the system of runrig, by which grazing land was common, and arable land was periodically reallocated among the clansmen, persisted right into the nineteenth century. Comparable examples may be quoted freely from other societies. Broadly speaking, the further back a country's legal system is traced, the sharper becomes the distinction between land and other kinds of property, and the clearer the recognition that no particular man had a better title to own land than any other, save insofar as he was rendering some special service to the community as a whole in consideration of that title.

When Huxley proceeds to amplify his own views of early landholding, he declares: "The particular method of early landholding of which we have the most widespread traces is that in which each of a great number of moderate-sized portions of the whole territory occupied by a nation is held in complete and inalienable ownership by the members of a family or a small number of actual or supposed kindred families. . .These circumstances were in the main. . .that there was plenty of land unoccupied; that population was very scanty and increased slowly. . ."[19]

If, contrary to present indications, the validity of Huxley's contentions about early landholding be established, it will be observed that the workings of that system turned on there being "plenty of land unoccupied." In that case it would not be a matter of great importance whether the "complete and inalienable ownership" of cultivated sites was recognized or not, for the landless man could always secure as much land as he wanted for the mere taking; while, conversely, there was no advantage for a family to hold any more land that its own members could work. The evil against which George protested was a system under which some men owned far more land than they could work, and others were almost or completely without land. While the matter on which Huxley and George disagree is of historical interest, they seem both to accept the practical and vital point that within early societies all men had access to as much land as they required.

Yet, while George confutes the morality of the landowner's original title, he does not regard this as good enough reason, in itself, for overriding the claim of the present incumbent. This point is discussed admirably in his second great book, *The Irish Land Question* (1881). If, argues George, I am able to prove that the remote ancestor of another man robbed my own remote ancestor of some money or chattel, this does not give me a reasonable claim against the title of the present holder. Conversely, however, if the profession of the remote ancestor was piracy, it does not give his descendant the right to continue the business, even though the intervening generations have done so. "The past is forever behind us," wrote George. "We can neither punish nor recompense the dead. But rob a people of the land on which they must live, and the robbery is continuous. It is a fresh robbery of every succeeding generation—a new robbery every year and every day; it is like the robbery which condemns to slavery the children of the slave. To apply to it the statute of limitations, to acknowledge for it the title of prescription, is not to condone the past; it is to legalize robbery in the present, to justify it in the future. . ."[20]

A more serious moral difficulty confronts the land reformer when he comes to face the next question: if the landowner has no moral right to the economic rent of land—then who has? Huxley quotes George's magisterial declaration: "The Almighty, who created earth for men, and men for the earth, has entailed it upon all the generations of the children of men by a decree written upon the constitution of things—a decree which no human action can bar and no prescription determine."[21]

Huxley does not so much challenge George's hypothesis as draw his own conclusions therefrom: "Hence it follows that the London infant has no more title to the Duke of Westminster's land, and the New York baby no more to Messrs. Astor's land, than the child of a North American squaw, of a native Australian, or of a Hottentot."[22]

W. E. H. Lecky, in the somewhat later work *Democracy and Liberty*, embellishes and develops Huxley's point. Referring to the condition in the United States, he observes:

It is at least quite certain that the original owners of the soil, whoever they may have been, were not the members of the Anglo-Saxon race. If there is no such thing as prescription in property; if violent dispossession in a remote and even a prehistoric past invalidates all succeeding contracts, the white man has no kind of title, either to an individual or to a joint possession of American soil. The sooner he disappears, the better. Against him, at least, the claim of the Red Indian is invincible.

But in truth the principle of Mr. George may be carried still further. If the land of the world is the inalienable possession of the whole human race, no nation has any right to claim one portion of it to the exclusion of the rest. . . . And what possible right, on the principle of Mr. George, have the younger nations to claim for themselves the exclusive possession of vast tracts of fertile and almost uninhabited land, as against the teeming millions and the over crowded centres of the Old World?[23]

Not without force, Huxley points out that many landless Britons, who joyfully acclaimed George's assertion that they were entitled to a share in the land currently owned by a small indigenous class, would have repudiated with considerable indignation the contention that people of other nationalities had a claim equal to their own.

This line of criticism has been examined in particular by two writers, one a contemporary of Lecky and Huxley, the other modern. Max Hirsch, writing in 1901, declares that: "Admitting that all men, without distinction of race or colour, have equal rights to all the earth, it by no means follows that none of them may take possession of any part of it; what does follow is, that no one of them may take more than his equal share of land, without compensating all others for the special privilege which he assumes."[24]

Perhaps the purist would challenge the implication that only men with "more than [their] equal share of land" ought to compensate the others, but the general argument is at least consistent with George's proposals insofar as they concern the internal arrangements of states. George does not seek to displace existing landowners from their holdings; he merely asks that they should pay the community for the benefits which they receive, through a tax on land values.

Hirsch goes on to argue that "if all mankind formed one social body, the contention would be true, that this social body must frame regulations safeguarding the equal rights of all men to the use of the whole earth. As long, however as men are associated in several and distinct social bodies, justice is satisfied, if each of these social bodies frames regulations safeguarding the equal rights of all its members to all the land which each of these social bodies controls. As between the members of each social body, justice requires such regulations to be framed, whether they are or are not equally framed by other social bodies."[25]

Robert V. Andelson, writing in 1971, develops this theme a little further:

> While the application of Lecky's argument might give every Mauri-tanean Bedouin and Albanian peasant a moral share in the wheat-lands of Kansas, it would also give every Swiss banker and Scottish shipbuilder a moral share in the oilfields of Iran. Lecky's objection, however, possesses only *prima facie* validity. That is to say, it would be valid if all mankind were a single covenant community in which respect for rights was everywhere and equally implanted. Since this is not and will not be foreseeably the case, the covenant community, where it exists, can only protect itself from dissolution by insisting upon territorial sovereignty.[26]

Hirsch used a further argument, which was losing validity even in his own day and has now become even more questionable. The young nations, he suggested, "prefer no claim to. . .exclusive possession, in the only sense in which the term can be legitimately used here; i.e., that they deprive the members of the older nations of the use of such land. Unable, even if they were willing, to bring the land which they control to the inhabitants of the older world, they have no objection to the latter coming to that land; nay, are anxious for them to do so. When, therefore, they have appropriated rent for common purposes, they will have recognised the equal right of all men to their land."[27]

Andelson, with the baleful record of the intervening seventy years before him, sees this condition as an ideal rather than an actuality: "If the inhabitants of poorer regions are not arbitrarily excluded from immigration, their right is afforded the fullest possible recognition consistent with the geographically-uneven social progress of the race."[28]

Modern experience had laid much stress on the essentially inequitable distribution of land between nation-states, and the tremendous influence of quite accidental considerations, like the discovery of minerals, on the prosperity not merely of individuals or classes, but of whole communities. Furthermore, nation-states of economic blocs have become less and less willing to accept immigrants from outside during the course of this present century; indeed, they have often set restrictions on the free movement of ethnic groups among their own subjects. In an absolute sense, there can be no convincing defence for the proposition that nation-states are entitled to arrogate the economic rent of land for their own exclusive use—particularly when those nation-states deny outsiders free access to their resources. The argument in favor of the collection of land-rent by nation-states is not that it is an ideal arrangement for the whole future of mankind, but that it represents a very great improvement upon the present condition of affairs. Yet it seems to carry the implication that the more fortunate nation-states have some kind of moral obligation towards others who are less well endowed.

The writing of Huxley leaves us with a curious impression of the man, very different indeed from that which we receive of Mallock. Huxley was a controversialist so committed—so bitter, even—that although in one sense he was a sincere and fearless seeker after truth, yet, once he had entered a quarrel he took Polonius's famous advice completely to heart. The winning of that immediate controversy became for him a more important matter even than the furtherance of the ideas which lay at the root of his social thought.

The present author has written of Mallock that he won some battles against George, but lost the war. The same could be said of Huxley, though in a very different sense. Mallock started from principles irreconcilable with those of George. He lost his war because he was fighting on the wrong side. Huxley lost his war, at least in the biological field, because he took issue with a man who need not have been treated as an enemy at all; because he entered a wholly unnecessary conflict through a mistaken understanding.

Notes

1. T. H. Huxley, "Natural Rights and Political Rights," *Collected Essays* (1890; London: Macmillan, 1894), 1:338.

2. T. H. Huxley and Herbert Spencer correspondence, *The Times*, 7, 11, 12, 15, 18, 19, 21, and 27 November 1889. Huxley, "On the Natural Inequality of Man," *Collected Essays,* 1:290 ff.; "Natural Rights and Political Rights," ibid., pp. 336 ff.; "Capital the Mother of Labour," *Collected Essays*, 9:147 ff.

3. Huxley, "Inequality," *Collected Essays*, 1:295.

4. Ibid., pp. 304-5.

5. Ibid., pp. 305-7.

6.   Ibid., p. 309.

7.   Huxley, "Natural Rights," *Collected Essays,* 1:345-46.

8.   Ibid., p. 354.

9.   Ibid., p. 355.

10.   Michael Flürscheim, "Professor Huxley's Attacks," *Nineteenth Century* 27 (1890); 639 f. and 648.

11.   Samuel B. Clarke, "Criticisms upon Henry George, Reviewed from the Stand-Point of Justice," *Harvard Law Review* 1, no. 6 (1887-1888): 265-93, at 266-67.

12.   Huxley, "Natural Rights," *Collected Essays,* 1:362.

13.   Ibid., pp. 366-67.

14.   Charles F. Collier, "Henry George's System of Economics: Analysis and Criticism," Ph.D. dissertation, Duke University, 1975, pp. 127-218.

15.   Huxley, "Natural Rights," *Collected Essays,* 1:356.

16.   Ibid., p. 369.

17.   Huxley, "Inequality," *Collected Essays,* 1:323.

18.   Leviticus 25:23.

19.   Huxley, "Inequality," *Collected Essays,* 1:324, 327.

20.   Henry George, *The Land Question* [and Other Essays] (New York: Robert Schalkenbach Foundation, 1965), p. 51. This work was originally published as *The Irish Land Question.*

21.   Huxley, "Natural Rights," *Collected Essays,* 1:380-81. The quotation is from an early edition of *The Land Question* and corresponds, with minor differences in wording, to a passage on p. 52 of the edition used here.

22.   Ibid.

23.   W.E.H. Lecky, *Democracy and Liberty* (London: Longmans Green & Co., 1896), 2:293-94.

24.   Max Hirsch, *Democracy versus Socialism* (London: Macmillan, 1901), p. 362.

25.   Ibid., p. 362.

26.   Robert V. Andelson, *Imputed Rights* (Athens, Ga.: University of Georgia Press, 1971), p. 110.

27.   Hirsch, *Democracy versus Socialism*, p. 363.

28.   Andelson, *Imputed Rights*, p. 110.

10

Rae: A Journalist Out of His Depth

BY AARON B. FULLER

I

John Rae (1845-1915) was a successful British journalist and author who is best known to students of economics as Adam Smith's principal biographer.[1] For many years he was associated in an editorial capacity with *The Contemporary Review*, which was one of the leading British journals of fact and opinion. In addition to these activities and dozens of articles in *The Contemporary Review* and the *British Quarterly* he authored *Eight Hours for Work* (1894) and *Contemporary Socialism* (1884). It is in this latter work, which was so successful that it went through four editions (1884, 1891, 1901, 1908), that Rae turned his capable literary talents to describing and criticizing "the two main types of existing social democracy—the Centralist, which is usually known as Communism, Socialism, or Collectivism, and the Anarchist, which—though also Communist, Socialist, or Collectivist—is generally known as Anarchism or Nihilism."[2] An entire chapter was devoted to Henry George because "although he is not a socialist, . . .his doctrines are in many respects closely allied with those of socialism, and because he has done more than any other single person to stir and deepen in this country an agitation which, if not socialistic, at least promises to be a mother of socialism."[3] This explanation provides us examples of Rae's great strength as an expositor and social critic and of his great weakness as a theorist. He was precisely correct that the agitation created by George's ideas would stimulate the growth of British socialism, but he was precisely wrong that George's doctrines were allied with socialism. It is characteristic of journalists to be long on social commentary and perception and short on conceptual analysis, and Rae is no exception. It is from the perspective that Rae was a journalist criticizing George an economist that we investigate the substantive contents of Rae's chapter, "The Agrarian Socialism of Henry George" in his book *Contemporary Socialism.**

*The present writer is, of course, aware that George himself spent most of his professional life in journalism, and that he had no formal training in economics. His *intellectual* life, however, displayed in his major written works, was spent largely as an economist—an economist whose scientific efforts were inextricably bound up with his intense involvement in questions of ethics and social reform, but an economist nonetheless. (See the judgment expressed in Joseph A. Schumpeter's conclusively authoritative *History of Economic Analysis*, p. 865, that George "was a self-taught economist, but he *was* an economist.") Whatever his limitations in this field, the appellation could scarcely be withheld from one to whose insight John Bates Clark admittedly owed the inspiration that led to his development of marginalism.

153

II

Rae devoted separate chapters to Karl Marx, Ferdinand Lassalle, and Carl Marlo in addition to Henry George, and this provides us with an index of the significance he attached to George's influence. Already in 1884 Marx's ideas were influential enough to require special attention in any survey of the status of contemporary socialism. Lassalle's famous phrase identifying an "iron law of wages" and his pivotal role in the formation of the General Association of German Workers (later to evolve into the German Social Democratic Party), qualify him as a major symbol of practical socialist activism.[4] Carl Marlo is no longer well-known, but in the mid-nineteenth century his writings contributed much to the popular conception of competitive capitalism as an inherently oppressive system of organization, and his political recommendations of industrial nationalization and cooperative corporate organization strikingly resemble the commercial structure of Western Europe in the mid-twentieth century.[5] Rae's implied elevation of George's influence to an approximate equality with these three socialist standardbearers testifies to the seriousness with which he viewed George as a potential molder of British opinion.

Rae's criticisms of Henry George were uncompromising because he viewed George as a dangerous voice that had to be stilled to preserve the good order of British society. To achieve this purpose, it did not necessarily matter to Rae what the contents of George's theories were; whatever George said had to be refuted because it contributed to popular unrest. Discussing George's self-proclaimed search for an explanation of why poverty accompanies material progress, Rae clearly establishes his categorical rejection of George's reasonings.

He first tormented his brain with imaginary facts, and has then restored it with erroneous theories. His argument is really little better than a prolonged and, we will own, athletic beating of the air; but since both the imaginary facts and the erroneous theories of which it is composed have obtained considerable vogue, it is well to subject it to a critical examination.[6]

Rae's critical examination is divided into three parts. In part one he challenges George on the empirical evidence of advancing poverty, denying that poverty was increasing and arguing that in proportion to population poverty was "considerably less in the more advanced industrial countries than in the less advanced ones."[7] Reasoning by analogy, Rae described George's view of advancing poverty amidst advancing wealth as like riding on a moving train that is passed by a faster train on a parallel track. The slower train seems to be moving backward only because the faster train is moving farther and farther ahead, but in fact both trains are moving ahead. Rae explained that like the motions of the two trains, the incomes of the poor and wealthy were both moving ahead, but the more rapid progress of the wealthy made it seem as if the poor were losing ground when in fact they were not. Phrased more precisely, Rae agreed with George that real income growth was disproportionate among high- and low-income classes, but disagreed with what he interpreted as George's view that the rate of growth was positive for the rich and negative for the poor.

In part two Rae discounts George's theoretical analyses and mistakenly suggests that George proposed his own version of the Malthusian population theory and "a new wages fund theory." This is Rae at his worst. Not only does he misstate what he offers as the then current contents of economic theory, but he also badly misunderstands the foundations and implications of George's analytics. This failure to capture the theoretical essence of his subject is characteristic of Rae's writing, and it is evidenced perhaps even more sharply in his *Life of Adam Smith* than in his *Contemporary Socialism*. In his biography of his Scottish countryman he spends more than four hundred pages reconstructing the intimate details of Smith's life through hundreds of letters and notes, and yet nowhere in the narrative does he provide even the barest analysis of Smith's ideas. Even granting Rae an unusual restraint not characteristic of biographers, it is difficult to explain how he could write about Adam Smith and not relate the man to his ideas. As an example, to Rae *The Theory of Moral Sentiments* is nothing more than Smith's first great work that brought him "immediate and universal recognition, in the first rank of contemporary writers."[8] No hint is offered that he understands the significance of the concepts in *The Theory of Moral Sentiments* as the groundwork for what was to come later in *An Inquiry Into The Nature and Causes of the Wealth of Nations*. The best that Rae can manage is that *The Theory of Moral Sentiments* "is an essay supporting and illustrating the doctrine that moral approbation and disapprobation are in the last analysis expressions of sympathy with the feelings of an imaginary and impartial spectator."[9] Rae entirely misses Smith's identification of passion, not reason, as the means to self-preservation. For Smith reason is the agent of substantive right, and by rejecting reason as the means to advancing self-preservation, Smith rejects the notion that the end of nature is a debatable proposition.[10] Concerning the roles of reason and passion in human affairs, Smith elaborates that the passions direct us to self-preservation whether we seek that end or not, and the proper view of nature is that it is an inner-directed impulse to survive. The passions will coordinate survival regardless of what we reason, providing us with an appetite both for the end of self-preservation and for the means to bring it about. Relating this to the fundamental propostions in Smith's *Wealth of Nations*, it is clear that even at this fundamental level of human motivations Smith structures his analyses around his advocacy of the unintended results of human action as preferred to the intended results of human design.[11] It is an important part of Smith's genius that his system of natural liberty, expressed in the ruling passions in *The Theory of Moral Sentiments* and in commercial economic society in *The Wealth of Nations*, utilizes an explanation of the ideal foundations of human behavior that is posterior to human nature and derivative from society. Had any of this occurred to Rae, he could have understood George's analytical foundations better than he did, because George was an accomplished student of Smith's ideas and much of the character of the analyses in *Progress and Poverty* reflects the character of Smith's conception of commercial economic affairs as the embodiment of natural liberty. But it did not occur to Rae and it probably could not; if he did not understand the ideas of the man whose biographer he was, it is exceedingly unlikely that he would understand the ideas of a man whose influence on the British people he feared.

In part three Rae rejects George's proposals for land-rent taxation and denies the optimistic results that George claims for their adoption. Rae is more on his own ground here, using his literary talents to counter the rhetorical exaggerations that George attached to his practical policy proposals. But in addition to pouncing on George's hyperbole, Rae attempted some analytical comments on land rent, the nature of land as a unique economic commodity, and property rights, and because these comments are contradictory and inconsistent Rae introduced additional elements of confusion into his critique.

Rae's three-part critical examination of George's ideas is presented much like a set of "even-if" arguments encountered in the formal argumentation of a legal brief. He first rejects George's ideas because they are inconsistent with the empirical evidence—poverty is not increasing with progress. But, he contended, even if poverty were increasing, a second reason to reject George's ideas, independent of the empirical evidence, is George's alleged theoretical error and confusion. Finally, he maintained that even if the empirical evidence and the analytical arguments were on George's side, a third independent reason to reject George is that his solutions to the problems he identifies are either incorrect or inadequate. Such a scattered array of independent arguments is sometimes called the "shotgun" approach to argumentation. Potentially deadly at the close quarters of journalistic and legal persuasion where the form of the argument may be more important than its contents, it is less effective at the longer range of analytical scholarship where logical and factual consistency weigh more heavily than persuasiveness. Rae's journalistic shotgun approach to criticism, composed of scattered independent arguments, did little serious analytical damage to George's analyses. But serious analytical damage may not have been Rae's intent; instead, he may have been trying to persuade his readers that George was a dangerous agitator who, like the socialists discussed elsewhere in *Contemporary Socialism*, threatened to disrupt British institutions.

In what follows we shall examine Rae's specific criticisms of George's vision of poverty, his economic analysis, and his land taxation proposals.

III

Rae challenged and denied George's fundamental proposition that poverty increases with progress. He cited empirical evidence that, to him, proved the error of George's claim. There are three assessments that are relevant here: First, was Rae's criticism unique? Second, was Rae correct about the empirical evidence? Third, was Rae's criticism related to George's fundamental proposition? Let us examine each in turn.

Rae's denial of George's proposition that poverty accompanies progress was a commonplace criticism of George during the late nineteenth century. Perhaps the two leading critics among professional economists were Arnold Toynbee and Alfred Marshall. Both denied George's assertion of poverty's accompanying progress as part of their more general denials of the claims of socialists, radicals, and others that growing poverty was an inherent concomitant of expanding industrial capitalism. Marshall began a series of lectures on Henry George in 1883 with the judgment that *Progress and Poverty* "is the last outcome of the feeling that we ought not to be content with our progress as long as there is so much suffering in the world."[12] He admits that "Mr.

George's book is the latest outcome of this yearning after a better state of things," but rhetorically asks if "we are sure that with the increase of wealth want has actually increased?"[13] Citing historical evidence, Marshall answers his own query in the negative. Among his examples to disprove increasing poverty he cites increasing agricultural wages over the prior thirty years, rising per capita income among the working classes, and better food in the diets of the working population.

Toynbee declared that "economists have to answer the question whether it is possible for the mass of the working classes to raise themselves under the present conditions of competition and private property. Ricardo and Henry George have both answered, No." Citing evidence from various sources, including the *Contemporary Review*, of which Rae was an associate editor, Toynbee counters the idea of increasing poverty by noting that "it is a fact that though the cost of living has undoubtedly increased, wages have risen in a higher ratio," that there has been "strong proof of a rise in agricultural wages," and that "the facts make it clear that the working classes can raise their position, though not in the same ratio as the middle classes."[14]

It is almost certain that Rae was aware of these criticisms made by Marshall and Toynbee. Marshall was already a well-known professor and his lectures were published in various newspapers in 1883. Toynbee's citations of evidence to prove that poverty was not increasing relied heavily on articles appearing in the *Contemporary Review*. In effect, Rae's challenge to George's proposition that poverty was increasing with progress amounts to a summary of one of the standard criticisms of George's ideas readily available to Rae in the accessible literature. Rae's challenge was not unique.

Unique or not, a separate question asks who was right concerning the empirical evidence. Was poverty in fact increasing or decreasing? The empirical evidence is contradictory, and even in the 1970s it is impossible to determine with a high degree of certainty whether poverty, expressed as changes in the standard of living and changes in real wages, was increasing or decreasing in the decades immediately prior to the 1880s.[15] Rae claims to have defeated George's assertion of increasing poverty because George failed to cite the wage and income data familiar to Rae and others like Toynbee and Marshall. But these data were fragmentary and subject to criticism even in the 1880s, so that Rae cannot lay claim to empirical superiority compared to George when the data turn out to be unreliable.

Rae's reiteration of the idea that George was wrong about increasing poverty's accompanying progress failed to address the central issue of what George meant by his claimed observation. Rae correctly noted that at times George seemed to refer to absolute income levels and standards of living, while at other times George seemed to refer to relative differences between and among income classes. But Rae reads the mixture of absolute and relative income differences as confusion on George's part, and does not attempt to analyze the implications of George's treatment of poverty. In fact, George's observation of progress's accompanying poverty may be interpreted as an early assessment of the structural changes that occur when an economy shifts from dependence on individual self-sufficient landownership to a dependence on interdependent specialized divison of labor. In absolute dollar income terms, poverty emerges with progress because progress entails the growing division of labor with its associated dependence of one specialized producer on the products of other specialized producers, and the producers who do not own specialized factors of production like land will not enjoy the increased rents owing to the specialized factors from increased usage. According to George, progress creates poverty that did not exist in nonmarket or limited-market economies because it creates rental premiums for the specialized factors of production like land. Thus, as economies become industrialized and specialized in the name of progress, they evolve a real, absolute difference between those individuals who own specialized factors and those who do not. This is the nature of the "wedge" that is driven between different elements in an economy, a wedge between those which own specialized factors and those which do not.

In relative terms, the emergence of a market economy where individuals are dependent upon one another for varieties of products also signals the growth of human wants. A greater variety of products produces desires by individuals to enjoy the greater variety. These culturally determined wants become real elements in the standard of living, and their satisfaction becomes a measure of how well off an individual is relative to other individuals. Given that the set of culturally determined wants is much larger in a specialized market economy enjoying industrial progress than in a less-specialized premarket economy without industrial progress, there seems to be little question that relative poverty, that is, relative nonsatisfaction of culturally determined wants, will be greater in the market economy.

Seen in the light of George's vision of industrial progress as a product of market specialization and the division of labor, where culturally determined wants grow dramatically with the specialization and division, both absolute and relative income differences become relevant to an identification of the character of poverty amid progress. Rae failed to understand any of this, and instead chided George for the seemingly simplistic error of confusing absolute income differences with relative differences.

IV

Rae attacks George's economic analysis with respect to population theory, the wages-fund theory, and the concept of economic rent. Although Rae claims and attempts to demonstrate that George is confused with respect to Malthusian population theory and its relationship to diminishing returns, and misunderstands Ricardian rent theory, it is in his treatment of the wages-fund theory that Rae assigns the broadest range of analytical failures to George. This is curious and indicative of Rae's own failures analytically, because George's treatment of the wages-fund theory is one of his soundest analytical exercises.

Rae's failure is highlighted first by his mistaken impression that the wages-fund theory was a dead letter. He criticized George for bothering with the theory because it "was refuted by Mr. Thornton in 1869, was almost instantly abandoned by the candid mind of Mr. Mill, and is now rarely met with as a living economic doctrine."[16] Rae is again performing as a journalist faithfully reporting what he has heard or read of others but not bothering to assess for himself the validity of his reporting. It is correct that the wages fund was refuted by Thornton in 1869, refuted in the limited sense that Thornton offered arguments of refutation, but not refuted in the sense of its being shown as false.[17] George correctly judges Thornton's essay as a more formal than real attack upon the wages fund, and he accurately notes that Thornton rejected only one element of the theory, the presumed existence of a predetermined wages fund.[18] George's implication was that Thornton's attack left the wages-fund theory fundamentally intact, and Rae to the contrary, George was correct.[19] Feeling that previous writers, including Thornton, had attacked the wages-fund theory but were unsuccessful in destroying its logic, George set out to do it on his own.

Rae's statement that the wages-fund theory was abandoned by Mill in response to Thornton's strictures is not in every sense correct. Mill, it is true, thought these strictures so persuasive that he acceded to them in his review of the book in which they were advanced.[20] Yet he did not delete the theory from the seventh (1871) edition of his *Principles*, the last to appear in his lifetime, although in a footnote to his preface to that edition, he did direct attention to Thornton's book, his review, and Thornton's reply, without, however, indicating that his review contained a repudiation of the theory. Neither was it deleted from subsequent editions. The active debate over the wages fund had begun in earnest in 1879 with the publication of Henry Sidgwick's "The Wages Fund Theory" in *The Fortnightly Review*, and it continued throughout the 1880s and into the 1890s in the journal articles produced by a host of economists including Walker, Carver, Clark, Commons, Davenport, Hadley, Hollander, Johnson, Laughlin, Macvane, Veblen, Taussig, Edgeworth, Webb, Marshall, and others.[21] Rae's claim that the wages fund was not to be met as a living economic doctrine is an indictment of his appreciation of the status of the concept when George attacked it in 1879, and provides an explanation of why he thought George was wasting his time on a long-settled issue. Rae himself did not understand that the wages fund was alive and well.

V

Rae discussed George's proposal for a tax on land rent in the final section of the chapter. Contrasting George's expansive claims for the effects of such a tax with the dictates of common sense, Rae suggested that George expected too much to flow from the imposition of a tax on land rent. Rae's moderation, with which we can agree, is not carried over into his analysis of the land-rent proposal. In general, Rae misrepresents and misinterprets the implications of a tax on land rent. As an example, he is astounded at George's "scheme" to destroy individual ownership but not individual occupation. What Rae fails to recognize through the veil of the rhetoric is that it is not the property right to utilize a piece of land that George's taxation will change, but the right to acquire the economic rent of the land. There is nothing inconsistent in proposing that physical ownership of land be preserved while the property right to acquire, buy, and sell the expected future rental increments is appropriated to a central authority. Given that individuals attempt to make themselves as well off as possible, and do not attempt to make themselves worse off, the removal of the property right to acquire economic rents will encourage land to be utilized in its highest valued uses, that is, those uses where its contribution to the real product of economic activity is greatest. This is the fundamental basis for George's rhetorical claims of advantage under a system of land-rent taxation.

VI

John Rae's criticisms of Henry George's ideas are surprisingly unsophisticated for someone who could have been expected to be familiar with Adam Smith's conceptual foundations in *The Theory of Moral Sentiments* and the *Wealth of Nations*. George was a student of Smith's ideas, and much of the structure of the concepts in *Progress and Poverty* as well as George's other works is derived from George's understanding of Adam Smith. The Smithian connection has not been extensively pursued here because Rae did not pursue it, even though we could have expected it of him as Smith's principal biographer. If Rae had understood Smith's conception of commercial society as the embodiment of natural liberty, which is in turn an embodiment of Smith's conception of the passion for self-preservation, he would have had the perspective from which to view George's ideas in their proper context. But Rae was not aware of the fundamental elements of Smith's conceptual foundations, and in turn could not be aware of the elements of George's foundations. Instead, he was caught up in George's rhetorical dash and sought to combat the impact of the rhetoric with rhetoric of his own. This caused him to misread George's doctrines as closely akin to those of socialism, when in fact George was a thoroughgoing free-market advocate.

Notes

1. John Rae, *Life of Adam Smith* (1895; reprint ed. New York: Augustus P. Kelley, 1965), with an introduction by Jacob Viner. Rae's biography is the major source for what we know of Smith's life. It replaced Dugald Stewart's *Biographical Memoir of Adam Smith* (1811) as the standard Smith reference. Economists may be familiar with the name John Rae in another context. There was an economist named John Rae who was born in Scotland in 1796, migrated to Canada in 1822, and in 1834 published *Statement of Some New Principles on the Subject of Political Economy Exposing the Fallacies of the System of Free Trade and Some Other Doctrines Maintained in the Wealth of Nations*. This other Rae made important contributions to capital theory and directly influenced the builders of modern capital theory, Böhm-Bawerk, Irving Fisher, and Knut Wicksell. As far as I know, the John Rae of this inquiry, the journalist and author, was not directly related to the earlier economist John Rae.

2. John Rae, *Contemporary Socialism* (London: S. Sonnenschein and Co., Ltd., 1908), p. 57.

3. Ibid., p. 446.

4. Joseph A. Schumpeter, *History of Economic Analysis*, ed. Elizabeth Boody Schumpeter (New York: Oxford University Press, 1954), p. 650.

5. Ibid., pp. 459-60.

6. Rae, *Contemporary Socialism*, p. 445.

7. Ibid., p. 446.

8. Rae, *Life of Adam Smith*, p. 141.

9. Ibid, pp. 141-42.

10. Adam Smith, *The Theory of Moral Sentiments*, (1759; reprint ed., ed. E.G. West; New Rochelle, N.Y.: Arlington House, 1969), p. 110.

11. Aaron B. Fuller, "The Passions of Adam Smith," History of Economics Society Conference Paper (Chicago, 1976).

12. George J. Stigler, "Alfred Marshall's Lectures on Progress and Poverty," *Journal of Law and Economics* 12, no. 1 (1969):181-226.

13. Ibid., p. 184.

14. Arnold Toynbee, *Lectures on the Industrial Revolution in England* (London: Rivingtons, 1884), pp. 121-22.

15. T. R. Gourvish, "Flinn and Real Wage Trends in Britain, 1750-1850: A Comment," *Economic History Review*, 2d ser., 29 (1976):136-45; Eric Hopkins, "Small Town Aristocrats of Labor and Their Standard of Living, 1840-1914," *Economic History Review*, 2d. ser., 28 (1975):222-42; M. W. Flinn, "Trends in Real Wages, 1759-1850," *Economic History Review*, 2d ser., 27 (1974):395-411.

16. Rae, *Contemporary Socialism*, p. 464.

17. William Breit, "The Wages Fund Controversy Revisited," *Canadian Journal of Economics* 33, no. 4 (1967):510-28.

18. Henry George, *Progress and Poverty*, 75th anniversary ed. (New York: Robert Schalkenbach Foundation, 1954), p. 18.

19. Aaron B. Fuller, "Henry George and the Wages Fund," History of Economics Society Conference Paper (Chapel Hill, N.C., 1974).

20. Mill's review of Thornton's *On Labour* appeared in *Fortnightly Review* of May and June 1869, and was reprinted in John Stuart Mill, *Dissertations and Discussions* (London: Longmans Green, Reader and Dyer, 1875), 4:25-85.

21. H. Scott Gordon, "The Wage-Fund Controversy: The Second Round," *History of Political Economy* 5, no. 1 (1973):14-35.

Part III

Nineteenth-Century American Critics

11
Dixwell: Animadversions of an Admiring Adversary

BY GEORGE BABILOT

I. Introduction

In the decade that followed the appearance of Henry George's *Progress and Poverty,* the range of economic thinking in this country perceptibly broadened. It was a time when proponents of competing theories and advocates of alternative policy proposals successfully challenged the traditional boundaries of American economic thought and exercised a powerful influence on the direction as well as on the scope of economic inquiry. On issues typical of that day—free trade and protectionism, economic crises and unemployment, restrictive monopolistic practices, monetary instability, inequitable distribution of income and wealth, individual and social welfare—radical remedies competed freely with moderately heterodox ones for popular acceptance; then in turn, both radical and heterodox proposals had to contend with the more firmly entrenched orthodox prescriptions. This was a time of ferment, of economic unrest and uncertainty that could be discerned not only by the number and diversity of theories that vied for attention but also in the wide-ranging and also diverse policy proposals that circulated in quest of political support. In the midst of this turbulent time George Basil Dixwell (1815-1885) chose to set down his views on political economy.

In 1875, at the age of sixty, Dixwell decided to abandon a lifelong career in international commerce and diplomacy to try his hand at something that for him was entirely new and different. At an age in life when most persons are expected to slow down and give increasing thought to retirement and leisure, Dixwell, in contrary fashion and with astonishing energy, turned his full attention to the pursuit of scholarly research and writing. His contributions to economics were produced in an impressively short period of time. All of his published works appeared during the decade 1875-1885.[1] He devoted the last seven years of his life exclusively to studying and writing on topics in political economy.

Most of Dixwell's adult life was spent outside the United States. He lived for many years in China, where he held various commercial and diplomatic positions, including service as consul-general for Russia at Hong Kong and chief municipal officer at the foreign concession at Shanghai.[2] He was a member of a prominent, wealthy New England family. A generous inheritance provided him with financial independence and relieved him of the necessity for continuing his business career. He returned to the United States in 1875 to devote his full time to research and scholarly writing.

Dixwell's views on political economy are probably best described as heterodox.[3] While he readily accepted the orthodox position regarding private enterprise, private property, and the market system, he did not accept the orthodox position on free trade nor the orthodox position on the impossibility of general overproduction. He was a staunch advocate of tariffs and protectionism. Dixwell not only recognized the possibility of general overproduction, but he also set out to identify what he regarded as the significant causal factors involved. His position on protective tariffs, like that of other influential protectionists of his day, was not unrelated to concern about general overproduction and the causes of economic crisis.[4] He expressed his views on political economy through a series of journal articles and pamphlets. Dixwell did not publish in book form, although he did make available in a single bound volume some of his previously published articles and he also included in this collection a critique of the economics of Henry George titled *"Progress and Poverty." A Review of the Doctrines of Henry George.* This review, initially published as a forty-six page monograph in 1882, contains as complete a statement of Dixwell's economics as can be found anywhere, besides being a noteworthy contemporaneous critique of *Progress and Poverty.*

Although Dixwell's economic views differ markedly from George's, and therefore the temptation for derisive statement was understandably present, he nevertheless used restraint in his critical comments, paying scrupulous attention to the phrasing of his remarks to ensure that they not have the slightest taint of irony or contain even a hint of sarcasm. He in fact begins the review with a gracious statement of praise. "In *Progress and Poverty* Mr. Henry George has given to the world a brilliant work, admirably written, full of eloquence, radiant with the noble aspiration of diminishing human suffering. . ."[5] Then at the conclusion of his critique he again is generous with high praise: ". . .it is a brilliant book glowing with noble philanthropy, courage, and self-devotion. All that we have read in fable, or history, or the records of science, is brought again to mind in admirable sentences, and there is much of most interesting and suggestive thought and speculation."[6] What is written in the space between those beginning and concluding expressions of the high esteem in which he held Henry George and his work, however, is the product of what Dixwell terms "the disagreeable task of picking flaws in *Progress and Poverty.*" This task, though perhaps reluctantly assumed, is carried out in systematic fashion. His critical remarks are directed seriatim to (1) George's Position on Free Trade, (2) George's View of the American Problem, (3) George on the Malthusian Doctrine, (4) George on Wages, Rent, and Capital, and (5) George on the Remedy and the Meaning of Justice.

II. Henry George On Free Trade

The free trade versus tariff protection debate was in full swing in this country during the 1870s and 1880s. On this issue Dixwell sided with those of his contemporaries who favored protection and who disputed the orthodox free-trade arguments.[7] To Dixwell protectionism was a necessary step in order to counteract the economy's tendency toward overproduction with its accompanying unemployment and general crisis conditions. Evidently because of his own intense interest in the free trade-protectionism controversy and possibly because it was an issue with current popular appeal, he chose to defer discussion of the fundamental problem to which *Progress and Poverty* addresses itself, and, in its stead, seized the opportunity to engage first in a discussion of the free-trade question.

A year earlier, in 1881, there had appeared a review article of the English-language version of Frédéric Bastiat's book *Sophisms of Protectionism*, in which Dixwell defends the protectionist position against the criticisms of the recognized exponent of free trade, Bastiat. His comments on Henry George's arguments for free trade seem a continuation of what he wrote in that earlier review.[8] For example, he quotes a passage on free trade not taken from *Progress and Poverty* but from an article written by Henry George for the *Popular Science Monthly*, and his response to this argument is similar to, though less succinct than, that given earlier in his review of Bastiat's book. In the quotation referred to, Henry George writes:

> The effect of a tariff is to increase the cost of bringing goods from abroad. Now if this benefits a country, then all difficulties, dangers, and impediments which increase the cost of bringing goods from abroad are likewise beneficial. If this theory be correct, then the city which is the hardest to get at has the most advantageous situation; pirates and shipwrecks contribute to national prosperity by raising the price of freight and insurance; and improvements in navigation, in railroads and steamships, are injurious. Manifestly this is absurd.[9]

In citing this quotation Dixwell intends to alert the reader to the "absurdity in Mr. George's reasoning" and to warn that this is representative of the bad logic that occurs throughout *Progress and Poverty*. Dixwell proceeds to correct for George's "absurd reasoning" by substituting what he claims is the true (logical) statement.

> One of the effects of a tariff is to increase the cost of bringing *certain kinds* of goods from abroad. Nevertheless a tariff is said to be beneficial. If so, then everything which increases the cost of bringing from abroad not only those certain goods, but all goods, must likewise be beneficial. The obstacles he mentions not only raise the price of a particular kind or kinds of goods, but of all goods, and that of passage also, and they diminish the value of all exports. The railroad and the steamship facilitate every sort of exchange, but this does not prove that every sort of exchange is beneficial. Rum, opium, small-pox, and leprosy do not become desirable because distributed by rail and steamer! A tariff does not stop all exchanges, but only some.[10]

By stopping some exchanges through tariffs Dixwell visualizes a beneficial effect on the home country in the guise of increased employment, incomes, and overall demand. Elsewhere he wrote, "But restrictive laws [tariffs] have for their object to produce abundance, and they effect their object: if they raise the price, they increase in a much greater degree the effective demand—the ability to pay the price."[11] As to George's expressed concern for what happens to the consumer in all of this (". . .the robbery involved in the protective tariff, which for every twenty-five cents it puts in the treasury takes a dollar and it may be four or five out of the pocket of the consumer. . . ."[12]), his reply is that "Production is the condition precedent of consumption" and that *"poor consumers* are consumers only in consequence of their being able to produce."[13] In other words, protective tariffs create jobs, which create incomes, which, in turn, make possible greater consumption. Prices do rise, but the ability to purchase increases at an even faster rate because of the new jobs created and the greater income flow. Dixwell's argument, of course, is premised on the assumption that the exporting countries do not engage in retaliatory tariffs. If they did, this could mean a diminution in exports, and, depending upon the significance of foreign sales to the economy of the home country, conceivably the result could be a net increase in unemployment as exports fall off. George Dixwell evidently ignores the possibility of retaliatory-tariff behavior in his efforts to link greater consumption to greater production by way of protective tariffs. On the issue of the need to sustain domestic employment, opponents of protectionism could just as convincingly argue the alternative free-trade case. Conceivably effective demand and real income could be increased just as readily as a consequence of the lower prices from the removal of all levies on imported goods. Lower prices on imported goods would mean, in effect, a greater amount of household income available for spending on all goods, domestic and foreign. One might expect, therefore, that the rise in expenditures resulting from the overall increase in effective demand, induced by lower prices, would lead to an expansion in employment. Dixwell makes no mention of this theoretical possibility in his discourse on free trade and protectionism.

In his criticism of George's position on the subject, Dixwell notes that the great folly of free trade is the dependency status of the importing country, which makes it vulnerable to monopolistic behavior by the exporting country. Because of its dependency status the home country must accept terms of trade much to its disadvantage and perhaps at the cost of indebtedness and capital outflow. Dixwell throughout the review questions the validity of George's logic and his penchant for "droll syllogism." But here surely one must question the logic of Dixwell when he assumes the presence of monopolistic elements in a free-trade paradigm. Proponents of free trade meant exactly that, free trade. To cite the presence of restrictive monopolistic elements as an argument against free trade is little different from arguing against free trade because of the existence of tariffs! Henry George was talking about free trade. He opposed obstacles to free trade, whether in the form of protective tariffs or in the form of other monopoly practices.

It seems somewhat puzzling in a review of *Progress and Poverty* that Dixwell would give so much attention to the question of free trade. Henry George's views on the subject are better represented in his other writings.[14]

There is not that much on free trade in *Progress and Poverty* to warrant so much comment, and what little there is makes clear that it is of secondary importance to the central problem being dealt with by the book. Free trade, according to George, cannot in itself solve the basic problem confronting the economy. He notes, for example, that "free trade has enormously increased the wealth of Great Britain without lessening pauperism. It has simply increased rent."[15] As George saw it, free trade, without also the elimination of the private receipt of ground rents, could do little to eradicate the fundamental problem of inequitable distribution of income and wealth. Dixwell, for reasons of his own, chose to discuss George's veiws on free trade and protectionism independently of what George saw as the fundamental problem.

III. Henry George's View of the American Problem

Perhaps one reason Dixwell decided not to discuss the fundamental problem first is that he flatly denies that it even exists. By use of empirical data and by offering his own version of what the "real" American problem is, he tries to show that the one with which *Progress and Poverty* is concerned—deepening poverty accompanying society's material advance—is not in accord with the facts. In other words, George's proffered solution is for a problem that really does not exist. Like a vaccine prepared for a nonexisting disease, *Progress and Poverty* provides a remedy for a nonexisting societal illness. The statistical evidence adduced by Dixwell, however, provides flimsy support for his contention. He uses product per capita by ten-year intervals in an attempt to prove Henry George wrong. Dixwell's figures show that per capita product would have allowed each individual in the United States $61 in 1840, $69 in 1850, $83 in 1860, $110 in 1870, and $140 in 1880. These data show that product per capita rose in each of the ten-year periods, actually more than doubling between 1840 and 1880. Dixwell therefore infers from these statistics: "Wages, fees, salaries, emoluments of every kind, have risen every ten years. . .At each period there was more to divide and every portion of the community obtained a larger dividend—every portion, that is, in which no exceptional or temporary causes overcame the general swing of financial events."[16] This also prompts him to the conclusion: "The problem, then, for the solution of which Mr. George wrote his eloquent book seems not to exist."[17] Dixwell's conclusion is not warranted by the data he cites as evidence.

Data based solely on the statistical abstraction of per capita product (income) cannot constitute evidence in refutation of Henry George's contention of growing poverty amidst plenty. Income or product per person tells absolutely nothing about the *actual* distribution of income and product and, of course, inequitable distribution was the crucial point of Henry George's argument. Dixwell's statistics obviously show "progress," that is, growing material output—output increasing at a rate faster than population growth—and that is not inconsistent with George's view of the problem. What these data fail to reveal is how the fruits of this "progress" are actually divided up among persons, families, and income classes. Dixwell seems not to have considered the possibility that a more equal distribution of actual income (product) in 1840, when statistical per capita income was only $61, might conceivably mean less poverty than a more unequal distribution of a statistical per capita income twice that amount, such as in 1880 when it was $140.

Other statistical evidence Dixwell offers includes an estimate of the amount of gross product that annually goes into profits and rents. He claims that out of a gross annual product of $7,000,000,000 in 1880, only $2,400,000,000 (calculated by allowing a six percent return on an estimated total property value of $40,000,000,000) went to profits and rents.[18] He maintains that practically the total sum goes to create jobs by the consumption and investment activities of the recipients. To determine the portion going to ground rents alone, Dixwell makes what he considers appropriate adjustments in his estimate and concludes that the sum is so little as to be of no significance. "The reader will then see that ground rent from the abolition of which Mr. George expects the return of the golden age is altogether too minute to produce any perceptible harm."[19] If, as according to Dixwell, the amount going to ground rents is so insignificant, then what possible harm could be done by society's appropriating so "minute" a sum? George does not regard the portion of product going to ground rents as insignificant by any standard. But the size of rent is really not the issue. The nature of ground rent does not change with changes in its size. Whether large or small, rent represents an unearned increment to personal income—a surplus element that makes income greater than that warranted by the productivity of the recipient.

Dixwell exhibits a benign regard for the private receipt of rent and he is certainly not disposed to treat it as an unearned increment. He views it rather as a functionally necessary return. However, he seems confused about how to interpret George's rent concept, for he implies that it also includes the return to improvements. He claims that practically all the value of land in the United States is, in fact, the product of capital amassed by self-denial. Then, by way of illustration, he cites the case of a farmer and his wife enduring lifelong sacrifices to make their farm essentially

> their bank, in which many years of labor might under the laws of their country, be safely deposited. They looked forward to an independent old age and something with which to give their children a start in life. Even now, in their declining years, their farm has no rent which can be distinguished from the rent for improvements. Then, says Mr. George, let the rent of all be taken. And this in the name of justice![20]

If, in his illustration, what he says is true, that there is no ground rent, then nothing could or would be taken. Dixwell evidently overlooked Henry George's statement in *Progress and Poverty* that "the complete recognition of common rights to land need in no way interfere with the complete recognition of individual right to improvements or produce."[21] Almost as if George anticipates Dixwell's rhetorical illustration, he states,

> It is not necessary to say to a man, "this land is yours" in order to induce him to cultivate or improve it. It is only necessary to say to him, "whatever your labor or capital produces on this land shall be yours.". . . Give a man security that he may reap, and he will sow; assure him of the possession of the house he wants to build, and he will build it. These are natural rewards of labor. . . .The ownership of land has nothing to do with it.[22]

Dixwell's belief in the functional role of rent in the economy is not unrelated to his version of what constitutes the "real" American problem; his version differs considerably from George's. The difficulty, as he sees it, derives from the fact that progress is not continuous but rather comes about in waves, and, although each wave runs higher than the previous one, "during the reflux, there has been distress enough to wring the heart of anyone who observed it at its focus in the poorer quarters of a great city."[23] According to Dixwell, the "real" problem is to determine why, when society moves from one level of opulence to another, this movement is accompanied by periods of depression. He offers an explanation for this phenomenon, noting that "at the bottom of the whole trouble lie the imperfect information and consequent imperfect judgment of individuals."[24] Depression is ushered in by an episode of overproduction, a condition brought on by the formation of capital, in response to the desire to save, at a rate faster than population and effective demand can accommodate. Despite the fact that he defends the private receipt of rent because it provides a ready source of saving for capital accumulation and the fact that he acknowledges the greater desire to save as a major factor in the tendency toward overproduction, Dixwell nevertheless maintains that rent is in no way a contributing cause. Quite the contrary, he warns that "to lay all taxes upon real estate would give government enormous revenues during periods of excitement, when to use them would be prejudicial and leave it without a large portion of its necesssary revenue during periods of depression when expenditures would be beneficial."[25] As Dixwell sees it, when misery and poverty are not the result of "vice, crime, ignorance, and brutality"—note that the cause-and-effect relationship here is directly opposite from that held by George—it is a transient condition, the result of cyclical fluctuations in economic activity. All that is necessary to overcome misery and poverty, then, is for society to avoid recurring episodes of overproduction, and the problem evidently will disappear automatically. George does not share this cyclical view of the problem. For him the cause of poverty is far more deeply rooted in the structure of the economy—the inevitable consequence of an institutional arrangement that permits the private appropriation of socially created rents.

IV. George on the Malthusian Doctrine

Citations of recurring economic crises (gluts) as the problem, of the efficacy of protective tariffs as a remedy, and of the treatment of landowner spending behavior as a mitigating factor—all have a familiar ring. Each points to the unmistakable influence of Thomas Malthus on the thinking of Dixwell. When he discusses the issue of population growth, it is not surprising, therefore, that he should look to the same source of support. George, of course, felt that the Malthusian theory of population growth was at the basis of the erroneous wages-fund doctrine. He also felt that it incorrectly suggests that the cause of misery and poverty, being the inevitable consequence of natural instinct, was outside the influence of social control. In *Progress and Poverty*, George attempts, by appeal to facts, to disprove the Malthusian population doctrine. Dixwell, not unexpectedly, defends the population doctrine against George's criticisms. For this, he finds it convenient to focus on George's rejection of John Stuart Mill's adaptation of the doctrine. George quotes John Stuart Mill:

> A greater number of people cannot, in any given state of civilization, be collectively as well provided for as a smaller. The niggardliness of nature, not the injustice of society, is the cause of the penalty attached to over-population. An unjust distribution of wealth does not aggravate the evil, but, at most, causes it to be somewhat earlier felt. It is in vain to say that all mouths which the increase of mankind call into existence bring with them hands. The new mouths require as much food as the old ones, and the hands do not produce as much.[26]

Then George proceeds to deny all this, claiming the opposite to be true: "I assert that the very reverse of these propositions is true. I assert that in any given state of civilization a greater number of people can collectively be better provided for than a smaller. I assert that the injustice of society, not the niggardliness of nature, is the cause of the want and misery which the current theory attributes to over-population."[27] His resort to facts leads to the conclusion "that wealth is the greatest where population is densest."[28] Dixwell maintains that George's appeal to facts appears to contradict Mill only at first blush. On closer inspection, he argues, the facts as presented are not inconsistent with Mill's position, for Mill had acknowledged that an increase in population could result in a more than proportionate increase in wealth in areas that were "underpeopled" relative to the land available. Where he differs with George is in the attempt to extend this to the generalization that wealth would uninterruptedly continue to increase at a rate faster than the growth in population. Mill thought great increases in population, unaccompanied by significant improvements in the arts of production, would because of the operation of diminishing returns result in output's increasing at a rate slower than that of population growth, bringing with it human misery and privation. The facts cited by George draw heavily on the experience of the previous four decades when, asserts Dixwell, conditions were atypical. It was a period of time characterized by great advances in the arts of production, which propelled the rate of increase in output to exceed the rate of increase in population. He is quick to point out that the unusual experience of the previous forty years, therefore, was a transitory, temporary phenomenon, and clearly one anticipated by Mill in his statement on the consequences of overpopulation. The events of the immediate past, according to Dixwell, do not provide George with sufficient proof to establish what he intends—the universal fact that the power to produce wealth increases faster than the increase of population. In the words of Dixwell, what George's facts actually show is: "wealth has increased in consequence of these improvements—not in consequence of the greater population. The greater wealth and the greater population are joint effects; or rather the improvements brought greater wealth and this brought greater density of population."[29] Then in response to the second point of George's wherein he draws a comparison with countries that have a low density of population, Dixwell proceeds along lines that suggest a vague recognition of George's confounding of returns to scale and diminishing returns: ". . .it is quite true that greater wealth would ensue from greater population up to a certain not very well defined point. More capital can be used to advantage as population increases."[30] Where he thinks George goes astray is in "concluding that what is true to a certain point is true indefinitely." But if George fails to establish the "universal fact" that the power to produce wealth does not decrease with increases in population, Dixwell does little better in his attempt to establish the universal truth of the population doctrine of Malthus and Mill. He sees little possibility, anywhere in the world, of technological advances proceeding at a rate faster than population for very long. In forecasting the future of the United States he concludes: "It seems probable, then, that in the course of another century, or half a century, population with us will press upon the means of subsistence."[31]

V. George on Wages, Rent, and Capital

Since Dixwell rejects the argument that with increases in population the combined output of labor and capital increases at a faster rate, he also denies the corollary that workers are robbed when in densely populated areas the wages paid them are less than in areas where land is more freely available. His rejection is based on acceptance of the Malthusian population doctrine and the principle of diminishing returns, which comes into play because of the relative scarcity of land as population increases. As indicated above, he holds little hope that technological advance will proceed at a rate fast enough to be other than a temporary offset to the inevitable consequences of diminishing returns. From this perspective, coupled with his concern about general overproduction, he is prompted to view wages, rent, and capital differently from George.

While he, like George, rejects the wages-fund doctrine—that wages are determined by the ratio between capital and the number of workers—he finds George's proposition that capital does not employ labor but that labor employs capital equally unacceptable. In a modern monetary-exchange economy, the real wages of labor, which include food, clothing, and shelter, among other things, on which wages are spent, according to Dixwell, are produced before they are used. Labor that produces certain capital is not necessarily supported by that same capital. In response to George's claim "that since labor is the producer of capital, therefore, labor cannot be dependent for support upon capital," Dixwell maintains that capital produced by labor in one time period is available to use by labor of another time period. Crops of a previous year may be used as food for labor of a subsequent year. Though the wages-fund doctrine is not a valid explanation, nevertheless the capitalist, in this sense, does make an advance to labor, asserts Dixwell.

Consistent with his general overproduction viewpoint, Dixwell sees industry not limited by capital, but instead both industry and capital limited by the *field of employment*, which means that even in a country with enormous underdeveloped resources, at each stage in the development of the industrial community the rate of progress is limited by effective demand. When the normal limit to the *field of employment* has been exceeded, the desire to save forms capital faster than the population and its effective demand increases.[32] The situation is one of excess employment which, in turn, creates an excess production of commodities. Unlike George, the problem as Dixwell sees it is not related to the distribution of wages, profits, and rents. Returns to labor, capital, and land divide up the gross annual product, so that wages, profits, and rents all increase when gross product increases and all decrease when gross product decreases. In contrast to George, he claims that the proportion of gross product that actually goes to labor, capital, and landowners is determined by supply and demand. That factor which is relatively scarce receives a larger percentage of gross product and that factor which is relatively abundant receives a smaller percentage of gross product. For these reasons, Dixwell thinks George's algebraic formula—Produce = Rent + Wages + Interest, therefore, Produce - Rent = Wages + Interest—is meaningless. "As long as men and capital, taking the whole country together, are scarcer than land, they must be paid first, and rent must take what they leave. When, in the far future, men and capital are the more plenty, and land the less, then, and then only, will his interpretation of the formula be true."[33]

Dixwell sees the limit to the *field of employment* determined by the effective demand of the population, and he observes that if too much is saved and not enough spent on consumption, general overproduction is the result. He argues the beneficial effect of rent receivers on the economy through their purchaces of convenience and luxury goods, which help sustain effective demand, and through their savings, which help make capital available. Though he admits that overproduction is caused by capital formations taking place at too rapid a rate relative to effective demand, he makes no causal connection between this and the spending-and-saving patterns encouraged by the private receipt of rents. In terms of his own theory, he does not see the possibility of redistribution of income and wealth, via public appropriation of rents, as having a remedial effect on periodic oversaving and underconsumption. Moreover, while extolling the spending-and-saving virtues of landowners, he again overlooks George's major point that rent is a socially created, unearned increment to income. The manner of its disposition by the recipient can in no way alter that fact.

VI. George on the Remedy and the Meaning of Justice

Dixwell's reaction to George's remedy and sense of justice is predictable, for he refuses to assume that the value of land is the product of society. He evidently believes that practically the whole of the value of land is the result of improvements brought forth by labor, capital, and thrift. "But for this antecedent labor and thrift no piece of ground would command any rent. The whole value then would seem to belong of right to those who are here."[34] Nowhere, however, does he offer an explanation for the spectacular rises in the value of *unimproved* urban and rural lands. On the contrary, he seems to assume that all landowners are concerned capitalists, who, if they are not setting society's standards for convenience and luxury goods by their habits of consumption, are providing, by their abstinence, the savings used for capital improvements. In either instance Dixwell finds landowners (rent recipients) beneficial to society. In his defense of landowner's against George's remedy, he overlooks the fact that public appropriation of ground rents would not leave labor and capital uncompensated for their productivity. The return for the landowner's provision of labor and capital should ensure sufficient funds to him to maintain both his capital and his standard of living.

Dixwell notes two possible exceptions to the beneficial behavior of landowners, where, in fact, rent of land and "the rent of capital" may become oppressive and the source of poverty. One case is when the owners are absentee landlords, a situation toward which George directed attention, and the other, which George did not do much with, is when the landowners do not buy at home but purchase their luxuries and conveniences abroad. He cites the landlords of Ireland, and offers this solution for Irish misery and poverty: "Native landlords living on their estates and using Irish products would speedily change the whole aspect of that island. The abolition of landlords will indefinitely postpone her resurrection."[35] Again he points to the protective tariff as a necessary device to encourage consumption of domestic commodities and to discourage landlords from purchasing foreign-made, luxury items. It is doubtful that the very high income groups could so easily be dissuaded, by tax-induced higher prices, from purchasing what they view as desirable foreign-made convenience goods.

Dixwell has a very high regard for private ownership and he treats the subject at times as though George advocates its total elimination. This is his reaction to what he interprets as George's notion of justice:

> It appeals at once to our natural and laudable compassion for the poor, and to our natural but not laudable envy of the rich. To pillage the latter and pass the plunder over to the former, gratifies at once two strong passions. But how if, in thus gratifying our blind inclinations, we should miss our aim, and prevent that development of society to which alone the puny infant can look for a chance of unfolding its faculties and rising in the world? How if, in robbing the rich, we rob a thousand times as many deserving persons who cannot afford to be robbed?[36]

Henry George most certainly would not agree that his remedy in any way qualifies as an act of robbery. Since he does not see rent as an unearned addition to income, Dixwell assumes that society would be taking something that rightfully belongs to the landowner. George, on the other hand, sees the matter differently—that appropriation of economic rents would be an act by society of merely receiving what it itself had created, and therefore not one of taking something that an individual could lay claim to as a reward for productivity. If some are harmed through implementation of the remedy, then George's quest for justice and equitable treatment suggests the proper rule to apply: "It is the greater that swallow up the less not the less that swallow up the greater."[37]

It is apparent that Dixwell looks upon *Progress and Poverty* as a stimulating, and at times a disturbing, challenge to his own outlook on political economy. From the outset, his view of the basic American problem as a cyclical one, his protectionist notions, his acceptance of the Malthusian population doctrine, and the beneficent functional role he ascribed to landowners precluded any possibility of reconciliation of his position with George's. It is obvious that he admires Henry George in every way except, ironically, for his views on political economy. He in fact said as much: "If political economy could all be strained out, there would remain a volume which every critic would applaud and which the general reader would turn to again and again as a source of improvement and pleasure."[38]

Notes

1. A number of his articles were published in the *Bulletin of the National Association of Wool Manufacturers*. Six of his articles appeared in the *Bulletin* over a three-year period between 1881 and 1883. Three of his works appeared in a single volume (vol. 12) in 1881. From 1875 until his death in 1885 his contributions appeared in a number of other journals, including the *American*, published in Washington, the *Protectionist* and *Issue*, published in New York, and the *Journal*, published in Boston.

2. Biographical data are provided in "Obituary," *Bulletin of the National Association of Wool Manufacturers* 15 (1885):96-99.

3. Joseph Dorfman, in *The Economic Mind in American Civiliations, 1865-1918* (New York: Augustus M. Kelley, 1969), 3:123-36, associates Dixwell's views with a group of nonacademic American contemporaries whose outlook he describes as "heterodox" because of their questioning of the classical economic notion of the impossibility of general overproduction. In this group Dorfman includes: Carroll D. Wright, Uriel H. Crocker, Frederick William Henshaw, Frederick B. Hawley, and David A. Wells.

4. The most notable are Frederick William Henshaw and Frederick B. Hawley.

5. George Basic Dixwell, *"Progress and Poverty." A Review of the Doctrines of Henry George* (Cambridge: John Wilson and Son. University Press, 1882), p. 1. Hereinafter referred to as *A Review*.

6. Ibid., p. 46.

7. The names of some of the more prominent spokesmen for protectionism include Henry C. Carey, David A. Wells, Frederick William Henshaw, and Frederick B. Hawley.

8. Dixwell, "Review of Bastiat's Sophisms of Protection," *Bulletin of the National Association of Wool Manufacturers* II (1881):233-57. Hereinafter referred to as "Bastiat."

9. Dixwell, *A Review*, p. 1. This quotation is taken from Henry George, "The Study of Political Economy," *Popular Science Monthly* (March 1880), p. 606.

10. Dixwell, *A Review*, p. 4.

11. Dixwell, "Bastiat", p. 236.

12. Henry George, *Progress and Poverty*, 75th anniversary ed. (New York: Robert Schalkenbach Foundation, 1954), p. 300.

13. Dixwell, "Bastiat", p. 237.

14. Dixwell's *Review of the Doctrines of Henry George* appeared before the publication of Henry George's *Protection or Free Trade*(1885). Besides the *Popular Science Monthly* article cited by Dixwell, other sources of Henry George's views on free trade include his speeches, parts of his book *Social Problems* (1883) and sections of his book *The Science of Political Economy* (1898). Excellent information on the subject is scattered throughout Henry George, Jr., *The Life of Henry George* (1900; reprint ed. New York: Robert Schalkenbach Foundation, 1960).

15. George, *Progress and Poverty*, p. 254.

16. Dixwell, *A Review*, p. 12.

17. Ibid.

18. Ibid., p. 9.

19. Ibid., p. 11.

20. Ibid., pp. 42-43.

21. George, *Progress and Poverty,* p. 399.

22. Ibid., p. 398.

23. Dixwell, *A Review*, p. 13.

24. Ibid.

25. Ibid., p. 18.

26. George, *Progress and Poverty*, bk. 2, chap. 4. The quotation is taken from John Stuart Mill, *Principles of Political Economy*, bk. 1, chap. 13, sec. 2.

27. George, *Progress and Poverty*, p. 141.

28. Ibid., p. 144.

29. Dixwell, *A Review*, p. 24.

30. Ibid.
31. Ibid., p. 31.
32. Ibid., p. 18.
33. Ibid., p. 35.
34. Ibid., p. 41.
35. Ibid., p. 10.
36. Ibid., p. 42.
37. George, *Progress and Poverty,* p. 343.
38. Dixwell, *A Review,* p. 46.

12

Walker: The General Leads the Charge

BY STEVEN B. CORD

Francis Amasa Walker, the son of a noted political economist, followed illustriously in his father's footsteps, also achieving eminence as a leading statistician and educator of his time. After taking his baccalaureate degree at Amherst and reading law with a distinguished firm, he enrolled as an enlisted man in the Union Army, rising through the ranks as an adjutant, to retire, after sustaining severe wounds, with the brevet rank of brigadier general at the ripe age of twenty-five. Soon afterward he was appointed to the Bureau of Statistics, where he gained further acclaim by reorganizing it on an efficient and scientific basis. At various points in his career he served as superintendent of the census, commissioner of Indian affairs, and professor of political economy and history at Yale. In 1881 he became president of the Massachusetts Institute of Technology, modernizing and enlarging that institution until his death in 1897. Recipient of numerous honorary degrees both at home and abroad, when the American Economic Association was organized in 1885 he was made its first president virtually by acclamation.

As an economist, Walker published extensively. In his book *The Wages Question* (1876), he was the first professional economist to oppose John Stuart Mill's wages-fund theory, which maintained that wages were wholly dependent upon the amount of preexisting capital. Three years later, in *Progress and Poverty*, Henry George cited Walker's attack upon this theory as the most vital that he knew, but criticized it for conceding too much.[1] Although generally conservative, Walker was capable of intellectual courage: he favored international bimetallism despite adverse attitudes in his home state of Massachusetts and in his profession.

The controversy between Walker and George began with a skirmish over figures when George, in an article in *Frank Leslie's Illustrated Newspaper* entitled "The March of Concentration" (later included as a chapter in his *Social Problems*), challenged certain statistics about landholding that had just appeared in the *Compendium* of the Census of 1880, and for which Walker was responsible. This elicited a contemptuous but careless rejoinder in *Leslie's* by Walker, followed by a devastating counterthrust by George, another effort by Walker at rebuttal, and a coup de grâce by George. Six months later, in the preface of a new census volume, Walker was obliged to admit that his earlier statistics had contained disparity and error.

In 1883 Walker published a book, *Land and Its Rent*, which contains some of the most detailed criticism ever presented of the economic analysis in *Progress and Poverty*, and which was admittedly written for the express purpose of refuting George. It was based upon a series of lectures delivered by Walker at Harvard University.

The argument begins inauspiciously with a misrepresentation of George's proposal. According to Walker, George contended for "the natural and inalienable right of all individual members of the human race indiscriminately to enter and enjoy at will each and every lot and parcel of land upon the globe, and every building which may have been or may hereafter be erected thereupon."[2] In point of fact, George asserted that each man's equal right to land could be achieved if the government would only appropriate the land rent by taxation, and he vigorously opposed government seizure of land titles. He constantly defended private property in buildings and other improvements, even insisting that they should be subject to no taxation whatsoever.

Walker did not really warm up to his argument until later in the book, when he plunged into a lengthy attack upon George's economic system. "How much is there in the view," he wrote, "that commercial disturbance and industrial depression are due chiefly to the speculative holding of land?. . .Mr. George makes no point against private property in land unless he can show that it is, of all species of property, peculiarly the subject of speculative impulses."[3]

Max Hirsch rightly observes that George's position does not require that he show anything of the sort. For "is it not possible that whereas speculation in [unmonopolized] labour-products might inflict little or no harm on the community, speculation in land might inflict infinite harm, though land were no more subject to speculative impulses than labour-products?"[4] In any case, George had, in fact, stressed at least one peculiarity of land speculation—that it withholds a vital inelastic factor from production, whereas the higher prices induced by speculation in produced commodities attract additional producers, and the increased supply causes prices to adjust themselves back downward. Furthermore, as Hirsch remarks, the problem is not merely one of agricultural land, to which Walker confines it, but of all land. "Which are the main objects of speculation at Stock Exchanges? Railways, tramways, mines, gas and water shares and similar securities based on the ownership of land or special privileges to land, easily come first. Moreover, any inflation, whether it be a paper-money inflation, or any large addition to capital seeking investment, results first and foremost in the speculative rise of urban properties. . . .By far the greater part of land values, therefore, are not merely 'peculiarly the subject of speculative impulses,' but are pre-eminently the object of speculative transactions and excesses."[5]

Today's economists would stand with Walker in asserting that land speculation is not the main cause of depression; rather, the main cause is a sudden diminution in the money supply, and particularly the credit supply, resulting either from sudden mass pessimism about the short-run future of business, or from mistaken government action (e.g., the constriction of bank credit from 1929 to 1931 by the Federal Reserve Board to such an extent that the money supply fell by two-thirds).

But that land speculation can be *a* cause of depressions, there should be no doubt, either logically or empirically. Logically, because increasing speculation increasingly withdraws one of the vital factors (land) from the productive process, and imposes an ever-heavier speculative rent burden upon labor and capital, the active factors in production. Empirically, because increasing land speculation has, in fact, preceded every depression in the United States.

Walker then maintained that the amount of land that was, or ever would be, held idle for speculative purposes was negligible: "Because, forsooth, a man is holding a tract of land in the hope of a rise in value years hence, does that constitute any reason why he should refuse to rent it, this year or next, and get from it what he can, were it not more than enough to pay his taxes and a part of the interest of the money borrowed, to 'carry' the property?"[6]

This touches a somewhat weak spot in George's analysis, for throughout his writings George seems to assume that all land held for speculation would be kept absolutely idle. Collier, who is otherwise not impressed by Walker's treatment of George, thinks that this argument "constitutes a valid and very serious criticism."[7] But Hirsch successfully combats it by pointing out that it really makes relatively little difference whether land held for speculation is kept wholly idle, on the one hand, or put to some use well below its optimum capacity, on the other: "For if valuable land, fit for cultivation and near to markets, is largely used for this inferior purpose, then the arguments urged by George and which Mr. Walker endeavors to disprove must follow; labour and capital must be driven to the cultivation of poorer and more distant soils."[8] Thus, while George may perhaps be mildly faulted for often speaking of "idle" when he might better have spoken of "underused" land, in terms of its effect upon the margin this is a distinction without much of a difference. After giving some telling examples that bear out his contention, Hirsch extends the argument to encompass urban and mineral lands (which Walker ignored), remarking:

> Around all cities, much land fit for the intensest culture, is kept idle for speculative purposes. Users will only take it on long leases, owing to the valuable improvements which intense culture demands. Owners refuse to grant such leases, because it might deprive them of the opportunity to sell the land for building purposes. . . .
> Similarly, large areas of mining land are everywhere held out of use for speculative purposes. To such an extent is this practice carried, that a special term "shepherding" has been invented for it. . . .
> Fixing his gaze upon the least valuable land, agricultural land, alone, Mr. Walker has overlooked all these cases in which speculation induces the idle holding of much of the most valuable land in the community, enormously increasing rent, reducing wages, and intensifying many of the worst evils of our civilization.[9]

Walker next proceeded to attack another of George's theses, namely, that "irrespective of the increase of population, the effect of improvements in methods of production and exchange is to increase rent," this effect being carried so far that "all the advantages gained by the march of progress go to the owners of land, and wages do not increase."[10] This, he contended, is

George's "main proposition, the proposition to which the others are subsidiary." Hirsch, while conceding it to be "the most debatable point in *Progress and Poverty*,"[11] does not accept Walker's view of its indispensability to George's system. For he holds that even if Walker is successful in showing that rent does not increase through progress in methods of production when population remains stationary, an *increase* in population is the actual condition accompanying progress in production. He goes on to assert, moreover, that while George may have "somewhat exaggerated the facts of the case," Walker's contention is false even when population is stationary as far as *permanent* increase in wages is concerned.[12]

Walker commenced this line of attack on the ground that *qualitative* improvements in production enhance the demand for labor without enhancing the demand for land, thereby raising wages but not rent. He adduced several examples, of which the following may be taken as characteristic: "Here is the rude furniture of a laborer's cottage, worth perhaps $30. The same amount of wood may be made into furniture worth $200 for the home of the clerk, or into furniture worth $2,000 for the home of the banker. . .The actual material derived from the soil which would go into a picture by a master, worth thousands, makes a smaller draught upon the productive essences of the soil than a chromo of the Prodigal's Return, sold from a cart for $2, frame included."[13]

However, as Hirsch comments, none of Walker's examples are to the point. They do not even illustrate that a greater production of wealth has taken place:

> For obviously, had the same labour been devoted to the production of a greater quantity of. . .goods of inferior quality instead of making a smaller quantity of superior quality, the production of wealth might have been the same or greater. What he has shown, therefore, is that labour may be directed to produce the same amount of wealth from a smaller quantity of raw material, thus reducing the demand for land and for labour in the cultivation of land. That has not been disputed, nor is such a change in the direction of labour an "improvement in the methods of production."[14]

Walker's discussion of this point is subjected by Collier to even more devastating analysis. He calls attention to the fact that George's argument, and Walker's own summary of it, refer explicitly and exclusively to labor-saving innovations. From the context of George's work it is quite clear that by "improvements in production" he meant innovations that "literally saved, or used less labor, or at least increased the demand for labor less than the demand for other factors. George's proposition when viewed in that context becomes a virtual tautology which is irrefutable."[15]

If Walker had shown that there are qualitative improvements that enhance productivity without saving labor or increasing the demand for land, he could at least have scored a hit against George's general idea that rent tends to absorb the rewards of material progress, although it would not have demolished the specific argument in support of that idea which he thought he had addressed. "But, as Walker's own argument shows, he did not choose this alternative. Rather, he chose to argue the absurdity that labor-saving innovations are labor-using."[16]

Walker went as far as to claim that innovations have actually *decreased* the demand for land. He classified them under three headings, according to whether they improve manufacture, transportation, or cultivation of the soil.[17] With respect to the first category, he asserted that although manufacturing innovations do tend to increase the demand for land, they increase the demand for labor even more. This is simply presented as an *ipse dixit*, without supporting evidence or proof.

With respect to the second category, he stated that "whatever quickens and cheapens transport, acts directly in the reduction of rents, and cannot act in any other way, since it throws out of cultivation the poorer lands previously in use for the supply of the market, enabling the better soils at a distance to take their place, thus raising the lower limit, or, as it is called, the 'margin' of cultivation, and thus reducing rents."[18] Walker was true to Ricardo's Law of Rent here, for he assumed that rent is the difference between what can be produced on good land over what can be produced on the most inferior land with the same application of labor and capital. He maintained that this rent difference would be reduced by improvements in transportation because outlying lands, previously of little use, would now become more productive.

This stance, however, is highly questionable. After all, do not improvements in transportation greatly increase the value of many urban lands? Are not wharves and land surrounding them made more valuable by improvements in shipping? Do not better highways usually make city land more valuable? Improvements in transportation may in some cases have, as Walker claims, the effect of reducing rent, but certainly not "absolutely and exclusively" as he asserts, and not for the reason that he states; rather, because such improvements might sometimes reduce the difference between what can be produced on good land and on marginal land, respectively, *with the same application of labor and capital*. Yet since this land-rent difference is nonmeasurable (because no one would ever apply the same labor and capital to both good land and marginal land) Walker cannot prove via the Law of Rent that improved transportation reduces land rent. The contention must be demonstrated empirically.

There yet remains the last category, agricultural innovations, of which Walker recognizes two types: those which yield a constant product with less labor, and those which get more product with a fixed amount of labor. Collier contends that Walker slipped into a "subtle error" (too technical to go into here) in his analysis of the first type, and failed to demonstrate, in his anaylsis of the second type, an adequate understanding of "the relationship of differences in fertility in the determination of rent."[19]

Hirsch admits that Walker "was justified in the statement that some agricultural improvements reduce rent, *i.e.*, those which result in an increased yield without an equivalent increase in labor, and which are applicable to all land,"[20] but concludes that "while George, therefore, was to some small extent in error when he alleged that 'irrespective of the increase of population, the effect of improvements in methods of production and exchange is to increase rent,' inasmuch as there is one rare class of improvements which fail to do so in the long run, Mr. Walker's absolute denial of this generally true fact was a far greater error."[21]

To give Walker his due, we must note that he did present statistics to show that poverty had not increased with progress, that wages had not fallen over the years, and that rent had not increased faster than total production. His factual evidence was strong, and current statistics continue to support his case. (See the *U.S. Statistical Abstract*.) But it may be defensibly submitted that what George describes—namely, rent squeezing wages and interest to the wall—is the *natural* tendency when production is free of government interference and of all monopoly save that of land. Since his time, monopoly-union wage increases and taxation for such unproductive purposes as defense, crime-fighting, welfare, and the like, have lessened the share rent takes from total production. George himself foresaw that such factors could theoretically reduce rent,[22] and since then they have actually done so. Who could doubt, for instance, that if taxes were reduced (particularly the property tax on buildings) and if union-induced wage increases were abolished, rent would increase even if total production remained static? Who could doubt that if these factors were nullified, the rental difference between what the same application of labor and capital could produce on good land over marginal land would rise without any concurrent rise in wages and interest? If this be so, then George's analysis is still, with some slight modification, relevant and important.

We observe with some surprise that Walker did not concern himself in *Land and Its Rent* with the merits or demerits of George's famous tax proposal, but only with George's economic analysis of poverty and depressions. The question to which Walker addressed himself was: Are these two economic evils to be attributed solely or largely to private landownership and land speculation? In the 1880s most people were interested in learning whether George had really isolated the causes of these grand economic problems; only later did they begin to think of land-value taxation chiefly as a possible solution to more limited economic problems such as inflation, urban congestion, and the need for tax reform.

The arguments set forth in *Land and Its Rent* were reproduced almost verbatim in several other books by Walker, including the later editions of his widely used text *Political Economy*. It was in this work that he characterized George's practical proposal to tax away land values without compensating the owners as a "precious piece of villainy," and stated: "I will not insult my readers by discussing a project so steeped in infamy."[23] Eventually, however, his attitude altered in a way that mirrored the general academic change of view. In 1890, when he presented his address "The Tide of Economic Thought" before the annual meeting of the American Economic Association, Walker was able to treat George in a calmer and more impartial manner. He continued to insist upon compensation to the end, but a shift of emphasis may be detected in his 1890 speech, evidenced by his statement that "conceding compensation to existing owners, the proposition is one which an honest man can entertain."[24] He personally still had objections to the scheme, but it seemed to him that economists at large "have rather been inclining to the view that somewhat more of the economic rent than is now taken by the State might be brought into the treasury."[25] Walker, however, doubted that practical politicians could get the votes from small farmers and village lot-owners for such a plan.

His position on the subject was spelled out more completely in the 1893 edition of *First Lessons in Political Economy*, a high school textbook (but not significantly easier to read, one notes, than were the college texts of the period). Wrote Walker: "There can be no question, I think, that if the community chooses to claim rent, it has a clear and full right to it."[26] Nevertheless, the government must pay compensation, because if it had recognized the individual's legal right to land and its rent, to suddenly deny that right would be sheer robbery. Landowners have a vested interest that society is bound to protect even though, with economic progress, "a larger and still larger share of the product of industry tends to pass into the hands of the owners of land, not because they have done more for society, but because society has a greater need of that which they control"[27] (It should be remarked that this statement represents a sweeping contradiction of the thesis in *Land and Its Rent* that rent does *not* absorb the benefits of material advance!)

Numerous arguments may be put forth against the claim to compensation. First, government is constantly making adjustments that harm some people but benefit society at large, yet no claim to compensation is recognized or even broached. Utility rates are lowered by public service commissions, tariffs are reduced, military installations are shut down, yet no compensation is offered to those whose vested interests are adversely affected. The Eighteenth Amendment was imposed, yet the liquor interests were not compensated. Slavery was abolished, yet slaveowners were not compensated. Are we never to reduce farm subsidies because by now the farmers have obtained a vested interest? It is not usual for the government to compensate anybody when the rules of taxation are changed. Are we never to change the rules? Is not property legally held subject to changing laws? After all, we are faced with the choice of having government "confiscate" land rent, an income (or potential income) that, since land values are a social product, rightfully belongs to all, or having it "confiscate" personal incomes which are individually produced. Which alternative is ethically preferable?

Second, landowners receive from society a privilege—the exclusive use and disposition, at the expense of its other members, of a good that is the product of no human effort but without which production is impossible. Yet, through the years, society has received only a minuscule fraction of the value of this privilege; most has been appropriated by landowners. Hence, if any compensation is in order, it should be paid to society.

Finally, imposition of the land-value tax, if sufficiently gradual, would be only mildly confiscatory; it would be financially tantamount to gradual compensation without interest. Assuming a parcel of land worth $10,000 and a capitalization rate of five percent, the annual rent would be $500. If this annual rent were appropriated by taxation gradually over a period of forty years, the average annual *unappropriated* rent during this period would be $250, which, at the end of the period, would total $10,000—the full value of the land. These are only a few of the arguments against compensation; he who wishes others may read, for example, George's *A Perplexed Philosopher*, part 3, chapter 11.

Walker, in *First Lessons in Political Economy*, informed his young readers that an increasing number of educated and experienced gentlemen believed in the nationalization of land, although they were still in the minority. He advised his students to place themselves with the majority until the opposite side had been proved beyond the shadow of a doubt.

To lengthen that shadow, Walker then listed two principal objections to the national ownership of land, under which rubric he erroneously included the single tax. First was the administrative objection that the amount of political machinery required to administer all the lands, and the immense opportunities for corruption and favoritism involved, would make the scheme unworkable. An army of officials was pictured crossing the land, fixing and refixing rentals, and making the individual ownership of improvements insecure.

Like the necessity for compensation, this was to become a familiar theme. In rebuttal, supporters of George's proposal pointed out that it could be administered locally rather than nationally, and would in no way require any more officials than already administered the general property tax. In fact, the opportunities for corruption would be narrowed, since buildings would no longer be taxed. Land titles would remain in private hands, thus safeguarding the ownership of improvements.

Walker's second objection concerned the conservation of the fertility of agricultural land. He said that conservation was of great historical importance, citing several ancient territories that once supported rich civilizations but because of soil exhaustion could no longer do so. He maintained that land nationalization would be harmful to soil conservation, for what farmer, he asked, would take care to conserve the fertility of soil he did not own?

This argument reflected the growing interest in the conservation of natural resources, and would be heard frequently in the years to come. But it lacks cogency. Even under the existing system of land taxation, the fertility of the soil had been carelessly exploited. Vast areas of the United States, fertile not so long ago, are now wastelands. Absentee farm ownership was an important contributory cause of this, for wherever it existed the tenant farmer was truly not farming his own soil, and was indeed likely to take an indifferent attitude toward long-run fertility. Under land-value taxation, however, since the speculative water would be squeezed out of land prices, thus bringing them within reach of the cultivator, absentee farm ownership would tend to disappear, thereby abetting the cause of soil conservation.

Perhaps most important of all, under land-value taxation land would be assessed and taxed according to its optimum use. In the case of agricultural land, optimum use would reflect the application of fertilizer. If a farmer did not fertilize or otherwise conserve his soil, he would still be assessed and taxed as if he did. Thus he would be encouraged to conserve his land properly in order to derive the maximum income out of it, so that he could have a profit from it after paying the tax. Not only that, but there would be no tax on his fertilizer or other conservation investments, hence such investments would be stimulated.

One more point: a prudent farm owner who cultivated his own land would not be likely, under any tax system, to deliberately ruin the fertility of his soil; farm improvements are not easily moved, and if the soil became worthless or severely depleted, they would sharply depreciate in value. And, of course, proper soil-conservation practices could be mandated by law, as much under land-value taxation as under the current system.

So much for the strictures of General Walker, George's earliest, and superficially most formidable, serious academic adversary. On close examination he seems somewhat of a paper tiger!

Notes

1.   Henry George, *Progress and Poverty*, 75th anniversary ed. (New York: Robert Schalkenbach Foundation, 1954), pp. 18, 36.

2.   Francis A. Walker, *Land and Its Rent* (Boston: Little, Brown, 1883), p. 141.

3.   Ibid., p. 162.

4.   Max Hirsch, *Democracy Versus Socialism*, 4th ed. (New York: Robert Schalkenbach Foundation, 1948), p. 427.

5.   Ibid., p. 428.

6.   Walker, *Land and Its Rent*, pp. 164 f.

7.   Charles F. Collier, "Henry George's System of Economics: Analysis and Criticism," Ph.D. Dissertation, Duke University, 1976, p. 167.

8.   Hirsch, *Democracy Versus Socialism*, p. 429.

9.   Ibid., pp. 430-31.

10.   Walker, *Land and Its Rent*, p. 167.

11.   Hirsch, *Democracy Versus Socialism*, p. 432.

12.   Ibid., pp. 432-34.

13.   Walker, *Land and Its Rent*, p. 172.

14.   Hirsch, *Democracy Versus Socialism*, p. 436.

15.   Collier, "Henry George's System," p. 169.

16.   Ibid.

17.   Walker, *Land and Its Rent*, p. 175.

18.   Ibid.

19.   Collier, "Henry George's System," pp. 172-73.

20.   Hirsch, *Democracy Versus Socialism*, pp. 445 f.

21.   Ibid., p. 446.

22.   See *Progress and Poverty*, p. 310, and *Protection or Free Trade* (1886, reprint ed. New York: Robert Schalkenbach Foundation, n.d.), pp. 267 f.

23.   Walker, *Political Economy*, 3d ed. (New York: Henry Holt and Company, 1888), pp. 418, 419.

24.   Walker, "The Tide of Economic Thought," *Reports of the Proceedings of the American Economic Association, Fourth Annual Meeting*, 1890, p. 24.

25.   Ibid., p. 27.

26.   Walker, *First Lessons in Political Economy* (New York: Henry Holt and Company, 1893), p. 208.

27.   Ibid., p. 209.

13

Harris and His Anachronistic Attack

BY CHARLES F. COLLIER

William Torrey Harris (1835-1909) is best known as an American educator, editor, and philosopher. He served as a teacher in, and superintendent of, the St. Louis, Missouri, school system, and later as the United States Commissioner of Education. He edited Appleton's *International Education Series*, Webster's *New International Dictionary*, and the philosophy section of *Johnson's Encyclopedia*; he wrote numerous reports, papers and articles, and books. He was (with Emerson and Alcott) a founder of the influential School of Philosophy in Concord, Massachusetts, founder and editor of the *Journal of Speculative Philosophy*, and a promoter of Hegelian idealism. Yet, on several occasions, Harris took time from these activities to offer his critique of George's *Progress and Poverty*. (None of George's other works were discussed.) Harris believed that his basic arguments against George's ideas were never refuted.[1]

It is not surprising that Harris emerged as a critic of George since, on matters of economic theory, Harris was a disciple of Henry C. Carey.[2] Carey was a critic of the deductive method of analysis and the Ricardian rent theory in particular. Further, his theory of income distribution was quite different from the theories of the classicists and George.[3] Carey's ideas provided the foundation for Harris's critique.

Harris's attack began in September 1886 in an address to the Saratoga meeting of the American Social Science Association.[4] The speech was important for several reasons. First, it set the pattern for all of his other attacks. Since Harris believed that his arguments were devastating and that they had not been refuted, he did little to revise them. Second, as Barker noted in his definitive biography of George, with this speech Harris became "the most famous person to speak against [George] in this period."[5]

After some preliminary remarks, Harris, following Carey, attacked all of the classical economists, including George, for their use of the deductive method of reasoning. Carey claimed that the axioms of the classicists (wealth-maximizing behavior, drives to reproduce, etc.) simply did not adequately represent actual human behavior. He also claimed that when classicists applied deductive logic to these inadequate axioms they inevitably got

187

inadequate results. Further, he charged that the classicists never detected the flaws because their test of their theories' validity was logical consistency, not the ability to explain and predict "real world" behavior. He maintained that if the classicists ever tested their theories against actual data, they would have had to reject most of their theories.[6] Harris, in similar fashion, said that classicists failed because they "set up principles for absolute ones which serve only for a nation of mere shopkeepers."[7] He too believed that empirical tests would lead to the rejection of most of classical political economy. Carey felt that one of the worst errors produced by the classicists was the Ricardian rent theory, a theory that postulated that the most fertile land would be settled first and that the margin of cultivation would then extend downward and outward as more land was needed. Carey said that the historical evidence of England, the home of most of the classicists, revealed that the *reverse* was true, namely, that the first settlements were in the hill country and that settlement extended to, not from, the richer soil of the river bottoms.[8] That pattern, insisted Carey, was quite general. Harris, in turn, argued that the Ricardian view was obviously incorrect because, if the best land had been settled first, the lush Amazon basin would have been settled before most other parts of the world.[9]

In reiterating Carey's arguments, Harris apparently never realized that leading economists had refuted them twenty years before. John Stuart Mill reasoned that in areas of new settlement, in which labor and capital were scarce relative to land, people might not settle on land that would eventually prove to be the most fertile *if* initial cultivation of that land required more capital and labor than cultivation of another plot that would eventually prove less fertile. But, said Mill, once societies had become well populated by people with adequate capital, it would be nothing short of absurd for them to let the more fertile plots remain idle while they lived on the less fertile plots. Mill claimed that *after a certain state of development had been reached*, societies did act in accordance with the Ricardian view.[10] Francis Amasa Walker, perhaps the foremost American economist of the era, also had written a lengthy and devastating analysis of Carey's ideas before Harris reiterated them.[11] Finally, Alfred Marshall, the greatest economist alive at the turn of the century, also had refuted Carey's arguments. He accepted Mill's analysis and then added that the first settlers in a country may settle on hills and not on river bottoms since hills can be more defensible positions against enemies and wild animals. Further, he noted that many river bottoms are places in which one was more likely to catch diseases such as malaria. Marshall argued that since such risks must be taken into account, it would be quite logical to delay settlement of the river bottoms until medical technology and defense capability were developed.[12] Mill, Walker, and Marshall all agreed that the Carey-Harris objections were valid when they were directed at careless statements of the Ricardian theory, but they argued that the Carey-Harris objections were entirely irrelevant or incorrect when they were directed against careful statements of the theory. Harris's failure to deal with, or even acknowledge, these arguments indicates that he was not so conversant with the literature as he should have been.

Harris's main objection to George's method of procedure was that the method was entirely deductive and that George had not applied a single reliable statistical test to his theories. Harris believed that such tests would reveal that the problem that George proposed to solve was entirely specious and that George's proposed remedy would actually be detrimental to the interests of the classes it was designed to help. He sought to prove that with the available census data.[13]

In some senses, Harris was correct. George did often tend to assume things that could have been tested empirically, and rejection of these assumptions would greatly weaken George's analysis. For instance, George did assume that land speculators would hold their land idle while they waited for its value to increase. Also, George did assume a good deal more than he had a right to about the links between progress and poverty. But these were not the things that Harris proposed to test. Harris proposed to make statements about rent, land value, real wages, and so on based upon census data, and to use those statements to refute George's arguments. The problem, however, is that the data that Harris had at his disposal were so unreliable and Harris's handling of that data was so poor that all of his conclusions must be regarded as highly suspect. Moreover, there seems to be no way to treat the data so as to make them reliable.

It is not possible here to provide a detailed analysis of Harris's statistical techniques. The following should, however, indicate the basic nature of the problem. The fundamental problem is that the data that Harris needed did not exist in the form in which he needed them. Neither the United States nor the United Kingdom had accurate data on rent or land value—or if they did, Harris never cited them.

Harris proposed to use the 1880 national census as his basic source of data for the United States. And yet the census reported only the total value of all "property," including land, buildings, machinery, raw materials, manufactured goods, and money. The value of such "property" was, clearly, of no special interest in this context. To ascertain the magnitudes of the relevant variables, Harris undertook four steps. First, he noted that in Massachusetts, the only state that reported land value and building value separately, the ratio of the value of buildings to the value of land was 56 to 44. He assumed that the same ratio applied to all "Eastern states." And he assumed that an approximately inverse ratio, 40 to 60, applied in the "Southern section" and in all "Western States and Territories." He used those ratios to calculate the value of all of the land and buildings in the country.[14] Second, he used a statement by Henry Gannett, that while the ratio of assessed value to market value varied greatly among districts (from 40 to 100 percent), the average ratio was 65 percent.[15] That figure was used to estimate the market value of all of the land in the United States. Third, Harris argued that annual rent would be four percent of the value of the land. He concluded, "Counting rent at four per cent. on the actual valuation (which would be 6.1 per cent. on assessed value), we have the sum of $400,000,000 as the total rental of land in the United States. Four per cent. is probably a larger average rent than land brings in because land-owners raise prices on land when it produces more than three per cent. after paying taxes."[16] Fourth, he argued that since the population of the United States was about fifty million people, rent only amounted to about 2.2 cents per day per person and that such a sum was far too small to cure the problem of poverty even if "it were all distributed."[17]

Harris's procedures are open to at least some question at each step. The assignment of the ratios of building values to land values was, after all, quite arbitrary. All ratios were based upon a comparison or contrast with Massachusetts. Even if one were to grant that the Massachusetts estimates were accurate, it is very unsafe to apply that one estimate to the entire country. Further, the context does not make it clear that the estimate supplied by Gannett applied to "land" and not "real estate" in general. The several kinds of property are assessed differently and the distinctions must be *clearly* drawn. Further, the "average" is, technically, inaccurate unless it is a weighted average, since land value is not uniformly distributed across all districts. The statement that rent will tend to be four percent of land value is simply analytically invalid. When land is subject to an ad valorem tax, the kind that George proposed, its value is given by the equation

$$V = \frac{R}{i + t}$$

where V is post tax-market value, R is gross rent, i is the interest rate used for capitalization purposes, and t is the tax rate. It is clear that V rises *whenever* R rises (i and t held constant), no matter what percentage R is of V. Rent is simply not a fixed percentage of the capitalized value of land. The issue of the "distribution of rent" will be discussed below.

Apparently, Harris himself eventually realized that most of his original statements about the United Kingdom were severely flawed. Many of these statements were based upon the work of Michael Mulhall. From the beginning, Harris understood that Mulhall's use of the term *land* was very imprecise, meaning "agricultural capital in land" including farms, farm buildings, and fences, but excluding all urban land.[18] At other times, however, he seems to have forgotten that imprecision, for he made statements about "land" which, if true at all, were true only for rural land.[19] He also cited a Parliamentary study as giving the total rent of land in the United Kingdom after *explicitly* noting that the study ignored all land holdings of less than one acre and that the study ignored the entire city of London.[20] In his final article on this topic, Harris expressed realization of the fact that Mulhall's use of the term *houses* was as vague as his use of the term *land*. In his earlier articles, Harris followed Mulhall and kept "houses" separate from "land." He later realized, however, that Mulhall's "houses" included "city houses and the lots on which they stand. . ."[21] The new finding did not cause him to revise his conclusions in any important way, although it should have. He also made calculations that indicated that rent in the United Kingdom was between one-twenty-fifth and one-eighteenth of the gross national product and that it amounted to only 2.5 cents per person per day. It seems clear that since Harris's data for "land" includes rural buildings and since his data for "houses" includes urban sites, and since he never adjusted the data to account for that, his findings cannot be accepted as accurate.

There does not seem to be any way, even in principle, to put order into the data. The categories under which the data were gathered preclude that. The point is important to an analysis of the structure of Harris's argument. Harris claimed that an examination of census data would lead a reasonable person to reject George's ideas. In fact, however, Harris had no reliable data; he had only several overly aggregated and/or ambiguously classified observations and a lengthy sequence of dubious assumptions as to how to process the data. One can only conclude that neither George nor Harris was at all convincing on this point. Neither writer produced any acceptable work on the issue and it must be said that the issue was unresolved after each side had stated its case.

For present purposes, it is important to note that even if Harris's data were accurate—or even if they could be made accurate—they would not have been relevant to his argument. Harris appeared to have felt that his strongest argument against George's proposal was that over time the rental share of annual income had declined so much that it represented between one-twenty-fifth and one-eighteenth of that income or about 2.2 cents per person per day in the United States and 2.5 cents per person per day in the United Kingdom.[22] He argued that even if all of the rent were taxed away and divided equally among the population, the amount that each person would receive would be too small to eliminate poverty.[23] It was this objection that Harris considered to have been unrefuted.[24]

While Harris may have believed that this objection escaped refutation, there were actually several important refutations produced in his lifetime. Within weeks of the publication of Harris's first article, Mary E. Beedy, in an otherwise laudatory review of Harris's career, noted: "It is quite possible that Dr. Harris may not fully have comprehended Mr. George's views, or that his statistics may be in some degree faulty; but this we must all feel: that the question is now ably opened on both sides, and Mr. George will be compelled to meet Dr. Harris with the weapons of facts and figures."[25] Later, in 1892, E. Benjamin Andrews, President of Brown University and a moderately sympathetic critic of George's, commented that many of the "flaws" that Harris felt he had uncovered were "in a way recommendations instead."[26] Beedy and Andrews apparently realized, as Harris never did, that George never proposed to cure poverty through an equal division of rent among all of the citizens of the country. Instead, he envisioned his tax as the vehicle for the removal of obstacles to production and employment. He saw the results of these incentive effects, not cash disbursements from the government, as the cure to the problem of poverty. One might conclude, along with Andrews, that George's proposal, if implemented, would not accomplish two-thirds, or even one half, of the things promised. One might even conclude that George had greatly exaggerated the impact that private ownership of land has upon the production process. Yet one might still favor the imposition of heavy taxes on goods available in perfectly (or almost perfectly) inelastic supply, and one might favor the removal, or reduction of taxes on goods available in more elastic supply.[27] And, perhaps more to the point of this discussion, one must analyze and accept or reject George's proposal as George wrote it and intended it. An effective critique cannot be based upon a misunderstanding as thorough as Harris's.[28]

After Harris had delivered what he felt to be his irrefutable objections to George's proposal, he moved on to discuss "The Cause of Mr. George's Error."[29] The error was said to stem from George's alleged failure to distinguish between the several kinds of land. Harris argued, "Land for building purposes is prevented from demanding high prices by competition with suburban agricultural land. The rapid transit of the railroad produces this competition, offering to the laborer in the city a cheap building lot carved out of a country farm, in a healthful locality. On the other hand, capital in the form of cheap transportation keeps down the price of farming land on the Atlantic coast by bringing into competition with it the border lands of the west."[30] That point is true, if ever, only under certain circumstances. Even if the marginal land was to be had rent free, or at zero price, as even Carey supposed, the very process discussed by Carey and Harris would raise the rent on all hitherto marginal and intramarginal plots. Harris appears not to have considered that point, and that oversight is the potentially fatal flaw in the argument. For Harris's purposes it was not sufficient to look just at the reduced rate of increase in rent on urban land and Atlantic-coast farm land. He should have considered the *total* rent paid throughout society. If the rents on hitherto marginal and intramarginal plots rose enough, the total effect might be quite different from the effect on any isolated plot or group of plots.

Harris next attempted to demonstrate that the problem of poverty was becoming less and less serious over time because real wages were rising continuously.[31] While that claim may well be true, Harris's method of demonstrating it is flawed. He began by citing some income and wage data for the United States and the United Kingdom. He then proposed to show that since consumer prices had risen less than money wages, real wages had risen. Following Mulhall, Harris claimed that he planned to reject all of the consumer price index numbers calculated by economists in favor of "the volume of trade method."[32] Although Mulhall is not precise in his description of his method, it appears that he wished to calculate the ratio of current output to past output, assuming that base-period prices prevailed.[33] It is worth noting that neither Mulhall nor Harris realized that, contrary to their plans, the "volume of trade method" yields a Laspeyres quantity index. The important issue, however, is that such an index introduces an important bias into the argument. As Franklin Fisher and Karl Shell have shown, over time periods in which tastes and production-possibility maps change, the consumer price index should be calculated using a Paasche index for the Laspeyres quantity index understates the correct value.[34] Thus, if Harris's chosen index understated the price-level increase, it would overstate the real-wage increase because the price index appears in the denominator of the fraction that indicates the real wage. While real wages had surely increased, arguments such as Harris's will overstate the amount of the increase.

Harris next discussed his own theory of "progress and poverty." The great increase in production was said to be due to the utilization of enormous amounts of "labor-saving machinery," which increased the productivity of the employed labor. But, he added, the problems of poverty and unemployment were related to the same tendency. The fact that technological advance was continuous implied that new machines would be developed to do more and more jobs. This would, inevitably, tend to replace human laborers. Those who were reemployed would gain, for there would be more goods and services for them to consume, but those who could not readjust their skills would become unemployed. And those who could be replaced by machinery would have to accept very low wages in order to make themselves more attractive than machinery. The cure to the problem, said Harris, was to develop a system in which people would become flexible enough to readjust their careers as required.[35]

Harris next turned his attention to "the function of property" and argued that the institution of private property was of paramount importance. With it, the rights of all individuals were well-defined and accepted by all. Social conflicts were held to the minimum levels as each individual accepted the rights of others to treat their property as they saw fit. Without it, there would inevitably be conflicts over the use of any existing objects. But, said Harris, the scope of individual liberty would be drastically limited unless private ownership extended to land. He asserted, without elaboration, that unless private property extended to land, "there must be one absolute will which limits all others, and deprives them of perfect freedom to that extent."[36] There is no explanation as to the identity of the "absolute will" and no discussion of the way in which it inhibits personal freedom. A paradoxical feature of this criticism is that it was made of a Jeffersonian individualist by a Hegelian who had, on another occasion, enthusiastically anticipated the emergence of a national consciousness in which "each individual recognizes his substantial side to be the State as such."[37]

In expatiating upon the supposed loss of individuality that would accompany the abolition of "free" (fee simple) ownership of land, Harris raised aesthetic considerations with an argument that we have not encountered elsewhere in relation to the thought of George: "The owner of a leasehold is careful if he builds, to study how to build so that in case the land passes away from his possession he may get the most for his building. Hence, he adopts a conventional style, and there is no self-revelation in his work and no culture that comes from it."[38]

This is an interesting observation, but it ceases to hold good in proportion to the greater length of the lease. The Chrysler and Empire State buildings and Rockefeller Center are but three familiar examples of innovative construction on leased land; others, of more recent vintage, would be many of our most distinctive shopping malls and plazas. Since what George proposed was tantamount to a *perpetual* lease at a variable figure reflecting income potential, the observation obviously has no bearing on it.

Harris next argued that it would literally be "killing the goose that laid the golden egg" for society to tax the "unearned increment." It seems, however, that he misunderstood the meaning of the term. He repeatedly noted that individuals incurred risks and invented new goods and new production techniques because of the prospective gains associated with success. To tax the rewards of such success would be to create a disincentive effect that would lead to little or no innovation.[39] One need only note that Harris's conclusions are quite true but that they have nothing whatever to do with the "unearned increment." George, like all other economists, used the term *unearned increment* to apply to increases in value that occurred *separately* from the things discussed by Harris.[40]

Finally, Harris turned his attention to the impact of George's tax. Again Harris appears to have misinterpreted George's proposal, for he repeatedly refers to it as a "land tax."[41] Of course, George proposed a land-value tax, not a land tax. The distinction is important because in both the Georgian and the Carey-Harris framework there was a no-rent margin. Thus, in both frameworks, there was land that had no value. Then Harris claimed, without proof, that the tax would be shifted and that it would be shifted in an undesirable way. He asserted that the tax would soon be shifted to the occupants of the houses on the land. And, without explaining why it would be so, he claimed that the shift would lower the rent of the houses lived in by the rich and raise the rent of the houses of the poor. Thus, said Harris, the proposal would actually hurt those whom it was intended to help.[42] It only needs to be said that there is nothing in economic theory which insures that those conclusions are necessarily true. Indeed, the lack of any theory in support of his views may explain why Harris was content to merely assert his conclusions.

It must be said that Harris did begin with an excellent idea. It is necessary to examine the empirical findings related to this issue. And it would be necessary to reject or revise George's ideas if the empirical findings dictated that. The problem with the specific case of Harris, however, is that the data that he had available were not those he needed. Further, it is clear that Harris never understood George's proposal and hence he never really tested it; instead he tested only his misstatement of the proposal. It is also clear that Harris's proposed alternative system, based on the work of Henry C. Carey, was obsolete at the time that Harris wrote. One can conclude only that while Harris may well have been a competent and innovative educator, and an able (if not especially original) philosopher, he was not at all adequate as an economist and he was not equipped to handle the task he set for himself. For these reasons the specific critique he offered must be judged quite ineffective.

Notes

1. Kurt F. Leidecker, *Yankee Teacher: The Life of William Torrey Harris* (New York: Philosophical Library, 1946), pp. 540-41.
2. Ibid., p. 540.
3. Henry C. Carey, *Principles of Social Science* (Philadelphia: Lippincott, 1858), 1:104-46 and 3:109-70.
4. William T. Harris, "The Right of Property and the Ownership of Land," *Journal of Social Science* 22 (June 1887):116-55.
5. Charles Albro Barker, *Henry George* (New York: Oxford, 1955), p. 556.
6. Carey, *Principles*, 1:28-32.
7. Harris, "Right," p. 119.
8. Carey, *Principles*, 1:170.
9. Harris, "Right," p. 119 and Carey, *Principles*, 1:28-35 and 104-46.
10. John Stuart Mill, *Principles of Political Economy: With Some Applications to Social Philosophy*, ed. W. J. Ashley, 9th ed. (1885; reprint ed. New York: Kelley, 1965), pp. 181-83 and 430-33. Ashley assures us that all cited arguments appeared in all editions since the edition of 1865 (the sixth edition). They were therefore available to Harris, who wrote and spoke on the topic from 1886 to 1897.
11. Francis A. Walker, *Land and Its Rent* (Boston: Little, Brown, 1883), pp. 75-108.
12. Alfred Marshall, *Principles of Economics*, 4th ed. (London: Macmillan, 1898), 1:240-44.
13. Harris, "Right," pp. 120-22 and his "Henry George's Mistake about Land," *The Forum* 3 (July 1887):433-42.
14. Harris, "Right," pp. 122-24.
15. Ibid., p. 123.
16. Ibid., p. 125.
17. Ibid., pp. 122 and 125.
18. Ibid., p. 128, n. 1.

19. In "Mistake," p. 439, he reported the value of land in the United Kingdom as 1,737,000,000 pounds sterling. Yet, in "Right," p. 128, n. 2, that figure is given as the value of agricultural capital in land.

20. Harris, "Right," p. 129. n. One of the first people to have noticed that this problem existed was Thomas G. Shearman. See his *Natural Taxation* (New York: Doubleday, Page, 1916), p. 137.

21. W. T. Harris, "Statistics versus Socialism," *The Forum* 24 (October 1897):190.

22. Harris, "Right," pp. 125-28; "Mistake," pp. 437-38; and "Statistics," p. 196.

23. Harris, "Right," p. 122.

24. Leidecker, *Yankee Teacher*, pp. 540-41.

25. Mary E. Beedy, "Dr. William T. Harris and His Reply to Henry George," *Education* 8 (October 1887):111-12. The article first appeared in *The Chicago Tribune* of 10 July 1887.

26. E. Benjamin Andrews, "Economic Reforms Short of Socialism," *International Journal of Ethics* 2 (April 1892):281-83.

27. Ibid., p. 281. For a statement that a tax on the "unearned increment" will not distort production incentives or efficiency, see Paul A. Samuelson, *Economics*, 10th ed. (New York: McGraw-Hill, 1976), p. 564.

28. It may be worth noting that Harris repeatedly made this kind of error. In "Statistics" he wrote, "I consider the most important item of economic statistics to be that which shows the total product of the State or nation in the form of the average per day for each inhabitant. This item helps the individual citizen to compare his daily wages or his annual income with the quota which he would receive in case the total product of his State or nation were distributed to each inhabitant without any deductions for capital, for land, or for supervision" (pp. 192-93). Earlier he had spoken of an equal division of rent, so he tended to report all of his data in those terms. While per capita or per day data may be useful for some purposes they are not especially useful for others. Specifically, neither of the major groups criticized by Harris—the single taxers and the Marxist socialists—proposed an equal division of rent or total product. Thus Harris's critique of both groups was badly misdirected.

29. The phrase is the title of a section of "Right." See pp. 129-30.

30. Harris, "Right," p. 129. See "Mistake," pp. 439-40 for a similar statement. This point, like so many of Harris's points, appears to have been derived from the work of Carey. See Carey's *Principles*, 1:168-69. And, as was often the case, John Stuart Mill had alrady furnished a demonstration that Carey's point was theoretically unsound. See Mill, *Principles of Political Economy*, p. 432.

31. Harris, "Right," pp. 130-35.

32. Ibid., p. 132 and the sources cited there.

33. Michael G. Mulhall, *History of Prices Since the Year 1850* (London: Longmans, Green, 1885), p. 122.

34. Franklin Fisher and Karl Shell, *The Economic Theory of Price Indices: Two Essays on the Effects of Taste, Quality and Technological Change* (New York: Academic, 1972), pp. 58-59.

35. Harris, "Right," pp. 134-46.

36. Ibid., pp. 146-47. The quoted passage is from p. 147.

37. William Torrey Harris, "To the Reader," *Journal of Speculative Philosophy*, (January 1867).

38. Harris, "Right," p. 148.

39. Ibid., pp. 148-51.

40. It should be noted that the passage seems to be aimed at Marx more than at George. It must be said, in fairness to Marx, that Harris appears to have misunderstood Marx's economics and that his objection to it is irrelevant.

41. Harris, "Right," p. 152.

42. Ibid., pp. 152-55.

14

Gronlund and Other Marxists

BY FRED HARRISON

The paradoxical relationship of the Jeffersonian individualist, Henry George, to the history of general socialism is a familiar story, well summarized by the following oft-quoted statements by Sidney Webb and George Bernard Shaw, respectively: "Little as Henry George intended it, there can be no doubt that it was the enormous circulation of his *Progress and Poverty* which gave the touch that caused all the seething influences to crystallize into a popular Socialist movement."[1] "When I was thus swept into the great Socialist revival of 1883, I found that five-sixths of those who were swept in with me had been converted by Henry George."[2]

But when we examine the convoluted tale of George's relationship to Marxism as distinguished from socialism in the broader sense, we find ourselves on less familiar yet even more paradoxical ground.

Marx and George never met. Upon receiving three copies of *Progress and Poverty* from various friends, Marx "looked it through" and dismissed it contemptuously as "the capitalist's last ditch,"[3] characterizing George in a letter to F. A. Sorge as "behind the times" theoretically, and marked by the "repulsive presumption and arrogance that invariably distinguish all such panacea-mongers."[4] George's estimate of Marx was equally uncomplimentary; he regarded him as "a most superficial thinker, entangled in an inexact and vicious terminology,"[5] and as "the prince of muddleheads."[6] Despite Marx's low opinion of it, H. Hessel Tiltman observes that George's book "achieved the undoubted feat of making Karl Marx into a popular author, for chapters of *Das Kapital* were published and read as sequels of *Progress and Poverty*."[7]

During George's lifetime his views were publicly attacked in Marxist circles, not, ironically, by Marx himself, who, as we have seen, considered him "repulsive," but mainly by two men with whom he had maintained friendly connexions, Henry Mayers Hyndman and Laurence Gronlund. Hyndman, a founder of the British Social Democratic Federation and the first British popularizer of Marx's thought, was introduced to George in 1882 by John Stuart Mill's step-daughter, Helen Taylor. Shortly thereafter, George and his wife accepted Hyndman's invitation to be houseguests at his elegant London home. Although the invitation was extended, according to the host's own account, "because I hoped, quite mistakenly as it afterwards appeared, to convert him to the truth as it is in Socialist economics,"[8] Hyndman entertained a genuine, if rather condescending, feeling of affection toward George long after it had become clear that their theoretical differences could not be reconciled.[9] These differences emerged with increasing sharpness in two published exchanges between them: the first, a dialogue, in 1885; the second, a full-scale debate, in 1887.

George first heard of Gronlund in 1883, when the latter was earning ten dollars a week and saving three of them to defray the cost of publication of his *Cooperative Commonwealth*, which came out the following year. According to Barker, George "admired and encouraged" the impecunious Danish immigrant,[10] and Gronlund reciprocated with generous references in his book to George, which were, however, interspersed with others that announced the principal points of disagreement which he was later to elaborate.

Educated as a lawyer in both Copenhagen and Milwaukee, Gronlund left that profession as his socialist convictions ripened, in favor of an economically precarious career as a journalist and political lecturer. Eugene V. Debs, the labour leader and perennial Socialist Party candidate for president, acknowledged him as his ideological mentor.[11] During the period which concerns us Gronlund was a thorough Marxist, although he sought to play down the more incendiary aspects of the doctrine in order to make it less distasteful to the average American. In time he was to renounce the class struggle, and to move in the direction of Christian socialism.

Gronlund's two tracts against Henry George were issued during the struggle between George and the socialists for control of the United Labor Party in 1887—a struggle which culminated in the expulsion of the socialists. These tracts, *Insufficiency of Henry George's Theory* and *Socialism vs. Tax Reform: An Answer to Henry George*, slight though they be, represent the most considerable effort ever made, so far as I have been able to discover,* to refute George on Marxist grounds. For this reason they will, in some measure, constitute the focus of this chapter.

Yet, curiously, Marx's own posthumous writings indicate that before his death he had arrived at analyses in many respects similar to those of George—analyses which, although he of course never repudiated it, run counter to what is generally understood as "Marxism." Hence I shall have occasion to cite passages from Marx in opposition to the principal Marxist critique of George. As we examine these passages, I shall also explore the question of why, in the light of them, Marx did not abandon his earlier conclusions, and shall venture an evaluation, based on evidence which Marx himself laboriously compiled, of the status of socioeconomic systems built on Marxist tenets as the only and historically inevitable alternative to monopoly capitalism.

*George R. Geiger (*The Philosophy of Henry George* [New York: Macmillan, 1933], p. 238n.) maintains that the socialist position against George is most effectively presented not only in Gronlund's two pamphlets but also in Algie M. Simons's twenty-nine-page attack, *Single Tax Versus Socialism* (Chicago: Charles H. Kerr & Co., 1899). This work, unfortunately, has become so scarce that it is not to be found even in the British Museum or the Library of Congress. Copies do exist in the Henry George Collection of the New York Public Library and in the Harvard University Library, but they are too fragile to permit loan or duplication. The present writer is unwilling to evaluate Simons's work on the basis of someone else's summary, and cannot now make a transatlantic journey to examine it in person.

I

In arguing for the transformation of rights to capital as well as to land, Gronlund had to claim that George's analysis of the effects of monopoly ownership of land was inadequate: that it could neither wholly explain the existence of, nor finally abolish, poverty. Gronlund informed George: ". . .your teachings that private property in land is *the* cause of our social evils and that abolition of land ownership would remedy them are false."[12]

George's central problem, the coexistence of economic progress with poverty, can be broken into two parts. The first embraces those issues which deal with income distribution. The second concerns the dynamics of the mode of production itself, the facility with which each factor helps or hinders the growth of wealth, and the cyclical crises which Marxists regard as the inevitable result of the alleged internal contradictions of capitalism.

Gronlund attacked George for suggesting that the landowner was the main beneficiary of the growth of the economy. Preposterous, he declared. ". . .George comes to the conclusion, affirms and reaffirms, that only landholders grow richer and richer by our material progress, while capitalists do not get their proper share and are, in fact, in the same boat as the wage workers. But how, may be asked, can he come to such a preposterous conclusion, since if he but glances at the other side, he will see that landholders constitute but a small portion of our monied class, and by no means the richest portion."[13]

George does not come to this conclusion at all. He explicitly stated: "When I say that wages fall as rent rises, I do not mean that the quantity of wealth obtained by laborers as wages is necessarily less, but that the proportion which it bears to the whole produce is necessarily less. The proportion may diminish while the quantity remains the same *or even increases.*"[14] The same applied to interest. George is thus not guilty of the "self-deception" with which he is charged by Gronlund, that "only landholders benefit from our material progress."[15]

As if anticipating this rebuttal, Gronlund switched to a discussion of the declining rate of interest; still, however, he remained on the offensive. "Well, that the rate of interest constantly diminishes, is, of course, a fact: but what of that? This does not at all , as every schoolboy knows, prevent the income of the capitalist from constantly growing, from growing at a tremendous rate, from *growing much faster than the income of the landlord* from increasing rent."[16]

Marx would have sided with Henry George on this issue: ". . .in the same proportion as [surplus product] develops, landed property acquires the capacity to capture an *ever-increasing portion* of this surplus value by means of its landed monopoly and thereby, of raising the value of its rent and the price of the land itself. The capitalist still performs an active function in the development of this surplus value and surplus product. But the landowner need only appropriate the growing share in the surplus product and the surplus value, without having contributed anything to this growth."[17]

Nor did Marx share Gronlund's dismissive approach to the problem of the rate of interest. The ordinary interest rate directly affects the buying price of land. If it fell from five percent to four percent, then an annual ground-rent of £200 would represent the annual realization from a capital of £5,000 instead of £4,000. Thus the price of the same piece of land would have risen by £1,000, or from twenty years' to twenty-five years' purchase. Therefore, given that the growth of loanable capital had the long-term effect of reducing the interest rate, "it follows that the price of land has a tendency to rise, even independently of the movement of ground-rent and the prices of the products of the land, of which rent constitutes a part."[18] The consequences for people wanting to start new job-creating businesses, or build homes for themselves, are evident.

Marx was also willing to concede the possibility that rent in its aggregate may increase proportionately more than industrial profit, by which he meant the "profits of enterprise," that is, after the interest on capital had been deducted from gross profits.[19] If correct, this would have important effects on investment decision-making. It would help to explain the speculative buying of land, which is often kept unproductive until the owners consider the time ripe to "make a killing" by selling out. This behaviour, held George, was a fundamental reason for the periodic crises in an industrial economy. Gronlund rejected the claim, and placed the blame on capitalist plutocrats. "It is to the rule of these selfish plutocrats, and to their wage-system, competition and 'private enterprise' that the so-called 'over-production' and our crises are due, and *not at all* to the speculative rise in the value of land, as George declares."[20] To judge by the vacillations of politicians today in industrial societies, the causes of economic depression are still not determined; this disagreement is reflected in ambivalent policy formation. It would therefore be useful to accord the problem an extended treatment, in the hope of clarifying live problems.

George did not advance a monocausal explanation for cyclical crises. He cited the complex interdependence of the interlocking parts of industrial economies, such as monetary policies and restrictive trade practises. But the speculative advance of land values was "the great initiatory cause."[21] Before we evaluate this key proposition, we must briefly consider the competing Marxist explanation that crises were caused by the "overproduction" caused by the unplanned output by individual manufacturers all working to advance their private interests and oblivious of social needs, and the converse phenomenon of "underconsumption" arising from the maldistribution of income.

Associated with the early stages of the slow-down of an industrial economy there is a rise in the pile of goods held in manufacturers' warehouses. But far from causing the crisis, this is a response to it. Manufacturers hope that by building up their stocks they will be able to continue their operations and be well placed to meet the demand in the upswing of the cycle. When, however, the depression continues, there comes a point where they have to either contract their scale of operations (causing unemployment of labour and capital) or cut their prices (reducing profits), or both. When the market is swamped with "surplus" goods, this is interpreted as overproduction based on the miscalculation of effective demand by individual entrepreneurs. This "flooding" of the market, linked with a cutback in output, is then held to be the cause of the crisis; ergo, the need for socialism, to inject rational planning into the system. But the socialist interpretation fails to explain why individual entrepreneurs continually act against their private interests by overproducing in cyclical—and predictable—fashion.

There is an element of truth in the Marxist argument that the division of income causes underconsumption. Some people receive incomes which they do not earn by a simultaneous creation of wealth. Their incomes tend to be high, and their propensity to spend on staple consumer products—those produced by the majority of people—tends to be proportionately low. On the other hand, the mass of people who work for a living, as a direct result of having to hand over part of their wealth to nonproducers (and another slice in taxation to public authorities who do not always spend their revenue productively), consume less of the goods they produce than would otherwise be the case.

This bifurcation in the pattern of consumption, production, and income distribution has a distorting effect on the productive processes. It is seen in its most unambiguouis form in Third World countries which are struggling to industrialize, where "conspicuous consumption" of imported luxury goods is at its most deleterious extreme. A major problem experienced by these countries is the shortfall in the size of the domestic market, allied with unfavourable trade balances and foreign exchange difficulties which arise to an important degree from the import of luxury foreign goods.

Who are the idle income receivers? Henry George said they were the landlords; Gronlund and Marx agreed, but wanted to add the capitalists. The latter, they said, also creamed off part of "surplus value," and so created the conditions for underconsumption. Yet, despite Marx's propaganda, he was willing to concede that capitalists played an active role in the production process—a role for which, according to George, they were entitled to receive their income (which they were normally disposed to reinvest in a productive form). This isolates the landlord class, the rent-appropriators who contribute nothing to the process of wealth-creation beyond granting, for a fee, permission to others to use natural resources which they, the landlords, did not produce.

But this is only part of the problem. What about the involuntary nature of most unemployment? Why, asked George, did men and machines stand idle when both could be working for the mutual benefit of all? His answer—speculation in land. This, he found, resulted from the expectation of profit from population expansion (which increased demand for land) and *future* economic growth as a result of technical innovations and capital accumulation. Once people observed a rise in land values, they too wanted to get in on the act; this had the cumulative effect of pushing up buying prices even further.

How does this cause unemployment and human misery? At a certain point in the land boom, buyers realise that the yields on their investments are not keeping pace with the rise in the graph of land values. In other words, current income—the rent paid out of current production—cannot rise as fast as the expectations of the speculators, no matter how hard the land users are squeezed. There follows a levelling off of prices, and panic selling as the speculators appreciate that their investments could earn more elsewhere, find difficulty in financing loans which they took out to make the speculative purchases, and realise that their property is grossly overvalued. The only way out for them is to sell quickly before prospective buyers realise that the bottom has dropped out of the market.

From this we can see how money is sterilized (buying land does not create machines or jobs), land is kept idle while there is a demand for it, and the less efficient (or least protected) firms and individuals are put out of business. Henry George saw that this situation could not be sustained indefinitely. Eventually, speculative rents had to come into line with "normal" rent as a result of one or a combination of three reactions: (1) a fall in speculative land values, evident in the reduction of rents; (2) the increased efficiency of labour arising from, for example, a change in what Marx called the organic composition of capital—a shift from labour to machine—thereby increasing productivity; and (3) reduced income to labour and capital.[22]

How does this theory stand up to empirical testing? Two French authors, Flamant and Singer-Kérel, have summarized the major economic recessions.[23] Throughout the nineteenth century, speculation in land, or in the shares of companies owning natural resources, is isolated as being directly responsible for the periodical panics which caused economic crises. This was so in 1816: speculation in British land; 1825: speculation in South American natural resources; 1836-39: speculation in land in the Middle West of the United States; 1847: speculation in the French metallurgical industry; 1853-57: speculation in U.S. government land and railway shares; 1866: speculation in German railway shares, land and building developments; and so on.*

To break the monotony of this list, Flamant and Singer-Kérel note that France escaped an economic depression in the 1870s because war reparations to Germany "had absorbed capital resources that might have been devoted to speculation."[24]

Linked with each or most of these crises were phenomena which make up a consistent pattern: governments using the printing presses to increase the money supply, in desperate attempts to stave off the seemingly inevitable crises (and in doing so, causing inflation); the exploitation of monopoly power to artificially boost profits when these were sagging (the United Kingdom Corn Laws after 1816, the U.S. tariffs in 1825); and the shock waves feeding into the manufacturing sectors, causing unemployment.

Economists believe that the origins of twentieth-century economic crises have become more complex. If true, this would diminish the contemporary relevance of much of Henry George's work. But the causal effect of land speculation is still transparently clear. The events which culminated in the Wall Street slump in 1929 were triggered by the great Florida real estate speculation in the mid-twenties.[25] What of the economic collapse of the Weimar Republic, which led to Hitler's electoral elevation to the chancellorship? This has often been ascribed to various obscure psychosocial causes.[26] But the role of land speculation, which weakened industry and led to distortions in the economy—which were then exploited by the Nazis—has been carefully preserved for us by Bruno Heilig, an Austrian journalist. Heilig saw the

---

*Speculation in the shares of the most important leading sector of the early industrial age—the railway companies, especially in the United States—was only superficially associated with the regards of real capital accumulation. The speculators expected to make their biggest and quickest gains from capitalisation of the land acquired by these companies. In the United States, the railway companies received federal and state grants totalling about 380 million acres, nearly twenty percent of the whole country!

workings of the dark side of the German economy as well as (for thirteen months) the inside of Buchenwald and Dachau concentration camps.[27]

The two foregoing cases were individually the most fatal for this century. I cannot review all the others, but it would be instructive to digress just a little further and introduce a contemporary example.

The most depressed economy in Western Europe in the mid-seventies was Britain's. The case is worth studying. After a cautious start, the Conservative government which came into power in 1970 decided on a "boom or bust" strategy. Under Chancellor Anthony Barber the money supply was allowed to forge ahead of the economy's full employment potential. There was a new surge in speculation, and land values boomed. Stuart Holland, a leading British socialist economist, noted the impact of property speculation. "The City of London has been more concerned to invest in office blocks than in manufacturing companies—for the small firms in the microeconomic sector, such disproportionate investment outside manufacturing means the difference between expansion and relative or absolute decline."[28]

The way land speculation hit the private housing market gives us a broad hint of how personal spending power was reduced. Families taking out new mortgages during the boom had less to spend on consumption.

GROSS REPAYMENT FIGURES OF NEW MORTGAGES
AS PERCENTAGE OF HOUSEHOLD INCOME

1969 . . . 17.9	1973 . . . 24.3
1970 . . . 18.1	1974 . . . 22.5
1971 . . . 18.0	1975 . . . 21.1
1972 . . . 21.1	

SOURCE: United Kingdom Dept. of Environment

Added to the domestic trends was the fourfold increase in the price of oil which resulted from the exercise of oligopolistic power by the Organisation of Petroleum Exporting Countries. This had a thoroughly depressing impact on the world economy. The exercise of power over a scarce natural resource is as clear an example of "initiatory" influence of such power as one could wish to find. The huge oil price increases triggered an immediate redirection of income, and so altered the pattern of domestic consumption in the U.K. The oil-rich countries lengthened the order books for Rolls Royce and five-star hotels in London's West End; but the effect on the factories of Bolton and Barnsley was depressing.

By the mid-seventies the British economy was experiencing precisely those adjustments which Henry George predicted as necessary preconditions for a revival of trade. There was a drop in land values, with owners experiencing difficulty in selling their plots. The owners of buildings had to drop their rents to attract new tenants, especially in London, and the construction industry cut back severely on the purchase of new land for their "land banks."[29] Private sector house prices declined sufficiently to take a smaller proportion of personal incomes by 1975.

As for those measures implied in the need to increase the efficiency of labour, Socialist Premier James Callaghan made it clear that his government would sacrifice its social objectives to give priority to the needs of industry.[30] On George's third point—the lowering of living standards—this was accomplished as a deliberate aim of the U.K.'s economic strategy; it is one of the greatest ironies that the central element in that strategy—the restrictive incomes policy which went by the name of the Social Contract—was proposed by a Socialist government and policed by the Trades Union Congress.

Thus we can see that the impact of speculation in land does have a crucially destabilising impact on an industrial economy, an impact which is grievously neglected by the economic analysts who advise governments. George's analysis, far from being "far-fetched," as Gronlund put it,[31] is crucially relevant. With the decline in the popularity of Keynesianism, which amounts to dissatisfaction with the mixed-economy approach, an alternative model for action is required. This would have to be either a free market system shorn of the impediments of private monopoly of ground rent, or a state socialist economy which would meet with Marx's approval.*

II

Gronlund levelled one of the stock charges at George: a land tax would not cover all governmental spending. He calculated that in 1880 gross rental income would have been $1,100 million, with federal and state revenue at $610 million. From the first figure, said Gronlund, three deductions would have to be made to conform to George's proposals:

(1) To allow for the element of improved value.

Gronlund does not say how much he would allow for improvements. One-fifth would be a roughly fair proportion for his day; a deduction of two-fifths would have left $660 million, which would have been more than sufficient to meet public spending. But for purposes of argument, let us err in Gronlund's favour and deduct half of the value, to leave us with an economic rent—what Marx called ground-rent—of $550 million, a deficit of $60 million.

(2) To allow for the speculative component in the price of much land, which would disappear with the introduction of a land tax.

This was necessary, thought Gronlund, because he based his figure of $1,100 million annual rental income on the capital value of real estate in the U.S. ($23,000 million). The latter sum, he judged, included an element of speculative value which would be destroyed by a one-hundred percent tax on land values, and which therefore would have to be allowed for when calculating rental income. In fact we need not make any allowance here. Certainly there was an element of speculative value incorporated in the total value of real estate. This, however, would have been offset in part by the undervaluation of

---

* Henry George would have forecasted that the Keynesian model, which seeks to offset underconsumption in the private sector by increased public sector spending, was destined to failure precisely because it ignored land speculation. Keynes did not take this factor into account because he explicitly saw no problems. He relegated the deleterious impact of land speculation on economic growth to earlier, agricultural-based social organisations (J. M. Keynes, *The General Theory of Employment Interest and Money* [London: Macmillan, 1967], p. 241). The land question, he told the Liberal Summer School at Cambridge in 1925, was no longer a problem thanks to "a silent change in the facts."

land arising from individual errors of judgement, and zoning laws which comprised restrictions on land use and so reduced the market value of affected sites. Of greater significance, however, under the regime which George prescribed, the level of economic activity would have been very much higher. Aggregate land values, therefore, would have risen in line with the higher level of demand for land, and this would have compensated for the removal of speculative values. Thus for present purposes, total land values (and therefore the rental income which Gronlund calculated at at five percent per annum) need not be reduced.

(3) To allow for the loss of revenue from agricultural rents which, Gronlund claimed, George said would not be levied.

George did not exempt agricultural land. Where, as Gronlund notes, George said the tax burden on farmers would be reduced, he was referring to taxes which were a burden on capital and labour. But in one of his *Standard* articles, which Gronlund quotes, George stated explicitly that agricultural land would be "subjected to the same just system."[32] So there would be no deduction from total revenue to the advantage of agricultural landowners.*

Our generosity, however, has encumbered the single tax with a deficit of $60 million. This could have been made up out of new increments in land values following the introduction of land-value taxation. For workers would have been left with their full wages, thereby increasing both consumption and savings. Untaxed profits would have left entrepreneurs with resources to be formed into new capital, thereby increasing productivity and employment. The net effect would have been an economy operating at a higher level of activity, thereby pushing up land values, and so land taxes. From this one would expect that the relatively small sum of $60 million could have been easily raised, and more besides. In any event, higher disposable incomes would have permitted lower federal and state expenditure, since many supportive governmental measures could have been met by citizens out of their own pockets, exercising their free choice.[33]

Gronlund further argued that labour would still be at the mercy of privately owned capital, and therefore still vulnerable, even if we had land-value taxation. Henry George held that land was the primary instrument of production, and that people would prosper if they enjoyed the kind of access to it which was so difficult under conditions of monopoly control. Gronlund replied by claiming that there was no difference between land and capital, which were twin sisters.[34] He was obliged to take this stand in order to sidestep the demand for differential treatment for these two factors, whether in fiscal policy or physical appropriation.

Precisely because both land and capital were undifferentiated in being means of production, said Gronlund, "that is the reason why progress demands that both land and capital be placed under collective control."[35] Land may be prior in time (it being there before man and the capital created by

---

*Gronlund, in fact, was an opportunist. His socialist programme it seems, was not so bold as to upset American farmers. "True, land should be nationalized; as part of a comprehensive programme such nationalization is the right thing, but to commence the programme with such demand is, in the United States, *commencing from the wrong end*; it is antagonizing the very class, the farmers, whom we want to benefit, for they, in the first place, will lose the grip on their farms. Why, the nationalization of agricultural land is here the very last thing to be thought of" (*Insufficiency of Henry George's Theory* [New York: New York Labor News Co., 1887], p. 12). Original emphasis.

man), but "suppose a normal man had land to stand in and absolutely *nothing else*? He, undoubtedly, would be just as sure of dying by starvation, as if he was suspended in mid-air. If land therefore is said to be primary in *importance*, we deny it."[36] In what can only be seen as an attempt at intimidating George in future debates, Gronlund proceeded to caution him that "you may put it down as an axiom to bear in mind in all your further encounters with Socialists, that no class in the community are so logical as Socialists. Logic is their forte."[37]

Marx would not have been impressed by this particular demonstration of socialist logic. In his *Critique of the Gotha Programme*, Marx states that nature *was* "the primary source of all instruments and subjects of labour."[38] In the end even Gronlund had to contradict himself by accepting that people were not so helpless as he would have us believe. He declared that "even half-savages learn sometime or other to manufacture for themselves."[39] Then imagine what "civilized" men could do, given access to natural resources!

Gronlund used distortion in his attempts to thwart the single-tax campaign at one of its critical historical points. We see this in the following statement:

> When we object that free land will not enable the workers to become their own employers, because they still have not that other thing which is equally important: Capital, what does he say then? It is almost incredible the answer he gives. He verily refers us to the fact that—"we see the poorest class of labourers building themselves some sort of shanties" whenever they can find some free land. So, thus, that the poor can go down to the river and fish out old, rotten boards with which they build most miserable "shanties" is here to be an answer, worthy of a philosopher, to the most difficult of problems, to the great stumbling block to the execution of his ideas, to the lack in the working classes of capital of *large amounts* of capital!![40]

We need only read George in context to see the meaning he attributed to his words, which were originally published in the *Standard*.[41] George made two points. The first was that the union of men and land would be sufficient to lead to the creation of capital. The second was that, even under oppressive monopoly conditions, men had the enterprise to put a roof over their heads provided they had access to land, even if they had to do so as squatters (we see this in the Third World urban centres today). What, then, George invited his readers to consider, might men be able to do if land were not monopolized, the economy grew without hindrance from speculators, and wages were not taxed?

Nonetheless, Gronlund raised a fair point when he emphasised the need for "large amounts" of capital to start up a business in industrial society. But this was not the problem which he assumed. Marx showed how the capital-owning class was not a closed one. "The circumstances that a man without fortune but possessing energy, solidity, ability and business acumen may become a capitalist in this manner [receiving credit]—and the commercial value of each individual is pretty accurately estimated under the capitalist mode of production—is greatly admired by apologists of the capitalist system. . .this circumstance continually brings an unwelcome number of new soldiers of fortune into the field and into competition with the already existing individual capitalists. . . ."[42]

III

Gronlund's view that there was an identity of interests between the owners of capital and of land was not one which Marx shared. Indeed, a careful examination of *Capital*, vol. 3, reveals that Marx came very close in places to George's analysis of the problems of industrial society.

Landowners, said Marx, were as much in "mutual opposition" to industrial capitalists as labourers;[43] indeed, landed property was an "alien force,"[44] tending to impede capital formation.[45] Where investment was undertaken, as with house building, "it is the ground-rent, and not the house, which forms the actual object of building speculation in rapidly growing cities, especially where construction is carried on as an industry, e.g., in London."[46]

The necessity of having to buy land, to produce wealth, "is a hindrance to agriculture, even where such purchase takes place in the case of large estates. It contradicts in fact the capitalist mode of production."[47] Landed property can and does enforce the underutilisation of labour and capital resources.[48] "The mere legal ownership of land does not create any ground-rent for the owner," wrote Marx.

> But it does, indeed, give him the power to withdraw his land from exploitation until economic conditions permit him to utilize it in such a manner as to yield him a surplus, be it used for actual agricultural or other production purposes, such as buildings, etc. He cannot increase or decrease the absolute magnitude of this sphere, but he can change the quantity of land placed on the market. Hence, as Fourier already observed, it is a characteristic fact that in all civilized countries a comparatively appreciable portion of land always remains uncultivated. Thus, assuming the demand requires that new land be taken under cultivation whose soil, let us say, is less fertile than hitherto cultivated—will the landlord lease it for nothing, just because the market-price of the product of the land has risen sufficiently to return to the farmer the price of production, and thereby the usual profit, on his investment in this land? By no means. The investment of capital must yield him rent. He does not lease his land until he can be paid lease money for it. Therefore, the market price must rise to a point above the price of production, i.e., to P + r [price of production plus rent] so that rent can be paid to the landlord.[49]

This evidence catalogued by Marx was the same evidence which was synthesised into an explanation for economic crises by Henry George, and which formed the foundations for a theory which Gronlund shrugged aside as "most far-fetched."[50]

Yet the material accumulated for vol. 3 was not sufficient to change Marx's mind about a capitalist society shorn of land monopoly. He saw clearly that by defining property one was also defining extant social relations in a given historical epoch,[51] and that the appropriation of land rent by taxation would divest private possession of its noxious power to dominate and exploit.[52] Thus, according to his own propositions, such a rearrangement of property rights would radically alter social relations. Parasitism, and the corrosive influence of envy, would evaporate. Yet right up to the end he was unwilling to take a more benign view of the potential for a capitalist society reformed along the lines delineated by Henry George.

Let us try to penetrate behind this anomoly by reviewing Marx's views on land-value taxation in more detail. This opportunity arises from the hostility which Marx developed for his one-time friend from the Latin Quarter of Paris, P.-J. Proudhon. The split between the two ideologues occurred finally when Proudhon published his *Systeme des contradictions économiques ou philosophie de la misère*. Marx replied with *The Poverty of Philosophy*. In this he noted that Proudhon was in fact equating the concept of property with landed property.[53] Proudhon viewed landed property as the original cause of economic instability. In the fifth of ten propositions concerning property ("Property is impossible, because, if it exists, Society devours itself"), he showed how tenant farmers and manufacturers toiling under the burden of the rental claims of monopoly landlords had to turn on each other in attempts to create monopoly conditions which provided them with abnormal profits—in order to continue to meet the landlords' demands. Workers, as a result, were rendered vulnerable. For to cut production costs, labour-saving machines were introduced. "Under the rule of property, the flowers of industry are woven into none but funeral wreaths. The labourer digs his own grave." And: "It is when labourers, whose wages are scarcely sufficient to support them from one day to another, are thrown out of work, that the consequences of the principle of property become most frightful."[54]

"Property is theft," declared Proudhon, and his solution was a simple one: a tax on rental income. Rent, he wrote, was a measure above the costs of production, yet it could operate as an instrument for distributive justice, serving a higher interest than the private ones of idle landowners.

Marx replied: "We understand such economists as Mill, Cherbuliez, Hilditch and others demanding that rent should be handed over to the state to serve in place of taxes. That is a frank expression of the hatred the industrial capitalist bears toward the landed proprietor, who seems to him a useless thing, an excrescence upon the general body of bourgeois production."[55]

This was the use of psychology in economics which, when it was employed by Proudhon, called forth a rebuke from Marx! But Marx did advance concrete objections. One was against Proudhon's claim that rent bound men to nature. Marx became pedantic. He showed that rent merely bound the use of land to competition. Proudhon would not have dissented, but was arguing that a tax on rental income followed by a redistribution—thereby also benefiting those not deriving their living directly from the land—would reestablish a harmonious relationship between ALL men and the land of their community.

Marx also marshalled a list of technical problems. Rent, as paid by tenants to landowners, was money that incorporated interest paid on the landowners' capital which had been invested in and on the land; location, as well as fertility, determined rent—and anyway, rent was not an invariable index of fertility since advances in chemistry and geology constantly altered our appreciation of relative fertility; and the pattern of land use may be a function of social tastes rather than soil fertility.[56]

These represent no difficulty to a Department of Inland Revenue. Pure economic rent can be calculated, for, as Marx himself noted, capital invested in land was a measurable phenomenon which exhausted itself and had to be renewed—and so was capable of being distinguished from the contribution to production made by land per se.[57] Marx was well aware that it was practicable to separate land from capital, rent from interest;[58] why, then, should there be any difficulty for tax inspectors?

If, as he said, "rent is a product of society and not of the soil,"[59] this draws us into a game of semantics which does not alter the facts. Economic rent reflects a surplus above the costs of production, and is greater or less depending on where people chose (or were forced) to live, and the composition of all they chose (or were forced) to consume.

Nor need we be daunted by Marx's mischievous assertion that "for any land valuation based upon rent to be of practical value, the conditions of present society must not be departed from."[60] This is the technique of innuendo: all good socialists, aware of poverty among the proletariat, would of course reject a solution which retained "the present society." In fact, all that would be required was an efficient market which allocated land according to optimum uses based on social preferences. This would then meet Marx's objection that land valuations were constantly changing; such changes could be computed annually with the aid of a land register and computers, and so constitute no argument against land-value taxation.

Marx's final objection is perhaps the most interesting, because it poses the question of the Marxist alternative to the model of individualism, private property in wealth produced by identifiable people, and exchange through the exercise of free choice in the market.

Rent, he said, "is constituted by the *equal price* of the products of land of *unequal fertility*, so that a hectolitre of corn which has cost ten francs is sold for twenty francs if the cost of production rises to twenty francs upon soil of inferior quality. . .but first to make the price of the hectolitre of corn twenty francs in order then to make a general distribution of ten francs overcharge levied on the consumer, is indeed enough to make the *social genius pursue its zigzag course mournfully*—and knock its head against some *corner*."[61]

An absurd, long-winded process for equalising wealth, thought Marx.

Let us suppose for a moment that the price of corn is determined by the labour time needed to produce it, and at once the hectolitre of corn obtained from the better soil will sell at ten francs, while the hectolitre of corn obtained on the inferior soil will cost twenty francs. This being admitted, the average market price will be fifteen francs, whereas, according to the law of competition, it is twenty francs. If the average price were fifteen francs, there would be no occasion for any distribution, whether equalised or otherwise, for there would be no rent. Rent exists only when one can sell for twenty francs the hectolitre of corn which has cost the producer ten francs.[62]

The advantage of bourgeois economics is that it enables one to calculate the relative contributions of various factors, and so maximise efficiency. Such calculations and relative performances, however, become obscured if—as Marx suggested—the hectolitre should be sold at the average price of fifteen francs. His solution is put forth in cursory fashion, but on it is built all of socialist economics, bureaucratic administrations, and centralized political control.

This opens up the whole question of political liberties. Gronlund denied that socialist control of the economy would erode personal freedom. He attacked the competitive market economy as planless, anarchic, and so liable to periodic crises;[63] hence the need for collective, planned action. The state would merely take on the role of General Manager, General Statistician, and General Arbitrator—thereby determining how much to produce, distributing the work and ensuring that it was performed, and arbitrating to guarantee justice between various associations of men.

Russian critics of the Soviet Union have amply demonstrated the brutalities and economic deficiencies of such a rigid social system as developed and operated by fallible human beings. Whether one can fairly compare the economic foundation of this imperial power with George's reformed capitalism depends on whether one accepts the U.S.S.R. as an example of what happens when men seek to structure society along Marxist principles.

IV

Why did Karl Marx oppose capitalism as reformed by land-value taxation? The detailed objections examined above hardly constitute a sufficient case against Georgeism for a man of his intellectual capacity. The answer has to be sought in his personal psychology and his dialectical materialism. These combined to predetermine his concept of civilized man and the structure of property ownership which he could find acceptable. George, in the strong tradition of nineteenth-century individualism, desired the freedom of people to work under conditions which matched their personal preferences. This made for a decentralized system, in which the actions of all men found their aggregate expression in the market place. Within that framework, George had faith in the ability of most individuals to provide for all their own needs. Those who, as with the infirm, could not support themselves, could be looked after by society, and their claims would be on the basis of right, not of the charity which came to stigmatize the Poor Laws. For they, too, were entitled to claim a share of natural resources realised through the medium of state expenditure based on revenue derived from a tax on land values.

This process of decentralization was unacceptable to Marx. Societies—according to his reading of history—were constantly moving in the direction of centralization, and the units of economic activity were growing in size. (This theme was also emphasised by Gronlund both in *The Cooperative Common-wealth* and in his last book, *The New Society*.) The idea of people living on family-sized farms was anathema to Marx. In the *Communist Manifesto* he referred to the "idiocy of country life,"[64] and he claimed that it was impossible for "isolated' rural labour—which he contrasted with "social" labour—to develop spiritually.[65] The value of the capitalist mode of production was its development of the productive powers of "social labour," which thereby abolished "private labour."[66] The dispersal of free labour onto its own land was a brake on the formation of new capital (independent producers, it seems, consume but do not save).[67] Ergo, farming had to be organised on a factory basis; and capital, which according to his theory was produced by social labour, must therefore be owned socially, that is, collectively in large aggregations.*

The problem of clarifying Marx's position intensifies when we consider his specifications of the preconditions for capitalism. We have seen that he regarded landed property as a hindrance to the capitalist mode of production. "Landed property has nothing to do with the actual process of production. Its role is confined to transferring a portion of the produced surplus value from the pockets of capital to its own."[68] "It is true. . .that landed property differs from other kinds of property in that it appears superfluous and harmful at a certain stage of development, even from the point of view of the capitalist mode of production," which contrasts with "the capitalist [who] performs an active function in the development of this surplus value and surplus production."[69]

Despite this, Marx concluded that the landlord played a role in the capitalist mode of production "particularly because he appears as the personification of one of the most essential conditions of production."[70] But why must land be personified by an individual or class rather than by the whole community? In fact, private property in land was not a necessary condition for the emergence of capitalism. In practice, it was an obstacle to that mode of production, as Marx showed. Nonetheless Marx argued that landed property arose as a necessary precondition of, and yet somehow as a result of, capitalism[71]—a most improbable situation (even if it were not self-contradictory), since the transformation of rights to land along the social-individual continuum began in the thirteenth century, and was well advanced by the sixteenth century, the period from which Marx dates the rise of capitalism.

The precondition stipulated as necessary by Marx—a market reallocating land—would have been more efficiently met by the refinement of an ancient fiscal system (land value taxation). Instead, during the Industrial Revolution at the turn into the nineteenth century, income tax was introduced in Britain by the landlord-dominated Parliament in order to shift the burden from the land. Conceived within the Georgeist model of society, economic relations would have been dramatically different: harmonious, cooperative, prosperous. But Marx was not prepared to entertain this outcome, which he chose to dismiss as just a ploy by capitalists to get rid of landlords who were "a limitation on profit, not a necessary requirement for production."[72]

The outcome which we can predict, using the Georgeist model, cannot be fully elaborated here. But consider the nature of the labour market in a society in which people were not forcibly rendered landless by, for example, mass enclosure of common land. Industrialists, to get the labour they needed, would have been compelled to *attract* rural labour. So wages would have had to have been higher than what a farmer could get by working for himself: conditions

* Quite apart from the metaphysics involved, there is also the alleged economic problem of being able to apportion individual ownership to value created in the productive process, where a large number of workers were involved in a complex operation. Marx was not the only one to see this alleged difficulty. It was stated by Bertrand Russell, who thereupon drew the conclusion that "the principle that a man has a right to the produce of his own labour is useless in an industrial civilization" (*History of Western Philosophy* [London: George Allen & Unwin, 1967], pp. 612, 613). I can reply only that tax inspectors charged with levying a value-added tax have no difficulty in identifying incremental value added at each stage of the production process, and that individual workers have no problem in specifying their personal contributions to each stage of that value-creating process.

would have had to have been acceptable (how many would have voluntarily swapped green pastures for urban society if the best things on offer were slum dwellings and dark satanic mills?). Marx's argument that capitalism *needed* a vulnerable class of landless labourers in the first place—which it somehow created by inducing the inception of landed property—in order to realise higher profits at the expense of wages, is a superficial analysis born of his metaphysics. In the Georgeist model, profits would have been as high, if not higher, along with higher wages, because landholders could not have deterred economic investment and growth for personal reasons.*

Evidence in support of this interpretation can be derived from Marx himself. In attacking those who dared to espouse a form of socialism which differed from his own, he was led to admit that without land monopoly there would be no monopoly of capital. His *Critique of the Gotha Programme* contains these words: "In present-day society the instruments of labour are the monopoly of the landowners *and* the capitalists."[73] He added in parentheses: ". . .the monopoly of property in land is even the basis of the monopoly of capital. . . . " To understand what he meant, note his further observation: "In England, the capitalist is usually not even the owner of the land on which his factory stands." From this we derive several illuminating points. First, the original monopoly power inhered in land ownership. Second, the power wielded by capital was derivative, of a secondary nature, and *not* intrinsic to itself: if labour was vulnerable to capital, then, it was because workers did not have access to land of their own.

This interpretation is consistent with Marx's account of the vulnerability of capital in colonies where there was plenty of free land for migrant labour: ". . .the capitalist finds that his capital ceases to be capital without wage labour, and that one of the presuppositions of the latter is not only landed property in general, but modern landed property; landed property which, as capitalized rent, is expensive, and which, as such, excludes the direct use of the soil by individuals. Hence Wakefield's theory of colonies, followed in practise by the English government in Australia. Landed property is here artificially made more expensive in order to transform the workers into wage workers, to make capital act as capital. . ."[74]

Marx appreciated that if land were not privately monopolized, men would be able to live as free individuals. This was the conviction behind the following statement: "The nationalization of land will work a complete change in the relations between labour and capital, and finally, do away with the capitalist form of production, whether industrial or rural."[75]

Marx, of course, saw the next step as being in the direction of socialism. But Henry George insisted on an alternative path forward. For land-value taxation was more than a mechanism for redistributing income; it also destroyed what Marx called "the monstrous power wielded by landed property, [which] when united hand in hand with industrial capital, enables it to be used against labourers engaged in their wage struggle as a means of practically expelling them from the earth as a dwelling place."[76]

---

* Speculation in future capital gains was only one motive for acquiring land. There were strong social reasons as well. The urban merchant sought status by buying a manor, and the landed class required large tracts for sporting pursuits.

Marx's account of the redistribution of power following a change in the structure of property rights in land alone is not consistent with his refusal to accept capitalism reformed along the Georgeist model. But the facts, telling though they were, could not override his preconceived notions. A. J. P. Taylor, the British historian, puts it thus: ". . .his later observations, though extremely laborious, were fitted into a system which already existed, a system moreover which was treated as complete once and for all."[77] (Taylor's use of the term *fitted* is unfortunate: these "later observations" never could be really made to fit.)

Marx's philosophy, based on dialectical materialism, promised an end—communism—which would constitute the resolution of all human conflicts. The discontinuities of which epochs are made would come to rest finally in the termination of history itself. Communism, the promised land, the final synthesis, would arrive. Clearly, then, Marx could not allow a realistic appreciation of the economic facts—the relationship between capital and labour, and the distortions interposed by landed property—to disturb his nirvana. To go along with Georgeist reforms, which he saw were sound in relation to the prevailing mode of production, was impossible; for that would delay the day of judgement, when the proletariat would dictate. Such reforms would enhance the conditions of labour, but would consequently protract the life of capitalism!

A further problem for Marx arose with interest, the returns on capital. Marx admitted that in precapitalist modes of production a portion of the surplus-labour product of the worker could be retained by him and congealed into his "ownership of the conditions of labour as distinct from land, such as agricultural implements, and other goods and chattels"[78]—that is, into capital. Why then, one might ask, in a capitalist society, could not a man who embodied his own labour into the form of a machine be at liberty to employ others to work it (assuming that they willingly agreed to do so, with an eye to their advantage), and enjoy rewards accruing to his embodied labour without being accused by Marx of being exploitative?

Marx might have answered that the prerequisites for a truly free agreement did not exist, since enclosures and other land usurpations had created an industrial reserve army without bargaining power—a proletariat. This, however, was precisely the situation for the correction of which George's remedy was calculated, so such an argument would not be relevant to capitalism on the Georgeist model.

The fact is that to concede a right of this nature would have ruptured Marx's vision of a communist harmony. Men would still have been unequal, in some sense—the employers and the employed. Their wealth would have been unequal; emotions would allegedly be disturbed. Much better that everybody should have everything (more precisely, and utopian, they should altruistically contribute that of which they were capable, and take as much as they needed), to remove all emotions which might conceivably portend further struggles. Hence all land, capital, and labour had to be conflated into the category of "social"; the uniqueness of individuals had to be dissolved into the homogeneous mass called "social labour"; society, rather than the individual, would direct social intercourse, thereby necessitating central control, the better to avoid the prospect of individuals unilaterally going their own sweet ways. . . .Current realities, practical or theoretical, had either to be fitted into this system or ignored.

But, while Marx was a collectivist, it would be a mistake to counterpose Henry George at the other extreme—as an individualist of the atomistic variety. Gronlund, in propagating Marx's scheme—"We belong to each other, and this rests upon the contention that ALL men are created to work for other men"[79]—sought to distort George's political philosophy. "George would, if he could, separate the Individual entirely from society. But Society is an organism. . . ."[80] Yet, while George held that "whatever savors of regulation and restriction is in itself bad, and should not be resorted to if any other mode of accomplishing the same end presents itself," he too insisted that "society is an organism," and ended book 6 of *Progress and Poverty* by approvingly quoting from Marcus Aurelius: "*We are made for co-operation—like feet, like hands, like eyelids, like the rows of the upper and lower teeth.*"[81]

V

Marx thought that he had checkmated Henry George when, in a letter dated 20 June 1881, he asked why it was that America—the nation of relatively abundant land—should have rapidly produced an exploited proletariat when, according to George's theory, the workers should have been independent producers.[82]

In rebuttal we can turn to evidence produced by none other than Marx's friend and collaborator, Engels, who reviewed the labour question in the preface to the American edition of *The Condition of the Working Class in England*. Up till 1885, wrote Engels, public opinion was almost unanimous in proclaiming the absence of a European-style proletariat on American soil. From that point on, however, a proletariat rapidly developed. What caused this change? Engels had no doubts: the drying up of cheap land on the western frontier.

While land was readily available, the great mass of the native American population could "retire" in early manhood from wage labour and become farmers, dealers, or employers of labour, "while the hard work for wages, the position of the proletarian for life, mostly fell to the lot of immigrants." Immigrants were vulnerable—dependent upon employers—during the early phases of each wave of migration, when the newcomers sought to recover from the Old World and adjust to the New; yet as long as land out West was there for the taking, the immigrants too could expect to lead a good and independent existence. "But America has outgrown this early stage," wrote Engels in the mid-eighties. "The boundless backwoods have disappeared, and the still more boundless prairies are faster and faster passing from the hands of the Nation and the States into those of private owners. The great safety-valve against the formation of a permanent proletarian class has practically ceased to act."

Engels prided himself in foreseeing the consequences of this process. Henry George, however, had anticipated events at an earlier date. An account similar to the one by Engels, published six years earlier, appeared in *Progress and Poverty*,[83] although the predictions and analyses can be traced back to 1871, when he issued *Our Land and Land Policy* as a pamphlet.

Engels, of course, was not interested in lending credence to Henry

George. In his account he argued that George's contention that expropriation of people from their land was the great and universal cause of the division of society into two classes—rich and poor—was "not quite correct historically."[84] As evidence, Engels cited the case of slavery in the ancient world. Slavery was "not so much the expropriation of the masses from the land as the appropriation of their persons." The subtlety of the relationship between man and land in a system based on slavery was not lost on Marx, however, and the crux of that relationship was the private appropriation of land. Marx cites evidence from Rome, where the rich appropriated land and *then* sought and used slaves to till the ground and tend the cattle.[85]

So anxious was Engels to qualify George's analysis that he further cited the serfs of the Middle Ages. These were exploited as part of a system which, far from throwing them off the land, actually tied them to it. This does not count against George, but it does reveal a confusion in Engels. The burden of George's analysis was not that people were dispossessed physically from their land, but that the surplus which they collectively created (economic rent) was privately appropriated. It did not matter, therefore, whether people were tied to, or thrown off, land—the end result was the same: an unjust distribution of wealth, and a malfunctioning economy.

Engels declined, on tactical grounds, to deal extensively with George, for he felt that to do so then would only create dissension within the nascent proletarian movement in America. There is a suggestion (in a letter to his American translator) that he hoped to undertake a full and exhaustive critique of George at some later, more propitious, time.[86] Had he done so, he might have been obliged to reexamine and perhaps alter some of his own key beliefs!

Since Marx and Engels never met or corresponded with George, the opportunity for a sustained colloquy between them never arose. Nevertheless, we do have access to a reasonable second-best: the record of an exchange of views between George and his one-time London host, Henry M. Hyndman, who was for a while a confidant of Marx. In 1889 the two met for a celebrated debate on The Single Tax versus Social Democracy at St. James's Hall, London. (Two years previously, they had engaged in conciliatory dialogue in the pages of the *Nineteenth Century*.) Before examining the report of this event, we must note that in 1882 Hyndman—with the encouragement of Henry George—had edited and published the lecture delivered in 1775 by Thomas Spence, who had proposed that rent should be appropriated for the benefit of the whole community. In his introduction Hyndman referred to "my friend" Henry George, whose book *Progress and Poverty* had shown that the capitalist's power of exploitation had its foundation in "the monopoly of the soil in the first instance."[87] By 1906, when he wrote an introduction to the St. Jame's debate, this and other insights had become mere "attractive error."[88] I shall examine three key criticisms advanced by Hyndman during the debate.

Who would benefit from land-value taxation and the concomitant reduction of taxes on earned income? Hyndman contended that the workers would not be any better off—"the capitalist class would pocket every six-pence" of reduced taxation.[89]

His argument suffered from confusion at two distinct levels. First, the new fiscal structure. If taxes on wages were reduced to offset, in part, the revenue from the land tax, would that not increase the real value of wages?

And if taxes on goods and customs duties were also reduced, would this not reduce prices and therefore further increase real living standards?

Hyndman apparently did not see this. He might have wished to reply with an argument which he did advance against George: that, because of competition for jobs, workers would continue to be vulnerable to employers, and that therefore a reduction in taxes on wages would simply (through the labour market) result in a reduction of wages to their former levels. Hence there would be only a temporary benefit to workers. This reply would fail on two counts (1) Immediately a land tax were instituted, it would increase the supply of land, making its use available to a wider group of people and so contracting the supply of hired labour: wages, therefore, would tend to rise! (2) As Hyndman had earlier noted—and Marx before him—the ability to exploit workers rested on the prior monopoly of land, the removal of which would alter the relative distribution of economic power in favour of greater mutual cooperation.

Hyndman's second major criticism concerned George's theory of rent. He said that an increase in rent in capitalist economies did not necessarily reduce the rate of wages.* Two pieces of evidence were produced. Rent and wages had simultaneously increased in Australia, he declared. This was no problem for George; for as Marx himself had noted, a land-abundant continent like Australia left workers in a very strong bargaining position. Undaunted, Hyndman noted that real wages in the United States had risen over the previous twenty-five years. This constituted no problem for George, either. "I have, in the first place, never stated anything more than that the increase of rent produces a *tendency* to the decrease of wages, and by wages in all such parts as that, I mean that proportion which goes to the labourer."[90] Furthermore, technical progress in an advancing capitalist economy, which required higher operating skills from workers, would drive up wages. But as Henry George noted: ". . .while land everywhere has been increasing in value in the United States, so everywhere have we become accustomed to what a few years ago we knew nothing about—the tramp and the pauper."

Hyndman's third criticism was potentially the most damaging. He claimed that the land tax was directly responsible for extensive poverty among the peasants of India. Here was a challenge on which the whole Georgeist movement could collapse, since the central economic case for land taxation was the enrichment of all members of a community who were willing to work.

"The full economic rent of the land is taken to the amount of £22 m. or £23 m. a year, and is the sheet-anchor of the taxation of India—yet there is no such poverty in the world as in our great and glorious Empire of India," declared Hyndman. "The land in Madras was nationalised in accordance with Mr. George's views, and was assessed annually to the amount of its full rental value. The result was such an enormous increase of poverty that the Government of India was absolutely obliged to give it up as a complete failure."[91]

Some of the main problems with the Indian agricultural system were

---

* If this were true, and given the long-term decline in the rate of profit, where was the inexorable process of exploitation of surplus value which Marxists claimed would impoverish the proletariat to the point of revolution?

described to the Fabian Society in 1902 by S. S. Thorburn, who had accumulated considerable experience as financial commissioner of the Punjab.[92] He made the following points:

(a) The British landlords who went to India to administer this part of the Empire transformed traditional land-use rights into proprietary rights. This destroyed the communal, cooperative ethos of village life.

(b) The authorities, in the form of the East India Company until the 1860s, levied a fixed "land tax" irrespective of the effect of the weather on any season's crop. This forced peasants to borrow to make the tax payments after droughts had produced famine.

(c) The salt tax was severely regressive, since it fell heaviest on the peasants who needed salt to feed to their cattle.

Central to any solution, said Thorburn, was a more elastic land revenue-collecting system. There had to be remission of taxes on rain land which suffered from drought.[93]

It would, he said, be easy to devise a system which operated a sliding scale of tax rates based on the harvest and the prevailing prices, and which therefore fell on economic rent only. Henry George anticipated all this in *Progress and Poverty*.[94] But what of the seemingly devastating example of Madras—where land was "nationalised in accordance with Mr. George's views"*—which Hyndman marshalled in the debate with his American opponent? The tax was a high one on the gross produce rather than the net produce (economic rent). It was therefore a disincentive to capital improvement, and it undoubtedly impoverished the peasants under what became known as the Ryotwari Settlement introduced in Madras by Sir Thomas Munro in the 1820s. Dutt reviewed the consequences of this settlement, and explained the nature of the tax: "What is the Land Tax? The Court of Directors [of the East India Company] declared in 1856 that the right of the Government is not a rent which consists of all the surplus produce *after* paying the cost of cultivation and the profits of agricultual stocks, but a land revenue only."[95] So much for Hyndman's knowledge of fiscal policy in India, and the influences which fashioned it.

The British would have done well to have operated a land tax of the sort George prescribed, for land which failed to produce a crop because the rain did not fall consequently produced no economic rent; thus, there should have been no tax exaction. Where taxes were levied in such circumstances, these fell not on economic rent but on the ability of peasants to borrow by mortgaging land. This in turn led to indebtedness and eventual loss of land. There were other injurious features of the tax system, such as fixing assessments in perpetuity. As economic rent increased, this surplus remained in private hands; where it decreased, the tax burden fell on the returns to capital and labour, with all the impoverishing effects that this entailed. A sensitive land tax which appropriated for public use that part of a season's actual production which could be attributed to nature could easily have been implemented, according to

---

* Actually, Ricardo was the economist who had had some influence of a theoretical nature over the early nineteenth-century British administrators in India. See F. G. H. Anderson, *Some Facts, Fallacies and Reflections Concerning the Land Revenue Systems in India*, Paper no. 24, Fourth International Conference to Promote Land Value Taxation and Free Trade, Edinburgh 1929, London International Union for Land Value Taxation and Free Trade.

Thorburn; had this happened, the peasants would not have suffered. As it was, the tax fell on the cultivator, not his land.

But Hyndman was not particularly interested in the details of the Indian land tax, for he was anxious to show that capital was the culprit in the subcontinent. His misdiagnosis was consistent with the failure of the Left in Western politics to perceive (or where it was perceived, as initially it was by Hyndman, to consistently follow through to the logical conclusion) the original cause of exploitation within industrial society.* Hence it suited him to erroneously claim that "the land was being taxed up to its full economic value. . .therefore there are very much greater causes of poverty than merely the monopoly of the land."[96] The role of privately owned land was thus carefully neutralized out of the picture, leaving the Marxist free to single out his favorite target: the capitalist.

After Hyndman, twentieth-century critics in the Marxist tradition had little to say about Henry George. Presumably they thought there was little left to add: this would seem to be a reasonable conclusion after examining Arthur Lewis's attempt in 1919 in his *Ten Blind Leaders of the Blind*,[97] which embodies certain phrases which appear to have been taken straight from Gronlund's tracts. Lewis resorted to vilification (George "rails like a fishwife," and was "a true lackey of capital"), but he provided little fresh analysis. The only point of substance he raised concerned George's mistaken account of the mechanism by which interest rates were established—but which, as Lewis acknowledged, not even George's followers accepted.

For the rest Lewis seemed most anxious to demonstrate (as with Gronlund before him) his superior logical faculties. Why, observed Lewis, certain simple-minded persons had argued that if rent was robbery, the thing for the robbed community to do was to take the land away from the landlord and thus put an end to his income from rent. "But Henry George refused to be a party to any such proceedings."[98] Lewis failed to explain why this drastic action of physical appropriation was necessary, if land-value taxation approaching one hundred percent deprived landlords of rental income. After all, Henry George would have replied, having taken the land away, it would then be necessary to finance a bureaucracy to lease it back and administer its use—a wholly unnecessary solution since better results could be achieved more cheaply (and with no risk to political freedom) by permitting the market to do the job.

Thus we have come to the end of this examination of the Marxist critique of Henry George. Before I conclude, however, it is worth taking a brief retrospective view of the historical developments of the century since George wrote *Progress and Poverty*, to see which of the two social science traditions has proved to be the more useful in analysing the affairs of men.

Gronlund, in *The New Economy*, confidently asserted that "because our goal is predestined, it is futile to argue as Henry George does, not very successfully, in the volume, published after his death, that Collectivism is unworkable."[99] But surely events have vindicated George! For he did not deny that collectivism could be made to work—at a price. Was he not right to warn, in

---

*This was true not just of political theoreticians. Time and again the workers who suffered deprivation during economic crises blamed technology rather than land speculation. Hence the cases of destructive reaction, such as the Luddites of 1816 and the weavers in 1827; and the promises of socialist salvation, as from the Chartists after 1836.

Progress and Poverty, that in that kind of system "instead of an intelligent award of duties and earnings, we should have a Roman distribution of Sicilian corn, and the demagogue would soon become the Imperator"?[100] The price of collectivism, as we all know, has indeed been great.

Marx fared no better than Gronlund in his predictions. The most celebrated of these related to the mechanism which he said would cause the transformation of societies from capitalism to socialism. The greatest alienation, said Marx, manifested itself within societies where capital was concentrating in ever-larger aggregations, and it was within these that the proletariat would develop the solidarity and class consciousness which would equip them to effect the most dramatic socioeconomic changes. Henry George, by contrast, held that it was rather in societies where there was a concentration of land ownership that such changes would occur.[101] George was obviously the better prophet. Where the Marxist ideology has successfully reinforced revolution—from Russia and China to Cuba and Vietnam—these social transformations have been in peasant societies heavily or totally dependent upon agrarian economies. And the major non-Marxist upheavals of the twentieth century, beginning with Mexico, have also been in land-based peasant societies.

VI

Thus we are entitled to entertain serious doubts about the value of Marxism as a guiding philosophy. With equal confidence we can assert that, if human existence is dependent on evolutionary adaptation to new social forms in keeping with the needs of man and his natural environment, the Georgeist model has to be regarded in the main as the most attractive and feasible alternative.

Notes

1.   Sidney Webb, *Socialism in England* (London: Swan Sonnenschein & Co., 1890), pp. 20, 21. Marx explained the cause of the excitement stimulated by *Progress and Poverty* to his friend Sorge, who had sent him a copy: "George's book, and also the sensation it has created among you, is significant because it is a first though unsuccessful effort at emancipation from orthodox political economy." Karl Marx and Frederick Engels, *Selected Correspondence*, trans. I. Lasker (1955; 3d revised ed. Moscow: Progress Publishers, 1975), p. 323. Cf. the estimate by R. S. Moffat as revealed in the title of his book, *Mr. Henry George the "Orthodox"*, which is examined by Babilot in chapter 7 of the present volume.

2.   Cited in Anna George de Mille, *Henry George: Citizen of the World* (Chapel Hill: University of North Carolina Press, 1950), p. 2.

3.   Henry M. Hyndman, *Record of an Adventurous Life* (New York: Macmillan, 1911), p. 268.

4.   Marx and Engels, *Selected Correspondence*, p. 324.

5.   In a letter to Hyndman, 22 June 1884, quoted in George R. Geiger, *The Philosophy of Henry George* (New York: Macmillan, 1933), p. 239.

6.   In a letter to Thomas Walker, 25 September 1890, quoted in Charles Albro Barker, *Henry George* (New York: Oxford University Press, 1955), p. 564.

7.   H. Hessel Tiltman, *J. Ramsay MacDonald* (New York: Frederick A. Stokes Co., 1929), p. 18.

8.   Hyndman, *Record of an Adventurous Life*, p. 226.

9.   See Hyndman's obituary article on George in the *Saturday Review* (London) 6 (November 1897): 485-86.

10. Charles Albro Barker, *Henry George*, p. 495.

11. See Stow Persons's introduction to the Harvard Library edition of Gronlund's *Cooperative Commonwealth* (1884; reprinted ed. Cambridge, Mass.: Harvard University Press, 1965), p. xxii.

12. Laurence Gronlund, *Socialism vs. Tax Reform: An Answer to Henry George* (New York: New York Labor News Co., 1887), p. 15.

13. Laurence Gronlund, *Insufficiency of Henry George's Theory* (New York: New York Labor News Co., 1887), p. 3. Hereinafter referred to as *Insufficiency*.

14. Henry George, *Progress and Poverty*, 75th anniversary ed. (New York: Robert Schalkenbach Foundation, 1954), p. 216; emphasis added. In the preface to the fourth edition, written in 1880 but reproduced in the edition cited, George said: "What I have done in this book, if I have correctly solved the great problem I have sought to investigate, is to unite the truth perceived by the school of Smith and Ricardo to the truth perceived by the schools of Proudhon and Lasalle; to show that *laissez faire* (in its full true meaning) opens the way to a realization of the noble dreams of socialism. . ." (p. xv).

15. Gronlund, *Insufficiency*, p. 3.

16. Ibid.; emphasis added.

17. Karl Marx, *Capital,* trans. not indicated (Moscow: Foreign Languages Publishing House, 1962), 3: 623; emphasis added.

18. Ibid., p. 609.

19. Ibid., pp. 237, 366.

20. Gronlund, *Insufficiency*, p. 15; emphasis added.

21. George, *Progress and Poverty*, p. 264.

22. Ibid., p. 281.

23. Maurice Flamant and Jeanne Singer-Kérel, *Modern Economic Crises* (London: Barrie & Jenkins, 1970), chap. 1.

24. Ibid., p. 31.

25. J. K. Galbraith, *The Great Crash 1929* (Harmondsworth: Penquin, 1975), pp. 32-35.

26. "In a word, the explanation of Hitler's success both in attaining power and office and in carrying out a programme laid down in 1925 can only be found in psychology" (J. A. R. Marriott and C. G. Robertson, *The Evolution of Prussia*, rev. ed. [Oxford; Clarendon Press, 1968], p. 486).

27. Bruno Heilig, "Why the German Republic Fell" in A. W. Madsen, ed., *Why the German Republic Fell and Other Studies of the Causes and Consequences of Economic Inequality* (London: Hogarth Press, 1941).

28. Stuart Holland, *The Socialist Challenge* (London: Quartet Books, 1975), p. 394.

29. Articles by J. C. Cook, D. S. Sayer, and E. L. Norman in *Chartered Surveyor: Urban Quarterly* (London) 4, no. 2 (1976).

30. *The Times* (London), 16 November 1976.

31. Gronlund, *Insufficiency*, p. 15.

32. Gronlund, *Socialism vs. Tax Reform*, p. 10.

33. Thomas Spence anticipated this last point as early as 1775 in his lecture *The Nationalization of the Land*, ed. H. M. Hyndman (London: E. W. Allen, 1882), pp. 17, 18.

34. Gronlund, *Insufficiency*, p. 7.

35. Ibid.

36. Gronlund, *Socialism vs. Tax Reform*, p. 18; original emphasis.

37. Ibid., p. 23.

38. Karl Marx and Frederick Engels, *Selected Works* (Moscow: Foreign Languages Publishing House, 1951), 2: 17.

39. Gronlund, *Insufficiency*, p. 16.

40. Gronlund, *Socialism vs. Tax Reform*, p. 29; original emphasis.

41. Ibid., p. 10.

42. Marx, *Capital*, 3: 587.

43. Ibid., p. 604.

44. Ibid., p. 743.

45. Ibid., p. 792.

46. Ibid., p. 755.

47. Ibid., p. 790. Ernest Mandel, a leading contemporary European Marxist, states: "private property in land, far from being a condition for the penetration of the capitalist mode of production *into agriculture*, is a hindrance and brake upon it" (*Marxist Economic Theory* [London: Merlin Press, 1968), p. 286]. Original emphasis.

48. Marx, *Capital*, 3: 603, 630, 727, 732.

49. Ibid., p. 739; emphasis added.

50. Gronlund, *Insufficiency*, p. 15.

51. Karl Marx, *The Poverty of Philosophy* trans. not identified (Moscow: Progress Publishers, 1966), p. 134.

52. Marx, *Capital*, 3: 771 f.

53. Marx, *The Poverty of Philosophy*, p. 134. See also George Woodcock's introduction to P. J. Proudhon, *What is Property?* (New York: Dover Publications, 1970), p. xiv.

54. Proudhon, *What is Property?*, p. 192.

55. Marx, *Poverty of Philosophy*, p. 140.

56. Ibid., p. 141.

57. Ibid., p. 144.

58. Marx, *Capital*, 3: 755. See also pp. 608, 729, 762.

59. Marx, *Poverty of Philosophy*, p. 144

60. Ibid., p. 141.

61. Ibid., p. 140; original emphasis.

62. Ibid.

63. Gronlund, *Insufficiency*, p. 16.

64. Karl Marx and Friedrich Engels, *Communist Manifesto*, trans. Samuel Moore (1888; reprinted., intro. A. J. P. Taylor, Harmondsworth: Penguin Books, 1968), p. 84.

65. Marx, *Capital*, 3: 792, 793.

66. Ibid., p. 261.

67. Karl Marx, *Grundrisse* trans. Martin Nicolus (Harmondsworth: Pelican Books, 1973), p. 279.

68. Marx, *Capital*, 3: 801.

69. Ibid., pp. 608, 623.

70. Ibid., p. 801. Gronlund, in an attempt to contrast himself with George, also ascribed teleological value to landlords. He claimed that "private ownership of land was instituted, when it was, because it was an advantage to society at large and is not such an *absolute*, universal evil as George wants to make it out" (*Insufficiency*, p. 14; original emphasis). Mandel (*Marxist Economic Theory*, pp. 286, 287) also repeats Marx's point: "The private appropriation of *all cultivable land*, which prevents free settlement of new peasants on the land, nevertheless remains an absolutely indispensable condition for the rise of *industrial capitalism*. So long as there are vast expanses of land available, urban labour-power has a refuge from the factory prison, there is practically no industrial reserve army, and wages may well rise in consequence of competition between industrial and agricultural employment." Mandel undermines his case, however, by conceding in the next sentence: "The high wages which existed in the U.S.A. before the disappearance of the Western 'frontier,' which definitely established a wage scale higher than any in Europe, are to be explained to a large extent by this factor." The high wages, of course, did not retard the industrial system—they merely recognised that a weak monopoly of land worked in the bargaining favour of labour!

71. Marx, *Grundrisse*, p. 278; idem, *Capital*, 3: 582, 602, 603, 792, 801.

72. Marx, *Grundrisse*, p. 279.

73. Ibid., p. 19; original emphasis.

74. Ibid., p. 278. See also Marx, *Capital*, 1, trans. from 3d German ed. by Samuel Moore and Edward Aveling and ed. by Frederick Engels. (Moscow: Foreign Languages Publishing House, 1962) chap. 33.

75. Karl Marx, *The Nationalization of the Land*, in *Selected Works*, (Moscow: Progress Publishers, 1973), 2: 290.

76. Marx, *Capital*, 3: 754. Marx, in also thinking that a redistribution of property rights would fundamentally alter the distribution of economic power, contradicted himself when he claimed that those who supported land-value taxation were trying "to bamboozle themselves or the world into believing that by transforming rent of land into a tax payable to the state *all the evils* of capitalist production would vanish of themselves" (Marx and Engels, *Selected Correspondence*, p. 323; emphasis added). Not all the evils, perhaps, but the remaining ones would be tolerable!

77. Taylor's introduction to Marx and Engels, *Communist Manifesto*, p. 10.

78. Marx, *Capital*, 3: 776, 777.

79. Gronlund, *Insufficiency*, p. 19.

80. Ibid.

81. George, *Progress and Poverty*, pp. 320, 321, 330.

82. Marx and Engels, *Selected Correspondence*, p. 323. This argument is repeated by Sir Eric Roll in his *A History of Economic Thought*, rev. ed. (London: Faber & Faber, 1973), p. 424. The superficiality of Roll's knowledge can be gauged from this statement on page 423: "Nor was George's impression on the working-class movement very profound."

83. George, *Progress and Poverty*, pp. 390-94.

84. Preface to the American edition of Frederick Engels, *The Condition of the Working-Class in England,* in Karl Marx and Frederick Engels, *On Britain,* 2nd. ed. (Moscow: Foreign Languages Publishing House, 1962), p. 10.

85. Marx, *Capital*, 1: 680. See also p. 86, where Marx says of the Roman republic that "its secret history is the history of landed property."

86. Marx and Engels, *Selected Correspondence*, pp. 376-77.

87. Spence, *Nationalization of the Land*, p. 6.

88. *The Single Tax versus Social-Democracy: Which will most Benefit the People?* Debate between Henry George and H. M. Hyndman (London: Twentieth Century Press, 1906), p. 3.

89. Ibid., p. 27.

90. Ibid., pp. 14, 15.

91. Ibid., pp. 11, 12.

92. S. S. Thorburn, *Problems of Indian Poverty*, Tract no. 110 (London: Fabian Society, 1902).

93. Ibid., p. 14.

94. George, *Progress and Poverty*, pp. 117-21.

95. Romesh Dutt, *The Economic History of India*, 2d ed. (London: Routledge & Kegan Paul, 1906), 1: 169; emphasis added.

96. George and Hyndman, *The Single Tax versus Social-Democracy*, p. 20.

97. Arthur M. Lewis, *Ten Blind Leaders of the Blind* (Chicago: Chas. H. Kerr & Co., 1919).

98. Ibid., p. 33.

99. Lawrence Gronlund, *The New Economy: A Peaceable Solution of the Social Problem* (Chicago: H. S. Stone & Co., 1898), p. 297. The posthumous volume to which Gronlund refers is, of course, George's *Science of Political Economy*.

100. George, *Progress and Poverty*, p. 321.

101. Ibid., p. 327.

15

Rutherford: The Devil Quotes Scripture

BY CHARLES F. COLLIER

Reuben C. Rutherford's only book, *Henry George versus Henry George*, is fascinating for several reasons.[1] First, it is a full-length, 326-page critique of *Progress and Poverty*. Second, each of the major elements of George's system of political economy—capital, interest, labor, wages, property rights, progress, and so on—is examined at length. Third, Rutherford's approach to the critique is intriguing. As the title of his book suggests, Rutherford proposed to demonstrate that George's system was logically inconsistent and filled with contradictions by juxtaposing passages of George's. That is, he proposed to show that George contradicts almost all of his own ideas and "that all he builds up at one time, he pulls down at another" (p. vi). Fourth, the time element associated with the book is interesting. It was published in 1887, yet Rutherford says that almost all of it was written in 1882, when he first read George's book. He explains the delay in publication by stating that he was persuaded by friends that the fame of *Progress and Poverty* would be transitory and that, hence, the book was not worth criticizing. When it appeared that the fame of George's book would endure, Rutherford issued his critique. From an analytical viewpoint, however, several of Rutherford's main arguments had become obsolete well before 1882. Rutherford was a staunch defender of the unmodified classical wages-fund theory.[2] It is, however, generally agreed that the unmodified classical version of that theory disappeared from the mainstream of analysis when John Stuart Mill recanted it in 1869. There were, to be sure, numerous efforts to modify the theory to salvage some parts of it.[3] Rutherford seems to have been unaware of the "second round" of the controversy. At least he never cited, or even alluded to, any of the discussion.*

---

*A search of all the standard biographical sources yields only fragmentary information about Rutherford himself. He was born in 1823 to a prominent New York State family that numbered the discoverer of nitrogen among its forebears. Like his ancestor, he seems to have been of scientific bent, for his published writings, apart from the book to which this chapter is addressed, consist of an article on the diffusion of odors and a treatise on the healthful properties of woolen, as opposed to linen, garments. He served in the Union Army, attaining the rank of brigadier general, as did his brothers, Friend and George. His profession remains an enigma to me, and I have not been able to ascertain the date of his death.

The prerecantation version of the wages-fund theory, defended by Rutherford, presupposed an agricultural economy. (Indeed, it was precisely as agriculture ceased to be the main sector of the economy that the theory encountered the most devastating criticism.) It is interesting and perhaps suggestive that when Rutherford speaks of people's being paid for a job, he speaks of boys who were paid in apples, an agricultural commodity, for their labor. Later, farming is explicitly mentioned as a characteristic industry (pp. 2, 7, 63). The classical theory assumed that there was a fixed production period—however long it took the crops to grow. Further, it assumed that once the harvest was in, the amount of food available was fixed. No more would be available until the next harvest. That food had to provide for needs of all agricultural laborers until the next harvest since there was simply no other source of food. It then seemed to the classicists that the real wages, or means of subsistence, had to be *advanced* to the laborers. That is, the product of current labor would not be available until the next harvest. But since the laborers had to live day-to-day from one harvest to the next, the food they received could come only from the last harvest. "Last year's" crops, then, maintained labor until "this year's" crops were harvested. Since real wages were paid to the laborers before the product of their current labor was harvested, the term *advanced* seemed appropriate. Although Rutherford does not always use the word *advanced*, he surely does speak of labor's being maintained out of a previously accumulated fund while the product is being produced (p. 8). Once the total amount of food, or real wages, was known, the average amount per worker was found by dividing that total by the number of workers. Here Malthusian population theory seemed to fit perfectly. If the means of subsistence were fixed and divided among a larger number of people, the average must decrease. It seemed to be a simple arithmetic problem—and we do find Rutherford claiming it to be just that. "Given so much wood to be pitched into the cellar, and so many apples with which to pay the boys for pitching it in, why is it that if twelve boys do the task, each will get a smaller share of the apples than if two boys had performed it? Is there anything labyrinthian or mysterious about that? And yet that is all, absolutely all that is involved in Mr. George's problem from a purely politico-economic point of view. . ." (p. 2; also pp. 9, 11, 92). Finally, classicists claimed that their model was generally applicable to the entire economy. That assumption was, as later critics indicated, very unsound and misleading. Still, it is the assumption that was generally made. And we find Rutherford claiming that labor in any sector of the economy can never be employed without a prior accumulation of capital from which to make advances (p. 5).

Rutherford used the above model as the basis for his first attack upon George's system. The first page of his book reproduces what he felt to be George's statement of the problem to be investigated: "Why, in spite of the increase of productive power, do wages tend to a minimum which will give but a bare living?"[4] Rutherford immediatley ridicules George for posing such a seemingly simple problem as if it were profound.

That George was always an ardent critic of the wages-fund theory is well known. All of book 1 of *Progress and Poverty* was dedicated to a refutation of the theory. But George did more than criticize the wages-fund theory; he

offered a well-developed alternative theory—a well-developed marginal-productivity theory of wages.[5] Marginal-productivity theorists claim that the wage
paid to the worker is equivalent to the value of the product produced by him
during the production period. That, of course, completely contradicts the
wages-fund theory, since it makes the wage paid per period depend upon the
productivity of labor, not upon the quotient of the wages fund and the number
of laborers.

Before marginal-productivity theory can be made operational, there must be
some way, at least in principle, to measure the product of a single laborer apart
from the contributions of other factors. George's proposed method was really
quite ingenious. First, he imagined a Robinson Crusoe alone on an island. He
argued that such a person could always pick wild berries and gather birds'
eggs. Those berries or eggs would be the product of labor and hence the real
wage for Crusoe. "Surely no one will contend that in such a case wages are
drawn from capital. There is no capital in the case. An absolutely naked man
thrown on an island where no human being has before trod, may gather birds'
eggs or pick berries."[6] Naturally, a more advanced version of the theory was
required to explain the marginal land that served as the basis of classical rent
theory. Almost by definition, the no-rent marginal land was the least fertile
land cultivated or the least favorably located land built upon. Since that land
would not be totally barren or completely isolated, it would yield some
product. But precisely because it was no-rent margin land, all advantages that
could be eliminated would be eliminated. If a laborer were to be a "squatter"
on the no-rent marginal land, his income or wealth would never be influenced by
increases in the value of the land—assuming, of course, that future
developments would eventually give value to the land. If, further, the laborer
were to have no special skills and no capital with which to work, there would
be no payments for special skills and no interest payments. The product
produced, then, would be ascribed to "raw labor power" since all special
advantages of land, land ownership, and capital were eliminated. It followed
that since all other factors of production were eliminated, all other factor
payments would be eliminated. The total product would be the wage of that
laborer. That wage, moreover, would become the general wage for all
unskilled laborers in the economy because of an unimpeded market
mechanism. George always contended that there was a "fringe" of laborers in
any occupation who could and would shift from one occupation to another
whenever there was any incentive to do so. Thus, if the wages to be earned at
the no-rent margin were to exceed the wages in any intramarginal occupation,
laborers would move from those occupations to the no-rent margin and
cultivate it. Conversely, if the wages to be earned in any intramarginal
occupation were to exceed the wages at the no-rent margin, laborers would
flow from the no-rent margin to intramarginal activities. Thus George claimed
that the wages of unskilled laborers in any occupation could be identified with
the product of laborers at the no-rent margin. The wages of skilled laborers
would be higher, said George, because those laborers produced more than did
the unskilled laborers. That, in essence, was George's theory of wages.[7]

George also denied that there was any "fixed period of production," or that
the value produced by the laborer was, in any sense, "crystallized" at harvest
time, or when the product was finished. Instead, said George, the creation of

value was continuous. He argued that even in the most complicated industrial enterprises, the creation of value was continuous. Even in the construction of the largest of steamships, which required several years for their construction, value was created every day—in fact, with every blow of any hammer used on the job.[8] There was a second sense in which George viewed the creation of value as being continuous. In any economy that had many industries and a variety of agricultural activities, finished products would appear on the market every day. After all, there was no reason to believe that every activity had the identical production period. But if each of a large number of productive activities had its own production period, goods from one industry or another would become available every day. That point is important for two reasons. First, it had a direct bearing on the payment of wages. It meant that laborers, especially those employed in long-term projects, did not have to be paid directly out of the goods they produced. It meant only that they were paid amounts *equivalent to* but not identical with the product that they created. George wrote, "The series of exchanges which unite production and consumption may be likened to a curved pipe filled with water. If a quantity of water is poured in at one end, a like quantity is released at the other. It is not identically the same water, but is its equivalent. And so they who do the work of production put in as they take out—they receive in substance and wages but the produce of their labor."[9] Once that point is understood, Rutherford's claim (p. 26) that the Georgian theory implies that people who haul away ashes should be paid in ashes seems rather foolish. Second, this difference on the period of production is illustrative of a more fundamental difference in views on economic activity. When Rutherford and other wages-fund theorists argued that the average wage was determined by dividing a fixed amount of crops among a fixed population, they made wages a *stock* concept, or a quantity without a time dimension. When George and others argued that wages depended upon continuous productivity and that products became available continuously, he made wages a *flow* concept, or a quantity with a time dimension. The difference between stocks and flows is vital in economic analysis since it involves the role of time in the production process.[10] As economists know, the failure to distinguish between stocks and flows has produced a great many errors.

Rutherford criticized George's "law of least exertion," although he probably never understood it and certainly never saw its analytical significance. Rutherford interpreted the law as being a "law of selfishness" that set each individual against all others. It was that conflict of interests, said Rutherford, which was primarily responsible for the unequal distribution of income and which was responsible for poverty (p. 107). He later contended that if poverty were ever eliminated and all income were equally distributed, the "law of laziness," as he so called it, would lead individuals to stop working. That would clearly hurt society. Further, Rutherford claimed that poverty was not entirely bad since it was often an effective incentive for people to create and produce. Since Rutherford perceived disincentive effects in George's system, he believed that he had found a reason to reject it (pp. 263-73). Aside from the obvious fact that George never proposed to distribute income equally, Rutherford's objections misinterpret the law. As George made quite clear, his intention was merely to claim that people will attempt to gratify their desires with the least possible exertion—or, simply, that people will not waste effort by working harder than they have to. The law has a corollary that George implies if he does not state: for a given amount of exertion, people will try to get as much product as possible.[11] It is that corollary which is the most vital part of the market mechanism that makes the wage-theory operate. As stated above, the product of laborers on the no-rent margin was to become the general wage for unskilled labor because laborers will flow to, or from, the marginal land whenever wages in other occupations are less than, or greater than, the wage at the margin. It is the corollary to the law of least exertion that leads those laborers to seek the highest reward for their exertion. Rutherford never discussed that issue at all.

It is accurate to say that George won each point in the dispute over wages. Economists have rejected the wages-fund concept and they have accepted marginal-productivity theory. It is customary—and very justifiable—for historians of economic analysis to claim that the *complete* marginal-productivity theory was developed by John Bates Clark. (Clark's version was complete because it was generalized to all factors of production.) It is not always realized that Clark's version of the theory was heavily influenced by George. Clark explicitly stated, "It was the claim advanced by Mr. Henry George, that wages are fixed by the product which a man can create by tilling rentless land, that first led me to seek a method by which the product of labor everywhere may be disentangled from the product of cooperating agents and separately identified; and it was this quest which led to the attainment of the law that is here presented, according to which the wages of all labor tend, under perfectly free competition to equal the product that is separately attributable to labor."[12] Economists also deny Rutherford's claims about one fixed period of production for all economic activity. We do believe that production is continuous. Scott Gordon claims that the only important economists of the era who advanced the view that there was no lag in production were Clark and the great English economist Alfred Marshall.[13] Clark, in fact, did write of a "full-pipeline of production" such that labor input at one end instantaneously and automatically forced product out of the other end.[14] The idea, its function, and even the figure of speech are strikingly similar to George's "curved pipe filled with water," discussed above. And economists do accept the idea, if not the name, of the "law of least exertion" as an element of the market mechanism. This law implies self-interest, not selfishness at all. The difference is far more than a matter of semantics. In sum, George was quite advanced in his analysis of wage theory. He was an important participant in the debate over the wages fund, and his views were correct. Rutherford, who defended the orthodox version of the theory after other defenders abandoned orthodoxy for more flexible positions, was ineffective in his criticism of George's views.

Rutherford next turned his attention to George's capital and interest theories. These sections are, quite frankly, depressing and contribute little or nothing to economic analysis. It must be said that both men were quite wrong in all of their main ideas on the topics. Rutherford, as would be expected, adhered to a capital theory that was compatible with the wages-fund theory.

He wrote, "The accepted doctrine is, that capital is anything saved or reserved for the payment of labor not employed in, or devoted to the production of the immediate necessaries of life. Capital is anything that may be used to support the laborer while performing his task—using the word 'laborer' in the sense of a hired person" (p. 31).

There are at least two major objections to Rutherford's procedure. First, as George noted, it is circular to argue that "labor is maintained by capital because capital is that which maintains labor." Second, from the viewpoint of logic, Rutherford's position was untenable. In his critique of the wages-fund theory George, in effect, challenged the wages-fund theorists to justify their views. But all Rutherford did was repeat, and reassert as true, the old definitions. Since he never did more than reassert definitions, he really evaded the issue entirely.

George's treatment of capital theory is more involved, but equally unsatisfactory. George was often inconsistent and not infrequently simplistic. Rutherford, who was not completely inept as a critic, seized each opportunity to indicate these inconsistencies. At times George defined capital as "wealth devoted to production."[15] Rutherford realized that such a definition differed from his in several important ways. Later, Frank Taussig also accused George of a redefinition of terms and argued that since his refutation of the wages-fund theory relied on that redefinition, it was invalid.[16] That criticism, however, misses the point that George's definition entailed substantive differences from the old definition. If capital were narrowly defined to include only those items of wealth which were used to produce more wealth, then the food and clothing consumed by the laborers during the production period would not be capital. Moreover, George's new definition can be viewed as similar to the now-accepted definition as any input that is itself an output of the economic system.

The problem with George's capital theory is simply that George had many other definitions of capital in addition to the one cited above. Rutherford was, in fact, able to fill four pages of his book with lists of George's definitions of capital (pp. 78, 159-61). He was then able to score a goodly number of points against George by showing that the definitions were inconsistent. To consider only one such instance, George *did* state that capital was "wealth in the course of exchange."[17] Rutherford was able to show that such a definition was not really very different from the wages-fund theorists' definition to which George objected elsewhere. After all, if laborers were engaged in a lengthy project, they would have to live on goods equivalent in amount to their productivity, as discussed above. Such goods, according to George's own definition, would be "wealth." But since these goods were not produced directly by the laborers involved, they could be obtained only by exchange. That, then, would make the goods on which the laborers lived "wealth in the course of exchange"—or capital, as a wages-fund theorist would argue. There are, in fact, so many problems and inconsistencies in George's capital theory that modern economists have rejected his ideas.

Given the fact that neither man had an adequate capital theory, it is hardly surprising that neither man produced an adquate theory of interest. Rutherford's theory was, at very best, old-fashioned. Interest to Rutherford was payment for borrowed capital—and for borrowed capital only (pp. 12,

18-19). That is simply unsatisfactory by modern standards, which recognize that interest is the return to any capital, borrowed or otherwise. George's theory is also unsatisfactory according to those same standards. George argues, in essence, that since labor produced wealth and capital was just a special kind of wealth, capital was nothing more than "stored-up" labor. It then seemed to him that, since labor and capital were related, wages and interest ought to be related. George tried to argue that the ratio of wages to interest was always a constant. The problem was that he so vastly over-simplified that he never even hinted at how we could determine the value of the constant of proportionality.[18]

It is easy to explain Rutherford's failure in these matters; it is harder—and much more interesting—to explain George's failures. Rutherford's definitions were simply obsolete when he wrote them. Those definitions relied upon the prerecantation version of the wages-fund theory. But since Rutherford wrote during the postrecantation, "second-round" era, his ideas lost any credibility they might ever have had. George's failures are not so simple to explain. As outlined above, George's wage theory was remarkably accurate and sophisticated. But George did not generalize his marginal-productivity theory of wages to make it a complete marginal-productivity theory applicable to all factors of production; he simply did not transfer his penetrating insights into wage theory to interest or rent theory.[19] That means that George was really a *proto*marginalist, with a marginal-productivity theory of wages but no other marginal-productivity theories. That, in turn, means that his interest and capital theories were also old-fashioned. It was precisely the old-fashioned elements of the theories upon which Rutherford seized to claim that George's theories were inconsistent and to claim that even George accepted the concepts of the wages-fund theory despite his denials.

Next Rutherford turned his attention to George's critique of Malthusian population theory. Rutherford spent most of his time trying to show that the Malthusian theory was correct and that George's objections were invalid. He overlooked, however, the main flaw in George's arguments—the fact that the only fully valid point that George raises in his discussion of the dynamics of income-distribution theory implicitly assumes a Malthusian population theory. In book 4, chapter 1, of *Progress and Poverty* George conceded that increasing population would force the margin of cultivation downward and outward and thereby raise rent. He immediately attempted to qualify that statement by arguing that the impact of increasing population has been greatly misunderstood. The second chapter of book 4 attempts to argue that increasing returns to labor occur as population increases. He wrote, "For increased population, of itself, and without any advance in the arts, implies an increase in the productive power of labor. The labor of 100 men, other things being equal, will produce much more than one hundred times as much the labor of one man, and the labor of 1,000 men much more than ten times as much as the labor of 100 men; and, so, with every additional pair of hands which increasing population brings, there is a more than proportionate addition to the productive power of labor." In the next paragraph he repeats his claim that these increasing returns continue without limit, even after increased population has extended the margin as far as it can go.[20] Clearly, George is arguing that labor is subject to unlimited increasing returns. Equally clearly, his argument is thoroughly invalid since the laws that state that factors of production are subject to decreasing returns, at least after some point, are among the most frequently verified laws of all economics. Chapter 3 of book 4 argues that the effect of any laborsaving improvement will be to extend the margin of cultivation and raise rent. The problem here is that George's analysis is simply wrong—his framework of analysis is incorrect and, not surprisingly, his conclusion is invalid. Interestingly enough, David Ricardo, from whom George derived his rent theory, provided a correct analysis and perfect counterexample to George's argument. Ricardo noted that when a technological advance of the kind discussed by George occurred, the margin of cultivation would contract inward and upward and not extend downward and outward as George assumed. As a result, rent may very well fall both as a share of the product and as an amount. Further, Ricardo claimed that such innovations would automatically raise real wages—again, a result in contradiction to George's.[21] These points greatly damage George's case since they disprove several of the major contentions of the Georgian system—that rent always rises and wages always tend to fall as progress occurs. The final chapter of book 4 takes for granted that progress and technological advance will increase rent and argues that once it becomes known that rent will increase, expectations of further increases arise. Those expectations lead speculators to buy land, evict tenants, and hold the land idle while waiting for its value to increase. That idle holding of land itself forces the margin to be artificially extended and thereby brings about the very rent increase that was expected. There are, it seems, three major flaws in George's arguments on this matter. First, there is simply no reason why land speculators will hold their land idle. There is a wide range of circumstances, including all of the usual cases, in which it would be beneficial for a speculator to use his land productively while waiting for its value to increase. Second, even if one were to assume, with George, that speculators did hold their lands idle, it is not difficult to produce a counterexample, one faithful to all of the Georgian principles, especially the principle of least exertion, that demonstrates that rent may fall as both a share and an amount, under the conditions specified by George.[22] Third, given the fact that George was wrong in his analyses of increasing returns to labor and technological advance, it follows that his theory of expectations must be invalid. No reasonable person could expect land values to increase for the reasons George gave. It seems, then, that all of George's arguments are invalid *except* the one that relies on population pressure's forcing an extension of the margin of cultivation. And since George believed that rent increases would be continuous, the pressure of population against the margin must be continuous. That, however, constitutes the core of the Malthusian population theory.

Given that the dynamic theory, as written by George, relies upon a (perhaps implicit) assumption of Malthusian population theory, it is interesting to attempt to explain why George so vehemently rejected the idea in his explicit statements. First, it is undoubtedly true that much of George's hostility to the doctrine rested upon an unwillingness to accept the ethical-religious conclusions that seemed to follow from the theory. George, who was always a religious man, could never believe that a beneficient Creator of the world would ever have created the poverty and desolation that followed from the Malthusian theory. And, since his belief in the beneficent Creator was unyielding, he was almost compelled to oppose the Malthusian theory on ethical grounds. Second, on an analytical level, George apparently never realized that there are really *two* Ricardian rent theories—one for the extensive margin and one for the intensive margin. George's analysis relies exclusively upon the theory of the extensive margin.[23] That, in turn, meant that George had to try to show that all progressive developments extended the margin. The trouble is that much of his discussion, especially that relating to technological advance and local improvements in intangibles, should have been in terms of the intensive margin. Further, many of George's assertions about the extensive margin are simply invalid unless there is a continuous population increase. Thus the only argument presented by George that is correct is the one that presupposes a Malthusian population theory. It is for this reason that it is stated that the Georgian model, as built by George, requires an assumption (perhaps implicit) about Malthusian population theory.[24]

Rutherford then attempted to show that the existing distribution of wealth was quite proper because it was the result of a long series of voluntary decisions made by reasonable economic factors acting according to their own self-interests. To try to prove that, Rutherford developed his own "historical model" and contrasted it with George's. Rutherford, as did George, began with a single hypothetical family and then imagined that more and more families came and settled in the neighborhood. According to Rutherford, inequalities in wealth emerged from the very beginning, or as soon as there were two or more families with different preferences. Suppose, he said, that there were just two families, one headed by Andrew and the other headed by Peter. Suppose further that one morning Andrew lingers behind to kiss his wife while Peter goes out to work gathering clams. Peter, by virtue of his early start, is able to find a particularly favorable location, stake a claim, and make the land his property. Then, by virtue of hard work, he is able to become wealthier than Andrew, and may under certain circumstances eventually employ Andrew as a laborer (pp. 114-19). That is all as it should be, said Rutherford, because those who wish to become rich can do so while those who are more interested in family affairs can spend their time in other ways. Each person gets the things in which he is most interested; hence, Rutherford concluded, the distribution of wealth is optimal. The entire example fails, however, since it presupposes private property in sites. Surely part of Peter's wealth is derived from the fact that he could claim private property in the desirable site. Obviously, however, it is just such private-property rights whose legitimacy George questioned. Clearly, it is entirely unsatisfactory to attempt to answer such questions by hypothesizing that such rights are justifiable.

The same theme is pursued in a chapter entitled, "Wages, Interest and Profit" (pp. 120-51). All that should be said about wages and interest has been said above. It is interesting here to note that there is no discussion of rent theory in the chapter. One can only speculate as to whether or not Rutherford accepted the theory. Since his book was dedicated to discussing disagreements with George, the absence of discussion might well indicate agreement on the issue. Rutherford does spend a good deal of time trying to resurrect the classical theory of profit as a fourth, independent, factor payment. This contrasted sharply with George's view that profit was not a separate payment at all and that anything called profit could really be broken down into some combination of wages, rent, or interest. While George was by no means the first to argue that profit was not a separate factor payment, he was among those who so argued. It is sufficient to note here that modern economists have accepted the view of George and others on this issue. Today there is no fourth factor payment called profit—at least not in the classical sense of the term.

Rutherford's inquiry concludes with an alternative view of human nature and its role in social progress. George, of course, believed that if society implemented his land reforms and fiscal reforms, poverty would be abolished. Then, since immorality was said to result from poverty, it seemed that immorality would also vanish. That is to say, George believed that moral reform would be a result of property reform. Rutherford, as might be supposed, took exactly the opposite view and argued that there was nothing good to be gained from a revision of property rights until there had been moral reform. The problem as Rutherford saw it was simply that the vast majority of individuals in society had no sense of responsibility and no social conscience (p. 188). He agreed with George's claim that moral character was degenerating, but he denied that private property rights in land were responsible. Instead he saw the evil as stemming from the perceived selfishness of individuals. (p. 308). That selfishness was said to pit one individual against all others and to lead each individual to think that he was separate from the social whole. Poverty resulted from that conflict and from the fact that all individuals were not equally gifted in talent or ability. Therefore, in the competition among the individuals, some would win and become rich as others would lose and become poor. What seemed worse, the dominant social attitudes were such that those who became rich felt no responsibility to those who became poor. It then seemed to Rutherford that George was quite wrong in advocating more personal liberty, because individuals would simply use that liberty to do unjust things (p. 317). Instead, Rutherford chose to move in exactly the opposite direction. That is, he proposed to add more and more restrictions on all private property and on all individuals to compel people to act in desirable ways. These restrictions were designed to force moral reform before any Georgian revision of property rights in land was implemented. It seems that the men disagreed because they had fundamentally different views about human nature. George's view, essentially "optimistic," was that people would readily become moral if they were given the opportunity; Rutherford's view, essentially "pessimistic," was that people would resist becoming moral and therefore they must be forced to become so.[25] It is probably impossible for scholars to decide which view is correct. The issue is really one of differences in values and outlook, which cannot be resolved in any objective fashion. One might note, however, that if Rutherford were correct in his pessimistic view of human nature, it still would not be clear that governmental officials should be given broad powers to restrict personal freedoms. For such officials might well be as fallible and selfish as anybody else.

While the main issue discussed above may be unresolvable, there is one subpoint that can be resolved. Rutherford insisted that liberty and equality could not cure poverty until there was moral regeneration. The point is that Rutherford used the word *equality* in a sense quite different from George's and that led Rutherford to attribute to George ideas that he did not hold. Specifically, Rutherford argued that in the absence of moral reform it would do no good to try to augment wages by distributing rent equally among all of the laborers in society (p. 253). Of course, George never proposed any such equal division of rent. George viewed his proposals as a way to free all supramarginal land for use, thereby raising the margin of cultivation, thereby increasing the yield to labor on the marginal plot, thereby raising wages. That, not any equal division of rent among the workers, was the way in which wages were to rise. Since Rutherford never understood that, and since he attributed to George ideas that he never had, his critique is invalid.[26] The same comments apply, almost without modification, to Rutherford's charge that equality, in the sense of giving everyone the same income, would stifle progress because poverty often inspires people to be especially productive and innovative (p. 299). The point, of course, is that any faithful reading of George's work would show that George never proposed "equality of results." Instead, he proposed only "equality of opportunity." Even Rutherford seems to have realized that at one point (p. 322 n.). Rutherford's claim is, therefore, misdirected.

It is probably reasonable to conclude that Rutherford vastly overstated his critique of *Progress and Poverty*. He literally set out to refute every major point in George's book. He was destined to fail because there are many points in the book that are analytically valid, or that were accepted at the time they were written. Rutherford did, in fact, find some flaws in George's analysis. Interestingly, however, the ideas that Rutherford proposed to substitute were often obsolete or wrong. Much of the force of the critique was therefore lost. For these reasons Rutherford's attempt to refute George's ideas was not very effective.

Notes

1. Reuben C. Rutherford, *Henry George versus Henry George* (New York: D. Appleton and Co., 1887). Because this is the only work of Rutherford's cited and because it will be cited often, subsequent page references to it are in parenthesis in the text.
2. That theory will be discussed below.
3. The most useful account, and one that notes but perhaps underestimates George's role, is Scott Gordon, "The Wage-Fund Controversy: The Second Round," *History of Political Economy* 5 (Spring 1973): 14-35. The best summary statement by a defender of the modified theory is made by Frank W. Taussig, *Wages and Capital: An Examination of the Wages Fund Doctrine* (New York: Appleton, 1896).
4. Rutherford does not specify the edition of George's *Progress and Poverty*, but his citations always agree with the Appleton edition of 1882. Since the 1882 edition may be uncommon, all subsequent citations of *Progress and Poverty* will be given in terms of the 75th anniversary edition (New York: Robert Schalkenbach Foundation, 1954). See p. 17 for the passage cited here.

5. For a more complete discussion of George's wage theory and its place in his system of political economy, see Charles Collier, "Henry George's System of Economics: Analysis and Criticism," (Ph. D. dissertation, Duke University, 1975), esp. pp. 16-22. Hereinafter cited as "George's System."

6. George, *Progress and Poverty*, p. 51.

7. This whole paragraph relies heavily upon Collier, "George's System," pp. 16-22.

8. George, *Progress and Poverty*, p. 65, and Collier, "George's System," p. 18.

9. George, *Progress and Poverty*, p. 79.

10. See Scott Gordon, "Second Round," for a discussion of stocks and flows.

11. George, *Progress and Poverty*, p. 204; idem, *The Science of Political Economy* (1898; reprinted ed. New York: Robert Schalkenbach Foundation, 1968), p. 91; Collier, "George's System," pp. 14-16.

12. John Bates Clark, *The Distribution of Wealth: A Theory of Wages, Interest and Profits* (London: Macmillan and Co., 1924), pp. v, 9. The work first appeared in 1899. For a fuller discussion of the George-Clark relation, see Collier, "George's System," pp. 108-15.

13. Gordon, "Second Round,", p. 28.

14. Ibid.

15. George, *Progress and Poverty*, p. 47, and Rutherford, *Versus*, p. 46.

16. Rutherford, *Versus*, p. 48, and Taussig, *Wages and Capital*, pp. 26-27.

17. George, *Progress and Poverty*, p. 78, and Rutherford, *Versus*, pp. 31, 49.

18. George, *Progress and Poverty*, pp. 216-22, and Collier, "George's System," p. 23.

19. It remained for P. H. Wicksteed and others to show that Ricardian rent theory is equivalent to the marginal-productivity theory of land and for J. B. Clark to develop the complete theory.

20. George, *Progress and Poverty*, pp. 229-30.

21. David Ricardo, *The Principles of Political Economy and Taxation* (New York: Dutton, 1965), pp. 43-44, and Collier, "George's System," pp. 252-59.

22. Collier, "George's System," pp. 247-51.

23. George, *Progress and Poverty*, pp. 169, 239, 243, 247, 248, 249, 250, 253-58.

24. It seems to me that any arguments other than those written by George himself cannot be considered in this inquiry, which deals with George's writings and the critics' reaction to them.

25. The use of the words *optimistic* and *pessimistic* implies nothing about which is the better description of reality.

26. Interestingly, William Torrey Harris made the same mistake. See my analysis of Harris's critique in chapter 13 of this collection.

16

Ingalls, Hanson, and Tucker: Nineteenth-Century American Anarchists

BY JACK SCHWARTZMAN

This chapter essays an analysis of the attacks made upon the thought of Henry George by three individualist American anarchists—Joshua K. Ingalls, William Hanson, and Benjamin R. Tucker.

To one historian of the movement, American anarchism had a "double tradition." The native tradition, running from the beginning of the nineteenth century, was "strongly individualistic" and suspicious of the state. The immigrant tradition, begun in the 1870s, "was first collectivist and afterward anarchist communist."[1] The three critics of George were part of the native tradition.

The individualist anarchism of Joshua K. Ingalls reflected his two tenets: free individuals and free land. Born in Massachusetts in 1816, he was a Quaker, a social reformer, a minister (for a short time), and a strong champion of "land limitation." All his life he attacked land monopoly and urged the repeal of laws that protected land titles not based on personal occupancy. In 1850 he helped organize a utopian colony in West Virginia (The Valley Farm Association), which shortly thereafter failed. In 1878 he began to denounce "capitalism," identifying it with land monopoly. He lost faith in organized labor, continued to assail the state, criticized the growth of moneyed corporations, castigated the entrenched land monopoly, and finally endorsed the doctrine of individualist anarchism. He opposed what he termed the Henry George advocacy of State landlordism, as well as George's "failure" to recognize capital as the enemy of labor. Ingalls's book *Social Wealth*[2] became a noted anarchist classic. His antipoverty remedy was the "occupancy and use" formula of land distribution. (More about that later.) Like Henry George, Ingalls ignored the money question, and disagreed with Tucker, who stressed it. Ingalls regarded the monetary approach as superficial. He preferred to deal with "causes" and "remedies" of social ills. He did not believe in revolutions or legislation, and urged, characteristically, reform through education. Toward the end of his life, which coincided with the end of the nineteenth century, he became extremely pessimistic.[3]

Very little is recorded of William Hanson. He was a contributor to Tucker's *Liberty*, and was highly regarded as an individualistic anarchist in the nineteenth century. His adverse analysis of Henry George is found in a well-written book, *The Fallacies in "Progress and Poverty."*[4] Like Ingalls, Hanson believed in the "occupancy and use" formula. He took George to task for defending capital and interest, for proposing state landlordism, and for the comments about "unearned increment." Hanson believed in natural law, and his book is deeply religious and sincere.[5]

The most famous of the three anarchists presented in this chapter was Benjamin R. Tucker. Born in Massachusetts in 1854, of Quaker background, he was, at various times, a Unitarian, "an atheist, a materialist, an evolutionist, a prohibitionist, a free trader, a champion of the legal eight-hour day, a woman suffragist, an enemy of marriage, and a believer in sexual freedom."[6] He finally became an individualist anarchist. He was, for a time, the "boy lover" of the notorious Victoria Woodhull, herself a professed rebel.[7]

After traveling extensively in Europe, Tucker settled down, first in Boston and then in New York. He became a journalist, and finally established his reputation with the magazine *Liberty*, which he founded. Most of his writings from that publication were gathered in a volume entitled *Instead of a Book.*[8] A later variation of *Instead of a Book*, with some additional writings of Tucker, was titled *Individual Liberty.*[9]

Accepting some of the dogmas of the socialists, Tucker nevertheless adhered firmly, or so he claimed, to the basic principles of philosophical anarchism. He devoted his entire productive life to exposing and attacking what he considered the four prime monopolies: money, land, tariff, and patent.[10] Tucker called the monopolists "a brotherhood of thieves."[11]

Tucker, who according to a prominent social historian "won the attention and sympathetic interest of the American people more than any other anarchist in the United States,"[12] edited *Liberty* in his own characteristic fashion for a quarter of a century. He solicited articles even from opponents of his thought. In 1908 his printing shop burned down, and he departed for Europe, to remain there for the rest of his life. His remaining years were spent in pessimistic lethargy.[13] He died in Monaco in 1939.

When Henry George in 1887 changed his mind and refused to support the convicted anarchists in the so-called Haymarket Affair (because he believed them guilty of murder), Tucker lashed out at George, abusing him orally as well as in a vituperative pamphlet *Henry George, Traitor.*[14] Tucker accused George, who was running for public office, of allowing his political ambitions to influence his behavior. George's refusal to support the anarchists caused a rift among his followers. The debate as to whether George acted "properly" or not continues to this day.[15]

To return to Tucker's philosophy of anarchism: the state, he declared, was the enemy of humanity. "He who attempts to control another is a governor, an aggressor, an invader."[16] Liberty was always preferable to security. Anarchism was always preferable to socialism. "The people cannot afford to be enslaved for the sake of being insured." Answering the Marxists, who accused him of not seeing that the state and society were one, he stated that they were one in the sense "that the lamb and lion are one after the lion has eaten the lamb."[17]

Taxation had to be resisted at all costs.[18] The Henry George single tax was just as vicious a tax as any other, and had to be opposed. He advocated the "occupancy and use" formula as his panacea.[19]

Describing individualist anarchists, Tucker said that they were "not only utilitarians, but egoists in the farthest and fullest sense." The statement was not made apologetically.[20]

It is now necessary to turn to the writings of these three thinkers insofar as such writings pertain to and criticize the various views of Henry George.

Henry George in his works presented the concepts of *rent* and *unearned increment* as synonymous terms. He likewise defined *land value* as a capitalized form of rent. By means of the *inevitable* operation of the "law of rent," George stated, rent or unearned increment would always exist as a mathematical differential. Since rent was unjustly appropriated by monopolistic "landlords," George proposed that the state take it through taxation for the betterment of society. Not only would each person then receive the benefit of his share of such increment but, more important, land, with the speculative shackles removed, would be opened up to individual enterprise, thus creating the condition of true freedom.

The individualist anarchists saw land economics differently. They visualized rent and its "laws" as artificial concepts having no permanency, mathematical certainty, or any validity except as an exploitative gun pointed at the producers. The *true* synonyms for rent, the anarchists claimed, were "interest," "profit," "usury," "tax," or any other "confiscation." There was no limit to such confiscations. Only when the "exploiters" were permanently gone would land be opened up to *true* individualistic endeavor, and each person would take as much land as he desired, provided it be used in keeping with the "occupancy and use" formula. Since the state was the supporter of the exploiters, to give it more power to tax (as George allegedly advocated) was to augment its might and bring about permanent poverty and slavery. The *true* solution would be to get rid of the landlords *and* the state.

Thus each side stressed individualism, liberty, and the removal of land monopoly—yet each side took a sharply opposed position as to how these goals should be achieved. Which one was right? Before a detailed discussion of the controversy is begun, the reader must first be made aware of one more anarchistic criticism of George and the rent question. The individualist anarchists attacked George for his supposed "Malthusianism." Even though they applauded him, on the one hand, for writing a masterful "exposé" of the Malthusian doctrine, they claimed, on the other, that George actually revived the doctrine by his espousal of the Ricardian law of rent. He contended, for instance, that "the pressure of population" drove the margin of land to the zero point, thereby causing rent to rise. George, according to the anarchists, should have "demolished" *both* the Malthusian and the Ricardian theories.

The topic of rent and its allied concepts will now be more thoroughly examined.

Henry George, in his classic *Progress and Poverty*,[21] stated that private property in land was the cause of maldistribution of wealth and the resulting poverty and misery. "Historically, as ethically," he asserted, "private property in land is robbery."[22]

Ingalls accused George of inability to see that "landlordism" was no longer the main oppressor of labor but only a tool of "capitalism." George was especially criticized for adhering to Ricardo's law of rent, which was declared to be but a "buttress of the Malthusian theory" of overpopulation.[23]

In 1817 David Ricardo had defined rent as "that portion of the produce of the earth which is paid to the landlord for the use of the original and indestructible power of the soil."[24] George followed that definition when he wrote that rent "is the share in the wealth produced which the exclusive right to the use of natural capabilities gives to the owner."[25]

"Nothing can raise rent," wrote Ricardo, giving the world its first glimpse of his famous theory, "but a demand for new land of an inferior quality. . . .It is this necessity of taking inferior land into cultivation which is the cause of the rise of rent."[26] Again, George, in paraphrasing what he called the "sometimes styled 'Ricardo's law of rent,' " declared "*The rent of land is determined by the excess of its produce over that which the same application can secure from the least productive land in use.*"[27]

Was Ricardo's "law" a "buttress" of the Malthusian doctrine, as the anarchists claimed? Ricardo himself gave due credit to Malthus, but did so for the latter's *theory of rent*, not for his theory of population. "Whatever cause may drive capital to inferior land," stated Ricardo, "must elevate rent on the superior land; the cause of rent being, as stated by Mr. Malthus. . .'the comparative scarcity of the most fertile land.' "[28]

The anarchists pointed to George's own comments to prove that he was a "Malthusian." George had written that the Malthusian doctrine received support "from the current elucidations of the theory of rent," and that the population theory of Malthus and the rent promulgation of Ricardo were "made to harmonize and blend."[29] George had also said that the increase of population tended to increase rent, and, at the same time, "to diminish the proportion of the produce which goes to capital and labor."[30] When George further stated that "the most valuable lands on the globe, the lands which yield the highest rent, are not lands of surpassing natural fertility but lands to which a surpassing utility has been given by the increase of population,"[31] he was again reproached for his "Malthusian" remark. Ingalls replied that it was not the increase of population that caused the margin to be pushed down, thus raising rent, but, on the contrary, it was the "artificial" creation of rent that pushed labor to the marginal lands.[32] This artificiality of rent, Ingalls complained, was created by the landlords' arbitrary demands caused by "exclusive land ownership," and *not* by some mathematical difference or some "mysterious power" that created value "independent of labor." Rent, as he defined it, was an "immoral tax," paid as tribute to landlords, and was synonymous with interest, profit, usury, and tax. Landlords could draw "fabulous wages" without regard to any (nonexistent) economic law.[33]

George's statements that rent did "not arise spontaneously from land," and was "due to nothing that the landowners have done," being only "the price of monopoly,"[34] sparked off another controversy. The anarchists claimed that they were bewildered by George's "dual" definitions of rent. Did he not say, they questioned, that rent was a "difference" or an "excess"? (That it was, they violently denied.) Did he not now say, they inquired, that rent was "the price of monopoly"? (That it was, they heartily accepted.) What *did* George mean?

The anarchists seemed unable to comprehend George's view: that rent actually *was* a "difference," but that monopoly of land placed this "difference" in monopolists' hands.

Hanson defined rent as the "cause" of "profit," which in turn was the "cause" of "interest." All of these (rent, profit, interest) came into being because of the existence of state-enforced land monopoly. Like Ingalls, Hanson believed that rent was an "immoral tax." If the protective power of the state were taken away, the landlords would not be able to enforce the collection of rent. The so-called law of rent was a myth.[35]

Tucker's criticism of George's concept of rent seems ironic, since Tucker actually believed in a "dual" concept of rent. He claimed that there was such a thing as "economic rent," which would persist even under "Liberty" (his term for his proposed utopia of the future), but, he stated, such "economic rent" was different from "moneyed rent," his name for arbitrary exaction. Liberty, Tucker rapturously declared, would do away with moneyed rent and other iniquities; and, eventually, *all* rent (including economic rent) would become merely nominal because of genuine competition.[36]

(An evaluation of the anarchists' views of rent will appear at the end of the discussions of "unearned increment" and "land value.")

A term equivalent to the concept *rent* bothered the anarchists even more. Hanson was annoyed by George's use of the term *unearned increment*, which Hanson attributed to John Stuart Mill. George, claimed Hanson, wanted the state to "become the landlord, and then tax the unearned increment and appropriate it as rent paid to the State."[37] Tucker, too, ridiculed George for his acceptance of the term.[38]

What was meant by *unearned increment*?

John Stuart Mill spoke of it as an "increase in land values."[39] "There is," he declared, "a kind of income which constantly tends to increase, without any exertion or sacrifice on the part of the owners." It was this "increased income" or "unearned increment" that he proposed to tax because "it would merely be applying an accession of wealth, created by circumstances, to the benefit of society, instead of allowing it to become an unearned appendage to the riches of a particular class."[40]

Arthur Nichols Young believes that although the idea of taxing the "unearned increment" was favorably discussed by Adam Smith, the earliest thorough consideration of the concept should be credited to James Mill, John Stuart's father.[41] "This continual increase," the elder Mill had written, "arising from the circumstances of the community, and from nothing in which the landholders themselves have any peculiar share does seem a fund peculiarly fitted for the appropriation to the purposes of the State."[42]

Henry George's definition of "unearned increment" was the same as that of the Mills: it was another name, he declared, for rent.[43] "Here is a fund," George pointed out, "which the State may take while leaving to labor and capital their full reward."[44]

Hanson, referring to George, inquired: "Has he not proven that the monopoly of land is the cause of rent? Why then, does he now assume that it is the unearned increment which is the cause of rent?"[45]

(One may point out, in passing, that George never did say that unearned increment was the *cause* of rent. He stated, as was seen, that it *was* rent. The *cause* of rent, for George, was to be found in Ricardo's law.)

There *was* no such thing as "unearned increment," Hanson reiterated. Whatever "excess" there existed in the produce of one land over another, belonged, in a free society, to the producer on the superior land. "The produce of work is the natural recompense of work."[46]

Yet it is interesting to note that a modern writer remarks that historically "landowners themselves accepted the charge of John Stuart Mill and Henry George that rent was an 'unearned increment.' "[47]

Concurrently used with the concepts of *rent* and *unearned increment* was the term *land value*. George commented: "It is this capacity of yielding rent which gives value to land. Until its ownership will confer some advantage, land has no value." He repeated: "The value of land is at the beginning of society nothing, but as society develops by the increase of population and the advance of the arts, it becomes greater and greater. . . .The demand for land fixes its value."[48]

The anarchists, after criticizing George for his "population" remark, responded. "Land value," declared Ingalls, was an "artificial capitalization of the land," not based on "values of utility or service," but on the power to monopolize land. Such value embraced the entire product of labor "minus the necessary amount required to keep the stock of labor supplied."[49] (Shades of Marx's surplus-value theory! Compare that remark with a similar one by Tucker.)[50] It was labor, emphasized Ingalls, that gave value to land, not some imaginary law of rent.[51]

Criticizing George somewhat differently (especially for his single-tax proposal), Hanson emphatically denied the concept of land value altogether. Land was free and had "no value in economics, any more than man has. Land values are purely arbitrary. . . .How then are land values ordained of God for taxation?" They were "flagrant violations of God's natural laws."[52]

In attempting to elucidate the meaning of land value (while justifying the single tax), George emphatically declared that a tax on land values was "the taking by the community of that value which is the creation of the community,"[53] causing Hanson to answer: "As well think of selling lightning by the *ohm*; or air by the cubic foot; or light by the square yard. Because there is a demand for these things have they 'a value which is created by the community as a whole?' "[54]

(Hanson should have lived a century later. He would have been shocked by the "values" of air space and air time.)

It was already seen that Tucker recognized two different kinds of rent. Even though he protested that land had no value, he did concede that under "Liberty," some people would get "superior" and some "inferior" land. Thus there would be differences, and even "favoritism" in land distribution. However, said Tucker, "free" competition would tend to reduce the differences.[55] "Equality," he proclaimed, "if we can get it, but Liberty at any rate!"[56]

Let me now try to summarize and evaluate the arguments dealing with the rent question.

The individualist anarchists attacked the concepts of rent, law of rent, unearned increment, and land value. Yet, even among themselves, they could not agree. There were contentions that only labor gave value to land; that land value was an artificial capitalization; that land value was basically surplus value; that land value was another name for economic rent; and, finally, that there was no such thing as land value altogether. Confusion reigned in anarchist ranks. Even more confusion prevailed when they attempted, without justifiable evidence, to "synonymize" rent with interest, profits, and tax.

However, they all agreed that rent was an arbitrary demand by monopolists, and not some eternal "differential."

The anarchists' rent philosophy appears naive and (if one may pardon the pun) valueless. Glance where one may, rent (land values) exists (and has existed, and will exist). Should this statement appear to be one that merely justifies the status quo, another example may suffice and possibly be more clarifying. The demand for today's oil, for instance, has given fabulous valuation to Arab lands. Once the demand for oil is replaced by a demand for another commodity, the current land value of Saudi Arabia may plunge to zero. It is communal demand and need that give rise to rents (land values). No amount of anarchist denials will disprove the apparent facts of economic history.

By claiming that the producers on superior lands (in a "free society") would be entitled to the "excess" produce as their "wages," the anarchists merely gave another name to the term *rent*. The "producers" would become "land-lords." (The Ricardian law of rent would operate even in anarchist utopias.)

Concerning the anarchist's contention that George's advocacy of Ricardo's law of rent was an extension of Malthusianism, one can only repeat what George had often observed. In an unjust condition of land monopoly, population would be compelled to push the margin to zero. As George once stated: "The phenomena attributed to the pressure of population against subsistence would, under existing conditions, manifest themselves were population to remain stationary."[57]

Ricardo's law of rent appears to be (at least to this writer) as valid as ever.

In any case, to the anarchists the main problem lay in the "strife" between "capital" and "labor." Even if land were freed from monopolistic control, insisted Tucker, it would be useless to the workers without capital.[58]

It is to the discussion of capital and interest, therefore, that one must now turn.

More than for any other economic utterance, George was excoriated by the anarchists for his definitions and stand on capital and interest. Since he recognized capital as a necessary factor of production, and justified interest as a valid return to capital, he was bitterly attacked by his three critics.

To the anarchists capital was a parasite on the body economic. Accepting the socialist view, they both defined and condemned capital as a monopoly or as an inert substance that had no right to be included in any economic partnership. Interest was identified with usury or rent, or merely charged off as robbery.

George had written that "land, labor, and capital" were the factors of production. He termed capital "wealth in course of exchange," explaining that exchange was not only the passing from hand to hand but the fact of reproductive transmutation. He summarized his viewpoint by defining capital as "all wealth used to produce more wealth." That part of the produce "which constituted the return for the use of capital" he called "interest."[59]

The anarchists were angered. There were only *two* factors of production, Ingalls retorted, and capital was not one of them. Capitalists were usurers and enemies of labor; capitalists and landlords were one and the same. The ownership of capital was just as oppressive as that of land. In fact, it was the capitalists who foreclosed on small property holders.[60]

One could answer the last criticism immediately by stating that, in the economic sense, the foreclosers (mortgagees) were the true landlords and the "small property holders" (mortgagers) merely tenants.

Agreeing with Ingalls, Hanson claimed that without the "superintendence of labor," capital was as powerless to produce as "stone." Since capital was but inert matter (Hanson's definition), it was labor alone that was the producer; therefore, it was labor alone that was entitled to the produce.[61]

Capitalism, added Tucker (identifying it with monopoly), abolished the free market, but labor was forced to depend on capital in order to survive.[62]

The anarchists (using *capital*, *capitalist*, and *capitalism* interchangeably) called the capitalist an arch-villain, and denounced him. Their argument was circular.

A capitalist, according to Ingalls, was "one who becomes clothed with legal rights over the land, or over the man, which authorize him to take from the laborer or from the land the fruits of industry to the production of which he has not contributed."[63] A capitalist, to Hanson, was an idler;[64] to Tucker, a usurer.[65]

Being thus defined by the anarchists (sometimes with great inconsistency), the capitalist became a monopolist, a usurer, an idler, a parasite, a landlord, a robot, and a robber. Small wonder then, that, according to George's three critics, the capitalist was entitled to nothing. Imagine their indignation, therefore, when George, propounding his "reproductive modes" theory of interest, not only justified interest as a valid return to capital, but gave it a "life" of its own.

George commenced his presentation by denying that interest was simply "the reward of abstinence." Abstinence in itself produces nothing. Also, if all wealth consisted of but "inert matter," and production were but the "working up" of "this inert matter into different shapes," then "interest would be but the robbery of industry." But all wealth is not inert. "It is true that if I put away money, it will not increase. But, suppose, instead, I put away wine. At the end of a year I will have an increased value, for the wine will have improved in quality." Now, this "increase," although it required "labor to utilize it," is "yet distinct and separable from labor—the active power of nature; the principle of growth, of reproduction, which everywhere characterizes all the forms of that mysterious thing or condition which we call life." "It is this," argued George, "which is the cause of interest, or the increase of capital over that due to labor." Speaking "metaphysically" (as he was accused of doing), George stressed that there were "certain vital currents" in "the everlasting flux of nature" that aided man "in turning matter into. . .wealth." Since wealth is interchangeable, "the power of increase which the reproductive or vital force of nature gives to some species of capital must average with all."[66]

In another book George observed that "the principle that time is a necessary element in all production we must take into account from the very first."[67] "Time," writes Geiger in paraphrasing George's argument, "is also essential in production, for it makes possible taking advantage of the reproductive power of nature. As applied to capital it justifies interest."[68]

George's theory of interest not only antagonized the anarchists but caused disagreement in the Georgist ranks. Some thought that his theory of interest was not so clear as his concept of rent. Others set forth their own theories. Still others felt that since capital was a valid factor of production, it was entitled to a return, and there was no need for any intricate or elaborate explanation (except, possibly, that capital was stored-up labor).[69]

As far as the anarchists were concerned, Ingalls questioned George's presentation of capital and on that account also his consequent theory of interest, and asked whether capital, in its nature, was competent to give increase, or "borrowed" such power from other means. The implication was that only nature—land—was capable of "increase," and therefore, since there *was* an increase (as in wine), the return was not interest but *rent* (and thus unjustified).[70] Ingalls devoted an entire chapter of his book to attack the "time" theory.[71] He felt that labor should get any "increase" in capital production, since labor "initiated" the production process. Savagely tearing into George for justifying interest by saying: "The seed in the ground germinates and grows while the farmer sleeps or plows new fields,"[72] Ingalls contended that "nature everywhere repudiates the crudity, born of capitalistic assumption, that anything can be obtained for nothing. Only at the expense of labor can this be realized."[73]

Obviously agreeing with Ingalls, Hanson stated: "Idleness produces nothing, and is therefore entitled to nothing."[74] Tucker called an "idle man" a "parasite," and assailed the "proposition that the man who for time spent in idleness receives [justifiably] the product of time employed in labor."[75] "The services of time," he added, "are venal only when rendered through human forces; when rendered exclusively through the forces of nature, they are gratuitous."[76] Hanson concluded: "The theory of interest, promulgated by Henry George, . . .is thereby utterly overthrown."[77]

The anarchists, in their turn, proceeded to define interest. Ingalls named it "a fraudulent claim of one party to an exchange, by which a charge is made for the 'flight of time' between the inception and the completion of an exchange."[78]

Tucker called interest usurious, and labeled it "a deduction from the earnings of other men." Tucker also attacked George for the latter's "silly and forced distinction between interest considered as the increase of capital and interest considered as payment for the use of legal tender."[79]

Tucker further criticized George for the latter's "failure" to see that capitalists controlled currency, thus "causing" high interest to exist. His utopia of the future would feature "free money" and "free competition in currency," thereby insuring "both low interest and high wages."[80] To George, on the other hand, the solution of economic problems through regulation of money was only a superficial means toward the solution of the ills of society. Admitting that money was "conveniently important," he warned that it was easy to "over-estimate that importance and to forget that men lived and advanced before money was developed." In any case, true interest was not derived from any monetary manipulation, and capital was not to be confused with money.[81]

Hanson contended that rent, profit, and interest were all "caused" by land monopoly, and would vanish once it were removed.[82] He concluded: "But as no moral reason can possibly be adduced why interest should be paid, it logically follows that interest is *robbery*."[83]

As if in anticipation, George had already explained: "The belief that interest is the robbery of industry is. . .in large part due to a failure to discriminate between what is really capital and what is not, and between profits which are properly interest and profits which arise from other sources than the use of capital." He devoted almost three pages to demonstrate that the term *profit* had no meaning in economics, and was used interchangeably and confusedly with interest, wages of superintendence, and insurance.[84]

Before a summary and critique of the capital-interest controversy are attempted, the reader must be made aware of one more topic (related both to the rent and the interest problems) that agitated the anarchists. They criticized George for his "equilibrium" presentation: namely, that interest and wages were naturally "related"; that both represented "equal returns to equal exertions"; that both varied directly with each other and inversely with rent; that both rose as rent fell, and that both fell as rent rose.[85]

Ingalls, especially, reproached George for the latter's "inability" to see that interest and wages varied inversely.[86]

Commenting on the fact that George's equilibrium theory, when tied to the Ricardo theory of rent "caused bitter criticism" in economic circles, a prominent Georgist wrote that "much of this criticism has slighted the significance. . .of George's synthesis of the laws of distribution," noting that the "synthesis" prompted John Bates Clark (as the latter readily admitted) to develop his influential views on diminishing returns and marginal productivity.[87]

To the writer of this chapter, George's equilibrium observations appear quite valid. In hard times wages and interest fall, men lose their jobs, and businesses fail. In good times both interest and wages rise. In the long run rent always rises.

Capital and labor ride up and down the same elevator, kicking each other in the shins. The question is: *Should* they?

Invisibly behind the apparent contestants stands the land monopolist, controlling the elevator ride.

The basic reason for the controversy between George and the anarchists is the failure to agree on definitions. Since capital, according to the anarchists, included all forms of oppression, it was almost an impossible task for George to make the anarchists really *understand* that the source of social inequity lay in land monopoly—even though Hanson, as we have seen, had said it did.

To George, nothing could have been more simple than the theory, which he set forth with great clarity, that both capital and labor (partners in production) were victimized by the inability to utilize land for production. This was owing not so much to the fact that landowners controlled land privately (George was basically an individualist who strove for each person's right to control his share of the universe) as to the fact that land monopoly *prohibited* labor *and* capital from using natural resources to produce goods and services.

The word *capitalist* has so deeply seeped into the unconscious layer of public awareness that most people today probably think of the capitalist as a sinister being of incalculable wealth whose power over human destiny is autocratic and well-nigh infinite.

On the other hand, nothing supports George's justification of capital and interest more than the obvious operations of lending and borrowing. Who would lend to a stranger any part of one's wealth, or who would borrow, knowing that he would have to repay the loan with interest, unless the two parties were aware that a benefit would accrue to *both* from the transaction? From where would interest come? Is there not an "increase" somewhere? Interest is not a subtraction, as Tucker claimed; it is an addition. The anarchists were poor mathematicians.

Harry Gunnison Brown once stated (and the writer of this chapter very much agrees): "There is no intention, here, of expressing the slightest sympathy with the socialist notion that interest on capital. . .is an unearned income or the gain of exploitation. . . .The person who works and saves and who thus is instrumental in bringing capital into existence, does more to increase the output of industry than does the person who works with equal efficiency but does not save. If, doing more for production, he receives a larger part of what production yields, this does not rob anyone else. The socialist view that interest is an illegitimate income cannot be endorsed."[88]

Another topic that occupied the attention of George and the anarchists pertained to copyrights and patents. Originally, George argued that the "temporary monopolies created by the patent and copyright law," since they were "recognitions of the right of labor to its intangible productions," would be "unjust and unwise to tax." They were "necessary" monopolies, and should be left alone.[89]

Ingalls attacked such "exclusive right in invention,"[90] and Hanson claimed that patents and copyrights contravened "the Law of Nature which has ordained that the utility of all products. . .shall be had without price." Invention could be measured only by work. Patents and copyrights were "robbery."[91]

In 1888 George, acknowledging that he had made a partial mistake, now felt that a patent was "in defiance" of man's "natural right." "Discovery," he wrote, "can give no right of ownership, for whatever is discovered must have been already here to be discovered."[92] A copyright, on the other hand, was a right "to the labor expended in the thing itself," and was "morally" right.[93]

Tucker sardonically attacked this distinction, contending that neither copyrights nor patents should exist. "The same argument that demolishes the right of the inventor," Tucker emphasized, "demolishes the right of the author."[94]

As usual, the controversy that had begun a century ago still continues. The argument rages in Georgist ranks as well. This author, as editor of a magazine, has specifically forsworn the principle of copyright in the masthead of his publication. To each his own!

The most important "debate" revolved around George's proposed "sovereign remedy." The anarchists were horrified when they read George's words: "To extirpate poverty, to make wages what justice commands they should be. . .*we must make land common property*."[95] George proposed to accomplish this "remedy" by utilizing the method of the "single tax." There are indications that George was not too pleased with the name,[96] but he himself had written that "the advantages which would be gained by substituting for the numerous taxes by which the public revenues are now raised, a single tax levied upon the value of the land, will appear more and more important the more they are considered."[97]

Ingalls was indignant. To him George's remedy smacked of state socialism. It was merely another "land nationalization" scheme, he cried, "minus the fixity of tenure, and limitation by 'occupying ownership.' " The single tax to him was just a tax: a supertax. "The power to enforce taxation is the power to take the earnings of labor and make such return as it pleases, or none at all." Furthermore, he claimed, the single tax would not work.[98]

To Hanson the single-tax idea was abhorrent. "If an individual can not have property in land," he questioned, "how can the community or the State?" Since there was no land value, "Mr. George's grand panacea," the single tax, would fall on the poor: "on my neighbor's potatoes." And since there was no "unearned increment," he concluded (somewhat contradictorily), "the State will have nothing to appropriate."[99]

George's plan would bring land nationalization, Tucker exclaimed, that would cause "a concentration and hundred-fold multiplication of the landlord's power."[100] To Tucker the municipality to which people had to pay "tribute" was "not a bit more defensible than the State itself,—in fact, is nothing but a small State."[101]

Tucker, seeing in the single tax nothing but "robbery," characterized the single taxers as future "inquisitors." He preferred, he said, "if I must be robbed. . .to be robbed by the landowner, who is likely to spend it in some useful way, rather than by an institution called government, which will probably spend it for fireworks or something else which I equally disapprove."[102]

The anarchists never understood George's plan. The abolition of all taxes on production and exchange, he stated, would result in a tremendous spurt of economic activity. The placing of the one tax on land values would likewise result in an economic upsurge. It would do away with land withholding and speculation. Thus production would be aided in two different ways.

George did not favor the term *nationalization of land* as the name for his proposed remedy. His leaning was toward individualism. "In form," he declared, speaking of his plan, "the ownership of land would remain just as now."[103]

"It must be stated at this point, clearly and emphatically," writes Geiger, "that George's 'common property' in land did not mean common ownership in land. That is to say, George was in no sense a land nationalist and did not suggest. . .that land was to be owned by the State, or that it should be held in joint ownership by the citizens. . . .All such concepts were distinctly repudiated by him."[104]

In a later book George made his meaning quite clear: "To make a redivision every year, or to treat land as a common, where no one could claim the exclusive use of any particular piece, would be practicable only where men lived in movable tents and made no permanent improvements, and would effectually prevent any advance beyond such a state. No one would sow a crop, or build a house. . .so long as any one else could come in and turn him out of the land in which or on which such improvements must be fixed. Thus it is absolutely necessary to the proper use and improvement of land that society should secure to the user and improver safe possession."[105]

In actuality George regarded the state with the same suspicion as did the anarchists.. "The more complex and extravagant government becomes.," he wrote, "the more it gets to be a power distinct from and independent of the people."[106]

His "remedy" did not imply government aggrandizement. It was merely a method to open up land and opportunities for all. George was attacked because his critics did not understand him. "I myself am classed as a socialist by those who denounce socialism, while those who profess themselves socialists declare me not to be one."[107]

His own mind was crystal clear.

To the individualist anarchists, the most unanswerable criticism of the single tax was that the tax would simply be shifted to the backs of the poor.

"The successful capitalist would then, as now," asserted Ingalls, "be able to shift the tax to shoulders of toil, plus the profits upon the capital necessary to meet his dues to the government."[108]

"The merchant, tradesman, or manufacturer," declared Hanson, "who is obliged to pay rent for the use of land, will necessarily put the rent, or distribute it in the price of merchandise he sells."[109]

"When I reflect that under a Single-Tax system," mused Tucker, "the occupants of superior land are likely to become the politicians and to tax back from the people. . .what the people have taxed out of them as economic rent. . .I prefer to leave it in the pocket of the landowner."[110]

"A tax on rent," John Stuart Mill had once written, "falls wholly on the landlord. There are no means by which he can shift the burden upon any one else. It does not affect the value or price of agricultural produce."[111]

The anarchists paid no heed to Mill's utterance. Their persistent complaints caused George to write an editorial, subsequently reprinted as a booklet. After cautioning the reader not to confuse a tax on land with a tax on land values (or rent), George added that it "was conceded by all ecnomists of reputation" that the tax on rent could not be shifted. "Rent," he pointed out, "is the highest price that anyone will give. . . .Now, if a tax be levied on that rent or value, this in no wise adds. . .to the ability of the owner to demand more. To suppose. . .that such a tax could be thrown by landowners upon tenants is to suppose that the owners of land do not now get for the land all it will bring; is to suppose that, whenever they want to, they can up the prices as they please. This is. . .absurd."[112]

Even more than when George wrote, the nonshiftability of a tax on land values is regarded by professional economists as virtually beyond dispute.[113] To George's critics, however, he indulged in "sophistry." To them, the most important "remedy" was "occupancy and use." That will be the next topic of discussion.

The only way to establish justice, Ingalls claimed, was to abolish land ownership, repeal all laws that protect it, encourage true education, and distribute land according to the principle of "occupancy and use." As much land as was necessary for each person, that is how much land each person would get. How would this be accomplished? He explained: "I find nature. . .gives or parts with no thing. . . .Her invariable price for its use is the labor necessary to avail oneself of its benefits. She [neither] exacts nor permits rent, interest, or taxation, but repudiates them wholly. . . ."[114]

"Nature," as thus personified and deified, was a creation of Ingalls. There would be no state to supervise any division or occupancy. Education would accomplish this, just as education brings about cooperation necessary to build bridges. Ingalls attacked George and his followers because they were "ignorant" of "the law of use" and, instead, relied upon the mandatory appropriation of land values by society through government. Like George, Ingalls believed in natural rights but he repudiated the use of organized physical force in their protection.

Similar to Ingalls's approach to "occupancy and use" was that of Hanson. He felt that the state would "wither away" once true education prevailed. "Ignorance is the bane of mankind. And the rich are as ignorant as the poor in their relation to these vital questions." His plan envisioned a utopia where rents and interest would tumble to zero; land would be chosen by lots; and the state would have nothing to tax, especially since there would be no state and no tax. "There should be a voluntary relinquishment for the public weal of land monopolized for speculative ends. . . .This should be done as a social and religious duty, just as one should voluntarily refrain from highway robbery, stealing, perjury or murder. Landlords should also voluntarily cease taking unrighteous rent." "Occupancy and use" would not guarantee equality, but inequality of production would teach thrift, management, and better production.[115] Hanson, like George and Ingalls, believed in natural law and natural rights.

Both Ingalls and Hanson might be labeled "visionaries," since both believed in accomplishment through education only. There could be no solution, they claimed, until the mind first grasped the necessary idea. Yet they did not fully understand George's ideas; and he, in turn, could not argue with people so trustingly childlike in their faith in human nature.

A more cynical approach was taken by Tucker, who summarily pronounced: "All economic reforms, including the Single Tax, are a delusion and a snare."[116]

Most of the individualist anarchists, including Ingalls, Hanson, and Tucker, followed the "occupancy and use" formula of Josiah Warren, which was in turn based on the views of the New York land reformer of the 1820s, George Henry Evans.[117] The anarchists' vagueness in attempting to define *occupancy and use* was best exemplified in the correspondence between Tucker and Stephen Byington (who subsequently became a "disciple" of Tucker's). Byington wanted to know what would happen to occupiers of land or buildings when they would be away from their premises for a period of time. Tucker, reducing his answer to an absurdity, replied that the very last user and occupier would not only lose his land but his personal property as well.[118]

Trying to explain to Byington (in still another controversy) what *occupancy and use* meant, Tucker wrote: "Occupancy and use is the only title to the land in which we will protect you; if you attempt to use land which another is occupying and using, we will protect him against you; if another attempts to use land to which you lay claim, but which you are not occupying and using, we will not interfere with him; but of such land as you occupy and use you are the sole master, and we will not ourselves take from you, or allow any one else to take from you, whatever you may get out of such land."[119]

The "we" sounds ironic, coming as it does from an antistatist!

Concerning the single tax, Tucker may have deliberately distorted its meaning. That is what Henry George would say to a prospective land occupier, Tucker told Byington. "You may hold all the land you have inherited or bought. . .and we will protect you in such holding; but, if you produce more from your land than your neighbors produce from theirs, we will take from you the excess of your product over theirs and distribute it among them. . .or we will make any use of it, wise or foolish, that may come into our heads."[120]

Deliberate or not, it was not only a cruel distortion of George's meaning, but it turned an individualistic proposal to spur production into a socialistic deterrent!

In one more important respect did Tucker and George differ. Starting off as a believer in natural rights, Tucker subsequently embraced the egoistic philosophy of Max Stirner. This in turn led to utilitarianism and opportunism,[121] as well as to pronouncements that smacked more of nihilism (such as a mother's right to throw her baby into a fire[122]) than of libertarian individualism. The man who had once chanted ecstatically that "the first of all equities is not equality of material well-being, but equality of Liberty"[123] later declared: "In times past. . .it was my habit to talk glibly of the right of man to land. It was a bad habit, and I long ago sloughed it off. . . .Man's only right over the land is his might over it."[124]

Tucker's utterance about "rights" should be compared with the one made by George when he said: "There can be to the ownership of anything no rightful title which is not derived from the title of the producer and does not rest upon the natural right of the man to himself."[125]

I cast my vote for Henry George.

The time has come to summarize the respective philosophies of George and his three critics. The following "table" may be helpful:

HENRY GEORGE	INDIVIDUALIST ANARCHISTS
1. Capital, a specialized form of labor ("stored up labor"), is one of the three factors of production. Only two of the three factors are entitled to shares in the produce: labor and capital.	1. Capital is a parasite feeding on the produce of labor on land. Only one of the two factors of production is entitled to a share in the produce: labor.
2. Interest is justified, as explained by the "reproductive modes" theory, but also by the concept of capital as "stored-up labor."	2. Interest is never justified. It is robbery.
3. Private appropriation of land is the great iniquity. Land monopolists prey on labor and capital.	3. Capitalism is the great evil preying on labor. Landlordism is but a species of capitalism.
4. Rent is payment made to landowners because of the relative value of monopolized land. However, even under the "sovereign remedy," rent will continue to exist, but will be paid to the community as a premium for the privilege of exclusive possession.	4. Rent, as payment to any landlord, private or public, is always robbery. In a free commonwealth, according to Ingalls and Hanson, all rent will be abolished. According to Tucker, only "economic" rent will remain.
5. Under the "sovereign remedy," land will become common property (but not socialized).	5. Under "Liberty," land will become private property (but not monopolistic property).
6. Private property in land will assume a different form. Rent (except for a small "brokerage fee") will be paid to the community.	6. Private property in land will exist and be practiced, within the limits prescribed by the "occupancy and use" formula.
7. Government will be utilized as the arm of the community for the purpose of some services and the collection of rent. Monopoly landlordism will be abolished.	7. The state will be abolished and so will capitalism and landlordism. Community and society, as used by Henry George, are vague and ambiguous terms.
8. Patents, as long-range monopolies, will be ended. Copyrights will remain.	8. Both patents and copyrights will be abolished.
9. Private enterprise will exist, with labor and capital free to pursue their own aims because land will become more readily available to those who wish to use it. There will be no equality, in the socialistic sense, only liberty.	9. Free land will exist, with labor free to pursue its own aims. An attempt will be made toward equality. Liberty, however, will be the prime goal.

Notes

1. George Woodcock, *Anarchism: A History of Libertarian Ideas and Movements* (New York: The World Publishing Co., 1962), p. 453.

2. Joshua K. Ingalls, *Social Wealth: The Sole Factors and Exact Ratios in Its Acquirement and Apportionment* (New York: Social Science Publishing Co., 1885).

3. For a summary of his life and ideas, see (besides *Social Wealth*) Joshua K. Ingalls, *Reminiscences of an Octogenarian in the Fields of Industrial and Social Reform* (New York: M. L. Holbrook, 1897). See also James J. Martin, *Men Against the State: The Expositors of Individualist Anarchism in America, 1827-1908* (DeKalb, Ill., 1953), pp. 142-52. For a comment that labeled Ingalls a "disciple" of Josiah Warren, see Corinne Jacker, *The Black Flag of Anarchy: Antistatism in the United States* (New York: Charles Scribner's Sons, 1968), p. 63.

4. The complete reference title is: William Hanson, *The Fallacies in "Progress and Poverty," in Henry Dunning Macleod's Economics, and "Social Problems," with the Ethics of Protection and Free Trade and The Industrial Problem Considered a-Priori* (New York: Fowler and Wells Co., 1884).

5. For scattered comments about him, see Martin, *Men Against the State*, pp. 225, 267, and 286. On p. 246 Martin called Hanson "next to Ingalls the most competent of anarchist critics of Henry George."

6. Jacker, *Black Flag of Anarchy*, p. 120; Charles A. Madison, *Critics & Crusaders: A Century of American Protest* (New York: Henry Holt and Co., 1947), pp. 194-95.

7. Johanna Johnston, *Mrs. Satan: The Incredible Saga of Victoria C. Woodhull* (New York: G. P. Putnam's Sons, 1967) various pages; Jacker, *Black Flag of Anarchy*, pp. 121-22; Madison *Critics & Crusaders*, p. 195; Martin, *Men Against the State*, p. 223.

8. Benjamin R. Tucker, *Instead of a Book By a Man Too Busy to Write One* (1897; reprint ed. New York: Gordon Press, 1972).

9. Benjamin R. Tucker, *Individual Liberty* (New York: Vanguard Press, 1926). (It was edited by "C.L.S."—Clarence Lee Swartz.)

10. Atindranath Bose, *A History of Anarchism* (Calcutta: The World Press Private Ltd., 1967), p. 380.

11. Madison, *Critics & Crusaders*, p. 204.

12. Eunice M. Schuster, *Native American Anarchism*, quoted in Madison, pp. 197-98.

13. Madison, *Critics & Crusaders*, pp. 211-12.

14. Benjamin R. Tucker, *Henry George, Traitor* (New York: Benjamin R. Tucker, writer and publisher, 1896).

15. Ibid., pp. 1-16; see also Madison, *Critics & Crusaders*, p. 209; Martin *Men Against the State*, p. 221; Charles Albro Barker, *Henry George* (New York: Oxford University Press, 1955), pp. 503-6; Henry David, *The History of the Haymarket Affair* (1936; reprint ed., New York: Russell & Russell, 1958), pp. 400-3; Henry George, Jr., *The Life of Henry George* (1900; reprint ed. New York: Robert Schalkenbach Foundation, 1960), p. 498 n., and pp. 501-2 n.

16. Bose, *History of Anarchism*, p. 382; Jacker, *Black Flag of Anarchy*, p. 124; Martin, *Men Against the State*, p. 212.

17. Bose, *History of Anarchism*, pp. 383, 387, 382.

18. Ibid., pp. 388-89.

19. Madison, *Critics & Crusaders*, p. 205; Martin, *Men Against the State*, p. 220.

20. Bose, *History of Anarchism*, p. 389. For a thorough discussion of the biography and thought of Tucker, the reader is directed, in addition to his three texts here mentioned, to idem, pp. 378-90; Madison, *Critics & Crusaders*, pp. 194-213; Martin, *Men Against the State*, pp. 202-73; Jacker, *Black Flag of Anarchy*, pp. 117-27; Woodcock, *Anarchism*, pp. 459-60; Johnston, *Mrs. Satan*, pp. 185, 207-16, 265, 269-70; Carl Watner, "Benjamin Tucker and His Periodical, *Liberty*," *Journal of Libertarian Studies* (Fall 1977), pp. 307-18.

21. Henry George, *Progress and Poverty*, 75th anniversary ed. (New York: Robert Schalkenbach Foundation, 1954).

22. Ibid., pp. 336-46, 328, 370.

Ingalls, Hanson, and Tucker: Nineteenth-Century American Anarchists 251

23. Ingalls, *Social Wealth*, pp. 31, 68.
24. David Ricardo, *The Principles of Political Economy and Taxation* (London; 1817), chap. 2.
25. George, *Progress and Poverty*, p. 166.
26. Ricardo, *Principles*, chap. 32.
27. George, *Progress and Poverty*, p. 168; italics original.
28. Ricardo, *Principles*, chap. 32.
29. George, *Progress and Poverty*, pp. 230-31.
30. Ibid., pp. 234, 243.
31. Ibid., p. 242.
32. Ingalls, *Social Wealth*, p. 69.
33. Ibid., pp. 68-9, 316, 71. For further criticisms of George's views of rent, see Ingalls's *Reminiscences*. He devoted the entire chap. 12, written in dialogue form, to "expose" George's rent concept.
34. George, *Progress and Poverty*, pp. 421, 167.
35. Hanson, *Fallacies*, pp. 76, 77, 92, 97, 99, 100, 36.
36. Tucker, *Instead of a Book*, pp. 343-48; Tucker, *Individual Liberty*, pp. 190-91.
37. Hanson, *Fallacies*, p. 88.
38. Tucker, *Individual Liberty*, pp. 238-39.
39. George Raymond Geiger, *The Philosophy of Henry George* (New York: Macmillan, 1933), p. 203; Edmund Whittaker, *A History of Economic Ideas* (New York: Longmans, Green and Co., 1940), p. 231.
40. John Stuart Mill, *Principles of Political Economy, with Some of Their Applications to Social Philosophy* (London, 1848), bk. 5, chap. 2, sec. 5.
41. Arthur Nichols Young, *The Single Tax Movement in the United States* (Princeton University Press, 1916), p. 22
42. James Mill, *Elements of Political Economy* (London: 1826), chap. 4, sec. 5.
43. Henry George, *The Science of Political Economy* (1897; reprint ed. New York: Robert Schalkenbach Foundation, 1968), pp. 150-51.
44. George, *Progress and Poverty*, p. 436.
45. Hanson, *Fallacies*, pp. 88-89.
46. Ibid.
47. Spencer H. MacCallum, *The Art of Community* (Menlo Park, Calif: Institute for Humane Studies, 1970), p. 100.
48. George, *Progress and Poverty*, pp. 166, 406, 437.
49. Ingalls, *Social Wealth*, pp. 253, 282.
50. Tucker, *Individual Liberty*, pp. 87-88.
51. Ingalls, *Social Wealth*, pp. 73-75.
52. Hanson, *Fallacies*, pp. 108-10, 99.
53. George, *Progress and Poverty*, pp. 421, 365.
54. Hanson, *Fallacies*, p. 110.
55. For a prolonged discussion of the subject, see Tucker, *Instead of a Book*, pp. 343-48; idem, *Individual Liberty*, pp. 181, 191, 197, 217, 239; Martin, *Men Against the State*, pp. 220-21.
56. Tucker, *Individual Liberty*, p. 217.
57. George, *Progress and Poverty*, p. 231.
58. Tucker, *Individual Liberty*, pp. 197, 239.
59. George, *Progress and Poverty*, pp. 48, 162.
60. Ingalls, *Social Wealth*, pp. 191, 105, 172, 165, 57, 285.
61. Hanson, *Fallacies*, pp. 79-80.
62. Tucker, *Instead of a Book*, p. 202.
63. Ingalls, *Social Wealth*, pp. 313, 14.
64. Hanson, *Fallacies*, p. 166.
65. Tucker, *Instead of a Book*, p. 275.
66. George, *Progress and Poverty*, pp. 176, 180-82.

67. George, *Science of Political Economy*, p. 370.
68. Geiger, *Philosophy of Henry George*, p. 116, n. 44.
69. For a thorough discussion of the theory of interest among Georgists, see ibid., pp. 114-19; Gaston Haxo, *The Philosophy of Freedom* (New York: Land and Freedom, 1941), p. 63 n.; Max Hirsch, *Democracy Versus Socialism*, 4th ed. (New York: Robert Schalkenbach Foundation, 1966), p. 143; Harry Gunnison Brown, *The Economic Basis of Tax Reform* (Columbia, Mo.: Lucas Brothers, 1932), pp. 103-4.
70. Ingalls, *Social Wealth*, p. 168.
71. Ibid., chap. 5.
72. George, *Progress and Poverty*, p. 184.
73. Ingalls, *Social Wealth*, pp. 66-67.
74. Hanson, *Fallacies*, p. 165.
75. Tucker, *Instead of a Book*, pp. 208, 202.
76. Ibid., p. 204.
77. Hanson, *Fallacies*, p. 166.
78. Ingalls, *Social Wealth*, p. 315.
79. Tucker, *Instead of a Book*, pp. 202, 208.
80. Tucker, *Individual Liberty*, pp. 190-91.
81. George, *Science of Political Economy*, pp. 505-6.
82. Hanson, *Fallacies*, pp. 75-77.
83. Ibid., p. 79; italics original.
84. George, *Progress and Poverty*, pp. 156-58.
85. Ibid., pp. 199, 203.
86. Ingalls, *Social Wealth*, pp. 191, 61.
87. Geiger, *Philosophy of Henry George*, pp. 118-19.
88. Brown, *Economic Basis of Tax Reform*, pp. 103-4.
89. George, *Progress and Poverty*, pp. 410-11.
90. Ingalls, *Social Wealth*, p. 85.
91. Hanson, *Fallacies*, p. 163.
92. George, *Progress and Poverty*, p. 411 n.
93. George, Jr., *Life of Henry George*, p. 593 n.
94. Tucker, *Individual Liberty*, pp. 287-88.
95. George, *Progress and Poverty*, p. 328; italics original.
96. George, Jr., *Life of Henry George*, p. 496 n.; Young, *Single Tax Movement*, pp. 109-11; Geiger, *Philosophy of Henry George*, pp. 43-44 n.; and Barker, *Henry George*, pp. 519-20.
97. George, *Progress and Poverty*, p. 433.
98. Ingalls, *Social Wealth*, pp. 258, 261-64, 281-83.
99. Hanson, *Fallacies*, pp. 86, 90, 95.
100. Tucker, *Instead of a Book*, p. 300.
101. Ibid., p. 306; idem, *Individual Liberty*, pp. 185-86.
102. Tucker, *Individual Liberty*, pp. 232, 238, 188-89.
103. George, *Progress and Poverty*, p. 406.
104. Geiger, *Philosophy of Henry George*, p. 130.
105. Henry George, *Protection or Free Trade*, (1886; reprint ed. New York: Robert Schalkenbach Foundation, 1962), p. 279.
106. George, *Progress and Poverty*, p. 303.
107. George, *Protection or Free Trade*, pp. 302-3 n.
108. Ingalls, *Social Wealth*, p. 282.
109. Hanson, *Fallacies*, p. 75.
110. Tucker, *Individual Liberty*, p. 189.
111. J. S. Mill, *Principles of Political Economy*, bk. 5, chap. 3, sec. 2.
112. Henry George, *Why the Landowner Cannot Shift the Tax on Land Values* (New York: Robert Schalkenbach Foundation, n.d.).

113. See Brown, *Economic Basis of Tax Reform*, pp. 57-60, 155-56; Whittaker, *History of Economic Ideas*, pp. 236-37; Geiger, *Philosophy of Henry George*, p. 154.

114. Ingalls, *Social Wealth*, pp. 287, 186, 261.

115. Hanson, *Fallacies*, pp. 92, 141-42, 93-94, 110-11, 138.

116. Tucker, *Individual Liberty*, p. 221.

117. Martin, *Men Against the State*, pp. 27, 142.

118. Watner, "Benjamin Tucker and His Periodical," p. 315.

119. Tucker, *Instead of a Book*, p. 351.

120. Ibid.

121. Martin, *Men Against the State*, pp. 237-50.

122. Watner, "Benjamin Tucker and His Periodical," p. 312.

123. Tucker, *Individual Liberty*, p. 207.

124. Tucker, *Instead of a Book*, p. 350.

125. George, *Progress and Poverty*, p. 335.

17

Atkinson: An Ill-Informed Assailant*

BY WILLIAM B. TRUEHART

Edward Atkinson, Boston laissez-faire liberal of the nineteenth century, delivered what he believed was a staggering blow to Henry George's single-tax theory in an exchange with George in the *Century Magazine* in 1890.[1]

Atkinson (1827-1905) shared *some* concepts and ideals with George, including limited government, free trade (or at least low tariffs, for revenue only), and a genuine nineteenth-century liberal optimism that reform is possible, resulting in making the world a much better place in which to live.[2] Besides delving into economics and politics, Atkinson was engaged in the cotton and fire insurance businesses, and was an avid inventor.

Atkinson held, and tried to show, that the single tax, even if it could be applied, would not abolish poverty, and would so disrupt the economy of the nation that very probably chaos would result. He used statistics—Gross National Product and taxes—to try to support his arguments. I shall deal with his arguments one at a time.

Using the United States Census of 1880, Atkinson estimated the Gross National Product of the U. S. to be $10 billion, or $200 per capita—which averaged $600 per person gainfully employed. He broke this down to equal 55 cents per capita per day. He estimated total taxes, national, state, and local, to be seven percent of the Gross National Product, or $700,000,000 per year, or $14 per capita, which equaled four cents per day per capita.[3] He estimated that about twenty percent, or $140,000,000, was raised from taxes on land values. From this he deduced that if taxes on land were to substitute for all government revenue, the land-tax rate would have to be increased fivefold. He said:

> It might happen that the burden would become too great to be undertaken, except by persons who already possess ample capital from which they could advance the taxes. . . .
> Could the poor farmer, the mechanic, or the artisan of moderate means, or in fact could anyone who did not possess ample capital, afford to accept

---

*The reader will be well rewarded by examining another critique (or refutation) of Atkinson's arguments against the single tax, in Max Hirsch's *Democracy Versus Socialism,* 4th ed. (New York: Robert Schalkenbach Foundation, 1948), pp. 414-25.

the conditional possession of land under such terms? Each one who now occupies land can answer this question for himself by multiplying the present tax upon his land by five or at least by four.[4]

Atkinson apparently ignored two important things. One is the fact that people of low or moderate means rent homes or shops, and as a result pay the full market rental-value of the land sites involved. Substituting a single tax on land values for all other taxes would not result in taxes any greater than the rental value of land. In fact, George suggested that the tax be slightly less. The second point is that the abolition of all other taxes, including all indirect taxes as well as taxes on improvements, would in most cases amount to more than the increase in land taxes on persons of low or moderate means. One reason is that such individuals cannot afford to own valuable land, whereas their improvements are often worth several times the value of the underlying land. I shall have more to say about the burden of indirect taxes below.

Atkinson made a statement that shows a total ignorance of the incidence of taxation. He said:

Does it follow that if the whole tax of the country were assessed in a single tax imposed in the first instance upon land, this would be but an indirect method of deriving the whole tax from all products of labor and capital combined, without discrimination? If so, this would be but an indiscriminating mode of taxing all consumption.[5]

Henry George himself answered this point in the same issue of the magazine, and quoted John Stuart Mill (*Principles of Political Economy*, bk. 5, chap. 3, sec. 3) to the efect that taxes on land rent fall wholly on the landowner. Mill said: "A tax on rent falls wholly on the landlord. There are no means by which he can shift the burden to anyone else."[6] Of course, if he leases the land to someone else, that other person ultimately pays the tax, for it comes out of his rent, but his rent cannot be increased to accommodate the tax and still give the landlord the same net return.

This point can best be made in the context of modern economic theory. Tax shifting can occur, other things being equal, if the supply elasticity is very great. But since the elasticity of supply of land is essentially zero (supply is strictly limited), there is nothing in an increased tax on land that can decrease the supply of land. Neither will it increase the demand. Consequently, the equilibrium rent before the tax is the equilibrium after the tax is increased, and there is no way the landowner can pass it on. It stays squarely where it is placed. George himself recognized this principle.[7]

Atkinson went on to say (p. 387) that the land tax has to come out of the "joint produce of land, labor, and capital, by due process of law, from the people who do the actual work by which men subsist." In this he inferred that the earnings of labor and capital are reduced, as a result.

He ignored the economic facts of distribution. The rates of wages, interest, and rent (rewards respectively for labor, capital, and land) are determined by market forces. The active factors of production (capital and labor—including, if you wish, entrepreneurship) must already pay the market-set rent to private landowners, whether annually or in a capitalized (selling price) form. If government takes part or all of this rent in taxation, it would in no wise decrease the rewards of the active factors (land is the passive factor, being acted upon). If an individual or firm owns land, it changes nothing, since part of the income is implicit rent, and should be so distinguished. Taxing owner-used land takes nothing from the earnings of either labor or capital.

Atkinson did admit that indirect taxes are largely regressive, and that eliminating them would increase effective disposable income. He said:

> To the extent to which the necessary cost of living is increased while wages are reduced by these taxes, they are without question a cause of poverty. To the extent to which [they] may be removed poverty may be alleviated; but that is all. This is something very different from the extravagant expectations of the Antipoverty societies that advocate the single tax on land valuation as a panacea for all poverty.[8]

George answered this by pointing out that taxes pyramid as they go from one stage of production to another, with each firm or entrepreneur adding a markup. He cited the case of the whisky ring that "spent money like water" to oppose the reduction of the whisky tax, and the cigar maufacturers "working like beavers" to prevent the repeal of the cigar tax. George estimated conservatively that such profits on indirect taxes amounted to *at least* as much as the taxes themselves, and so made the burden of indirect taxation twice as great. Speaking of their regressive nature, he said: "Considering that indirect taxes fall with greatest weight on the poorest of our people, this direct saving ought to be quite an alleviation of poverty."[9]

Another scholar of the period, Thomas G. Shearman, estimated, partly with the aid of data previously compiled by Atkinson, that indirect taxes amounted to about twenty-five percent of national income, over a twenty-five year period, including the pyramiding mentioned above. And, assuming that such taxes reduce savings by this much, he estimated that they represent seventy-five percent of the savings of the masses of the people, as against only three percent of that of a few multimillionaires.[10]

Atkinson asserted, quite correctly, that land, labor, and capital are the three factors of production. He said, however:

> Is it not. . .manifest that it may be injudicious to put the whole burden of taxation in the first instance upon only one of the three necessary factors of production? Why not put part of it on the other two factors? Why not tax, at least in part, the result or income—i.e., the product which has been derived from land by the application of labor and capital to its use and occupancy—when such product is in the process of consumption rather than to tax the source of all production at the point where such taxes may prove to be the greatest obstruction to an abundant result?[11]

This statement shows practically no knowledge of tax incidence and effects. If you tax labor directly, you discourage it or make working people poorer. If you tax capital, you tend to drive it away or discourage its production. And if you tax consumption with indirect taxation, taxes often pyramid, with resultant price increases of a regressive nature.

But if you tax the value, or economic rent of land, the result is complete neutrality in taxation. This is because the land-value tax is in effect a tax on a surplus, and has no effect on marginal cost. What would be the optimal use of given land sites, without any taxes at all, remains the optimal use with the land-value tax. This is the only major source of taxation of which this is true. A tax on buildings or other improvements is definitely nonneutral, and does affect the marginal allocation of resources. It discourages construction, reduces the supply of buildings, and raises rents to consumers. The land-value tax cannot raise rents, as explained above; and, in fact, it may initially lower them by discouraging land speculation and encouraging land sites to be put to their highest and best use. This, coupled with the stimulus to construction resulting from the elimination of the improvement tax, may even result in lower rents.

Atkinson went on to claim that neither land area nor land value bears any proportional relationship to the final product. Then, through his illustrations, he proceeded to ignore land *value*, and concentrated only on land *area*. Since farmers occupy a larger proportional land *area*, he concluded: "If land only is taxed, the farmer must pay the larger part of the tax and recover it from consumers in the best way he can devise. If he cannot recover it, he must stop work."[12]

George himself answered this point quite well in his reply to Atkinson in the same publication by pointing out that it was land *value*, not land area, that he proposed to tax; and that farmers owned relatively lower land *values* compared to urban landholders. This is still true today. It is also true that farmers are burdened, by and large, by mortgages based often on speculative land values, which values would tend to fall, under a land value tax, because of the tax capitalization effect. Further, farmers are also burdened with indirect taxes on practically everything they buy and use. Under land-value taxation farmers could acquire land a great deal more cheaply, and with the elimination of all other taxes would be relieved of the indirect levies they now pay.

As far as their property taxes are concerned, often their taxes on houses, barns, fences, livestock, orchards, vineyards, and the like are today as high as, or higher than would be a land-value tax based on land rent. The great mass of nonowning farmers—tenants and sharecroppers—would be infinitely better off. They already pay rent, which in many cases is higher than the land tax would be, besides all manner of indirect taxes. With the fall in land prices, they could afford in many cases to acquire land of their own.

The next criticism of the single tax advanced by Atkinson concerned the problem of correctly valuing all land within the country at a uniform rate so that all levels of government, including federal, could be funded from the tax. He alleged that land assessments would have to be equalized nationally by a board of assessors. He siad: "At this point, the theory begins to break down by becoming impracticable. Such a national assessment could not be made."[13]

He then went on to say that if the land-tax rate appropriated the entire rental value of land in taxation, the selling price would disappear and it would be difficult, if not impossible, to value land—that such valuation, tax, rent, or whatever it was called, would have to be made arbitrarily by assessors appointed by the national government. The implication was that this would give rise to all manner of favoritism and corruption.[14]

First, it is theoretically true that if one hundred percent of land rent is taken in taxation, the tax will be completely capitalized, and the selling value will fall to zero. George admitted this in what he called the application of his theory to the point of "theoretical perfection." He did say, however, in his answer to Atkinson, that if such point were reached, all that would be necessary would be to adopt the British system of valuing the annual, or rental, value, instead of the selling, or capitalized, value. He said, "With speculative values gone, and with public attention concentrated on one source of revenue, there could be no difficulty with this."[15]

George, however, in *Progress and Poverty*, proposed leaving to landowners a small percentage of rent (somewhat like a real estate broker's commission) for their service in collecting and turning over rent to government. He said: "By leaving to land owners a percentage of rent which would probably be much less than the cost and loss involved in attempting to rent lands through State agency, and by making use of this existing machinery, we may, without jar or shock, assert the common right to land by taking rent for public uses."[16]

If this were done, land would retain a small capitalized, or selling, value, which, even if it were taxed up to one hundred percent, would still fall slightly short of the entire economic rent. And the assessment of such value could be done as easily as—in fact, *more* easily—than is currently the case with combined land and improvement values.

In Australia and New Zealand most municipalities and some higher levels of government tax land values only, and exempt improvements and personalty from property taxes. The rate, however, is not high enough to capture for public use anywhere nearly all of the economic rent. Their assessors, however, vastly prefer to value land only, claiming that it is easier and cheaper than to assess both land and buildings, according to J. Bruce Brown, valuer-general of New Zealand.

> The assessment of the unimproved [land] value only, involves by far the least amount of work, both administratively and in terms of time spent in making each valuation. For one thing, the value of urban land can generally be updated without recourse to regular inspections of the property. In arriving at an assessment of capital or annual value [meaning, respectively, the capital value of both land and improvements, or the rental value of both], however, the position is very different. A great deal more work is involved. . . .The technical content of the valuation process is much more detailed than for land alone.[17]

J. F. N. Murray, prominent assessor and author of a leading textbook on appraising in Australia, said that: (1) equity in valuation is much more easily achieved when assessing land only rather than both land and buildings, (2) considerable economies are possible if land only is valued, and (3) most of the errors in valuation involve buildings, not land.[18]

Atkinson contended that the single tax would redound to the benefit of large capitalists, who could then invest all of their capital in improvements on the land. He said, further:

> If land should be taxed at its "site" value, without regard to the capital or value of the buildings or improvements upon it, then the poor man who may now be in possession of a small house must pay as much as the rich man who owns a large house in the next lot of the same site value, or an expensive warehouse in the immediate neighborhood on another lot of the same site value.[19]

In claiming that large capitalists can get land cheaper, or without purchase price, under land-value taxation, Atkinson would have to admit that entrepreneurs or capitalists of lesser means would also benefit, even more in proportion. This is because those of small means may not be able to afford expensive land at all now. But, granted that large capitalists would be able to devote *all* of their capital to improvements on the land, what is wrong with that? The building and maintenance of such improvements create jobs and benefit the community, whereas the mere ownership of high-priced land by some titleholder does not.

Modern research, including that of the writer, gives the lie to Atkinson's assertion that land-value taxes are regressive. The opposite is true, as the following should indicate. The writer's doctoral dissertation in economics included a computer simulation of a switch from real and personal property taxation to a base of land values only, which would have raised for each of the 1,800 taxing agencies in Los Angeles County the same total revenue for the 1971-72 fiscal year. The percentage change in tax impact was summarized for some ninety land-use categories in seventy-seven cities and the unincorporated area. The following results were noted for Baldwin Park, a working-class Los Angeles suburb, compared with Beverly Hills, an upper-middle-class and wealthy suburb.

In the 1971-72 tax year, the total tax rate in Baldwin Park, owing to a relatively low tax base, ranged from fourteen to fifteen percent of assessed value. The twenty-five percent assessment ratio (to full value) listed land at $19.3 million and improvements at over $42 million. As a result, Baldwin Park homeowners would have experienced an average tax *de*crease of almost thirty-four percent, with over ninety percent of them having their property taxes fall by forty percent.

In contrast, consider Beverly Hills. Owing to a high tax base, the tax rate there ranged from slightly less than 9 up to almost 12 percent. Assessed land values were almost $162 million, with improvement values assessed at only $132.5 million. The shift to site-value taxation would have resulted in the average homeowner in Beverly Hills having a property tax *in*crease of 15.4 percent, or $546.[20] This is a case in point to indicate that land-based property taxes are progressive. Other studies have tended to show that ownership of land *value* tends to increase in greater proportion than income.

Another case in point, from the same source, concerns the community of Watts, a south-central Los Angeles neighborhood, almost entirely black, and generally poor. Assessed values for land were almost $4 million, while those for improvements were about $7 million. The result of land-value taxation would have been an average property tax *de*crease, over *all* types of land use, of over 19 percent.[21]

One of Atkinson's final arguments is that the single tax was tried in France before the French Revolution, under the physiocrats, led by Turgot, and proved a miserable failure.[22] However, in a slightly later issue of the *Century*, replying to a communication from James Middleton, he admitted that he had been incorrect, and that the single tax had never been tried in France.[23]

Atkinson was sincere and well-intentioned, even if much of his reasoning proved shallow and ill-informed. In retrospect, he joins the long list of those who verbally dueled with George and came out worsted.

Notes

1. Edward Atkinson, "A Single Tax Upon Land," *Century Magazine* 40 (July 1890): 385-94, 403-5.

2. Harold Francis Williamson, *Edward Atkinson: The Biography of an American Liberal, 1827-1905* (Cambridge, Mass.: Riverside Press, 1934).

3. Atkinson, "A Single Tax Upon Land," pp. 385-86.

4. Ibid., p. 386.

5. Ibid., p. 387.

6. Henry George, "A Single Tax on Land Values—Reply to Mr. Atkinson" *Century Magazine* 40 (July 1890): 396. Hereinafter cited as "Reply."

7. Ibid., p. 399.

8. Atkinson, "A Single Tax Upon Land," p. 387.

9. George, "Reply," p. 399.

10. Thomas G. Shearman, "Henry George's Mistakes," *The Forum* 8 (September-February 1889-90): 44-45.

11. Atkinson, "A Single Tax Upon Land," pp. 388-89.

12. Ibid., p. 389.

13. Ibid., p. 390.

14. Ibid., p. 391-92.

15. George, "Reply," p. 401.

16. Henry George, *Progress and Poverty*, 75th anniversary ed. (New York: Robert Schalkenbach Foundation, 1954), p. 405.

17. J. Bruce Brown, "The Incidence of Property Taxes under Three Alternative Systems in Urban Areas in New Zealand," *National Tax Journal* 21 (September 1968): 251.

18. A. M. Woodruff and L. L. Ecker-Racz, "Property Taxes and Land Use Patterns in Australia and New Zealand," *Tax Executive* 8 (October 1965): 57.

19. Atkinson, "A Simgle Tax Upon Land," p. 392.

20. William B. Truehart, "The Impact of Real Property Versus Land Value Taxation in Los Angeles County," Ph. D. dissertation, Claremont Graduate School, 1973, pp. 108-9.

21. Ibid., pp. 112-13.

22. Atkinson, "A Single Tax Upon Land," p. 393.

23. Edward Atkinson, "Mr. Atkinson's Correction," *Century Magazine* 41 (November 1890): 158.

18

Clark and Patten: Exemplars of the New American Professionalism

BY CHARLES F. COLLIER

I

In many ways the reactions of John Bates Clark[1] and Simon Nelson Patten[2] to the thought of Henry George epitomize, almost perfectly, the main developments in American economics at the turn of the century. The period was the one in which this country produced its first internationally known economic writers and theorists, and surely George and Clark were among them. The period was also the one in which American economics "came of age," in the sense that there were sufficiently large numbers of economists to justify, or even make necessary, the formation of professional associations. Clark and Patten were both instrumental in founding the American Economic Association, and each served as its president. Moreover, the period was the one in which American economics, particularly as presented in academic institutions, became increasingly a specialized discipline. Up until about 1870 or 1880 American economics was written and taught by men who were often trained in other fields, such as law, political science, and philosophy. After about 1880 professors tended to have advanced degrees in economics and *tended* to concentrate their teaching efforts in it.[3] In this regard, George seems to be a particularly good example of the kind of self-educated "layman" economist whose era was fading away, while Clark and Patten are illustrative of the new generation of those with formal, advanced training in the subject. (Both Clark and Patten did their advanced study in Europe. They had to go to Europe for the simple reason that American universities did not have recognized graduate programs in economics at that time.) And this was a period during which economists in many parts of the world were making devastating critiques of classical economics.

Again, George, Clark, and Patten are of interest since each criticized classicism from a different viewpoint. George's writing is best viewed as an attempt to correct the flaws of classical economics and to resuscitate it. Clark's early writings called for a rejection of the classical *homo oeconomicus* on the grounds that "he" did not adequately represent humanity, and because Clark felt that the perfect competition assumed by the classicists did not exist. Although his later works illustrate his "conversion," especially on the issue of competition, they still differed enough from the classical works to place them in the neoclassical tradition.[4] Patten rejected the classical view that the events that controlled humanity's destiny (events such as the increases in land rent predicted by Ricardo) were largely beyond man's control. He was generally far too optimistic to accept such premises. Also, he advocated far more governmental intervention than the classicists.[5] Then too, this was a period in which the very subject matter changed so much that the discipline's name was changed from (classical) political economy to (neoclassical) economics. Patten was generally a neoclassical economist, and certainly Clark was one of the founders of the school. George, in contrast, always viewed himself as a classical political economist in the vein of Adam Smith and he always viewed the new science of economics as a bastardization of the true science, political economy. In fact, he always used the word *economics* in a pejorative sense.[6]

In sum, each of the writers wrote on most of the major topics of concern at the turn of the century. It is not too much to say that George, Clark, and Patten *created* many of those topics of concern. And it is not too much to say that Clark and Patten developed many of theirs as reactions to the ideas of George.

II

One major area on which the three differed was the kind of analysis that could be, or had to be, carried out. Specifically, the three writers adopted three different views with respect to the time period, and the changes that could occur in the time period considered. Here Clark's treatment was the simplest—and the one that best realized the limits of the then current tools. His analysis was *basically* static. Static analysis, as Clark used the term, referred to the analysis of a society in which the production techniques, tools, organization, distribution of income, population, amount of capital, and desires of consumers all remained unchanged.[7] He, of course, recognized that such states never had existed, and never will exist in the "real world," since all societies contain numerous dynamic elements. Still, he said, static analysis had served, and would continue to serve, several important purposes. First, and a matter of historical importance, Clark contended that many of the most important classical principles rested on static analysis. He argued, for instance, that when classicists sought the natural laws that governed the prices of goods, or when they sought the natural wage or the natural rate of interest, they were using the term *natural* in a sense that made it equivalent to Clark's term *static*.[8] Second, Clark argued that even in a dynamic society, the transactions that occur at any instant, or on any given day, are governed by precisely the same forces that, if acting alone, would bring society into permanent rest, or into a static state.[9] Third, Clark wrote, "It is my belief that students should become acquainted with the laws of Economic Dynamics, and that they can approach the study of them advantageously only after a study of Economic Statics."[10] His point seems to have been that one can understand changes in the levels of variables (dynamics) only if one understands the levels themselves (statics). Fourth, Clark seems to have realized that it is incredibly difficult to develop a dynamic theory that allows everything to vary at once. Given the state of the science of economic theory as it then existed, the best that one could do was attempt to approach dynamics by a series of successive approximations involving more and more complex static states.[11] Clark thus developed a static analysis and confined his dynamics to inferences from the static analysis.

Patten's economics, in contrast, was primarily dynamic. His analysis was that of a society in which progress was the primary characteristic. Patten, for example, never assumed that the state of the art of production or the level of technological sophistication was constant, as Clark so often did. He also believed that all living organisms, human institutions, and societies tend to evolve continuously. He argued that once any environment becomes occupied by organisms, each having an appetite for food, a struggle tends to begin and each individual tries to appropriate, sometimes using physical power, a part of the region. Eventually, however, people realize that the food furnished by nature is only a small part of the amount that can be produced. Patten believed that attention then turns away from aggressiveness to cooperation in an attempt to increase the total food supply. That, however, introduces new moral codes, tending to impose sanctions upon those who now undertake the very actions that were once the primary actions taken to survive. Under the new codes the ultimate aim was said to be to increase *the group's* ability to maximize pleasure and minimize pain. Those who are too weak or too lazy to work will not survive in the new competitive struggle to aid the group. And, much more to the point of this discussion, Patten argued that those who continue their aggressive actions designed to monopolize the food supply will ultimately be destroyed by their own selfishness.[12] Moreover, Patten argued that as these developments occurred, people would discover more and more desires that could not be gratified by the natural food supply. As a result they would tend to devote more and more of their labor to the production of commodities that would satisfy these desires. In a statement using the ideas, if not the exact terminology of marginal utility theory, Patten argued that people will continue to work to produce these goods up to the point at which the marginal pleasure gained from the consumption of one more unit of a good equaled the marginal pain of producing it.[13] Patten argued that during some phases of economic development the general rate of wages would tend to fall, if everything else were held equal. He claimed that in any society the wants first satisfied will be those where gratification provides the highest level of utility to the consumers. Patten argued that since the highest level of utility was derived from gratification of these desires, consumers would pay, and laborers would earn, a great deal from production. But after these desires were gratified, less "important" desires would be gratified. Gratification of these less important desires would provide less utility to consumers, and consumers would, accordingly, pay less to have them gratified. This sequence would continue with the "importance" of the desires steadily diminishing, the amount of utility diminishing, and the amount consumers would pay diminishing, hence the amount producers would earn would also diminish accordingly.[14] Patten felt, however, that actually observed wages probably would not fall because technological advance and improvement in the arts of production would more than offset the above-mentioned developments. And if it should occur that the population of any community exceeded the limits of the food supply to support it, some individuals would leave that community to settle a new one. But, it was argued, the new settlement would represent a higher level of civilization and a higher phase in the evolutionary process of humanity.[15] Patten's economics was, therefore, a dynamic, evolutionary economics.

George, in contrast to both Clark and Patten, chose to approach economics in both its static and its dynamic aspects. Readers of this essay are presumably familiar enough with *Progress and Poverty* so that a detailed explication of it is not needed. It will perhaps suffice to note that in book 3 of that work George attempted to survey essentially the same ground as Clark later did. Chapter 1 of that book is devoted to the (quite correct) proposition that the static laws of income distribution ought to have more unity than the classical system gave them. And, chapters 2 through 6 do attempt to provide a discussion of the several factor payments in turn. That George intended that all of book 3 be interpreted in a static framework is probably best shown by the fact that chapter 8, the final and summary chapter, is entitled "The Statics of the Problem Thus Explained." Then, in book 4 George attempted to consider the same topics that Patten considered. In that book George began with a chapter entitled "The Dynamics of the Problem Yet to Seek," and proceeded to analyze the effects of increasing population, improvements in the arts of production, and the effect of expectations raised by progress. Later chapters and other books attempt to explain the business cycle, the dynamic aspects of poverty amid increasing wealth, and "The Law of Human Progress." Clearly, these are attempts to dynamize the earlier discussion.[16]

III

If one were to compare, contrast, and evaluate the views of the three writers, he would have to say that the task that George set for himself was at once the most ambitious and the most *potentially* fruitful. The economy can, after all, be analyzed both at one point in time and as it varies through time. And one may believe, as Clark clearly did, that ideally one *should* try to develop both a static and a dynamic analysis. Yet, one would also have to accept Clark's judgment that it was simply too difficult to develop both statics and dynamics, given the then available tools. One would have to conclude that Patten's dynamic theory—implying that people come to believe that the group's welfare is the most important concern, and implying that all new settlements represent progress to higher levels of civilization—was quite naive and quaint. It must also be stated that George's dynamic theory—relying in a crucial way on a wholly untenable theory of land speculation and a demonstrably incorrect analysis of dynamic rent theory[17]—was a less than happy aspect of his analysis. It is probably accurate to say that Clark, who always kept the limits of his tools in mind, was the most successful in his efforts.

The differences in the level of analysis also produced differences in the kinds of issues investigated. Clark was interested primarily in the issue of income distribution. Indeed, his most famous work was *The Distribution of Wealth*. Clark's decision to concentrate on distribution theory was quite logical, given the static framework that he adopted. When Clark held population, organization, amount of capital, and the state of the art of production constant, it followed that the amount of wealth produced per unit of time would be unvarying. It then followed that the principles underlying the distribution of that wealth or income were the most important issues to investigate.[18]

Since Clark explicitly stated that the mechanism underlying his theory was derived by following up on a lead advanced by George,[19] it seems wisest to turn attention to George's theory first. As is well known, George's rent theory was the undiluted classical Ricardian rent theory extended to all, not merely to agricultural, land.[20] The only especially interesting feature of George's handling of the concept was the fact that his version of the theory applied only to the extensive margin of cultivation. He had no theory of the intensive margin at all.[21] George's static wage theory was perhaps his single most important contribution to economic analysis. He imagined a worker with no special skills, no capital, and no previously accumulated stock of goods, and placed that worker on a plot of marginal land. The point was that since the land would not be totally barren, the worker would produce some product. But since George had given the laborer no advantages of any sort, it seemed entirely reasonable that the entire product should be ascribed to raw, unskilled labor power.[22] That product, said George, would become the wage for that particular worker. Moreover, the perfectly working market mechanism would insure that that wage would become the wage for all unskilled labor in the economy, if everything else were held equal. Skilled laborers, who supplied more units of exertion, would produce more units of product in a given time period. Since the product produced and the wage received were thought of as equivalent, the skilled laborers would receive a higher wage.[23]

George's static theory of interest, in contrast, was the weakest component of his system. George argued, in the first place, that since capital was, among other things, "stored up" labor, interest could be viewed as another form of wages. From this he deduced that the ratio of wages to interest must be constant.[24] Second, in order to account for the mechanics of the return to capital, he advanced his ingenious but generally discredited concept of the "reproductive modes" of interest[25]—which never gained widespread acceptance even among his adherents. It would scarcely be profitable to attempt here to summarize this concept or to review the reasons why it has been so universally rejected, but at least one commentator has noted its incompatibility with the rest of George's system,[26] while another has remarked upon its superfluity.[27] Whatever the philosophical merits of George's notion of capital as "stored up" labor, and of interest as thus a specialized form of wages, it has rarely been discussed in economic literature. One senses that many writers thought it too simple to warrant comment. In any case, George's deduction from it is without empirical support. The ratio of wages to interest is, in fact, not constant, and, even if it were, George never indicated any way to determine the value of the ratio.

George's dynamic theory of income distribution was derived from the Ricardian rent theory applied to the extensive margin, and from some of his own ideas about speculation, increased population, improvements in the arts of production, and material progress. Briefly, George argued that once population increased, the arts of production improved, and/or the amount of material wealth increased, the demand for land would also increase, causing rent to rise. Speculators, anticipating even further increases, would purchase land, and hold it idle or underused while waiting for its value to increase even more.[28] Laborers, barred in large measure from the chance to work these speculative holdings, would either go to the city and become a class of urban poor, or move to hitherto submarginal plots of land and settle on them. When the new plots were settled, the rent on all plots already inside the margin would increase and rent would arise for the first time on the former marginal plots. Hence aggregate rents would rise. Moreover, since all wages ultimately were based upon the productivity of labor applied to marginal land, wages would inevitably fall as long as the margin of cultivation or building continued to extend downward and outward. And since the ratio of wages to interest was supposed to be constant, it seemed to follow that the amount of interest would fall as the amount of wages fell.

Clark's theory of income distribution shared at least two very important points with that of George. Clark, like George, believed that the classical distribution theory lacked unity since each factor payment was determined by a different rule in the classical theory. To correct that flaw Clark sought one general principle that would simultaneously determine all factor shares. Further, in his greatest work, *The Distribution of Wealth*, Clark explicitly acknowledged that the one principle he finally found was based upon a principle of the static Georgian theory.

> It was the claim advanced by Mr. Henry George, that wages are fixed by the product which a man can create by tilling rentless land, that first led me to seek a method by which the product of labor everywhere may be disentangled from the product of cooperating agents and separately identified; and it was this quest which led to the attainment of the law that is here presented, according to which the wages of all labor tend, under perfectly free competition, to equal the product that is separately attributable to the labor. The product of the "final unit" of labor is the same as that of every unit, separately considered; and if normal tendencies could work in perfection, it would be true not only of each unit, but of the working force as a whole, that its product and its pay are identical.[29]

Clark's truly brilliant achievement was the generalization of that rule to *all* of the factors of production. Each factor contributed to the production process and each got as its compensation an amount equal to its contribution to the process. An analyst could estimate the contribution of any particular factor by adding or subtracting one unit of that factor and noting what happens to the total product. Under an exceedingly wide array of circumstances it is accurate to attribute the change to the addition or subtraction of the dose of the factor. That change, then, is a measure of the factor's productivity and in the Clarkian theory it serves as the basis for compensation.

While it is undeniable that Clark's theory was similar to, and derived from, George's, there were also critical differences. Clark's theory rested squarely on the law of diminishing returns to the factors of production, a law that George categorically rejected in *Progress and Poverty* and did not accept until he wrote his unfinished *Science of Political Economy*.[30] (The law states that as additional doses of a variable input are added to a constant amount of fixed inputs, after some point the product produced will increase at a decreasing rate, and that if even more doses of the variable input are added, after another point the total product will actually decline.) Clark reasoned that since, after some point, the per dose productivity of the variable factor fell, since all doses of the factor were assumed to be homogeneous, and since pay and productivity are identical in pure competition, the pay to each dose of the factor would fall as more doses were applied. The reliance upon the law of diminishing returns to factors gave Clark's theory two immense advantages over George's. First, since the law is stated in terms of additional doses of a variable input being added to a fixed input, Clark was able to apply his theory to both the extensive and intensive margins, while George could apply his theory only to the extensive margin. Second, since any factor can be the variable one when the others are fixed, Clark's theory can be applied to any factor and is therefore quite general.

Clark then went on to make a crucial distinction that reflected a major difference with George—the distinction between capital and capital goods. Capital goods, said Clark, were specific and often immobile, and they had only a temporary existence. Capital, in contrast, was a general, mobile, and permanent fund. That is, capital goods were the specific tools employed in any productive process. Such goods are often immobile since they are often too large to be moved or since they may possess attributes that restrict the number of processes in which they can be used. And, since such goods depreciate and eventually wear out, they are only temporary. Capital, in contrast, is the complete fund of all capital goods, of any form, available now or in the future. Since it contains all capital goods of any form, capital is the general, amorphous, concept of investment opportunity. Since it contains goods available now or in the future, it can be moved or transformed in any way and is, therefore, completely mobile. And, since it consists of the "endless succession" of capital goods, it is permanent.[31]

Clark used the distinction between capital and capital goods to argue that there was really no important difference at all between land and capital. Clark argued that the claim that land was absolutely fixed in supply was true, but very misleading. He contended that in the static state, which he analyzed, the supply of *all* factors would be fixed, by definition. (Clark argued, correctly, that changes in factor supplies are part of dynamics, and hence excluded from his consideration.)[32] Moreover, the claim that land was unique because its earnings were differential returns or surpluses was also true, but again misleading. Part of Clark's great contribution stemmed from the fact that he saw that his whole theory of marginal productivity was a generalization of Ricardian rent theory. But that meant that the returns to *any* factor could be viewed as a differential return or surplus.[33] (In fact, Clark explicitly referred to such things as no-rent machines.)[34] There was, then, nothing especially unique about land, and Clark regularly wrote of "units of capital in land" to emphasize that fact.[35]

There seems to be no doubt that Clark's views evolved (and his views did evolve over a period of several years), at least in part, as a direct reaction to George's views. Frank A. Fetter, a contemporary of Clark and a close observer of his development, has advanced the idea that the "single-tax agitation" was probably the source of "immediate stimulation" for Clark's reformulation of capital theory.[36] More on this point will be said below.

Patten seems to have been the least concerned of the three with income distribution theory. In a significant sense that was logical, given Patten's concern for dynamics. While there is, of course, a dynamic income distribution theory, it is not uncommon for those who are primarily concerned with the growth of income to give relatively little attention to its distribution.

Patten's distribution theory, such as it was, showed several crucial differences from the theories of George and Clark. In essence, Patten's rent theory was closer to Malthus's than Ricardo's in the sense that it placed heavy emphasis on social factors in rent determination. Like George, but for a different reason, Patten believed in a social law of increasing returns to factors of production. He contended that social innovations and mechanical inventions would more than offset the diminishing returns that applied to the factors considered separately.[37] Patten also seems to have rejected the classical idea that rent and profits vary inversely. And, unlike Clark, Patten did not believe that profits would tend to zero in competitive long-run equilibrium. His conclusion seemed to follow from the fact that he considered a dynamic economy. Since new industries were always developing and firms were always introducing new inventions, there was always some profit accruing to somebody somewhere. That, it was argued, was sufficient to prove that profits do not tend to zero.[38] It is not, however, perfectly clear that Patten realized that the traditional statement was to hold only in equilibrium and was never intended to hold in the case that he considered. He was, in fact, discussing a different proposition, not refuting a classical one. Interest was not felt to be a cost of production. Instead, Patten adopted what was essentially a time-preference theory of interest, which stated that when one saved, he gave up a certain amount of goods today for a preferred bundle of goods in the future. Given the fact that people tend to prefer goods in the present, one could be enticed into saving only if he were offered more goods in the future.[39] It is hard to find in Patten a definite statement of a law of wages that is of comparable analytical quality with the statements of Clark and George. Instead, Patten devoted most of his discussion to consideration of the social factors that caused changes in wages. These factors included the rate at which new job opportunities opened up, laborers' preferences for present over future goods (labor produces goods that will become available in the future, but it must be paid in the present; hence the wages paid were said to be some function of the present value of the future goods), the consumption habits of the citizens, the state of the arts of production, the foreign trade policy of the nation,[40] and, as discussed earlier, the rapidity with which diminishing returns to labor apply.

It seems reasonable to conclude that Patten's theory was a good deal less unified than were the others. George had a somewhat unified theory based upon the productivity of labor applied to marginal land and upon marginal rent theory. But it was Clark, with his marginal productivity theory, who had the most unified theory. And it was Clark who, in the final summary, has made the greatest contribution to the mainstream of economic analysis. Yet, it should not be forgotten that he built upon foundations laid by George.

IV

Each of the three thinkers also considered the ethical issues involved in income distribution. George's *Progress and Poverty* is, in fact, as much a moral as an economic treatise. Clark's first published response to it—the transcript of his presentation in the single-tax debate at the 1890 conference of the American Social Science Association at Saratoga—put strong emphasis on ethical objections. These objections were elaborated in an article, "The Ethics of Land Tenure." which appeared later that year in the initial number of *The International Journal of Ethics*. In April of the following year Patten published in the same journal "Another View of the Ethics of Land Tenure," in which, while rejecting George's program, he took issue with some of Clark's objections to it, and accepted certain of its ethical assumptions. Later, however, his opposition to the single tax became so ferocious that, as we shall see, he was led to advocate a breach of intellectual honesty in order to combat it.

George considered the private appropriation of land value to be unethical as well as inefficient. The basis for that belief was, of course, his theory of property rights—a theory that held that an individual had valid property rights in anything he had created or acquired through voluntary transfer from one who legitimately owned it. Since no human being created the "original and indestructible powers of the soil," nobody could ever claim legitimate property rights in them. Nor could the state confer such rights, because to do so would be to arrogate to some persons the natural opportunity made by God as a patrimony for all. It seemed to follow that the private appropriation of rent or land value was unethical. (This was not to say that landlords, personally, were to be morally condemned, but rather that the system itself was inconsistent with moral law.) Wages and interest, on the other hand, were quite properly subject to private ownership, being payments for productive services legitimately rendered.

Clark's position should not be surprising, given the discussion earlier. He argued, as has been shown, that there is really nothing special about land, and that land is really just part of the investment concept called capital. Since he felt that this was so, he saw no reason to classify the private appropriation of rent or land values as unethical or in any way improper. In fact, he argued for just the reverse view, asserting that since the state had allowed, and sometimes even encouraged, private investment in land, it would be unethical to modify any of the rules regarding such investments after the investments had been made. Moreover, he said, it was simply efficient, from an economic point of view, to allow private investment in land, and private appropriation of rent or land value. Competitive market forces, he insisted, would operate to insure that the land was used in the most efficient way by the most efficient producers. In a passage directed at some "agrarian socialists," Clark wrote that "pure capital, when invested in land, has the same rights that elsewhere belong to it." To infringe upon these rights or to confiscate rent or land value would, he said, be not just robbery but "the quintessence of robbery."[41]

While Patten was interested in social reform, he favored retention of the traditional structure of property rights, although modified by governmental intervention. Specifically, he condemned the single-tax proposal as unethical since it threatened to nullify what he understood to be valid private rights.

There is yet another way in which the question of ethics enters into this discussion—namely, the professional ethics of Clark and Patten in responding to George. It has always seemed to me that neither Clark nor Patten was entirely beyond reproach in this connection, although Patten was by far the worst offender. Patten's opposition to the single tax grew so extreme that he ultimately came to favor restructuring the whole science of economics so as to exclude it as a logical deduction. Patten explicitly conceded that many of George's propositions and conclusions did, in fact, follow logically from classical economics. Then, after citing George as one who attacked the classical harmony of interest theory (in which Patten believed), he wrote:

> If the new group of thinkers called themselves sociologists or historians they might be disregarded. But they openly claim to be economists; and the worst of the matter is, they have, so far as statement goes, the mass of the older economists on their side. Nothing pleases a socialist or a single taxer better than to quote authorities and to use the well-known economic theories to prove his case. The economists rubbed their eyes in surprise when this assault first began; but they soon realized that their favorite authors were not so perfect as they supposed and that economic doctrine must be recast so that it would rest wholly on present data. This, I take it, is the real meaning of the present movement in economic thought. It will not accept socialism; and to free itself from the snares into which it has fallen through the careless statements of its creators, it must isolate itself more fully from history, sociology and other disciplines that give undue weight to past experience.[42]

Patten thus proposed to radically reorganize the entire science so as to eliminate the propositions that George (and others) used to develop their arguments.

It really does appear that, from a purely scholarly standpoint, Patten committed a very serious crime. He literally proposed to pick his ethical conclusions in advance, pick the body of propositions that would lead to those conclusions, call that body of propositions "economics," and isolate himself from anything that might lead to other conclusions. This procedure amounts to nothing more than the rationalization of preconceived biases, and is clearly a travesty of scholarship.

Clark's procedure was more sound that Patten's because Clark was engaged in a many-sided discussion of capital theory. (Other participants included the Austrian marginalists, the remaining classicists, and the members of the German historical school.) In fact, the old concept of capital *was* flawed and did need to be revised. Still, one would feel more confidence in Clark's new definition of capital were it not for the fact that it gives the appearance of being specially tailored to lead to arguments for use against George.

V

As stated in the opening paragraphs, the participants in this discussion wrote on—indeed, were responsible for formulating—most of the major topics of concern in economics at the turn of the century. The two later writers, Clark and Patten, often did not refer explicitly to George, and some of their references were indirect (such as the arguments that Clark directed against the "agrarian socialists"). Yet, there can be no doubt that both Clark and Patten were heavily influenced by George, although in different ways. Patten seems to have developed many of his ideas as a negative reaction to the work of George. Clark, although rejecting George's "remedy" and much of his analysis, did not hesitate, as we have seen, to state that his own major contribution to economic theory was the direct result of following up a lead found in *Progress and Poverty*.

Notes

1. John Bates Clark (1847-1938) received his undergraduate training at Brown and Amherst and his graduate training in Heidelberg and Zurich. He taught at Carleton College, Smith, and Amherst before permanently settling at Columbia University. His reputation was established with the publication of *The Philosophy of Wealth* (1885), a collection of essays written during the 1870s. *The Distribution of Wealth: A Theory of Wages, Interest and Profits* (1899) presented, formally, the complete marginal productivity theory, and advanced Clark to the front ranks of economists in the entire English-speaking world. His *Essentials of Economic Theory* (1907) was an attempt to build on his earlier foundation, but one that was not so successful as he hoped it would be. He is also famous as one of the founders of the American Economic Association, still the most prestigious of all professional associations of economists in this country. At the time of his death he was regarded as the "dean of all academic economists in America."

2. Simon Nelson Patten (1852-1922) received a doctorate from Halle (Germany) in 1878. However, he was unable to secure a university teaching position until 1889, when Edmond Janes James helped him to obtain an appointment at the Wharton School of the University of Pennsylvania, where he eventually became head of the economics department, and remained until his mandatory retirement at the age of sixty-five. His publications include 18 books (some on topics other than economics) and 130 articles. He is best known for his advocacy of protectionist policies.

3. One must say *tended* to concentrate on economics, because their specialization was often incomplete. At Carleton, Clark, for instance, was employed as the librarian, and as professor of political economy and history. But his actual duties also included teaching in so many other areas, such as rhetoric and moral philosophy, that he described himself as "Professor of Odds and Ends." See Joseph Dorfman, *The Economic Mind in American Civilization* (New York: Viking, 1949), 3: 189.

4. For a much more complete discussion of these and other points related to Clark's change of views, see Joel Jalladeau, "The Methodological Conversion of John Bates Clark," *History of Political Economy* 7 (Summer 1975, 209-26.

5. Patten's economic writings are analyzed in James L. Boswell, *The Economics of Simon Nelson Patten* (Philadelphia: Winston, 1934). A detailed analysis of Patten's differences with classicism appears in the first chapter.

6. See especially Henry George, *The Science of Political Economy* (1897; reprint ed. New York: Robert Schalkenbach Foundation, 1968), particularly pp. 128-29 and 207-9.

7. See John Bates Clark, *The Distribution of Wealth: A Theory of Wages, Interest and Profits* (New York: Macmillan, 1899), p. 28 and passim, and his *Essentials of Economic Theory, As Applied to Modern Problems of Industry and Public Policy* (New York: Macmillan, 1907), pp. 203-6, and Jalladeau, "The Methodological Conversion," pp. 216-19.

8. Clark, *Essentials of Economic Theory*, p. vi, and "The Dynamics of the Wages Question," *American Economic Review: Papers and Proceedings* 4 (February 1903): 131. Clark went on to add that in the classical system the main, if not exclusive, example of a dynamic theory was Malthusian population theory.

9. Clark, *Essentials of Economic Theory*, p. vii.

10. Ibid., p. ix.

11. Jalladeau, "The Methodological Conversion," p. 219.

12. This paragraph has thus far relied quite heavily upon Boswell, *Economics of Simon Nelson Patten*, pp. 25-27.

13. Simon Nelson Patten, *The Consumption of Wealth* (Philadelphia: Ginn, 1901), pp. 28-30.

14. Simon Nelson Patten, "Another View of the Ethics of Land Tenure," *International Journal of Ethics* (April 1891), especially pp. 357-60.

15. Boswell, *Economics of Simon Nelson Patten*, pp. 25-26.

16. The references to the book and chapter titles in *Progress and Poverty* apply to any unabridged edition.

17. Charles F. Collier, "Henry George's System of Economics: Analysis and Criticism," Ph. D. dissertation, Duke University, 1975, especially pp. 247-60.

18. Jalladeau, "The Methodological Conversion," p. 209.

19. Clark, *The Distribution of Wealth*, p. xiii.

20. See George, *Progress and Poverty*, bk. 3, chap. 2.

21. Note that George always wrote in terms of displaced workers, or increased population, moving to the frontier and settling on hitherto submarginal plots. They were never permitted to become additional workers on already cultivated plots. The original Ricardian version of the theory correctly allowed for both cases.

22. Technically speaking, since the land was not totally barren, its productive powers would contribute something to the productive process. But since the land considered was marginal land, George had eliminated as much of the productive powers as he could have.

23. For a further discussion of this topic, see Collier, "George's System of Economics," pp. 16-22.

24. See George, *Progress and Poverty*, 75th anniversary ed. (New York: Robert Schalkenbach Foundation, 1954), pp. 198 f.

25. Ibid., pp. 180-88.

26. James Haldane Smith, *Economic Moralism: An Essay in Constructive Economics* (London: George Allen and Unwin, 1916), p. 73.

27. Irving Fisher, *The Rate of Interest: Its Nature, Determination and Relation to Economic Phenomena* (New York: Macmillan, 1907), p. 28.

28. In fact, as Francis A. Walker pointed out, there is no valid reason why speculators should hold their land idle. But George assumed that they would.

29. Clark, *The Distribution of Wealth*, p. viii.

30. For Clark's acceptance and statement of the universality of the law, see ibid., p. 49. For George's rejection, see *Progress and Poverty*, bk. 2, chaps. 3-4; for his acceptance, see *The Science of Political Economy*, especially pp. 357-64.

31. Clark, *The Distribution of Wealth*, chaps. 9-11, especially pp. 116-20 and 156.

32. Ibid., p. 338.

33. Ibid., p. 345.

34. Ibid. "The lowest grade of every instrument produces nothing, and is a no-rent article."

35. Such as ibid., p. 344, to cite but one instance.

36. Frank A. Fetter, "Clark's Reformulation of the Capital Concept," *Economic Essays Contributed in Honor of John Bates Clark*, ed. Jacob Hollander (New York: Macmillan, 1927), reprinted in *Capital, Interest and Rent: Essays in the Theory of Distribution* by Frank A. Fetter, ed. Murray N. Rothbard (Kansas City: Sheed, Andrews and McMeel, 1977), pp. 126-28.

Fetter is, no doubt, correct. For an early, not completely developed, version of this argument, see Clark, "The Ethics of Land Tenure," *International Journal of Ethics,* (October, 1890), pp. 62-79. Interestingly, in this article Clark never mentioned George by name. It is clear, however, that the "special assailants of the land system" discussed by Clark were George and his followers.

37. Boswell, *Economics of Simon Nelson Patten*, p. 30.

38. Ibid., pp. 30-31.

39. Ibid., pp. 60-63.

40. Ibid., pp. 102-13.

41. Clark, cited by Fetter, "Clark's Reformation," p. 127. See also Clark's "Ethics of Land Tenure," pp. 62-79.

42. Simon Nelson Patten, "The Conflict Theory of Distribution," *Yale Review,* (August 1908), reprinted in *Essays in Economic Theory*, ed. Rexford G. Tugwell (New York: A. A. Knopf, 1924), p. 219.

19

Seligman and His Critique from Social Utility

BY ROBERT V. ANDELSON
AND
MASON GAFFNEY

Edwin R. A. Seligman (1861-1939), a long-time doyen of American tax economists, criticized the single tax with such unrelenting vigor that of the six sentences comprising his biographical sketch in the *World Book Encyclopedia*, one is devoted to setting forth this fact. Louis F. Post, an ardent Georgist who served as assistant secretary of labor in the Wilson administration, speaks of him as "the chief antagonist of our Prophet's cause, the most influential in scholastic and also in business circles. . . ."[1]

Seligman was the son of a prominent banker, philanthropist, and Jewish leader who, on one occasion, declined President Grant's offer of a major Cabinet post. Upon graduation from Columbia University, young Seligman spent three years studying history and political science in Germany and France, returning to Columbia to earn both a law degree and a Ph.D. In 1885 he was appointed a lecturer at his alma mater; by 1891 he was full professor of political economy and finance; in 1904 he was named to the McVickar chair. Author of more than a dozen books, he originated and edited the *Political Science Quarterly* and served on numerous advisory commissions, as a consultant to the League of Nations, and, in 1931, as financial adviser to the Cuban government. Seligman's *The Income Tax* (1911) expounded principles that Congress embodied in the income tax law of 1913. He was active in New York City reform politics, and was chairman of the mayor's tax commission, 1914-1916. His distinctions included five honorary doctorates and several foreign decorations. He took pride in owning the largest private library on economics in America, rich in rare sixteenth and seventeenth-century volumes.

When not yet thirty and already of professorial rank, Seligman took the lead in opposing George at the 1890 conference of the American Social Science Association in Saratoga, which was wholly devoted to a debate on the merits of the single tax. Their eloquent but acerbic exchange was the high point of the proceedings.

At this event Seligman provoked all of George's combative instincts, which were never far below the surface, with the assertion that "there is not a single man with a thorough training in the history of economics, or an acquaintance with the science of finance, who is an advocate of the single tax on land values. In biology, in astronomy, in metaphysics, we bow down before the specialist; but every man whose knowledge of economics or of the science of finance is derived from the daily papers, or one or two books with lopsided ideas, thinks that he is a full-fledged scientist, able to instruct the closest student of the markets or of the political and social organisms."[2]

To this broadside George replied that the antagonism of the professors toward his teaching was attributable to the domination of the universities by vested interests, condemned Seligman for his elitism, and asked: "If our remedy will not do, what is your remedy?" He went on to say that palliatives would not avail. "You must choose between the single tax, with its recognition of the rights of the individual, with its recognition of the province of government, with its recognition of the rights of property, on the one hand, and socialism on the other. . . ." He accused the professors of proposing "more restrictions, more interference, more extensions of government into the individual field, more organization of class against class, more bars to the liberty of the citizen. In turning from us, even though it be to milk-and-water socialism, you are turning to the road that leads to revolution and chaos. . . ."[3]

Seligman's rejoinder ended with a peroration that summed up the attitude of most academic economists of his day:

> Mr. George, you ask us, if the single tax is not the remedy, what is the remedy? Ay, that is the question. . . . If we thought that you had solved the problem we would enthrone you on our council seats, we would reverently bend the knee and acknowledge in you a master, a prophet. But when you come to us with a tale that is as old as the hills, when you set forth in your writings doctrines that have been long exploded, when you in the innocence of your enthusiasm seek to impose upon us a remedy which appears to us as unjust as it is one-sided, as illogical as it is inequitable, we have a right to protest. All careful students beware of the man with the *ism*. This is not the first time that the enthusiast has supposed that he has discovered a world-saving panacea. The remedy lies not in any such lop-sided idea: the remedy is the slow and gradual evolution in a hundred ways of the moral conscience of mankind.[4]

The acrimonious encounter at Saratoga initiated a long series of criticisms that appeared in many books and articles by Seligman. Yet he was not altogether unappreciative of George and George's followers: "It is undoubtedly true," he wrote in one of his most celebrated works, "that the single tax agitation has been of great value. It has in some countries served to direct attention to the abuses of a medieval land system. It has in the United States helped to disclose the shortcomings of the antiquated general property tax. It has everywhere done yeoman's service in emphasizing the question of unjust privilege."[5] Especially did he prize the cooperation of single-taxers in his efforts to secure the abolition of taxes on personalty, which he regarded as particularly obnoxious. In point of fact, Seligman favored the taxation of land values as part of a more inclusive system, because, as he put it, "it reaches one of the elements of taxable ability.''[6] But he felt that all save the most modest incomes, from whatever source, should, for the same reason, be subject to exactions at progressive rates.

Seligman's influential *Essays in Taxation* may be considered his fullest and most definitive critique of Georgist doctrine. In it his animadversions are presented under two main headings, theoretical and practical, and within the latter heading under four subdivisions: fiscal, political, moral, and economic—in that order. However, it has been deemed expedient in the present chapter to commence with a treatment of his theoretical and moral objections by a specialist in social ethics, followed by a section on the other three categories by a specialist in land economics and public finance.

I*

In the distribution of wealth, the just satisfaction of individual claims requires that society's claim be also justly met. Such is the general crux of Henry George's message. But where does society's claim rightly stop? George's answer to this question set forth boundaries sharp and well-defined. In the hands of others, the boundaries of society's claim have been so far extended as to constitute no boundaries at all, and the claims of individuals proportionately reduced to nothing.

Among these others, few have had the influence of Seligman. As one who advocated an extended view of society's claim, Seligman overlooked no opportunity to challenge the restricted view of George. While most of his objections along this line had been advanced in one form or another by earlier writers, they achieved their greatest impact under the aegis of his authority. Such attempts as have been made to counter them have mainly taken place outside the normative stream of economic literature and have hence been but little felt despite their cogency.

One conclusion that emerges from Steven B. Cord's valuable study, *Henry George: Dreamer or Realist?*, is that the revived appreciation of George that has been manifest in recent years tends to be limited to certain rather superficial aspects of what George proposed, and does not preclude the concurrent acceptance of ideas antithetical to some of his most fundamental premises. This may be viewed, at least in part, as a testimony to the durability of attitudes that Seligman helped greatly to engender.

The moral rationale for George's system rests upon two logically independent but complementary arguments, one primary and the other secondary. The first of these is the argument that since God created the earth for the use of all men, no one has the right to arrogate to himself exclusive access to any portion of it without indemnifying those thereby denied access. The indemnity, amounting to the market value of the advantage, namely, ground rent, is seen as a divinely provided fund that should be used by the community to meet general social needs.

The secondary argument is that inasmuch as the market value of raw land is wholly a social product, that value should be appropriated by society as the

*Section I, by Dr. Andelson, is adapted from his article "Where Society's Claim Stops: An Evaluation of Seligman's Ethical Critique of Henry George," *American Journal of Economics and Sociology* 27, no. 1 (January 1968): 41-53.

most "natural" and equitable source of public revenue. The primary argument is directed, at least initially, against private ownership of land and espouses the public appropriation of ground rent simply as a mechanism whereby such ownership may be rendered ethically and practically innocuous. The secondary argument, on the other hand, bypasses the matter of land and attacks the question of ground rent directly.

Both arguments, it should be noted, assume the labor theory of ownership, which in turn is rooted in the doctrine of natural rights. Given classical expression in Locke's *Second Treatise of Government*, the labor theory of ownership asserts that since the individual has an inherent right to his own person, he has a right to his labor as an extension of his person, and therefore a right to whatever that labor produces when applied to the opportunities afforded by his natural environment. This product he may consume, save, give away, bequeath, destroy, or exchange at will. But inasmuch as land is not a product of human labor, it may legitimately be treated as private property only so long as there is "enough, and as good, left in common for others."[7] Translated into economic terms, this means only as long as it has no market value. Implicit in Locke's position is a corollary upon which George laid emphasis: ". . .as labor cannot produce without the use of land, the denial of the equal right to the use of land is necessarily the denial of the right of labor to its own produce."[8]

Seligman's ethical critique of George begins with the misleading statement that "the essential feature of the Single Tax is the singleness of the tax. . . ."[9] In his essay "The Classification of Public Revenues" he defines a tax as "a compulsory contribution. . .to defray the expenses incurred in the common interest of all, without reference to special benefits conferred."[10] George's proposal for the public appropriation of ground rent is not in this sense a proposal for a tax at all, but rather for a public or quasi-public price to be placed upon the special benefit received from society by the holders of land titles. As a concession to popular usage, he sometimes referred to it as a tax, but he never considered the term descriptively accurate.

Nor did George regard the "singleness" aspect of his proposal as its essential feature. He rejected all true taxes as arbitrary and unjust because not proportionate to benefits. But his system does not exclude the theoretical possibility of public charges for special benefits other than the privilege of monopolizing the "opportunities which nature offers impartially to all," although he viewed such other benefits as comparatively trivial. Neither does his system exclude the theoretical possibility of a uniform charge for socially conferred benefits available to everyone; he merely held that those who enjoy such common benefits should not be made to pay for them until those who enjoy special benefits at the expense of all have paid for these in full.[11] He anticipated that if this were done, the revenue would be sufficient to render a more general levy superfluous, and there is evidence that, at least for his time, he may have been correct in this. Insofar as monopolistic privilege begets social evils that give rise to public expense, his reform, to the extent that it would extirpate such privilege, would concurrently reduce the need for public revenue. Furthermore, the potential ground-rent fund is much larger than is commonly supposed.[12]

Seligman gets his critique under way with a sweeping indictment of the doctrine of natural rights, which he claims has been proved incontestably by modern jurisprudence and political philosophy to be mistaken.[13] This claim he grounds upon the fact that *belief* in the doctrine has been demonstrated to be a phenomenon lacking in historical catholicity—a fact that actually, of course, in no way invalidates the doctrine itself. However, this non sequitur need not occupy us further, for Seligman contends that even if the natural rights doctrine could be accepted, the labor theory of ownership would still be false.

Individual labor, he asserts, has never by itself produced anything in civilized society.* The very conditions that make production (save at the most primitive and rudimentary level) possible are the result of the contributions of the community. Civilized production depends upon a general fund of knowledge that has been built up through generations of technological experimentation. It depends upon opportunities for transportation, marketing, and the like that the individual finds already at hand, a legacy from others. It depends upon the materials and tools he uses, made available by countless men and women, the specific identity of most of whom he cannot but be ignorant:

> Take, for example, the workman fashioning a chair. The wood has not been produced by him; it is the gift of nature. The tools that he uses are the results of the contributions of others; the house in which he works, the clothes he wears, the food he eats (all of which are necessary in civilized society to the making of a chair), are the result of the contributions of the community. His safety from robbery and pillage—nay, his very existence—is dependent on the ceaseless cooperation of the society about him. How can it be said, in the face of all this, that his own individual labor wholly creates anything?. . .No one has a right to say: This belongs absolutely and completely to me, because I alone have produced it. Society, from this point of view, holds a mortgage on everything that is produced.[14]

All private ownership is justified, therefore, only because and to the extent that it has social utility. Since all property is preeminently a social product, what a man owes society should be measured by how much he owns, and the amount of his tax governed by his ability to pay.

The above reasoning really consists of three separate lines of argument, for it is clear that three distinct factors have gone into the making of the chair apart from the labor of the chairmaker. First, there is the wood. Although, as Cord points out, only as uncut virgin timber is wood, strictly speaking, a gift of nature,[15] we may, for purposes of discussion, regard it as representing the element of natural opportunity, namely, land, upon which all production ultimately rests. Second, there is the mental and physical labor of other individual producers, signified by the chairmaker's tools, his clothes, his food, and so on. Finally, there is his safety from robbery and pillage, guaranteed by government. Only this last may be considered the contribution of society as an organized body not separable into its component members.

Perhaps Henry George's most distinctive offering to social thought is his insistence that the cost of governmental factor should not be drawn from wages and interest, but rather met from the natural factor as an inevitable

---

*This argument was rudimentarily anticipated in Richard T. Ely's *Taxation in American Cities* (1888), pp. 16 f.

accompaniment of the full exercise of the protective function. By appropriating ground rent, government would not only acquire the means (he believed sufficient means) for its own support, but also perform one of its most vital duties—that of protecting citizens from pillage in the form of the monopolistic private expropriation of natural opportunity. From that which no private labor has produced, he taught, arises a social fund which, if taken by society as an organized totality, should prove adequate to sustain its operations as an organized totality. Why should the chairmaker pay tribute to a private landowner for his wood, George would have asked, when the landowner did nothing to produce it? Instead, let him make his payment to society, for the wood is a natural opportunity in limited supply, and the market value of timberland delineates the degree to which that opportunity is not available to all who wish to use it. His payment (made via the landowner, who could retain a small percentage of it as a collection fee) would reimburse the other members of society for the opportunity of which his acquisition has dispossessed them, and at the same time support the protection that society, through government, affords to him and them alike.[16] George would concur with Seligman that society holds a mortgage on the chair for the wood of which it was fashioned and the protection under which it was produced, but he would say that the expense of the latter can and should be met by the payment of the former.

This leaves the middle factor that went into the making of the chair—the mental and physical labor of other producers, drawn upon by the chairmaker in his use of tools, housing, clothes, food, and the like. As Cord incisively remarks:

> the chairmaker satisfies his obligations to the society that provided him with these things by paying for them. Should he pay twice, once by reimbursing the original owners of these goods and services and then again by turning over a share. . .of his own chairmaking income? It would seem that one payment to society and its members should be morally and practically sufficient.[17]

But, it may be argued, the middle factor includes not merely those goods and services for which the chairmaker pays, but also a host of others for which he does not—the general cultural and technological advantages, both tangible and intangible, built up through the centuries by the efforts of individuals upon whose shoulders we all stand. Yet, if not paid for by the chairmaker, these advantages have been paid for nonetheless, in whatever returns for which they were initially exchanged. If, because of monopoly or other form of exploitation, these returns were in many instances more meager than they would have been under a free market, the chairmaker is not placed under obligation for this reason. The modern tourist who thrills to the sight of the pyramids does not incur a debt because they happened to be built by slaves! Although perhaps an unintended beneficiary of exploitation, he was not its agent; its victims are, in any case, beyond the possibility of recompense, and it is to no one's detriment that he avails himself of the advantage for which he does not pay.

In contending that this middle factor constitutes a justification for a mortgage by society upon production, Seligman repeats a fallacy that may stem from a misreading of Mill[18] and was spread in this country by Edward Bellamy,[19] namely, that the division of labor imposes upon the individual who is its beneficiary an obligation that extends beyond that which he satisfies in the ordinary process of exchange.

The division of labor assumes by definition the reciprocal satisfaction of its participants, for by division, rational division is implied, and without reciprocity division must in the last analysis rest upon arbitrary elements. Society does not exist apart from concrete individuals, and its function (however much perverted in historic practice) is to permit them the reciprocal satisfaction of their wants. If, therefore, they are not free to exchange goods and services on a voluntary basis, it is evident that social institutions obtain that thwart the function of society itself. If they are free to make such voluntary exchanges, they will do so only in terms of mutual satisfaction as determined by supply and demand. When once, under such conditions, an exchange has been consummated, its participants have no further claim to a return. Although others, not parties to the exchange, may benefit incidentally from it, no liability is thereby incurred by them, for (1) they did not enter into the transaction, and (2) those who did enter into it have already been fully recompensed according to the stipulations upon which the exchange was based.

This is not to say, of course, that the exchange may not anticipate the involvement of additional parties, but the obligation of such parties does not arise unless and until they agree to meet whatever terms are set by the makers of the original transaction. In other words, while an initial transaction may lead to new ones, it does not of itself impose a liability upon anyone not a party to it. The division of labor as manifested in the marketplace affords no justification for a social mortgage on production, for, if unimpeded, the operation of the market automatically provides for the reciprocal satisfaction of its participants. This is brought out in more detail by Max Hirsch, who also effectively refutes another line of argument against the labor theory of ownership—that ability and the value of services are social products, and that their reward therefore rightfully belongs to society as a whole.[20]

Since the labor theory of ownership does not purport to justify the private ownership of nature, Seligman's point about the wood used by the chairmaker is irrelevant. Since the labor theory can be enforced only by the protective activities of government, it is in no way invalidated by the recognition that the cost of those activities represents a lien on ownership. By refusing protection, an individual may theoretically divest himself of such a lien, but in thus placing himself outside of the protective system he makes himself presumptively its enemy, forfeiting his claim to the right of ownership by declining to assume its correlative responsibilities. However, since the costs of protection can be met, at least in part, by a charge for the privilege of treating as private property something not produced by labor, society's lien on ownership to pay these costs does not become morally operative until the full rent-yield of nature, as determined by the market, has been collected and applied against them.

Cord adverts to Seligman's repetition of the time-worn notion that "since land is bought with the fruits of human labor, the labor theory [of ownership] can justify the private ownership of land."[21] Like the proposition just dealt with, that the labor theory can justify the ownership of producible goods (e.g., chairs) by society, this is an attempt to discredit the labor theory as self-contradictory. Cord answers it succinctly: "Exchange or purchase cannot make an unjust title just; after all, one might buy stolen property or a slave, and yet a rightful title would not be acquired by such a purchase."[22]

Cord believes that "although George's labor theory [of ownership] merits respect, recent developments regarding taxation force some short-run modification of it."[23] Yet his suggestions in this connection do not really touch the labor theory of ownership as such, but merely George's application of it as embodied in the proposal for a levy falling exclusively upon ground rent. I have already shown that George's theory does not actually exclude the possibility of other benefit charges should the rent fund prove inadequate to meet such obviously legitimate expenses as the cost of public safety. Since such things as police protection and national defense are benefits vital to the common weal, and upon which every member of society may lay equal claim, it is patently right that each should bear an equal share of any cost that may exceed that which can be financed from the rent fund. The same principle obtains from a perhaps more local standpoint with respect to the expenditures necessary for safety requirements like fire and flood control and the control of communicable disease.

However, Cord goes further, suggesting that still other expenditures are needed to maintain "that essential condition of true democracy, equality of opportunity."[24] In this category he mentions expenditures for free medical care for the indigent, and compulsory unemployment insurance, and remarks that "many people argue" that the list should include expenditures for farm price supports, public housing, tariff protection, and post office deficit—additions that he is evidently not himself inclined to accept.

Even if all these things were demonstrably requisite to equality of opportunity, their legitimacy might well be questioned on the ground that whereas the function of insuring *equal freedom of opportunity* falls properly within the role of government, the function of insuring equality of opportunity does not. If government seriously undertakes to insure equality of opportunity, it must go beyond preventing predation and the unequal advantages that arise therefrom and seek to redress inequality resulting from differences in native endowment. It can do this only by conferring special privileges on some at the expense of others, and this is precisely what it does when it uses tax money for the purposes just listed. But, as Cord comments, from a moral standpoint "the taxing of one individual to benefit another cannot be condoned."[25] Coercive monopolization of opportunity could be largely obviated by the public appropriation of ground rent. For, as stated in the eloquent prose of Winston Churchill, the land monopoly, while not the only monopoly, "is by far the greatest of monopolies—it is a perpetual monopoly, and it is the mother of all other forms of monopoly."[26] It seems probable that if freedom of access to natural opportunity were thus guaranteed, the number of deserving indigent would be so reduced that their needs could be cared for without recourse to compulsory support.

In his impressive study *The Philosophy of Henry George*, George Raymond Geiger essayed to reconcile the labor theory of ownership with the social-utility theory.[27] In like vein, Cord asserts that in the last analysis "there may be no real difference between the social utility and labor theories of property, except in the matter of emphasis,"[28] because "what is best for society is that each man should receive the fruits of his labor."[29] While advocates of the utility theory might accept this notion of what is best for society as a very general long-run proposition, most would allow for so many exceptions in specific cases as to render it useless as a regulating principle. Furthermore, to say that in the long run justice promotes utility is not the same as saying that utility ought to be the standard for justice. In fact, the two theories cannot be reconciled, for each asserts a different norm as ultimate. Yet to accept utility as ultimate is to follow a will-o'-the-wisp, for it always presupposes something else in terms of which it is defined.

Allied with Seligman's attack upon the labor theory of ownership is his attack upon the concept of ground rent as a uniquely social product. Whereas according to the former attack, inasmuch as nothing is the product of unaided labor, social utility and not labor constitutes the proper criterion for ownership; according to the latter attack, inasmuch as nothing can be long produced for sale without social demand, society holds a mortgage upon all commodities. Thus George's secondary argument—that because ground rent is socially produced it constitutes a distinctively appropriate basis for public revenue—comes under fire.

In his book Cord concedes, albeit reluctantly, this point,[30] insisting that the justification for the public collection of ground rent can be made to rest squarely upon George's primary argument and is weakened by appeal to the secondary one, which he dismisses as untenable despite its facile and seductive nature.[31] However, he has since abandoned this position. As Geiger remarks in his defense of the secondary argument, economic value is determined, not by demand alone, but by the relationship between supply and demand:

> the press of population and all the amenities of civilized society express themselves in the demand for land—as they do in the demand for everything else—but whereas the demand for land *must* raise land rent and land value, the value of consumer goods and capital goods will rise *or* fall, not merely as demand varies, but also in proportion to the elasticity of a reproducible supply in meeting that demand.[32]

This he illustrates by pointing out that in large centers of population, where rent is invariably high, the value of labor products, all other things being equal, is comparatively low. Land is supremely characterized by its inelasticity of reproducible supply.

> Given an unmonopolized supply of any economic element, in the production of which there is some measure of competition, increased demand and higher societal organization may not result in increased value. But since there is essentially a monopoly of land and since it is fundamentally irreproducible, increasing demand and social organization *must* raise land values.[33]

It must be noted that the reasoning just quoted hypothesizes an unmonopolized supply of consumer and capital goods. However, Seligman maintains that "if there is one thing that distinguishes the modern age, it is the development of economic monopolies of all kinds," and that the " 'unearned increment' of land is only one instance of a far larger class."[34] For purposes of example, he draws a parallel between increase in land values and the rising earnings of a newspaper because of the growth of a community. Jackson H. Ralston comments that in order for such a parallel to be valid, "the newspaper plant must be closed, the machinery left in place and all labor employed in it discharged. In that case, how much unearned increment will the newspaper building and the machinery, now idle, put into the pocket of the owner because they are surrounded by an industrial community?"[35]

The pertinence of Seligman's thrust as to the ubiquity of monopoly in consumer and capital goods is dispelled by a consideration of the seminal and pervasive character that land monopoly reveals to anyone who looks beneath the surface. The recognition of this character, dramatically proclaimed with Churchill's castigation of land monopoly as "the mother of monopoly," finds somewhat more sedate expression in the following statement by John R. Commons, an economist contemporaneous with Seligman: "If the size of fortunes is taken into account, it will be found that perhaps ninety-five percent of the total values represented by these millionaire fortunes is due to those investments classed as land values and natural monopolies, and to competitive industries aided by such monopolies."[36] Geiger concludes that:

> no matter how complete may be the capitalistic control of machinery and all the actual instruments of production, any significant separation of that "capital" from mineral, timber, fuel, railroad "land," would be fatal to monopoly. . . .It seems that, Antaeus-like, capital derives its strength from land, and it would appear that the breaking of land monopoly—which must follow once the value of land has been socialized—might operate upon the very foundations of capitalistic monopoly.[37]

More formidable than Seligman's objection to the secondary argument is one raised by Charles B. Spahr, another economist of the period. Even if land values are socially created, he insists, not all members of society are equally responsible for creating them. Some, in fact, may actually decrease them. Why, therefore, should ground rent be equally enjoyed, as George proposed, by all members of a given community?[38] Yet this objection, too, loses force when subjected to the following considerations:

To begin with, the extent to which an individual increases or decreases the value of a site has little or no relationship to whether or not he owns the site. Hence, however valid it may be otherwise, Spahr's objection constitutes no argument that rent should necessarily be appropriated by the owner. Second, everyone adds an equal unit to site-value merely by adding a population unit to the community where a site is located, even though, over and above this, individuals may differ in their effect on rent. Whereas the former effect is measurable, the latter is not and should therefore accrue to the community at large. Third, land values are in part due to the presence of good government and valuable public services. In a democratic community these things must be attributed to the general voting public, rather than to specific individual citizens. Finally, even where an individual contributes nothing to (or even decreases) land values, he still has a legitimate claim to be indemnified to the extent that private land ownership has denied him equal freedom of opportunity in the use of nature. Thus even if George's secondary argument were rendered nugatory by Spahr's objection, his primary argument would still vindicate the public appropriation of ground rent.

To return to Seligman—in the last analysis his attack upon the concept of land value as a uniquely social product represents an approach more forensic than substantive. For behind his effort to extend the notion of social increment as a source of public revenue beyond the limits defined by George lies an organismic theory of the state, which ultimately justifies the public confiscation of any kind of income, regardless of its source, his view of equity demanding only that the confiscation be proportioned to ability to pay. He sees the state as a unity that transcends the sum of its component members:

> [the individual] does not choose the State, but is born into it; it is interwoven with the very fibres of his being, nay, in the last resort, he gives to it his very life. . . .We pay taxes not because we get benefits from the State, but because it is as much our duty to support the State as to support ourselves or our family; because, in short, the State is an integral part of us.[39]

> The government, indeed, must do something for the community in return for the support which it receives. But this reciprocal obligation on the part of the government is not toward the individual as such, but toward the individual as a part of the greater whole. The special benefit is swallowed up in the common benefit. . . .In its ideal form, at all events, the State must be likened not to a joint-stock company, but to a family. The citizens are not stockholders but brethren, animated, if they are patriots, by the same ideals and by the same fine sense of cooperation in the common interest.[40]

This romantic theory, doubtless carried back by Seligman from his student sojourn in Germany, is grounded upon an interpretation of human nature that comports ill with the hardheaded empiricism affected by him as fitting to a social scientist. Seligman takes repeated potshots at George's "utopianism,"[41] yet what is more utopian than the notion that such exalted motives can be safely made the foundation of a political order? In actual application its effect has ever been to undergird the hegemony of authoritarians who declare with Robespierre, "Our will is the general will."

As an authority both restraining and restrained, the state is necessary and legitimate. As an absolute and omnicompetent power, from the standpoint of psychological realism it is both an ethical travesty and a practical absurdity. That personal fulfillment comes only as the individual loses himself in a preoccupation with some goal beyond himself is a truth that has been recognized by moral and mental theorists for centuries. But this truth cannot without unconscionable risk be made the foundation of a political philosophy. Considering the difficulty of finding men who can be trusted not to abuse the relatively modest function of insuring the reciprocal freedom of citizens to choose and follow their own separate goals, it is fatuous to suppose that any leader, elite group, or majority of men is so virtuous and wise as to qualify for the task of choosing goals to which all shall be compelled to give allegiance. Reciprocal freedom is the only goal the acceptance of which can safely be made operatively incumbent upon every citizen. Although George, in words attributed to Helen Keller, displayed "a splendid faith in the essential nobility of human nature,"[42] his system does not depend upon that faith. Instead of relying upon the beneficent use of unchecked power, it envisages its limitation and dispersion through decentralization and the extirpation of monopoly. As one examines George's thought against the horrors that manifest themselves increasingly as the final outcome of the logic of the total state, one cannot but conclude that he should be reckoned the realist, and Seligman, the dreamer.

II*

In addition to opposing the single tax on theoretical and moral grounds, Seligman had a number of pragmatic technical objections to it. As we review these, it should be borne in mind that, like the others, they were directed against the *single* tax, not against land-value taxation as merely one component of a public revenue system also embracing other levies such as Seligman's choice, the progressive income tax.

Under the rubric "fiscal defects," he cites, to begin with, the inelasticity of a sole tax on land values as a source of public funds. By this he means, first of all, that under it the fisc cannot increase revenues at will, because it has but one source and is already by assumption taking all that that source will yield. Second, he means that revenues based only upon that source will be unstable, since the unimproved value of land is "subject to far more fluctuations than in commodities where the supply may be altered at pleasure."[43]

Against the charge of inelasticity considered in its first aspect, the following points may be raised:

(a) The same charge is leveled routinely but mindlessly against the property tax in general. It flies in the face of the fact that the value of land is rising faster than income or almost anything else, and the property-tax base is in fact highly elastic. Income tax revenues rise in part because rates keep rising as inflation puts more and more people in higher and higher brackets; property taxes rise because the base rises, with fixed rates.

(b) An unbridled power to tax is not necessarily desirable. The history of the decline of civilizations is not one of inadequate powers to tax, but of topheavy parasitic bureaucracies. Today, the movement for revenue limitations in several states reflects widespread belief that government profligacy can be controlled in no other way.

(c) Governmental units with bonding and borrowing power can handle temporary bulges in needs without increasing taxes, as long as they have sufficient discipline to retrench when capital needs have been met.

(d) At present, most governments collect considerably less than the full land rent, raising the percentage from time to time as required and often lowering it too. They could just as well collect it all and distribute part of it in the form of social dividends, reducing dividends when faced with mounting needs.

(e) A small local community cannot tax more than the rent anyway, by whatever means, because other taxes are shifted into lower rents—that is, they reduce land values. (If this were to continue to the point where land ceased to have value, the community, and hence the need for taxes, would disappear.) Taxing rent directly is simply a more efficient means of doing this, without the "excess burdens" of indirect taxation. A corollary of this is that a local government can collect more revenue by taxing land values than in any other

*Section II is the work of Dr. Gaffney.

way. Inefficient taxes create unacceptable hardships for marginal lands and producers while the best lands are still yielding lots of rent for their owners. (A marginal community will not be uniformly marginal, but have better and worse parcels.)

(f) Efficient government will generate more rents (although fewer speculative values).

Issue may also be taken with the charge of inelasticity in its second aspect:

(a) Historically there have been some wide boom-and-bust swings in land values in frontier areas, to which Seligman evidently alludes. But these have occured in the absence of heavy land taxes. As he points out later[44] with respect to Western Canada, even where buildings were exempt, tax rates on land were so low as to bear scarely any resemblance to what George proposed (Charles H. Shields found they were lower than in the average U.S. city[45]). One of Seligman's inconsistencies is to pillory the full single tax, and use the negligible single tax as a case in point.

(b) Local governments rely upon property taxation because of its stability and reliability, which many of them need because of their weak credit ratings. Short-term variations in activity-based taxes are not matched by equal variations in property taxes. The land part of the property base is normally the more stable. This may be seen frequently in decaying central cities, where the land retains a renewal value even where buildings have become worthless. After a whole neighborhood declines, the land also loses value; but at the fringes of the blighted neighborhood there is still land value, and the renewal that would result from taxing land instead of buildings would sequentially restore the renewal value of land from the outside inwards. In marginal areas with minerals, the property tax on mineral values provides a stable revenue, while the severance tax is turned on and off at the convenience of the owners. Indeed, owners criticize the property tax for imposing risk on them. It follows that it reduces risk for the fisc.

(c) A compact and orderly city and region, growing outward sequentially, would not be subject to boom and bust. This is the objective of land planning cum land taxation. The wild swings that Seligman deplores have occurred in the absence of significant land-value taxation, and should hardly be cited as the results of, or as arguments against, it—whether it be proposed as the sole source of public revenue or otherwise.

Another alleged fiscal weakness of the single tax is that land is difficult to assess accurately. Seligman gives no authorities or data, but much vigorous affirmation. Extended discussion by economists and assessors of this point may be found in *The Assessment of Land Value*, edited by Daniel M. Holland.[46] The weight of opinion there is that the accurate assessment of land values is feasible but that of buildings, less so. There is, of course, a problem of undertrained assessors, but it tends to solve itself as we increase reliance on this tax base. The tax on which we rely most heavily will get the brains and personnel to handle technical difficulties.

Seligman concedes in a qualified way that land values in cities can be distinguished from building values, but he thinks that in rural districts the separation of land values from improvement values constitutes an insuperable problem because agricultural improvements are so largely *in* rather than *on* the land. As a farm economist at the University of Missouri, the present writer looked into this question and found little to support Seligman's position.[47] Léon Walras, too, examined this question in his *Théorie d'économie sociale*, although his treatment of it is omitted from Jaffe's English translation. The farmland apologists, he says, see the manure going into the soil; they do not see the yield coming out of it each year. Artificial fertility in fact turns itself over economically in a short time.

With respect to the matter of agricultural improvements, as elsewhere, Seligman assumes the worst: a perverse, destructive assessor who seizes upon any soil improvement to confiscate, and violates the spirit of the laws he is administering. This smacks more of hostile rhetoric than of careful analysis.

Seligman next introduces three "political defects." The first of these is that the adoption of the single tax would necessitate the abolition of import duties. Most economists favor free trade anyway, as George did. But if protection be regarded as desirable, nothing says we cannot tax both land and imports, or use quotas and marketing agreements. Seligman suggests that, quite apart from protection, there may be political or fiscal advantages in having import duties. Most economists have noted, on the other hand, that Britain's era of political and economic hegemony coincided with its era of free trade.

The second "political defect" is that the single tax would preclude sumptuary taxes. But sumptuary taxes, although sometimes prolific revenue producers, often fail in their intended function; when set high enough on a commodity to deter legal sale, they are evaded on the black market. If, however, a cigarette tax, for instance, be viewed as a rent charge for the use of air at the expense of others, it can be justified on Georgist grounds. Taxes on activities that pollute the environment are rents for the use of a natural resource.

The third political weakness is that the single tax would take away "from the vast majority of citizens the sense of their obligation to the government, and. . .divorce their economic interests from those of the state," since a relatively small segment of the population would pay the taxes.[48] This rings strangely coming from an advocate of ability to pay as the prime criterion of taxation, and is one of Seligman's many inconsistencies. (Incidentally, it should be noted that he concedes, in asserting this position, that land is not very widely held.) "Since the 'unearned increment' would flow of itself, silently and noiselessly into the treasury, there would be no need of a budget; and the sense of responsibility in the citizens would be perceptibly diminished."[49] There is an inconsistency here, too, for the statement does not jibe with his earlier concern about the elasticity of revenue, which suggested that the problem would be lack of enough money for government. Here he worries that there would be too much. In fact, the ability to tax almost anything, which he favors, seems more likely to encourage public extravagance than does the limitation of taxes to land values. Certainly, the ability of landowners to slough taxes onto others turns them from watchdogs of the treasury into raiders, since so much of public spending creates new unearned increments to land value.

The remainder of Seligman's objections to the single tax are "economic defects." The first is that marginal communities would have practically no public revenue if they were restricted to taxing land. "Since land values [in such communities] are insignificant, a tax imposed on an insignificant basis must be insignificant."[50] Under such circumstances, the maintenance of roads, schools, and so on would become impossible. In fact, in order to be marginal rather than submarginal, a district must have land that yields enough to pay not merely the private costs of production but also the costs of government, however taxes may be levied. Labor and capital are mobile in comparison with land, so they will move around until their returns are equalized after taxes; they will not remain in a marginal district if the burden of taxes is placed upon them.

He next asserts that under the Henry George proposal, the taxes of the farm population would increase. He presents data showing that the value of improvements per dollar of land value is, on the whole, greater in cities than on farms. A missing link in his argument is whether these data come from within the same tax jurisdiction, but they clearly do not and so miss the mark. Actually, as to land/building ratios, both farms and cities are heterogeneous. There are land-intensive farms, and capital-intensive ones. It is between these categories that the shift of the tax burden would occur. (The present writer has data showing that the capital-intensive farms are, for the most part, smaller.) Where cities include "farms" today, they would be valued primarily as speculations and only incidentally as farms. Getting more taxes from their owners would not be increasing the burden on working farmers.

But if some farmers did have to pay more, so what? It is bad enough to make cows sacred, and worse to add the owners of their pasture. Intensive farmers would not pay more. "The efficient farmer with his heavy investment in capital equipment would certainly benefit by a shift of taxation from improvements to land; the inefficient might not, but perhaps he should be persuaded by every means, including that of taxation, to switch to more economically desirable endeavors."[51]

Seligman's final point has to do with the effect of the single tax on urban communities. Here he seeks to refute the contention that the inhabitants of slums would be benefited because the abolition of taxes on improvements would cause "vacant lots to be built over as if by magic,"[52] thus making more housing available, and forcing down tenement rents.

He asks "where all this additional capital which is to be invested in houses is coming from. There is no fund floating about in the air which can be brought to earth simply by the imposition of the Single Tax; the amounts to be laid out in houses must be taken from the capital now invested in some other form of productive enterprise."[53] Seligman contradicted himself in an article written a few years later, by stating that the imposition of a land-value tax would cause a building boom that would last until a new equilibrium between dwellings and population had been reached.[54] Still, it could be instructive to pursue his idea.

His contention in the *Essays* that capital would not be available for building represents an unstated change of focus from the local to the national or world economy. Any small jurisdiction, obviously, can import capital from outside, and will do so if it exempts buildings and taxes land. Today, economists speak routinely of "open" and "closed" economies, to indicate what is assumed about the possibilities for migration of capital and labor. One is supposed, in a discussion of this sort, to stick with one or the other; Seligman makes points by moving back and forth without saying what he is doing. Georgists have not always been consistent either, but here I am reviewing Seligman.

He correctly states that the Georgist premise that building taxes are shifted forward to tenants assumes implicitly that what is at issue is a building tax levied partially and selectively on rental buildings. This is known now as partial equilibrium analysis. But if taxes are levied on all capital, and the supply of capital is *not* fixed (an open economy), then the tax must rather be shifted into lower land values. Where else could it lodge? The other inputs can all cut and run.

Seligman, however, has moved in his discussion, without saying so, to a closed economy. If all capital is taxed uniformly, he states, the supply, like that of land, is fixed, and so owners of capital bear the tax in lower rates of return.

Seligman fails to consider that even in this closed economy there is a fund of capital, not "floating about in the air" but stuck in the ground. This is the huge and ever-growing waste of public and utility-industry capital in the over-extended infrastructure demanded by urban sprawl, and private trucks and autos required to survive in scatter land. These diversions of capital from housing and industrial needs result from the land speculation that George's policies are designed to prevent and remedy.

Also, even in a closed economy, taxing capital means a lower rate of return to capital after tax, which might reduce saving, investment and capital formation. This is a major issue today. Nor does Seligman look at the allocation of capital between taxed private uses and tax-free public ones. Public agencies generally overuse capital, in part because they pay no property taxes on it. Nor does he consider that even the whole national economy is not really entirely closed. Capital is imported and exported. Lower returns here have caused it to emigrate on a grand scale.

Nor does Seligman consider that lower after-tax returns to capital mean lower capitalization rates applied to land incomes. Land value is income/interest rate. Higher land values thus result from taxing capital, where capital bears the tax (granting the assumption that it does). This higher land value is an asset to the owner, constituting a substitute for real capital, and weakening his incentive to save. Thus lower after-tax returns to capital do indeed reduce capital formation.

Seligman now raises the objection that the single tax could not reduce inner-city congestion, because slum inhabitants are necessarily limited to small areas by their preference for living in proximity to their work and, since virtually all the land in these areas is already developed and in use, nothing will increase the effective supply. He cites a tenement neighborhood on Manhattan Island, saying that "not seven-tenths of one percent of the building lots lie idle."[55]

Two of his assertions now contradict each other. First, he alleges that the exemption of improvements from taxation would cause landowners to erect higher tenements, creating worse congestion. Second, he says that taxation has relatively little impact upon land-use decisions. (The evidence he gives for this consists of instances in Western Canada where improvements were exempt, while the land tax was kept low in the face of a tremendous surge in land values.) By now his hostile rhetoric has carried him beyond the self-discipline of consistency, and he becomes merely quarrelsome and captious. Perhaps he was reacting to careless overstatements by others, but we cannot say, because he never identifies or cites his antagonists, simply lumping the whole bad lot as "single taxers."

Seligman ends with a proposal to stop the underassessment of unimproved city lots, and another for the imposition of a special or higher tax on vacant lands in or near the city. While these proposals are oriented in the right direction, they suggest a very limited understanding of the problem of land speculation, for urban real estate that is completely unimproved and vacant is just the tip of the iceberg.

Notes

1.   Louis F. Post, *The Prophet of San Francisco* (New York: Vanguard Press, 1930), p. 231. Chapter 23 of Post's book is almost wholly devoted to the refutation of Seligman's arguments.

2.   Edwin R. A. Seligman, Henry George, et al., "The Single Tax Debate," *Journal of Social Science: Containing the Transactions of the American Association,* no. 27 (October 1890), p. 85.

3.   Ibid., p. 98.

4.   Ibid.

5.   E.R. A. Seligman, *Essays in Taxation,* 9th ed. (New York: Macmillan, 1923), p. 96. The first edition appeared in 1895.

6.   Ibid., p. 74.

7.   John Locke, *Second Treatise of Government,* chap. 5, par. 27.

8.   Henry George, *Progress and Poverty,* 75th anniversary ed. (New York: Robert Schalken-bach Foundation, 1954), p. 341.

9.   Seligman, *Essays in Taxation,* p. 68.

10.   Ibid., p. 432.

11.   See George, *Progress and Poverty*, p. 20.

12.   See Steven B. Cord, *Henry George: Dreamer or Realist?* (Philadelphia: University of Pennsylvania Press, 1965), pp. 122, 191-93.

13.   Seligman, *Essays in Taxation,* p. 69.

14.   Ibid., p. 71.

15.   Cord, *Henry George,* p. 83.

16.   The foregoing analysis accepts, for the sake of argument, the adequacy of Seligman's illustration, if not the logic of his inferences. It should, however, be remembered that the incidence of payment finally rests upon the chair's ultimate purchaser, regardless of whether the payment goes to the landowner or to society. One sometimes hears it said that the landowner cannot shift a public charge ("tax") on land to the consumer. This is a loose way of phrasing a proposition with which almost all economists, including Seligman, agree—that such a charge cannot increase ground rent and raise commodity prices. (See E. R. A. Seligman, *The Shifting and Incidence of Taxation,* 4th ed., [New York: Columbia, 1921], pp. 281-87.) In fact, it tends to decrease prices by "squeezing the speculative water" out of land values, for if a high enough percentage of ground rent is taken by the taxing authority, the incentive to hold land off the market disappears, along with the inflated prices owing to artifical scarcity.

17.   Cord, *Henry George,* p. 83.

18.   John Stuart Mill, *Principles of Political Economy,* 7th ed. (1871), bk. 1, chap. 2.

19.   Edward Bellamy, *Equality* (New York: Appleton & Co., 1897), chap. 13, pp. 88-91.

20.   Max Hirsch, *Democracy versus Socialism*, 4th ed. (New York: Robert Schalkenbach Foundation, 1948), pp. 221-27.

21.   Cord, *Henry George,* p. 83.

22.   Ibid. See also a vigorous and extended discussion in Hirsch, *Democracy versus Socialism,*

chap. 7.

23.   Cord, *Henry George* p. 230.

24.   Ibid.

25.   Ibid., p. 231.

26.   Winston S. Churchill, *Liberalism and the Social Problem* (London: Hodder & Stoughton, 1939), p. 318.

27.   George Raymond Geiger, *The Philosophy of Henry George* (New York: The Macmillan Company, 1933), p. 138.

28.   Cord, *Henry George*, p. 83.

29.   Ibid., p. 231.

30.   Ibid., p. 232.

31.   Ibid. See also p. 127.

32.   Geiger, *Philosophy of Henry George*, p. 108. See also p. 96. Geiger's defense is somewhat blurred by his characterization of capital as a social product (p. 108). But the burden of his discussion is to demonstrate that this is only partially the case, whereas it is wholly true of land values. When he speaks of the supply of capital as being socially determined, he does not mean that it is primarily a social product, but that it expands and contracts in response to social demand.

33.   Geiger, *Philosophy of Henry George*, p. 108.

34.   Seligman, *Essays in Taxation*, pp. 81, 83.

35.   Jackson H. Ralston, *What's Wrong with Taxation?* (San Diego: Ingram Institute, 1932), p. 58.

36.   John R. Commons, *The Distribution of Wealth*, p. 253. Cited by Cord, *Henry George*, p. 72.

37.   Geiger, *Philosophy of Henry George*, pp. 260 f.

38.   Charles B. Spahr, "Single Tax," *Political Science Quarterly* (December 1891). Cited by Cord, *Henry George*, p. 70.

39.   Seligman, *Essays*, p. 73.

40.   Ibid., p. 337.

41.   Ibid., pp. 69, 97. Also his concluding remarks at the Saratoga convention of the American Social Science Association, reported in *Journal of Social Science: Containing the Transactions of the American Association*, no. 27 (October 1890), p. 98.

42.   This quotation was cited for many years in the annual brochure of the Henry George School of Social Science; its source is a letter written around 1930 by Miss Keller to the Robert Shalkenbach Foundation.

43.   Seligman, *Essays*, p. 76.

44.   Ibid., p. 94.

45.   Charles H. Shields, *Single Tax Exposed*, 7th ed. (Seattle, Wash.: Trade Register, Inc., 1914), chap. 9.

46.   Daniel M. Holland, ed., *The Assessment of Land Value* (Madison: University of Wisconsin Press, 1970).

47.   See M. Mason Gaffney, "Soil Depletion and Land Rent," *Natural Resources Journal* 4, no. 3 (January 1965): 537-57.

48.   Seligman, *Essays*, pp. 78 f.

49.   Ibid., p. 78.

50.   Ibid., p. 84.

51.   Cord, *Henry George*, p. 86.

52.   Seligman, *Essays*, p. 92.

53.   Ibid.

54.   Seligman, "Halving the Tax Rate on Buildings: The Argument in Opposition," *Survey* 31 (17 March 1914), as reprinted in Edna Bullock, comp., *Selected Articles on the Single Tax*, 2d ed. (New York: H. W. Wilson Co., 1917), p. 164. Cited in Cord, *Henry George*, pp. 88 f.

55.   Seligman, *Essays*, p. 93.

Part IV
Twentieth-Century Critics

20

Davenport: "Single Taxer of the Looser Observance"

BY AARON B. FULLER

I

Herbert Joseph Davenport (1861-1931) was a prominent, early twentieth-century American economist whose contributions to economic analysis include a sophisticated opportunity-cost theory and a series of lucid presentations of marginal-utility theory.[1] Something of an iconoclast, he criticized many of his fellow economists and befriended his former teacher Thorstein Veblen at a time when most economists had lost interest in Veblen's theatrical personality and sweeping denunciations of economic principles.[2] In addition to these accomplishments, Davenport is cited by George R. Geiger in his important book *The Philosophy of Henry George*, as a major critic of George's theory of capital. Geiger argues that the "classical" distinction between land and capital was "a crucial one for George's economic system," and that "Professor Davenport was perhaps the most characteristic critic of this type of distinction."[3] But following these forthright assertions about George's system and Davenport's criticism of it, Geiger equivocates and severely qualifies his initial declaration that Davenport was "perhaps the most characteristic critic." His qualification is that Davenport's criticism is mentioned "not because his interpretation of economics—one which repudiates the classical attempts to make the science primarily a logical or ethical discipline and which instead stresses a strictly 'cost' approach—is felt to be necessarily representative of modern economic theory, but simply because of his decisive treatment of this particular [*capital theory*] problem."[4] Geiger has introduced a contradiction with his "most characteristic critic" description followed by his denial that Davenport's ideas are necessarily representative of modern economic theory, and this contradiction is present throughout Geiger's discussion of Davenport's views. Geiger offers no explicit clues as to why he decided to circumscribe the relevance of Davenport's views, but it is clear that by his equivocation he severs those views from any role that they might have played as representative of how then contemporary economic theorists viewed George's ideas.[5] As we shall see in the ensuing discussion of

293

Davenport's criticisms, Geiger's equivocation was as unnecessary as his basic point is incorrect; that is, Davenport's views on capital theory were very representative of contemporary economic theory, particularly as it was presented by Irving Fisher, and Davenport's capital theory was not a criticism of George's.

Geiger's view that Davenport was a critic of George's theoretical soundness is not absolute, because in a footnote he recognizes that Davenport favored a policy of land-rent taxation, and he correctly paraphrases Davenport's suggestion that "economists have been wrong in looking upon the single tax as a fad or hobby offering no practical discussion possibilities."[6] Even stronger recognition of Davenport's positive view of George's theoretical soundness is offered by Geiger's quotation in the same footnote of Davenport's explicit statement that "the economists have never seriously attacked the theoretical validity of the single tax program." In another footnote, Geiger cites Davenport's inclusion of himself (in the concluding paragraph of his *American Economic Review* essay, "Theoretical Issues in the Single Tax") among the "single taxers of the looser observance."[7] However, Geiger never reconciles Davenport's clear defense of the theoretical legitimacy of land-rent taxation, cited in these footnotes, with Geiger's own textual claim that Davenport is a major negative critic of George's theoretical structure. This contradiction between the main theme of Geiger's textual discussion of Davenport and the substance of the footnotes provides further evidence of Geiger's equivocal treatment of Davenport as a critic of George's theoretical soundness.

In addition to assessing the implications of Davenport's alleged criticisms of George's capital theory, we shall also examine Davenport's criticisms of land-rent-taxation proposals. Davenport expressed much sympathy with the basic principle of taxing land rents, declaring that "the truth is with the single-taxers in principle but not in method."[8] The "method" to which he particularly objected was the taxation of rents already accrued at the moment of the adoption of a land-rent tax program. He argued that those economic decision makers who enjoyed the gains from past increases in economic rents should not be deprived of those fortuitous increases.

Finally, it is necessary to examine two fundamental elements of the economic ideas of George and Davenport, opportunity cost and economic methodology, in order to see that there are compelling similarities between their ideas, leading to the implication that, to the extent that Davenport was a sound economist, George was also.

Geiger's discussion of Davenport is the sole basis in the literature for the claim that Davenport was a negative critic of George' theory. Geiger was simply wrong, and a suitable explanation for his error cannot be reconstructed from the textual evidence. We may hypothesize several speculations: that Geiger, a philosopher and not an economist, simply misread what Davenport and George wrote; that Geiger did not intend to introduce equivocations and contradictions, and they were simply missed in the editorial process; and that Geiger had an ax to hone, and Davenport's ideas provided a convenient rough edge against which he could sharpen his own preconceived ideas. These and other speculations must remain unresolved because it is not the present concern to engage in a historiographical reconstruction of Geiger's motives. In fact, the issue of whether Geiger's error is the result of deliberate intent or whether it was purely accidental is irrelevant to assessment of the contents of Davenport's ideas as they relate to Henry George. But Geiger's error (that Davenport was a negative critic of George's theoretical soundness) is relevant in a broader context, the issue of whether Henry George was a competent economist. Since Geiger's book (in the main an able and valuable study) is basically a defense of George's thought, the implications of this error tend to vitiate the work's essential thrust, and, were he aware of them, could not fail to be distressful to its author.

Geiger's initial identification of Davenport as a theoretical critic of George establishes a perspective in which George's conceptual foundations are viewed as being in conflict with the ideas of prominent economists. Geiger states that George's distinction between land and capital "has been severely attacked by more recent economic critics," and then he goes on to identify Davenport as the "most characteristic" of these severe critics.[9] Geiger's presentation is symptomatic of a major presupposition that underlies much of the literature that presents George's ideas—the preconceived, untested notion that George's ideas stand on one side of the issues he addresses and that the ideas of respected economists stand on the opposite side. Geiger to the contrary, Davenport was not a critic of George's economics. Davenport's and George's concepts of capital are different but compatible because they addressed different analytical needs, Davenport's the capital budgeting (optimal investment decision) problem and George's the theory of production and distribution. Extending beyond Geiger's presentation, Davenport did object to the retroactive taxation of accrued land rents, but this is an objection grounded in normative differences about what "ought" to be, not in positive differences based on theory about what "is." There is no basis here for arguing that Davenport was a negative critic of George's economics, because different policy prescriptions based on different value judgments are perfectly consistent with simultaneous agreements about the objective analytical facts. Finally, in two major conceptual areas Davenport and George were in agreement (opportunity cost and methodology), and this provides a far more substantial basis for arguing that Davenport and George shared similar analytical conceptions than Geiger's error does for arguing that Davenport and George were conceptually opposed. Geiger's error is unimportant in and of itself, but when related to the larger issue of whether George's ideas are outside the framework of accepted economic analysis, it deserves to be exposed. Such an exposure cannot prove that George was a good economist, but it can prevent false proof from being tendered that he was not.

II

It is in chapter 3, "George's Economic Solution," that Geiger presents what he interprets as the differences between Davenport and George: Davenport "broadly" defines capital as "all durable and objective sources of valuable private income," while George "narrowly" defines capital as "wealth used in the production of more wealth." In Geiger's view these definitions are radically different, with Davenport's representing "the continual shift away from the classical separation between land and capital. . .which is becoming more and more a characteristic element of present-day theory," and with George's representing the traditional classical position stated in the works of Adam Smith, David Ricardo, and John Stuart Mill. In order to assess Geiger's interpretation of the conflict between these concepts of capital, we must simultaneously address several related issues. First, is Geiger correct that these concepts of capital conflict? Second, what does George's definition mean in terms of his analytical approach? Third, what does Davenport's definition mean in terms of his analytical approach?

Geiger is incorrect that Davenport's view of capital is a criticism of or is in conflict with George's view of capital. Geiger fails to recognize that Davenport's concept of capital is intended for a different analytical purpose from George's, and that different definitions of capital are appropriate to different analytical contexts. Davenport's concern with capital is in terms of what is currently called the capital budgeting problem, or alternatively, the problem of optimal investment decisions.[10] This modern capital budgeting theory relies heavily on Irving Fisher's seminal analyses of capital theory, where consumption is viewed as the final aim of economic activity.[11] Davenport was well aware of Fisher's work, and he footnotes his discussion of the theory of capital and interest in *Value and Distribution* (1908) with the comment that "Professor Irving Fisher's admirable treatise upon *The Rate of Interest* appears as the present work is passing through the press." The footnote then continues over six pages of close type, taking up nearly all of the pages with a careful exposition of the basic elements of Fisher's capital and interest theories. Based on the Fisherian view, the balancing of consumption opportunities over time becomes the central economic allocation problem and it is broadly conceived as encompassing all rational economic choice.[12] The time element is a critical feature of this balancing process because it means that rational economic decision-making revolves around choices to consume income now or to abstain from consumption now and to wait to consume income in the future. Capital is then defined as current income that is not consumed but is "invested" to provide for consumption in the future, or in Hirshleifer's elegant phrasing, "capital is the present embodiment of future-dated consumption goods."[13] This view of capital emphasizes what economists call "capital value," and it is this capital value, the present market value of future income streams, that solutions to the capital budgeting problem are intended to maximize over time.

Davenport's definition of capital cited by Geiger, "all durable and objective sources of valuable private income," is in fact a definition of "real capital" or "capital goods" that is consistent with the Fisherian view of capital, shared by Davenport, which identifies capital as the present embodiment of future-dated consumption goods. The durable and objective capital goods provide the sources of the income streams that are allocated over time to maximize consumption over time. The source of these income streams is irrelevant to the capital budgeting (optimal investment) decision; what is important is that these income streams exist. Geiger's emphasis on Davenport's definition of capital goods is used to demonstrate that Davenport would include land in the definitition of capital goods, and Geiger is correct. But Geiger's implication is that the inclusion of land in the category of capital goods is evidence of an attack on the traditional distinction between land and capital, and this implication is incorrect. Land was included in the category of capital goods because it yields an income stream that can be allocated over time, and this allocation process is what Davenport was interested in describing and analyzing. Davenport does not deny that land has unique physical properties and that it can earn rents that are payments in excess of opportunity costs, but he does deny that these features of land are relevant to the decisions regarding the maximization of consumption opportunities over time. Maximizing consumption over time through the allocation of various income streams is not influenced by the sources of the income streams.

Geiger never realizes in his narrative that Davenport's definition of capital goods refers to sources of income, while Davenport's concept of capital refers to capital values that can be allocated over time to maximize consumption opportunities. As Davenport explains, "The value of any instrument of production is the present worth of all the future income attributed to it," and this value is the capital value to which the sources of income streams are irrelevant.[14] These income streams can come from land, machinery, buildings, inventories of goods and services, and all things that can be "traded in, or valued, or rented, or capitalized."[15] In fact, Davenport's list of durable and objective capital goods includes items that are durable and objective only in the sense that they can provide allocatable income streams over time: they are durable in the sense that they persist across alternative time periods, and they are objective in the sense that they provide allocatable income streams. Some of these less obvious capital goods besides land, buildings, machinery, and inventories are "patents, copyrights, trade-marks, business connections, reputation, good-will, privilege, government favor, franchises, royalties, rights of toll and tribute, rents, annuities, mortgage rights, personal claims; and further it includes monopolies of no matter how various kinds and degrees, so far as they may become the subject of invested cost in obtaining them, so far as they are bought and sold as steps in competitive-productive investment, or are vendible upon the market as capitalized dividend-paying properties."[16] All of these capital goods are legitimate objects of capital budgeting (optimal investment) decisions, and Davenport makes this quite clear in his description of the capital budgeting process. "Actual business computations of the expenses of production include a wide range of expenditures made out of what, in the individual reckoning, stands as the total business investment, and functions in the terminology and reckoning of the business world as business capital. . . . The manufacturing entrepreneur or the corporation manager would find it a novel and perplexing doctrine which should restrict the capital investment to the buildings, machinery and raw materials of the undertaking; the corporation really possesses nothing that is not capital."[17]

Davenport's presentation of a Fisherian view of capital is not necessarily inconsistent with George's narrower view of capital as produced means of production. In the Fisherian sense, capital is anything that yields valuable services over time, and in such a circumstance "the theory of capital becomes a theory of general economic growth."[18] *Capital* simply becomes a general term denoting consumption that is put off until a later time period, and the rate of interest is the exchange rate between present and future-dated consumption. Such an approach permits various solutions to the problems of intertemporal choice and the maximization of consumption over time, but if one is interested in a different problem, such as the problem of substitution in production and distribution, then a different concept of capital might not be inappropriate. These latter words are carefully chosen, because my argument is not that the Fisherian theory of capital is incapable of yielding answers to the issues surrounding production and distribution theory (primarily substitutability among productive resources)—in fact, this broad conception of capital can be used to provide such answers; instead, my argument is that George's conception of capital is not incapable of yielding these answers either. Thus the broad Fisherian capital concept advanced by Davenport has multiple analytical applications because it is so broad, while the narrower, produced-means-of-production concept advanced by George has fewer applications, but those to which it is relevant are just as legitimate as the Fisherian applications. There is no necessary conflict between the theories of capital advanced by Davenport and George, and Geiger's perception of conflict is mistaken.

As a final note on this capital theory issue, we should recognize that George did work through a rudimentary marginal productivity theory of production and distribution, and it is to this theory that the produced-means-of-production concept of capital is relevant. Although it is possible to develop a marginal productivity theory without the distinctions between land, labor, and capital that are present in George's analysis, it is also possible to develop such a theory with them, and this is what George did in a preliminary way. The critical requirement for a theory of marginal productivity is the recognition of the substitutability condition among resources in production, and George recognizes the necessity of substitutability at the margin.[19]

III

In two articles dealing with single-tax proposals, Davenport does provide some evidence that he is a "critic" of Henry George, but a critic of specific policy applications of land taxation, and not a critic of George's theoretical soundness.[20] Although George is not mentioned explicitly, Davenport objects to all single taxers who would tax both the existing accrued rents and the future increments of rent. He advocates only the taxation of the future increments, arguing that the taxation of previously accrued rents constitutes "a program which shall impose on any casual present owner of original natural bounty the penalty for a general and institutional blunder."[21] This objection is not a quarrel with the idea of the single tax on theoretical grounds; instead, it is a normative objection based on differing ethical standards. Davenport makes this clear when he declares that the "truth is with the single-taxers in principle but not in method," and that "it may be said with approximate accuracy that the economists have never seriously attacked the theoretical validity of the single tax program."[22] Davenport's strong normative views are well summarized by his rhetorical claim that "surely wholesale confiscation of existing land values is wholesale robbery."[23] In this, Davenport's rhetoric sounds similar to George's, although the objects of their rhetoric are different. To George it was robbery to permit landowners to retain the rights to accrued rents, just as surely as it was robbery to permit them to accumulate future rental increments. George rhetorically asks, "Why should we hesitate about making short work of such a system [of land rent]? Because I was robbed yesterday, and the day before, and the day before that, is it any reason that I should suffer myself to be robbed today and tomorrow? Any reason that I should conclude that the robber has acquired a vested right to rob me?"[24]

Although this difference in normative value judgments between Davenport and George provides evidence of a legitimate context in which Davenport is a negative critic, it is hardly the sense in which Geiger views Davenport as a critic. Differences in value judgments may exist between individuals who share identical scientific analytical conceptions, and the existence of such differences cannot be accepted as evidence that the individuals differ concerning their basic theoretical approaches to issues.

IV

Thus far I have rejected Geiger's claim that Davenport's advocacy of a Fisherian capital theory constituted a criticism of George's analytical soundness, and I have acknowledged that Davenport and George differed with respect to the value judgments attached to the taxation of accrued rental values. Although neither of these discussions leads to the conclusion that Davenport and George were at odds on basic economic principles, they also fail to provide any strong evidence that they shared any fundamental conceptual ground. To provide some evidence of conceptual similarities, let us briefly examine what each man had to say about two central elements of economic reasoning, the idea of opportunity cost and the methodology of economics.

Davenport is widely recognized as a major contributor to the notion of opportunity cost.[25] In fact, Davenport's contribution was quite sophisticated in that it went beyond the traditional concept of the predictive theory of opportunity cost and explored the concept of choice-influencing subjectivist cost. The traditional predictive theory views costs as quantifiable values that can be determined following the act of choice, while the choice-influencing subjectivist theory views costs as subjective constraints existing in the mind of a decision-maker prior to the act of choice and determining the direction of choice.

Davenport emphasized "entrepreneur's cost," which characterized cost as a "margin determinant" purely within the personal aspects of entrepreneurship, "a managerial fact, a subjective phenomenon, in which all the influences bearing upon the psychology of choice between different occupations or between occupation and leisure have their place."[26] Davenport's basis for the psychology of choice is "the psychological law valid for all human activity: men follow the line of least sacrifice."[27] This sounds remarkably similar to George's "fundamental law of political economy" that "men always seek to gratify their desires with the least exertion."[28] Although George's presentations of opportunity cost are clearly in the traditional mold, based on measurable values sacrificed after the act of choice, there is an element of subjective choice implied in the examples he gives to illustrate the idea. George's image of the marginal workers seems to rely on an implied subjective choice context, where these decision-makers are evaluating their opportunities before the act of choice and basing their decision on their attempts to "gratify their desires with the least exertion." As George describes the framework of opportunity cost,

> It is, indeed, evident from observation, as it must be from theory, that whatever be the circumstances which produce the differences of wages in different occupations, and although they frequently vary in relation to each other, producing, as between time and time, and place and place, greater or less relative differences, yet the rate of wages in one occupation is always dependent on the rate in another. . . .Thus, on the verge of each occupation, stand those to whom the inducements between one occupation and another are so nicely balanced that the slightest change is sufficient to determine their labor in one direction or another.[29]

These marginal decision-makers "on the verge of each occupation" seem to be engaging in subjective evaluations of the costs to themselves of remaining in their present occupation compared to changing to another occupation. While I am not trying to suggest that George's concept of opportunity cost included the same awareness of the distinction between choice-influenced objective costs and choice-influencing subjective costs that is explicitly developed by Davenport, it is accurate to suggest that the basic notion of choice-influenced opportunity cost is present in George's ideas along with a hint of the subjectivist element. Davenport and George are discussing the same ideas with similar conceptual language, and in this respect there is common conceptual ground upon which their ideas rest.

George's methodology emphasizes that the nature of economics is as a positive science as opposed to a normative science, and he advises that in commencing to study economics (political economy) we should consider "the nature and scope of political economy."[30] This is a similar admonition to the one offered by John Neville Keynes in his classic consideration of the character of economic methodology, *The Scope and Method of Political Economy* (1890). In Friedman's equally classic article on "The Methodology of Positive Economics," Keynes is quoted with regard to the methodology issue, where he identifies a positive science as "a body of systematized knowledge concerning what is; a normative or regulative science" as a body of systematized knowledge concerning what ought to be, and an art as "a system of rules for the attainment of a given end."[31] These characterizations are quite similar to those offered by George with respect to the methodology issue.

> There is found among economic writers much dispute not only as to the proper method of political economy, but also as to whether it should be spoken of as a science or as an art. There are some who have styled it a science, and some who have styled it an art, and some who speak of it as both science and art. Others again make substantially the same division, into abstract or theoretical or speculative political economy, on the one side, and concrete or normative or regulative or applied political economy on the other side.[32]

George leaves no doubt about his views of the proper method of political economy.

Into this matter, however, it is hardly worth while for us to enter at any length, since the reasons for considering a proper political economy as a science rather than an art have already been given. It is only necessary to observe that where systematized knowledge may be distinguished, as it sometimes is, into two branches, science and art, the proper distinction between them is that the one relates to what we call laws of nature; the other to the manner in which we may avail ourselves to these natural laws to attain desired ends.

Thus, consistent with Keynes's admonition of 1890 and Freidman's contemporary version of it, George advises us that the methodology of economics involves the determination of laws that describe "what is," that is, economics is a positive science. Davenport also sought to rid economic theory of any dependence on ethical value judgments, and the entire character of his major works is infused with the attempt to make economics as value-free as possible. In this, George and Davenport are alike, and their methodological approaches are consistent with the standard approach in the economic literature as represented by Keynes and Friedman.[33]

V

Herbert Joseph Davenport turns out not to be a theoretical critic of Henry George at all. Contrary to George R. Geiger's claim with respect to their different conceptions of capital, Davenport's Fisherian capital theory is not necessarily antagonistic to George's more traditional, produced-means-of-production concept. The two articles in which Davenport does disagree with George are evidence of differing normative value judgments between them, not of opposing theoretical structures. Their thoughts on opportunity costs and economic methodology reveal fundamental similarities. Geiger's error concerning their capital theories is relatively unimportant when taken in isolation from wider implications. The danger is that if it is permitted to stand uncorrected, it could lend unwarranted support to the mistaken impression that George's contribution is somehow outside the accepted boundaries of economic theory.

Notes

1. Davenport's major ideas are presented in *The Economics of Enterprise* (New York: Macmillan, 1913), and *Value and Distribution* (Chicago: University of Chicago, 1908).

2. Philip Charles Newman, *The Development of Economic Thought* (New York: Prentice-Hall, 1952), and Joseph Dorfman, *The Economic Mind in American Civilization, 1865-1918* (New York: Viking Press, 1949).

3. George R. Geiger, *The Philosophy of Henry George* (New York: Macmillan, 1933), pp. 99-100.

4. Ibid., pp. 100-101.

5. A purely speculative explanation might be that Geiger, a philosopher and not an economist, did not regard his own assessments of eocnomic theory as definitive, and he was not willing to commit himself to an unequivocal declaration that Davenport was a mainstream representative of economic theory. In fact, such a commitment was fully justified by Davenport's contributions.

Another speculative explanation is that Geiger wanted to use Davenport's material as a straw-man basis for his own ideas.

6.   Geiger, *Philosophy of Henry George*, p. 105 n.

7.   Ibid., p. 157 n.

8.   Herbert J. Davenport, "The Single Tax in the English Budget," *Quarterly Journal of Economics* 24 (1910): 6.

9.   Geiger, *Philosophy of Henry George*, p. 100.

10.   Jack Hirshleifer, "On the Theory of the Optimal Investment Decision," *Journal of Political Economy* (August 1958).

11.   Irving Fisher, *The Theory of Interest* (New York: Macmillan, 1930), and *The Rate of Interest* (New York: Macmillan, 1907).

12.   George J. Stigler, *The Theory of Price*, 3d ed. (New York: Macmillan, 1966), p. 286.

13.   Jack Hirshleifer, *Investment, Interest and Capital* (Englewood Cliffs, N.J.: Prentice-Hall, 1970), pp. v-vi.

14.   Davenport, *Value and Distribution*, p. 242.

15.   Ibid., p. 152.

16.   Ibid., pp. 152-55.

17.   Ibid., p. 148.

18.   Stigler, *Theory of Price*, pp. 275-86.

19.   Henry George, *Progress and Poverty*, 75th anniversary ed. (New York: Robert Schalkenbach Foundation, 1954), pp. 168-72.

20.   Herbert J. Davenport, "The Single Tax in the English Budget," and "Theoretical Issues in the Single Tax," *American Economic Review* 7 (1917). Davenport especially focused his policy criticism on ad valorem land taxation, which he viewed as destructive of individual investment incentives and as contrary to his conception of ethical justice.

21.   Davenport, "Theoretical Issues in the Single Tax," p. 2.

22.   Davenport, "The Single Tax in the English Budget," p. 279.

23.   Ibid., p. 287.

24.   George, *Progress and Poverty*, p. 365.

25.   Edmund Whittaker, *A History of Economic Ideas* (New York: Longmans, 1940), p. 456.

26.   Davenport, *Value and Distribution*, p. 273.

27.   Davenport, *The Economics of Enterprise*, pp. 59-61.

28.   George, *The Science of Political Economy* (1897; reprint ed. New York: Robert Schalkenbach Foundation), 1962, p. 86.

29.   George, *Progress and Poverty*, pp. 210-11.

30.   George, *The Science of Political Economy*, p. xxxviii.

31.   John Neville Keynes, *The Scope and Method of Political Economy* (London: Macmillan, 1890), and Milton Friedman, *Essays in Positive Economics* (Chicago: University of Chicago, 1953).

32.   George, *The Science of Political Economy*, p. 101.

33.   See also *Progress and Poverty*, p. 13. This is not to deny that George believed that, from an ultimate perspective, "economic law and moral law are essentially one." Ibid., p. 560.

21

Carver: Reluctant Demi-Georgist

BY ROBERT V. ANDELSON

In 1954, just prior to becoming a nonagenarian, Dr. Thomas Nixon Carver, who had retired from the Harvard faculty more than two decades before, began a new career as a weekly columnist for the *Los Angeles Times*. The vigorous and trenchant pieces that appeared under the by-line of this remarkable man until his death, seven years later, at the age of ninety-six, are well remembered by the present writer, who was then pursuing doctoral studies at the University of Southern California—coincidentally, Carver's alma mater.

Iowa-born, educated at U.S.C. and Cornell, Carver was the author of eighteen books (on sociology, social philosophy, and even religion, as well as on economics), including *Essays in Social Justice*, which contains a unique chapter, "The Single Tax." In 1915, when this work appeared, he was David A. Wells Professor of Political Economy at Harvard, and had just spent two years as a high official in the United States Department of Agriculture. The following year he served as president of the American Economic Association.

What makes the chapter unique is that in it Carver firmly endorses a large measure of land-value taxation for reasons of his own, while at the same time attacking, sometimes scathingly, many of the arguments advanced for its adoption by Henry George and his followers. Let it never be imagined that this crusty scholar was not an independent thinker!

Carver was a Darwinian empiricist, who had no use for what he regarded as abstract metaphysical ideas of right and justice, and who defined morality as the facilitation of human adjustment to the material universe.[1] That social group the members of which best manifest such qualities as industry, frugality, enterprise, fortitude, and mutual helpfulness, will be best adapted to the inexorable and universal laws that govern the material universe, will be strong, and will survive in the inevitable competition with other groups:

> Instead of saying that nature is non-moral or that science is unable to discover the moral order of the universe, we should say that nature is the final authority on morality, and that our opinions, likes and dislikes, approvals and disapprovals, must be modified to suit that final authority. . . . If we once perceive that morality is merely social hygiene, and that anything is

moral which works well for society in the long run, which prolongs its life and enables it to grow and flourish and hold its own in competition with other societies, and beat out all those which are organized on immoral bases, we should think no more about questioning the moral order of the universe than we do now of questioning the hygienic order. We should then say frankly that whatever the order of the universe is, that, *per se*, is the moral order, likes and dislikes, approvals and disapprovals to the contrary notwithstanding. We should then say that whatever social customs and conventions are found to fit into the order of the universe, and whatever private conduct is found to permanently strengthen the social group, that is *per se* morality.[2]

Let it be immediately noted that this formulation exhibits the so-called Is-Ought Fallacy: one cannot get an *ought* solely out of an *is*, cannot derive a value judgment merely from a factual one. But this is an issue about which logicians are by no means in agreement, and, in any event, Carver would doubtless retort that if his formulation is deductively invalid, then so much the worse for the deductive method; he prefers to rest his case at the bar of induction.

Despite his stated antipathy for metaphysical abstraction, Carver sees no conflict between his Social Darwinism and "the highest form of religious thought which the world possesses today,"[3] asserting that "the laws of natural selection are identical with the laws of divine approval; and. . .the process of exterminating the unfit or the unadapted is only a manifestation of divine disapproval." Behind the material universe is the divine energy and will, which not only created it but sustains and re-creates it continuously every moment. This belief is stated only in passing in the *Essays*, and is not the dominant theme even in Carver's slim volume *The Religion Worth Having*,[4] which seems to make utility in promoting human prosperity the ultimate criterion for religious value. Yet it may help to provide the answer to what would be otherwise a mysterious element in Carver's thought—the individual's motive for embracing the work ethic. Carver sometimes speaks as if the stern code of natural selection operates undeviatingly upon individuals, so that industrious and provident persons automatically prosper and survive while the idle and profligate suffer and are doomed. But, as Job protested, in this world such inevitability of personal desert does not obtain. Although it may be that the Puritan virtues make the possibility of individual prosperity and survival greater, still, as Carver recognizes, many a man has been so circumstanced as to be able to enjoy a life of luxurious indolence with no ill effect other than perhaps an occasional attack of gout. Apart from a theological impetus, it is difficult to understand why such a one would be moved to abandon his parasitic existence for the strenuous "worldly asceticism" Carver would have him embrace in order to make a productive contribution to his nation or race. True, Carver endorses social arrangements that would remove, to a considerable extent, opportunities for luxurious indolence. Moreover, he does not consider human nature wholly selfish. But he places immense stress upon the cultivation of a kind of sacrificial patriotism which, when not informed by powerful religious sentiment, one normally observes only in wartime or other periods of extraordinary national emergency.

Actually, it is this insistence upon rigorous personal sacrifice for the sake of the well-being of the group that exculpates Carver's religion (which invokes no promise of transcendental reward) from the charge of low prudentialism. Nevertheless, although I do not wish to stray any farther than necessary into theological excursis, there is an objection that I feel constrained to raise. Henry George's faith in God revived when he came to believe that the grim doctrine of Malthus described the results of human error and perversion, and was not ingrained in the created natural order. For George, a Malthusian order was not just, and only a just creator could be God. Carver did not address himself specifically to this aspect of George's thought, but had he done so there can be little doubt that he would have taken him to task for presumptuously making his own subjective sentiments the standard to which God must conform. This, he would have insisted, is to worship man and his emotional predilections, not God. But is not Carver's approach at least equally man-centered? To define morality (and hence justice) as whatever facilitates the group's survival and prosperity, is to at least give the impression that human survival and prosperity are the ultimate values. And to simply equate the will of God with that to which the social body must conform if it is to survive and prosper, is to make human survival and prosperity the final criteria of goodness, not goodness, that is, God, an end to be reverenced and cherished for its own sake.

Although it may seem as if we have come rather far afield before I even commence discussion of the topic of this chapter, the foregoing review of the broad framework of Carver's thought may help to illuminate the background and therefore some of the details of his critique of George.

For Carver, the state's most essential role in promoting social justice is to encourage and protect producers, and to restrain predators—to channel human conflict into competitive production, where success depends (to a much larger extent than in other forms of conflict) upon service rather than upon destruction or deception. Property rights are nothing more than a tool for the furtherance of this end, and their validity in each case depends upon whether, in the long run, their recognition fosters or obstructs it.[5]

Carver divides wealth into three categories: "earnings," "stealings," and "findings." Under the last of these he places the site value of land (land rent). Since the only valid property rights are those which rest upon long-run social utility, whether or not it would be unjust for the community to confiscate rent becomes simply a question of whether or not it would be practically desirable for it to do so. In other words, does the social appropriation of rent foster socially useful production more effectively than does the individual appropriation of rent? Against the same criterion, the applicability of which Carver takes for granted, he measures all "findings," not merely land rent—and, for that matter, every form of wealth. But the social utility of earnings and the social disutility of stealings are sufficiently obvious to render unnecessary a lengthy justification of private property rights in one and not in the other.

Before subjecting the question of rent to the pragmatic test specified above, Carver launches into two digressions somewhat hostile to George and his followers.

First, he proceeds to demolish the single taxers' supposed contention that land is not productive. He deduces this curious conclusion from their view that a site would have no economic value were it not for the community around it, assuming that this implies that the community is the sole producer.

> In the first place, this proves too much. All that is said respecting land could be said of any other factor of production. If it were not for the community round about, neither the buildings on the land nor the labor of the lawyer, the doctor, the merchant and the manufacturer would be of any great value. In the second place, if we begin at another link in the chain and follow the same method of reasoning, we could prove that land produces everything. If it were not for the land there would be no productivity, or any community either.[6]

Actually, of course, neither George nor any of his followers ever claimed that land is unproductive. Like all economists in the classical tradition, they viewed it as one of the two primary factors of production.[7] That it is productive only when conjoined with labor and (usually) capital, Carver himself would scarcely deny. As for its value, it is perfectly true that nothing would have value without the presence of a community to provide a market for it, but since the supply of land is inelastic, this leaves the community (with its public services, its aggregate improvements, its cultural, industrial, and commercial enterprises, and, above all, its demand) the only active factor in determining what land is worth. Therefore there is some force to the Georgist argument that land value is a social product in a way that is not true of the value of other basic goods. In the quoted passage, it may be remarked, Carver appears to conflate value and productivity, two ideas that, although often related, are conceptually distinct.

After completing the supererogatory task of proving that land is a productive agent, Carver observes that "it does not follow by any means that the landowner is a productive agent"—which is all that George or any knowledgeable Georgist ever contended. Carver, however, goes on to say that just because the landowner, as such, is not a producer, one ought not to assume that he is necessarily a parasite. He fulfills, at least to some extent, a useful function, that of conserver of exhaustible resources. Carver concedes that landowners may be receiving more in the way of rent than they deserve for this, but he feels that under an unmodified single tax the function might not be performed at all, for the nominal owner would be a virtual tenant to the public. Having no interest in the future increase or decrease of the value of his land, his inclination would be to rapidly exploit the land's productive powers to the point of exhaustion and then move on. To prevent this the state would be obliged to institute controls, involving close and detailed regulation and inspection by an army of paid officials.

> Possibly a refined form of the single tax could be devised which would tax only site value and not soil or anything else which could possibly be exhausted or destroyed. In that case the public would be the virtual owner of the site alone, and the private owner would be the real as well as the nominal owner of everything else, including the soil. He would then have the same motive as now for conserving the value of everything which might

be exhausted and which therefore needs conserving, leaving to the state the virtual ownership of the site, the only thing which cannot be exhausted and therefore needs no conservation.[8]

The specter of reckless exploitation had earlier been raised by Francis Amasa Walker. In chapter 12 on General Walker in the present volume, Professor Cord points out that absentee farm ownership, an important contributory cause of soil depletion, would tend to disappear under land-value taxation. Further, since land would be assessed and taxed according to its optimum use as determined by the market, and optimum use for farmland reflects the application of fertilizer, it would scarcely be economically feasible, says Cord, for the farmer to fail to keep his soil enriched. As for mineral resources, their depletion could be discouraged by combining a severance tax with the land-value tax, the total not to exceed the site's economic rent.

Carver's second hostile digression invidiously compares the single taxer with the hardy, enterprising pioneer: "They who desire land know where they can get it; what the aggressive single taxer wants is not *land*, but a share in the value of the land which somebody else has. . . . Moreover, it must be said, this modern movement is promoted, not by appealing to the pioneering, colonizing spirit of a sturdy, conquering race, but too often by appealing to jealousy, covetousness, and other of the less commendable motives which actuate mankind."[9] Be this as it may, since it would eliminate speculative withholding, the Georgist proposal *would* make land more readily available to those who actually wished to use it, not just to share in its value. If Carver momentarily ignores this, his next remark could not fail to delight the most rabid partisan of George, for he comments that since urban landowners find it profitable to encourage metropolitan congestion, no sympathy need be wasted on them if the masses who flock to cities should vote to confiscate land rent. The landowners will have simply paid the penalty for gambling with economic and political forces.

Carver, however, believes that such matters should be decided, not by sentiment but by constructive statesmanship, and that, from this point of view, the issue to be considered is whether priority of occupation constitutes a sufficient ground upon which to base a legal right to land and its rent, and if so, what limitations might be reasonably placed upon that right.[10]

In clearing the way for such consideration, Carver quickly dismisses "metaphysical" doctrines of human rights in general, and of property rights in particular, instancing Locke's labor theory of ownership (upon which George relied) as an example of the latter. Its major premise asserts that a man has a right to himself; its minor premise, that when he has worked upon a thing, he has put a part of himself into it; and its conclusion, that therefore he has a right to that upon which he has worked. In Carver's judgment the minor premise is "absurd and meaningless, and that is enough to spoil the argument."[11] He asked rhetorically: "If, after he has parted with the thing he has as much of himself left as he had before, can he be said to have put a part of himself into it?"[12] To which the rejoinder might be made that he can indeed, although it may have been his *past* rather than his present self. He has lost the time and effort that he would probably have expended differently were it not for the anticipation of owning the thing. Besides, he may have impaired his health or vital powers in producing the thing, in which case he has literally diminished his present self.

Long-run utility, it will be recalled, is Carver's touchstone: "Is it useful in the long run, i.e., does it work well, to allow the first occupant of a piece of land some rights in it which we deny to those who come later and want a part of it or its value? Of two communities otherwise equally favored, one of which recognizes this right while the other does not, which is likely to become the more comfortable, prosperous, and powerful?"[13]

Since he largely equates nation-building with pioneering, with subduing and cultivating new lands, and expanding productivity, Carver holds that constructive statesmanship must address itself to the question of how pioneering is affected by the present system, on the one hand, and how it would be affected by the Georgist proposal, on the other. The desire to get the future "unearned increment" of land is doubtless one stimulus to pioneering in the sense of opening and settling new territories, but the opportunity for such activity had ceased to be very significant when Carver's book appeared, giving his concern a somewhat anachronistic flavor. Intellectual and spiritual pioneering can also take place (and a strong case can be made for the proposition that they are more likely to take place) in metropolitan areas. Carver implies that a sharing in "the enormously inflated value of land in overcrowded urban centers" would induce the landless to remain in them instead of spreading out to where land is cheaper and more abundant, evidently forgetting that such sharing would tend to reduce the inflated value by taking the profit out of speculation.

Under frontier conditions, observers Carver, the distinction, so crucial to George's position, between property in land and property in other things, seems nugatory:

If one settler saw a tree which seemed to contain certain possibilities, and chopped it down and made it into a table, it would be in accordance with social utility that the table should be his. If another settler saw a piece of land which seemed to contain certain possibilities, and cleared it and ploughed it and reduced it to cultivation, on the same reasoning the land would be his. Each settler would have found a free gift of nature, each would have worked upon it, each would have changed its form from the raw state in which he found it to a form which would suit his purpose. The mere fact that the result of one's labor happened to be a farm, and that of the other's a table, would not have appeared at the time to be a real difference. This aspect of the case is recommended to the consideration of those who believe that the private ownership of land is forbidden by a moral law ordained from the foundation of the world. . . .

In view of all these considerations it will be difficult for any reasonable man to lash himself into a state of moral indignation against the private ownership of land. If a pioneer settler were brought face to face with a certain type of radical single taxer who makes a moral issue of the ownership of land values, and makes free use of certain formulae, such as the equal right of all to access to God's earth, the moral indignation would not be all on the side of the single taxer.[14]

This sardonic passage (which well illustrates its author's unadorned but effective literary style) contains at least one misleading implication, for not even the "radical single taxer who makes a moral issue of the ownership of land values" really objects to private ownership of land where land is so abundant that it has no value in its raw state. The Georgist stress upon the right to private ownership of labor products justifies security of improvements. It is only where land becomes so scarce that it acquires a value independent of its improvements that the moral objection to private ownership arising from first occupancy comes into play, and this objection is focused upon private retention of that value rather than of the land itself.

Curiously, Carver then develops his argument in such a manner as to arrive at much the same place as the single taxer, although, of course, basing his conclusions upon long-run social utility, and eschewing moralistic formulae of the type that serves as target for his irony. However, it should not be overlooked that his understanding of social utility is, in its way, itself profoundly moralistic: "Justice is mercy writ large. It is benevolence with a long look ahead, a look which takes in the most distant generations of the future and places them on an exact equality with the present generations; which has as much regard for an as yet voiceless individual to be born a thousand years hence as for any individual now alive and clamoring for his rights."[15] It is in the light of this that one should consider his account of what occurs when frontier conditions cease to exist:

A real difference between the table and the land would begin to appear. In the first place, it would be found that the owners of the land held control of the original raw material for the manufacture of tables and all other produced goods. When the maker of the first table [or his descendents] wished to make a new one to replace the old one when it was worn out, he would have to pay the landowner for the privilege of cutting a tree from which to make it. In the second place, the value of the land would increase in proportion to the number of persons wishing to make use of its products either for purposes of consumption or for the purpose of producing other goods. The fortunate owners of the limited supply of land would find themselves in possession of a growing income far in excess of anything which the land might have cost them [or their ancestors], whereas the owners of the tables and other goods would find themselves always compelled to expend approximately as much in the making of them as they were worth. As time goes on this difference increases, especially in a growing city, while the value of tables continues to bear a fairly close relation to their cost of production.[16]

Since pioneer conditions no longer obtain in established communities, the problem of landownership, said Carver, really becomes largely a problem of inheritance, and the issue to be resolved is whether or not there are any modifications of the right of inheritance that may logically be expected to improve social and economic conditions, stimulate the productive energies of the population, or lead to such a distribution of wealth as would foster the virtues of hard work, frugality, and useful investment.

On these grounds, the land-value tax (which falls to a considerable extent upon inherited property) has much to commend it in Carver's eyes. He specifies three distinct advantages that would result to modern society through an increase in the taxation of land values: (1) Such an increase would discourage the holding of valuable land out of use for speculative purposes. By thus bringing land into best use, it would stimulate the demand for labor and capital, augmenting the returns for working and productive saving. (2) Taxation on active industry would be reduced in proportion as the burden is placed on the site value of land. This would invariably encourage business and industry, since people would not be penalized for production or improvements, and there would be no incentive to hold a site vacant or to put it to some use below its optimum. All this would make goods more abundant for everyone in the community. (3) It would tend to eliminate the waste of the labor power of those who live upon the unearned increment of land, devoting themselves to idle self-indulgence, to what Carver caustically refers to as "the ornamental professions," or to the dissipation of their investing talent in land speculation, which is not only sterile but actually detrimental to the creation of national wealth. Because Carver believed that, "generally speaking, the leisure class is made up of the most capable members of the community,"[17] he heavily underscored the importance of diverting its ability (as well as its material assets) into productive channels. This argument for land-value taxation, which he considered probably the most important of the three, was wholly novel; even George himself does not seem to have hit upon it—perhaps because he had a less favorable impression than did our Ivy League professor of the capabilities of the leisure class.

Because of the reasons just cited, and in spite of the reservations and objections he had raised earlier in his essay, Carver concluded that a considerable extension of land-value taxation "would work well for the nation."[18]

The reader will recall that Carver had insisted upon the distinction, so strongly emphasized by George, between land and goods produced by labor, although he held that its effects do not emerge until an area is settled, and that on no account is it in any case a moral issue. He admitted that land (in the non-technical meaning of the term) is sometimes "made" in the sense of being reclaimed from the sea or desert, whereas there are some produced goods, such as antiques and rare works of art, that resemble land (as defined in classical economics) in that their supply cannot be increased in response to market forces. But these exceptions he regarded as of little consequence. The fact that whereas nonreproducible land is the rule and reproducible land the exception, and reproducible goods of other kinds the rule and nonreproducible ones the exceptions, may be called a difference of degree only, but it is a difference of degree so great as to constitute for scientific and practical purposes a difference of kind: "As a matter of fact, nearly all scientific differences are differences of degree. It is not denied, however, that there are many resemblances between land and other goods. There are also certain resemblances between a man and a clothes-pin, but the differences are sufficiently important to warrant our placing them in different classes."[19]

The above discussion, as well as part of that to which I previously alluded on the same topic, is reproduced in Carver's *Essays* from his *Distribution of Wealth*, published eleven years earlier. This earlier work also contains an argument against the contention that though geographic land (land surface) may not be materially increased by labor, economic land (land capital) may. His treatment of this point is quoted in chapter 22 on Richard T. Ely.

The last chapter of Carver's *Essays*, "The Distribution of Taxation," sets forth in addition two rather standard arguments for land-value taxation as a permanent levy. The first is that a tax on land values cannot be shifted, since it neither lowers supply nor raises demand. The second is that such a tax tends to be capitalized, and, hence, if it lasts over a long enough period, becomes burdenless. "It is paid once and for all when the tax is taken out of the capitalized value of the thing taxed."[20]

Of course, neither Carver's espousal of these two arguments, his defense of the key distinction between land and other goods, nor his outright advocacy of a very sizable degree of land-value taxation makes him a single taxer—as he is by no means hesitant to point out.[21] For he also recommends a stiff tax upon inherited wealth, regardless of its source or nature, and, moreover, somewhat less emphatically, a moderately progressive income tax.[22] He further maintains that a tax that is easily shifted and thus diffuses itself throughout the community (such as a sales tax), is the most suitable means of raising temporary emergency revenues, which must be gathered without "too nice a regard for absolute justice."[23]

Yet he urges that among permanent taxes preference should be given to those which fall upon natural rather than upon produced goods, and upon increments that come to individuals through natural causes over which they have no control rather than upon incomes earned by the individuals themselves.[24] A land-value tax, be it noted, is the only tax that uniformly satisfies *both* of these criteria. Thus Carver may at least be ranged alongside the single taxers in the order of his priorities.

It would probably be correct to say that Carver's aversion to Georgism had more to do with style than with substance, with presentation than with program. In spite of his extreme distaste for reasoning that he considered "metaphysical," "sentimental," or "demagogic," in the end his sturdy intellectual honesty compelled him to acknowledge, albeit with some reluctance, the merits of essential aspects of what George proposed.

Notes

1. Thomas Nixon Carver, *Essays in Social Justice* (Cambridge, Mass.: Harvard University Press, 1915), p. 24.
2. Ibid., p. 25.
3. Ibid., p. 26.
4. Thomas Nixon Carver, *The Religion Worth Having* (Boston: Houghton, 1912).
5. Carver, *Essays*, p. 93.
6. Ibid., pp. 283 f.
7. See Henry George, *Progress and Poverty*, 75th anniversairy ed. (New York: Robert Schalkenbach Foundation, 1954), pp. 38 f.
8. Carver, *Essays*, p. 287.
9. Ibid., p. 289.
10. Ibid., p. 290.
11. Ibid., p. 291.

12. Ibid.

13. Ibid., p. 292.

14. Ibid., pp. 295 f. The first part of the extract is excerpted by Carver from his *Distribution of Wealth* (New York: Macmillan, 1904), pp. 108 f.

15. Carver, *Essays*, p. 292.

16. Ibid., pp. 295 f.

17. Ibid., p. 300.

18. Ibid., p. 303.

19. Ibid., p. 296.

20. Ibid., p. 410.

21. Ibid., p. 303.

22. Ibid., chap. 12 and p. 408.

23. Ibid., pp. 409 f., 429.

24. Ibid., p. 429.

22

Ely: A Liberal Economist Defends Landlordism

BY STEVEN B. CORD
AND
ROBERT V. ANDELSON

Richard T. Ely was a member of that small yet growing group of advanced economists who, even during Henry George's lifetime, advocated a substantially greater role for government in the economy. After earning his baccalaureate degree at Columbia, he pursued graduate study for three years in Germany, receiving the doctorate from Heidelberg in 1879. Following a little more than a decade on the faculty of Johns Hopkins, he became director of the School of Social Science, History and Economics at the University of Wisconsin where, in 1920, he founded the Institute for Research in Land Economics and Public Utilities. Later he moved this organization to Northwestern University and ultimately to New York, changing its name, after the first move, to the Institute for Economic Research.

Under his direction, the Institute, which was privately funded and which at one time had a staff of twenty-five or thirty, conducted graduate courses, produced a considerable amount of economic literature including a quarterly journal, and engaged in adult education through an arrangement with the United Y.M.C.A. Schools. One of the founders of the American Economic Association, Ely was author of more than twenty-five books, and co-author or editor of many others. His potency was by no means confined to scholarly efforts; not least of his accomplishments was that of fathering two children after his second marriage at the age of seventy-seven. He had wide influence as a teacher and adviser clear into the 1930s. Msgr. John A. Ryan, the subject of chapter 24 in the present volume, was among his many protégés, and Woodrow Wilson, Frederick Jackson Turner, and John R. Commons studied under him. His circle of personal friends included such luminaries as Theodore Roosevelt, Robert M. LaFollette, Oliver Wendell Holmes, Jr., and Cardinal Gibbons, not to mention numerous leaders in academe, on the one hand, and the world of commerce and industry, on the other. Raised in a strict Presbyterian home, he retained a strong lifelong Christian involvement, and lectured frequently to diverse denominational gatherings, and also to meetings of the Chautauqua Society, which was religious in its origins and overall atmosphere.

While at Wisconsin, Ely was the subject of a sensational trial before the Board of Regents, stemming from charges of socialism by the state superinten- dent of education. The assault upon him turned into a fiasco, and, as part of their statement of exoneration, the regents issued a famous declaration upholding academic freedom, which was inscribed on a tablet in Bascom Hall. Before he left for Northwestern, they conferred upon him an L.L.D. and other honors.

Despite his rejection of laissez faire, Ely did not regard himself as a socialist. He held that only certain areas of business are inherently monopolistic,[1] and he did not, by and large, consider land ownership to be among them. Psychological reasons for his generally sympathetic attitude toward land ownership may perhaps be revealed by his autobiographical remark that "a strong attachment to the land is characteristic of nearly all the Elys and of most New England families. . . .We, in Connecticut, loved the land we owned and would not let it go."[2] While he nowhere essayed a thoroughgoing critique of Henry George's writings, he did devote some adverse paragraphs to the single tax, and doubtless displayed his antipathy toward it orally in such a way as to inculcate his students, most of whom came to occupy positions that enabled them to further disseminate his unfavorable opinions.

In spite of his antipathy to the single tax, Ely, to his credit, was capable of generous sentiments concerning George's broader contribution:

> Perhaps the greatest service of all which Mr. George has rendered is to be found in the discussions of right and wrong in economic affairs and institu- tions which he has provoked. There have always been plenty to advocate the economic rights of the individual, and it is very fortunate that now, at least, a few leaders of thought are urging us to look at rights from the standpoint of the public as well as the individual. . . .The question is frequently asked: "Are property rights safe?" I have no fear about the property rights of the individual, but I have much fear that the property of the public will be stolen in the future as it has too frequently in the past. Henry George and others like him are helping to protect the property of the public, and for this the millions whose rights are too often overlooked ought to be grateful.[3]

Ely's most extensive criticisms of the single tax are contained in his *Outlines of Land Economics* and his *Outlines of Economics*. The first of these, which was originally published in three volumes in mimeographed form in 1922, was written to set forth fundamental principles upon which the more specialized monographs of the Institute would be grounded. In 1928, 1931, and again in 1940, its subject matter was revised and rearranged with the co-authorship of George S. Wehrwein, and brought out in a single volume, *Land Economics*. The foreword to the 1964 reprint of this work by the University of Wisconsin Press opens with the statement: "In the history of land economics, the Ely- Wehrwein volume is probably the single most influential book."[4]

In 1925 Ely, his Institute, and his *Outlines of Land Economics* were the targets of a 205-page attack by a Georgist, Emil O. Jorgensen, the vitriolic tone of which is typified by its cumbersome but pugnacious title. *False Education in Our Colleges and Universities: An Exposé of Prof. Richard T. Ely and His "Institute for Research in Land Economics and Public Utilities"* was published in Chicago by the Manufacturers and Merchants Federal Tax League, of which Jorgensen was information director. It accuses Ely of bias, hypocrisy, and mendacity, and strongly implies that the policies of his Institute were tailored to accommodate the landed interests prominent among its donors.[5] While this implication may seem uncharitable, it is perhaps worthy of remark that as soon as Ely moved his Institute away from the University of Wisconsin, the regents of that school resolved "that no gifts, donations, nor subsidies shall in future be accepted by or in behalf of the University of Wisconsin from any incorporated educational endowments or organizations of like character"[6]—as if the Institute's dependence upon vested interests had threatened the integrity of its erstwhile host.

Whether or not Jorgensen was justified in impugning Ely's motives, he could scarcely have chosen a better way to vitiate the effectiveness of his offensive. One finds it difficult to escape the conclusion that, were it not for Ely's prestige, many of his postures would be dismissed as perverse by most economists, regardless of their estimate of George, and that these postures fairly invited Jorgensen's intemperate response. Had Jorgensen been content to concentrate his fire on these without resorting to personal invective, his book might have been more successful in accomplishing its purpose. However, in his attempted refutation of the thirty-two chief fallacies that he purports to find in the *Outlines of Land Economics* and, to a lesser extent, in other works by Ely, Jorgensen does manage to score some telling points. Space does not here permit a review of his treatment of all thirty-two "fallacies," so the present authors will occupy themselves only with the thirteen most pertinent objections. Of those with which we shall not deal, some are trivial; others cast aspersion upon Ely's intellectual honesty; others merely assert dogmatically propositions contrary to those of Ely; while still others reflect what appear to be misreadings or distorted interpretations of the passages in question. Our method will be to state each "fallacy" in Jorgensen's words, to present a citation from Ely substantiating that he actually held the position ascribed to him, and, finally, to summarize in each case Jorgensen's rejoinder, with sometimes a comment of our own. The "fallacies" are numbered here as they originally appeared.

"3—*That Land CANNOT be Monopolized, While Capital and the Products of Industry CAN be Monopolized*": "Of all the factors of production land is the most difficult to monopolize. . . .In land ownership there is usually the freest and fullest competition, so that the returns yielded by land are reduced to a lower level than the returns to fluid capital. Land requires more care and gives smaller returns in proportion to what is put into it in the way of capital and enterprise, than standard investments of other kinds. . . .It is a curious thing that people speak of land as a monopoly when it, of all things is the least monopolizable."[7]

Jorgensen's rejoinder: "Land cannot be duplicated, but capital can be duplicated indefinitely," and, indeed, "must be constantly duplicated to keep it from returning to. . .the dust of the earth. Competition, therefore, cannot affect land in the same manner and in the same degree that it affects capital. . . ." "Land has no cost of production, capital has. And whereas in civilized society land always starts at zero and *appreciates* in value, capital—minor disturbances apart—always starts at its cost of production and *depreciates* in value."[8]

"*6—That Invention, Discovery and Material Progress Have the Effect of REDUCING Land Values Instead of RAISING Them*": "Progress brings economy in the use of land, making the same area go farther toward satisfying the need for land. With a stationary population, if society progresses, a land supply, though constant in area, increases relatively through improvements in the utilization of agricultural land and through improvements in transport in the case of urban land. As a result land will fall in value."[9]

Jorgensen's rejoinder: The reverse of the above is true because human wants are insatiable. Improvements elevate the standard of consumption. This constantly increases the demand for land (even when population is stationary) and hence land values. To support his argument, Jorgensen quotes from various authorities, including Adam Smith and Thorold Rogers.[10] Later, he administers the coup de grâce by quoting another passage from the same volume (p. 111) in which Ely, asserting that a progressive society that increases in prosperity "inevitably adds to the selling price of the land,"[11] takes a stand directly opposite to that under discussion.

"*7—That the Rent of Land Has Not RISEN During the Last Hundred Years, But Has Remained STATIONARY*": "Henry George and others hold that the rent of land absorbs the increase in wealth. The history of the world in the last hundred years, however, shows wealth increasing and the rent of land remaining fairly stationary. In the period from 1850 to 1910 the rent of land never amounted to as much as ten per cent of the annual wealth of the United States, while in England the rent of land has decreased."[12]

Jorgensen's rejoinder: Contrary to Ely's contention, rent has been steadily rising over the last hundred years, even in England. For example, farm rent that two hundred years ago stood at zero, now absorbs from twenty to sixty percent of the farmer's annual income. Urban residential site rent, next to nothing in the days of Benjamin Franklin, now takes from twelve to forty percent of the earnings of the people who live on the sites. Royalties for coal-bearing sites are as much as twenty-six percent of the price the coal sells for at the mouth of the mine; oil royalties, from twelve to twenty percent of the price of oil at the well. "In short, we know that the rent of land, which, in the seventeenth century absorbed nothing from the wealth produced by capital and labor, now absorbs twenty, thirty, forty and sometimes sixty percent of that wealth, instead of less than ten per cent as claimed by Prof. Ely."* Dr. Sun Yat-sen is quoted (New York *Independent* 13 June 1912) as saying that the value of land in Shanghai had increased ten thousandfold (100,000 percent!) during the past century.[13]

"*8—That Unearned Increment is Not to Be Found in Land RENT, But Is to Be Found in WAGES and INTEREST*": "Unearned increments. . .are due to two great causes; namely, monopoly and conjecture. In the case of land ownership the first is eliminated, whereas in many other parts of the economic field both operate."[14]

---

*If it be objected that, by going back to the seventeenth century or to the days of Franklin, Jorgensen does not really speak to Ely's point that rent has not risen over *the last hundred years*, the truly immense appreciation in land values over the past three decades certainly supports his general position.

Jorgensen's rejoinder: Jorgensen offers the standard Georgist reply, pointing out that wages and interest are, by definition, earned, while rent, not being the product of individual effort, cannot be earned by individuals. He quotes John Stuart Mill's observation (*Principles of Political Economy*, bk. 5, chap. 2, sec. 5) that landlords "grow richer as it were, in their sleep, without working, risking or economising."[15] We would add that Ely simply calls speculative profits (which certainly apply to land) "rent of conjecture" instead of monopoly rent, ignoring the fact that without some element of monopoly, conjecture would seldom yield rent, which results from the combination of a monopoly of location and/or subsoil assets with population increase and improvements in the area. He says (p. 55) that this speculative profit should be called "conjectural surplus" or "rent of conjecture" rather than the unearned increment of land, yet on the next page (p. 56) he explicitly classes it as an unearned increment.

"10—*That the Amount of Good Land Held Out of Use Is Not LARGE, But Very SMALL*": "The idea that good land is held out of use in large areas is a fiction."[16]

Jorgensen's rejoinder: The table of vacant land in thirteen U.S. cities, compiled by a staff member of Ely's Institute, and upon which he bases the above statement, actually does not support it, for it shows Spokane to be 63.5 percent, St. Paul to be 51.9 percent, Chicago to be 31 percent, St. Louis to be 29.8 percent, San Francisco to be 26.7 percent, and so on, unimproved. "But the situation is emphatically worse than the table indicates. For one thing, its accuracy in several places is rather doubtful—Chicago, for instance, having, according to the assessment officials, approximately 55 per cent of its land vacant instead of 31 per cent." Furthermore, even if the table were correct, it would be misleading because of the vast amount of land which is classified by public officals as improved, but which is so underdeveloped as to be practically vacant—where the "improvement" (which may be nothing but a billboard) bears no relation to the value of the site. Ely seeks to substantiate his claim only with respect to urban land, but Jorgensen documents the existence of immense tracts of desirable coal, mineral, waterpower, timber, and agricultural land that were either undeveloped or underdeveloped, citing figures from the Forestry Department, the 1914 federal report on *The Lumber Industry*, and Gifford Pinchot.[17]

"11—*That Speculation in Vacant Land Is an ASSET to a Community Instead of a LIABILITY*": "It should be apparent that the owner of vacant land supplies these conditions (available land for gardens, lawns and open air spaces) at a rather low cost. . . .Did we not have the public revenues yielded by vacant land privately owned while undergoing the ripening process, the tax rate would have to be raised. . . .He (the owner of vacant land) has made an investment: he has performed economically desirable functions, he has taken great risks, he has paid significant sums in taxes and assessments. Very uncertain and often inadequate are the gains that finally come to him."[18]

Jorgensen's rejoinder: The vacant lots in question do not in the main consist of gardens, lawns, and so forth, as Ely implies, but largely of weed-patches, mud puddles, and dumping places for junk and garbage. Their price is too high for those who would like to beautify them. This high price forces congestion on the land that is improved, *reducing* the availability of fresh air and sunlight. As for taxes, "if it were not for the chronic undertaxation of vacant land everywhere there would be no resultant overtaxation of improved land." Land ventures, it is true, do not always turn out profitably. But Ely thinks that speculators are entitled to a profit for making such investments and taking such risks. "Figs! The bandit who purchases a revolver and waits all night for his victim to come by is not always successful either. He, too, has made an 'investment,' has 'worked hard' and has 'taken great risks' and if the vacant land monopolist whose object is to hold up the land user is fairly entitled to a profit, so is the bandit." But the chief loss that the withholding of land imposes on the community is: (1) in the greatly increased cost that it lays on government, first, by making it more expensive to obtain land for public improvements, and second, by compelling states and municipalities to build and keep in repair an enormous amount of unnecessary improvements because of "suburban sprawl"; and (2) in the immense obstacles that it puts in the way of the legitimate production and distribution of wealth, because land available for use is not compactly situated.[19] These two points, it may be parenthetically remarked, were never put more dramatically than by Winston Churchill in 1909, on the stump in Lancashire. What he said there on the topic was published as the fourth chapter of his book, *The People's Rights*,[20] and is heartily commended to the attention of the reader.

"13—*That Most Land is Owned by POOR People, and Not by RICH People*": "Few of the men of great wealth whose names are familiar to us have made their money in land. . . .Land is the poor man's investment and should be such."[21]

Jorgensen's rejoinder: Jorgensen presents a table showing that ten percent of the U.S. population owns ninety percent of the total land values, forty percent owns ten percent of the total land values, and fifty percent owns no land values whatsoever. He then points out that the names of very few wealthy persons are "familiar" to the public at large, since they are chiefly nonproducers and therefore have no pecuniary reason to advertise their names. In any case, he says, it is not true that few of the famous multi-millionaires made their money in land, and he backs this assertion with various citations, including the following from John R. Commons (*The Distribution of Wealth* [New York: Macmillan, 1893], p. 253): "If the size of fortunes is taken into account, it will be found that perhaps 95% of the total values represented by these millionaire fortunes is due to those investments classed as land values and natural monopolies, and to competetive industries aided by such monopolies."[22]

"15—*That the Separation of Land and Improvements is NOT PRACTICABLE, But IMPRACTICABLE*": "Among the many reasons why we should not tax separately the value of the land and the value of improvements is the difficulty of separating the two values."[23]

Jorgensen's rejoinder: Jorgensen denies that such a difficulty exists, instancing the successful application of the Somers System in Cleveland and Columbus, Ohio; Springfield and Joliet, Illinois; Des Moines and Dubuque, Iowa; Phoenix, Tucson, and Prescott, Arizona; Houston, Beaumont, Waco, Galveston, San Antonio, and Corpus Christi, Texas; Denver, Colorado; Augusta, Georgia; and Redlands, California; and elsewhere; as well as the separation of land from improvement values in Australia, New Zealand,

South Africa, Canada, Denmark, and Hungary, together with New York City and the California Irrigation Districts. In further support of his position he cites the authoritative *Principles of Real Estate Appraising* by John A. Zangerle, and *The Taxation of Land Values* by Louis F. Post, a Georgist who served as assistant secretary of labor under Woodrow Wilson.[24]

"*22—That Consumption Taxes Will Not HURT the Poor People, But Will HIT the Rich People*": "The 'masses' have a surplus that can be taxed. . . .On every hand can be seen an enormous surplus of income over needs of subsistence. The expenditures of the public for prize fights, 'movies,' ice cream, candy, tobacco, chewing gum, perfumery and beverages of all kinds run into the hundreds of millions, yes, even billions of dollars every year. . . .Taxes on consumption and various indirect forms of taxation must be employed to a larger extent."[25] "Now, we have a great many people of large means who own tax-exempt securities and the aggregate of these securities runs into many billions of dollars. We can reach these people, and that without violation of faith, by indirect taxes."[26]

Jorgensen's rejoinder: If there really is a margin that allows the workers to indulge in "movies" and ice cream, and if they earned it by rendering useful services, it properly belongs to them, and should not be sucked away from them in order to "enable the owners of our natural opportunities to put in their pockets a still larger amount of ground rent which they do not earn."[27] As for indirect taxes being a means of reaching the rich, "There is no way in which indirect taxes can be placed upon the food, clothing and luxuries of the people that will not strike the poor, in proportion to their means, infinitely harder than they will strike the rich—not if they are intended to raise any substantial amount of revenue." For to raise much revenue, they must be levied upon such articles as are in wide and common use, and the millionaire does not consume a significantly larger quantity of these than does the day laborer.[28]

"*23—That to Take the Socially-Created Rent of Land is CONFISCATION, But to Take the Earnings of Capital and Labor is NOT Confiscation*": "Many are disturbed because property in land yields income. Our attention is frequently called to a corner lot in a city, from which the owner derives, let us say, $30,000 a year. Taxes and all improvements are paid by the owner of the building erected on the lot. The owner of the lot may live in idleness, and it is said that he makes no return to society for what he receives. . . .Unless we are prepared to go over to Socialism and abandon private ownership of productive property, we must expect to find men receiving an income from property, and using this income sometimes wisely and sometimes ill. . . .The solution of our land problems is not at all to be sought in confiscation of land values."[29]

Jorgensen's rejoinder: To the above, Jorgensen juxtaposes Ely's passage on consumption taxes for the masses, quoted under the last heading. The obvious conclusion to be drawn from comparing the two passages is that Ely maintains that it is the landowner's own business what he does with his income, but that if workers spend money on such nonessentials as ice cream and "movies," they should be penalized by indirect taxation. It could, of course, be objected that such taxes would apply to landowners as well, but Jorgensen contends that the landowners's income, being a social product, is something that "justly belongs to the whole community," whereas the wages of labor and the interest on capital are returns for human effort expended and useful services rendered, and therefore rightfully belong to those who have earned them. "Hence, if any portion of these funds of wages and interest be appropriated by taxation, it is—so long as government has its own source of revenue—nothing less than robbery, robbery under the forms of law."[30]

"*24—That the Singletax Means, Not INDIVIDUALISM, But SOCIALISM and COMMUNISM*": "According to the single tax theory all land is a gift of nature to society; consequently all the returns from utilizing land belong to society, not to any individual owner."[31]

Jorgensen's rejoinder: Jorgensen correctly asserts that "the singletax theory *does* hold that 'all land is a gift of nature to society,' but it *does not* hold that 'all the returns from utilizing land belong to society, not to any individual owner.' The singletax holds just the opposite of this; namely, that 'all the returns from utilizing land' belong to individuals and not to society."[32] Upon analysis, Ely's statement would indeed appear, as Jorgensen complains, to place the single tax "in the same class with socialism and communism." Whether this was, as he charges, Ely's design, is less clear. Yet Ely's treatment of George in his *Recent American Socialism* lends a degree of credence to the charge, for in that work George is presented as a harbinger and abettor of socialism (which to some extent he unintentionally was), with scarcely a hint that he was also a firm believer in the rights of capital and in free market competition.[33]

Ely's *Outlines of Economics* went into six editions over a period lasting from 1893 to 1937. Most of these had various co-authors, and the views expressed in them were not always uniform, but Ely, as senior author, was ultimately responsible for the content of each edition. While all the editions tended to be unsympathetic to the single tax, the fullest discussion of it is contained in the two last ones, and it is therefore to these that we shall primarily refer.

"On what ground of justice or ethics," asked Ely, "shall the landowner be singled out for taxation?"[34] Why should the rich merchant or stockholder go tax free while the landowner, who may be either rich or poor, is taxed to the point of confiscation? Ely maintained that the only just basis for taxation is ability to pay, and so was a strong exponent of the progressive income tax (although, as we have seen, he also favored taxes on consumption).

Ely's objections to the single tax were practical as well as moral. Allusion has already been made to his belief that the tax would be difficult if not impossible to implement, because of the problem of trying to separate the value of land from the value of improvements on or to it. Unlike General Walker, who advanced the same objection, Ely concerned himself with urban as well as with rural land, and asked how we could separate from the bare land value the value of such capital improvements as grading, landscaping, drainage, and the installation of sewers, streets, and utilities.[35] Curiously, this flatly contradicts his stand in earlier editions, where he raised the problem with respect to agricultural land only, and acknowledged that "it is easy in cities to separate economic rent from rent for improvements, and it is done a thousand times a day."[36] The final (6th) edition, published in 1937, and coauthored by

Ralph Hess, does not take a definite position one way or the other on this issue.

Ely was one of the first to broach the charge of inelasticity, which was to appear again and again in the writings of opponents of the single tax. He felt that the amount of land rent in a community did not necessarily equal the amount of revenue required for public purposes. At times the land-value tax might yield more than the government needed, but at other times it might yield less. In periods of emergency, such as depression or natural disaster, the land rent fund would tend to diminish just when more public revenue was called for.[37]

To this indictment the single-taxers replied that the land-value tax would collect so much revenue that all possible governmental needs would be satisfied. Although, on both moral and economic grounds, George advocated collecting all but a small fraction of the land rent, some of his more moderate followers (notably, Thomas Shearman and Charles B. Fillebrown) pointed out that any of it not needed for legitimate public expenditures would not have to be collected. All of the single-taxers argued that the government should live off its own rightful income just as any individual or corporation is expected to do, and should therefore limit its expenditures according to the capacity of the socially produced land-rent fund. They reasoned that a government expenditure should create an equivalent amount of land value because it presumably increases the desirability of living in the area served by the government; this increased desirability is reflected in location value, that is, land rent. Hence, if a government expenditure did not increase land rent by an amount at least equivalent to the expenditure itself, it should be condemned as wasteful and ill-advised.

Although it is widely conceded that in George's time land rent would have met the cost of government at all levels, and although after three decades of geometrically increasing land values, the most informed estimate is that U.S. annual land rent is now probably double U.S. corporate after-tax profits,[38] it may well be doubted whether even this would yield a sum sufficient to support today's gigantic public budgets. As for the single-taxers' "rightful income" argument, while it might hold true in a utopia where all men are rational and no one infringes upon the just claims of his fellows, its applicability to our present nonutopian world seems rather dubious. In a utopia, huge outlays for defense and police would not be necessary. But today the size of such outlays is determined by urgent practical need rather than by the amount of land values they might generate. On the other hand, Georgists would be quick to point out that the effect of land-value taxation with respect to employment, housing, and numerous other domestic problems might well be such as to eliminate or at least drastically reduce the requirement for public spending in these and related areas.

Furthermore, it should be realized that the inelasticity criticism applies only to the single tax, not to a land-value tax imposed as one tax among others. Somewhat unaccountably, Ely, in most of his writings, refused, as did many other professional economists, to consider the land-value tax as anything else than a single tax.[39] Yet there is no real reason why the land-value tax, if insufficient for justifiable government expenditures, could not, consistent with George's premises, be supplemented by other levies based on the concept of payment for benefits received.[40] And even most contemporary economists (who reject the benefit theory) recognize the peculiar advantages of land-value taxation as one source of public revenue.

Ely's argument that it is practically impossible to separate urban improvement values from bare land values was not borne out by the experience of many municipalities that even in his day were assessing land and improvements separately. This may be why the argument does not appear in the final edition of his book. Assessors were and are doing what he claimed was impossible. To the examples instanced by Jorgensen, we may add Kiao-chau during its period as a German protectorate prior to World War I, Jamaica, Hawaii, and the Pennsylvania cities of Pittsburgh, Scranton, and Harrisburg. Only the costs of grading, drainage, and other types of site development that "merge with the land" present a genuine difficulty, but solutions do exist. One good method is to permit tax deductions, spread over a number of years, for the increase in land values resulting from these site-development expenses.

What about Ely's contention that ability to pay (as an application of the more general social utility theory) is the most just criterion for a tax? Like other "liberal" economists who reflected the influence of study in Bismarck's Germany, he was contemptuous of the idea that people should be obliged to pay only for specific benefits received from the community, holding that the individual has no rights apart from society, and that the privilege of being part of society is a general benefit for which he should be made to pay whatever he is able.[41] To George, an uncompromising Jeffersonian individualist whose social philosophy was squarely grounded on the doctrine of natural rights, this approach was, of course, anathema. He maintained that all true taxation was morally wrong, and that the so-called single tax was not really a tax at all. It was merely the public appropriation of a publicly produced phenomenon, land rent, for public purposes.[42]

But when he used the word *tax* in the broader and more conventional sense (as he often did as a concession to common parlance), George maintained that it was better to tax a special privilege like the exclusive use and disposition of a site (a portion of that earth which God created for the habitation and sustenance of all His children) than an ability such as business acumen or inventiveness. Why fine a man by taxing his ability when by using it he cannot help but benefit society? A contemporary proponent of land-value taxation might add that we should adopt it because it fulfills better than any alternative the canons of taxation generally accepted ever since the days of Adam Smith. While no Georgist would ever advocate "soaking the rich" as a matter of principle, if for some reason this were still deemed necessary or desirable by the elected representatives of the public, other taxes could be added for the purpose.[43]

The sixth (last) edition of the *Outlines of Economics* contains a criticism that we have not yet considered, which also appears in germinal form in the fifth edition and is similar to arguments earlier advanced by Carl C. Plehn, John Bates Clark, and Frank Fetter:[44]

Henry George's social philosophy was based. . .on the fundamental distinction he drew between land and capital. . . .But modern economic thought has come to recognize that land, like capital, is an agent of production which owes its usefulness to human toil. Land, in the economic sense, can be said to exist only in so far as it is brought into use by man, and, in this sense, the supply of land, like the supply of capital is susceptible of increase in response to demand.[45]

But decades before Ely gave it currency, this point had been forcefully addressed by Thomas Nixon Carver, who stoutly upheld the distinction between land and capital in the following words:

Now land capital [economic land as distinguished from mere geographic land] cannot possibly mean anything else than land *value*, since it is used in a way which excludes improvements placed on the land such as buildings and fences. But to argue that though land surface may not be increased, land value may, is to beg the whole question. One might as well say that during the supposed coal famine of the winter of 1902-1903, it was not coal in the economic sense, but only in the material sense, which was scarce; that though there were few coal-tons there was much coal-value; and that therefore there was as much coal, in the economic sense, as ever: but that would be a travesty on the science of economics.[46]

Carver went on to point out that although there are certain ways (such as improved transportation facilities) by which the scarcity of land can be alleviated when the pressure becomes great enough to furnish inducement, they cannot do so sufficiently to prevent land from "rising to enormous values in thickly populated centres"—which is manifestly the case with capital only temporarily when at all.

George Raymond Geiger, expanding upon remarks by Harry Gunnison Brown, subjects Ely's argument to yet another line of contravention, with which it seems appropriate to bring this chapter to a close:

We are told, by Ely *et al*, that the utilization of land is possible only through labor, since the use of land demands accessiblity, and that therefore in this sense land is *produced*. "How utterly irrelevant is all this to the real problem about land rent! If landowners alone paid the entire cost of 'creating means of access' to their land, such as bulding all the railroads, roads, bridges, and wharves required, maintaining them, and replacing them when worn out or obsolete; if the various owners paid, each in proportion to the increased land value received by them; and if the total capitalized land value did not exceed the reproduction cost, minus depreciation and obsolescence, of these 'means of access,' then Ely's discussion would have relevancy to the problem of private enjoyment of land rent." We are told that bridges and dams and irrigation projects are irreproducible, and that therefore to distinguish between land and capital is old-fashioned! In other words, we are indirectly informed, by an argument like this, that depreciation of *all* capital can be neglected. Or perhaps we are supposed to believe that land *site* depreciates just as much as manufactured articles. (That *fertility* does decline is obvious, but what "land economist" is prepared to argue that the depreciation of farm land *in general* is commensurate with that of buildings and improvements?) This is the type of argument that is used to overthrow the classical contention that land space is set by natural forces, that man can *in no signficant way* amend that work of nature or extend it, and that man can and does produce and reproduce goods— wealth and capital. Is it any wonder that some of us become very impatient with our emancipated economic theorist?[47]

Notes

1. Richard T. Ely, *Ground Under Our Feet* (New York: Macmillan, 1938), p. 268.

2. Ibid., p. 4.

3. Richard T. Ely, "The Single Tax," *Christian Advocate,* 25 December 1890, p. 856. Cited in Arthur N. Young, *The Single Tax Movement in the United States* (Princeton, N.J.: Princeton University Press, 1916), p. 318.

4. Richard T. Ely and George S. Wehrwein, *Land Economics* (1940; reprint ed. Madison, Wis.: University of Wisconsin Press, 1964), p. v.

5. According to Ely himself, contributors included the Carnegie Corporation of New York, the Laura Spellman Rockefeller Memorial Foundation, railways, public utility companies, land companies, lumber companies, etc. "An Open Letter," *Institute News*, October 1924.

6. Resolution of the Board of Regents, August 1925.

7. Richard T. Ely, assisted by Mary L. Shine and George S. Wehrwein, *Outlines of Land Economics* (Ann Arbor, Mich.: Edwards Bros., 1922), 2: 52, 53, 73.

8. Emil O. Jorgensen, *False Education in Our Colleges and Universities: An Exposé of Prof. Richard T. Ely and His "Institute for Research in Land Economics and Public Utilities"* (Chicago: Manufacturers and Merchants Federal Tax League, 1925), pp. 38 f., 40.

9. Ely et al., *Outlines of Land Economics,* 2: 58. See also Richard T. Ely and Edward W. Morehouse, *Elements of Land Economics* (New York: Macmillan, 1924), p. 262.

10. Jorgensen, *False Education*, pp. 43-50.

11. Ibid., p. 72.

12. Ely et al., *Outlines of Land Economics*, 2: 74.

13. Jorgesen, *False Education*, pp. 51 f.

14. Ely et al., *Outlines of Land Economics*, 2: 56.

15. Jorgensen, *False Education*, p. 53.

16. Ely et al., *Outlines of Land Economics*, 3: 98.

17. Jorgensen, *False Education*, pp. 61 f.

18. Ely et al., *Outlines of Land Economics*, 3: 105 f.

19. Jorgensen, *False Education*, pp. 64 f.

20. Winston Spencer Churchill, *The People's Rights* (1909; reprint ed. New York: Taplinger Publishing Company, 1971).

21. Ely et al., *Outlines of Land Economics*, 3: 98.

22. Jorgensen, *False Education*, pp. 75-78.

23. Ely et al., *Outlines of Land Economics*, 3: 115.

24. Jorgensen, *False Education*, pp. 85-87.

25. Ely et al., *Outlines of Land Economics*, 3: 93.

26. Richard T. Ely, *Taxation of Farm Lands* (St. Paul: Webb Publishing Company, 1924), p. 25.

27. Jorgensen, *False Education*, p. 107.

28. Ibid., pp. 109 f.

29. Ely et al., *Outlines of Land Economics*, 3:102 f., 105.

30. Jorgensen, *False Education*, p. 113.

31. Ely and Morehouse, *Elements of Land Economics*, p. 323.

32. Jorgensen, *False Education*, p. 117.

33. Richard T. Ely, *Recent American Socialism* (Baltimore, Md.: Johns Hopkins University Press, 1884), part 2.

34. Richard T. Ely, Thomas S. Adams, Max O. Lorenz, and Allyn A. Young, *Outlines of Economics*, 5th rev. ed. (New York: Macmillan, 1930), p. 462.

35. Ibid., pp. 444, 460.

36. Richard T. Ely, *Outlines of Economics* (1893; reprint ed. New York: Macmillan, 1905), p. 366.

37. Ely et al., *Outlines of Economics*, 5th rev. ed., p. 460.

38.   Mason Gaffney, "Adequacy of Land as a Tax Base," in *The Assessment of Land Value*, ed. Daniel M. Holland (Madison: University of Wisconsin Press, 1970).

39.   An exception would be *Land Economics*, coauthored by George S. Wehrwein, in which taxation as a land-use control is sharply distinguished from the single tax. See p. 477.

40.   This is implied by Ely and Wehrwein, ibid.

41.   See, for example, Richard T. Ely, *Property and Contract in their Relations to the Distribution of Wealth* (1914; reprint ed. Port Washington, N.Y.: Kennikat Press, 1971), 2: 504. For a discussion of this position as advocated by E. R. A. Seligman, see chapter 18 on Seligman in the present volume.

42.   Henry George, *Progress and Poverty*, 75th anniversary ed. (New York: Robert Schalkenbach Foundation, 1954), p. 421.

43.   The income tax is not so much of a "soak the rich" tax as many people think. There are many loopholes in the income tax law, and rich men can employ able accountants and lawyers to find them. Most large incomes are derived from capital gains, only forty percent of which are subject to taxation for individuals and twenty-five percent for corporations. Income splitting among family members, a loose interpretation of business expenses, income from tax-exempt government bonds, profit-sharing trusts, stock options, etc., are legal means of tax avoidance. In addition, it is well-known that tax evasion is widespread at the high and medium income levels, whereas salaried employees must pay their full share and more of the tax load.

In 1955 eighty-four percent of the income tax revenue was derived from the twenty percent basic rate that all taxpayers pay on taxable income, and only sixteen percent of the revenue was derived from the progressive rate (which ranged from twenty-two to ninety-one percent) How much more progressive (i.e., based on income) is the income tax when compared with a national sales tax?

Census figures indicate that in 1955 the highest income-tenth received twenty-nine percent of the national personal income before federal income taxes and twenty-seven percent after. The highest income-fifth received forty-five percent before and forty-three percent after. (See Gabriel Kolko, *Wealth and Power in America* [New York: Praeger, 1966], p. 34.) These figures have not changed appreciably since then.

Since the more valuable land is owned almost entirely by rich people, a land-value tax would fall much more on them than upon the poor. In the light of the above statistics, it is certain that the land-value tax would be more progressive than the income tax!

44.   Plehn's criticism was presented in a paper read before the Massachusetts Single Tax League, 8 December 1902; Clark's argument is found in his *Distribution of Wealth* (1900), and Fetter's in "The Relations Between Rent and Interest," *Publications of the American Economic Association*, 3d ser., 5, no. 1, pt. 1.

45.   Richard T. Ely and Ralph H. Hess, *Outlines of Economics*, 6th ed. (New York: Macmillan, 1937), p. 465.

46.   Thomas Nixon Carver, *The Distribution of Wealth* (New York: Macmillan, 1904), pp. 113 f.

47.   George Raymond Geiger, *The Theory of the Land Question* (New York: Macmillan, 1936), pp. 76 f. The interior quotation is from Harry Gunnison Brown, *The Economic Basis of Tax Reform* (Columbia, Mo.: Lucas Bros., 1932), p. 115 n.

23

Alcázar's "Most Voluminous
of All Assaults"

BY JAMES L. BUSEY

In 1917 there appeared in Spain the most voluminous of all assaults upon the teaching of Henry George—a 383-page tome by Father Juan Alcázar Alvarez, bearing the appropriately ponderous title, *Estudio filosófico crítico del libro "Progreso y miseria," de Henry George, en sus cuestiones fundamentales y el alivio social*. It was published by Perlado, Páez y Compañía of Madrid, with the imprimatur of the bishop and ecclesiastic governor of Madrid-Alcalá.

By now it is doubtful that many people are much influenced by or would take the trouble to wade through this tedious and rambling work, but the *Estudio filosófico* is of some significance because (1) it indicates that during a period of several decades in which sustained literary discussion of George was extremely rare, there were individuals in far away Iberia who deemed him to be so potent a thinker that he deserved 383 published pages of response; (2) it draws together most of the more notable misconceptions about Georgist theory into one albeit too-lengthy book, and thus becomes a useful if dreary compendium of anti-Georgist absurdities; (3) it does point up important areas where George left himself open to unnecessary attack; and (4) it offers some insight into the curious contest that went on during the 1880s between Henry George and prelates of the Catholic Church. This chapter will be organized around these four major points.

Perceived Significance of Henry George

Father Alcázar left no doubt that he considered Henry George's philosophy to be worthy of the most serious consideration. The *Estudio filosófico* fairly bristles with expressions indicating the importance that Alcázar attached to Georgism. The first, introductory chapter asks (p.2):[1] "What do I believe regarding the single-tax theory, today so much in vogue? What does the inexorable tribunal of pure reason tell us about the significance of this theory propounded by the eminent George?"[2]

There are several verbose and irrelevant excursions into intricate questions of philosophy and metaphysics (e.g., pp. 128-35, about the difference between the *possible* and what *ought* to be); but in general, Alcázar devotes the first of two parts, eleven chapters and 178 pages, to a drumbeat attack on what he alleges to be the proposals of Henry George. On page 66 he announces that "now we have pulverized the arguments of Henry George...,"and after 117 more pages of "pulverization" promises on page 183, at the beginning of the second part (eleven more chapters, 200 pages) that he will no longer attack Henry George's theories directly, but will present positive proposals for alleviation of social distress. This he succeeds in doing only in part. In chapter 3 of part two (pp. 198-206), the author urges that world peace be assured by creation of Supreme International Tribunal, designed to arbitrate and settle disputes among nations. Unlike the Permanent Court of International Justice, created three years after publication of the *Estudio filosófico* and now known as the International Court of Justice, Alcázar's Supreme International Tribunal would be directed by the Pope.

Chapter 4 (pp. 207-16) expresses sincere concern over the huge military expenditures incurred by governments, and stresses that if these could be reduced, thus lightening the burdens of taxation, the ravages of pauperism would be lessened. With settlement of disputes and conflicts under guidance of a papally directed international tribunal, and achievement of divinely inspired mutual human love among peoples, wars and dangers of wars would diminish and so would the terrible burdens of huge armaments, armies, and navies, and the dangers of aerial bombardment.

An improbable chapter 5 (pp. 217-36) within part two follows the theme that " the civil State ought to subordinate itself to the Catholic Church," a concept that antedates the Doctrine of the Two Swords, propounded by Pope Gelasius I at the end of the fifth century.[3] Pope Gelasius, in contrast to Father Alcázar, contended that the political state should be left to handle matters of a temporal nature, with the Church held responsible for spiritual affairs. It is doubtful that many Catholics today, or even in 1917, would adhere to such a premedieval point of view as that of Father Alcázar; but this does not prevent him from contending that all the problems of the world result, not from the maldistribution of property, but from the failure of mankind to put itself under the headship of the Roman Catholic Church.

Chapter 6 (pp. 237-53), on "Liberty and Libertinism" (*libertinaje*) is in much the same vein, and points out that moral, religious guidance must be the controlling force in society; that the world will be saved from calamity only when subjected to direction by God, Jesus Christ, and the Pope.

Chapter 9 (pp.314-331) includes a section on agricultural collective syndicates that were appearing in Spain at the time, and Father Alcázar indicates his support for these and his hope that the State will stand out of their way; and chapter 10 (pp. 332-44) expresses considerable agreement with George on the subject of free trade, though with an admixture of mutual aid, cooperation, and conceptions of universality.

Otherwise, much of part two of the *Estudio filosófico* lambastes Henry George and Georgism as much as does part one. Chapters 7 and 8, "Wages" and "Rent," and sections throughout other chapters continue the attack on Henry George and all his works. The book is supposed to conclude on page 351, with the statement that the author does not doubt that if a man "so valiant as Henry George" were to follow less sterile principles, the economy would receive a gigantic protective force. But this is not all. A two-part appendix (pp. 353-83) comments in detail on the debate between Henry George and the Duke of Argyll;[4] and, apparently after having read *Protection or Free Trade* subsequent to his preparation of chapter 10 on the same subject, Alcázar makes it clear that he agrees with Henry George somewhat, but not too much.

To Juan Alcázar Alvarez, in other words, Henry George was a dragon to be thrice slain. Later I shall have occasion to comment on the obvious fact that at one time the theories of Henry George were vastly more prestigious than they are now; and on the factors that may have contributed to the decline of public awareness of Henry George and his philosophy.

To the Attack

Like his fictional compatriot, the knight of LaMancha, Alcázar seems to have had a penchant for tilting at windmills. The *Estudio filosófico* never comes clear as to exactly what Henry George did propose. Chapter 2 of part one, "The Single Tax Opposed to Reason" (pp. 4-9) comes somewhere near the mark when it charges that George would unjustly make only one sector of society, the landlords, support all the rest of the population. Alcázar finds this to be a form of slavery, an unjust punishment without trial, and returns elsewhere (pp. 136-170 and passim) to the theme that taxation should be imposed equitably on all classes, not on just one. This iniquitous tax scheme would pick out a single class as social pariahs, a state of affairs that Father Alcázar finds to be intolerable.

Alcázar never bothered to explain why George would allegedly single out this particular economic class for taxation, and offers no explanation of the nature of unearned increment from economic rent, or its effects on the society.[5] Instead, the *Estudio filosófico* moves quickly to the implication that the single tax would fall especially on the agricultural classes and small, productive, middle-class elements, "the proprietary agricultural classes...." (p.17). Again and again Alcázar returned to the theme that to single out the "agricultural" element for this sort of treatment would be very wrong and would deny it recompense for past labors and sacrifices. According to Alcázar, it would be manifestly unjust that the "opulent classess" should live off taxation imposed on the "humble, honorable worker on the land" (p. 17), or that big industrialists, who after all only improve products secured from the land, would be so exempted from taxation at the expense of the hard-working agricultural producers (p. 28). There is no doubt that such an arrangement would be the very epitome of injustice, but of course Henry George never proposed anything of the sort. George was talking about unearned economic rent, most of which arises in heavily populated and urbanized areas. Of all the people Henry George had in mind, farmers and ranchers would be less taxed than any, simply because their unearned economic rent per acre is almost nil.[6] Whether deliberately or otherwise, Alcázar persisted throughout his book in conveying the impression that the whole Georgist proposal was directed against the agrarian sector, which is, of course, exactly opposite to the truth. It is for this reason that, in an attempt at making positive proposals for the alleviation of social distress, Alcázar wrote the later section to which I have alluded, wherein he advocated encouragement of the agrarian collectives that were appearing in Spain at the time. Alcázar called George a "communist" (pp. 119, 133, and passim) but turned out to be more of a communist than the individualist Henry George.

Alcázar's book is completely misleading about the single tax and its purpose. More than this, the book soon moves away from any allusion to the *impuesto único*, and contends variously and inconsistently that Henry George proposed collectivization or state ownership of the land, or simple division of it among the whole population. On the matter of collectivization (which Alcázar seemed to favor if in the form of agricultural syndicates), the author argued (p. 55) that if it is wrong for the individual to own property or use it for his own purposes, it is just as wrong for the state to do the same; that according to Georgists, "the State, not the individual, should be the master of the land" (p.237); that Henry George would turn over the land to state functionaries, deputies, and bureaucrats, who would try to work the lands themselves or more likely put them into hands of vagabonds and political favorites (pp.75, 76); that maybe man did not make land, as George said, but neither did society or the state, which therefore has no special right to its possession (p. 374); and that Henry George nowhere proves that collective use is better than individual use of the land (p. 125).

Apparently unaware of the inconsistency, Alcázar contended elsewhere that George advocated the equal division of the land (p.46); and the *Estudio filosófico* argues at some length that because of differing aptitudes of individuals, such division or distribution of the land would not make everyone equal, but that some would remain poorer than others (p. 164).

Of course, George never proposed either the collectivization or the equal or any other kind of distribution of land.[7] Though the long disquisitions in *Progress and Poverty* against private property in land, including his statement that "we must make land common property,"[8] had the unfortunate effect of misleading many readers about George's ultimate proposal, what he advocated was the socialization of land values or economic rent, not of the land itself[9]—and, as I shall have occasion to point out later, there is a fundamental difference between the two.

Henry George was by no means the first to contend that the right to property arises out of one's own exertions.[10] Theorists such as Adam Smith and John Locke held to an identical view; and in an odd sort of way, even the Marxist labor theory of value and its denunciation of private collection of "surplus value" are in the same tradition.[11] Alcázar agreed that "the fundamental principle of the right of property is labor" (p.21), and further, admitted that everyone has a "right" to land, but that this "right" can only be implemented by "labor and worthiness" and more to the same effect (part one, chap. 8, pp. 81-109).

From that point Alcázar not only moved far away from the Georgist position, but also revealed a profound misunderstanding of the philosophy and proposals of Henry George. He persisted in supposing that land values arise out of labor performed on the land, and that it would therefore be unjust and despotic for the state to abuse "agrarian property" after its owners had acquired it by their hard work and given value to it through their strenuous efforts while leaving "other elements free of tribute" (p. 42); and the denial of private land ownership would deny this right. It would be terribly wrong, he contended, to take land with which the owner has mixed his life, his labor, and his sweat, and divide it among other individuals (p. 44). The result of imposition of land tax would be that agricultural proprietors would cease to work, since they would be more oppressed and vexed the more they produced (pp. 26-27). He argued that the value of land is given to it by those who work it, who should therefore enjoy recompense for their labors.

Vaguely aware that Henry George might have been saying something he did not comprehend, Alcázar asked (p. 153): How can the value of land be separated from its improvements? If land is worth nothing at first, but made more valuable by improving it, then the collectivization of such land is especially wrong (p.74). In a chapter devoted entirely to the subject of rent, which Alcázar obviously did not understand at all, he contended that the single tax would fall on work performed on the land; and stressed over and over that rent can arise only out of labor performed on the land. Thus, he argued, land is no different from capital, both of which are made valuable by labor; and wages are paid to labor after deductions for returns to capital, including rent (part two, chap. 8 pp. 285-313). In the same chapter Alcázar thought he had caught George in an inconsistency: If land has no value until labor is performed, how is it that rent can rise steeply though the owner does no work?[12]

Of course, the labor to which George was referring was labor contributing to productivity throughout the community, not labor on a specific piece of land. What George was saying, and what Alcázar either could not or would not understand, was that the value of land results from labor on the part of the whole society, not labor on the part of the individual landowner. The point that George emphasized repeatedly, and that was the whole basis for his contention that private collection of economic rent is unjust, was precisely that land values are irrelevant to and not affected by labor performed on the land in question.[13]

Alcázar never admitted to an understanding of the concept of economic rent; nor did he conceive that there is a distinction between the income arising from unearned economic rent and that arising from labor on land, nor that Henry George was bent upon socializing unearned economic rent but not the products of labor. Even John Locke, though favoring the private ownership of land, saw clearly that this could depend only upon actual use of and labor upon it, and could not extend to unused land allowed to go to waste.[14] Alcázar assumed that all privately held land, of whatever condition, represented an admixture of "labor and sweat," and that therefore all its income should accrue only to its owner. It is conceivable that some hard-working early American frontiersman might hold to such a belief, but difficult to understand how such a contention could come out of Spain, of all places.

Alcázar understood that George based his theory on conceptions of both justice and utility, but pointed out that even if private ownership of land were incompatible with its best use, it might still be compatible with justice—which, in the view of Alcázar, was obviously the case (pp.110 ff.); and, certainly, justice must prevail over utility. In the mind of Alcázar, however, the George proposal did not even have utility to recommend it. Because soils differ so much in their composition, the problems of assessment would be unbelievably complex (p.137). Also, how could the state determine what part of production from the land was of material worth, arising out of the largesse of the earth, and what was the result of labor and intellectual effort, which should be rewarded? Alcázar offered the example of a mine. How could one know how much metal is contained within it? Or, as would be more likely, the tax would have to be imposed after extraction had occurred. How could the state determine what had been extracted as a consequence of intelligence and ability, and what had simply been taken because it was lying around (pp.171-78)?

Such confusion about George's proposals boggles the reviewer's mind. Again, Alcázar was revealing his incomprehension that economic rent is something to be determined by general market value as a reflection of community demand, not by labor or extraction performed on the land. The last thing that Henry George would propose would be to assess a tax on production. Alcázar saw the *impuesto único* as some kind of severance tax to be determined by the value of crops or minerals or timber or whatever else could be extracted from the land. The gap between this idea and the idea of land value as arising out of general societal demand or need, and as occurring in large measure because of the efforts of the whole community, was too great for the *Estudio filosófico* to bridge; but this is not an unusual source of confusion about Henry George's thought, and may be central to much public misunderstanding of his proposals. The single tax was deceptively simple in appearance. People do not turn conceptual corners easily, and many have been bewildered by the same misconceptions that plagued Juan Alcázar Alvarez.

It was in this connection that Alcázar did pose a problem that could be quite real for the application of Georgist devices in many countries where conceptions of public probity are not of a high order. The *Estudio filosófico* points out that assessors and tax collectors could be bribed by landowners to adjust their fiscal impositions in proportion to subornations received (pp. 173-74). It is not surprising that such an idea would occur to a writer in the Hispanic world. As George himself readily conceded (in a letter in 1888 to William Lloyd Garrison, II) his system is not a panacea. No more than any other social theory can it succeed apart from supportive attitudes and institutions. It is therefore scarcely surprising that its modest triumphs of implementation have occurred almost exclusively in English-speaking and Scandinavian lands, with long traditions of responsible self-government. One could not realistically be very sanguine as to its chances for successful application in such states as Haiti, Nicaragua, Bolivia, or even Honduras.

Large parts of *Estudio filosófico* are devoted to the building up and knocking down of straw men, of views that Henry George never propounded. I have delineated several of these above. Another example deserves brief mention. Alcázar sees George as predicating individual happiness on the welfare of society, not the welfare of society on individual happiness (p. 165), and then fills three pages with an attack on this point of view. Of course, Henry George never took any such position, and Alcázar nowhere cites the section of *Progress and Poverty* that is supposed to argue in its favor.

Elsewhere (pp. 303-7) Alcázar reveals his total misunderstanding of the problems Henry George describes. In *Progress and Poverty* George tells the tale of the first immigrant who comes to a vast, unclaimed land; and of how, as new settlers come into the region, the value of the first colonist's property rises, not because of any improvement in its productivity or special effort on the part of the owner, but because of the interweaving cooperation of the increasing population. Years later, according to George, the land of the first immigrant is surrounded by a great city, and its owner is made wealthy by the increasing value of his land.[15] George says, "Our settler, or whoever has succeeded to his right to the land, is now a millionaire. Like another Rip Van Winkle, he may have lain down and slept; still he is rich—not from anything he has done, but from the increase in population."[16]

To Alcázar, who comprehends nothing about the sources of economic or ground rent, this could occur only because of the suffering and hard labor undergone by the original settler on the land, and his descendants are properly entitled to the resulting rewards. He quotes George accurately enough, but adds, "the man could be sleeping today, but the fruit of so many past sufferings continues giving optimum results. And everything is due essentially to the first colonist who was the most suffering and the hardest worker" (p.306). Everything else that George said about an increasing land value arising from the efforts and cooperation of others, is entirely lost on Juan **Alcázar Alvarez**.

In a paragraph that is often quoted by his adherents, George said:

> Place one hundred men on an island from which there is no escape, and whether you make one of these men the absolute master of the other ninety-nine, or the absolute owner of the soil of the land, will make no difference either to him or to them.
> In the one case, as the other, the one will be the absolute master of the ninety-nine—his power extending even to life and death, for simply to refuse them permission to live on the island would be to force them into the sea.[17]

Readers with a taste for irony will find it unintentionally gratified by Alcázar's grave reply to this. He says that to analyze such a situation, we must determine how these hundred people got onto the island. They could have arrived only (l) as a government colonization project, (2) by shipwreck, or (3) voluntarily. In the first case the government would set up rules and regulations and provide guards to prevent any one person from seizing full control. In the second, there would be no reason for the ninety-nine to submit to the claims of one individual, since they were all shipwrecked together; and in the third, they would certainly have drawn up rules and agreements before arriving. In any event, should such an island-owner somehow appear on the scene, he would be obliged by considerations of Christian mercy to provide alms and succor for the ninety-nine people without land; or, if worse came to worse, why should ninety-nine men put up with the demands of only one who is no stronger than any of them (pp.56-63)? This, of course, is exactly what George had in mind.

Alcázar was not entirely devoid of social conscience. He admitted that many *latifundistas* do indeed use their lands quite badly or not at all, and that when the national interest requires it, they have a social responsibility to their countries (p.320). He also declared that it would be permissible, *after* the state has utilized its own lands fully and has taken all other possible efforts to alleviate human distress, *then* to undertake measures to require that privately monopolized lands be put into more effective production (p.325): "The order of things is this: First, put into cultivation the diffuse State-owned fields; if this is not sufficient for the satisfaction of the needy elements of society, then resort to obliging private owners to cultivate their private *latifundios,* respecting their property rights, or indemnifying them for terrains which would pass to the social State for cultivation."

Where Alcázar found, or thought he found, similarities between the Georgist philosophy and his own doctrine, he offered lavish praise to the American theorist. The Spanish priest found much to his liking in book 10, "The Law of Human Progress," and quoted at length from a section of *Progress and Poverty* that he deemed to be critical of the Darwinian theory of evolution (pp.169-70).[18] In general, and despite his rejection or distortion of all Georgist concepts about private property in land and public collection of ground rents, Alcázar did not undertake a personal vendetta against Henry George, and for the most part referred to him civilly and even with some grudging admiration.

In the last section of this paper I shall discuss Alcázar's social views, which were drawn from the most conservative doctrines of the Spanish Catholic Church of the time. Suffice it to say here that Alcázar rejected the whole idea of equalization of individual opportunity that was implicit in all of George's writings. It was the view of the Spanish priest that any such scheme would tear down the whole structure whereby some social categories are preeminent over those which are inferior (p.184). It was his view, drawn straight out of medieval and even ancient Greek doctrine, that poverty and wealth, which vary from person to person, form a total and desirable equilibrium of forces (p.193): "From which I deduce that the existence of poor and rich carries within itself the true total beauty of material society. For that reason, it is not possible to point to a remedy which would put an end to *material* poverty and wealth."

Alcázar saw no way whereby the disparities between poverty and wealth could be bridged in this world, and indeed saw little reason why they should be. The next world was another question, which I shall consider in the concluding pages of this chapter. In any event, the *Estudio filosófico* came from a part of this world and a body of thought that were about as far away from those of Henry George as one could get and still be within the sphere of Western European culture and ideas. This vast difference between the world of Father Juan Alcázar Alvárez and the world of Henry George opens avenues for disturing contemplation regarding the possibility of acceptance of Georgist philosophy in many regions of the earth, several of which are even farther from the thinking or environment of Henry George than was the semi-medieval European, Hispanic culture of Father Alcázar.

Chinks in the Armor

Much of the Alcázar book inveighs against the thesis that private property in land must be abolished (pp.29-109 and passim).[19] Chapter 5 of part one (pp.29-48) questions the Georgist argument that private ownership of land is unjust.[20] Chapter 6 (pp.49-65) attacks George's view that private landlordism leads to the enslavement of laborers.[21] Chapter 7 (pp.66-80) argues that it would be unfair and unjust to refuse to indemnify landowners if their land were seized from them by the state.[22] Chapter 8 (pp.81-109) finds little empirical evidence to support the Georgist view that in earlier times land was held in common but was later obtained by force or fraud from the communities that previously enjoyed its use.[23] From Henry George's argument that private property in land has arisen out of military conquest, and the influence of a "sacerdotal class" and a "class of professional lawyers,"[24] Alcázar launches into a furious assault on the notion, invented by Alcázar himself, that Henry George would abolish or somehow eliminate soldiers, lawyers, and priests (pp.103-4).*

These are among the most stirring passages in *Progress and Poverty,* but as worded and placed in the book they also opened George to unnecessary attack. In his many pages on the iniquities of private property in land, Henry George seemed to be moving inexorably toward actual abolition of private titles to land, and some kind of general nationalization of land ownership—in other words, toward monopolization by the politically organized state of land and the resources beneath it.[25] Indeed, in one section he used the word *nationalization* where he declared that "by the time the people of any country such as England or the United States are sufficiently aroused to the injustice and disadvantages of individual ownership of land to induce them to attempt its nationalization, they will be sufficiently aroused to nationalize it in a much more direct and easy way than by purchase. They will not trouble themselves about compensating the proprietors of land."[26]

Phraseology of this sort created unnecessary difficulties for Henry George and provided a field day for critics such as Father Alcázar. Well before the days of Alcázar Alvarez, writers too numerous to cite fully here had clearly seen the potential authoritarian pitfalls that lay in the way of governmental monopolization of land or anything else.[27]

Had Henry George actually been talking about iniquities of land ownership per se, or been about to propose that private land titles should be confiscated and transferred to the state, his long and moving presentation on the subject would have been to the point and essential for the development of his final proposal. As it turned out about three-fourths of the way through *Progress and Poverty,* Henry George was agitated about the private collection of ground rent, not about private ownership of land; and he was intent, not upon confiscating land, but upon confiscating rent. After devoting seventy-four pages to the denunciation of private land ownership, proclaiming in italics that *"we must make land common property,"* and talking about nationalization of the land, and rejecting the idea that landowners should be compensated for loss of their titles, Henry George finally comes to the point: *"It is not necessary to confiscate land; it is only necessary to confiscate rent."*[28] Henry George filled the next sixty-eight pages of his book with a defense, not of confiscation of the land itself, but of confiscation of unearned economic rent arising out of ownership of the land. Owners would continue to hold title to their lands, and would enjoy the fruits of their labor and capital investment as applied to their lands; but their unearned economic rent, which is quite a different concept and arises out of the efforts of the community around them, would be taken by the state for the defrayal of public expenses.

Professor Andelson expresses the point quite well when he says that the public appropriation of ground rent would serve simply "as a mechanism whereby such ownership may be rendered ethically and practically

---

*In book 9, chap. 4, of *Progress and Poverty* George merely expresses the belief that the adoption of his remedy would so simplify the administration of justice as to dry up the demand for lawyers, and that it would foster such a growth of independence among the masses as to discourage the maintenance of standing armies. No mention at all is made of priests.

innocuous.''[29] The ownership would still be there, and the state would *not* nationalize the land. There is a vital difference between the concept of land and the concept of unearned economic rent derived via land ownership from the surrounding community. In taking so long to get around to this crucial point, Henry George did nothing to allay the concerns of later critics such as Juan Alcázar Alvarez. George's seminal proposal to confiscate rent, not land, could have been placed and justified at a much earlier point in *Progress and Poverty*, probably in his chapter, "The True Remedy,"[30] which instead included the unfortunate phrase that "we must make land common property"; and then, in presenting his arguments about the injustices of private property in land, he could have inserted enough references to the iniquities of private collection of rent, not ownership of land, to leave no doubt as to the position he was taking.

Alcázar himself noted this damaging inconsistency in Henry George's book, and pointed out the inherent logical conflict that lies between the Georgist claim that private property in land is unjust and not compatible with its best use, and the Georgist willingness to solve the problem by letting the state collect the rent (pp.125-26). Here Alcázar finds a further Georgist inconsistency, in that George attributes the miseries of India and China to the rapaciousness of governments, and specifically condemns the exorbitant land and salt taxes imposed by England upon the poverty-stricken producers of India.[31] Alcázar then launches into the indicated attack, and asks why George would suppose that governments, possessed of the power to collect economic rent as their only source of revenue, would be any more just or magnanimous with their subjects than was the imperial English government in India (pp.185-88). Alcázar is full of his own inconsistencies, and, as we have seen, never comes clear as to whether George advocated distribution or state nationalization of the land, or public collection of a land tax; but Henry George himself can be held partly responsible for some confusion on these points. (Yet see above, pp. 215 f.)

Alcázar, George, and the Catholic Church

As would be expected, Father Alcázar saw the problems of the world and their alleviation in the light of his devoutly religious point of view. To Americans of the 1970s, whether Catholic or otherwise, some of his expressions on this point seem to be extraordinarily quaint and drawn from much earlier epochs of Catholic thought. At the same time, the religious doctrine that is central to Alcázar's analysis is reminiscent of and may throw some light on the checkered pattern of relationships that prevailed among Henry George, Georgism, and the Roman Catholic Church.

Alcázar contended that social problems are far too complex and heterogeneous to be solved by a simple single tax (pp.314-15)—though of course, as we have seen, he did not consistently clarify that this was Henry George's central proposal. At the same time, a reading of *Estudio filosófico* reveals that Alcázar himself had his own simplistic moral and religious solution to the problems of the world.

Early in the Alcázar book, the reader detects where its message is likely to lead. It is not *property*, Alcázar tells us, that leads to individual enslavement, but the *abuse* of property by individuals not sufficiently guided by moral law (pp. 49-65, 351, and passim). "The social problem does not depend on distribution [of the land] but on good or bad men; it is licentiousness that brings human troubles in its wake" (p. 367). Are misery and decadence the consequences of maldistribution of property, or of moral depravity, the lack of moral conscience? The latter, of course (pp.49-65). Just because of the *abuse* of property ownership, private property should not altogether be eliminated (p.55). The only type of economy that can solve human problems is "moral economy" (p.349). According to Alcázar, the search for material rather than spiritual solutions is a sterile quest that will have no good effects in alleviation of the social condition (p.65).

This is by no means an unusual approach, even in contemporary times, and it is shared by religious and moral leaders of many faiths and points of view. The general phrase that covers this idea, and indeed is used as a title by a particular segment of the community of idealistic thinkers, is *moral rearmament*. It is not the purpose of this chapter to argue for or against this position, though something may be said in favor of an eclectic stand that would permit moral and material solutions to buttress each other.

But Alcázar goes much further than this, and as his argument develops it becomes more extreme. He argues, as might be expected, that under the guidance of moral law, just wages will be paid, and the concern of Henry George and other writers on this score will be without foundation (p.254). The moral law, according to Alcázar, is to (1) love God and (2) respect the lives of the underprivileged (p.61). People must love God, who loved the poor (pp.194-95); and poverty may be alleviated somewhat in this world through the introduction of divine love into the affairs of men (p.194). On a concluding page of his appendix, Alcázar unexpectedly argued that George was wrong in contending that any landowner can be the absolute master of land, since only God can be absolute master of anything (p.370); and in reality, only the reign of Jesus Christ can solve the problems of the world (p.189).

To this point Alcázar's argument is still not too surprising, and coincides with Geiger's finding that the typical response of certain circles in the Catholic Church was to argue for Christian loyalty and charity as the only real solutions to human suffering.[32]

According to Alcázar, social conditions may be bad; but they were much worse in ancient times, before the advent of Christianity—hence the replacement of all other faiths and beliefs by Christianity, under guidance of the teachings of Christ, offers the only means to remedy the human distresses that were the concern of Henry George (pp.49-65). Within the framework of Christianity, however, only the Catholic faith and the Catholic Church, and complete obedience to them, can resolve the multifold problems of mankind (pp.217-36, and passim).

Early in his book, Alcázar proclaimed (pp.45-46): "The only means that there are to put an end to these fears that someone may obtain not only exclusive right to 160 or 640 acres, but to a whole section, a whole state or to a whole continent, is to proclaim loud and clear [*predicar*] the Christian, Catholic, and Roman religion."

However, one can only accomplish so much in this material world. In the end we should not worry so much about what is mine and what is thine, for

God will ultimately take care of everything—not Henry George, even though he thinks himself to be some kind of God and to have the solution to everything (pp.79-80).

We move, then, to the inevitable but still startling conclusion: In this world there will always be problems. The remedy is not in this world, but in the one to follow (p.349); it is in the next life, not this one, where the solutions will be found (p.193): "In this material world, constantly variable in its phenomena, it is impossible to find stable good fortune; in the other, spiritual, varied but not variable, there does indeed exist that which we long for so much and dream of obtaining in this one."

As the old revolutionaries used to sing it, "You'll get your pie in the sky when you die!"

This was, of course, the most reactionary type of doctrine possible, and was by no means shared by all Catholics or even by all high Catholic prelates, during either the time of Alcázar or that of Henry George. However, an undercurrent of opposition to Henry George did appear in the highest councils of the Church, and it is likely that the expressions of Father Alcázar, who wrote under authorization by the bishop and ecclesiastic governor of Madrid-Alcalá, may have reflected a fear in some circles that George's proposals constituted a threat to the promises of the Church for ultimate salvation from despair.

As is well known to persons conversant with the Henry George years, one of his staunchest and most effective supporters in New York City, especially among the large Irish population, was Father Edward McGlynn.[33] Because of his support for Henry George, Father McGlynn was excommunicated in 1887, but in an unusual reversal of its act, the Holy See removed the excommunication in 1892 and restored Father McGlynn to his priestly functions.[34] The papal act of excommunication was much influenced by the pressures brought to bear by Archbishop Michael Corrigan of New York, whose views seem not to have differed very much from those of Father Alcázar.[35] However, there is much evidence that Catholic opposition to George went quite beyond the circles of Archbishop Corrigan and the temporary influence he could bring to bear. Other high prelates of the Church spoke out strongly against Henry George, and though not actually putting *Progress and Poverty* on the Index (which would have forbidden all Catholics to read it), the Holy Office did rule it to be "worthy of condemnation," which meant that any bishop could rule it to be prohibited reading for any Catholics within his jurisdiction.[36]

George saw this attitude as a "perverted Christianity to soothe the conscience of the rich and to frown down discontent on the part of the poor," and more to the same effect,[37] and in this instance he was, of course, attacking exactly the kind of Christianity that at a later date Juan Alcázar Alvarez was to vigorously espouse. George may have been more than half right when he perceived *Rerum Novarum*, Pope Leo XIII's encyclical "On the Condition of Labor" to be more directed against his views than against those of Marx or other assorted collectivists.[38]

But, as is true of many doctrines and institutions, Catholicism has not been on only one side of the Georgist question. Of course, there was Father McGlynn. There were other priests, such as Father Thomas Dawson, who gave George their full support,[39] and no doubt there were others who less conspicuously but no less strongly sympathized with his message. George received very warm support among the Catholic clergy of Ireland, including especially Thomas Nulty, Bishop of Meath;[40] and, of course, the reversal of Father McGlynn's excommunication was the work of many influential elements within the Church—including Archbishop Francesco Satolli, papal nuncio or ablegate who had just come to the United States as a direct representative of the Pope, and who carried on an impartial or even sympathetic investigation, as well as the theologians of Catholic University who helped prepare the favorable and decisive report that led to the reversal.[41]

In conclusion on this point, it is relevant to quote one of the strongest statements of support for Henry George to come from a religious source of high prestige and authority:

> After the Gospel, this is the book that I love and admire the most. It does not surprise me to learn that, after the Bible, it is the most widely published book in all the world. I think I do not offend God when I say that *Progress and Poverty* plays in the material realm the same role that the Gospel unfolds in the spiritual world.
>
> It is a profound book, of intense philosophical, moral and political radiance. It has simplicity and grandeur.
>
> No religion has been able to condemn it, because it is supported by the most profound and noble sentiment that God has placed in the heart of man: The sentiment of justice.
>
> And since this book, in the last analysis, preaches nothing but the application of justice to the economic activity of mankind, I think I can present it with this single phrase:
>
> Here we have the Gospel of Abundance!

The source? Dom Carlos Duarte Costa, Bishop of Rio de Janeiro, Roman Catholic Church of Brazil![42]

Catholic reaction to Henry George, it can be said, was quite mixed and by no means of one point of view. Had Bishop Carlos Duarte Costa of Rio de Janeiro, Brazil, instead of Father Juan Alcázar Alvarez of Spain, written the *Estudio* (or in Portuguese, *Estudo*) *filosófico*, the book would have turned out very differently from the way it did under authorship of the conservative Spanish priest.

The *Estudio filosófico* tells us something about the reaction of an important segment of the Catholic Church to *Progress and Poverty*, and may throw some light on the reasons for that reaction. Though the criticisms by Father Alcázar were often extreme, distorted, and unwarranted, they do remind us that in his haste to get his book into print, Henry George committed some errors of expression and organization that he could have corrected in a second edition—but instead of preparing a revised edition of *Progress and Poverty*, George went on to write other books.[43] At least this writer, who is sympathetic to the views of Henry George, would wish that he and his followers had concentrated more fully on the truly unique contribution of *Progress and Poverty*. No other works of Henry George were so original or so potentially radical as this one.

Because the Alcázar volume launches the attack against Henry George from every possible quarter, fair and unfair, accurate and hopelessly misleading, it enables the reader to see Henry George in the light of his most implacable critics. We all tend to be too uncritical of our heroes, and this can be a valuable exercise in itself.

One would wish that Alcázar's book had been written with less turgid, repetitious verbosity. But Henry George himself, though he wrote in a more moving and appealing style, was not given to undue brevity. Certainly one gets the impression from Alcázar that Henry George was not a theorist to be trifled with. From *Estudio filosófico* and from other clerical reactions to Henry George, we may deduce that influential elements within the great Catholic Church saw in Henry George a real challenger of its doctrinal and institutional hegemony over a large part of the Christian world.

One derives some satisfaction from knowing that Henry George was so important. One would be more gratified if his followers were more effective in translating his ideas into political reality. According to Henry George: "The truth that I have tried to make clear will not find easy acceptance. If that could be, it would have been accepted long ago. If that could be, it would never have been obscured. But it will find friends—those who will toil for it; suffer for it; if need be, die for it. This is the power of Truth."[44]

It is well to have friends who will toil for a worthy idea. It is even better that such friends have some awareness of the need for political organization and action.

In 1917, date of publication of the *Estudio filosófico*, Marxists seized power in Russia and soon after transformed it into the Union of Soviet Socialist Republics. One cannot but reflect that the success of Marxists in attracting the support of millions of followers, and in threatening the rest of the world with ultimate subjugation, results as much from their political strength as from any logic or reason in their philosophy. Marxism operates from a bastion of political power. Georgism does not.

In 1917, it would appear, Georgism seemed as likely as Marxism to sweep the world. That it did not, and that the fears of Juan Alcázar Alvarez did not materialize, may be attributed in large measure to that singular inattention to political action that has characterized Georgism almost since its inception.

Political Georgism was of short duration. In the view of Charles Albro Barker, it died when Tom Johnson left office as mayor of Cleveland in 1909.[45] Even Henry George himself, though he ran twice for mayor of New York, tended to reject political involvement and to prefer less boisterous speaking and writing activities. It was appropriate that Henry M. Hyndman, who had been both friend and socialist opponent of Henry George, said shortly after George's death, "He has died in a chivalrous attempt to accomplish the impossible without even organizing his forces for the struggle."[46] Georgists have only rarely organized their forces for the struggle. Juan Alcázar Alvarez need not have worried.

Notes

1.   Pages in *Estudio filosofico* will be cited parenthetically in the text, by number.

2.   I am responsible for all translations from the Alcazar book. This summary probably represents the closest it has ever come to being rendered into English.

3. George H. Sabine, *A History of Political Theory*, 3rd ed. (New York: Holt, Rinehart and Winston, 1961), pp. 194-96.

4. George Raymond Geiger, *The Philosophy of Henry George* (New York: The Macmillan Company, 1933), p. 69; Charles Albro Barker, *Henry George* (New York: Oxford University Press, 1955), pp. 196, 314, 331, 408-9, 529; Edward J. Rose, *Henry George* (New York: Twayne Publishers, Inc., 1968), pp. 82, 107, 108, 109-13.

5. Henry George, *Progress and Poverty*, 75th anniversary ed. (New York: Robert Schalkenbach Foundation, 1954), pp. 165-72, 218-24, 230-96, 333-57, and passim.

6. Ibid., pp. 438, 449-52. See also James R. Brown, *The Farmer and the Single Tax*, 4th ed. (New York: Manhattan Single Tax Club, n.d.).

7. In *Progress and Poverty,* pp. 321-27, Henry George specifically and categorically rejected the notion that land should be divided or distributed among the population.

8. Ibid., pp. 328-57, esp. p. 328, and passim.

9. Ibid., pp. 405-72, esp. 405-7.

10. Ibid., p. 334.

11. Geiger, *Philosophy of Henry George*, pp. 197-99; John Locke, *An Essay Concerning the True Original, Extent and End of Civil Government* (1690; in *Social Contract,,* intro. Sir Ernest Barker (New York and London: Oxford University Press, 1948), pp. 17-20; Adam Smith, *Wealth of Nations* (1776; New York: Random House [The Modern Library], 1937), pp. 121-22; Karl Marx, *Capital* (London: Swan Sonnenschein & Co., 1889), p. 6.

12. George, *Progress and Poverty*, pp. 165-68.

13. E.g., ibid., pp. 165-72, 333-46, and passim.

14. Locke, *Essay on Civil Government*, pp. 20-30.

15. George, *Progress and Poverty*, pp. 235-42.

16. Ibid., p. 241.

17. Ibid., p. 347.

18. Ibid., p. 476.

19. Ibid., pp. 328-30, wherein George proclaimed, in italics, *"We must make land common property"* (p. 328).

20. Ibid., pp. 333-46.

21. Ibid., pp. 347-57.

22. Ibid., pp. 358-67.

23. Ibid., pp. 368-84.

24. Ibid., p. 372.

25. Ibid., pp. 328-402, and passim.

26. Ibid., pp. 362-63.

27. E.g., and for example only, Max Hirsch, *Democracy vs. Socialism*, 4th ed. (New York: Robert Schalkenbach Foundation, 1966), pp. 263-336 and passim; or see the magnificent discussion of this fatal contradiction inherent in all socialist and collectivist theory, in Theodore D. Woolsey, *Political Science, or the State* (New York: Charles Scribner's Sons, 1877), 1: 314-23, or, Henry George himself, *Progress and Poverty*, pp. 319-21.

28. George, *Progress and Poverty*, p. 405.

29. Robert V. Andelson, "Where Society's Claim Stops: An Evaluation of Seligman's Ethical Critique of Henry George," *The American Journal of Economics and Sociology* 27 (January 1968): 41-53.

30. George, *Progress and Poverty*, pp. 328-30.

31. Ibid., p. 118.

32. Geiger, *Philosophy of Henry George*, p. 361.

33. This is a long and detailed story that cannot be recounted here, but is available in other sources. See Barker, Henry George pp. 457, 463, 513-14, 619, 621, and passim; Geiger, *Philosophy of Henry George*, pp. 69-70, 338-39, 343-60, 363, 368-72; Rose, *Henry George*, pp. 125-32; Charles Regal, "Father Edward McGlynn's Views on Land, Poverty, and the Church," unpublished paper reported in *Newsletter*, Henry George School of California, June 1975, p. 1.

34. Geiger, *Philosophy of Henry George*, 353-56.

35.   Barker, *Henry George*, pp. 126, 472, 476, 575; Geiger, *Philosophy of Henry George*, pp. 347-48, 353, 363; Rose, pp. 127-29.

36.   Barker, *Henry George*, pp. 489-90; for further substantiating evidence of this anti-Georgist Catholic attitude, see pp. 477, 486-91; and in Geiger, *Philosophy of Henry George*, the entire chap. 6, "Henry George and Religion," pp. 336-80.

37.   Geiger, *Philosophy and Henry George*, 339-42.

38.   Barker, *Henry George*, pp. 571-73.

39.   Ibid., pp. 121, 366, 574.

40.   Ibid., pp. 350-52.

41.   Ibid., pp. 576, 588; Geiger, *Philosophy of Henry George*, pp. 354-56.

42.   Henry George, *Progresso e pobreza*, trans. Americo Werneck Junior, 2d ed. (Rio de Janeiro: Gráfica Editora Aurora Ltda., 1946), flyleaf. My translation from the Portuguese.

43.   I.e., *The Condition of Labor*, 1881; *The Land Question*, 1881; *Social Problems*, 1883; *Protection or Free Trade*, 1886; *A Perplexed Philosopher*, 1892; *The Science of Political Economy*, publ. posthumously, 1898.

44.   George, *Progress and Poverty*, p. 555.

45.   Barker, *Henry George*, p. 633.

46.   Rose, *Henry George*, p. 153.

24

Ryan and His Domestication
of Natural Law*

BY ROBERT V. ANDELSON

Monsignor John A. Ryan (1869-1945), whom James Hastings Nichols speaks of as the chief theorist of social Catholicism in America,[1] devoted the bulk of three chapters in his great work, *Distributive Justice*, to a critique of Henry George's so-called single-tax doctrine.[2] Although Ryan, as a young man growing up amid agrarian ferment in rural Minnesota, was, if we are to give credence to Eric Goldman,[3] "electrified" by George's masterpiece, *Progress and Poverty*, his mature evaluation of George reveals no trace of this early enthusiasm.

George's system falls within the natural law tradition, and rests upon the Lockean premise that private property is ultimately justified by the right of the individual to his own person and to his labor as an extension thereof. Since land is not created by human effort but represents a fund of opportunity intended by God for the use of all, the argument for private ownership cannot apply to it. No one may justly arrogate to himself the goods of nature without fully indemnifying those who are thereby deprived of an equal chance to use them. Economic rent constitutes an exact measure of the disadvantage sustained by those who are denied the opportunity to use a given site because of its preemption by the titleholder; therefore it should be appropriated by the community as an indemnity to them, and applied to public services that would otherwise have to be paid for largely by a levy on the income from their labor.

George characterized this as "the taking by the community for the use of the community of that value which is the creation of the community,"[4] for he contended that rent is essentially a social product—the result of the presence of population, public demand, government services, and the aggregate activity of all the individuals in a given area, not of anything the owner, as such, may do to a particular site. He advocated that a tax (or more precisely, a public fee) approaching one hundred percent of the annual unimproved value of land be collected by the government, and that all other taxes be abolished.[5]

*This chapter was originally published in *The American Journal of Economics and Sociology* 33, no. 3 (July 1974): 273-86 under the title, "Msgr. John A. Ryan's Critique of Henry George."

I

Ryan begins his analysis by addressing himself to George's attack upon the idea that first occupancy establishes a valid original title to landownership.

> Priority of occupation [says George] gives exclusive and perpetual title to the surface of a globe in which, in the order of nature, countless generations succeed each other! . . .Has the first comer at a banquet the right to turn back all the chairs, and claim that none of the other guests shall partake of the food provided, except as they make terms with him? Does the first man who presents a ticket at the door of a theater, and passes in, acquire by his priority the right to shut the doors and have the performance go on for him alone? . . .And to this manifest absurdity does the recognition of the individual right to land come when carried to its ultimate that any human being, could he concentrate in himself the individual rights to the land of any country, could expel therefrom all the rest of the inhabitants; and could he thus concentrate the individual rights to the whole surface of the globe, he alone of all the teeming population of the earth would have the right to live.[6]

Ryan seeks to destroy this argument by saying that George attributes to the title created by first occupancy qualities that it does not possess and consequences for which it is not responsible. He claims that the correct interpretation of this title does not attribute to it, as George imagined, an unlimited right of ownership either extensively or intensively.

> There seems to be no good reason to think that the first occupant is justified in claiming as his own more land than he can cultivate by his own labor, or with the assistance of those who prefer to be his employees or his tenants rather than independent proprietors. . . .Though a man should have become the rightful owner of all the land in the neighborhood, he would have no moral right to exclude therefrom those persons who could not without extreme inconvenience find a living elsewhere. He would be morally bound to let them cultivate it at a fair rental.[7]

But is there any limit to the amount of land a man can cultivate with the assistance of tenants and employees, assuming a sufficient number? The King Ranch in Texas, the latifundia of Brazil, the estates of the Duchess of Alba—none of these would be proscribed under this rubric. Neither, in principle, would the ownership of an entire continent. So much for Ryan's "extensive" limitations. As for the "intensive" ones, we need only ask the question: What constitutes a "fair rental"? If determined by the market, in the case he gives (one in which one man owned all the land in the neighborhood) a fair rental would be so high as to reduce the tenants to the level of bare subsistence. Ryan would doubtless reject this criterion, and say that a fair rental should be determined primarily by the tenants' capacities and needs, and secondarily by the owner's right to a return on his investment. But here we enter into the realm of subjective valuations, which admit of no impartial formula for their quantification or reconciliation.

In any case, says Ryan, George overestimates the historical importance of first occupancy. Most abuses of private landownership have arisen, not from the appropriation of land that nobody owned, but from "the forcible and fraudulent seizure of land which had already been occupied."[8] Nothing could be more ludicrous than to imply that George was unaware of this. "Is it not all but universally true," he asked in his *Open Letter to Pope Leo XIII*, "that existing land titles. . .come. . .from force or fraud?"[9] But landowners do not ordinarily appeal to force or fraud to justify their titles! As Ryan himself tells us, "The prevailing view among the defenders of private landownership has always been that the original title is. . .first occupancy."[10] That, therefore, is the contention that George was at pains to refute.

Ryan is not satisfied with having shattered, as he supposes, George's argument against first occupancy; he goes on to try to show that the logic of George's own position itself leads to the conclusion that first occupancy creates the original title of ownership. His reasoning on this point is subtle and ingenious but also highly artificial and legalistic. Because, in George's theory, the individual producer, Ryan says, must agree to pay rent to the community before he can begin to produce, "his right to the use of natural opportunities is not 'free,' nor can his labor alone constitute a title to that part of them that he utilizes in production."[11] Consequently, labor does not create a right to the concrete product, but merely to the value that the producer adds to the raw material. His right to the raw material itself originates in the contract by which he is authorized to utilize it in return for rent paid to the community. So his right to the product does not spring from labor alone, but from labor plus compensation to the community. "Since the contract by which the prospective user agrees to pay this compensation or rent must precede his application of labor, it instead of labor is the original title [Ryan asserts]. Since the contract is made with a particular community for the use of a particular piece of land, the title that it conveys must derive ultimately from the occupation of that land by that community—or some previous community of which the present one is the legal heir."[12]

Now, as a matter of fact, it is not the temporal priority of the community to the individual that, in George's system, gives it the right to collect rent from him. If the individual were there before the community, that right would still obtain. It rests, rather, indirectly upon the title of labor. Only insofar as rent is publicly appropriated (or land nationalized, which George does not recommend) can the equal right of all men to the produce of their labor be assured, for otherwise a portion of that produce must be paid in tribute to the landowner.

Ryan notes that George argues against private landownership in the full sense of the term on the basis that it shuts out nonlandowners from access to the "reservoirs" of natural opportunity. He claims that in so doing, George has completely abandoned the principle that underlies the labor argument. "Instead of trying to show from the nature of the situation that there is a logical difference between the two kinds of ownership, he shifts his ground to a consideration of consequences. He makes the title of social utility instead of the title of labor the distinguishing and decisive consideration."[13] Actually, the passage in question does not represent an abandonment of the labor argument or its underlying principle; it is an indirect deduction *from* the labor argument. And justice, not social utility, is the ruling consideration (although George believes that whatever is just will always, in the long run, also be socially useful). The private appropriation of land and rent removes access to natural opportunity except upon such terms as the landowner may set, and therefore encroaches upon the title of labor—upon the equal right of every man to reap the harvest of his industry.

If the community had instituted the social appropriation of land values from the beginning, Ryan admits, it could have rightfully done so by virtue of priority of occupation. But "when it failed to take advantage of its opportunity to be the first occupant of these values, when it permitted the individual proprietor to appropriate them, it forfeited its own claim. Ever since, it has had no more right to already existing land values. . .than one person has to recover a gift or donation that he has unconditionally bestowed upon another."[14]

George would quarrel with this analogy, for he holds that, by virtue of its nature, land cannot be rightfully subject to ownership in fee simple. No more than private individuals has any community ever had a right to "own" land in the sense in which labor products may be owned; full ownership includes the right to alienate, and the estate of the community is inalienable. Thus no community ever had a right to grant to private parties absolute title to something created for the use and benefit of all—a concept dimly and imperfectly reflected in the principle of eminent domain.

But what of present owners who hold deeds to land innocently bought with the proceeds of honest labor on the assumption that both the land and its rent would be theirs in perpetuity? Here, according to the Georgist view, the land is comparable to a stolen watch that some unsuspecting person has purchased in good faith. Those who are deprived of their proper shares of land benefits have the same right to recover them from the existing owners that the watch owner has to recover his property from the innocent purchaser. To the objection that the laws of many countries would permit the innocent purchaser of the watch to retain it as long as enough time had elapsed to create a "title" of prescription, the Georgist would reply that the passage of time cannot turn a wrong into a right, and that furthermore the natural heritage of the race is both inalienable and too basic to human welfare to fall under the title of prescription. The argument based upon prescription was anticipated by George when he wrote: "Because I was robbed yesterday, and the day before, and the day before that, is it any reason that I should suffer myself to be robbed today and tomorrow? Any reason that I should conclude that the robber has acquired a vested right to rob me?"[15]

Ryan objects that the present private owners of land differ from the innocent purchaser of the stolen watch in that they have never been warned by society that the land might have been virtually stolen, or that the rightful claimants might some day be empowered by law to recover possession. This line of reasoning, if applied generally, would preclude any kind of legislation that might cause losses to some vested interest. Think, for example, of all the innocent investors who were never "warned by society" that strip mining or industrial pollution, the employment of child labor or the combination in restraint of trade, the indiscriminate sale of narcotics or the production of noxious foodstuffs might be prohibited by law!

II

As a general and abstract proposition, Ryan recognizes the equal right of all men to the use of nature, and he concedes that "private ownership of land can never bring about ideal justice in distribution" of natural opportunities.[16] But he claims that the institution is "not necessarily out of harmony with the demands of *practical* justice," because a community may lack the knowledge or the power to establish the ideal system. This observation is not so much faulty as irrelevant. Who would deny that practical justice is represented by whatever *situationally possible* course of action most closely approximates the ideal? As applied to the land question, all Ryan's point amounts to when analyzed is the truism that private landownership is just, as long as there is no possibility of replacing it with anything more just.

But, says Ryan, suppose that the Georgist system were instituted, and the rent of land appropriated by the community. This, he claims, would work an *injustice* on existing landowners, who, if not compensated, would be "deprived, in varying amounts, of the conditions of material well-being to which they have become accustomed, and. . .thereby subjected to varying degrees of positive inconvenience and hardship."[17] It does not seem to occur to Ryan that the same argument could be used to oppose the abolition of protective tariffs, to which he was himself committed.[18]

Actually, of course, few if any Georgists advocate the immediate appropriation of all rent, but rather the gradual implementation of the system in such a way as to militate against the likelihood of severe individual hardship. In his entire discussion, furthermore, Ryan virtually ignores the fact that under George's system the increase of the tax on land values would be accompanied by a corresponding decrease in other taxes, particularly in taxes on improvements. Hence any landowner who made efficient use of his land would actually benefit from the reform. In the state of South Australia, three-fifths of the landowners in a locality must approve any change from the old taxing system to land-value taxation; the law permits reversion to the old system if voted by a bare majority. Yet more and more localities have been switching to land-value taxation for a long time, and not one reversion poll has yet been successful.[19] Similar instances could be adduced from the experience of New Zealand and other places to show that, inasmuch as most landowners are also land *users*, the majority find themselves better off wherever an approach to George's system has been made.[20]

Ryan warns that the social consequences of the confiscation of rent would be "even more injurious than those falling upon the individuals despoiled."[21] The opposition of the landowners would threaten social peace and order, while the popular respect for all property rights would be greatly weakened if not destroyed, since the average man would not grasp George's distinction between land and other kinds of property in this connection. "Indeed," Ryan writes, "the proposal to confiscate rent is so abhorrent to the moral sense of the average man that it could never take place except in conditions of revolution and anarchy. If that day should ever arrive, the policy of confiscation would not stop with land."

It is simply not true that the confiscation of rent could never take place except in conditions of revolution and anarchy. Even when Ryan wrote, a substantial percentage of rent was being confiscated in Australia, New Zealand, and elsewhere under quite stable and orderly conditions. As for the United States, there is no reason why a nation that has come to take the Federal Income Tax for granted could not be educated to accept the confiscation of rent, which is, after all, *unearned* income.

After conjuring forth the injury to which George's proposal would presumably subject the landowner, Ryan goes on to state that, conversely,

> the persons who own no land under the present system. . .suffer no such degree of hardship when they are continued in that condition. They are kept out of something which they have never possessed, which they have never hoped to get by any such easy method, and from which they have not been accustomed to derive any benefit. . . .Evidently, their welfare and claims in the circumstances are not of the same moral importance as the welfare and claims of persons who would be called upon to suffer the loss of goods already possessed and enjoyed, and acquired with the full sanction of society.[22]

Elsewhere in his book Ryan contends that an employer has a moral obligation to pay his workmen "a living wage" (by which he means not merely a subsistence wage but one that would enable a man to support a good-sized family in modest comfort), and his various writings make it clear that he would have this obligation enforced by the state.[23] He qualifies this obligation by saying that it is not incumbent upon the employer who would be thereby driven out of business, or reduced to a standard of living little higher than that of his workmen. But no employer has a right to "indulge in anything like luxurious expenditure, so long as any of the employees fail to receive living wages."[24]

But suppose (as one may well do) that the employer had becomed used, with the full sanction of society, to a standard of living characterized by luxurious expenditure. And suppose (as one might well have supposed at the time the book was written) that the workmen were unaccustomed to what Ryan calls "a living wage." The relationship between employer and workman then becomes analogous to that between landowner and landless man, and in order to be consistent Ryan would be forced to say that, if obliged to pay a living wage, the employer would be deprived of conditions of material well-being to which he has become accustomed, and thus unjustly subjected to positive inconvenience and hardship, whereas, if he were not so obliged, the workers would suffer no such degree of hardship since they would merely be continued in their previous condition, and hence that the welfare and claims of the latter are not of the same moral importance as those of the former.

The decisive place the issue of compensation occupies in Ryan's thinking is suggested by the fact that while he condemns the confiscation of even future increments of land value as morally unjust without compensation,[25] he indicates that if landowners were compensated "with a sum equal to the present value, or the capitalized rent, of their land," the Georgist plan would be only *probably* inferior to the present system.[26] He maintains that "the moral sense of mankind recognizes that it is in accordance with equity to compensate slave owners when the slaves are legally emancipated. Infinitely stronger is the claim of the landowner to compensation."[27] The first half of this statement is a mere assertion, and the second, debatable for reasons that space limitations compel me to omit. But even if both were to be accepted, Cord observes that gradual imposition of full land-value taxation over a period of forty years is exactly equivalent to immediate compensation without interest. If three percent interest were given on the unpaid balance, then sixty-four years would be necessary.[28]

III

Ryan rejects the Georgist argument that rent should be appropriated by society because it is socially produced. He remarks, to begin with, that *all* land value is not socially produced; although no land can have value without being brought into relation with society, neither can it have value if it possesses no natural qualities suitable for the satisfaction of human wants.[29] George would not, of course, have denied this, but would have insisted that that portion of the value attributable to natural qualities is, like the land itself, an inalienable patrimony of the whole community, not properly subject to private usurpation.

But Ryan would not allow to society any right even to that portion of rent which he admits that it produces. He refuses to accept the proposition that the socially produced value of land ought to go to the social producer rather than to the individual proprietor, except in the case of future increments, and then only if the proprietor were indemnified for the loss of anticipated speculative increase reflected in his purchase price. He points out that "men do not admit that all production of value constitutes a title of ownership. Neither the monopolist who increases value by restricting supply, nor the pacemakers of fashion who increase value by merely increasing demand, are regarded as possessing a moral right to the value that they have 'created.' "[30] The ultimate basis of the producer's right to his produce, or to its value, is the fact that this is the only way in which he can get his just share of the earth's goods, and of the means of life and personal development. His right does not rest upon the mere fact of value production.

"Why," Ryan asks, "has the shoemaker a right to the value that he adds to the raw material in making a pair of shoes?" It is

> because men want to use his products, and because they have no right to require him to serve them without compensation. He is morally and juridically their equal, and has the same right as they to access on reasonable terms to the earth and the earth's possibilities of a livelihood. . . .To assume that he is obliged to produce socially useful things without remuneration, is to assume that his life and personality and personal development are of no intrinsic importance, and that his pursuit of the essential ends of life has no meaning except in so far as may be conducive to his function as an instrument of production. . . .
>
> As a producer of land values, the community is not on the same moral ground as the shoemaker. Its productive action is indirect and extrinsic, instead of direct and intrinsic, and is merely incidental to its principal activities and purposes. . . .The activities of which land values are a resultant have already been remunerated in the price paid to the wage-earner for his labor, the physician for his services, the manufacturer and the merchant for their wares, and the municipal corporation in the form of taxes. On what

ground can the community, or any part of it, set up a claim in strict justice to the increased land values?[31]

This last paragraph contains some truly astonishing assertions. The "activities of which land values are the resultant" have *not* already been remunerated, at least not in full, for a large part of what would otherwise be remuneration has had to go to landowners in the form of rent—landowners who, as such, contributed nothing positive to the production of those values. Only where rent has not yet arisen can the activities that lead to the production of future rent be said to have already been fully compensated, and physicians, manufacturers, and municipal corporations are seldom found in places where land has, as yet, acquired no value whatsoever.

Let it be granted that the community does not produce land values in the same direct and intrinsic sense in which the shoemaker produces the value that he adds to the leather. Does the landowner? The only value that the landowner, as landowner, produces is speculative value stemming from monopolistic scarcity, which Ryan specifically admits creates no moral title.[32] And the appropriation of land value by the landowner prevents both the community in its corporate capacity and its members in their individual capacities from enjoying the full benefits of the values that they do directly and intrinsically produce. It is they who are being compelled to serve the landowner without compensation, to divert to him by way of tribute a portion of their rightful recompense.

IV

We have seen that, according to Ryan, the community has no right either to land or to rent. The private owner, however, has a right to both. Ryan goes as far as to call it a *natural right*, but he uses the term in a sense different from that in which it is commonly understood.

He claims that it is a natural right because it is indirectly necessary for the welfare of the individual. By "indirectly necessary," he says he means necessary as a social institution rather than as something immediately connected with individual needs as such. Something is regarded as "necessary as a social institution" if, although neither an intrinsic good nor an indispensable means to the satisfaction of vital individual needs, it is capable of promoting the welfare of the average person or the majority of persons to a greater degree than any alternative.[33]

Thus, in the last analysis, Ryan, the spokesman of natural law and scathing nemesis of utilitarianism, rests his defense of private property in land upon what he considers to be its superior social utility as an institution. This judgment of superior social utility he derives, first, from certain pragmatic objections to the alternatives, socialism and Georgism, and second, from a view of private ownership in terms of its ideal potentialities.

I shall not review here Ryan's objections to socialism (objections with which I happen to concur) because they are not germane to the topic of this study. His pragmatic objections to Georgism are preceded by the acknowledgment of several important benefits to which the system would lead:

Since no man would find it profitable to retain control of more land than he could use himself, the number of actual land users would be increased. The land speculator would disappear, together with the opportunity of making and losing fortunes by gambling on the changes in land values. Owing to the removal of taxation from the necessaries of life and from industry, consumers would get goods cheaper, and some stimulus would be given to production and employment. Those monopolies which derive their strength from land would become weaker and tend to disappear.[34]

These benefits, however, would be counterbalanced, in his opinion, by the following fancied disadvantages:

1. *Many holdings would deteriorate because of those who would exhaust the land through careless or rapacious exploitation.* This has not occurred in practice. In fact, the Georgist system creates an incentive to *increase* fertility, since the tax would not reflect the value of improvement but only of land in its virgin state, and of location. Increased fertility through more careful cultivation has been the rule in Denmark, Australia, the California irrigation districts, and wherever an approach to Georgism has been instituted.

2. *The administrative machinery would inevitably involve a vast amount of error, inequality, favoritism, and corruption, for the land tax would be on the full amount of the annual rent instead of on a fraction, as at present.* This is absurd. There is no reason why, if all the rent were taxed, there should be proportionately any more error or corruption than when a fraction of it is taxed; in fact, there should be less, since public scrutiny would be keener. Furthermore, since land cannot be hidden, chances for error, favoritism, corruption, and the like are less than with other sources of tax revenue, and under George's system only land would be taxed. Virtually all current and most past authorities concede that a single tax on land would be uniquely free of these very ills. When one imagines the reduction in corruption that would accompany the abolition of the income tax, Ryan's objection becomes doubly curious!

3. *Cultivators would not have the inducement to make improvements that arises from the hope of selling both improvements and land at a profit, owing to the increased demand for land.* It is true that under a Georgist system improvements would not be made with an eye to speculative profits from land sales, but they would be made with the expectation of profit from the improvements themselves, and their making would be stimulated by the fact that it would not be penalized, as now, by a tax increase.

4. *The reform would lead to instability of tenure because, owing to misfortunes of various kinds (such as one or two poor crops), many landholders would be temporarily unable to pay the full amount of the rent and would lose their titles.* The tax is supposed to reflect current market value, determined by frequent reappraisal. Poor crops, if peculiar to a vicinity, would reduce the value of land in that vicinity, and hence the tax. Granted, marginal and less efficient producers might tend to be forced out (although their being taxed the full economic rent would be mitigated by the absence of other taxes, and the lower cost of commodities), but they would have a much better chance than at present of resuming their operations elsewhere because of cheaper land prices.

When we turn to Ryan's view of the ideal potentialities of private ownership, we come to an odd paradox. We find that he is not really interested in
defending landownership as it has existed historically, but only "in its essential
elements, and with its capacity for modification and improvement."[35] He
admits that "we should be tempted to declare that the most extreme form of
Agrarian Socialism could scarcely have been more productive of individual
and social injury" than private landownership as it obtained in certain
empirical instances. And the model he constructs in chapter 7 for a modified
and improved system has little in common with the institution as we now know
it.

The chapter is entitled "Methods of Reforming Our Land System." By the
time Ryan gets through reforming the system, he has moved about halfway
down the Georgist road. He would prohibit the alienation of lands now
publicly held, insisting that they be leased instead of sold. He would have
future increases in the value of land socially appropriated (with owners
compensated for positive losses of interest and principal). He would gradually
transfer the taxes on improvements and personal property to land. And he
would impose progressive supertaxes upon valuable mineral, timber, and
waterpower holdings, and upon certain agricultural lands not cultivated by the
owners. Practically speaking, in terms of the foreseeable future, today's
Georgist would probably be only too glad to settle for these reforms.

It is against this semi-Georgist model, not against landownership as historically practiced, that Ryan measures and finds wanting the full-scale George
proposal. He belittles the George proposal as an "untried system."[36] Yet
where has his own ideal system been tried in its totality? The George proposal,
as we have seen, has been given limited and partial application in many places.
To the extent that it has been applied, its social utility has been amply
demonstrated—even more conclusively since the time when Ryan's critique
appeared. Consider, for example, the Hutchinson Report, a survey comparing
the six Australian states in terms of the degree to which they use this method of
obtaining public revenue. Queensland, New South Wales, and Western
Australia have much heavier land-value taxes and much lower improvement
taxes than do South Australia, Victoria, and Tasmania. According to the
report, in the period considered the first group of states had increases in land
under crops, while the second group had decreases. The value of
improvements as compared to land was found to be 151 percent in the first
group, as against only 79 percent in the second, and was highest (198 percent)
in Queensland, which collects the greatest amount (54.4 percent) of economic
rent. Factory wages were higher in the first group and larger in purchasing
power. Last, it was discovered that population was flowing from the second
group to the first group, indicating that people in Australia found conditions
better in the first group. The inflow to Queensland, the state taxing land values
the most, was the greatest.[37] So even from a standpoint of social utility, the
criterion according to which Ryan proclaims private landownership to be a
natural right, the Georgist approach would seem empirically to be at least as
capable of vindication.

Notes

1.   James Hastings Nichols, *Democracy and the Churches*, (Philadelphia: Westminster Press, 1951), p. 131.

2.   John A. Ryan, *Distributive Justice* (1916; rev. ed. New York: Macmillan, 1927), chaps. 3, 4, and 5. Chap. 2 is reproduced, with minor omissions, in vol. 14 of the Modern Legal Philosophy Series. I refer to the single tax as "so-called" because its singleness is not its essential feature, and, strictly speaking, it is not a tax but rather a public fee.

3.   Eric F. Goldman, *Rendezvous With Destiny* (New York: Vintage Books, 1956), p. 85. For a more restrained account see Ryan's autobiography, *Social Doctrine in Action* (New York: Harper, 1941), p. 9.

4.   Henry George, *Progress and Poverty*, 75th anniversary ed. (New York: Robert Schalkenbach Foundation, 1954), p. 421.

5.   It should be emphasized that George did not regard his theory as a mere fiscal reform. He thought of it as a means whereby free enterprise, in which he ardently believed, could be rendered truly free by eliminating a fundamental and pervasive monopoly that interferes with the normal operation of the market and diverts a major share of wealth to those who make no positive contribution to the economic process. Rent, he taught, belongs to the community by right, and as long as it is privately appropriated, it serves as a fetter upon production and a barrier to the right of individuals to enjoy the fruits of their toil. Interest, on the other hand, he viewed as the capitalist's just return for that increase in wealth attributable to his saving and investment. If, he held, rent were taken by the public, the speculative element in land prices would disappear, and the consequent cheapness of land would place natural opportunity within the reach of all. Production would be stimulated, wages would rise, the cost of goods would be reduced, and with the extirpation of its basic cause, involuntary poverty would tend to vanish.

6.   George, *Progress and Poverty*, pp. 344 f.

7.   Ryan, *Distributive Justice*, pp. 25 f.

8.   Ibid., p. 26.

9.   Henry George, "The Condition of Labor: An Open Letter to Pope Leo XIII" (1881), *The Land Question* [and other Essays] (New York: Robert Schalkenbach Foundation, 1953), p. 36.

10.   Ryan, *Distributive Justice*, p. 24.

11.   Ibid., p. 28.

12.   Ibid., p. 29. The same kind of legalistic hairsplitting that characterizes Ryan's approach in the argument just cited also marks his treatment of a passage in which George speaks of travelers in the desert, saying that those who had had the forethought to provide themselves with vessels of water would have a just property right in the water so carried, against which the need of their less provident fellows could establish a claim only of charity and not of justice. "But suppose others use their forethought in pushing ahead and appropriating the springs, refusing when their fellows came up to let them drink of the water save as they buy it of them. Would such forethought give any right?" The obvius intent of this passage is simply to point up the distinction between "the forethought of carrying water where it is needed" (labor), and "the forethought of seizing springs" (first occupancy). Ryan, however, makes it the occasion for insisting that since the water in the vessels was originally abstracted from some spring, the right to it stems, initially, not from the labor of transporting it or filling the vessels with it, but from seizure of an ownerless good, quoting a paraphrase of Grotius to the effect that "since nothing can be made except out of pre-existing matter, acquisition by means of labor depends, ultimately, on possession by means of occupation." It is patent that the act of appropriation is temporally antecedent to productive labor, but it is far from evident why this truism should be accorded such overriding moral significance as to constitute the definitive factor in establishing ownership. Moreover, it should be noted that he who fills vessels from a spring does not (unless the spring is about to run dry) deprive others of the opportunity to use a natural good. George, "The Condition of Labor," p. 29; Ryan, *Distributive Justice*, p. 31.

13.   Ryan, *Distributive Justice*, pp. 31 f.

14.   Ibid., p. 49.

15. George, *Progress and Poverty*, p. 365. In 1967 the California Supreme Court answered this rhetorical question in the affirmative when it enjoined Sacramento Assessor Dr. Irene Hickman to cease assessing real property at 100 percent of market value as provided by the state constitution. The court declared, in effect, that previous assessors had ignored that constitutional provision for so long that real estate owners had acquired a vested right to its nonenforcement! No doubt, the court is privy to some arcane answer to Herbert Spencer's famous query: "At what rate per annum do invalid claims become valid?" Herbert Spencer, *Social Statics* (Original Version, 1850; reprint ed. New York: Robert Schalkenbach Foundation, 1954), p. 105.

16. Ryan, *Distributive Justice*, p. 35.

17. Ibid., p. 38.

18. See John A. Ryan, *Declining Liberty and Other Papers* (Freeport, N.Y.: Books for Libraries Press, 1927), p. 142.

19. Harry Gunnison Brown, Harold S. Buttenheim, et al., eds., *Land Value Taxation Around the World* (New York: Robert Schalkenbach Foundation, 1955), p. 11.

20. Ibid., pp. 13, 33.

21. Ryan, *Distributive Justice*, p. 41.

22. Ibid., p. 39.

23. See, for example, *Declining Liberty and Other Papers*, pp. 200 ff.

24. Ryan, *Distributive Justice*, p. 324.

25. Ibid., p. 103.

26. Ibid., pp. 54-56, 61, 66, 73.

27. Ibid., p. 39.

28. Steven B. Cord, *Henry George: Dreamer or Realist?* (Philadelphia: University of Pennsylvania Press, 1965), p. 65.

29. Ryan, *Distributive Justice*, p. 42.

30. Ibid., pp. 46 f.

31. Ibid., pp. 47 f.

32. Ibid., p. 45. I am willing to concede that *some* owners perform a useful entrepreneurial function in finding the best use for (and thus actualizing the latent value of) their sites. In this case, a portion of the rent is really wages, for it is attributable to mental labor rather than to mere ownership. But it would seem as if at least as many owners, through ignorant allocation or too prolonged withholding, prevent or inhibit optimal use, while the role of others is simply passive—responding to the entrepreneurial initiative of nonowners. The last instance demonstrates that the entrepreneurial function would continue to be performed (and not necessarily by public officials) even if all private land titles were extinguished.

33. Ibid., pp. 57-60.

34. Ibid., p. 54.

35. Ibid., p. 56.

36. Ibid.

37. A. R. Hutchinson, *Public Charges Upon Land Values* (Melbourne: Land Values Research Group, 1963).

25

Rothbard's Anarcho-Capitalist Critique

BY C. LOWELL HARRISS

Professional economists who were contemporaries of Henry George generally opposed his views. Other chapters in this volume discuss the leading examples. More recently, in academe as well as elsewhere, there has developed support for property-tax revision along the lines he so fervently advocated—much greater reliance on site values and a corresponding reduction in burdens on capital and other products of human labor.

Land-value taxation relates to countless issues of (local) government finance, including many types of distress in urban areas; land-use policies, the environment, energy, and "externalities" of endless variety are related in one way or another to present and potential taxes on land. For dealing with these and other matters, all potentially useful insights deserve attention—George's as well as those of his critics who have claim to competence.

Among contemporary economists, few if any have written more extensively in explicit criticism of George's work than has Murray N. Rothbard, widely recognized as a leading libertarian and student of Ludwig von Mises.[1] He explains in the preface to *Power and Market* that he devotes more attention than is now customary to this topic because "the Georgists are correct in noting that their important claims are never mentioned, much less refuted, in current works. . . ."[2] His critique draws heavily upon analyses made by two other writers—Frank H. Knight (1885-1972), in his day one of America's foremost economists,[3] and Spencer Heath (1876-1963), a successful inventor and patent attorney who published a book and several pamphlets in the field of social and political theory.[4]

Rothbard's statement of his basic position, that ". . .the very existence of taxation and the government budget is considered an act of intervention into the free market. . . ," alerts us to a general frame of reference—anarcho-capitalism, the belief that even such services as police protection and defense against external aggression should be supplied through voluntary contract. This extreme posture was also taken by Heath but not by Knight, although he too was strongly committed to the free market economy.[5]

Introductory Points: Words and Classifications

Recent occasion to examine many of George's writings brought me to some of them for the first time. The range is wide. Some have distinct value for today, but discrimination is needed. No effort to deal comprehensively with all of the published work could fit within the scope of this chapter. Even though none of the three above-named critics ranges so broadly, they touch upon more topics than can receive attention here.

George wrote so much, under a variety of conditions, over so many years, and responding to diverse impulses, that consistency among his statements is not always certain. Followers and critics can cite sources for items that do seem to conflict. Meanings are not always clear. We can mislead ourselves by yielding to a temptation to pick on what are essentially matters of secondary importance, even to quibble.

Our world differs from his. Although he was aware of urban growth and blasts the conditions of life in cities, and although he criticized Ricardo for viewing the law of rent merely in its relation to agriculture,[6] he lived at a time when the American population was largely rural, decades before the auto helped to transform land use and life in general. Inflation was not a widespread reality in the years in which he lived; quite the contrary. And he wrote long before federal income taxation became a determinant of decisions about land use and real estate investments.

Rothbard refers to "Georgists." Who are they? Unquestionably, more than one grouping would be defensible; each group would include people who, even though they hold key points in common, differ significantly on one or more aspects of policies involving land-value taxation. To write, as does Rothbard, "Georgists anticipate" or "single taxers do not deny," may be both correct and misleading. Persons who have informed interest in, and sympathy for, the leading ideas—and perhaps also, but not always fully, for the feelings and sentiments—expressed by George, are not a close-knit group. Great caution is required in generalizing about their views as of today, or probably as of any date in the past. On the crucial issue of how much of the fruits of land "should" remain for present owners, I expect that their conclusions would differ widely.

Nor can we know how George might write and speak today. In his own time he insisted upon rejecting what must be recognized as advances in economic theory. Would he have remained so adamant? If he had kept abreast of expanding knowledge, he could, I believe, have held to his chief policy position—and without serious modification—yet perhaps have avoided alienating so many economists. For example, his predictions of growing distress (in an era when standards of living actually rose) do not seem to me essential to the case for financing government more extensively by taxing land values. The rising demand for land (from whatever forces, not necessarily limited to those George cites) seems to me the economic element crucial to his policy recommendations.

George's treatment of population growth scarcely does him credit but is not a topic for major attention by Rothbard, Knight, or Heath.[7] Heath nevertheless applauds him for a "masterly and magnificent refutation"[8] of what might be termed a limiting case of Malthus's admonitions; the point involves the meaning of the implied "other things being the same" assumption in a world of improving technology, broadly defined, and capital accumulation.

George's efforts to define *wealth* and his uses of the term, the nature of *production* as he conceived it, his conclusions about the worth of the processes of exchange, and his understanding of the role of capital—these topics may have interest as part of the history of economic thought. Knight does not attempt to cover such points. Nor does Rothbard: "I will not deal with what I consider grave fallacies in capital and production theory because they take us too far afield from the main problem."[9] He has, however, cited as a deficiency in Georgist thinking, its view of capital as "the product of human energy," alleging that the exclusion of an essential element—*"and time"*—constitutes a fatal error.[10] Yet one finds clearly in *Progress and Poverty* and elsewhere words explicitly recognizing time and its importance.[11]

But George's usefulness as a source of helpful insight today stands or falls on other aspects of his writing. The extent of his originality on these points, if any, is not our concern because the three critics do not dwell on it.

Our responsibility is to use the tools of analysis available today. Rothbard and Knight utilize economic theory more complete than that of *Progress and Poverty* and the later writings of George. Emotions played a prominent role in his career; their relevance and influence must be recognized for what they were, and as not necessarily deserving of the same endorsement as conclusions reached by objective study. Rothbard speaks of a "confusion of economic and moral arguments." Let us accept the warning, noting that in neither George's writings nor those of a critic will the mixture of "scientific" with value judgments destroy, as a matter of course, the validity of the former judgments or the worth of the latter.

Major Criticisms

The selection of topics for comment here, and the exclusion of certain subleties, reflect to some extent judgments about importance.

"Single" Tax: Changing Conditions

The "single" aspect of George's tax proposals might have been adequate in some or most American communities in George's day.[12] The Census of Governments found total state-local spending on current operations in 1902 to be $796 million; debt service, $79 million; and assistance and subsidies, $15 million. Do such totals seem within the probable limits of a site-value tax? Property tax then yielded $706 million. The additional burden on land might have been well within the realm of feasibility. Gross National Product was around $20 billion. George devoted no effort to measure in the modern sense; at best, figures would have been scarce. Be that as it may, (local) government spending has probably outpaced the rise in "pure" land rent.[13]

Knight and Rothbard recognize that the "single" aspect can have become obsolete without invalidating other features. *Site-value* and *location-value* taxation are more appropriate terms for the essence of what George proposed.

His critics do make a point that commands attention. Knight especially emphasizes it. Land is by no means the only form of property whose value may reflect "unearned increments." Rothbard uses Rembrandts to illustrate. Other examples in various gradations could be cited. George would distinguish the painting from land because labor made the one and created a moral claim to ownership. Moreover, as Winston Churchill put it when he was president of the Board of Trade in Asquith's cabinet, "pictures do not get in anybody's way."[14]

Here it is enough to assert that in my view site values can rank high indeed on the scale of potential bases for at least local taxation without any presumption (1) that they would approximate the total revenue that the property tax raises in many localities, or (2) that they constitute the only elements of income for which the recipient may have done rather little in creating the value today.

Separability of Land Values

Can land values be distinguished from those of improvements on—and in—the surface of the earth to apply significantly different tax rates (with possibly a zero rate on man-made capital)? Rothbard in an essay published in 1957 recognizes that in urban areas the separation of land and improvement values *appears* to be done. But he denies the possibility of successfully implementing differential tax rates. More recently, he writes: "Ground-land taxation faces a further problem that cannot be solved: how to distinguish quantitatively between that portion of the gross rent of a land area which goes to ground land and that portion which goes to interest and wages. Since land in use is often amalgamated with capital investment and the two are bought and sold together, this distinction between them cannot be made."[15]

Knight seems to believe that human weaknesses would make the results too poor to be tolerable. Is he not, however, out of touch with what has existed for years? Land-value assessments resting on market tests underlie property taxes now. Two questions need to be made explicit: the most important in practical policy, "How high the tax rate?"; the second, "What quality of administration do we expect?"

If George spelled out in specific terms the tax rates he desired and the way the tax base would be computed, I do not remember the details. The kind of administration of assessment required to accomplish the goals and the means of achieving them are held to be those already operating; critics are on solid ground in calling attention to the need to separate land from other elements that make up real estate transactions. The practical issues mix with those involving the possible de facto "socialization" of land. A tax rate absorbing all of the yield *would* approach "socialization" in the sense of government ownership. Operation might be private, but what would be the purpose of private ownership? However, George envisaged that a small percentage of the yield be left to owners.[16]

Knight pictures a result in which market valuations would not in fact be usable. Reliance would of necessity be placed on human action; "some official, some 'bureaucrat' with power, would have to appraise it—subject to error, prejudice, and acute disagreement."[17] True, but not conclusive.

In the world as I see it, a tax absorbing much of the rent of land could be administered. In fact, persons who have compared property-tax assessment at present with the results attainable under a site-value system agree, I believe, that the assessment task would be simplified if land only were taxed. One must be cautious, of course, in speaking of conditions that would exist in circumstances quite different from those of actual experience. In any case, however, a decision should not hinge upon the probability or improbability of approximating perfection under a new system. Do we live with any institutions that are perfect? Appraisers and assessors have methods of doing what Knight and Rothbard seem to believe is impossible—valuing "land" as such even when it has buildings and other man-made improvements. The two economists are correct, however, in asserting that we could not go back through history to identify all inputs of capital (and the labor of pioneers and other settlers) that have gone into putting land in the present form. The worth in the original condition, free from all other kinds of inputs, could rarely be determined now. But we look to the future.

Most of the work of assessors today involves the nonland portions of real estate. Drastic reduction in reliance on taxes on buildings would lead one reasonably to expect a freeing of personnel and other resources for doing a better job on the land portion. One parcel of land generally differs rather little in worth per unit of area from those nearby. The linkages assist greatly in assessing on a mass basis.

In Taiwan, in parts of Australia and South Africa, and in some other places, the tax rests on land values. My own inquiries and those of others indicate no serious doubts about the separability of values. However, it should be remarked that the tax rates applicable in these instances are very much lower than would apply in American localities if the present total-revenue importance of property taxation were continued but a much higher fraction were imposed on land. Today American assessments do generally distinguish land from other portions of the total value. The accuracy of the results in separating the land from other values will differ from one assessment area to another. Where, as at present, the same tax rates apply, little significance attaches to the distinction.

If tax rates differed greatly—and under the "full" Georgist system one rate would be zero, the other very high—much more dispute than at present could be expected. The separation of the land from the other portions of selling price or lease terms would have considerable tax significance. Questions would demand more accurate answers than in fact is now the case. For income tax and other purposes there is now need to distinguish land from other elements of real estate. The rules that have been developed for these and other purposes would probably not be fully satisfactory. But there would be no need to start afresh; existing accounts would be of help.

Rothbard and the other critics are not obligated to prescribe means for solving transition problems. (George himself did not.) But to deny implicitly the possibility of effective solution seems to me to go too far. Most problems, I believe, could be anticipated as to their nature if not necessarily as to amounts.[18] *The changes in taxes would themselves alter both land values and the worth of existing improvements.* Any realistic approach would call for gradualism in transition—five years or more; one form of transition could be exemption or other favoritism for new structures or those of certain types.

The writings of George, and those of Georgists with which I am familiar, show little interest in the mechanics of implementing a separation of pure land values from those of man-made capital. Frequently, one senses a belief that land use is generally governed by rental agreements. In practice, of course, owner-occupancy is common. Rents are not the overwhelmingly typical form of payment. Rothbard and Knight are right in emphasizing that administration would of necessity rest on estimates of capital value made by fallible human beings. The conclusion, however, need not be that the present taxation of both land and buildings can be done tolerably well whereas a tax on land only could not be administered satisfactorily.

How High a Tax? Incentives

The height of the tax rate George would really have supported remains unclear to me.[19] He thought that the rent fund would yield a surplus over and above the public expenditures then existing, and that the greater part of this should be captured for public use.[20] Rothbard and the other critics typically write as if they believe that he favored taking *all* "pure" rent in taxation, and this conclusion seems confirmed by much of George's rhetoric, whereas his sentiments to the contrary are not prominently expressed and are therefore easily overlooked. Whatever George may have thought about the "proper" height of the tax rate, some points made by the critics ought to be considered. Rothbard writes:

> Suppose that the government did in fact levy a 100% tax on ground rent. What would be the economic effects? The current owners of ground land would be expropriated, and the capital value of ground land would fall to zero. Since site-owners could not obtain rents, the sites would become valueless on the market. From then on, sites would be free, and the site-owner would have to pay his annual ground rent into the Treasury.
>
> But since all ground rent is siphoned off to the government, there is no reason for owners to charge any rent. Ground rent will fall to zero as well, and rentals will thus be free. So, one economic effect of the single tax is that, far from supplying all the revenue of government, it would yield no revenue at all![21]

The extreme case of a one hundred percent tax is so far from experience that one has difficulty discussing the probabilities. Much would depend upon the structure of the tax. It would certainly be devised to raise revenue. Lawmakers would be smart enough to base tax on the *potential* yield. How would the market operate if the tax rate were one hundred percent? The responsibility, and the incentive, for getting the best price (yield) possible would perhaps lie overwhelmingly on government officials. Their concern for revenue would provide some incentive and involve the responsibility for getting whatever possible from the users of land. Differing productiveness of sites would exist. Rothbard seems wrong in asserting that one consequence would be no revenue. Locations would not become free if tax collectors were doing their job. Potential users would have reason to make the highest bids possible. Persons seeking homes, and businesses anxious for good locations, would be motivated to bid according to prospective usefulness. Payments would flow to government treasuries.

Rothbard may be on sounder ground, even though overstating his case, when he asserts that "economic havoc" would follow a tax of one hundred percent—but not because land producing no rent for the owner would be free. In an economy where owner-occupancy is common, a condition of land without price is not easily envisioned. Owner-occupants would pay differing amounts in taxes. But if government tried to take all, a significant change in conditions would be expected; the economizing forces of the price system would operate with less effectiveness. Would allocation become far less effective (though not necessarily chaotic) if government took all the yield? Or ninety-five percent?[22] Would waste from poor use become, if not enormous, at least enough larger than at present to cause real concern? Georgists cite improvements in land use as a benefit. Who would have both the knowledge and the incentive to get the best use if government took all? Gross yield would not fall to zero, but price could plummet. The form of tax we know, on capital value, might have to be converted into the British form of tax on yield—but not on the actual amount, as in Britain, but rather on the potential income, since under the former, idleness or gross underutilization brings in effect a kind of tax relief.

If government in fact became the owner of all the yield, would not politics and favoritism govern or at least play an inordinate role? Both Knight and Rothbard are apprehensive. If nongovernmental owners of land were left with no benefits, then one aspect of the demand-supply relationship would lose most of its force. Owners as suppliers would have less than the present incentive to strive for better terms, assuming that assessments reflected market conditions promptly.

Although such a condition can be pictured on the basis of some of George's statements, the picture seems to me quite out of line with anything reasonably to be advocated as site-value taxation today. Tax rates on land values could go up enough to permit constructive reductions in tax on man-made capital without reaching a height that would push land values to the near-zero level.

Two points relevant here are overlooked by both Rothbard and the other two authors: First, in some cases land values would benefit from rising demand as builders changed plans in response to lower taxes on new capital. Second, in many more cases, assuming that the change were not to alter the total revenue to be obtained from property taxation, present property owners would approximately break even; the decline in tax rate on improvements would bring advantages more or less offsetting the effects of an increase in tax on land.

Rothbard and the others are correct in pointing out that not all landowners are merely "idle," passively profiting as the community grows. Some devote time, energy, and skill—and serve usefully—in getting land into better uses. Land will not automatically move into the best use possible. Decisions must be made by human beings. The benefits to others that owners "produce" may sometimes include even the results of holding land apparently idle or under-utilized ("on speculation") waiting for "ripening," although, of course, speculative withholding may also delay or prevent wholesome development. The world as it exists often involves much that is uncertain. Real doubts intrude on the commitment of capital and other resources to a plot of land, usually for a period of many years. Views will frequently differ.

Added Pressures to Induce (Force) Land into Use

Advocates of land-(site-) value taxation usually claim that one advantage would be an improvement in land utilization. Owners, it is said, would face more pressure to use land more nearly at its full potential. Knight, however, seems to doubt that owners would have greater inducement or opportunity to try for the best use possible. The market creates the alternatives; the best one sacrificed is the cost of the existing use. Rothbard, too, sees a disadvantage. He writes that Georgists

assert the single tax will spur production. It will penalize idle land, and force landowners to develop their property in order to lower their tax burden.

Idle land, indeed, plays a large part in single tax theory, which contends that wicked speculators, holding out for their unearned increment, keep sites off the market, and cause a scarcity of land; that this speculation even causes depressions. A single tax, confiscating unearned increment, is supposed to eliminate land speculation, and so cure depressions and even poverty itself. . . .[Omitted are several paragraphs that deal with what Rothbard regards as gaps in George's theories stemming from his alleged failure to recognize the role of time in capital formation and in production using capital.]

Since labor is scarce relative to land, and much land *must* therefore remain idle, any attempt to force *all* land into production would bring economic disaster. Forcing all land into use would take labor and capital away from more productive uses, and compel their wasteful employment on land, a disservice to consumers.[23]

Rothbard seems to attribute to George an objective—"use" of "all" land—that appears quite out of keeping with the basic spirit of *Progress and Poverty*; certainly it is not articulated there or in any of George's other writings. Whether or not one could find half a dozen professed Georgists who would come close to advocating such an objective (forcing *all* land into use), it is not one meriting serious attention. Rothbard's treatment in *Power and Market* distinguishes a tax on current yield from one on capital value; the latter includes the present worth of future elements. The time factor enters. I do not see the inconsistency he does in taxing capital values of land on an annual basis, assuming real effort for good quality assessment.

What *would* happen? Actual results would, of course, depend upon a variety of conditions special to each particular locality. One consideration is the local tax rate that would apply. Another would be the effect of cuts in tax rates on improvements. In much of the country the tax rate on land could be a meaningful fraction of the gross potential yield from the land, conceivably a very large fraction.

Assessment should be realistic, that is, the responsible supporters of site-value taxation would endorse only assessments resting upon market valuations. Assessments would be related to the capitalization at going rates of return of what the land would produce. The tax would rest upon market values, but often at tax rates much higher than now prevail. Presumably capital values would change as the next tax structure became effective.

Interactions and changes from year to year could for a time be unsettling; the speed of transition would, of course, make a difference in the adjustment process.

George was, to say the least, lacking in precision in his statements about the most productive combinations of factors of production. Rothbard, however, seems to me to misunderstand the essence of site-value taxation as presently advocated. The market value (reflecting estimates of productivity under most favorable conditions) would determine the tax. Nothing in the system, even as George propounded it, would impose a current tax burden on sites with no worth. Labor and capital would be allocated by market forces as at present. The higher tax burden on supramarginal sites would tend to raise the availability of land as owners felt greater pressure to pay tax; but land that could not bid successfully in competition with other plots for labor and capital would have no value to bring tax liability. Nothing I can see would exist to draw labor and capital from land with higher to that with lower productive capacity.

The need to pay a tax in cash, generally at a rate much higher than at present—a tax based on the "highest and best use" (as reflected in market prices)—would discourage holding potentially productive land vacant or in a use below its optimum possibility. Determining that potential will typically involve uncertainty. Sometimes waiting for better conditions will be wise. The market by the process of discounting will distinguish present yields (excluding change of capital value) from those of equal dollar amount to be realized in the future. Today, of course, an owner not getting the best use of the land sacrifices an alternative that is a cost; this fact of economic life may occasionally involve larger values than any difference in tax proposed.[24] The tax change would be an additional factor leading to fuller use—*if the market would support the use*. If the market would not justify such a potential use, then the assessment and the tax would be "low." Nothing I can see in a "correct" restructuring would add incentive to put "idle" land to uses inappropriate to market realities.

The net effects in a community should be a readjustment of relative land prices. There would then be, on balance, pressures for uses of land closer to valuations reflecting current market opportunities. In challenging the exaggerated claims probably made by some Georgists, the critics do not weaken at all the fundamental point that reducing tax burdens on man-made capital and getting more revenue from a tax on land values would improve resource allocation and use. Although Rothbard recognizes that it would stimulate production,[25] neither he, Knight, nor Heath pays what I would consider adequate attention to the element of the Georgist plan consisting of the relief from taxes on improvements.

The total of capital funds available for investment in an area would presumably rise for the first communities to act. Funds would be redirected in the light of the relatively more favorable conditions. Demand for land would tend to go up.

The more localities adopting the change, however, the greater the spread of available new capital through the economy; unless new saving were to rise, the average increase in demand for land would be slight at most.

Service of Landowners

As already noted, the three critics, especially Rothbard, hold views that contrast strikingly with those of Georgists about the role of landowners in the determination of land prices. "Getting rich while sleeping" persists as the image of landowners as seen by some economists before George and by him and many of his followers. (I am speaking here of landowners per se, not of landowners insofar as they may also be improvers, developers, etc.) Just such extreme cases can be cited, while examples of more modest unearned gain abound. In many eras, in many countries, owners have profited from land-price increases they have done nothing positive to produce. The term *unearned increment* properly applies. Passivity, as nearly as can be seen, creates nothing but brings rewards. Not all increases in land values, however, result from the forces on which George focuses.

Another consideration has merit. It goes beyond the one emphasized by Rothbard. If the landowner seeking his own benefit tries to put his land to best use, he performs services in allocating this productive resource. Success can lead to rewards for others in the "neighborhood" (broadly defined) as well as for the owner of land.

A point consistent with the spirit of Rothbard, Knight, and Heath but not made explicitly by them deserves attention. Economic progress and rising (real) values of land depend upon more than population growth and the general accumulation of capital. One reality *is* passive "sitting by," waiting for others to accumulate capital, which increases the demand for land—presumably by doing something to satisfy consumers. But *active* effort to direct and to influence change constructively is also a reality. Innovation, risk-taking, entrepreneurship, do make a difference because things get done, things that sometimes are much better than routine (but sometimes flops!). Human beings act. The actions count. What will induce the most fruitful actions? The three critics have a low estimate of the likelihood of best results from bureaucrats administering a system that takes all, or virtually all, of increases in benefits as tax for government.

One element of progress involves better use of land—specific plots and larger areas. Part of the difference between high success and mediocrity depends upon the development of "community." The best results require more than the rather passive waiting for others to act, perhaps in semi-automatic ways. Leadership can make a difference. Some forms of community activity, some representation of the civic spirit, can be fruitful and productive without bringing direct monetary compensation (salaries) to the persons making the effort. Why will some persons try? The hope for a rise in land values can provide one positive incentive for getting desired and desirable things done. Such a hope will not, of course, provide a spur (and may even sometimes constitute a disincentive) to members of the community who do not own land. But those who do can be important.

Rothbard emphasizes a related element, one that contrasts markedly with the general focus of Georgist writings, with their concern about undue holding of land for apparently submarginal purposes (speculating on "unearned increments"). The landowner, or a developer acting as entrepreneur, benefits himself and others by putting land to higher-yielding uses. How much of the rise in land prices reflects the positive results of landowners' efforts to find the best uses? More of the increments than George would have conceded, but far from all those which have developed, have probably depended upon landowners' allocative actions. I see no way to measure the relative impact of the two conflicting forces.

In some cities today the preservation of value, the minimization of deterioration, and the reversal of retrogressive trends will constitute the difference between revitalization and eventual doom. Who will have incentive to engage in what can be a discouraging, unpromising, and uncertain activity? Who will have economic reason for sticking with the endangered area and trying to remedy matters as against moving to the suburbs and other newer spots? One group will be the owners of what must remain—the land. Their incentive may be enhanced, or threatened, by taxation.

The "good society"—good for present and future members—will have institutions that offer the owners of resources promising prospects of rewards from getting land, capital, and labor into the best uses possible (as well as for adding to the stock of productive capacity). Land can be distinguished from man-made capital. For one thing, unlike machinery, land in the physical sense is the product of nature. For another, the economic worth of land does depend to varying degree, often to large degree, upon what the "community" has done and is doing—upon what human beings as individuals and groups accomplish.[26] The fixity of location gives rise to special problems. It may be appropriate for the community both (1) to assure incentives to create value of location, to add to its social and economic attractiveness, and (2) to put pressure on the owner of this resource to induce more fruitful use than the owner acting alone might select.

One result of these considerations is the desirability of both carrot and stick.[27] The owner should have incentives, perhaps powerful ones, to get land into the best use. Moreover, he should have incentives to make a better community. In fact, today one of America's greater needs is inducement to make parts of some cities more inviting. The hope of rising land values offers promise. George's writings, and also those of the three critics, slight these matters; the untaxing of improvements would, of course, make a positive difference, but enhancement of the worth of location would seem to me desirable in addition. Mason Gaffney, incidentally, has stressed that the untaxing of improvements acts as a stimulus to such enhancement.[28]

The Ethical Issues

All three critics strike at George's advocacy of the expropriation of existing land values. To my knowledge, George did not suggest any specific timetable for the implementation of this proposal, but no present-day Georgists of stature urge that it be done except in gradual stages. Large, sudden, arbitrary changes in established rules do not belong in "the good society." But gradual change to achieve large results constitutes the responsible way to progress. Further, an element in George's plan that the critics slight deserves equal attention—the relief of man-made capital from taxation.

The issues involve elements that extend beyond the economic. Decisions as to what is "just" or "fair" or "equitable" in requiring persons to pay taxes for public services, rest upon more than the narrowly defined economic results to be expected from the various possible alternatives. By ethical criteria, which results are better? One consideration may be the legitimacy with which a person came into the income or property that the legal system now recognizes as his own. If there are degrees of legitimacy, then they may provide some basis for differential treatment. References are made by George to "natural law." Such references will help if gravity or molecular combinations are the subject under discussion. Land occupancy today, however, presents more complexity. Sincere differences of view about the propriety of right to occupancy of plots of ground can exist among persons who have equal claims to competence or confidence in the understanding of divine revelation.

George, as I and the three critics understand him, argued that no values in land as such (as distinguished from capital investments made in grading, drainage, etc.) belong by right to the present owner. Land was not created by humans. The persons who have, somehow, obtained title to land cannot, according to George, have legitimate ownership to value created by nature and the community. Therefore taxes to take the fruits of land are ethically proper.

Each individual has some basis by which to judge some things moral and others not. Frankly, I agree with the critics that it would be wrong to wipe out owners who have sacrificed other alternatives to acquire land values. Knight writes (and I agree; but for an ably argued contrasting approach, see Harry Gunnison Brown *Economic Science and the Common Welfare*, 2d ed. [Columbia, Mo.: Lucas Bros., 1925], pp. 217-24.):

> The allegation that our pioneers got the land for nothing, robbing future generations of their rightful heritage, should not have to be met by argument. The whole doctrine was invented by city men living in comfort, not by men in contact with the facts as owners or renters. How many preachers of single-tax doctrine would care to live their lives and bring up families under the conditions of the frontier, fight off the savages and other enemies, and occasionally be massacred, suffer the hardships, overcome the difficulties or succumb to them, do without the amenities of civilization, including medical attention for their families—for what the average pioneer got out of it? The question answers itself. Their heirs, near or remote, often got unearned wealth, but again that is not a sequel peculiar to land.[29]

Site values, however, do have characteristics that lend themselves to special taxation for local government, as Knight himself admits.[30] Not least among the reasons is the expenditure of governments on streets and other facilities that enhance the worth of land. In my view, there is a persuasive case on grounds of what is ethically "right" for capturing such increments in taxation for local government.

Present owners have acquired land according to rules long established and that have legal (constitutional) standing and overwhelming public support. The alternatives sacrificed in buying land as against other uses of savings represented opportunity costs. And the persons owning structures paid prices that assumed the continuation of property taxes. The "rules of the game" may have been less than optimal, but they prevailed. Suddenly to reverse them retroactively—and thereby quite arbitrarily to create gains for some and losses for others—conflicts with my sense of the morally desirable as well as of the politically feasible. (Such reasoning, however, would not be open to an anarcho-capitalist like Rothbard, by whom the fact that property rights have been decreed and sanctioned "by the very government which is condemned as a chronic aggressor"[31] could scarcely be cited either to justify them or to argue for gradualism in their modification or abolition.)

George uses the freeing of the slaves as an analogy. Slavery should never have existed. Destroying slavery without compensation he believes to have been justified. And he writes that private ownership of (most of) the income from land should "never" have developed; therefore, he argues, major changes in the conditions of landownership are warranted. An economist might, as a first point, suggest that the country would probably have been vastly better off during the last century if it had ended slavery by compensating owners rather than by fighting the Civil War. Be that as it may, possible means of revising property taxation will have different effects. Sudden, massive confiscation of property legally acquired would seem to me morally repulsive and economically destructive.[32] Nor would windfalls from sudden untaxing of man-made capital be the stuff of responsible public policy.

Tax laws, though, do alter the absolute and relative positions of taxpayers. Gradual change can accomplish much over the years. Such is the procedure of compromise. It is appropriate for a continuing society that has diverse values.

Rothbard admits that there is a land problem, and gives credit to George and his followers for calling attention to the fact.[33] But the problem, according to Rothbard, stems solely from the consideration that so many existing land titles have their origin in grants or sales by governments (to which the land never rightfully belonged from the beginning) rather than in first use, which he claims alone legitimizes title. His argument that first use creates a valid title simply extends to the land itself the rationale advanced by Locke (and accepted by George) for the ownership of produced goods: that he who mixes his labor with previously unused natural materials thereby abstracts the product from the common fund of opportunity and justly makes it his own property.

> no producer *really* "creates" matter; he takes nature-given matter and transforms it by his labor energy in accordance with his ideas and vision. But *this* is precisely what the pioneer—the "homesteader"—does when he brings previously unused land into his own private ownership. Just as the man who makes steel out of iron ore transforms that ore out of his know-how and with his energy, and just as the man who takes the iron out of the ground does the same, so does the homesteader who clears, fences, cultivates or builds upon the land. The homesteader, too, has transformed the character of the nature-given soil by his labor and his personality. The homesteader is just as legitimately the owner of the property as the sculptor or the manufacturer; he is just as much a "producer" as the others.[34]

In response to this George would probably point out that Locke qualified his willingness to recognize land ownership as just with the proviso that "there be enough and as good left in common for others,"[35] which, translated into economic terms, means as long as land has no market value. And indeed, it should be evident that the arrogation in perpetuity of the very ground of natural opportunity is not to be equated, either in logic or in ethics, with the mere abstraction of a renewable resource. As for nonrenewable resources, under George's system their value would presumably be reflected in the rent paid to the community, which would therefore have an obligation to spend it in ways that would compensate future generations for their loss.

Closing Comment

It is not to be supposed that the hostility exhibited toward much of George's thought by Rothbard and the other two critics dealt with here is necessarily characteristic of libertarians. George would probably have considered himself a libertarian had the term been current in his day, for he insisted that social ills could not be remedied by "weak projects for putting men in leading-strings to a brainless abstraction called the state. . . ."[36] And such twentieth-century libertarian champions as Albert Jay Nock and Frank Chodorov professed themselves outright Georgists.[37] It was Nock, in fact, who acclaimed George "the philosopher of freedom," "the exponent of individualism as against Statism," "the very best friend the capitalist ever had," and "the architect of a society based on voluntary cooperation rather than on enforced cooperation."[38] Something of the basis for this estimate may be seen in the following sentences from *Progress and Poverty*, which underscore the positive, constructive aspects of George's outlook, which the critics, in their alarm at his proposal to appropriate land values, tend to minimize:

To abolish the taxation which, acting and reacting, now hampers every wheel of exchange and presses upon every form of industry, would be like removing an immense weight from a powerful spring. Imbued with fresh energy, production would start into new life, and trade would receive a stimulus which would be felt to the remotest arteries. The present method of taxation. . .operates upon energy, and industry, and skill, and thrift, like a fine upon those qualities. If I have worked harder and built myself a good house while you have been contented to live in a hovel, the tax-gatherer now comes annually to make me pay a penalty for my energy and industry, by taxing me more than you. If I have saved while you have wasted, I am mulct, while you are exempt. If a man build a ship we make him pay for his temerity, as though he had done an injury to the state; if a railroad be opened, down comes the tax-collector upon it, as though it were a public nuisance; if a manufactory be erected we levy upon it an annual sum which would go far toward making a handsome profit. We say we want capital, but if any one accumulate it, or bring it among us, we charge him for it as though we were giving him a privilege. We punish with a tax the man who covers barren fields with ripening grain, we fine him who puts up machinery, and him who drains a swamp. . . .

To abolish these taxes would be to lift the whole enormous weight of taxation from productive industry. The needle of the seamstress and the great manufactory; the cart-horse and the locomotive; the fishing boat and the steamship; the farmer's plow and the merchant's stock, would be alike untaxed. . . .Instead of saying to the producer, as it does now, "The more you add to the general wealth the more shall you be taxed!" the state would say to the producer, "Be as industrious, as thrifty, as enterprising as you choose, you shall have your full reward! You shall not be fined for making two blades of grass grow where one grew before; you shall not be taxed for adding to the aggregate wealth."

. . .Every productive enterprise, besides its return to those who undertake it, yields collateral advantages to others. If a man plant a fruit-tree, his gain is that he gathers the fruit in its time and season. But in addition to his gain, there is a gain to the whole community. Others than the owner are benefited by the increased supply of fruit; the birds which it shelters fly far and wide; the rain which it helps to attract falls not alone on his field; and, even to the eye which rests upon it from a distance, it brings a sense of beauty. And so with everything else. The building of a house, a factory, a ship, or a railroad, benefits others besides those who get the direct profits. . . .

Well may the community leave to the individual producer all that prompts him to exertion; well may it let the laborer have the full reward of his labor, and the capitalist the full return of his capital. For the more that labor and capital produce, the greater grows the common wealth in which all may share.[39]

Notes

1.   Rothbard is professor of economics at the Polytechnic Institute of New York. His critique of George first appeared in 1957 in a ten-page essay, *The Single Tax: Economic and Moral Implications*, duplicated from the typescript and disseminated by the Foundation for Economic Education, for which it had been produced. This was followed by a three-page mimeographed *Reply to Georgist Criticisms* later the same year, also distributed by FEE. However, owing to criticism of Rothbard's analysis from within its own staff, FEE ceased to send out these pieces except when specifically requested to do so. Their argument was incorporated virtually intact into Rothbard's *Man, Economy, and State* (Princeton, N.J.: D. Van Nostrand, 1962) and *Power and Market: Government and the Economy* (Menlo Park, Calif.: Institute for Humane Studies, 1970), and continued on a somewhat different front in his *For a New Liberty* (New York: Macmillan, 1973).

2.   Rothbard, *Power and Market*, p. viii.

3.   Frank H. Knight, "Fallacies in the 'Single Tax,' " *The Freeman*, August 1953, pp. 809-11. Knight, Martin D. Hull Distinguished Service Professor at the University of Chicago, served as president of the American Economic Association in 1950. When mentioning George in *The Conquest of Poverty* (New Rochelle, N.Y.: Arlington House, 1973), Henry Hazlitt refers the interested reader to "the excellent analyses that have been made by Rothbard, Knight and others" (p. 121).

4.   His main commentary on George is the twenty-three-page pamphlet, *Progress and Poverty Reviewed and Its Fallacies Exposed* (New York: The Freeman, 1952). Spencer Heath was a man with wide-ranging interests. His pamphlet reveals familiarity with some economic materials. This discussion contains points that seem to me scarcely worth pursuing as well as several that have merit. An example of those deserving of respectful attention is the call to look at government's taxation and unwise spending; some of the unpleasant results that George and his followers attribute to landowners' demands for increasing rents (which absorb growing output) come really from the "take" of government. In challenging George's methodology, Heath notes that although George, in opening the discussion that proceeds for hundreds of pages, asserts a determination "to take nothing for granted," the conclusions set forth in *Progress and Poverty* had been reached long before it was written.

An erstwhile Georgist, Heath retained the idea that all public services should be paid for out of ground rent, but advocated that instead of being supplied by government they be supplied by landowners (individually and in association), holding that the market would attract renters to those locations with the best services—including defense. These proposals for social reorganization are developed in his *Citadel, Market and Altar* (Elkridge, Md.: Science of Society Foundation, 1957).

5. Rothbard, *Power and Market*, p. vii.

6. See George, *Progress and Poverty*, 75th anniversary ed. (New York: Robert Schalkenbach Foundation, 1954), p. 170. The editor of the present volume, drawing upon more extensive knowledge of George's writings than I possess, warns against any suggestion that George was merely an "agrarian reformer." Certainly true. The processes in urban land markets have similarities with, but also differences from, those of agriculture. The differences do not, I believe, have material significance for George's major argument except for magnitudes—the relatively greater importance in cities of man-made capital (and thus of reducing taxes on it)—and perhaps the complexities of useful as against wasteful "speculation."

7. George, in denying the principle of diminishing returns (variable proportions), took a position that I find difficult to understand. Perhaps he was misreading the history of his times with its extraordinary expansion of settlement on good land. The availability of such areas over the earth was inevitably limited. Improvements in technology—seeds, animal breeds, fertilizer and herbicides, machinery, communications, and so on—raise output per man and acre. But they involve capital.

8. Heath, *Progress and Poverty Reviewed*, p. 7.

9. Rothbard, *The Single Tax*, p. 3.

10. Ibid., p. 2. Original emphasis.

11. George, *Progress and Poverty*, pp. 183-85, 196; idem, *The Science of Political Economy* (1897; reprint ed. New York: Robert Schalkenbach Foundation, 1962), pp. 368-70. George seems to argue that abstention from consumption is essential for capital formation but not sufficient to account for the payment of interest. What he wrote about capital and the sources of new wealth might have some relevance to his main policy conclusions if measurement of dollar amounts to be taken as pure rent were to become a practical matter. But the discussion does not get to the practical issues of how to determine amounts of the returns that George would prescribe as appropriate for taxation.

12. Government finance was then overwhelmingly *local*.

13. Figures of "rental income of persons" in national income accounts—probably around $44 billion as of 1978—apply to elements significantly different from those appropriate for the tax base George had in mind. The annual estimate is by no means limited to land. And much that would belong in the base consists of the fruits of parcels of land that are not subject to lease—the homeowner's occupancy and the land owned and used by a corporation, as for factory, office space, or commercial occupancy, with the net yield appearing, presumably, as profit or in payment of interest on debt. The economic rent of much agricultural land appears as "farm income." Probably most of the land value in the country does not yield a rental appearing as such in the national income accounts. And, of course, in parts of the country property taxes *do* take more than a little of the pure rent. Moreover, taxes on capital gains absorb some of the land values George wished to capture; the revenues from capital gains go to federal and state, not local, governments—but federal-state grants to local governments far exceed yields from income taxes on capital gains and land rents.

14. Winston S. Churchill, *The People's Rights* (1909; reprint ed. New York: Taplinger Publishing Co., 1971), p. 118.

15. Rothbard, *Power and Market*, p. 92.

16. George, *Progress and Poverty*, p. 405.

17. Knight, "Fallacies in the 'Single Tax,' " p. 809.

18. For example, a decline in tax on structures would tend to encourage new building and raise the demand for land in some parts of the country.

19. If government spending were less than the total of annual rental values, the tax rate would not need to approach one hundred percent of yield. Thomas G. Shearman, one of George's staunchest associates, advocated taking no more in taxation than would be required for "the effective but economical administration of government," and calculated that, at the time he wrote, less than half of the net income from land would suffice for this. See his *Natural Taxation*,

2d ed. (New York: Doubleday & McClure, 1898), pp. 133, 157. George wrote long before the availability of statistical data we now take for granted. None of the three critics relies upon empirical gaps as the basis for challenging the argument.

20. The practical problems today seem to me to call for an approach more moderate than George had in mind. Confiscation of land-value rights seems to me subject to far more serious condemnation than it did to George. Using the term *socialization* does not dispose of the issue. What would be the results?

21. Rothbard, *Power and Market*, p. 95.

22. Would five or ten percent of (gross) yield be enough to induce smart men and women to exert themselves to devote skill and energy to get land into the most appropriate uses? Because of the importance of "location" and better as against poorer land use, the voting public should offer greater incentives than ten percent. But who can feel confident in recommending any specific amount? During the years of transition there would be opportunity for testing and gaining experience to use in settling on a "final" division.

23. Rothbard, *The Single Tax*, pp. 3-4; emphasis original.

24. Income tax considerations complicate calculations of the way the change in land tax would influence owners. The after-tax out-of-pocket costs of holding land for appreciation and capital gain may at times be modest relative to the after-tax benefits from a better current use. The relative few who are subject to very high federal plus state personal income tax rates would presumably be influenced differently from most owners, including corporations (especially those with income under $50,000). But any general conclusion is hazardous. Tax treatments of capital gains can be complex; they will affect decisions.

25. Rothbard, *Power and Market*, p. 92.

26. Governmental expenditures—for streets, schools, sewers, etc.—play a key role in adding to the market value of land in new suburbs and some other areas.

27. The "stick" as a symbol of deliberate governmental action carries, perhaps, an aura of intervention of a type inappropriate for a society that prizes freedom. My excuse for using the term is a belief that urban land values result in large part from community forces rather than from the creativity of the owner.

28. Mason Gaffney, "Adequacy of Land as a Tax Base," in Daniel M. Holland, ed., *The Assessment of Land Values* (Madison: University of Wisconsin Press, 1970), chap. 7.

29. Knight, "Fallacies in the 'Single Tax,' " pp. 809-10. Inheritance as an institution raises issues ranging beyond those of site values. The preservation of capital is itself involved.

30. Ibid., p. 811.

31. Rothbard, *For a New Liberty*, p. 29.

32. Governments in this country and abroad have failed to respect more traditional property rights. One result, I believe, is a weakening of the bases for personal security and capital accumulation for general progress.

33. Rothbard, *Power and Market*, p. 92.

34. Rothbard, *For a New Liberty*, p. 34.

35. John Locke, *Second Treatise of Government*, chap. 5, par. 27.

36. Henry George, *The Study of Political Economy* (March 1880; reprint ed. New York: Robert Schalkenbach Foundation, n.d.), p. 19.

37. While sometimes chiding Chodorov for his Georgism, Rothbard makes appreciative references to both these thinkers. See *Power and Market*, pp. 97, 172, 197, 205, 206, 211, and 215. Georgist sentiments are also expressed, although less explicitly, by two other libertarians mentioned appreciatively by Rothbard—Franz Oppenheimer and Bertrand de Jouvenel. See Oppenheimer, *The State*, trans. John M. Gitterman (New York: B. W. Heubsch, Inc., 1922), pp. 9-10, 14, 83, 278-79, 282-85, 290; and Jouvenel, *Sovereignty*, trans. J. F. Huntington (Chicago: University of Chicago Press, 1957), p. 162 n.

38. Albert Jay Nock, *Henry George* (New York: William Morrow & Co., 1939), p. 215.

39. George, *Progress and Poverty*, pp. 434-36.

26

Oser: Reservations of a Friendly Commentator

BY OSCAR B. JOHANNSEN

In 1974 Twayne Publishers, which six years before had brought out Edward J. Rose's biography of Henry George, issued, as part of its "Great Thinkers Series," a study of George by Jacob Oser, professor of economics at Utica College of Syracuse University and author of several well-known books on the history of economic thought. While also largely biographical, this work contains a chapter devoted to the critical analysis of the arguments in *Progress and Poverty*, George's magnum opus.

Oser's approach is generally sympathetic, and the chapter in question begins with a section endorsing George's rejection of the wages-fund theory, his development of Ricardo's Law of Rent, his contention that the landowner as landowner does nothing to earn his income, and his insistence that to tax away all economic rent would stimulate rather than retard production. However, Oser then goes on to find George's thinking defective in the following ways: (1) he was wrong in believing that the landlord's share of national income would rise and that of labor would fall with industrial progress; (2) he confused the law of diminishing returns, increasing returns to scale, and growing efficiency; (3) he was naively optimistic as to the fiscal adequacy of a single tax on land rent; (4) he misconceived the nature of capitalism, failing to realize that the private ownership of capital is a more powerful cause than is the private ownership of land in explaining the uneven distribution of income in industrial societies.

There is merit in some of Oser's criticism. Quite properly, he observes that George's generalization that wages and interest tend to rise and fall together is a dubious one. But issue must be taken with much of his analysis.

I

Oser contends that "George was wrong in believing that wages probably would fall as society progresses, and the percentage of the nation's income that goes to labor certainly would fall; he was just as wrong in believing that the share going to landowners would increase."[1] As proof he quotes data supplied by the U.S. Department of Commerce that list the value of privately held land in the United States to have been $27 billion in 1900, and indicate that its value as a percentage of Gross National Product decreased from 159 percent in 1900 to 66 percent in 1968, when its value was said to have been $571 billion. Although popular today in economic circles, the use of statistics to prove or disprove economic principles is a questionable technique. Ludwig von Mises, the celebrated economist of the Austrian school, in his attack on the substitution of "quantitative economics" for "qualitative economics," pointed out that "statistical figures referring to economic events are historical data. They tell us what happened in a non-repeatable historical case."[2] No doubt statistics may be useful in developing some corroborative evidence in analyzing a particular problem, but even in such an instance they must be treated with great circumspection. Controlled economic experiments being seldom possible, the statistics in use are rarely of the type that induce great confidence. Men, in their activities, do not bother to set down all the precise factors influencing their actions, hence the statistics that economists are forced to utilize, particularly if they are in terms of money, often are little better than proxies for what actually may have occurred.

In the ideal society, however, the real point at issue is not whether labor's share tends to decrease and the landlord's share to increase as society progresses. After all, if George's remedy were to be put into operation, the rent would all accrue to the people either indirectly through the provision of a multiplicity of services or directly through a per capita division. Under those conditions the division of income between labor and landlord (since the landlord, in effect, would be the people themselves) would probably not be nearly so important as it is today.

Now, however, since for all practical purposes the land, particularly in the Western World, is all enclosed, the real issue is that of the point at which a tendency to stabilization comes to exist, for this will determine how impoverished the mass of the people will be. That point tends to be where labor's share is at its subsistence level. Above this point it cannot remain, for competition among laborers for access to land will bring it down. Below this it cannot fall, for labor will starve or revolt.

Although Oser does not think it is possible, the absolute impoverishment of workers can occur if their subsistence point is low enough. In nations such as India the subsistence level is so low that many people actually starve. But the subsistence level in other nations, such as the United States, is far from being at that point. Long before starvation is reached, labor revolts. It may take the actual form of revolution, but often, instead of a bloody convulsion, the revolt is a demand for governmental interference to mitigate the effects of labor's decreasing share of the production pie. But this does not mean that George's analysis was in error, any more than the erection of a dam disproves the principle that water tends to flow downward.

Of course, the fact that there may be millions of landlords in a country does not mean that they do not act like monopolists, any more than the fact that there may be millions of patent holders prevents them from acting as monopolists. Just as each inventor holding a patent has a monopoly on the particular product involved, so the millions of landowners have a monopoly on the particular pieces of land they own. Ask any entrepreneur wishing to erect an office building on Wall Street in New York City if the owner of the land on which he wishes to construct the building acts as a monopolist when the entrepreneur approaches him with a request for the terms of sale.

II

Oser rebuts George's refutation of Malthus's theory on the grounds that George "was confusing increasing returns to scale and growing efficiency with the law of diminishing returns."[5] But he weakens his own charge subsequently, for toward the end of his book, in commenting on *The Science of Political Economy*, he notes that George was ahead of the orthodox economic thinking of his time in emphasizing that the law of diminishing returns applied to industry as well as to agriculture. And if book 3, chapter 7 of the cited work is read, one of the clearest and best explanations of the law of diminishing returns ever written will be found. As for the principle which has now come to be known as "increasing returns to scale," Oser himself points out that George noted that one hundred men will produce more than one hundred times what one man can produce. In view of all this, it is a mystery why Oser asserts that George confused these laws.

Oser appears to make a practice of vitiating his own criticisms, for after scoring "George's preposterous statement that the earth could support a thousand billion people as easily as one billion," he immediately goes on to say: "Only phenomenal, and as yet unseen, improvements in technology could make this possible."[6] Apparently, then, while the notion of the existence of a trillion people on the earth is an absurdity, it is still possible if technology develops sufficiently. No one, of course, knows whether a trillion people could be supported or not. But we do know that in America, under the impetus of the partially free economy existing, highly sophisticated machinery was invented in the nineteenth century (for example, the McCormick reaper) that enabled the United States to produce phenomenal amounts of food products. Just as no one in the seventeenth or eighteenth centuries could have foreseen such technological improvements, so we cannot foresee what new improvements may be made if needed and desired.

But the burden of George's attack on the Malthusian doctrine had nothing really to do with the maximum number of people who could possibly exist on our finite globe. The principal reason for attacking this theory was that it beclouded the whole issue of man's relationship to the land. It implied that an imbalance existed between man's sexual proclivities and his ability to produce. This imbalance was the cause of poverty amidst plenty and, because it was Mother Nature who was responsible, there was little man could do to remedy the situation.

Such an assumption was eminently satisfying to those possessing special privileges, such as landlords, particularly at the time that Malthus wrote, when people were beginning to question the absurdity of poverty amidst plenty. It is doubtful that George was particularly concerned with how many people could exist on the earth. What he wanted was to upset the theory, so comforting to privileged interests, that nature was to blame for the growing poverty with increasing productivity, and to redirect men's attention to attempting to discover what institutional arrangements might be the cause of this enigma.

III

Oser questions George's contention that a one hundred percent collection of economic rent would be sufficient to defray the expenses of government without the imposition of other taxes, claiming that while it was true in George's day, it is not so today. Again he resorts to statistics to prove his point, noting the fantastic increase in governmental expenditures within the past generation. But after doing so he undermines his own argument by noting that George believed that his fundamental reform would not only unleash productivity and growth, but would also result in a decrease in governmental functions. For example, in a peaceful world military expenditures would be unnecessary.

If an argument is to be leveled against the adequacy of the so-called single tax as a resource for governmental revenues, it would appear that logically one should first specify what the true functions of government are. If government is expected to supply every possible need or want of the people, then no amount of revenue not even total confiscation of all income generated, would be sufficient. If the socialists are correct in holding that all revenue, and not merely land rent, belongs rightfully to the state, then the question of the sufficiency or insufficiency of a tax on land values becomes meaningless. On the other hand, if the anarchists are correct in holding that no government is necessary, then whatever revenues are garnered would be actually superfluous.

But the question of the adequacy or inadequacy of the single tax for the raising of governmental revenues is not germane to what George was attempting to do. George was not interested in proposing a tax reform by means of which government might indulge itself in every form of do-goodism. Rather, he wished to establish those conditions predicated on the principles of justice wherein involuntary poverty would not exist and wherein the individual would attain his maximum potential. He wished people to be free to tread whatever paths they wished in order to give expression to the capacities with which they were born.

Man comes into this world with nothing but the ability to expend his physical and mental energy. But on what? Initially, in economic terms, the only thing in existence outside of man is land. If man is denied access to land, he is denied the opportunity to utilize his inborn talents to the utmost. Above all else, *Progress and Poverty* is a paean to justice and freedom, that even after a century, still has the power to quicken the hearts and kindle the souls of those who hold these values dear.

IV

Oser believes that George suffered from misconceptions about the nature of capitalism. Regrettably, because Oser does not explicitly state what he himself means by capitalism, much less capital, a comparison between his and George's views cannot be made directly. He does state that to George "capital includes those things that are not either land or labor...capital covers such things as buildings, cattle, tools, machinery—man-made goods used for further production."[7]

Although he derides George's assertion that labor is the actual employer of capital, the definition of capital that he attributes to George clearly implies that labor is the employer. If the above quotation is reduced to its simplest terms, does it not state that capital is but a synonym for tools? And who uses tools but labor? Oser scorns the idea of a workman's telling the chairman of

General Motors that he, the laborer, is the employer of capital. But such is unnecessary. The chairman has learned from sad experience that the workers are the actual employers, for when they go out on strike the capital lies idle awaiting their return.

In contending that George had mistaken notions about the nature of capitalism, Oser asserts that George was looking backward to a Jeffersonian agrarian democracy and not ahead to the problems of an industrial society. This presumption that George's view of the ideal society revolved around small-scale producers and craftsmen is an error that has been repeated over and over again and, no doubt, will be time and again in the future. It may be that this is because of the simple examples George used to explain his points, but because he was writing for general consumption, naturally he kept his illustrations as elementary as possible. But to imply, as Oser does, that George was blind to the startling growth of business and industry and what effect it might have, is to assume that George was not only insensible to his surroundings but was lacking in a grasp of the fundamentals involved. Oser himself states that in the introductory chapter of *Progress and Poverty* George noted the prodigious increase in wealth-producing power. This monumental increase in man's ability to produce wealth was part of the perplexing paradox he had determined to elucidate. Presumably, not only the necessities of life but luxuries undreamed of in previous times should be at the disposal of all with but a modicum of effort. Instead, horrendous poverty existed and was growing rather than decreasing as the mountains of wealth spewed forth from the gigantic industrial machine that man was building. It was this enigma that led George to focus his attention on economic phenomena.

That business and industry were increasing in complexity, requiring greater time and distances to accomplish their aims, did not becloud George's comprehension of the fundamentals in operation. Such growth did not affect the principles at work in the least any more than a twentieth-century jet liner is, in principle, different from the primitive plane of the Wright Brothers, which for the first time enabled man to realize his centuries-old dream of emulating the birds in flight. Oser believes that the great distances and time involved in modern production have made a difference—the difference being the importance of accumulating capital in advance. Implied in this assertion is that capital is money. It may well be that because this appears to be the major ingredient in his conception of capital, he attacks George's contention that wages are drawn from the product of labor and not capital. Parenthetically, it should be remarked that Oser's attack seems strange coming from one who earlier lauded George's perception in denying the wages-fund theory.[8]

Yet George does not restrict his definition of capital to the one attributed to him by Oser. George also included goods in the process of production and exchange. Thus he claims that in building a ship capital is being produced, and wages represent the purchase by the entrepreneur of the additional capital that the laborers had created. Since Oser apparently equates capital with money, he takes the position that, on the contrary, it is necessary first to have accumulated capital in order to finance the vessel's construction.

But it is clear that such is not the case when it is appreciated that, theoretically, laborers could cooperate with one another to build a ship without the necessity of any previous financing whatever. They could spend part of their time constructing the ship and the rest producing the necessities and luxuries they desired. When completed, the ship would be their property, which they could offer for whatever they thought it was worth. Even the materials and tools employed by them could be produced on the same basis by other laborers. Thus if one were to trace the production of all the materials and tools back to the land, from which all wealth comes, it is patent that it is not necessary for money first to have been accumulated. This is the method the Indians used in building their war canoes, for they did not bother first to accumulate the wampum they used as money before they commenced construction.

What modern business does is to eliminate the need for such cumbersome arrangements, thus permitting laborers to concentrate all their working time and effort on such a project as a ship. Instead of selling it upon its completion, they sell the part they have produced bit by bit as it is being constructed and use the funds obtained to purchase the necessities and luxuries they desire. This is precisely the point George expounded in his discussion of the building of the ship. If one assumes that only tools constitute capital, then George's error was in assuming that the laborers were producing more capital as they built the vessel, when all they were doing was producing wealth in the form of a ship.*

Of course, even under modern business conditions, if a project is of long duration—say five years— while financial arrangements may all be completed in advance, the actual finances need not be in existence. Instead, those financing the project will gear their investments so that the finances will be available as required.

Oser believes that George's view that labor is independent of capital sprang from his ignoring the fact that a certain amount of capital is necessary to establish even a small farm. Thus the Homestead Act, which granted settlers in the West 160 acres free except for some filing fees, was of little use to urban laborers. This was because, typically, one thousand dollars was required to obtain the equipment and livestock needed to get started and to feed their families until the first crop came in. Because apparently capital is money to Oser, he assumes that George could not admit that labor was dependent on capital's first being accumulated, for to do so would weaken the remedy George suggested.

But as for the necessity to have an accumulation of capital first, ask the American pioneers who landed on the forbidding shores of this continent what capital they had. It was practically nothing. Yet out of the forest they hewed their farms with only the minutest amount of capital—the few tools they had brought with them such as axes, shovels, and hoes. To the degree that they had even these simple tools they were at a great advantage. But had they waded ashore with nothing but their bare hands, it would have been only a question of time before they made whatever capital they needed, using the raw materials they found in the land. Naturally, however, because Europe with its huge quantity of capital existed, they exchanged their produce for the tools they needed from the Old World.

---

*That the article as a ship may subsequently be used as a tool and thus constitutes capital when so employed does not negate the fact that while it is being built it is merely an article of wealth that is being produced.

Surprisingly, without offering proof, Oser states that "the ownership of capital gives more wealth and power to a small group of people than the ownership of land."[9] One would assume that after having made such a sweeping statement he would give at least some arguments in support, but he neglects to do so.

To many it would appear that George, purely on the basis of logic, had proved quite conclusively that it is control over land that gives wealth and power to small groups of people. But even if his reasoning had made little impact, certainly the actions of the OPEC states, which own the land from which much of the world's oil comes, gave dramatic pragmatic proof of where power lies. As is well known, a few years ago they instituted a boycott, refusing to sell more than a trickle of their crude oil. If the ownership of capital gives more power than the ownership of land, why was it that the most powerful nation in the world, the United States, as well as all the nations of Western Europe and Japan, had almost to beg the OPEC states to end their boycott? As long as these nations did not wish to use military might, the fact that they owned most of the capital, that is, the refineries necessary to process the crude oil, meant nothing. Even if one considers money to be capital, they were helpless. The Western world no doubt has most of the world's money, but as long as the OPEC states refused to sell their oil, what power could money exert?

While Oser may thus be faulted for many of his criticisms, his evaluation of George is both objective and provocative. If only for this reason, his book should take its place as a welcome addition to the literature.

Notes

1. Jacob Oser, *Henry George* (New York: Twayne Publishers, Inc., 1974), p.54.

2. Ludwig von Mises, *Human Action* (New Haven, Conn.: Yale University Press, 1949), p.56.

3. Henry George, *Progress and Poverty*, 75th anniversary ed. (New York: Robert Schalkenbach Foundation, 1954), pp. 245-46.

4. Oser, *Henry George*, p. 55.

5. Ibid, p. 56.

6. Ibid, p. 62.

7. Ibid, p. 34.

8. Ibid, p. 51.

9. Ibid, p. 67

Part V
Conclusions

27

Neo-Georgism

BY ROBERT V. ANDELSON

I

Had Henry George created a system capable of withstanding in all its details a century of criticism, he would have been *sui generis* among social scientists and philosophers alike—not a mortal theorist but a veritable god. To recognize that some of his ideas are flawed does not destroy his stature as a thinker of the first magnitude whose economic methodology was, in fact, far more informed and sophisticated than is generally appreciated, and whose prescription for reform contains basic features that have enduring relevance.

Possibly he misconceived the problem, and was mistaken in assuming that, absent his prescription, poverty necessarily increases with industrial advance.* At least, so it might appear. Yet when we look behind appearances, we may discover that the expedients whereby this grim outcome has been forestalled give rise to ultimate consequences still more grim, consequences now presaged by rampant inflation and ever-mounting public debt. We may discover, in other words, the we have been living in a fool's paradise, that George was a better prophet than we realized, and that welfare spending, monetary tinkering, and union pressure have purchased temporary respite from the process he descried at the eventual price of a total and possibly irreversible collapse. This is, of course, a long-run augury; those who live only for the immediate present will dismiss it with Lord Keynes's flippant quip that "in the long run we are all dead."

Which is not to say that George's "all-devouring rent thesis" (to use Professor Cord's apt phrase) should be accepted unreservedly. Present-day statistical evidence has rendered it so dubious that even George's most assiduous academic proponent, Harry Gunnison Brown, was obliged to lay it aside.

One may nevertheless contend that land rent is a highly important economic factor and that George performed a real service in calling attention to this

---

*The reader should bear in mind that this assumption had to do with the *proportion* received by labor as its share of the product. In certain of his less flamboyant passages, George was careful to disclaim the notion that wages are universally diminished as an absolute quantity by industrial progress. (*Progress and Poverty*, 75th anniversary ed. [New York: Robert Schalkenbach Foundation, 1954], pp. 216, 233 f.) Because of his many paragraphs that fail to specify the distinction between proportion and amount, this disclaimer is apt to be overlooked.

truth, however extreme his inferences from it may have been. In 1948 the National Bureau of Economic Research estimated that land represented seventeen percent—in itself no mean amount—of the total wealth of the United States; since that time, a tremendous inflation (far exceeding that of general prices) has occurred in land values.* Commenting upon the N.B.E.R. report, Robert Clancy, then director of the Henry George School of Social Science, objected that it underestimated the value of commercial sites, vacant lots, and government-owned lands. He also pointed out that the report omitted all subsoil assets from the land inventory, neglected to include the land rent collected by local real estate taxes, and failed to take into consideration the notorious fact that corporations normally undervalue the land they own, and, indeed, seldom list it separately in their accounting procedures. Furthermore, urban rent controls, still significant at the time of the report but no longer in widespread operation, artificially held down land values. Clancy also noted that farm land values for 1952 were reliably placed at $70 billion by the Bureau of Agricultural Economics, a figure almost half that of the N.B.E.R. total of $157 billion. Since the value of urban is vastly greater than that of rural land per acre, he adduced this as added evidence that the N.B.E.R. total was much too low.[1] All of this strongly suggests that the role of land rent in the United States, even if overemphasized by George, is yet far from inconsiderable, and that in most other countries (where land monopoly is more acute) it must be still greater by no small degree.

For the most part, George's errors are, as in the case of his all-devouring rent thesis, errors merely of exaggeration. For example, descanting upon the growth of morality to be anticipated from the adoption of his proposal, he is not content merely to predict a marked diminution in crime and vice which stem from the brutalizing effects of poverty, but pictures a veritable Peaceable Kingdom in which greed has virtually disappeared along with the need for judges, police, and lawyers, and in which liberated human energies are spurred by pure and noble promptings to ever more exalted heights of creativity.[2] Alas! There is in human nature an intractable perverseness, which George's evangelical parents called "Original Sin" and which no social rearrangement can dispel. Material security and equality of opportunity, however desirable, will not usher in a moral paradise. Well-fed, well-housed, well-educated Sweden, with its disturbing incidence of alcoholism, suicide, and juvenile delinquency, may be cited as a case in point.

In keeping with the classical tradition, George insisted upon interpreting land rent as a monopoly price. For this he has been reproved by various critics from Marshall to Oser, who correctly observe (in Hébert's paraphrase) that "as long as land has alternative uses and many owners it comes to be supplied under conditions approaching competition." Again, however, George's error was essentially one merely of exaggeration. In the first place, landownership in much of the world, including many parts of the United States (e.g., Orange County, California, where the Irvine Estate holds approximately twenty percent of the land, and is a major factor in keeping up prices in the small areas it

*From 1950 to 1970 residential land prices in the United States rose 400-500 percent, while general prices increased only 60 percent. See Sylvan Kamm, "Inflation: Curbing Inflation in Residential Land Prices," *Urban Land*, 30, no. 8 (September 1971), p. 3.

develops and sells), is sufficiently concentrated that monopoly, or, at any rate, oligopoly, actually does obtain. In the second place, the fact that the supply of land is inelastic as respects location means that even where landownership is diffuse, land rent still involves a *monopolistic element* not characteristic of the price of capital goods (except for such economically insignificant items as antiques and works by famous artists). For although land may have alternative uses, and in that regard not be perfectly inelastic as to supply, its inherent inelasticity of location gives the owner a built-in advantage.

It is not the intention to suggest that the buyer or renter of land space has no alternative. He may use a smaller piece of land more intensively instead of a larger piece less intensively. Thus, he may put a twenty-story building on a small area instead of putting a ten-story building on a larger area. He may choose a poorer site instead of a better one. But the buyer or renter of capital has alternatives of these kinds and has *in addition* the alternative of becoming himself a producer of the sort of capital wanted.[3]

On this account, and for other reasons more ethical than economic, I am satisfied that there is a broad sense in which it is legitimate to speak of land rent as a monopoly price, even though, from a narrow, technical standpoint the phrase may be inaccurate.

It could, in addition, be charged that George exaggerated the revenue-generating adequacy of his proposal. But this would hardly be fair. Wilford I. King demonstrated that the land-rent fund would have been large enough before the Civil War to pay for all government expenses nearly twice over, and that it continued to be at least sufficient until 1915;[4] Steven Cord thinks that it could probably have been adequate until the 1930s.[5] During George's lifetime there would doubtless have been an ample surplus available for communal amenities or for distribution on a per capita basis, especially when one considers the savings to be looked for from his reform in reduced need for public assistance and government bureaucracy. This is one reason why his expectation that his remedy would "extirpate" involuntary poverty should be regarded as only mildly extravagant. Other reasons are, of course, the stimulus to productivity and the tendency toward equalization of opportunity that his reform might reasonably be anticipated—on the basis of both theoretical deduction and partial experiment—to engender. While the demands of national security make it today utopian to suppose that land rent could meet the total revenue requirements of government, let alone beget a surplus, its appropriation in taxes would substantially lessen the necessity for revenue from other sources, and would materially help to ameliorate involuntary poverty even if it did not wholly justify George's faith by extirpating it.

Closely related to the inadequacy argument is the objection that a single tax on land values (or on anything else if the full amount were taken) would be inflexible, incapable of adjusting to changing conditions. But Collier points out that this objection is valid only with respect to the *percentage* of the tax rate. The *amount* of the yield would vary in response to the business cycle.[6] Collier's rejoinder would not be employed by a strict Georgist, for George held that under the single tax the primary cause of the business cycle would be dispelled. Instead, the strict disciple would rely upon the claim, cited by Geiger,[7] that in a

fundamental sense a sole tax on land is highly flexible since it correlates directly with the progress and demands of any taxpaying and tax-requiring community—a point made by George in *Progress and Poverty*[8] and more particularly in his *Open Letter to Pope Leo XIII*[9] and in "Thy Kingdom Come,"
his Glasgow speech of 1889.[10] Whether it would be *sufficient* to satisfy extraordinary demands such as those of national defense in today's nuclear world, is
of course, quite another story.

The inflexibility, such as it is, of a sole land-value tax, has been accounted a
merit by some Georgists (and even some non-Georgists[11]), as constituting a
check upon the aggrandizement of government. Private individuals are expected to live within their proper means; why should not governments do the
same? When George envisaged public baths, dancing halls, shooting galleries,
and the like,[12] he was merely speculating as to ways in which a surplus rightfully belonging to the public might be spent, not advocating that such indulgences
be funded through coercive exaction. Although present conditions make the
question of the use of a surplus academic, per capita apportionment in the
form of dividends to be used according to private choice would seem to be
more consonant with his essential individualism.

Collier asserts that the benefits from a single tax on land values could be only temporary, since with the rise of population, settlement would extend to
(and probably beyond) the point that had been the margin of production prior
to the adoption of the tax. "Quite simply, the remedy would work once and
only once in any society because it relied in a special way on ending speculation
in land. That speculation can be ended once and only once."[13] Granting continuous population growth (or growth in productive activity and hence land
use), his point about the extension of the margin is well taken, and is one that
George, to my knowledge, did not anticipate. But his analysis disregards three
important considerations: To begin with, there is nothing inevitable about
population increase; the population of France has been stable ever since the
Great Revolution, long before the advent of modern birth control techniques.
Second, given the population increase assumed by Collier (or enhanced productive exploitation), the margin would have been pushed *much further*
downward and outward were it not for the halting by the tax of speculation.
Third, in a Georgist economy the extension of the margin is likely to be
postponed by the reduction, stemming from heightened productive efficiency,
of the actual acreage used. Finally, Collier overlooks a formidable advantage
that would continue to accrue regardless of the location of the margin—namely, the diversion of land rent to the public with the accompanying lifting of the
burden of taxation from wages and interest.

George's arguments on the population question suffer from such excesses as
his astonishing assertion that "the earth could maintain a thousand billions of
people as easily as a thousand millions[14]—a conceit that stems from his refusal
in *Progress and Poverty* to apply the law of diminishing returns to the employment of labor and capital on land.* Also, his inveterate environmentalism kept

---

*In the *Science of Political Economy*, his treatment of this matter is unclear. There, instead of
refusing to apply the law of diminishing returns to agriculture and the extractive industries, he
criticizes Mill and others for their failure to extend it to all modes of production, evidently thinking that he has thus weakened rather than strengthened the Malthusian position (bk. 3, chap. 4).
Had he lived to complete the book, he might have revised and clarified his treatment.

him from perceiving that even if increased numbers should, as he maintained, enhance productivity infinitely, there still might be a population problem of a genetically qualitative nature. (It is worthy of remark that Brown, the academic champion of George, was also a professed Malthusian.[15]) Genetically qualitative considerations aside, however, George's inordinate optimism with respect to population seems no more unwarranted than do the dire predictions of the latter-day disciples of Malthus. In our preoccupation with such horror-spots as Bangladesh, we tend to overlook he facts that Taiwan, with a populat-tion density matching that of Holland, has a net export of food, and that one hydroponic acre in Arizona produces 240,000 pounds of tomatoes annually. (This should not, of course, be taken as an argument against family planning or the conservation of natural resources.)

George has sometimes been faulted for inconsistency in relying on Ricardian rent theory while rejecting Malthusian population theory. That Malthusianism was assumed by Ricardo is a historical fact, and George accepts his view that rents are raised by "the increasing pressure of population which compels a resort to inferior points of production."[16] But he claims that this view really gives no countenance to Malthusianism, and has been enlisted in its support on-ly because of the misapprehension "that the recourse to lower points of pro-duction involves a smaller aggregate produce in proportion to the labor ex-pended."[17] And he holds that rent is also raised by other causes—the technological and social improvements that increase productive power. Now, his treatment of Malthusianism suffers (as I have already remarked) from his refusal to apply the law of diminishing returns to the division of labor. And his all-devouring rent thesis is weakened by his failure to adequately recognize that technological and social improvements are reflected in cheaper and better goods and hence in higher real wages. Yet, however unsatisfactory his analysis in these respects, he stands absolved of the charge of inconsistency to which I have alluded, for the pressure of population upon resources is not only offset, as he sees it, by the greater yield per person made possible by greater popula-tion, but is, in any case, merely one (and perhaps to him the least important) element in his version of the law of rent. Moreover, as Teilhac observes, "while George shows... that social evil is only the consequence of economic progress, contrary to Ricardo, he demonstrates that it is, nevertheless, only the artificial consequence of a natural law."[18] In other words, for George, unlike Ricardo, the law of rent *need not* culminate in an "iron law of wages"; pover-ty is not attributable to inexorable forces built into the order of nature, but to corrigible features of human economic arrangements.

At least two of the contributors to this volume agree with certain of George's critics that landowners and speculators (even when they are not themselves developers) sometimes perform entrepreneurial services that give them a legitimate, if perhaps qualified, claim on land values. George doubtless failed to recognize that part of the rise in land prices may at times reflect owners' constructive allocation efforts. (In terms of his classificatory system, that part would fall under wages rather than under rent.) Against this, however, must be placed the fact that constructive allocation has (to put it con-servatively) not infrequently been thwarted by withholding on the part of owners. At any rate, by permitting owners to retain a percentage of the value of their land large enough to induce them to retain title even when not developers or users, George's plan would provide a market premium for entrepreneurship, since the size of the owner's "brokerage fee" would depend upon his success in finding the most profitable use for his site. But even if all private titles were to be extinguished, I see no reason why there should be any diminution of incentive for skillful allocation, or why decisions as to allocation need become other than a private function (except perhaps where dictated by ecological or other public considerations). Not ownership but security of tenure is the decisive factor in encouraging optimum use—witness the phenomenon that so much intensive development occurs on leased land. The entrepreneur would have the same incentive as at present to find the most appropriate locations for development and use, but would simply lease them from the public rather than from a private owner.

One may freely grant that George omitted to give sufficient weight to the subjective element in value—a consequence of his failure to appreciate the considerable contributions of the Austrian school of economic theory. Also, one may recognize that government intervention in the marketplace, particularly federal manipulation of the supply of money and credit, has created aberrations and distortions not addressed by his analysis. His assumption that characteristically land held for speculation is kept absolutely idle is scarcely tenable. And it is patent that, for all its seductive neatness, his idea that wages and interest rise and fall in unison is not supported by the empirical data, although the situation might be different if the figures available represented only *real* wages instead of including transfer payments, and only *real* interest instead of including various extraneous elements that tend to be lumped with it. As for the "reproductive modes" aspect of George's theory of interest, it has been accepted only by his most doctrinaire followers. I confess that for me the concept holds a certain fascination, providing, as it does, an almost metaphysical basis for an explanation of why abstinence brings return, and I know of at least one person who was weaned away by it from Marxism because he considered that it definitively undercuts the theory of surplus value. Collier shows that some of the attacks upon it are invalid;[19] whether the reproductive-modes concept is itself invalid is of little moment here, since it is in no sense vital to George's system. James Haldane Smith, in fact, argues that it actually contradicts the remainder of the system[20]—a view that I believe could be refuted if doing so were worth the effort. In any case, a powerful justification of interest, wholly independent of that concept, may be readily inferred from George's general theory of capital.

The doctrines of natural law and natural rights undergird the entire framework of George's thought. There was a time when they were, in sophisticated circles, supposed to be hopelessly outmoded; more recently, they have undergone something of a revival.[21] These doctrines are not subject to empirical proof or disproof, since they are, in the last analysis, metaphysical, or at least axiological. The present writer, who subscribes to them wholeheartedly (without, however, regarding them as self-evident or self-contained), believes that they lend inestimable strength to George's teaching. Still, there have been those who, like Thomas Shearman, have embraced George's proposal solely on fiscal grounds; and those who, like George R. Geiger, have endorsed all the main elements of his system while recasting his view of natural rights in terms of John Dewey's instrumentalism. I am persuaded that the system, in its economic essentials, can stand without the doctrines of natural law and natural rights. I am equally persuaded that, for those who can accept them, they not only give it added logical support but also provide a motive, not otherwise entirely intelligible, for personal commitment to its furtherance.

On the tactical ingenuousness of certain of George's terminological idio-syncrasies we need not dwell. "We must make land common property"[22] has hung from the beginning like a millstone around the neck of the movement he created, notwithstanding that even as he used the phrase he took pains to explain that by "common property" he meant something very different from what it is ordinarily understood to mean. Similarly, "association in equality"[23] is a locution not altogether felicitous: it conjures up images of Dostoevski's "unanimous and harmonious ant-heap," which are dispelled only if one happens to note George's passing statement that he is using equality as a synonym for freedom.[24] And libertarians, reading his allusion to "the noble dreams of socialism,"[25] will deem the reference offensive unless they apprehend that in this context the word *socialism* signifies, not leveling collectivism but merely a cooperative order devoid of privilege.

II

The modern friend of George's thought who views the "Prophet of San Francisco" as a profound and perceptive guide rather than as an infallible oracle, will find the majestic symmetry of his system vitiated somewhat by the qualifications and adjustments dictated by candid analysis in the light of changed circumstances and refinements in economic methodology. "Neo-Georgism" will be less satisfying than the original article from an aesthetic standpoint. But aesthetic satisfaction must yield to intellectual honesty, and the basic truth of George's central thrust remains, in any event, intact.

What is that central thrust? It is the insight that natural opportunity should be open on the same terms to all, and socially created values socially appro-priated, while the fruits of private effort should be left inviolate to their producers or to the designees thereof. Here we find the authentic verities respectively inherent in socialism and individualism organically combined without detriment to the integrity of either. Here we see, not a confusing welter of compromises and half-measures, but a clear and logical relationship in which each pole is balanced and complemented by the other.

Fundamental to the application of this thrust is the idea that public fiscal burdens be distributed according to the criterion of benefits received from society. This idea has long been out of vogue, having been supplanted by the now-dominant position that taxes should be levied on the basis of ability to pay. In less polite words, they should "soak the rich." The ostensible justifi-cation for this position is that ability to pay is a gauge of equal sacrifice. Yet it is by no means clear why persons who do not make equal demands upon society should, in fairness, be expected to make equal sacrifices in its support. Furthermore, specialists in public revenue theory are not agreed as to what is really meant by equal sacrifice, or that it is actually best measured by progres-sive rates determined by ability to pay.[26] A free market can measure the marginal utility of relative satisfactions and therefore sacrifices as among its participants, but since taxes, being compulsory, do not reflect a market situation, it is difficult to see how they can be apportioned in terms of equal sacrifice. In view of these complications, some thinkers would assess the desirability of a tax system solely in terms of the system's efficacy in meeting broad social needs, without reference to its relative burden upon individual taxpayers except as that burden may have public consequences. (It was, in fact, upon just such grounds that Carver endorsed land-value taxation.) But social utility is, unless balanced by other considerations, a dangerous criterion for a tax or any other kind of compulsory system. Everything depends upon who defines society's needs, and the rights of the individual are all too likely to be swallowed by Leviathan.

The best surety for the protection of these rights, so far as the question of public revenue is concerned, is the restoration of the benefit principle. (Taxes based upon this principle are, technically speaking, not true taxes at all, but rather public fees; thus the term *single tax* is really a misnomer, and the proposal of Henry George has sometimes been spoken of by its adherents as a program for the abolition of taxation. George, however, reluctantly called it a tax as a concession to popular usage,[27] and I follow him in this.) Since the privilege of exclusive use and disposition of a site is a benefit received by the owner at the expense of the rest of society, the Neo-Georgist, like the Georgist, will insist that it be paid for in full, as measured by the value of the site. But he will not be a single-taxer, except in the sense of maintaining that (apart from genuine emergencies, such as war) payment for benefits should be the single criterion for taxation. Recognizing that, of all special benefits, land ownership is by far the most important, he will accord the land-value tax (which further commends itself because of its nonshiftability and benign effect upon production) premier place place in his table of priorities.* Second place will go to use taxes, of which the gasoline tax (assuming it be spent on highways or related functions) is a salient example. If taxes for special benefits prove insufficient to meet the cost of necessary services of a general nature, the Neo-Georgist will admit the legitimacy of general levies to take up the slack. But he will insist that the services in question be truly necessary and truly general (e.g., police and fire protection, national defense, the control of communicable disease, etc.). And he will demand that the obligation for their support be divided in terms of a formula that involves at least some approach to objectively equal payment—posssibly a nongraduated percentage of incomes. Finally, he will concede that really desperate exigencies, where the very survival of the community is at stake (and where, for instance, as Brown reminds us, millions of men might be "required to risk their lives at the fighting front"[28]) may temporarily justify whatever measures are capable of quickly raising the needed revenues, regardless of whether the burden be distributed with the same equity that normal conditions would enjoin.**

---

*Where, in the case of certain exhaustible natural resources, conservation is a prime desideratum, the benefit principle could be implemented through a severance tax in lieu of at least part of the land-value tax.

**A libertarian refinement of the program described above might be to distribute the revenue from land rent on a per capita basis, giving each individual the option of using his share to purchase domestic public services, or of doing without them. As a practical matter, this option could not very well extend to the support of national defense, since there would be no way of denying defense against foreign aggression to freeloaders. But the rent fund would not, in any event, suffice to support national defense in addition to legitimate domestic public services in today's world.

To recapitulate, the Neo-Georgist will neither claim that land value taxation should always be the sole source of public revenue, on the one hand, nor see it, like the Fabians on the other, as merely a highly desirable source to be employed as one tax among many without discrimination as to their ranking. He will have a definite order of priorities, governed by the regulating principle of benefit, which commands reliance, first, upon payment for special benefits by their recipients (the preference within this category being given to payments that cannot be shifted and that do not deter production); and second, upon general payments for general benefits,[29] with payments not geared to benefits exacted only as a temporary last resort in extraordinary crises. He will advocate the restriction of government spending to necessary protective functions apart from the first category, and also within the first subdivision of that category except for the hypothetical eventuality of a surplus.

Like George, and in contrast to the "single tax limited" of Shearman and Charles B. Fillebrown, Neo-Georgism will stand for the public appropriation of the *full* land rent, less a percentage just large enough to induce owners to retain private title. It will do so not only on the ground of public right, but also because legitimate government expenditure today would leave no excess in the land-rent fund, as might have been the case in Shearman's day. Yet, unlike George, it could accede to a policy of providing some form of temporary and limited compensation where the full public appropriation would cause extreme hardship to the owner; not, however, as a matter of justice but simply as a pragmatic gesture to smooth the way of implementation. Better, as Brown remarks, that special provision be made for the ubiquitous landowning "widows and orphans" whose anticipated distressful state has been made the basis for opposition to reform, than that a bad system be retained forever.[30]

III

Within less than two years of its publication by a commercial press, *Progress and Poverty* was a runaway best-seller, and its author's name, an international household word. By contrast, the only volume of *Das Kapital* that appeared in Marx's lifetime was scarcely noticed; just before he died Marx took pathetic pleasure when recognition of a sort came to him in the form of a biographical sketch in the British journal *Modern Thought*, probably arranged by Dr. Edward Aveling, his youngest daughter's paramour.[31] In Russia, especially, George's ideas had quickened the thought of social students and reformers long before those of his earlier contemporary gained any appreciable following.[32] Yet today George is relatively forgotten, while half the world calls itself Marxist.

Does this indicate that Marxism has proved itself a viable system, and that the thought of George is nothing but a burned-out meteor that once briefly lit the sky of social protest and reform? Scarcely. Marxism has not, in point of fact, demonstrated its viability as a system. It is rife with ambiguities and contradictions, both philosophical and economic.[33] (Indeed, vol. 3 of *Das Kapital* contains passages that suggest that, in the end, Marx had arrived at certain conclusions less in keeping with his better-known views than with the views of George.[34]) Where free scholarship prevails, Marxism has few orthodox adherents among reputable savants; where it is the official line, the various Communist blocs and factions are bitterly divided as to what constitutes its orthodox expression; while to the extent that it may be said to have been implemented with any degree of material success, its toll in human life and freedom has been so great as to render it utterly unacceptable to all but the most morally callous. For the effectiveness of Marxism lies neither in its cogency as an intellectual system nor in its utility as a constructive program; it lies rather in its propaganda value as a revolutionary myth—a myth with spurious but well-advertised pretensions to scientific authority and historical inevitability. It is these pretensions, providing as they do both an aureole of seeming dignity and a promise of triumph to the aspirations of the "have-nots," that give Marxism its potent appeal to the mass mind and cause it to be embraced, at least in name, by so many of the power-seekers who pose as saviors to the "wretched of the earth." Young accounts most perceptively for the way in which socialism has outstripped Georgism in prominence and numerical growth:

> A chief reason is that the former lends itself better to agitation. The socialist protest is more simple, being directed against the great inequalities in the distribution of wealth. But the single tax is a step more complex, since it undertakes to introduce a theoretical distinction between kinds of wealth, a distinction not readily grasped by the man on the street, to whom socialism makes a stronger appeal. A protest against the mere magnitude and economic power of individual wealth is simpler, and to the average mind appears more logical, than a protest directed against ownership of one form of wealth, and that not necessarily in the hands of the economically strong. The average man notices rather the amount of swollen fortunes than the kind of goods in which they happen at the moment to be invested.[35]

The image of Marx as "erudite doctor" has helped to buttress the scientific pretensions of his gospel. Actually, it may be doubted that, apart from his being multilingual (a faculty not uncommon among Europeans), his erudition was much superior to that of George. Most of his student years were spent in coffee houses rather than in lecture halls, and when he finally took his degree it was what we would call a "cheap" doctorate, from a university where he had never been in residence and that did not require its external students to undergo prolonged examination.[36] He had no formal training whatever in economics. Like George, he was fundamentally self-educated, a compulsive and omnivorous reader. Despite his pose of scholarly detachment, his approach was anything but detached: "All philosophies have sought to explain the world; the point, however, is to change it."[37] Insofar as he worked at all for a living instead of sponging on creditors and friends, Marx was, like George, a journalist, not an academician. Yet even among those who do not count themselves his disciples, he bears the reputation of a learned sage, while George is thought of as a talented but brash amateur.

I have depicted Marxism as a pseudo-science articulating a rationale for the crude *ressentiment* dumbly felt by the desperate multitudes, and holding out to them a messianic hope. No matter that it has everywhere turned out to be a false guide to history and a miserable failure in practice! It still exerts a powerful attraction, especially to the jobless intellectuals and semiliterate subalterns of the underdeveloped nations, who see it as the wave of the future and who fancy themselves the destined elite of a coming proletarian dictatorship.

Against it, the mélange of civil liberties and monopoly privileges miscalled capitalism can make no political headway in an increasingly populist age. As for the "pragmatic" economic mixtures that prevail in such places as Britain, they have succeeded merely in pricing their goods out of the world market and creating an exodus of brains and purchasing power. Only capitalism can provide the incentives imperative to keep production capable of satisfying needs. But only a *purified* capitalism in which the distribution of the product reflects unmonopolized natural opportunity, can commend itself to the disaffected millions upon whose allegiance the course of history could very well depend. Perhaps, as the lessons of experience become too obvious to ignore, these disaffected ones will apprehend that indiscriminate dispossession of the propertied is no real solution to social problems. Then the long-neglected doctrine of Henry George, pruned of questionable but inessential details and supplemented by fresh understandings and techniques, may come into its own.

Yet it is not only to emerging masses that George has something of profound significance to say. Exasperation with the arrogance of bureaucratic meddling, disillusionment with the bankruptcy of centralized planning, and disgust with the savagery of statist repression—all have engendered in the Western world a wholesome recrudescence of libertarian scholarship and propaganda. Who could have imagined, three decades ago, a Nozick at Harvard,* or the widespread vogue of Randian and Rothbardian teachings on college and university campuses? After so long a period of conformity to the interventionist establishment in academe, these are heartening signs indeed! The nonanarchist libertarian, however, needs to consider that even a minimal state must somehow be supported.** Shall it be supported by coercive imposts upon private earnings? Or shall it be supported, at least as far as possible, by a fund created by society itself, a fund that, if not taken for the common use, operates as a crippling gyve upon labor and capital alike?

---

*Nozick's acceptance of the "Lockean Proviso" commits him to the moral premises from which George developed his system. (See Robert Nozick, *Anarchy, State, and Utopia* [New York: Basic Books, 1974], pp. 174-82.) Doubtless increasing familiarity with George will in time move Nozick to acknowledge their affinity.

**Professor Milton Friedman, 1976 Nobel Prize winner in economics, and noted proponent of the free market, stated in response to a question at a recent anniversary banquet of the Americanism Educational League: "In my opinion the least bad tax is the property tax on the unimproved value of land, the Henry George argument of many, many years ago." Reported in *Human Events*, November 18, 1978, p. 14.

Notes

1. Clancy's comments are contained in the June 1952 Faculty Letter of the Henry George School, and in the *Henry George News* of July 1952, p. 7. A fuller summary of them than the one given here may be found in Steven B. Cord, *Henry George: Dreamer or Realist?* (Philadelphia: University of Pennsylvania Press, 1965), pp. 191-95.

2. Henry George, *Progress and Poverty,* 75th anniversary ed. (New York: Robert Schalkenbach Foundation, 1954), p. 456.

3. Harry Gunnison Brown, *Economic Science and the Common Welfare,* 6th ed. (Columbia, Mo.: Lucas Bros., 1936), p. 246 n.

4. Wilford I. King, *The Wealth and Income of the People of the United States* (New York: Macmillan, 1915), pp. 160-62.

5. Cord, *Henry George,* p. 234.

6. Charles F. Collier, "Henry George's System of Economics: Analysis and Criticism," Ph.D. dissertation, Duke University, 1976, p. 220.

7. George Raymond Geiger, *The Philosophy of Henry George* (New York: Macmillan, 1933), p. 157, n. 90.

8. George, *Progress and Poverty,* p. 456.

9. Henry George, "The Condition of Labor: An Open Letter to Pope Leo XIII," in *The Land Question* [and Other Essays] (New York: Robert Schalkenbach Foundation, 1953), p. 10.

10. Henry George, *Thy Kingdom Come* (New York: Robert Schalkenbach Foundation, n.d.), p. 13.

11. E.g., E. Benjamin Andrews, "Economic Reform Short of Socialism," *International Journal of Ethics* 2 (April 1892): 281-82.

12. George, *Progress and Poverty,* p. 456.

13. Collier, "Henry George's System," p. 261.

14. George, *Progress and Poverty,* p. 133.

15. See Harry Gunnison Brown, *Basic Prnciples of Economics,* 3d ed. (Columbia, Mo.: Lucas Brothers, 1955), pp. 403 ff., 416. The present writer vividly recalls hearing Brown make the flat announcement, "I am a Malthusian," to an audience of Georgists in 1960 or thereabouts.

16. George, *Progress and Poverty,* p. 228.

17. Ibid., p. 231.

18. Ernest Teilhac, *Pioneers of American Economic Thought in the Nineteenth Century,* trans. E. A. J. Johnson (New York: Macmillan, 1936), p. 141.

19. Collier, "Henry George's System," pp. 154-55, 158-60.

20. James Haldane Smith, *Economic Moralism: An Essay in Constructive Economics* (London: George Allen & Unwin, 1916), p. 73.

21. See Charles Grove Haines, *The Revival of Natural Law Concepts,* Harvard Studies in Jurisprudence, vol 4 (Cambridge, Mass.: Harvard University Press, 1958).

22. George, *Progress and Poverty,* p. 328.

23. Ibid., p. 508.

24. Ibid., p. 525.

25. Ibid., pp. xvi, 456.

26. See Walter J. Blum and Harry Kalven, Jr., *The Uneasy Case for Progressive Taxation* (Chicago: University of Chicago Press, 1953).

27. See Charles Albro Barker, *Henry George* (New York: Oxford University Press, 1955), pp. 519 f.

28. Harry Gunnison Brown, *Fiscal Policy, Taxation and Free Enterprise* (New York: Robert Schalkenbach Foundation, n.d.), p. 14.

29. Another source of public revenue, also second to the land-value tax in priority, might be escheatment to the community of all estates to which there are no immediate heirs in the direct line, unless the decedent has provided otherwise by will. I do not classify this, even nontechnically, as a tax, but simply as the public appropriation of property to which the title has become, from any standpoint of rational justice, vacant.

30.   Harry Gunnison Brown, *Economic Science and the Common Welfare*, 2d ed. (Columbia, Mo.: Lucas Brothers, 1925), pp. 251 f.

31.   See Robert Payne, *Marx* (New York: Simon and Schuster, 1968), pp. 484 f.

32.   See Barker, *Henry George*, p. 599.

33.   Leopold Schwarzschild presents a catalogue of contradictions in the thought of Marx himself. See *Karl Marx: The Red Prussian*, The Universal Library (New York: Grosset & Dunlap, 1947), pp. 398-401. The profound incompatibility between dialectic and materialism is arrestingly delineated by Nicolas Berdyaev in numerous passages, e.g., *The End of Our Time* (New York: Sheed and Ward, 1933), p. 240; and *The Bourgeois Mind and Other Essays* (New York: Sheed and Ward, 1933), p. 82.

34.   These are cited by Fred Harrison in chapter 14 on Gronlund in the present volume. See also Marx, *Das Kapital*, 1, pt. 7, and idem, "The Nationalization of the Land," in *Selected Works*, vol. 2 (Moscow: Progress Publishers, 1973).

35.   Arthur Nichols Young, *The Single Tax Movement in the United States* (Princeton, N.J.: Princeton University Press, 1916), p. 311.

36.   See Payne, *Marx*, p. 81.

37.   Karl Marx, *Theses on Feuerbach* (thesis 11).

Notes on Contributors

(Views expressed in this volume are not necessarily those of any organizations or institutions with which their authors are associated.)

ROBERT V. ANDELSON (Ph.D., University of Southern California) is professor of philosophy and a member of the graduate faculty at Auburn University. Current and past president of the Alabama Philosophical Society, his publications include *Imputed Rights* (University of Georgia Press) and numerous articles in ethics and social philosophy. He serves on the editorial boards of *The Personalist and The American Journal of Economics and Sociology.* His interest in the thought of Henry George extends over a period of more than thirty years.

GEORGE BABILOT (Ph.D., University of Oregon), professor of economics and director of the Center for Public Economics, San Diego State University, is author of monographs, essays, and articles on taxation, public finance, and welfare economics.

JAMES L. BUSEY (Ph.D., Ohio State University), professor and chairman of the department of political science, Cragmore Campus, University of Colorado, has many books and articles to his credit, including *Latin America: Political Institutions and Processes* (Random House), *Notes on Costa Rican Democracy* (University of Colorado Press) and *Political Aspects of the Panama Canal* (University of Arizona Press).

CHARLES F. COLLIER (Ph.D., Duke University) is assistant professor of economics at Hamilton College, Clinton, N.Y. He has previously published an article in the history of economic thought.

STEVEN B. CORD (Ed.D., Columbia University), professor of history, Indiana University of Pennsylvania, is author of *Henry George: Dreamer or Realist?* (University of Pennsylvania Press) and numerous articles. He serves as president of the Henry George Foundation of America.

ROY DOUGLAS (Ph.D., University of Edinburgh), senior lecturer in the department of general studies, University of Surrey, began his professional career in the field of biology, but his books have made him a recognized authority on modern political history. They include *The History of the British Liberal Party, 1895-1970* (Fairleigh Dickinson University Press), *Land, People and Politics* (St. Martin's Press), *In the Year of Munich* (Macmillan) and *The Advent of War, 1939-40* (Macmillan). He is also a barrister.

AARON B. FULLER (Ph.D., University of Virginia), formerly served as an assistant professor of economics in the California State University system, and since 1975 has been an economist on the staff of the Institute for Defense

Analyses, Arlington, Virginia. He is author of various articles and papers in the history of economic thought, and of monographs related to the economics of national defense.

MASON GAFFNEY (Ph.D., University of California at Berkeley) is currently professor of economics at the Graduate School of Administration, University of California at Riverside. His previous positions include executive director, British Columbia Institute for Economic Policy Analysis; senior research associate, Resources for the Future; professor and chairman, department of economics, University of Wisconsin at Milwaukee; and professor of agricultural economics, University of Missouri. A director of the Western Tax Association, he is the author of *Containment Policies for Urban Sprawl* (University of Kansas Press) as well as numerous monographs, chapters, and articles on taxation and land use, and editor of *Extractive Resources and Taxation* (University of Wisconsin Press).

FRED HARRISON (A.B., Oxford University; M.Sc., University of London) is an investigative reporter for the London *Sunday People*. He also finds time to edit *Land and Liberty* and (in emergencies) the British Liberal Party *News*, and to write monographs and articles in economics and social theory. His book on the distortion of the laissez faire economy by land monopoly should be nearing completion as this goes to press.

C. LOWELL HARRISS (Ph.D., Columbia University), professor of economics at Columbia, serves as consultant to the Tax Foundation, Inc., as associate with the Lincoln Institute of Land Policy, and on the editorial board of *The American Journal of Economics and Sociology*. He is author of *Gift Taxation in the United States* (American Council on Public Affairs), *Money and Banking* (Allyn and Bacon), *American Economy* (Irwin), and *Innovations in Tax Policy, and Other Essays* (University of Hartford Press); co-author of *American Public Finance* (Prentice-Hall); and editor of *Government Spending and Land Values* (University of Wisconsin Press). He is a past president of the National Tax Association.

ROBERT F. HÉBERT (Ph.D., Louisiana State University), is associate professor of economics and a member of the graduate faculty at Auburn University. Co-author of *A History of Economic Theory and Method* (McGraw-Hill), he has published a number of articles in the history of economic thought.

OSCAR B. JOHANNSEN (M.B.A., Ph.D. candidate, New York University), author of pamphlets and articles in economic and political theory, was awarded the grand prize for the best essay on the free enterprise system by the National Association of Manufacturers in 1975. After a long career in industry, he recently retired as secretary to the president of the United States Steel Corporation, to devote himself to doctoral studies in economics, and to service as vice-president of *The American Journal of Economics and Sociology* and contributing editor of *Fragments*.

JACK SCHWARTZMAN (J.S.D., St. Lawrence University; Ph.D., New York University), a native of Russia, has practiced law in this country for more than forty years. In addition, he is professor of English at Nassau Community College, State University of New York. In 1974 he won the New York State Chancellor's Award for Excellence in Teaching, and was subsequently appointed to the committee that recommends the awards. He is author of *Rebels of Individualism* (Exposition) and some three hundred articles, and chairman of the editorial board of the occasional journal *Fragments*.

WILLIAM B. TRUEHART (Ph.D., Claremont Graduate School), a lecturer in economics for the San Diego Community College District, formerly served as a staff executive with the Lincoln Institute of Land Policy. He is a member of the San Diego County Board of Assessment Appeals, and has written several articles and study guides in economics.

LOUIS WASSERMAN (Ph.D., University of California at Berkeley) is professor emeritus of philosophy and government, San Francisco State University. A past president of the Northern California Political Science Association, he is author of *Modern Political Philosophies* (Garden City—Doubleday; New Home Library) and many articles in political theory, joint author and editor of *American Institutions and Ideals* (Gutenberg), and co-author of *Self-Help Cooperatives in Los Angeles County* (University of California Press).

Index

cited with George by Toynbee as denying
possibility of improvement for the masses
under existing property system, 157;
theoretical differences with George, 229,
230; mentioned, 15, 16n, 219n14

Robespierre, Maximilien de: on the general
will, 283

Rockefeller Center: on leased land, 193

Rogers, Thorold: quoted by Jorgensen on
effects of progress on land values, 316

Roman Catholic critiques of George: by
Holaind, 21, Cathrein, 126-36, Ryan,
242-53, Alcázar, 326-41

Roman republic: Marx on historical impact of
landownership on, 214, 221n85

Roosevelt, Theodore: friend of Ely, 313

Rose, Edward J.: his biography of George, 371

Rothbard, Murray N.: biographical data, 354,
368n1; his appreciative references to
George, 25, 366; his anarcho-capitalism,
354; his critique of George, 354-70; justifies
ownership of *anything*, by same argument
Cooke used to attack labor theory of
ownership, 19, 366; mistakenly accuses
George of excluding time from his theory of
capital and interest, 356, 361; claims that
land and improvement values cannot be
adequately separated, 357; seems to believe
that George advocated confiscation of *all*
pure rent, 359; asserts that 100% socialization of rent would eliminate land value,
359; holds (together with Knight and
Heath) that many landowners perform a
useful allocative function, 360, 363-64;
mistakenly assumes that George intended
single tax to force *all* land into use, 361;
fails to pay adequate attention to George's
proposal to untax improvements, 362;
argument for vested legal rights of landowners not open to an anarchist like, 365;
his critique of George evaluated, 356-66
passim; his appreciative references to Nock
and Chodorov, 370n37

Rousseau, Jean Jacques: criticized by Huxley,
137-44; his views on land and natural rights
related to those of George, 137-38, 141; his
rhetoric reflected in Declaration of
Independence, 141; mentioned, 146

Russell, Bertrand: denies relevance of labor
theory of ownership to industrial society,
210n

Russia, 218, 339, 389

Rutherford, Reuben C.: biographical data,
222n; his critique of George, 222-33;
defends obsolete version of wages-fund
theory, 222-26; his critique of George's
wage theory, 222-26; his critique of
George's capital and interest theories,
226-28; his theory of income distribution,
230-31; defends classical view of profit,
231; his concept of human nature and social
reform, 231; advocates restrictions on
individual freedom, 231; misinterprets
George's use of term "equality," 232; misunderstands George's proposal, 232; his
critique of George evaluated, 222-32
passim, evaluation summarized, 232

Ryan, Msgr. John A.: biographical data, 342;
characterized by Nichols as chief theorist of
social Catholicism in America, 342; protégé
of Ely, 313; his critique of George, 242-53;
criticizes George's argument against first-
occupancy theory of ownership, 343-45,
352n12; argues that socialization of rent
without compensation would be unjust to
landowners, 346-49; claims that
confiscation of rent could never occur
peacefully, 346; claims that both
landowners and slaveowners have moral
right to compensation, 347-48;
distinguishes between *ideal* and *practical*
justice, 346; his extended definition of
natural rights, 349; defends landownership
on utilitarian grounds, 349; acknowledges
some advantages in George's proposal, 350;
asserts practical disadvantages of single tax,
350; views private landownership in terms
of its ideal potentialities, 351; his semi-
Georgist proposals for reforming land .
system, 351; his critique of George
evaluated, 343-53 passim

Ryotwari settlement, 216

St. Louis: percentage of vacant land in, 317

St. Paul: percentage of vacant land in, 317

San Antonio, Tex.: Somers system used in, 318

Sanford, Hugh Wheeler: criticizes George's
theory of rent, 24

San Francisco: percentage of vacant land in,
317

Saratoga Conferences, American Social
Science Association: (1886) 187; (1890) 269,
273-74

Satolli, Archbishop Francesco: helps reverse